The Seven Days of My Creation

Tales of Magic, Sex and Gender

Jani Farrell-Roberts

Writers Club Press
San Jose New York Lincoln Shanghai

The Seven Days of My Creation
Tales of Magic, Sex and Gender

Writers Club Press
an imprint of iUniverse, Inc.

For information address:
iUniverse, Inc.
5220 S. 16th St., Suite 200
Lincoln, NE 68512
www.iuniverse.com

ISBN: 0-595-23637-5

Printed in the United States of America

This book is dedicated to scary things
Like owning up to being
  A person who honours the moon
    Who hugs trees and talks to the plants
      A mystic, a wild woman, perhaps a witch
        Her birthright the shamanic gender-dance
      Who is proud to be a child
      Of the earth's dust
        But who is still nervous at
        Owning up to being
        Me.

Copyright Notice

Acknowledgement

With many thanks to my proofreaders, Alison Hall and Manek Rogers

NOTE—The names of the author's former partner and of their children have been changed to preserve their privacy.

Biographical Note on the Author

The author's human rights and environmental work has been funded or otherwise supported by Freedom from Hunger, War on Want, Community Aid Abroad, CIMRA, the World Council of Churches, Survival International, Anti-Slavery Society, the Methodists, Roman Catholics and the Geneva-based Frontier Internship Program funded by European and American Churches.

She worked for over 15 years for Australian Aboriginal support networks and their Civil Rights organisations—including as the Mining Advisor to the Federation of Aboriginal Land Councils.

She has authored several well-received books on Aboriginal topics including

Massacres to Mining: the Colonisation of Aboriginal Australia Launched by Aboriginal elders, with major media coverage, it tells what happened to the Aboriginal nations when the Europeans came, how the invasion was resisted in wars like to those of the American West and how genocidal policies were defended as helping the survival of the "fittest". She talks to survivors of the last massacres.

Jack of Cape Grim, the incredible story of the final armed stand on the outskirts of Melbourne of five Tasmanian Aborigines, two men and three women, including the famed Truganini, against three military expeditions sent to hunt them down.

The Mapoon Books (3 volumes) Editor and Co-Author. How an Aboriginal community triumphed against great odds. Money from these books helped the community return to tribal lands from which they were removed in irons some eight years earlier. It utilises Aboriginal oral history and many rare Presbyterian mission, State and mining company documents. It also helped the neighbouring Aurukun community evict Shell from over 500 square miles of tropical forest. The author was the only white person present when Shell's mining camp was occupied. The books were reviewed as a devastating exposure—but it is more—it is a success story.

She has also initiated, researched and produced investigative human rights television programs for major international broadcasters including

The Diamond Empire An investigative television series produced and written by the author for the BBC, the ABC and Frontline in North America. This describes how the De Beers diamond cartel aversely affected the lives of diamond mineworkers and diamond cutters throughout the world and exploited consumers. This ran at peak times in two parts on BBC2 while in the US and Canada it was shown as a feature length PBS Special. Well reviewed in the New York Times and other papers. Shot in six continents, it is the most international investigative movie every made.

Munda Nyuringu: he's taken our land, he believes it is his; he won't give it back. A dramatic account that weaves Aboriginal accounts with those of the first White settlers. It tells of the spiritual importance of land and of the impact of the invading cattle, gold and uranium industries. Set around Kalgoorlie, it uses original photographs, interviews at massacre sites and brilliant cartoons. Co-produced and co-directed with Aboriginal Elder Robert Bropho.

A Plain and Sacred Rite On Aboriginal spirituality and diamond mining. She initiated and researched this for the acclaimed BBC *Everyman* television series.

Monkey Business Co-Produced for Dispatches on Channel 4 in UK. Also shown in Australia on the ABC's Four Corners. It is based on peer-reviewed research and tells how a monkey virus contaminant in the polio vaccine injected into hundreds of millions is now turning up in thousands of human cancer cases. The virus switches off a key gene that protects us from cancer.

Strangers in Their Own Land Initiated and researched for World in Action, Granada TV, UK and televised worldwide. This documented how RTZ took over a thousand square miles of old tropical forest, still hunt-gathered by Aborigines, to strip it of bauxite, the raw material of aluminium.

The author also played a key role in stopping RTZ from pumping cyanide into 700km of underground rivers in southern Australia and worked with eco-warriors to successfully protect a forest near to where she grew up in Southern England.

She also writes and teaches on issues relating to public health, corporate responsibility, spirituality, sexuality, gender, mysticism and religion.

Reviews of works by the author

Humphrey McQueen, an Australian historian of high repute, reviewed the *Mapoon Books* she edited and co-authored as *"the finest, best researched and through study appearing in the Whitlam era."* (Gough Whitlam was a renowned Australian Prime Minister who led a renaissance of culture.)

Xavior Herbert, one of the greatest of Australian authors, wrote of her book *Massacres to Mining* in *The National Times*: "There is no doubt about Jan Roberts' feelings in the matter. Yet she handles her history with restraint that makes it a work deserving to be a classic in our history. Every revelation…is authenticated from official records but without marring the dramatic impact on the reader that is usual with objective writing."

John Pilger, a renowned British investigative journalist, used her work in his own films about Australia and lists her as one of his favourite journalists.

The **Australian Film Institute** awarded *Munda Nyuringu; they have taken our land, they believe it is their's, they won't give it back* a unanimous Nomination as one of the four best Australian documentaries of that year. It was co-produced and co-directed by the Aboriginal Elder **Robert Bropho** and **Janine Roberts**. When shown on the ABC, the Sydney Morning Herald wrote it up as the film of the week.

The Alice Springs Star of Central Australia said of her, "Jan Roberts does not look the sort of women you'd find sitting in the bush having a feed of goanna or a file snake for that matter. The only indication that the British-born sociologist showed that she roughs it, was a mass of mosquito bites on her legs. For the rest she was pretty much haute couture. Jan is the author of *Massacres to Mining, the colonisation of Aboriginal Australia,* an extensively documented work on the dispossession and exploitation of Aborigines and the destruction of their culture. Her book has already inspired the Granada Television film *Strangers in their own land.* Now it is to be the basis of a joint BBC-ABC television production for the prestigious BBC program *Everyman.*"

Contact

The Author may be contacted at 7days@witch.plus.com. Her websites include www.sparkle.plus.com on diamonds and human rights, www.vaccines.plus.com on childhood vaccination and www.witch.plus.com for her spiritual, Aboriginal and environmental work.

This book is a legacy for my daughters
And a sharing with my wider family

Prologue

I know my path to freedom. Writing this book is part of my way. I felt the wind of freedom as I quarried words from within and carved them to shape. I became lighter, freer, as images emerged from inner shadows.

On my journey I had to fall off pedestals of privilege; fight patriarchs and corruption, learn of the fate of women, of spirit and of magic, as I sought and found a vision and strength that no one could take from me.

Introduction

In my early years I was called "father" although I had not fathered. I then left this rocky prominence to descend to a rich fertile land in which I became a priestess and parent, investigative journalist and filmmaker.

On my journey I learnt about my nature, changed gender-roles, brought up children, survived male violence, wrote articles and books with the Aborigines among whom I lived and worked—as well as producing films shown on Australian, American and British television. During that time I did not speak publicly of my own unusual path for I wished to protect my children from being teased. But the children grew up, and into my life came a critical illness. I had no time to lose. I returned to what was most sacred to me.

Since then I have happily reclaimed my ancestral heritage, found my own place, travelled the full circle, renewing my dedication—but to Gaia, our Mother Earth, and to Macha, the mother of my Irish earth, as well as to the Christ who gave love primacy. Nowadays I simply try to serve what I see as the spiritual and magical inheritance of all earth's children, whatever one may call it; whether it be the Old Religion, the Human Craft, the way of Shamans or of Mystics. For me all Nature is imbued with divine energy, is living and is sacred. We are all part of it. We are a sacred family.

In this book I use my gender-journey as a metaphor for our society's journey out of patriarchy into a more balanced existence. I thus weave in stories of gender and sexuality gathered from Aboriginal and other ancient cultures, of magic and menstruation, circumcision, and childhood gender-typing, on how martyrdom became a route to heaven, of the suppression of the Gnostics and the Beguine women, on the witch-hunts, European shamanism, meditation and mysticism, child-welcoming and

Wiccan initiation rituals, the Final Rites—and much else. I think you will find this a richly textured book.

I knew that mine was not a unique gender journey. Only my route was rare. We each have our own male and female aspects to recognise and accept. We all have inner knowledge, strengths and destiny. We each inherit an inner great library, a collective unconsciousness that we make conscious; that unites us to each other and to our universe. This library is as much part of us as are our arms and legs. We learn from it through instincts, myths and dreams.

In my work as a freelance journalist for major newspapers, the BBC, WGBH, Channel 4 and other broadcasters, I investigated such dark topics as the arms-trade, child-labour and the plight of indigenous peoples. People thought me fairly fearless—but in truth my fear of rejection had made me hide much.

My spiritual work is today in the instinctive religion that needs no institution. I have had to learn from children and people of the road, from the Aboriginal elders with whom I worked for many years—as well as from the young eco-warriors with whom I shared a bender while protecting English woods. These experiences have helped me understand my world as it too emerges from a patriarchal age to regain its spiritual relationship with nature. This, then, is the story of my own and my world's transition, a tale of magic and religion, warfare and evil, sex and gender.

Contents

Monday

Birth Rites

Land mines and barbed wire entanglements protected our coastal village against an expected German invasion at the time of my birth. It was winter, mid-February 1942, in the silted ancient port of Winchelsea on the southern English coast. My parents had conceived me in the camouflaged huts of a radar station on nearby Romney Marsh between watching for German planes.

After birth I was whisked away by an alarmed midwife. When my mother's urgent pleas brought my return, she was alarmed to see my eyes peeping through bandages. The one-armed doctor who had delivered me then warned that I might be brain- damaged and not have long to live—for his forceps had squeezed my brain up into a cone above my fontanel. I can still see the dents he put in my cheekbones. My mother told me I looked like an Egyptian mummy. I have since learnt that Egyptian children destined for the priesthood had their heads bound to create the same high shape. My mother has speculated that brain damage might explain my gender change. I think her wrong—but that was her explanation for what I now delight in as a gift that has given me an extraordinarily rich life.

The midwife had decided that I was a boy when she looked between my legs. But she could not know that a rare event had given me a different path. I did not understand this when, as a child, I found I absurdly wanted to be a girl, nor did I when I told my mother at the age of three that I wanted to join the priesthood. I never varied in these seemingly utterly irreconcilable ambitions. It seemed so crazy to want to change my assigned gender. It took me until I was nearly thirty to discover that a person called in ancient times to walk between the genders might well be seen as having a gift that could make them a natural spiritual leader or Shaman. For them there was no contradiction between a calling to the priesthood and a desire to change gender roles. Slowly I began to suspect that I had been called, as they were called, through dreams and inner knowledge.

I then discovered that my own people once had their own "shamans", known sometimes as druids in the Celtic language and as witches (wiccae) in Anglo-Saxon. I explored these old nature-centred religious paths and found myself surprisingly at home.

So this is the story of what I discovered on a journey from an authoritative religion to an ancient way. It became for me a path of ecstasy, with my guide a loving Deity. I rejoiced, as I reclaimed a nature-centred spirituality and found others who shared my belief in the sacredness of nature. Many were spiritual healers. Some belonged to rural traditions. We all saw ourselves as on an ancient path in which Wisdom and Divinity were sought and found within nature and within ourselves.

As for my unusual gender path, it took me, a slow learner perhaps, a whole lifetime to understand just how important it is for everyone to recognise and integrate their male and female aspects. The alchemy of bringing these together is, I found, both a path to wholeness and part of the ancient craft of the Shaman.

My parents baptised me shortly after birth into the Roman Catholic faith in a Franciscan church in the nearby town of Rye. My mother had a very small role in this second birthing. She put me into the arms of a male priest who bloodlessly rebirthed me into a "sacred" life. It was the usual story. Mothers no longer gave a child its sacred life. They did the messy and painful business while males presided over the clean neat rites of higher life.[1]

There was an older birth rite in these islands that used milk instead of water, and recognised more the sacred role of the mother. A mother's milk was seen as sacred and as helping to form the spirit of the child. A monk's tale claimed that a milk baptism made a Christian of St. Bride, a Goddess once widely honoured in the British Isles. The Irish used milk for baptisms until the Church banned its use at the Synod of Cashel in 1172 .

We need rites that celebrate the arrival of sacred beings, not a rite that presumes babies arrive contaminated and sinful. All aspects of their being are divine, rich, natural—part of the beauty of creation. Children are divine sparks put into the temporary care of adults. The Creatrix does not need us to tell her who are her own and who she has to care for.

Birth rites are a matter for women among the Ngarrindjeri, an Australian people living by the mouth of the River Murray. The mother-child link is enshrined in their rituals. The birth cord, the "miwi", is still carefully preserved as a symbol of the sacred link between mother and child. It is tied, allowed to fall off naturally, then kept honourably. George Trevorrow of the Ngarrindjeri explained; "Our miwi is a very very strong spiritual thing, you know. We shouldn't be talking too much about it, but it's where everything comes from, that's the life force…the cord from the mother to child. It's the life-force that gives things life in our spiritual beliefs."[2]

Assigning Genders

My experience taught me that the gender of a child is ultimately its own business. It is the child's right to confirm the decision of the mother and midwife. As the child grows up, its instincts will tell it if the gender wiring of its brain does not match the gender assigned at birth. The old way and the old wisdom, preserved in many ancient societies, was to recognise the validity and truth of the child's instincts. Our less instinctive society has had to wait until this old wisdom was confirmed by post-mortems—but more about this later.

Our hospitals provide pink and blue blankets but life is not so easy to classify. One in five hundred newborn children do not have "standard issue" genitals. The midwife sometimes cannot decide if that is a large clitoris or a small penis.[3] Birth Certificates cannot be completed in such cases, as the gender cannot be specified.

In such cases, in British and American hospitals, a surgeon is quietly summoned who quickly makes most such children into "girls", since creating a vagina is easier than creating a penis. One child in a thousand is thus operated on at birth. Such children are known medically as "intersexed", meaning they were born with physical aspects of both genders—confusing to our gender rigid society. In their rush to perform this operation the surgeons and parents presume that gender is nothing to do with the structures of the brain.

But many of such operations go wrong for this very reason. Half of those operated on later claim to have been surgically assigned to the wrong gender. The surgeon had simply guessed the gender to assign on the assumption that later social conditioning would make his choice right. But new research indicates our gender is determined by quite a different factor. According to leading UK specialist, Dr Russell Reid, "recent medical evidence has demonstrated that transsexualism is a physiologically based condition rather than a mental disorder".[4] A child assigned at birth to a gender unlike that of their brain becomes potentially a "transsexual", a person who seeks gender reassignment later in life.

Today's scientists argue about what makes a person male or female. Some say it is the hormone shaped pre-birth brain. Others give the credit to social conditioning, peer pressure and our wish to conform. Some think gender equality requires there be no difference between genders that cannot be overcome by conditioning. But my experience teaches me that there is something deeper than conditioning, deeper than the evidence of mirrors, which makes us know ourselves as male or female.

When I first began to seriously consider changing my gender role, I read the pioneering medical works on transsexualism of Dr. John Money. It was from him that I first learnt of the old customs that once made transsexuals into shamans. His main thesis was that the best way to treat transsexuals was to help them live in their desired gender. He believed that children were gender-neutral at birth and gained gender by nurture while the brain was highly flexible in the first two years of life. My father had been absent during my first two years. Could I have taken on a female self-identity by identifying with my mother during those years? But boys brought up by single mothers do not have gender-identification problems—at least not in my experience. My instinct was that a pre-birth factor had gender-shaped my brain. My psychiatrist agreed—and in 1975 a letter from her saying that I was psychologically hermaphrodite enabled me to obtain a female passport.

Recent research indicates that it is not a "disjunction" or "abnormality" to be born between the genders, as intersexed or transsexual. It would instead be abnormal if none were so born. These varieties are not only found in humans—they naturally occur in many species and are physically determined prior to birth. In intersexed cases the genitals may not clearly indicate the gender of the brain. In transsexual cases, the genitals simply do not correspond to the brain's gender.

But for many years Dr Money's theories continued to hold vogue. He claimed his theory had been verified when he assigned "successfully" as "Brenda" a one–year–old infant boy who had lost his penis after a circumcision error. But "Brenda" had returned to living as a male at the age of fourteen, describing his earlier assignment to the female gender as a nightmarish mistake. His mother said as "Brenda" her child had constantly rebelled, not identified with girls and had changed gender-roles within months of learning what had been done to him in infanthood.

Ancient Cultures and Gender

Some of our oldest cultures believed a child's gender to be an aspect of its spirit. The Tjungundji, the Aboriginal people of Mapoon in NE Australia (with whom I worked 1974-6) saw children as formed out of the earth.[5] It was not just Adam but every child that was thus created. They held that the Creating Spirit formed the child's spirit from one of its parents' spirits. If formed from the mother's, then the child will be a girl, if from the father, then a boy. This gender-balanced theory was quite unlike that of Aristotle who could be stupid on occasion. He taught that the perfectly conceived child was always a boy—a doctrine that proved to have disastrous consequences for the status of women.

Amazonian Indian stories tell of an age before a gender-balanced society when women once ruled through spiritual power or magic. The Yamana-Yaghan told how women fooled men into honouring them by painting themselves as Spirits. But then one day the men came across girls without their paint. The men, angry at being deceived, stormed the women's hut, killing some women and magically transformed others into animals. The men then did women's magic in the captured women's hut, while the surviving women built a new hut in which to do their magic. Another Amazonian people, the Selk-nam, told a version in which the women were not attacked. In this story the men found the magic done in the women's hut scary—so built their own hut in which to do magic. These are cautionary tales, warnings of might happen if a gender claimed a role that put a society out of kilter. It is however curious that both tales depicted men as catching up with women. Similar Aboriginal stories have men capturing fire from women—or being given fire by women.[6]

All that I have read indicates that the societies that honoured and respected women also respected the transgendered and the homosexual. This was so in many religions that flourished in ancient times. It is still true, or was until very recent times, in the surviving hunter-gatherer societies that hold onto traditions going back perhaps over 100,000 years.

In these societies parents and elders would watch as the child grew, in order to discern, though its body language, behaviour and dreams, the rare cases when the child's appropriate gender was opposite to that of genitalia. Among the Inuit of North America, the Incas of South America, the Navaho of the south western US and the tribes of Siberia, a child that felt the call to change gender roles was said to have a gift that would teach it the secrets of both genders. Such a child was often trained as a spiritual leader—quite different from our society's presumption that such children need to be "cured" or made "normal." Nor did these older societies put the child into a "third" gender, as do some modern specialists in 'gender studies'. They saw them as a special type of female or male, thus honouring the child's choice of a male or female identity.

The Greek Herodotus recorded that among the Scythian nomads north of the Black Sea there were many former male warriors who "became impotent, do woman's work, live like women and converse accordingly...they put on women's clothes, holding that they have lost their manhood." They claimed that the Goddess had made them thus so they could devote themselves to sacred work. Such transformation may have been assisted by the use of oestrogen-rich herbs and an extract from the urine of pregnant mares. Ovid recorded that "witches" living near to the Scythians prepared this extract.

Vladimir Borgoras wrote early in the 19th century about the Chukchi transgendered Shaman of the far north of Russia. (He used the male pronoun of them because, unlike their community, he would not accept the validity of their female identity.) "He throws away the...lance, the lasso of the reindeer-herdsmen, and the harpoon of the seal-hunter, and takes to the needle and skin-scraper...Even his pronunciation changes from the male to the female mode. At the same time his body alters...his physical character changes. The transformed person becomes...fond of small talk and of nurturing small children".[7]

Among the Koniag Inuit of Russia's far north in the 18th century: "when the father or mother regard their apparent son as feminine in his bearing, they will often dedicate this child in earliest childhood to the vocation of Achnutschik (shaman or religious leader). Parents highly prized these children. Their mothers reared them as girls until they reached fifteen when an elder would start their training as shamans."

The Chukchi shaman made life-long marriages with the usual rites but their marriage was seen as very special, since they uniquely represented the divine marriage between humans and a supreme deity who possessed both genders.[8] Many of the Goddess-centred religions of the Mediterranean or Middle East similarly honoured the transgendered. They became priestesses in the temples of Innana, Isis and Cybele. They were said to be like the Creating Deity in knowing the energies of both genders. (This presumably was also true of those who travelled from life as a female to living as a male.)

In Okinawa in the Pacific there was a ceremony known as winagu nati "becoming a woman" in which the carefully prepared candidate went into the sacred grove in women's clothes to be trained as a "shamana".[9] The similarly transformed Ngaju shamans of Indonesia were recognised as women. Men expected them to act " as women sexually". They were not seen as "pretending" to be women.[10] In Angola gender identity was seen as residing in the spirit. A male-formed body might be " possessed since childhood by the spirit of a female". Such a person was known as a sacred Oma Essenge.[11] Inca parents in South America used to pray that they might be blessed with such a transgendered child.

Zulus, for all the image of them in feature films as fierce strong fighting men, believed that perfected souls normally return to live as female souls in female bodies. But there were exceptions. Sometimes these female souls would return to live in males. The latter were thus compelled to speak for a female spirit. The youth would experience nervousness and insomnia. They would dream that the female ancestors within needed a spokesperson. Typically the ancestors were heard to say: "We are your ancestors…We have long tried to make your people understand that we want you to be our house—to speak for us."[12]

The Zulu youth who felt called to change gender roles might also dream of being caught, torn to pieces and reassembled. (I had similar adolescent dreams in which I was forcibly remade into a female.) They would leave the settlement and spend time in the wilderness to see if these visions continued. They might be given tasks to fulfil such as catching a female snake and wearing it around the neck. When they returned from this ordeal, often exhausted and starving, they went to an elder to be healed and transformed, if that was what they still wanted. Only at this stage did they finally change gender roles.

It was not just a male to female process. Sometimes girls were magically transformed into men. Those becoming males among the Zulus were allowed to carry a shield and spear—the badges of malehood—and to enjoy beer and meat. Those becoming women had their hair plaited, their face and body painted, were given beads and their voice changed. These transformed male and female shamans worked in healing, divining, magic and performing sacrifices.[13]

The Omaha, an American Indian tribe of the Plains, examined dreams to recognise those called to change gender roles. A suitable candidate was said to dream of the moon deity asking him or her to chose between a bow and a burden strap. These were seen as emblems of gender. The next stage for one travelling to womanhood was when a passing elder woman stopped and called out "Welcome daughter." After this the youth would begin instructions in the mysteries of the Moon. Such a youth was henceforth seen as female and called a mesoga "instructed by the Moon."[14]

The Navaho Indians put such pubescent youths into the centre of a sacred fire circle where they were given the choice of a spear or digging stick. They would henceforth have the gender symbolised by the chosen tool. If the digging stick were chosen, she would be welcomed by the women, given female garb and name—and possibly trained as a shaman. They were known as nadles and thought to have the wisdom of both genders. Their training was in healing mental and physical illnesses and aiding in childbirth through the use of magical songs.[15] They were also said to be able to raise storms and to transform themselves into animals, plants and stones.

The ancient Greeks had theories on how such gender changes happened. Plato in his book *Symposium* had Aristophanes say: 'the male sprang from the sun and the female from the earth, while the gender of the one which was both male and female came from the moon, which partakes of the nature of both the Sun and Earth." Medieval Europe had another theory. Many of its doctors thought the uterus had seven cells: three cold cells for boys, three warm cells for girls and one for hermaphrodites.[16]

Childhood Dreams

In my childhood, I had no such knowledgeable elders around me and so was only able to transform myself into the equivalent of a boy. I can remember very little of my first three years between 1942 and 1945. Perhaps my brain has censored out the horror of living in wartime? While my father was away fighting the Japanese, my Mother and I lived in heavily bombed southern English coastal towns. I became a very sickly child and my Mother not much more than skin and bones as Dad's money failed to reach us. A journalist eventually wrote us up as a hard-luck story. This happily brought about Dad's return.

But the immediate consequence of this newspaper article was that our belongings were thrown into the street from an attic window as we were evicted by an angry landlady. We eventually found a refuge in a brothel, the only place that would give us a room. My Mother told me she admired the prostitutes for respecting her religious beliefs and her determination to remain faithful to my father. I remember only a dented aluminium colander I wore on my head when running to the bomb shelters.

My own earliest memories have no clear order but I can carbon-date them by the propensity of the giants within them of shrinking, as I grew older. Thus I calculate that my earliest memory must be walking hand in hand with my Mother when she was five times my height. Her ambitions for me were fuelled when I was three years old. I looked at a priest dressed splendidly in long skirts, my childhood world's poor equivalent of a shaman, and said; "I want to be like him". She immediately knew, with the inbuilt Geiger sense of the devout Irish, that I had a vocation to the Catholic priesthood. (The possibility did not occur to her that I might like to dress up like him.)

I also remember an early encounter with Mary, Christ's mother. When I was three my Mother left me in the care of nuns, sombre vast black creatures with heads enshrouded, who took me into my first schoolroom and told me to climb up black wrought iron legs onto a wooden desk seat. From this lofty perch I could see over a much graffitied desktop to a life-sized statue of a lady wearing a blue cloak and white tunic. She had arms outstretched and open hands. She was pastel faint, magically strange.

I knew my Mother revered her. Smaller statues of Mary were in every room at home. We were told that her divine Son could not refuse her so she was in practice as powerful. Jesus shared his Father's power, and she in love had His.

What is notable when we analyse our childhood memories? I clearly remember my first encounter with boys en masse. On my first day at a regular school I saw a group of them torturing wood lice by rolling them down an earthen bank. Why has this memory stayed so long? At that time I felt abandoned among aliens who had no sense of the preciousness of such tiny creatures. I hated that school so much that my parents soon shifted me to a more distant St. Francis Catholic Primary School under the walls of Maidstone Prison.

My brother Tony was born a year after the return from the war of my sandy-haired slender Dad. Tony's arrival was an epic-making event. In my earliest remembered dream, I watched while my fair-haired brother in a cream pram with black hood rolled through a gap in the side of a Maidstone bridge down into the Medway River. He then floated away

Moses-like past the old library. I then quietly walked on, hand in hand with my lofty four-times-my-height Mother, now her only child, to the centre where the red trolley buses congregated. When I recently described this dream to my Mother, she suggested it might have been triggered by a real life incident. She had walked out of a shop and down the street chattering with me, forgetting momentarily my brother in his pram.

When I dreamed this, our family lived in a post-war prefab—a low flat-roofed building of flimsy grey-white asbestos sheeting, clustering with others in a field, while we waited for a solid brick home on a housing estate. My few memories of this include watching hailstones bounce down our concrete front path and lying with measles behind curtained windows wondering why sunlight was bad for me. After about three years we moved to a two-story red brick council house at 30 Kent Avenue on the other side of town.

On the corner near our new home stood the grocery shop where we exchanged ration coupons, tiny stamps that I liked counting, for wartime shortages were still with us in the late 1940s. We also went to a government office to collect medicine bottles filled with concentrated orange juice or cod liver oil, part of an effort by the government to keep us kids healthy. They could stuff the cod liver oil. I remember vividly sickening teaspoons of it. However the orange juice nearly made up for it.

We played in the nearby Mote Park where we went tobogganing every winter. It had a mysterious cave shadowed by old trees in which we thought there were ancient bones. Nearby there was a lake and a stream with stepping-stones and, past this, a large old house shrouded in trees, the War Damage Commission, where Dad worked. Sometimes my brother and I timidly explored its gigantic rooms.

The government economised by not giving us inside doors downstairs. Instead hard breezeblocks edged the curtained doorways. One day my brother cracked his head against a corner of the entrance into the front room. My Mother, then still of relatively lofty height, put him in her lap as she sat on a kitchen stool. She stroked his blond hair. Underneath it was bright red, which made me very curious but not alarmed. He had to be rushed to hospital for stitches.

Then I dreamt that a lion escaped from a circus to make its den in our front room—a place reserved for formal occasions, such as Holy Mass or visits by relatives. Dad nailed planks criss-cross over the room's entrance to keep the lion in so it could not harm us. A jungle then grew behind the barricade. One day my brother Tony crawled under the bottom plank into the front-room jungle and presumably met the lion, for he never returned. I woke up convinced the lion was now on the giant wicker basket in my bedroom, ready to eat me. I woke the house, dispelled the lion, by screaming.

But when my second brother, Kevin arrived two years after Tony, I had no dreams in which he died or vanished. I no longer felt threatened by new arrivals, presumably because I had recovered from infantile jealousy, Mother remained close to me and chatted with me often and easily. We became a tightly knit happy family.

When I was about seven years of age, my parents told me they were thinking of us migrating to Australia. I dug in the back lawn towards Australia but found only a cracked drainpipe. I was later to have some of my most wonderful days travelling with the Aborigines that lived far below that drainpipe.

In this redbrick house I played a game in which I first tentatively explored my gender disquiet. I huddled with the next-door girl behind a redbrick wall in the front porch and secretly swapped clothes. I split her dress while struggling to get it over my head. She never told on me—and I never lost the secret feeling that I should be a girl.

Nowadays, my childhood seems to me to be a dream of a previous incarnation or perhaps a caterpillar existence. Looking back with the eyes of a woman, after spending most of my adult life as a woman, how else can I see my experience of "boyhood"?

Childhood Body Language

Although adult males never suspected me of being an infiltrator, young males were not so blinded by expectations. When I started at St. Francis, the Catholic primary school by Maidstone Prison, juvenile gender police ambushed me in the boys' playground, claimed I was a girl and tried to purge me violently from their midst

I don't know how I betrayed myself. Perhaps it was because I lacked male instincts. Maybe it was my body language. Whatever it was, the teasing boys had clearly a set of rules of which I was ignorant. I had no wish to compete but soon battlefield leaders approached to demand that I took part in their wars or else depart to the girls' playground.

One of them confronted me by the school door where I was waiting nervously for the bell to ring so I might escape their aggressive realm. "You goin' fight me. You yellow or somethin'?" Of course I did not want to fight. I knew it would be a massacre...

"No", I replied pragmatically. "Y'll beat me up."

Frustrated the bully said. "Yer fight me—or, or, yer let me punch yer"

"All right." I replied—quickly calculating that a single punch delivered cold would not hurt me as much as a full-scale battle. He pulled back his fist. Quizzed me once "You sure?" and when I nodded, I received just one surprised and lukewarm punch before the school bell allowed me to escape inside. My mother later told me she approved of this as a wise survival strategy. I do not remember my father's reactions to my un-macho behaviour—but I do not remember him as ever aggressive.

From then on I was teased mercilessly at school. The boys cruelly (and I now know accurately) called me "Patricia" instead of Pat, leaving me flummoxed, angry and confused. I protested loudly at their attempt to gender change me—while looking longingly over the playground wall that divided us from the girls. It seemed every bit as cruel as the wall that then divided Berlin.

However the adults did not share the bully's view of me as female for I could piss standing up. They thought this ability guaranteed me to be an authentic member of the ruling gender. They did not look for other indicators. They were thus more blinkered than the playground bully. They saw me as having a right to strut with men. I should have been pleased as so infiltrating the best paid of genders. My job prospects looked comparatively healthy. But instead I developed dreadful asthma and panted and gasped my way to school as I tried to cope with mysteriously feeling that somehow I was in the wrong playground.

My refusal to take part in male violence lasted throughout my youth. For example, seven years later, when I was fourteen, my brother Tony was caught by a gang of bullies in a wood under chalk cliffs near Folkestone. When I went back for him, these bullies demanded that I fight for his release. Instead I made a bargain. They could hit me once. This time my nose was broken and I was stretched upon the ground. But I got up, lied it did not hurt, and ran off with my brother, leaving behind a surprised and frustrated gang. For decades afterwards my nose had a tick inside it that only I could hear.

I puzzle still over the level of male aggression I experienced. "Male" hormones help create self-confidence in both men and women. But why are males seemingly uniquely pre-wired for physical aggression? It starts so early to affect boys that it seems that it cannot be completely accounted for by the social conditioning that reinforces, distorts and suppresses boys' instincts. Yet, when female brains are exposed to similar levels of "male" hormones, there are not the same aggressive reactions. (Except that both genders can be equally verbally aggressive.) Perhaps males have evolved a physical aggressive potential to protect the family? Biologists argue that aggression among male animals gives the strongest a better chance to perpetuate their genes, but I remain unconvinced that aggression among male humans has this effect. It seems more likely to repel the female.

Aboriginal Children and Initiation

Australia's Aborigines have their own ways of socialising boys. The central Australian peoples of the Warlpiri and the Arunta in the Northern Territory allow them to run free with little discipline during their first ten years. Then comes the time for them to be "turned around" into men through a circumcision ritual in which both men and women play a vital role. This rite gives the boys an adult set of responsibilities.[17]

The women's part in this ritual includes giving a boy his mother-in-law, thus complementing the action of the men who give the boy a "father-in-law" who circumcises him, all this before the boy obtains a wife or even a prospective wife! This is possible because Aboriginal communities have a kinship system of rights and obligations not based on blood relationships or even marriage. When a boy is given "in-laws", they say he receives adult responsibilities—and thus cannot continue to live as free as a child.

The Warpirri women's view of men is illustrated by their story of the legendary Rainbow Men who wooed women with dance and song and with brightly painted bodies. Sometimes a woman was thus persuaded to live with one of them—perhaps on her own land. But sometimes a Rainbow Man forced a woman to listen to him by spearing her in the leg. He would then woo her with all the skill he could muster. If he won her, she would go to live on his land. But sometimes his efforts were rejected and she went to live in the Single Women's camp from which men were banned.[18] (More about these camps later

Thus women said men were like the lightning storms of the Rainbow men, as changeable as the desert weather and as liable to do damage. (In their land there are sometimes the most violent of dry thunder and lightning storms.) Men might be kind; they might be violent. They were not to be completely trusted. Women believed that they should work with men to turn boys into responsible adults who would not inflict storms on them. Likewise men's legends depicted women as scary—but necessary.

Aboriginal communities are extended families formed by varying elegant systems of sections and subsections and sometimes of four or eight "skins". Members of one skin group are "brothers and sisters" to the members of a certain other skin, are not allowed to marry members of a certain skin, are "fathers or mothers" to members of a different skin and so on. It is a system that can give adult responsibilities and rights to even a stranger joining a community. Generally several boys of the same "skin" are initiated together in a ritual that may take ten days or more to complete.

Girls seemingly did not need such a large spectacular community ritual in order to make them an adult. (But Bell suggested that, since the Christian missions particularly targeted women, it might have been harder for them to continue their rituals.) There are many different Aboriginal nations and cultures in Australia so initiation rites can vary, but sometimes men may help dress the girls' hair before their menarche ceremonies. The senior women then take the girls to private women-only camps. The girls would be painted with elaborate signs linking them to their ancestral land. There would be special songs. Each girl might also have sacred signs burnt into an arm or incised onto the back while she stayed in the birthing squat. During this she will never cry out. It seems it may well be a ritual preparation for birthing children—which is also accompanied by a sacred woman's rite.[19]

Diane Bell, with the permission of the women, told of the male initiation rites in which she participated. She learnt how the mother of a boy tells the community when her son is ready for initiation. When the men collect a boy for the ritual, the mother sends her power with him by using a specific hand gesture. Later, during the men's ritual dances, women send their power out in gestures called "lifting up the business" and "sending out the power." They can stop the ritual if they are dissatisfied with the way the men are doing it. The selected "mothers-in-law" rub their ochred bodies against the boys' backs to transfer energy before the central ritual begins. Every night the "mothers" collect the boys from the men, carrying them to the women's camp where they are sat in the laps of the senior "mothers" while the "sisters" feed them. After the circumcision, the women erased the marks on the ground where they say the boys were "damaged". Finally the women completed the initiation process with a ritual in which the boys are given their mothers-in-law. Only after this final female rite is a boy "turned around" into a man.[20]

Whether such a ritual would have prevented my classmates from cruelly teasing me, I do not know—nor do I know how such a rite would have affected me. I remember having two significant rituals as a Roman Catholic child. The first was my first Holy Communion. I remember feeling left out and jealous in my seventh year when I saw the girls in pretty white dresses lining up before church. I had to wear the most boring of suits. As for my Confirmation, when the bishop put his hand on my head, this had nothing like the impact that an Aboriginal-style initiation would have had!

Boys and Aggression

I did not form any dislike of boys as a tribe, despite being teased. Yet asthma made my body treat the very air as a poison and dangerous to inhale from the time I started school. My body and my spirit then seemed like separate entities. I had to force air down my reluctant throat while coping with peer pressure that would force me into the male mould. It seems that I was not gagging at the invisible air but rather at the invisible social presumption that imprisoned me among males.

The boys enforcing gender law were as vigilant as the Chinese youths that denounced parents for behaving contrary to Mao's Red Book. I suspect this gender policing was particularly strong among males in cultures dominated by patriarchal religions. Girls rarely if ever reject another girl as too boyish, perhaps because tomboy behaviour is not a threat to them. So why is this gender policing more important to boys? Was it because boys are less secure in their socially mandated role? Was it because males have elevated their genitalia into a justification for supremacy and are frightened this theory will not stand the light of day?

Some explain male aggression by saying that males evolved with fighting skills so they could protect woman and children. But it was not chivalry these young boys were practising in my playground. These bullies despised girls rather than reverenced them. If they had learnt they should protect girls, it was because they believed that women were weak—and thought less of them for it. I was less than a boy in their eyes because I would not fight. I was perhaps a threat to their self-image.

Could it be that this male aggression be inherent with the possession of the phallus? Is a man naturally the aggressive partner because he has to penetrate the female? In my experience, many men seem to have no control over when they have erections and when they need to penetrate. The penis seems to have a life of its own. Some men talk as if a woman is but the ground they conquer and seed. But for me they over exalt their semen. It is but a half-life that seeks the half-life of the female egg. And the vagina too can be aggressive. It can seize, can hold and milk the male of his semen. Any sexually active woman knows that she is not passive.

But at that time I puzzled over why this boy in a scruffy fight-torn jacket should taunt me by changing my name into a female form. I felt compelled to deny the truth of his assertion in order to protect my social standing—and my sanity. I had learnt that if one had a penis, one was a boy. I thought my inner voice telling me I should be a girl was a minor form of insanity. Yet, I would have loved to be allowed to play with the girls at school. My playmate at home was the girl next door. We played much more interesting games than those played in the boys' playground. I could only observe other girls playing over the playground wall but they seemed to be playing games of co-operation, skipping, nurturing, singing and fussing about their clothes. I did not understand the fussing about clothes—I still am not fussed about clothes.

There is naturally anger in me at being ostracised, marginalized—not simply recognised as different. I would have loved it if boys had not been so aggressive and not typed me as a weakling. I would have loved it if I could have explored my strange girlish feelings without fear of taunt. In my secondary school I would be rejected apparently for Irishness, for being of the Catholic religion, for asthma, for girlishness and for religiousness. The fear of being rejected has haunted me ever since. It is the demon that I am hopefully exorcising in writing this book.

My parents decided not to force me to use a lazy eye by putting a patch on my good eye since it would make me liable to more teasing. They thought it was asthma that had made me an outsider, a target for taunts. But asthma was an effect, not a cause, of my being teased as "Patricia". My parents did not dream the children had diagnosed me correctly, that I could really be Patricia.

My severe asthma perplexed the doctors. They did countless tests in vast cream-walled hospital rooms. They administered eighty deep intra-muscular injections against allergies. The asthma continued. Then the white-coated men decided I had asthma because I was mentally hyperactive (I think this meant "thinking too much"), and this had to be stopped. It was true I spoke too fast. I had not learnt how slowly people heard. I can remember deciding to talk fast in order to share more ideas! So my brain was put under suspension orders. I was doped with phenobarbitone—a drug more suitable for epileptics if for anyone at all. For two or more key childhood years I was prevented from learning to read or write. Haze enveloped my life.

But thank God parental ambition impeded these fiendish white coats. My Mother's ambition was fine-tuned by her memory of how I said that I wanted to be in the priesthood. Anyhow, I really did want to be one of this spiritual elite. Catholic priests were for me androgynous beings of high prestige—and my parents highly approved of my ambition.

My Mother and Dad stopped my daily drugging when I was about nine years old because they felt these drugs might impede God's great designs. They determined that these would be fulfilled more easily if I made it to a Grammar School, since there I could study Latin and get the qualifications needed for entry to a seminary to study for the priesthood. I am glad they took this initiative. If I had been drugged for much longer, I would have been seriously educationally handicapped.

Shortly after I stopped taking the drug, I remember holding the hand of a teacher of lofty height as she led me from the dunce group to a top group as my mind raced in hyper-gear to tear to shreds the haze around me. My brother Tony recalls how astonished he was when his "silent brother began to talk and talk".

The most valuable gift my parents gave me was the lesson that I could do nothing better with my life than to give it to serving and loving others, fighting oppression and vanquishing injustice—and this I could do by becoming a priest. They also taught me the equally valuable lesson that it would be a blasphemy against our inner sacred nature to give priority to the earning of money over spiritual work.

I had three principal religious beliefs when I knelt small in church behind great wooden pews or trotted up to light candles. The first was that we had a very powerful and invisible Father God who cared for us. The second followed from this—that humans were one family. The third was that we should show we loved God by loving all as family. I did not wonder about such things, as how there could be a God the Father and no Goddess or Divine Mother. God was all-powerful therefore this was a silly question. God loved us all and therefore was to be run to—not run from.

My job at home on special days was to light the altar candles whenever God came symbolically into our living room. This happened when the priest came and consecrated the bread and wine during Holy Mass or when he brought us already consecrated bread as Holy Communion. These acts endorsed the sacredness of our family life. I thus saw God not as a stranger, but an honoured Guest.

I grew to love the idea behind the Mass, the sacred meal that bonds us together. I did not need, and thought complicated, the Church's teaching that God became one with the blessed bread and wine by a miracle of "transubstantiation" that made the substance of the food vanish. Surely the reality of God was always available for us to know and touch and share? I quietly dropped the idea of hell into a too hard don't really believe it's real basket. I did not see my parents as figures dispensing punishment, therefore my God did not dispense punishment.

After I came off the tranquillising drugs, I was not always that bright. One day, when I saw thick smoke coming out of a toilet block, I set out to save the school. Thus began my first great mission. I raced down the lane that led to the fire station. A vast burly man behind a lofty desk questioned me and then a red fire engine clanged out. Amazingly the headmaster was not that impressed. Next day he swept through the school asking what child had called the fire engine? When I raised my hand, he reminded me that the telephone had been invented. He explained that if I had come to see him first, the fireworks that had caused the smoke could have been extinguished much less dramatically.

I set fire to a Christmas tree too. This was merely a miscalculated scientific experiment. My parents parked me one morning by the front room window, gave me matches and told me to light the altar candles when the priest arrived with Holy Communion. Sitting there bored, I noticed a thin wisp of cotton-wool snow hanging down from the tree. I wondered if it burnt. My undrugged brain was unsafe with curiosity. The cotton burnt like lightning. My scream brought my Dad leaping down the stairs. For the next twenty years my parents had to hide under the settee the burn marks in the carpet made when the tree was wrapped in it to extinguish the flames.

When I was eleven, we all moved to Folkestone on the Kentish coast where I was to start at a grammar school since I was, surprisingly, one of the three boys in our class to pass the eleven-plus exam.

At this new school I was no longer taunted for femininity. I had discovered how to seem masculine. Soon puberty arrived—apparently sooner among my classmates than with me. I was now perplexed at the erotic visions that boys possessed that seemed to make them both deride women and be fascinated by them. I put my incomprehension down to my Catholicism. I was the only Catholic in the class so wondered if my religion protected me? The desire to masturbate also evaded me. I was not even curious.

The chronic asthma kept me out of the world of teams and competition that absorbed many of my classmates. I now think the asthma was due to the strain of living constantly in disguise. It would vanish totally when I changed my gender roles. In my teens my parents wisely insisted that I went to school even when racked by asthma. On the many bad days, I would manage to walk just twenty steps, satchel-backed and wheezing, then had to sit, steady my pounding chest, regain my breath, and repeat this again and again until I had covered the half-mile to the bus stop. Worried householders, seeing me sitting panting on their walls, sometimes came out to offer me cups of tea! But once I'd reached school and was distracted by study, the asthma would slide away and vanish. My parents did well in forcing me to keep going. The boy with asthma who lived opposite was not kept active and had a lung collapse. I was also never given asthma drugs to inhale.

In my years at the grammar school, I did not put up my nose at maledom. I accepted at my conscious level that I was a boy as my world told me. I believed my secret inner being was a fantasy to which I was mysteriously addicted.

I had escaped from female conditioning but male conditioning affected me. Looking back, I think it made me more centred on fulfilment through work than through relationships and more insensitive socially. I remember with shame how I was sometimes more concerned to teach others lessons rather than to understand them. Emotions were to be controlled. I was not to cry in public. I had to be tough towards myself. War also entered my fantasies. I dreamed of commanding artillery and putting a quick end to any who threatened our land. I learnt men fight to protect the weak. The supposed heroism of war justified my dreaming of violence. I had by now learnt through bitter experience that to be feminine in public was to be weak and soppy—so it was a wonder that my wish to become a girl survived.

These same gender stereotypes infiltrated the Macintosh computer program called 'Thunder" used to spell-check the early drafts of this book. Its thesaurus told me that "male" meant "characterised by the energy and drive considered typical of a male." Its synonyms and related words were "virile, decisive, forceful, potent". Its antonyms were "effeminate, womanish, weak, impotent." "Manly" was defined as showing no fear in danger. But female was defined simply as a "female human being" with no heroic associations. Its synonyms were women, lady, and gentlewoman and there were no antonyms. A "woman" had, as it's first meaning, "a man's regular partner" in sex. "Womanly" had no entry.

As a child I dreamed of fighting evil. I snuggled myself into the dugouts and old machine gun nests overlooking the English Channel, and imagined how I would have defeated the evil ones. I explored the Martello Towers built against Napoleon, one of which stood across the road from my home at 9 White Cliff Way in Folkestone. I played in the ruins of a Roman mansion a hundred yards from home, as well as in the ramparts of a prehistoric hill fort some five miles away. Much later, when I sought to cross the gender divide, I did not like admitting these fantasies to the psychologist who assessed my suitability for treatment, since I had believed for years that girls don't have such warlike fantasies.

On the way to school, in our black jackets and mandatory caps crowned with a red star, we were abused as 'grammar bugs' by the children who went to secondary modern schools after failing the eleven-plus exam. This teasing made me walk faster. My grammar school was founded by William Harvey. He had discovered, so we were told, that blood went round in circles within our bodies. Our school song did not celebrate this. Rather it picked some obscure relative of his that stopped French blood circulating at Trafalgar. The names of the French ships that fell victim to his iron balls resounded from our lips as we 'sung of the name and the fame of our time honoured school' on prize giving days, in Leas Cliff Hall in sight of the cliffs of France, a very British roar of defiance made in total disregard to the many French tourists in our town.

In my final years at this school, despite my secret wish to fight ogres, I wanted female mates. My parents saw this wish as originating from my pubescent hormones. They gently (but persuasively) told me I had the choice of either female company or of membership of the highest spiritual elite. Since I both wanted to be a priest and to please my parents, and had no phallic sexual drive, I gave up the opportunity to go to school dances and mix with girls. My own secret desire to be a girl was deeper buried in a corner of my mind.

The only man I really got to know was my father. He was a gentle man, red-haired, handsome and I loved him. I think with hindsight that I loved him as would most young daughters. I was disappointed to find him somewhat distant. He never understood how I wanted to be close to him. He sometimes showed me tried to fight. He once held me in a grip supposed to disable me and challenged me to escape. I bought my foot up sharply behind me and discovered how testicles made men vulnerable— much to our mutual shock and my total and apologetic horror.

A part of my male initiation was to learn from my father to put my mother and other women on a pedestal. I learnt that although women might be physically weaker, they were closely connected to the springs of life and therefore were the foundation on which the Church was built. Mother (we were forbidden to say Mum) was the mainstay of our Irish Catholic household. She not only controlled the purse strings, she gave us our religion. She had converted my father to Catholicism. We all took a full part in parish life, taking on as a family the task of transforming a local railwayman's club hall into a church every weekend by pushing the piano to the back of the stage and balancing a table on beer crates to make it into an altar.

Adolescent Sexuality

So what of my own sexuality? How did I deal with puberty? Surely a flood of testosterone overwhelmed my hesitations? No, this did not happen. I was excluded from this flood perhaps by some hormonal element, brain factor or gene. I was physically mature but unawakened sexually; a Peter Pan preserved in pre-puberty until I was nearly 30 years of age. Masturbation remained to me a totally foreign concept. However I was not so entirely neutered that my penis could not occasionally embarrass me by getting up to unordered manoeuvres, like an unruly younger brother that I had boringly to look after.

As my classmates moved through puberty, I found myself increasingly the alien. After gym classes most of the lads went into the communal shower. I never did. I did not want to display my body. I felt very shy about it. It was not that I felt any hatred or disgust for it. I felt it was a reasonable piece of creation, all right in its own way. But it did not seem true. I did not see my face in it. I was consequently as shy with boys as I would have been if my body then had been a girl's.

To my classmates it must have seemed that I was an innocent abroad. But there was no virtue in this. I was simply a mismatch—a girl not able to relate to boys as a girl, not treated as a girl, disinterested in being a boy among boys. I learnt by observing my male companions that women may have been put on pedestals in order to protect them. When the boys passed packs of cards depicting nude women they were clearly motivated by forces that I did not experience.

But other changes happened. I remember the fear I felt when I noted that my nipples were becoming darker and more sensitive. I went to my father for reassurance and he told me it was common in puberty. I did not know if he said this only to reassure me. I was secretly scared that my body was striving to mirror my private dreaded wishes.

Wounding Birth Rites

There are birth rites in other cultures that I am glad I avoided. If I had been born a girl in Sudan I could have been sewn up to keep me from any genital sexual act before I was very painfully unbound for my husband. If I had been born a Jewish "male", my infant penile flesh would have been cut with a sharp knife as if to brand my seed as Jewish! If I had been born Muslim or Aboriginal Australian it could have been later, at puberty, that I would be called on to demonstrate "manly" courage while enduring painful penile cuts. If I had been born among certain Aboriginal tribes I might have had to endure the practice of sub-incision. This entails the creation of a scar in the penile flesh called interestingly a vulva—but more about this later.

Why did so many cultures circumcise males? Some claimed that circumcision was carried out for cleanliness but this never convinced me. Why not then clip off our ears? They too can collect dirt. Labia have to be washed, why not the penile skin? But others said that men developed these puberty rites in an age when female menstrual blood was recognised as sacred, rich and fertile, so that men too might also shed sacred genital blood. There is a theory in anthropology that since women had a natural initiation at menarche that gave them power, some Aboriginal nations subjected their boys to a sacred genital blood shedding ritual so that they might also take on this same magic. A more sympathetic interpretation is that, for Aborigines, the blood of menstruation and the blood of circumcision unite the genders in the magic of creation. During these rituals, the bodies of participants are painted with ochre patterns—and this natural red pigment can represent the blood of the earth.

The anthropologist Chris Knight told the following story learnt from Aborigines. One day two women went to wash themselves in a waterhole. As the first was washing her period started and her blood went into the water. When the smell of blood reached the Rainbow Serpent that lives under the water, it started to wake up. Then the second woman began to bleed and the Serpent rose in full power and swallowed the two women alive. Some will stop the story here, saying this is a warning against polluting waterholes. But the real story goes further and much deeper. While the women were inside the Rainbow Serpent, it continued its work of creating the earth. When the women stopped bleeding, they left the Serpent and were unharmed—and often fertile. In other words, while women are bleeding they are united to the Creating Energy, one with the blood that is also shed at childbirth.[21]

When Aboriginal women shared stories with me at a sacred women's waterhole by Uluru (Ayers Rock) from which they said the Rainbow Serpent emerged, I could not be told by them what the men taught the boys about blood, so I am not sure if their nation had the story recorded by Chris Knight. He concluded by telling how the men of a particular Aboriginal nation taught boys that the reason for the blood shedding in circumcision was to give them a share in the spiritual power naturally possessed by women.

Poet and Law woman Daisy Utemorra, an elder of the Wandjina people of the Kimberleys in Northwest Australia, is reported to have said that only after men have obtained the highest degrees of male initiation "do they become eligible for initiation into women's law."[22] I myself was told at Uluru that only when men have grey hair could they learn the women's Law—and I think they said it was likewise for women.

The Aboriginal view of menstrual blood was thus vastly different from that of many early Christian leaders who saw naturally shed female blood as an impurity. The link between the menstrual cycle and the lunar cycle made menstrual blood even more dangerous in their eyes, for they saw all things natural as belonging to a "fallen" Satan-dominated world. Aborigines saw nature very differently. For them, their blood-like red earth symbolised the sacred power of life. The national Aboriginal flag has red for earth on its lower half, black for the people on the upper half—and in its centre a yellow sun.

In North America every Western Apache girl once had a puberty cere-mony, or na'ii'ees ('preparing her,' or 'getting her ready'), known popularly as the Sunrise Dance. During this ritual she was seen as embodying the Mother of all, the *Is dzán naadleeshe'*, the Changing Woman, who once lived all alone. Her power was transferred to the pubescent girl through songs sung by the *diiyin* ('one who has power') medicine man. The thirty-two or more songs were believed to have first been sung by Changing Woman and were collectively known as *gohzhoosih* ("songs of beauty and goodness"). This power resided in the girl for four days after the ceremony. During this period the pubescent girl personified the Changing Woman. She danced, ran to the cardinal points and was blessed with pollen. She was said to be able at the time of the ritual to cure the sick and bring rain.

I do not know why a medicine man was needed to pass on this female power to the girl. It could be that this was part of a gender balance or per-haps it was different earlier. The key point here is that the Power of Creation was seen as female and as possessed by the young woman. There is no hint that she was in some way tainted. The Celts similarly held that a woman at her marriage held the power of the Goddess—and thus called her "Bride", their name for the Goddess Mother of all.

Jews were prudishly gender-balanced in that they treated as unclean both male seminal fluid and the female monthly bleeding. But the Book of Genesis recorded a national Covenant in which men were given a unique role. "You must circumcise the flesh of your foreskin, and that will be the sign of the covenant between myself and you."[23] This was not a purely Jewish custom. The ancient Ethiopians and Egyptians practised "from the first" the circumcision of children, according to the Greek his-torian Herodotus, and may have taught the custom to the people of Palestine when their country was still called Syria.[24]

There is another interpretation of this. Women needed no initiation for they were of their nature part of the Jewish nation. This, with the power of the Jewish Mother, may indicate that once the Jewish nation was a matri-archy. But if so, that was a long time ago. Today it may be more related to the concept of women as merely the field in which a man puts his seed.[25] The women's birthing blood is now seen as a contamination. The Rabbinical practice is that "when a woman at childbirth bears a boy, she will be unclean for seven days, as unclean as she is during the time of her menstrual infirmity. On the eighth day the flesh of his foreskin shall be circumcised".[26] It does not matter if a man is born with little foreskin. The important part is the shedding of the boy's blood, for it represents the blood of the Covenant. The Mohel who does the cutting will ensure some of the boy's blood is removed. Again there is an Egyptian precedent. When the Sun God cut himself, the Gods Hu and Sia "sprung into existence from the blood that fell from his virile member."[27] It was said that circumcision increases virility. Abraham had his fertility restored by it in extreme old age. Philo held that "nations that practice circumcision greatly increase in population". He likened it to the pruning of a young fruit tree.[28]

It is clear that the possession of a penis is seen as a defining quality of male in religions that practice circumcision. I am not at all sure of how this affects their religious views on transsexuality. If it is true that our brains play the major role in defining our gender identity, then, in rare cases, they must be circumcising girls.

Some societies deliberately practice a female circumcision—it is still happening in closed communities in London's East End and in many parts of Africa. But this is no celebration of female sexuality. Rather it is a horrific practice designed to limit a woman's sexual pleasure by cutting off her clitoris. In Somalia this was said to enable her to focus on the "higher pleasures" of satisfying her husband and on vaginal sex. In 19th Century England, senior male doctors recommended it for girls to prevent hysteria, epilepsy and varicose veins. They cauterised clitorises with white-hot irons in order to prevent masturbation. Isaac Baker-Brown, a London surgeon who became the president of the London Medical Society, in 1858 published details on 48 cliterectomies he had performed. A French doctor and Catholic Trappist monk, J.C. Debreyne, recommended this practice, saying that the clitoris had no role in procreation and only helped stimulate lust![29] In 1998 an estimated 70% of Egyptian women had suffered this operation.

There is a vastly different attitude among the Australian Aborigines. The women of Uluru laughingly had told me one of their sacred caves "looks just like a vagina" when they took me into it to tell me their stories of creation.

Christians have no formal celebrations of menarche or of male maturity, but in western England I journeyed to see the Kilpeck church south of Hereford that has in its outside wall an ancient image of a woman holding her vagina open, a Sheila-na-gig. Some today interpret such sculptures as warnings against lust, but when they were put up "all the references to them indicate they were highly regarded, revered images".[30] There are hundreds of these in ancient churches and castles in Eire, England and France. The Kilpeck church also has a basin shaped like a pregnant woman's stomach, taken from a still older forest sanctuary. It thus seems there was a much more open attitude towards depicting female sexuality.

Gender role re-assignment may have been a sacred ritual in ancient cultures, but what has it been like since the Churches came to rule? Some Fathers of the Church, such as St Augustine of Hippo, made outraged attacks on the transgendered priestesses found in pagan temples, calling them "perverts" who had deserted the male sex. Then silence came to reign. In the first half of the 20th century electric shock therapy was used to try to "cure" people who said they were in the wrong gender. In the 21st century, as I have mentioned, children born with genitals that are not standard-issue are operated on before their parents take them home from hospital, so that they will hopefully grow up as standard-issue men and women. This is still happening—so let's look at this more closely.

Child Surgery and the "Intersexed."

The 1988 Standard Surgical Operating Guidelines allow our surgeons to define a newborn child's gender solely by the size of penis or clitoris. Their confidence came from the theory that infants are psychologically gender-neutral at birth. The presumption is that if we can be vaginally penetrated or penetrate, we then need nothing else but appropriate conditioning to grow up happily as men or women. (A theory pioneered in 1955 by John Money of Johns Hopkins University.) This operation is done soon after birth in conditions of a medical emergency, with the parents not always told what precisely is happening.[31] It has to be done quickly in the UK, because after the birth certificate is issued, the gender designated on it cannot be changed (unlike in most of the rest of Europe.).

Official medical guidelines in the US and the UK allow surgical intervention if a child has a penis less than 2.5cm (1 inch) long at birth—even if the child has testicles and XY hormones. The presumption is that a boy with a short penis is going to suffer from life-long inadequacy. They are "cured" by being given a vagina by surgery, for, as one surgeon accurately but crudely put it, it is easier to make a hole than build a pole. Female hormones are then given at puberty.

These same guidelines also allow surgery to the newborn girl if she is born with a clitoris over 0.9 cm in length. It may be surgically shortened, removing the most sensitive and erotic part, since a long clitoris is presumed to be a potentially embarrassing "deformity". Alternatively, some children may be assigned to the male gender because of the length of their clitoris. Such children have ovaries removed and are given male hormones at puberty.

These surgical guidelines run in the face of the old wisdom that the energy and dreams of a "different" child should be monitored while the child grows up to determine what is its appropriate gender—and also in the face of recent scientific discoveries that confirm this ancient wisdom. It is now known that the human brain is physically different in men and women—meaning that the surgeon sculpting a baby's genitals without regard to its brain may well be assigning it to a different gender than its brain. Post-mortem examination of the brains of transsexuals revealed that their brains are of the opposite gender-type to their genitals. Those growing up with this discordance seemed to know this instinctively. Their instincts are revealed through the dreams that the shamans of old were trained to recognise. The magic such unusual people then have to achieve is to learn to blindly trust their instincts, despite the evidence of mirrors. When they follow their instincts, their problem is nearly always resolved.

Those who change female to male roles are much less documented than are the reverse—perhaps because this change in less threatening to the system, perhaps because there are fewer of them, as is suggested by some studies. But there could also be a social reason for this discrepancy. Women can dress more freely in male clothes so the discordance may not be so visible.

It was an accepted modern theory until recently that all human embryos were by default female. The theory went that boys were formed in the womb when a gene triggered hormones to change a basically female body into male. It was thought that originally, in the early days of evolution, there was only one gender until the 'y" gene evolved to be different from the "x" gene. But this theory did not explain why some males have XX chromosomes, so a finer gene mechanism was sought.

Recent research suggested that the human embryo has initially the foundations for both sets of genitals. Then, at six to eighth weeks, a gene trigger prompts first the destruction of one foundation and then the forming of the other into a set of genitals. Some four weeks later another hormonal surge formed the brain along gender specific lines. This explained "transsexuals" as those whose brains formed on a different gender pattern to their genitals—or to put it another way; our Creatrix sang a different song when she formed us in the womb. This theory appealed to me, for it seemed to be the one that fitted best with my experience. The 'intersexed' were then those whose genitals were not clearly defined by their development within the womb. The gender of both the intersexed and the transsexual would be ultimately be determined by the gender of their brains.

Ill-advised modern theories have inflicted great suffering on those born "intersexed". An intersexed woman, Cheryl Chase, wrote: "Surgical and hormonal treatment allows parents and doctors to imagine that they have eliminated the child's intersexuality. Unfortunately the surgery is immensely destructive of sexual sensation and of the sense of bodily integrity...I find myself forced to wonder whether a concept of sexual normalcy that defines the sex organs of up to 4% of newborn infants as "defective" is not itself defective. Intersex specialists are busily snipping and trimming infant genitals to fit the Procrustean bed that is our cultural definition of gender...Those I have located have told me that they feel most lucky to have escaped with their bodies intact"[32]

A person surgically assigned at birth to the male sex stated: "Since I had been raised as a male I was given testosterone, to see how I reacted. I cannot describe the sense of horror and the feeling that my entire being was being raped, which I experienced from being endocrinologically mutated against my will. I reacted so badly that they decided it might be better if I were a girl and so now I was given that choice."[33]

Another wrote: "I call myself a lab rat because that is how intersexed kids are treated. Tested, photographed, examined, tested again, photographed some more...It was the experience of being so dehumanised, which was so damaging I never uttered a peep about being intersexed to anyone, not a word. Ever. It was something that I seemed completely incapable of doing. It was unthinkable to even think about doing such a thing. Talking means death. Intersexed people don't talk. It is one of the Mysteries. I never went on a date, had sex, or responded with anything but fear and anxiety to any man or woman who indicated that they might like to get close to me, either as a friend or a potential lover. They might find out about my terrible dark secret. I seemed normal, went to school and did well, had casual friends, all the time living in fear and shame."

In 1996 I visited in hospital a woman labelled a "transsexual", who was undergoing painful surgery to correct the surgery she had as an infant to make her look like a male baby. On another occasion I met a man who at birth was wrongly labelled female and given female hormones when female puberty did not occur. In mid-life both these victims were adjusting themselves back to what they believed was their true gender by means of so-called "sex-change" operations. In both cases they had instinctively known all their lives that something was very wrong. They were both victims of medical errors. Both were also victims of an official refusal to correct the gender given on their UK birth certificates.

In a 1998 UK legal case, it was decided that the birth certificate could be changed from male to female in the case of a child born with male chromosomes, testicles but no penis, assigned to the male gender at birth, but brought up as a girl from one year of age and given female hormones because of the lack of a penis. Hopefully her mother took note of her behaviour and found it female before taking this action. Otherwise it seemed it was solely the lack of a penis that made the authorities define her as female.

The study I briefly mentioned above carried out though post mortems on "male to female" transsexuals not only found they had female shaped brains, but also discovered that the brains of gay males were typically male-shaped.[34] It was also determined that this brain shaping was due to pre-birth factors, such as exposure to high female hormones at the time of the brain's formation within the womb.

It would be a mistake to consider "male" hormones exclusively male—simply because we have labelled them as male—and likewise for 'female' hormones. Androgens are at home in every female body but at a lesser level than in men. Pre-birth exposure to 'male" hormones, at lesser levels than those that change the gender of the brain, may help create women with good spatial perception and more aggression. "Female" hormones may also help a male express emotion and empathy.

Our bodies are delightfully complex. Why do we try to simplify? Chromosomes control the gift of hormones to embryos. If there were only two gender sets of chromosomes then deciding the gender of the child would be easier—but again nature loves diversity. There are more than just XX or XY humans—there are XXY and XYY and more. One human in 500 does not have XX or XY chromosomes. Some people have both.[35] There is a specific part of the brain that is a very differently sized in males and females. This is in the BSTc in the hypothalamus. In post mortems it was found to be the same size in "ordinary" females and "male to female" transsexuals. The research excluded both post-birth factors and hormone intake after birth and concluded that it must have been determined pre-birth. This part was found to have a major role in regulating certain hormones and gender behaviour but not one's sexual preference for a partner Males have about twice as much of this brain component, no matter if heterosexual or homosexual.

Another difference between male and female brains lies in the links between the brain hemispheres. Women have many more links than males, seemingly allowing women to use both hemispheres at once easier than can men. These links are in part of the brain known as the corpus callosum. The difference in brain structures between men and women is also witnessed by the discovery that injury to the same area of the brain typically robs women and men of different mental facilities. Again, "male to female" transsexuals brains are identical to female in this regard. The equivalent research seems not to have been done for "female to male" transsexuals.

This chromosome variety in humans proved a nightmare for the International Olympic Committee. From 1968 it required female athletes to produce a certificate that said they had XX chromosomes. No similar qualification was required for men. But this had to be reconsidered when the World Student Games was forced legally to reinstate Maria Martinez Patino, a woman they had disqualified in 1985 because she was XY, despite her having no outward signs of masculinisation. It became even more difficult to tell the genders apart when it was discovered that a person with XX chromosomes could look entirely male due to the AGS syndrome, in which an XX child is born sensitive to androgens rather than to oestrogens. The Committee ignored this finding, as it was not worried about "women" passing as "men". Scientists also thought males came about through a feature called SRY on the Y gene—but then found it could be on an X—and even be missing. Now they think other genes may be also involved such as SOX9 (as of 1999).

Women athletes were shocked when five women out of 2,406 tested "male" in the 1992 Barcelona Olympics, as did another eight in the 1996 Atlanta games. Many of those who tested "male| had thought all their lives that they were entirely female. Since then the Committee's Athletes' Commission has urged its parent organization to do away with sex analysis entirely and to discover impostors by observing urination during drug testing. Then, after a threat by women athletes to boycott the gender assessment team, the Committee decided for the Australian Olympics to drop universal compulsory gender testing for women athletes.

The discovery that humans grow up to be males or females in different ways was well known to ancients but sadly forgotten in Western society. In ancient times the elders knew of black cohosh, the oestrogen rich herb used in North America to help those whose bodies make insufficient of this hormone. In England the hops used for beer similarly contain oestrogens.

The idea that it is "abnormal" to be born intersexed or transsexual suggests that it would be good if such children could be "cured" in the womb. This ignores the functionality of societies that accept such people as healthy and normal. It also ignores the wide variety in gender expressions and sexualities that naturally occurs among birds and animals. Bruce Bagemihl documented over 400 species with wide ranging variation in his book *Animal Homosexuality and Natural Diversity*. He concluded that an exuberance of sexual expression is a natural feature of a healthy biological system giving it greater balance and vitality.

Our bodies may set our gender, but conditioning influences how we express our gender identity. One way is through bonding with others of the same gender. This did not happen to me. It was only in my mid-teens that I acquired a few gentle and intellectual young men as friends. I much regret I had no great bonding with my gentle father. I have no idea if this lack of bonding was caused by my different instincts. When I remember him now, I dearly wish it had been permitted to me to bond with him as a daughter.

Dreams of a Catholic Child

By my mid-teens I had become the eldest of five children. Three brothers had arrived and then finally a sister. We played together, stayed together, prayed together too. I was arrogantly proud of our close-knit family. In the Irish tradition my mother's ambitions dominated, so every one of us children wanted to give ourselves to God, seen inevitably as the Church. My three younger brothers were also to attempt the training to become priests. My sister would think to become a nun but would decide to become a surgeon and stay at home to look after Mother after Dad died. My brothers did not get as far as I did within the Church. I went further, perhaps because I was the most naive.

We had all the usual Catholic accompaniments at home to remind us of the sacred, such as blessed candles, St Christopher medals, holy water from Lourdes, pictures of the Sacred Heart. I remember my Dad used to be able to say a decade of the Rosary in a minute flat in our ever-expanding evening prayers. Blithely ignorant of attributed guilt, I remained unaware that every one else was praying "Holy Mary, pray for us sinners now." I was saying "pray for us since now." I did not feel like a sinner, and I was deaf to any allusion that I might be.

My mother also passed on to me the knowledge of spirits, specifically of the many angels who looked after us. They did so as part of the providence of the Creator. My mother gave them credit for many happenings—such as preventing clothes from falling off the clothesline into the mud. In the older traditions of these islands, different names were given to such guardian beings.

We were told to respect angels and dread devils. I learnt that priests had the power to throw out devils. But for me angels and devils were of no great importance. From what my parish priest explained, it seemed angels were bleached and faded effigies of spiritual power and devils were angels past their use-by-date. Today I understand they represent an ancient world-view that shaped early Catholicism by setting armies of good angels against armies of evil angels. A 1998 survey reported that 69% of Americans believed in angels with two thirds of these believing in personal guardian angels.[36, 37]

My mother helped forge me as a rebel. After carefully studying my father's genealogy, she told me that I was not just Catholic but five-eighths Irish. This made me the only Irish kid in my class as well as the only Catholic. Her father had been born in Falls Road in Belfast, in the heart of Irish nationalism. She took me to medieval churches and told me that King Henry VIII had stolen these from us. I learnt that the English had taken our Celtic land. The centuries that had passed since these injustices were as nothing to her.

At Grammer School I was thus an outsider on religious and nationalist grounds as well as being asthmatic. I had learnt by now to hide my secret gender identity and was no longer gender-teased, despite being slender built and smiling disconcertingly often for a boy—thus giving me the nickname of "Smiler". But many boys still perceived me as different and constantly besieged me. They told me the Irish were only good for labouring jobs—and that the Catholic faith was a mass of superstitions. I would fiercely defend my corner. I said it was scandalous to have a secular monarch as a head of a church. I defended the use of Latin in church, saying that a universal belief needed a universal language—no matter that I was bottom of the class in Latin, much to the despair of my teacher, coincidentally named Mr Latimer, alias "Crank".

These attacks pushed me to research my people's history. I looked for the ideals that inspired Catholics before the Reformation, when Europe was more united. I read in school corridors between classes Thomas More's sixteenth century *Utopia,* seeking my inheritance from the time before nationalism cut Britain from Europe and Thomas More lost his life to a self-important king. I found that Good Queen Bess killed more people than did Bloody Queen Mary, and that those who win the wars get to write the history books—a lesson that has stayed with me. My teacher applauded this. I took the school history prize.

There was no wonder that I was interested in history. Our home was set in history, in a land fit for imagination. The white cliffs of France could be seen from our bathroom window. Across the road stood a round tower erected against Napoleon. We played on the ruined walls of a Roman villa, a hundred yards away. A vast pre-Roman fortress crowned a nearby hill. An ancient trench ran for miles below the crest of the high chalk downs. Machine gun nests snuggled below this amid rusting barbed wire entanglements built against a much later foe. A great Norman castle stood above sheer protective cliffs just five miles away in Dover.

But socially our family looked inwards. I remember well the only girl I chatted to. We did nothing more than swap geography notes yet I would run to make sure we could briefly meet as she came home from school. We talked as she stood straddling her bicycle. I never could visit her at home. I wanted her as a peer, as a friend with whom I could explore different ideas. Even so these meetings received my parents' gentle disapproval. I was also solemnly warned against the coffee lounges that lurched suspiciously against the sloping cobbles of the High Street. I was told that they were invested with drugs, sex and vice. One day in curiosity I slipped wide-eyed into one of them. All that happened was that I had a milk shake. I had hoped for much more excitement.

However I did manage on Saturday afternoons to get into the company of girls without alarming my parents. I joined a mixed hockey team. It was simply companionship, fun. I enjoyed being on a team with girls. Sadly we met only at games. Despite the legacy of asthma, I knew how to position myself to score and did in nearly every match. But I scored goals, not girls. Nothing sexual ever occurred. In my school years I had utterly no sexual ambitions.

My sole adolescent female confidante remained my mother, the one woman who was not a threat to my vocation to the priesthood. We talked easily together, spent hours chatting on the nearby cliff top overlooking the harbour. She told me when young she once wanted to run away with a band as a singer. This wish, she intimated, was an aberration I should not imitate. But I could fulfil her other frustrated ambition by becoming a priest. There was a certain convenience to this. It helped sideline my gender confusion. But I could not talk to her about my inner mountainous dilemma. I knew it would be as incomprehensible to her as it was for me, and would give her pain for no good reason, as I then thought my gender role could never be changed. I hoped that one day I would learn how to bury my odd fantasy in a corner where it would rust away and bother me no more.

I found other safer worlds in books. Jane Austin provided a playground for my fantasies. I set my mind with Emma and other heroines against saturnine giants. I devoured these romances. Many I read several times. Men were exciting to me in fantasy. But in real life, when not dreaming, I did not see men as in any way sexually attractive. (Later I *was* to find them attractive but that was only when I could experience them as a woman).

As for my secret craving to live as a girl: I pondered this in church. Prayed half-heartedly for it to go. It would not. Eventually I rationalised this seemingly indestructible fantasy, seeing it as something sent by God to keep me humble. I imagined it as similar to the unnamed secret that St. Paul confessed kept him humble. I could not get rid of my secret craving.

It made me strangely happy to imagine myself a girl—and for this I sometimes felt very guilty. But I told no one.

One day lying reading on the sunken lawn behind the house, I had a sudden totally unexpected thrill of self-recognition. I found in a magazine the story of Christine Jorgenson who in 1952 leapt the wall to her long dreamed gender as surgeons re-adjusted her body. I remember kicking my legs with a whoop of pleasure. She was one of the first women to be so midwived by surgery. I thus learnt that the West had invented a technological way of achieving what other societies had done by other means. The Western way might be more technically advanced, but non-Western ways bestowed a far fuller social acceptance and appreciation.

But she was a rare case. In the 1950s and 1960s the western medical establishment nearly universally tried to "cure" those who said they were living in the wrong gender by submitting them to a barbarous amount of electric shock and aversion therapy to make them "want" to live in conformity with their birth certificate. The old knowledge had been forgotten. Narrow gender conformity was now king—and God help me if anyone discovered my secret!

One of my favourite adolescent fantasies was to imagine that I had been captured by evil scientists who forcibly changed me into a girl. I would resist but ultimately could not stop them—an odd twist to an ancient shaman initiate's dream in which he or she was dismembered and rebuilt. In this dream I was not responsible for what happened and had no need to feel guilty. I imagined how every part of my body was changed in a drug-induced puberty to that of a woman. I could not reverse the work of these scientists—nor in my dreams did I try to. Instead I became a beautiful Amazon who went on to defeat these neo-Nazi scientists and then proceeded to live happily ever after as a woman, thanking God for this strange providence.

I discovered hidden in the airing cupboard a year or more before my sister was born, a pink dress with puffed sleeves that my Mother had stored against a hoped for daughter. As her secret daughter, I dressed at night in this pretty dress, tied a scarf around my head, and cuddled myself to sleep while imagining stories in which I was a heroine and flirted lightly with men.

Sometimes, in the early hours of a summer day while all in the house were asleep, I would walk down the back garden as a girl, letting the wind swirl my skirt and scarf. My front lock of hair I grew as long as was permitted. The back and sides I could not get away with and thus the scarf. I felt as light as a grass seed when I secretly danced upon the lawn in the first light of the dawn.

Then, YUCK, I was revolted at myself. I thought in cold realism my fantasy utterly crazy. I knew that if discovered my priesthood ambitions would be doomed. I would be labelled a freak. One day I solemnly burnt the slip I had acquired from my mother's rejects, pushed the remains down the drain-trap and vowed hopelessly to bury and destroy these fantasies. This resolution only lasted weeks and then my pleasant dream of girlhood returned. I recovered the puffed sleeved dress from where I had thrust it—the back of the airing cupboard where I first found it. These fancies seemed so patently ridiculous.

Once my Dad became suspicious and shoved open my bedroom door despite my trying desperately to deny him admission. He found me in the puffed sleeve dress and told me to come to see him and Mother in their bedroom once I had changed. I was very scared, but it turned out to be only a very gentle and perplexed rebuke. I was told that I would not be able to proceed on to the priesthood if it were known what I had done.

But despite all the evidence of mirrors and parental advice, I continued to dream secretly of living as a female rather than a male. As a child I tried to understand why this seemingly futile dream was so strangely indestructible. I sometimes enjoyed it as a fancy but then cursed it. I was perplexed by it and wished I could destroy it.

Later, as a young adult, I buried my craving in an internal pit and built a life that ignored it. But in mature life I would come to know that it was part of my soul that haunted me; that it was the pattern of my soul's dance choreographed, some may say, by my double-helixed DNA—others by hormones or by destiny. Today I have embraced this phantom, put it in its proper place. I am no longer ashamed to dance my dance. No matter if it is a dance set for a few, it was and is my dance.

But at that time, I set myself other tasks, driven no doubt by my wish to escape from taunting. One day in an English class I was shocked when a student described me in a written piece as sickly thin and others recognised me from this. So I set out to demonstrate to myself that I was not incapable. As my asthma started to become more intermittent around my sixteenth year, I sometimes walked the miles to school bending over like a speed skater to give my legs more stretch. I carried my school bag in my left hand to strengthen my weaker arm, and developed an embarrassingly strong handshake so I wouldn't seem a sissy when I met someone new. One day, in a self imposed test of endurance, I peddled my bike from Folkestone to Canterbury, Herne Bay, Margate, Ramsgate, Deal and Dover, a distance of 105 miles—at least four times further than I had ever before ridden. The only sustenance I had was a plate of beetroot at my grandmother's, the only food she had in the house. She lived in Deal; a shingle protected town that smelt of seaweed and marshes some seventeen miles short of home.

Childhood Religion

An outsider at school, a religious deviant, sexually neutered by my gender confusion, the only Catholic in the class and highly teased, I found my private road. I spent hours in meditation, learning from the experiences of mystics. Again a traditional path for the transgendered but I did not know it. In my mediations I married my loving God for in this fantasy I could be the bride. I was thus happy with a male God. Only with this God could I be female. No one else knew me. I felt a bond of love with him.

This became the secret love that I still treasure, that kept me sane and was as real as the hands with which I type. It was of a person I call my Lover, the person who created me. This person has always been beyond names for me. I knew different religions give this person different names. This did not matter. My knowledge of this person also had little to do with the dry ascetic teachings of parish priests. They taught me a black-robed love, to love God humbly on my knees while doing penance for my sins. But something I inherited, perhaps my Irish blood, kept me from such sobriety. I could not conceive that this divine Lover was a God that I should fear.

I was taught by the priests that we were sinners and should feel guilty. This too I completely failed to understand. No loving relationship can be built on guilt. I later learnt that Christian missionaries in Australia had also tried to teach Aborigines to feel guilty. A 1961 Presbyterian mission annual report said their major "problem was to impart a sense of guilt or sin which is quite foreign to the native mind. They could not see that there was any wrong in themselves…it was a constant battle between darkness and light."[38]

Guilt and penance simply was not my kind of religion—so as a child I ignored them as irrelevant. I did not know of the suffering caused by such teachings or I might have been angry. But my parents and parish priests did convince me that God needed from me something sterner than just loving. My Irish mother taught me that I could be nothing finer than God's warrior. When I learnt that Jesuit priests were the missionary super-men of the Catholic Church, joining the Jesuits became my childhood ambition. I wanted to fight for justice for God's poor, for the family of God. I was often a fighter in my dreams. No submissive female role appealed to me.

When I walked and sang the hills, I did not sing to a patriarchal God. Rather He was for me a being that was part of the very hills, the wind, the larks, the tossed branch and waving grass. He was a spirit that loved me and held me, gave me security; a being that held us all, rocks, fossils, twigs, humans. Any attempt by sermonising priests to make me fear God perplexed me. I laughed with God. Loved God. Loved the wild world. God was the living presence in the wild. The students at my school noted the joy that I found in this relationship. They nicknamed me "Smiler" but I never explained to them why I often arrived at school with such a happy face.

As far as I can remember, I always understood the Deity contained both the male and the female but I knew that the Deity should be addressed as male. This was no problem for me. My secret female self loved the male side of the One, the sparkle in his eye, his gentle love for me, his protective arm around me. It was the male aspect I needed to complement my dreams. I was told his name was Jesus—the name was not so important. What was important was our relationship.

When I came to study books on mediation and spirituality, I found the love that bonded my God and I described as the "mystic marriage". I also learnt wisdom lay in uniting the male and female aspects of our personalities. A side benefit of my childhood spirituality was that my relationship with a male God ensured that I did not reject my male aspect as if it were tainted or cursed—as many transsexuals do after years of rejection and pain.

Some might say that I was sublimating sexual desires in loving so the Divinity. Maybe I was. Perhaps I endowed the Deity with the qualities I most needed. I certainly had few outlets for any sexual feelings. The possibility that one-day men might love me as female was beyond my understanding. I was totally uninterested in gay love. But I rejoiced in finding the divine one within me. He felt as real as anything in my life. This was one I could dance, laugh and be happy with.

On the high grasslands of the Downs I felt akin with the spirit that teaches men and women that they are part of God and of the Wild. A wilderness lay below the chalk cliffs between Folkestone and Dover, a world of tangled woods and thickets, of foxes and rabbits and chaotic games, where as a teenager I ran with my brothers down newly landslipped blue clay cliffs, leaping from ledge to ledge, playing hide and seek, finding fossils, exploring the rocks and sandy coves. Here I also found my

Lover God awaiting me. I searched out the remotest places in order to have uninterrupted time to dream and dance with him. I saw his face in the clouds, in the flight of a butterfly, in the alert rabbit ears, in the white cliffs themselves. Everything around me, rocks, grass, air, were alive and imbued with divinity.

Amid these games came ambition. Nothing would stop me. I would be a saint, a mystic, a missionary. The voice inside invited me. My parents reinforced it. I frequently walked after school a mile to the church to kneel in the dark to dedicate myself to my Creator and to the god-man that embodied divine wisdom, Jesus Christ, the martyr on the cross whose love transcended death. But I did not think of my Lover God as a victim on a cross. The tangible nature of our relationship seemed much more real.

My reputation grew, without my knowledge, among the keenly observant old women of the parish, who, fussing around the church, observed me and spoke of this saintly youth. My mother later informed me of this in her efforts to keep me unchanged within her own model of sanctity. When I later found my path lay outside the official church, my parents who had been glorified by these women as having a son a priest, fled the parish rather than face these women's tongues.

My path is my path. It has been rich and right for me. But I sometimes thought it might have been easier if I had been born into the Navaho or Siberian tribes. I could have been so much more open. My parents would have noted with pride and awe that they had been given a special child. They would bring me up with love as a daughter and before puberty give me to the community Shaman for instruction. I could have become a community healer, religious teacher—without suffering so much from the fear and reality of rejection.

But my parents did help me onto this sacred path by chance, or was it chance? My childhood imagining that I was married to the Deity was part of this old way. The Chukchi "transsexual" shaman in Siberia saw herself as married to the Deity. When she also married a husband, their marriage was seen by their community as symbolising her divine marriage—and thus as particularly blessed The shaman in her spiritual work was joyfully "en theos", in union with God, the old meaning of the word "enthusiasm." Their union with God transported them to the other world of spirit. They thus experienced "ecstasy"—a word that meant originally an "out-of-body" experience. These words came to us from the world of mystics and of shamans.

As a child I talked of a male God. Today I prefer to speak of a female— but this is only because the English language has only male and female singular personal pronouns. For me the divine energy encompasses both genders and can be manifested in many forms. I know of the ineffable infinite God of the Philosophers that helped shape our Western monotheism, but my experience was of a far more personal God. It was only later that I understood that people have named as Gods or Goddesses many different and personal manifestations of the same primal energy—but more about this later.

The Hermaphrodite Goddess

In many pre-Christian religions the Deity was depicted as hermaphrodite—as the hermaphrodite embodied aspects of both genders.[39] Thus the hermaphrodite human was also valued. The Goddess Cybele, whose temple stood where the Vatican now stands, in the ancient stories was the Creatrix who needed no husband to give birth to Creation because she had both genders (as do many trees). Then her male genitals fell to earth, became an almond tree and a nut of this tree fell by a river that was a Goddess and she conceived and gave birth to the male God. The ritual celebration of this Cybele myth was held on May the First—the very day that we once danced around phallic maypoles.

Another Middle Eastern Goddess was depicted as having both female breasts and a penis. She was known as the Bearded Aphrodite. She was also sometimes described as a woman warrior wearing horns and driving a chariot. In the old stories she gave birth to Hermaphrodite, after who are named all that are born with bodies that have both male and female aspects.

Around 2000 years ago, many pagan religions, including the Egyptian and Celtic, taught that the divine energy was one, but so rich that it was best explained and visualised in the form of a divine family. Thus evolved the idea of a divine trinity of father, mother and child. Christianity was shaped by these Mediterranean beliefs—and had to work hard in its early centuries to reconcile having a family of three Deities with Judaic and philosophical monotheism.

In early Christian days, many Christians of the gnostic persuasion, a major part of the Christian world before they were suppressed, taught a gender-balanced divinity. Their Gospels recorded a Christ who spoke of the divine Mother as well as the Father. They thus believed in a Trinity that included both male and female aspects. There was the Father, the Son and the Goddess Sophia, the "Holy Spirit", the Female Spirit of Love. Many Jewish mystics honoured Sophia. She was celebrated in the Biblical *Song of Songs*

The early Christian Gnostic book *On the Origin of the World* embodied a view of gender evolution surprisingly similar to modern ideas: "When Sophia let fall a droplet of light, it flowed onto the water, and immediately a human being appeared that was androgynous. That droplet she moulded first as a female body."

Gnosticism then embraced both Christians and Pagans. The best known of the Pagan Gnostics' books was *The Shepherd of Men*. It contained a more male-centred creation account: "And God-the-Mind, being male and female both…being Life and Light, did bring forth Man co-equal to Himself, with whom He fell in love, as being His own child; for he was beautiful beyond compare, in the Image of his Sire. In very truth, God fell in love with his own Form; and on him did bestow all of His own formations."

Some of the Gnostics wrote of the ultimate deity as 'the Primal Androgyne," the symbol of this being a couple embracing. The Hindus of

Indian similarly joined Shiva and Shakti and honoured "The Lord who is Half Woman".

But Sophia, the beautiful female aspect of the Jewish and Gnostic Deity, was to become at the hands of men who believed in the superiority of the male form, a faded, near invisible, sexless ghost, the Holy Ghost. All Christian books depicting a female divine person were excluded from the list of books selected for the New Testament by the Emperor Constantine before the 4th Century Council of Niceae. Yet these rejected books were from the heartland of the Christian faith. Those early Christians who honoured the female aspect of the deity also honoured women, allowing them into the Christian priesthood just as women were allowed into the Rabbinate. (More about this later.)

The Irish in pre-Christian times honoured those born with both gender aspects. Thus their great epic *The Tain* recorded that Queen Melb, a Goddess of Sovereignty, had seven offspring—all called Maine. They were called "sons" (at least in my translation) but three had male attributes, three female and one was androgynous. "There is Maine Mathramail the Motherlike, Maine Athramail the Fatherlike, Maine Morgor, the strongly dutiful, Maine Mingor the sweetly dutiful, Maine Moepirt of the honeyed speech, Maine Andoe the swift, and Maine Cotagaib Uli—the Maine with all the qualities, who took the likeness of his mother and father."[40]

The archaeologist Maria Gimbutas in her 1974 book *Gods and Goddesses of Old Europe* noted the wealth of female figures found in ancient sites in Europe. She deduced from this that there was once in Europe a strong Goddess centred religion belonging to a society in which women were of high status. However more recent work has revealed an aspect that she overlooked. Lauren Talalay at the Kelsey Museum of Archaeology in Ann Arbor, Michigan, reported that many of the "goddess" figures of the Neolithic are hermaphroditic. The latter display both female breasts and a phallic aspect—such as either a penis or a phallic shaped neck and head. (More on this below in "Saturday") The oldest carved image of a person yet found in the British Isles is that of a hermaphrodite with female breasts and penis—as once was I. Today, with the eyes of a crone, with my hair turning grey, I see my transexuality as a blessing that has helped me understand my people's ancient ways.

In societies that depicted the Deity as having both genders, sex with one of us in a temple or sacred place was seen as a very special joining with a person akin to the transgendered Deity. In a hymn written by the priestess Enheduanna, who served the Goddess Innana in Sumeria about 5000 years ago, the oldest hymn we have, she described her work as a priestess:

> "I erected a temple;
> Where I inaugurated important events:
> I set up an unshakeable throne.
> I gave out dagger and sword to…[word missing]
> I gave tambourine and drum to homosexuals,
> I changed men into women."

I do not however see myself as a male who became a woman. My instinct, my life experience, tells me that my spirit and brain were female from pre-birth. Others may be androgynous. I felt I was born with a female brain—or perhaps with a female spirit who informed and shaped my brain.

The Grecian legend about Hermaphrodites encompassed both the male fear of female power and of not being able to separate from a woman after intercourse. Hermaphrodites was born a boy and named for both his parents, Hermes and Aphrodite. When fifteen years old he discovered the Naiad, or Water Nymph, Salmacis swimming in a pool. She fell in love with him but he rejected her. She pretended to accept this, turned away and left him. Thinking he was now alone, he dived into the pool. But Salmacis re-appeared in the water, held him fast and stole kisses. The more he tried to escape, the more she clung to him. At the same time she prayed to the Gods that they might never be separated. The Gods heard her prayer and merged their two bodies into one. And from that day they were "not two persons, nor was it possible to call them man and woman any longer, but being one they seemed neither, and yet both".

There are several aspects to this story. One is that humans are not complete until they consciously unite in themselves both their male and female aspects. Another is that men have to yield to their female side to achieve this. The Jewish gnostic mystics expressed the first thus

> When Eve was in Adam,
> Death did not exist
> When we are complete again,
> A second Adam will appear called the Hermaphrodite.

There is much work to do in rebuilding our sacred world We need to recover or create again the lost myths and legends of heroes and heroines that are gay, that are lesbian, that are transsexual and hermaphrodite, so that our children gain a rich understanding of the divinely created tapestry of gender and sexuality—one that we share with many other species. We need the myths of a renewed world where women, gays and the transgendered have their proper place without a shadowing of fear. We need to rebirth sacred ceremonies for celebrating every kind of sexuality and for re-assigning gender roles, as once was the custom. We are the priestesses and priests of the future. If we are one with the Gods, then we have the strength needed to do this for the sake of our children.

But I did not know this so clearly when I was a child. I had much learning to do. The next stage of my journey saw me ensconced in a Castle studying to be a Catholic priest.

Tuesday

The Asexual God

My mother as a girl wanted to be a Catholic priest but her gender stopped her. Then she decided to be the mother of a priest who would be an alter-Christ teaching and leading in rituals. It was thus totally impossible to tell her I had a secret that could bar me from the Catholic priesthood as effectively as her girlhood barred her. If only the Catholic Church had allowed her to serve in its priesthood—and still to marry and conceive us! It would have solved part of my dilemma—and that of a thousand Irish sons.

The early Catholic teachers declared contradictorily that women were both the weaker sex and powerful as temptresses—and had been so since the Garden of Eden. The very concept of a priestess was anathema to them, although when they lived Pagan priestesses were respected members of society. They barred women from the Christian ministry, although women had headed local congregations in the Church's first centuries. Thus was the priesthood denied to my mother who so much wanted it.

So my mother charged me to fulfil her dreams, become a priest, bring Christ to the unbelievers, dedicate myself to my Lord like some apprentice knight in Camelot. I mock gently. Her dreams did charge me, did help lift me, and did help set my ambitions high.

Of course there were other reasons why I should pick a career that seemed asexual. I was not the ideal candidate for male parenting. My gender identity was so confused that I had no wish for a sexually active life. In my Catholic world an ethereal celibate priestly life seemed my destiny. But above all else, I thought I heard calling me the voice of my Lover-God.

If I were to be a priest, I had to choose what kind of priest. I decided early against the diocesan parish clergy although I served them as an altar boy in cassock and surplice, sometimes swinging an incense burner, sometimes holding tall candles and speculating how the melted wax would fall. I did not want to be one of those who constantly called for funds for parish complexes of presbyteries, schools, halls and churches. I dreamed of my ordination to the priesthood as my dedication as a knight of God, dedicated not to building an institution but to a deeper, more radical, service of the God of Love.

There was for me only one other path to the priesthood. I could join a religious order that specialised in aspects of the Church's work. Their members normally took vows of poverty, chastity and obedience. I had picked the Jesuits as I have mentioned, because of their reputation among Catholics as an elite renowned for intellectual pursuits and as warriors for Christ. I hoped they would provide a fertile ground in which I could fulfil my priestly and knightly ambitions.

Most Catholic clergy are committed to lives of celibacy—with the exception of some converts and Eastern Churches in communion with Rome. Celibacy had only become the universal rule in the West in 1139. It was not the rule in Jesus' time. The New Testament spoke of the Apostles travelling with their wives. But I lived after the 4th Century when St Jerome and the other Fathers had spread pessimistic ideas on women.

In my early teens my parents proudly invited a Jesuit recruiter to our family home. He sat on the settee that hid the carpet I had burnt, and said the Jesuits would welcome me, if I completed my sixth form with good results. But a year before I was to go to them, my parents showed me an advertisement for a free holiday. It read "Come to Highcliffe Castle in the New Forest and discover if God wants you for the priesthood."

My parents wanted to reinforce my ambition and persuaded me to go. Thus I set out in the August of 1959 to a distant castle on the Hampshire coast. On arrival I found it was a gothic fantasia with a vast arched entry portal sixty feet high. A statue of a rampant stag stood above on the summit of its roof. Its turrets lifted above cliffs that faced the Needle Rocks of the Isle of Wight. I was greeted by males of my age, then fairly boring to me. I should have been warned that I was entering a very different world.

In the chapel behind the entry portal an American was presiding, a Father Gamm. He sat behind altar rails beneath an enthroned statue of Mary Mother of God. He was not the spiritual leader I expected. He was the original high-pressure salesman. I was firm that I wanted to be a Jesuit—so he set out to undermine the resolve of this inexperienced youth.

He told me the Claretians were a sort of easy going Jesuits. I could reach the same intellectual heights that Jesuits could take me to—and save years in doing so. There was no need to get my A-Levels, a necessity for university entrance in England, for I would be sent to a Roman university. I could therefore start straight away. Why did I think God had got me to this Holiday-Retreat? Wasn't God telling me something? Let rip kid. God wants you NOW.

The Patriarchal Way to Holiness

I demurred slightly. I went home but he had me. The romance of it appealed; my parents were keen to see me on safe territory and encouraged me. If God wanted me now then I was ready. I deserted my A level studies. Two weeks later I drove up a narrow Somerset lane to Backwell Hill House, a Claretian Noviciate set in the midst of the wooded Mendip hills. Sombre dark oak panels clad the walls inside.

A noviciate was a place where those considering joining a religious order spend their first year without any commitment to remain. Only at the end of this year did they take vows. It was a place of prayer, of manual work, of lessons in spirituality and meditation.

I found it was also an institution that had changed little since the days when the Church's patriarchy was at its strongest. My noviciate was an introduction to a total world of men. Pope John XXIII in 1948 wrote in his spiritual diary; "After more than forty years I still warmly recall the edifying conversations that I had in the episcopal palace in Bergamo with my reverend bishop, Msgr. Radini Tedeschi. About the persons in the Vatican, from the Holy Father downward, there was never an expression that was not respectful, no, never. But as for women or their shape or what concerned them, no word was ever spoken. It was as if there were no women in the world. This absolute silence, this lack of any familiarity with regard to the other sex, was one of the most powerful and profound lessons of my young life as a priest…"[41]

This world was based on the model of a male God who lived apart from the world. We were told to detach our immortal souls from our corruptible body's needs so that we might be more God-like. Love without sex was the ideal since it was more God-like. The Claretians' full title was "Sons of the Immaculate Heart of Mary". We were sons of her heart since we were supposed to show a mother's love to all. Her love was immaculate, we were told, because she was uniquely uncontaminated by sex and sin.

Origen, a 3rd Century Father of the Church, wrote: "Everyone who enters the world is said to be affected by a kind of contamination. The very fact that he is placed in his mother's womb and that the source from which he takes the material of his body is the father's seed…[proves that] every man is polluted in father and mother. Only Jesus my Lord came to birth without stain since He was not polluted through his mother, for he entered a body which was not contaminated."[42]. Virgin birth thus meant for him that her womb was not "contaminated" by semen.

It was not only Judaic thought that influenced the early development of Christianity. It equally grew out of the Hellenic culture that influenced Judaism, as also had the ideas of Persians and Egyptians. Origin's ideas reflected a Persian dualism between spirit and matter, as also did the literature of the Essene Judaic sect recovered as *The Dead Sea Scrolls.*

The idea that Christ had been born of a virgin was due to a mistranslation into Greek. The author of the *Gospel according to Matthew* maintained that Christ had fulfilled the prophecy of Isaiah 7.14 by being born of a virgin—but the original Hebrew text of Isaiah had not said "virgin" but "young woman".[43]

But that was not the whole story, the whole meaning of "virgin". When Origen lived, some pagan religions saw virginity quite differently. The supreme Goddess was said to be a Virgin Mother—for she could create her children without a male.[44] This came from the idea of the Divinity as including both male and female powers, being ultimately beyond the need of gender to create. They thus taught that the Goddess could make love, be sexual, and remain a virgin. When fathers of Christianity gave Mary the title of Virgin Mother of God, they were knowingly giving her a supreme title of divinity among Pagans.

But when I first entered the noviciate I did not have time for such theological speculation. I was slung a black cassock and sash. I was very slim waisted then and others laughingly said it looked like a girl's dress on me. The androgyny appealed to me.

There were about seventeen of us novices. A Father Angel de Urrutia was our Novice Master and "Superior". He was a Basque, exiled from Franco's Spain for serving with the Basque nationalists; a genial white haired man, imbued with Iberian traditional ways of bringing up young priests and not at home in British ways.

I flung myself into the life of the noviciate. Sainthood here I come, or so I told myself! No time for fantasies about being a girl. I plunged into reading the lives of Christian heroes, saints, and mystics, exploring the territory of my European Christian inheritance

I skim read, adopting instinctively what complemented my teenage mysticism. I tossed aside books of spiritual rules that seemed irrelevant, including the plodding steps of the Exercises of Saint Ignatius, the founder of the Jesuits. He recommended starting with weeks of stern meditation on the sinful nature of the soul (and taught, in the usual human-centred way, that "the other things on the face of the earth are created for man"[45]). I felt that I did not need such a long approach to making God's acquaintance for He was already my mate. St. Ignatius' *40 Steps to Perfection* seemed mechanical and foreign. The idea that we had to struggle mightily against our sinful nature before we could attain friendship with God did not reflect for me the teaching that God truly loved us.

The Sacred Marriage and Mysticism

But the mystics I now read used sensual and loving imagery of God. Julian of Norwich in *The Wooing of Our Lord* spoke of a Christ "I can so sweetly kiss and embrace and of thy love have infinite delight." She saw Christ's "beauty and lovesome face, flesh white under clothing." The 12th century adventures of Bernard of Clairvaux, leaving all to bind himself to God, caught at my seventeen-year-old romantic soul. Father Angel deepened my knowledge of the Iberian mystics, John of the Cross and Teresa of Avila. I delighted in their passionate love affairs with God. John's writing was erotic. So too was the Biblical *Song of Songs*. I too could take a male God as my lover. It was all marvellous romantic stuff with transport in the beloved, dark nights of the soul, abandonment, self-surrender. For the mystics the parent God was also an archetypal lover.

A sacred marriage between God and human was the stuff of mysticism in many cultures. When the child Jesus went to Egypt, he experienced a land where the priests and priestesses of the Goddess Isis taught that human marriage was an apt symbol for the divine love that gave to the earth its fertility. In one story, Isis, described by Plutarch as "the female principle of Nature"[46] rescued her dead husband Osiris and made him breathe again by beating her wings while her tears caused the Nile's annual flood. I had been taught such myths were false history. Later I realised that these Pagans did not search for shrouds or relics to prove that Osiris really lived as Christians did of Christ. Their tales were simply myths that embodied wisdom.

I learnt much during that time that is still very precious to me. I frolicked in prayer. How could God be fearsome if he or she were a loving parent who instantly forgave the returning child? I plunged in, floated in God's ocean with the natural arrogance and presumption of youth. I felt suspended in vast open spaces of self-surrender and contemplation. I saw this state as a place that lovers can attain if both wish it.

There were some old customs of dubious wisdom taught to us by Father Angel. He provided me privately with a scourge, a short length of rope, so I could bring a stubborn fallen body into line. I never convincingly succeeded in using it. My Lover God seemed to laugh at me and ask what on earth was I doing to my sacred body? No matter that I was told such body punishing discipline came from the lessons taught by the Christian monks in 4th century Egypt (who founded Christian monasticism on the model of pagan Hermetic Egyptian communities). I soon discarded it in the conviction that such customs were no use to me. My Irish mother had taught me that my body was sacred so I could not see my flesh as an obstacle.

We were given diamond shaped grids with spikes protruding inwards to strap to our legs. The spikes were not sharp and did not make my legs even itch. They were stupid things. We were told not to let the points penetrate the skin. I only used it because it was supposedly dictated by some strange ancient wisdom. I was willing to try anything, to experiment, to explore this ancient way of life that was supposed to make me closer to God, but I soon found it an irrelevancy.

We were encouraged to take turns eating our meals while kneeling in the centre of the dining room or "refectory" as an exercise in humility. I tried out eating lying on the floor and kissing feet. I wore a scratchy hair shirt. None of it made much sense but I was on the move and would try out any idea recommended. These customs were supposed to liberate my spirit from a body prison, but none of these odd customs worked for me, and all were soon abandoned. I only indulged in them because my cynicism was not developed.

I undertook some strange experiments of my own. One day when I was in the walled vegetable garden a large insect settled on my forehead and bit me above an eye. In the interests of the insect and self-control I left it alone. Then another bit me above the other eye, so, for the next two weeks I went around with two lumps on my forehead as if about to germinate a devil's horns!

The Mendip forest around the noviciate preserved my sanity. Its every feature was part of the face of the Lover-Creator. I explored its glades, found havens underneath the heavy dipping branches of ancient yews and climbed lichen covered rocks. These seemed to be friends that welcomed me. The forest was divided by the cliffs of Brockley Combe, where a cave with an ancient smoke hole provided me with shelter. I brought books on prayer or sanctity and read them in its company. Sometimes I climbed down into the valley below, crossing outcrops of fossilised coral beds, to kick leaves on the valley's floor where beeches and horse chestnuts lived with hedgehogs, badgers and other denizens.

One of my tasks was to dig out the sewers and septic tank, watched one day by an enormous bloated toad. I also helped build with boulders a rough grotto enshrining a statue of the Mother of Jesus. Once a week we were allowed to go on afternoon bike rides, pups in Roman collars meandering through the countryside. We went to Cheddar and other gorges, to crystal lined clefts in rock, moist stalactite toothed caves, narrow lanes walled by high hedges, ancient villages and the nearby rounded ditches of supposed Camelot.

At the end of that year I took the vows of poverty, chastity and obedience that made me a member of the Claretians. I then saw this as a natural consequence of my earlier personal dedication. Obedience was for me a vow made primarily to God not to the Claretians. (They would have agreed—in theory.) Chastity seemed no trouble when my love affair was with a God. Poverty was a given since I had learnt that the seeking of material wealth was not in line with any sort of spiritual dedication. Again there was a romantic parallel. The lover leaves all to follow the beloved.

But this was also my initiation into a patriarchal world where the authority of the Religious Order came from the Pope. I leant our Order was ultimately part of the Papacy's army.

The celebration of my Vows was partly hijacked by my three-year-old sister. Assisted by our mother she convinced Father Angel that she knew all that was necessary to make her first Holy Communion at half the usual age. My mother told me that my sister saw and spoke to angels. I was a little sceptical but for us angels played the role that spirits or fairies had once taken. Once I left home, my mother replaced me with my sister as her confidante. Maryanne would still be her constant companion decades later.

Lithe and light, a professed religious in my black dress and sash, a neutral in the war between the sexes, I moved back to Highcliffe Castle in the New Forest to continue my studies as a hopeless romantic. I had to complete three years of philosophy and then four years of theology before I was ordained a priest. I had hoped to be sent to study at a Roman university, as Father Gamm had promised when he lured me, but the policy had changed. Students were no longer sent to Rome so I studied and lived in this castle for the next six years.

An eccentric English ambassador had built the castle in an 1830's consumer style later adopted by such Texans as the one who bought London Bridge. He rolled around France, gold coins at the ready, acquiring culture and status. He scrounged a genuine fifteenth century Gothic arch from one ruin, a statue-embellished bay window that had lit the last days of a King of Navarre from another, a sixteenth century window from a collapsed abbey and so on. These he landed on the English coast and built into a mansion extravaganza.

The Order thought the place marvellous. His lofty entrance hall with tall gothic windows enraptured them. They swiftly made it into a mock gothic chapel. In front of its far double doors they placed an altar. Above this, on the balcony from which string quartets had played for English royalty, they placed a larger-than-life statue of an enthroned Virgin Mary. As for the Louis XV styled reception rooms with Aesop's fables in gold leaf on the lofty ceilings; they were obviously meant to be study halls.

The library was long, with iron balconies reached by stairs concealed behind false bookcases. It was lit by windows adorned with the crests of nobility. A secret passage behind a bookcase led to the back of the fireplace in the Octagonal Room that opened to the rear gardens through a stately gothic porch. A large false bookcase at the furthest end of the library gave access to a conservatory where I spent many a recreation-period at the billiard and table tennis tables.

We were guarded carefully by the Order to make sure the Catholic laity who came to pray in our chapel did not corrupt us. Only a few vetted students were allowed to meet them after Holy Mass. The presumably more vulnerable students such as myself were only allowed to roam on the private side of the mansion down to the edge of the sea-washed sands. When my brother Tony came to test his own 'vocation' (much to my delight—we were always close), he too was excluded from the front-of-church danger zone.

Every year the Provincial, the head of the Order in England, came to review the house and the state of the community. At one such visitation he solemnly warned us from the altar steps that the beach was a spiritual minefield and that expulsion from the Order awaited any of us who stepped onto it. We could gawk at its denizens from above and be safe from heavenly lightning bolts. But one footprint in the sand and we were a goner. So ruled Father Emaldia, who was in charge of the six or so Claretian houses in England. He was a white-haired stocky Basque akin to our novice master.

But when he retired, under a new regime we were allowed onto the sands and even to swim. The bikini-clad girls watched, as laughing young men dragged medieval black cassocks over their heads to reveal bathing trunks. Despite all the earlier predictions of sexual mayhem, no sexual liaisons resulted, not at least as far as I observed. We were mostly a very highly motivated community.

I returned to the escape of intellectual pursuits as I had done at the Grammar School. I buried myself in philosophy. I delighted in striving to understand intriguing dead and living minds. I sparred with Descartes, romped with Maritaine, jostled with Hegel got bored with Russell, leapt with Heiderger, dived with Spinoza. This helped me escape from caring about most of life's hassles. I had a rival fellow-student and we fought for supremacy. I finished Philosophy three years later just one mark ahead of him with a Summa cum Laude.

One of the philosophers I then encountered told a most amusing story about the human genders. Plato in his *Symposium* wrote:

"For our original nature was by no means the same as it is now. In the first place, there were three kinds of human beings not merely the two sexes, male and female, as at present: there was a third kind as well, which had equal shares of the other two, and whose name survives though, the thing itself has vanished. For the hermaphrodite 'man-woman' was then a unity in form no less than name, composed of both sexes and sharing equally in male and female; whereas now it has come to be merely a name of reproach."[47]

Then Plato wrote a tongue-in-cheek description of these humans.

" Secondly, the form of each person was round all over, with back and sides encompassing it every way; each had four arms, and legs to match these, and two faces perfectly alike on a cylindrical neck. There was one head to the two faces, which looked opposite ways; there were four ears, two privy members, and all the other parts, as may be imagined, in proportion. The creature walked upright as now, in either direction as it pleased and whenever it started running fast, it went like our acrobats, whirling over and over with legs stuck out straight; only then they had eight limbs to support and speed them swiftly round and round."[48]

Plato's narrator went on to explain why such creatures no longer existed. They were too powerful and challenged the Gods themselves. So Zeus weakened them:

'Methinks I can contrive that men, without ceasing to exist, shall give over their iniquity through a lessening of their strength. I propose now to slice every one of them in two, so that while making them weaker we shall find them more useful by reason of their multiplication; and they shall walk erect upon two legs."

So saying, " he sliced each human being in two, just as they slice sorb-apples to make a dry preserve". Thus the tale explained our varying sexual appetites. The males sliced apart are today's gays—yearning to be united with other males. The females sliced are the lesbians. The hermaphrodites sliced apart are today's heterosexuals striving to unite themselves with the opposite gender.

Zeus finished his work with a final threat: "If they continue turbulent and do not choose to keep quiet, I will do it again…I will slice every person in two, and then they must go their ways on one leg, hopping."'

When I studied these things it was the early sixties, a time when it seemed Latin was entering its death throes inside its last redoubt, the Catholic Church. We started our studies with Latin textbooks. We attended lectures given in Latin and took notes in Latin. After two years we went to working in English because of a decision by the bishops at the Second Vatican Council. It was good providence that led me to study Catholic theology at a time when it was more open to new ideas than it has been at any time earlier or since.

Two rival spiritual traditions were then clashing within the Church. Pére Chenu, an "expert" to this Council, called these "creation spirituality", which saw nature as good and as reflecting God, and "fall-redemption" which saw nature as fallen and corrupted. The latter was a direct descendent of the Persian dualism between matter and spirit. The battle between it and nature spirituality was clearly unresolved within the Church. Chenu wrote the first draft of the Council document *The Church in the Modern World,* which he later said in disgust, was "drowned in holy water".[49]

Soon after starting theology, the time came for me to be induced into the lower orders of the clergy. In a solemn ceremony a bishop made by a bishop in a lineage reportedly going back to the time of Christ, gave me a place in this female-less ancestry. I progressed over four years through the seven sacred orders, Acolyte, Reader, Exorcist, Thurifer, Sub-Deacon, Deacon and Priest. I was thus initiated into a supernatural order that had seemingly replaced the natural order where women dwelt.

I remember when a sister of a student played him at tennis. Our moral guardians noticed her tennis dress. They announced at prayers next day that she would be the last woman to play on our court. I saw no reason for the fuss. It seemed irrelevant. She looked OK to me. Even normal. But I made no protest. I did not allow the fuss to distract me. I had a goal. I drove on towards it. I was determined to allow nothing to bar me from the priesthood. (But sex would have been the last thing to distract me.)

The very early Church did not share this attitude towards women. Women rallied the apostles after Christ's death. St Paul credited women as preachers and gave them the same title he gave himself. He praised Junia, as "outstanding among the apostles" For long time incredulous male translators "corrected" her name to the male form, Junias.[50] (Scholars now believe those of "Paul's" epistles that told women to be subservient and to keep quiet in church were not written by him but composed after his death. In his own work he stated women and men were equal in God— but more about this later.)

I found myself a refuge in the castle where I could be alone, out of sight and unsupervised. I took up the job of mending its roofs. These were constantly springing leaks. I would take a pot of black tar roof-medicine and a book or two, and spend many an hour lying on slates, reading in the sun. With equal pleasure I would fix the roofs in storms, even climbing up to the stone stag rearing on top of the chapel. Here my imagination could run riot as it had done as a child on the summits of the Downs.

At other times I worked in the gardens, always trying to get myself into the less tamed woods. I cleared leaves, weeds, observed vipers, lizards and rabbits, cut paths through bamboo thickets, interrupted once by a beautiful bluish-black mole that tunnelled across my levelled path. I liked to work by myself. I was awkward with my male peers and never quite at home with most of them.

As in the novitiate, we were allowed to go out on a recreational bike ride for a couple of hours once a week. The bikes were kept hanging like carcasses from old meat hooks in a cellar. Another cellar held a crop of mushrooms, growing amid broke-down central heating systems and decaying lawn mowers. On our days of escape, we mounted our bikes, rode through the cellars for about thirty yards then up a ramp into the civilian world. These rides were absolutely vital for my survival. I found remote places within the New Forest where I could briefly wander alone.

The seminary had a hothouse atmosphere. We took it in turns to wake the community of about forty. We would race from door to door, calling out a Latin jingle to which the inmates had to sleepily respond in Latin. Our days were tightly organised around the recitation of the Divine Office in choir plus the rituals of the Holy Mass in the mornings and Benediction in the afternoons, with spiritual readings during breakfast, lunch and supper, with study periods and lectures. We could chat only in the half-hour breaks every three hours or so. The evening break was longer—and was a time when we could watch authorised TV programs such as the Eurovision Song Contest. (I particularly remember when Sandie Shaw's *Puppet on a String* won.) Outside these breaks we had to maintain silence.

In the early morning, when we knelt in the chapel beneath the great statue of Mary, we would keep our ears half cocked to catch the noise of any car. When one was heard, we would quickly look around to see if anyone was missing. For this was how expulsions would happen. Rumours would afterwards spread. Had the Superior expelled him for being gay? Had he met with a girl on the weekly bike-rides? Had he stepped upon the beach?

Meditation and Magic

We were taught perfection in prayer was being able to hold ourselves in undivided attention, transfixed, before the ineffable Godhead. We learnt that the imagination was a tool of childhood to be disregarded as the mutterings of the lower self. I tried to do this—but found my imagination hard to conquer. My "lower" self protested at being barred from the sacred. From what I later learnt, it was like holding a conversation blindfolded.

I found the prayer discipline taught to me handicapping and disempowering. It was based on a concept of a Creating God who was outside his Creation judging it. In prayer we had to put ourselves outside creation to the best of our ability. We were helpless, so we were told, and had to beseech Him to have mercy on us as sinners. We learnt we were His children, but were told this did not mean we could relax and enjoy being part of a divine family. We had to be constantly aware that we were unworthy of our Parent.

If any strangers to Catholicism entered our chapel, the dominating statue of the enthroned Mary would have convinced them that they were in the presence of a religion with a Goddess. This originally was a deliberate stratagem of the Catholic Church. Pope Gregory I (590-604) wrote to Melitus, the archbishop of Canterbury, urging that the holy days of the pagan British be "sanctified' by becoming Christian feasts. Later Pope Sergius (687-701) ordered the festivals be celebrated on the pagan holy days—such as May 1st, the feast of Beltaine when the sacred rites of spring were celebrated.[51] This later became the International Workers' Day—so the Church made it also the feast of the carpenter, St Joseph. I also suspect converts did much the same by renaming their favourite Goddess statues after Mary rather than disposing of them.

Other older rites influenced us. Thus we garlanded the walls of the chapel with holly every Christmas. The holly with its evergreen leaves and food for birds in winter has been from pagan times a symbol of everlasting life. Long ropes of holly leaves were draped along the chapel sides and up to the statue of Mary above the altar.

As an Order dedicated to Mary we prayed to her many times a day. But, although I did not know it then, a man who lived in the village in which our college stood, a Gerald Gardner, would one day become famous for reviving rituals that honoured the Goddess and God in what he called pagan witchcraft or Wicca. He must have known our Castle before it became a centre for training priests, for it is likely that he was initiated into witchcraft in a nearby house purchased from the Highcliffe Castle estate.[52] I knew this house well—I had often explored Chewton Glen in which it was hidden. I would then have found incredible the idea that one day I would work as the high priestess and magical partner of a member of the coven that Gardner founded.

The Church had claimed that witches needed the devil's help to do magic. I then knew little of modern witches who saw themselves as working only with natural forces, including the Divine, to bring about change. I thought killing women as demon-allied witches a piece of medieval stupidity and wickedness committed by both State and Church, but I did not look into what was really believed by the people that were killed. I presumed them to be mostly hapless victims.

But in the first centuries of the Christian era, the debate had waged fiercely over magic versus prayer. The Magi who visited the baby Jesus came from a Persian people well known for their magical skills—the very word "magic" came from them. The writers of this Gospel story did not dislike the Magi because of their magic but rather respected them.

But others used the word "magician" quite differently. Jewish writers in the Second Century described Jesus disdainfully as a "magician" who learnt his great skills in Egypt. A Jewish document written prior to 220CE[53] alleged that Jesus was accused of being a sorcerer. "There is a tradition [in a Barraitha document]: They hanged Yeshu on the Sabbath of the Passover. But for forty days before that a herald went in front of him [crying], "Yeshu is to be stoned because he practised sorcery and seduced

Israel and lead them away from God. Anyone who can provide evidence on his behalf should come forward to defend him." When nothing favourable about him was found, he was hanged on the Sabbath of the Passover."

Christians likewise alleged Simon Magus was a magician. He was a miracle-worker seen by some as a rival to Jesus. Eusebius, the author of one of the first histories of Catholicism, admitted Magus "performed some mighty acts of magic" and had, with his partner Helena, attracted many followers but he explained away these feats by declaring disdainfully that they were done through the power of "demons". He damned Simon as "the author of all heresy", ignoring any good he did. The Acts of the Apostles alleged that Simon tried to buy the magic of Jesus—a sin that later became known as "Simony". I do not know what manner of man Simon was—save that he inspired many and was a famous follower of John the Baptist.

Early Christians—Catholics versus Gnostics

The Christians of that time were divided, to put it simplistically, into Catholics and Gnostics. The Catholics believed in a centralised authority defining doctrine and practice, the Gnostics looked within to find their guide in personal inspiration and the voice of the Spirit. The Catholics saw this as undermining the authority of the Church—and thus spent much of their time attacking the Gnostics.

Thus the Catholic Eusebius venomously accused the Gnostic Christians of using magic. "It was an artifice of the devil to endeavour by means of such sorcerers, who assumed the name of Christians to defame the great mystery of Godliness by magical art." The Gnostics replied by saying they were working both with Jesus and with Nature's gifts. The Catholics said Nature was corrupted by the "Fall" and thus in the domain of the Devil, and poured scorn on the wealth of different ideas among the Gnostic groups, saying this showed a lack of discipline.

Behind these accusations lay a struggle by a "Catholic" elite to establish a religious power-base. The Christian Gnostics on the other hand believed in local groups working out their own practices in a spirit of freedom and love for God; they looked to Christ for inspiration but were not ashamed to admit that they shared many spiritual insights with the Pagan Gnostics who looked to the God Hermes for inspiration. He was a winged Greek God of thought and wisdom who had monastic Pagan Gnostic communities dedicated to him in Egypt. Both Pagan and Christian Gnostics saw human perfection as a process of freeing oneself from material concerns in order to achieve knowledge of and love for God. Both believed in a long process of training, initiation and growth and both had sacraments to help this process.

The Catholics shared much of this, but said their ministers held their power to teach from God and that no others were so authorised. They instead demonised the spiritual work of others, including that of the Gnostic Christians, saying it derived its effectiveness from Satan's rival Evil Empire. In this the Catholics teaching reflected the dualism of the Persian Zoroastrian religion that held the earth was governed by two rival spiritual forces, one evil and one good—as also was influenced the Essenes, a Jewish sect influential in Israel in Christ's time. Judaism drew from many sources in this period. It was only after the destruction of the Temple by the Romans that Judaism became much more narrowly defined under the Rabbinate.

Among the Catholics this matter-spirit dualism created a world-view in which there were rival Divine and Satanic empires—with Satan dominating Matter and God ruling Spirit. The victory for this Catholic view would shape Western culture for millennia—but it was only achieved with great difficulty and it was never complete.

But their victory led to magic being banned from the Roman Empire by state edict in 319CE, just seven years after the Emperor Constantine made the Catholic version of Christianity an official Empire religion. The "first great persecution of the Christian era" was ordered in 367CE with death prescribed for all that practised magic. This is largely forgotten today, but at that time "large numbers of people were put to death…and a veritable panic swept through the eastern world."[54]

The victory was greatly helped by Emperor Constantine, despite him being only baptized a Christian on his deathbed. He did much to forge Catholicism into a strong unified body. He thought the wealth of Christian books with varying interpretations of Christ's teaching then available undermined the authority of the Catholics, so in 233CE he ordered the Catholic historian Eusebius to select out a collection of "authorised" texts. He commissioned him to deliver to his palace fifty bound copies of those selected. It was this selection that became today's *New Testament*.

Eusebius explained how he selected books for inclusion. He did not choose by studying which were the more accurate, the oldest or most uplifting but according to how often the authorities of the Catholic fraction had cited them. The Gospels of Matthew, Mark, Luke and John were an easy choice. They had been endorsed by the Catholic Irenaeus of Lyon around 180CE. They encompassed a worldview shared by most Catholics, for they depicted Christ as dying in a fight of global significance against the devil—rather than in a struggle against local authorities. This was a universal message that would have much appeal outside Judea.

Those books quoted more by Gnostic Christians were summarily rejected by Eusebius. Out went the *Gospel according to Philip* that did not mention the devil[55]. He also ignored the Gospels attributed to the apostles Thomas and Peter, to Mary Magdalene and many more. It did not matter that Thomas's Gospel was written nearer to Jesus's time than the books he selected. He omitted the Gospel linked to Mary Magdalene, despite her being exceptionally close to Jesus. All the non-selected works would be destroyed when Catholics gained power A few copies of Gnostic Christian books were however hidden in Egypt to be rediscovered by archaeologists in the 20th century. Some Pagan Gnostic or Hermetic books were preserved in the libraries of remote desert towns. Copies of the latter would find their way to Europe in the Middle Ages.

Elaine Pagels asked in *The Gnostic Gospels* why the Gnostic Christian writings were so thoroughly suppressed? The Gnostics were also puzzled at the hatred the Catholics showed towards them. Pagels concluded that it was probably because of the importance given to women in some of these books and among the Gnostics. "By the year 200 virtually all the female imagery for God had disappeared from orthodox [Catholic] Christian tradition."[56]

Some of the Gnostic Christian texts recorded that Jesus spoke not just of the divine Father but also of the divine Mother. Thus in the *Gospel to the Hebrews* Jesus spoke of "my Mother the Spirit." In the *Gospel of Phillip* the Holy Spirit is called "the Mother". The Gnostic teacher Valentinus taught the Deity is essentially beyond knowledge but can be imagined as both the Primal Father and the Womb and Mother of All. The *Gospel of the Egyptians* taught a Trinity consisting of "The Father, the Mother and the Son" which emanated from the supreme Godhead whose name 'cannot be uttered."[57]

Pagans, Jews and Gnostic Christians lost many of their most treasured books to this devastating Catholic purge. The Codex Theodosianus of the late 4th Century declared, "the privileges which are bestowed for the cultivation of religion should be given only to followers of the Catholic faith. We desire that heretics and schismatics [including the Gnostic Christians] be subjected to fines." It also declared: "All temples should be closed at once." Anyone who sacrificed in them in future would be put to "the sword". It said this edict was "against [both] the madness of Jewish impiety and the insanity of foolish Paganism."

While I first learnt of such things, I thought such intolerant acts had little to do with Christ. Instead I focused on the fine spiritual works that I found preserved within the Church. I was not disturbed by the intolerance and genocide supposedly authorized by the Old Testament Jehovah as we were taught that our faith was not based on a book but on the living presence of God within us and within the community of His Church. This was an idea shared between modern Catholics and Gnostics so it seemed that Gnostic ways had not been entirely eliminated. This led to seeming contradictions—such as being taught both that our conscience was our prime guide in spiritual matters—and the Pope could make "infallible" declarations we must believe.

I thus came to know the great mystic writers of my fellow-Europeans and to understand the historical roots and limitations of the Bible. I learnt of the hermits and of those who dedicated themselves to serving the oppressed, saying the face of God could be seen in them. I was inspired by stories of priests who lived in poverty while fighting against social injustice. I wanted to be such a priest.

My focus was on the goal, not on steps towards it. I sought Ordination as a consecration of myself to a God I knew and loved. When I were ordained, then I would have fulfilled a dream or calling and have the status to inspire and teach—or so I thought. There was also a distraction. My fantasy of womanhood was again secretly on the loose. Intellectual sublimation had its limits. In the chapel my thoughts often went to what it would be like if by magic I woke up a woman. These dreams were strangely hard to ignore.

But to my great surprise, seminary life provided me with safe opportunities to express this secret dream. Every year we had festival days when we were allowed to wear fancy dress and be a bit crazy. Many of us would not have survived without these days. On the feastdays of St George and of St Patrick, after the solemn High Mass celebrating the great exploits of these saints, killing dragons and driving snakes out and the like, we had treasure hunts for silly prizes in the woods, played four-a-side soccer on the tennis pitch, held table tennis tournaments and other games.

In the evening when fancy dress was permitted I would let loose the fantasy that still plagued me. I dressed up as a girl, carefully, realistically. I relaxed, changed and was female on such days, much to the surprise of fellow students and supervisory priests, who would sometimes cross-dress but in a way that lampooned women. I caught their startled stare when suddenly I seemed to them more naturally female than they thought possible.

I would extend the time I wore a dress as long as possible. After the festivities, late at night I would walk in the woods alone and ridiculously happy as a young woman, singing to my creator and the trees. I would even sleep in the dress. Only morning prayers made me resume my devotee's garb of a black cassock and sash with a white Roman plastic collar around my neck. At such times I would thank God for the pleasure of the night before and then bury my impossible and strange fantasy.

The seminary thus gave me the support I needed to maintain the status quo. Outside I would have been challenged in my sexuality. Inside the seminary I never saw the males around me as possible sexual partners—for no one, not even I, saw me as a woman in reality. Rather I left such desires to the realm of dreams and drove blindly and asexually towards my target of the priesthood. I was not unhappy. I did not crave sexual freedom or sexual partners. I strove for inward conquests.

We studied an ethics that did not teach us how to be humane but which existed solely in the intellect. We were taught from a textbook that dissected human motives and assigned degrees of sin. It was one of the first books I disposed of when I finished at the seminary. The teachers were not so knowledgeable. I remember being ridiculed by a lecturer because I suggested there was such a thing as female circumcision.

Naturally inferior women

Celibacy was not a practical problem for the asexual me—but it was increasingly an intellectual problem. Hans Kung, a radical Catholic theologian then much read in seminaries, was developing ideas that would lead him to teach that the celibacy laws 'led directly [in the church] to the devaluation of sexuality and indirectly to a devaluation of women."[58]

This was very different from what I read in our massive white paper-backed theological textbooks written by the 13th Century master St. Thomas Aquinas. He dominated my first years of theology—as he had dominated the training of Roman Catholic priests for seven hundred years. He had re-discovered the pagan Aristotle and endorsed with enthu-siasm Aristotle's view that male bodies are superior to the female. This did not prevent my seminary teachers from praising Aquinas for his use of Aristotle—as if the church had thereby taken on enlightened Grecian thinking. A positive aspect to Aquinas' teaching was that he held we had rights and duties based on natural law. The negative aspect was that he held that women were inferior under this natural law.

Aquinas's view did not match what I had learnt at home, where my mother presided and was much honoured. I preferred Hans Kung's teach-ings—yet the Holy Office, formerly known as the Holy Inquisition, sus-pected his orthodoxy and was always interrogating him. In contrast Aquinas was enthusiastically endorsed by the Vatican. It acclaimed him as a saint and "the Angelic doctor".

Much of what Aquinas taught about women was skipped over when I studied him in the Seminary. I later learnt his teachings included "because of the higher water content in women, they are more easily influenced by sexual pleasure"[59]. And that: "nothing drags the mind of a man down from its elevation so much as the caresses of a woman and the bodily contacts without which a man cannot possess his wife."[60] He added, because of "the defect in her reasoning ability" which is "also evident in children and men-tally ill persons" a "woman cannot serve as a witness in testamentary mat-ters."[61]

He also maintained as had Aristotle; "the father should be loved more than the mother because he is the active principle of generation".[62] He took this further: "the husband has the nobler part in the marital act" therefore "it is natural that he needs to blush less."[63] For him "woman is intended for procreation…not for perfection of mind." He concluded that the natural inferiority of women barred them from the priesthood, teaching; "Because women are in a state of subordination", they cannot receive holy orders."[64]

When, in the last years of the 20th century the Vatican solemnly declared that it could not ordain women because of a long and inspired tradition of ordaining only men—it conveniently forgot to mention the sexist theories that helped create this long tradition.

But I was then over-optimistic, for I expected the Catholic Church to be permanently changed by the radical and reforming Second Vatican Council of the 1960s. It would not be long before the Council's legacy would be sidelined by the bureaucrats of the Roman Curia—just as it did not take long for the Roman Curia to re-establish Papal supremacy after the 15th Century Council of Constance put the authority of Church Councils above the Papacy.

I still found it extraordinary that the men honoured as the "Fathers of the Church", the men Aquinas quoted as authorities, were not rejected as heretics when they started to teach that women were both inferior to men and uniquely susceptible to Satanic temptations.

The Jesus of the Gospels was accompanied by women; worked closely with them, protected them from zealous priests and respected them—but the "Fathers" taught that pious men should avoid the company of women. Surely that should have been seen as heresy? Sadly it was not. The Father of the Church Tertullian (who is not honoured as a saint since he finally changed his tune and left the Catholic Church) wrote to women: " You are the devil's gateway, you are the unsealer of that forbidden tree: you are the first deserter of the divine law: You are she who persuaded him whom the devil was not valiant enough to attack. You destroyed so easily God's image, man. On account of YOUR desert—that is death—even the Son of God had to die. And do you think about adorning yourself over and above your tunic of skin?"[65]

Even the *New Testament* suffered at the hands of these chauvinists. The "Fathers" based their arguments on certain of St. Paul's epistles—picking letters now thought by scholars to date from when Paul had been dead for many decades. "Paul's" letter to Timothy which blames women for the Fall, was written 50 years after Paul's death, at around the time the Church in Rome had started to exclude women. Likewise the Letter to the Ephesians, that told women to be veiled and quiet in church, is thought to date from some 60 years after Paul's death.

Galatians, an authentic letter of Paul's, spoke instead of the equality of men and women in Christ; "There is neither Jew nor Greek, there is neither slave nor free, there is neither male nor female: for you are all one in Christ Jesus".[66] It was such texts that made the Gnostic Christians claim that Paul was really one of the greatest of the Gnostic teachers.[67]

Tertullian justified his diatribe against women by quoting the Adam and Eve story, saying the first woman deserted her God-given role of helping Adam to form an alliance with the Serpent against Adam. Tertullian took little notice of the other creation account in Genesis where the Deity created humankind "in his own image", both "male and female"—and in which Eve had a sacred role. He also rejected other Christian creation myths in which Eve enlightened Adam and gave him a soul. If you have not heard of these other accounts, this is no surprise. Shortly after the Catholic Church gained official status in the Roman Empire, these accounts were among those ordered burnt and expunged from records.

The anti-woman views of the Fathers of this Church influenced the Protestant Reformation over a thousand years later. In the 16th Century the Reformer John Knox quoted Augustine and Tertullian to justify a claim that the rule of a woman over men was utterly unnatural and an insult to God. He was so indignant about Queen Mary's enthronement in England that he wrote *The First Blast of the Trumpet against the Monstrous Regiment of Women*.[68]

Tertullian was part of the Catholic school of Christians that claimed more power than did the Emperor. Clement, one of the first to claim the title of the Bishop of Rome, declared that Almighty God had not only delegated His authority to him, God had empowered him to delegate the divine authority to all his officers, whether bishops, priests or deacons. All of them could command the laity in the name of God. It was a major sin to disobey. He added that anyone who disobeyed his clergy would "receive the death sentence."[69] Clement's claim was amazingly made only seventy years after the death of Jesus and while the books of the New Testament were still being written. The Catholic Bishop Ignatius of Antioch, who lived a generation later, warned the laity to obey every bishop "as if he were God." This was not just in doctrinal matters. In 170CE Victor, Bishop of Rome, demanded that Christians stop celebrating Easter at Passover, as was common in many places, but on the date set by Rome. If they did not, they would be thrown out of the Church.

Gnostics, Catholics and Women

When I studied theology in the Seminary the Christian Gnostic books, although discovered hidden in Egypt in 1945, had not yet become publicly available. They were to be first published during the 1970s.

These books were "gnostic" in that they taught we should trust in the inner voice of the Holy Spirit or Sophia rather than in the voice of authority, even if that voice were that of the Bishop of Rome. "Gnostic" came from the Greek word "gnosis", meaning inner knowledge or wisdom. Hans Kung described Gnosticism as a religious school "characterised by striving for knowledge seen as widespread and not limited to Christians".[70] They thus did not demonise the pagans among whom they lived. They looked for wisdom both in Christ's teaching and their people's inherited Pagan wisdom. We know of this from Tertullian. He was bitterly critical of the Gnostic Christians for "they listen equally, they pray equally—even with pagans, if any happen to come…they share the kiss of peace with all that come."[71]

It was the party line among Catholic Christians that its own antecedents lay entirely in Judaism and the Old Testament, but this was not entirely true. It was also influenced by the teachings of Pagan religions. The Gnostic Christians were more open about this, but the Catholics were equally influenced, and not just by the dualism they inherited from Zoroastrianism through possibly the Jewish Essenes. When the books of Hermes came into the hands of later Christian authorities, they were so amazed by their similarity to Christian teaching that they said Hermes must be a prophet foretelling Christ. In fact he was a Pagan God. The similarity arose because Hermetic ideas had helped shape Christianity.[72]

The Catholics were so determined to destroy the power of women teachers and ritual leaders among the Gnostic Christians that they issued edicts against women's rights that helped shape Europe for the next two millennia. Tertullian declared of Gnostic Christian women: "These heretical women—how audacious they are! They have no modesty; they are bold enough to teach, to engage in argument, to enact exorcisms, to undertake cures, and, it may be, even to baptise!" He added: 'it is not permitted for a woman…to offer [the Eucharist] nor to claim a share in any masculine function—not to mention any priestly office."[73]

The Gnostics did not impose uniformity on their groups. For them wisdom was multifaceted like a jewel reflecting infinity. Tertullian thus attacked them for being "without authority" and "without discipline".[74] In recent times the Catholic Encyclopaedia has attacked them for fostering a "wild confusion of gnostic systems". Some taught that the body was a prison while others taught that the body was a sacred temple. They wrote about the primal fertile chaos from which life emerged, seeing this as female and as dark as the inside of the womb. Later churchmen thought of this darkness as evil, even though the Gnostics had said it sparkled with divine life.

The Gnostic Christians held that God was in all creatures. The Catholics attacked them also for this, calling it pagan "pantheism".[75] Many Catholics then saw nature was a vale of tears dominated by Satan. The spirits of nature, *daemons* in Greek, became the demon servants of Satan.

The Gnostics had no laity for they believed all members were part of a sacred priesthood. Thus Tertullian protested; "Even on the laity they impose the functions of priesthood." Some of the Gnostic groups cast lots to see who would serve as the priest or priestess for the day. This outraged the Catholics but the Gnostics believed they were following Jesus every bit as much as did the Catholics.

Until recently we only knew of the teachings of the Gnostic Christians from the distorting words of their enemies. The Catholics had triumphed over the Gnostics when Emperor Constantine made Catholicism a recognised state religion. Perhaps the Catholic views appealed to him because they were similar to his own on authority and on women? In 325CE, a year after he summoned and presided over the opening session of the Nicene Church Council called to give a single enforced Creed to Christianity, he had his wife Fausta boiled alive—and killed his eldest son Crispus.

He not only commissioned the book collection that we now know as the *New Testament*, he gave the Catholic faction a powerful empire-wide organisation supported by his Imperial Administration. He summoned its Councils, helped enforce its authority, funded it and endorsed its decisions. Eusebius, the man he commissioned to create the *New Testament*, praised Constantine in his *History of Christianity* as "the mightiest victor, adorned with every virtue of piety [who], together with his son Crispus, a most God-Beloved prince,…formed one united Roman Empire as of old." It is not known what Eusebius thought when Constantine killed Crispus.

Around the time of these murders, protests broke out in Rome against Constantine for refusing to take part in an official Pagan procession. He then left Rome never to return, living instead in Constantinople. He rebuilt this city using funds obtained by sacking ancient Pagan temples He gave the Catholic bishops juridical status and declared that Satan's influence lay behind any disobedience to a bishop's order. Gnostic Christians were forbidden to hold meetings and possession of Gnostic texts became a criminal offence.

Our subsequent ignorance about the Gnostics continued for over 1,500 years. Then in 1945 a peasant farmer called Muhammad Alí al-Sammán went out with his camels to obtain good topsoil from land near the town of Nag Hammadi in Upper Egypt—and unearthed with his brothers' help a large earthenware jar . The brothers were at first scared to open it, fearing that a spirit, a jinni, might be hidden within. Then the idea came that it might contain gold. They gathered their courage and broke it open.[76]

Much to their disappointment it was full of ancient documents written on papyrus, including thirteen books bound in leather. The farmer returned to his home in al-Qasr and dumped them on the straw piled next to the oven. Muhammad's mother, 'Umm-Ahmad, later admitted to burning some in the oven along with the straw she used to kindle the fire. Fortunately many were rescued. These are now known as the Nag Hammadi texts (an English transliteration of the town's name).

These documents, hidden to save them from destruction, have revolutionised our ideas about the early Christians. Several came from the same period as the official New Testament's Gospels—and were written by Christians with as close a knowledge of the life of Christ as had the Evangelists. The oldest parts of one of these, the *Gospel according to Thomas*, date back to around the year 60CE while the earliest New Testament gospel texts date back to around 65CE.[77]

These revealed to us a Gnosticism very different to that portrayed by its enemies and by scholars who had relied on texts written by its foes. For a start, Gnosticism turned out to be much less dualistic than they had imagined. Gnostics wrote of the material universe as essentially good and as still retaining the spark of divinity, although some held it had been much corrupted by humankind and by powerful spirits or demi-gods.[78]

One of these suppressed accounts was surprisingly blunt and feminist in its comments on the Adam and Eve story. The author of the book *On the Origin of the World* said that a demi-god inspired this story in order to justify the subjection of women. The author imagined the words said by the demi-god: "And let us instruct him in his sleep to the effect that she came from his rib, in order that his wife may obey and he may be lord over her." But this failed to deceive a powerful Eve. 'Then Eve, being a force, laughed at their decision."

A surprising insight into the relations between the Apostle Peter and women is also to be found in these documents. The *Gospel according to Mary*, perhaps linked to Mary Magdalene, reported: '(Peter) questioned them about the Saviour. "Did he really speak privately with a woman (and) not openly with us? Are we to turn about and all listen to her? Did he prefer her to us?' Then Mary wept and said to Peter, "My brother Peter, what do you think? Do you think I made this up in my heart or that I am lying about the Saviour?" Levi (Mathew) answered and said to Peter, "You have always been hot tempered. Now I see you contending against the women like the adversaries. But if the Saviour made her worthy, who are you indeed to reject her? Surely the Saviour knows her very well. That is why he loved her more than us.""[79] After this Mary was recognised as a divinely appointed teacher.

In another document, *Pistis Sophia*, Mary admits to Jesus that she scarcely dared talk freely to him in front of Peter for "Peter makes me hesitate. I am afraid of him because he hates the female race."[80] But the Gnostic *Gospel according to Thomas* was not so woman-friendly. It had Christ say that women have to become men in order to become perfect! This could have been a reference to the need we all have to embrace both sides of our nature, anima and animus, but as I said, the Gnostics did not enforce a uniform line.

These documents contained other ancient creation myths rejected by the Fathers and destroyed, perhaps because they did not blame women for the Fall. The book *On the Origin of the World* depicted Eve as the daughter and messenger of the Goddess Sophia. Eve was given the mystical name of Zoe, meaning life. Sophia sent her to give Adam a soul and to instruct him so that his children might become vessels of light. When Eve saw Adam in his cast down condition she pitied him, and exclaimed: "Adam, live! Rise up upon the earth!"

Many Gnostic Christians agreed with the Fathers and with Plato that there was ultimately only one ineffable deity—a very non-dualistic theory.[81] They held with Plato that from this supreme Deity flowed the gendered Deities, the divine Father and the Mother Sophia. She was at that time widely honoured among the mystically inclined Gnostic Christians and Jews

Some, including the Catholics, had another theory, also developed from Platonic ideas. In this Father was identified as the Ineffable and Transcendent One—from whom came both Christ as the Rational Word immanent in Creation and the Holy Spirit as Love immanent in Creation. This can be found at the start of John's Gospel.

It had been no easy matter for the advocates of a patriarchy to purge Judaism of its Goddess. The Bible recorded earlier attempts. When the prophet Jeremiah led the charge, he met with resistance. 'A great crowd answered Jeremiah as follows; "We have no intention of listening to the word you have just spoken to us in Yahweh's name, but intend to go on doing all we have vowed to do; offering incense to the Queen of Heaven and pouring libations in her honour, as we used to do, we and our ancestors, our kings and our chief men, in the towns of Judah and the streets of Jerusalem We had food a plenty then, we lived well, we suffered no disasters. But since we gave up offering incense to the Queen of Heaven and pouring libations in her honour, we have been destitute and have perished either by sword or by famine. Besides…[the women said] do you think we make cakes for her with her features on them and pour libations to her without our husbands' knowledge?"'[82]

But 100 years after Jesus' birth, the Jewish philosopher Philo provided an intellectual escape route for Jews and Christians who were uncomfortable with seeing the Holy Spirit, Sophia, as female. He queried whether Sophia was really female: "Is it because while Wisdom's name is feminine, her nature is manly?…Pre-eminence always pertains to the masculine. The feminine always falls short of and is less than it, Let us then pay no heed to the gender of the words and say that the daughter of God, even Wisdom, is not only masculine but father." This argument played a major role in developing a Christian religion deprived of a Goddess. Sophia, the Mother, the Spirit of Love and of Wisdom, was to become faded, near invisible, a sexless ghost, the Holy Ghost.

In 2000CE I was surprised and delighted when I discovered that the official British celebrations for the Millennium at the 'Dome' were centred around a pageant in the main arena that amazingly told a story in which the Goddess Sophia joined with a young God who had first got things wrong by rejecting her and creating a materialistic unnatural world! When they eventually mated, a green and beautiful world ensued. I thought this extraordinarily appropriate and wondered why the Press had not described it. It was clearly intended as a myth for today. The very choice of the name "Sophia" betrayed its inspiration. The Press had instead described the controversy over the shape of the 'spirit zone'. Apparently some Christians had objected to its original design as a pyramid, seeing this as a pagan shape, so it was redesigned as a spiral—an ancient Celtic pagan symbol!

Creation Myths

St. Augustine was a convert from a pagan religion called Manichaeanism with a matter-spirit dichotomy. Western scholars once only knew of Manichaeanism through the accounts of its enemies but in the twentieth century Manichean scriptures were discovered in Asia and a living Manichean-based religion, Mandean, found surviving in Iraq. The word *Manda* is the Semitic for "Gnosis".[83] It was probably present in the Jordan valley during Jesus' lifetime. This religion turned out not to be as miserable as portrayed by Augustine after he had left it—and it was surprisingly unflattering to men in its creation myth.

Their myth, as taught in Iraq, was that there emanated from the ultimate Deity lesser male and female deities who created this world. A female deity made Adam—but was appalled at the results. "He was like a man, but moved about on all fours, had a face like an ape, and made noises like a sheep." She went to ask the supreme Deity that lived in the House of Life why she had failed. The House of Life saw that Adam had no soul— so sent a Son to ask a Soul to go into the man. But when the Soul saw Adam, she was horrified and exclaimed, "What! Must I dwell in this flesh and blood, this house of uncleanness?'" She refused to go. The House of Light pleaded with her. She then agreed "on one condition only, and that is that everything that is in the world of light shall be in this world— including flowers, trees, light, pure air (ajar), running water (yardna) and baptisms." And so it was. Later, the lesser female deity who had created Adam mated with him, and thus the human race was started.

The Sleeping Beauty myth encapsulated some of the Gnostic teaching. The soul is the sleeping beauty that is awoken and transformed by the kiss of the Divine Lover. They taught that a divine spark existed in nature, is in each of us and only needed awakening.

But St. Augustine did not put his faith in any such spark but in a City of God that existed outside nature, or so he claimed. He depicted the universe dualistically as two rival cities—one of God and one of Satan. He developed his theory after being shocked by the sacking of the Eternal City, Rome, by Alaric, the King of the West Goths in 410CE.[84] In his last great work, *The City of God* Augustine wrote of history as a battle between the natural state, seen as the Devil's kingdom of Babylon, and the City of God, seen as the supernatural world of the Predestined Elite.

Catholic Christians at that time saw little point in looking after nature, whether it was tainted or not, for many thought the world was about to end. Tertullian even suggested that procreation be left to Pagans, as Christians need not engage in such a dangerous activity with such little time to go! They saw history as linear, beginning with an act of Creation, bearing fruit with Christ, and ending with the Apocalypse. This was a dramatic change from the normal pagan spiral or circular view of history, developed from the experience of a continuous cycle of life and death and of the seasons.

It was said by Catholics such as Tatian that the sacrament of baptism delivered Christians from being part of nature. After baptism the Christian stood outside of nature alongside God.[85] The consequent rejection of all the daemones or nature spirits as "demons" or devils shocked Pagans.

But as previously mentioned, Christianity was not a complete system that suddenly appeared. It was formed from pre-existing Pagan and Judaic philosophical and religious systems that it had adapted and made Christ-centred. Thus we can find in Christianity many Pagan and Judaic beliefs.

It is likely that the contemporary Jewish sect of Essenes, whose library was found hidden in Dead Sea caves, and who may well have been influenced by Zoroastrianism, had helped give Christianity its dualism. One of its principal texts, *The Scroll of the War of the Sons of Light against the Sons of Darkness,* told of a "Prince of Light" who would help them fight "Satan" who 'rules in darkness" in a spiritual war of cosmic proportions.[86]

Christian initiation or baptism soon came to include an oath to forsake Satan and an exorcism banishing Satan and all his works. But this doctrine of a Satanic rival to God was foreign to most Pagan religions—and many Pagans took strong exception to it. Celsus wrote "that what made the Christian message dangerous is not that they believe in one God but that they deviate from monotheism by the 'blasphemous' belief in the devil."[87]

Augustine's book on the rival cities was enormously influential. Charlemagne was said to read some of it every day while extending "the City of God" by armed force—in one case by having a bishop bless a river while his soldiers forced the local inhabitants though it downstream at sword point, thus "baptising" them. Charlemagne saw his authority as coming from God via the Pope who had anointed him as King of the Holy Roman Empire. This again was a very different concept of kingship from that prevalent in earlier pagan kingdoms where the King was seen as coming from the land and being responsible to the land.

Augustine's theory influenced the more fundamentalist forms of Christianity present today, and perhaps even President Ronald Reagan's naming of the Soviet Union as "the Evil Empire" and in President George W. Bush naming of Iraq, Iran and North Korea as 'the Axis of Evil". It fostered a very black and white view of the world, with one side Evil, and the other side, our side, Good.

But when Augustine and other "Fathers" undermined the prestige of women by saying they were the prime causes of the Fall and therefore of original sin, women still had leading sacred roles in temples. He was still more vehement against the priests and priestesses of the Goddess Cybele in Rome—because in her priesthood there were those who were sexually 'different", the gays and the transsexuals.

The Priestesses who served Cybele were known as Gallae and her Priests as Gallus. Some of these were transsexuals gender-reassigned in the temple by means of a sacred operation.[88] Augustine fumed against these priestesses, saying they were "foully unmanned and corrupted"; adding that Cybele herself was a "demon"[121] and that she as "the Great Mother surpassed all the Gods…not for reason of her divine power but in the enormity of her wickedness." His vehement attack on her priestesses and priests helped bring about their torture and deaths under the first Christian emperors.

Yet many other aspects of the cult of Cybele made their way into Christianity. She had her main temple in Rome where now stands the Vatican. The Sacred Marriage was celebrated among her mysteries. Roman coins had on them an inscription calling her "Mater Dei", the very title soon to be given to Mary. Her priestesses wore mitres and stoles, as do today's Bishops. They were said to "vaticanate" when they divinated. Her symbols were tablets with a fish and a chalice carved onto them—the fish would become a Christian symbol. Fish were a food sacred to her. Her special day of the week was Friday—and still to this day some Christians eat fish on Fridays.[89]

Statues of Cybele have been found in Ukraine, the Crimea, Romania and Bulgaria. The Greeks said the Amazons honoured her. She was represented in her temple by a black meteorite brought to Rome from her original shrine in Anatolia. Similar goddess symbols were the cube shaped black stone at Poetra and the meteorite stone of the Ka'aba at Mecca. The latter was honoured before the rise of Islam as an image of the creating goddess. The priests who tended this shrine were still known as 'the sons of the Old Woman' after the rise of Islam.

Once Christianity became in the 4th Century the official religion of the Roman Empire, the temple of Cybele, the Mother Goddess of Rome, was razed and the Vatican was built upon its ruins. Images of Mary now appeared decked in the same symbols as were previously reserved to pagan goddesses—perhaps because this was the only legal way for people to retain an image that symbolised their Goddess and the old ways. A sculpture of the boat of Isis became the boat of Mary still present before a church in Rome. Mary was depicted with twelve stars around her head after the *Book of Revelations*. "And there appeared a great wonder in heaven, a woman clothed with the sun and the moon under her feet, and upon her head a crown of twelve stars".[90] This image was taken from a millennia old image of Innana, a Middle Eastern Goddess.

It was not forgotten by those who suppressed women that the male body was also part of nature and thus also an enemy to be subdued. The Catholic ascetics and Fathers believed that the body should be forced into line by starvation, penance and hardship. This teaching was based on the dualism that saw matter as a realm of Satan but it may have been also partially inherited from the warrior ethos. A warrior conquered both other nations and himself.

They believed self-inflicted pain showed how seriously they took their faith. Ascetic schools of monks and nuns set up settlements on remote islands, on headlands and in barren places around Europe. Their ideas had helped shape the very institution in which I lived, the Claretian Order.

It took centuries for these puritanical ideas to prevail in Europe. The 8th Century missionary St Boniface wrote in disgust of the British that they "totally despise matrimony" and had sexual relations outside marriage "after the manner of neighing horses and braying asses." A century later the monk Alcuin wrote that Britain "has been absolutely submerged under a flood of fornication, adultery, incest, so that the very semblance of modesty is entirely absent."[91]

In Ireland the clash between the Christian ascetic world and older values was reflected in stories about Bridget, also known as Bride. She was the Goddess most celebrated in Ireland at the time when St Patrick arrived. One story had him given to spending his nights in icy pools of water as a penance. When Bridget went to do the same, the pools promptly dried up. The lesson taken was that she was not to engage in the body punishing spirituality of Patrick.[92] When she had trouble with Coemgen of Glendalough, who punished himself by holding his palms up for seven years, she predicted that he would soon be driven indoors by a snowstorm. She evidently thought little of such asceticism.

There was not much room for sex in the Christian world of .the early Middle Ages. It was officially banned on Thursdays in honour of Christ's arrest, on Fridays because of his death, on Saturdays because it was Our Lady's day, on Sundays because of the Resurrection and on Mondays in commemoration of the dead.[93] (No doubt couples stayed home on Tuesday and Wednesday nights!)

Training for the priesthood

But to return to the story of my life in the Seminary at Highcliffe Castle, I had not yet come to the point of actively questioning my male privileges. After three years I had completed my studies in Philosophy and had started Theology. I would soon be ordained an Exorcist in a step towards the priesthood. I would thus become one of those officially authorised to deal with spirits—under the Church's direction.

Around this time, for some reason that was never specified, Father Mahon, who was responsible for discipline among the students, called me to his study and insisted that I should see a psychiatrist. He did not mention the cross-dressing. I was puzzled. I had only one secret. What else could make him so concerned? I watched him, bent over in his chair, wringing his hands but he would not say why he was giving this instruction.

I was told I had to see the 'shrink' if I wished to continue studying for the priesthood so I went. The psychiatrist invited me to sit in a large armchair and then gently probed me with questions. He seemed to have no target. Nothing was said about cross-dressing. Normality guided my careful responses. My sexual identity problem remained buried.

"Why have you come to see me?" he finally asked.

"Because my Father Prefect wanted me to come."

"Why did he think you should see me?"

I gave my theory. "He is a nervous and highly strung man and I think he misinterpreted me because of his own problems."

"Ah."

A few days later at morning prayers Father Mahon literally went off his head. He raved about our collective faults to an uncommon degree. As a result he was relieved of his duties and went off to recuperate. I survived and carried on working towards becoming a priest—ready to survive anything to reach this goal.

It was a long training, eight years in all. As the years passed in that greenhouse world, I had much time to dream of the kind of priest I would be. I learnt about the Worker-Priest movement in France. I liked how they worked in ordinary jobs, sharing whatever they earned. They fought as trade union members for justice for the poorly paid. They seemed to me true Christians. They inspired me. Thus I sought any opportunity to do such work. Around 1964 came my first small chance. Some of us were allowed day release to work as nurses for two weeks in a geriatric ward.

The following year we were allowed out on longer leashes. I went to a London Catholic hospital and nursed for about three weeks, returning at night to a Claretian parish. I was allowed to watch two caesarean operations. In one a tiny baby was stillborn. They attempted to resuscitate with fingers softly squeezing each side of its tiny chest. They blew gently in its mouth—but failed. The child was extraordinarily beautiful, but under handsize. The other operation was like a conjuring act. The surgeon, master magician, leaned forward and presto a child came from a slit in the cloth over the mother. The moment was extraordinarily the surgeon's, with the woman reduced for the moment to being simply the container. The evenings in the parish after these sessions at the hospital were frustrating. Parish life seemed like that of a gentleman's club in comparison.

The year after this, I went with another student to work at a state hospital, the Lambeth at Elephant and Castle, in one of the roughest areas of South London. This saw our leash stretch nearly to vanishing point. We were allowed to find our own accommodation. I stayed in a students' flat, sharing with young men and women. I nursed in Casualty, learning to take out stitches, to cope with drunks, children and panicked people. Humanity entered deeper into my life. Romanticism did not leave it. I served my Lover-God, I moved with female company but without romance, simply as the friends I had always wanted.

I found a window into another world by working in the evenings with a Catholic lay organisation called the Legion of Mary. They contacted the women of the street in Soho to offer them friendship and any help they needed. It was exciting to work through the night, go to small cafes up fire escapes; to visit people in their homes, down back-lanes, sometimes in the street by sex parlour or brothel doors. The most disturbing (and wanted) experience was when I met a young woman who was then far advanced in the course I would later take. She had been brought up as a boy and yet was in every way feminine. Her flat was soft with cuddly toys. Lace covers decorated the dressing table. She had adopted all the stereotypical symbols of femininity, perhaps because once they had been banned from her life, perhaps because she did not want anyone to doubt her gender, perhaps simply because that was the kind of girl she was. She was the first person I met that shared the dream I hid. I was sorry at the time that we did not have the chance to speak—but I would have feared exposure of my fantasy so perhaps would never have mentioned it.

Between these sojourns in the real world, I moved through the four-year course in a theology that was stiffened with canon law, laced with psychiatry, psychology and social studies. I did not find these studies boring for the old edifice was cracking and taking in fresh air. Iconoclastic theologians had taken advantage of the fissures provided by the Vatican Council to question the borders of Catholic belief, setting themselves against the elitism of the hierarchy, the compulsory celibacy of priests, the primacy of edict over conscience. I swam in these same fissures and read *Concilium*, the professional journal of the theological left, and a thousand articles and books by Karl Rahner, Hans Kung and many more.

Many of my fellow students were of radical inclination. One weekend, we were asked to accompany a priest to help with a service at the elite military academy of Sandhurst. We were to stay overnight and thus were allotted by Sandhurst a "batman", of the sort assigned to all officers in the British army so they could feel they were members of the upper class. He showed us to our bedroom and then respectfully asked us to leave our shoes outside the door so he could take and polish them.

Well, one of my companions thought this highly undemocratic. No one would clean his shoes for him he declared, as he firmly stuffed them under his bed. I, much less principled, thought it appropriate that the British army should clean the shoes of the child of an Irish rebel and so put my shoes outside the door as requested.

We were woken in the very early hours by the batman crawling between our beds, seeking the shoes my friend had hidden, so he could properly service us as honorary officers! We made up for this later by making a mess of their golf course. They had assumed that we had been initi-ated to this game, then, I think, dominated by "gentlemen".

After six years at the Castle I was sent for my final year of theology to the Jesuitical bastions of Heythrop College in Oxfordshire. My early dream of studying with the Jesuits thus came true. I enjoyed the company of their witty and unassuming tutors and exploring their great library. Nuns came to study with us. I rode a broad hunter horse through the fields and lanes, got a driving license, helped rewire our hall of residence and gained a master's degree in Theology from a Roman university linked to Heythrop—a degree at that time denied to the women who studied with us. My own gender troubles remained suppressed.

Ordination to the Priesthood

I then achieved my long-term goal. At Easter in 1967 I happily went to be ordained a priest in my family's parish church in Folkestone, accompa-nied by friends from the college and admired by the local women who remembered how I prayed for hours in the church after school. The Bishop presided but he was for me not much more than the official wit-ness. I felt I was dedicating myself in an intensely personal act, receiving powers and responsibilities from my Lover, witnessed by the community. The Bishop would not have seen my ordination in quite the same light. For him I was dedicating myself also to serving an institution under the directions of the Bishop and of Rome

Lying prostrate before the altar during my vigil and ordination I dedi-cated myself to my Lover. When the chalice was put into my hands I took it with joy and awe, wondering at the marvel of being able to handle the blood of my Lover, the bread, the flesh of my Lover. I shared my Lover with all in communion, united in an oneness that encompassed all creation

Afterwards my Mother, glowing with pride, gave me a gold-coated chalice, the gold coming from her rings. The names of family members were engraved upon it. I now had spiritual elite status and found it odd and uncomfortable. I did not see my ordination as making me a privileged mediator between humans and God but that was what many presumed. My church work would also include witnessing forgiveness in the confessional. I would not be forgiving but witnessing, for I believed sins were forgiven, forgotten, as soon as a human came in love to God. But I was at odds with the beliefs of the many Catholics who presumed that if I refused to forgive sins they were retained by a God who was bound to be as unforgiving as myself. It was "Father, can we do this, Father can we do that" and it was into the confessional to assure a thousand scrupulous people that masturbation was no sin.

The Catholic Church teaches that the priesthood once received cannot be removed or even given up, for it places a sacred mark upon the soul, sealing it as God's own. This sounded to me like a claim to have worked magic upon my soul. And in a sense this was right. But it was not the bishop but my Lover God working in conjunction with me that had worked this magic. This is why the Church cannot remove it. In their law I am still an ordained priest.

Ordination should not have made me a member of an elite. I never believed that a separated clergy was part of divine revelation. The Jesus of the New Testament did not recommend to his followers the creation of a priestly mediating class. Instead he was critical of the Jewish priesthood and said that there was no need for a mediator between a loving God and us. The only mention of a Christian priesthood in the New Testament is where Paul said that all men and women were part of the priesthood. This challenged those who thought God a preserve of a dedicated elite. It challenged none more than the Fathers of the Church and the Bishop in Rome.

With such beliefs, why was it important to me to be ordained a priest? Why did I need to be ordained at all, if all were in the priesthood?

I thought much about this at the time. I decided that it was because I wanted to celebrate as solemnly and publicly as I could my self-gift to God and his acceptance of my service. I thought I was not gaining the priesthood, but simply becoming its servant, the trained enabler and empowerer, master of ceremonies, who would work with others to strengthen their relationship with their Lover-God.

I knew there were no boundaries when working with a God who is a Lover of all. For me the priesthood reached beyond Christendom to all humans. Ultimately it is part of our very nature as human creatures. We are all priests and priestesses. One in gender, one in race, one in kind, one with nature, one with the very power of creation.

Pope Pius XI in the 1936 encyclical *The Catholic Priesthood* stressed "Since God is spirit, it seems appropriate that everyone who consecrates and devotes himself to the spirit should also in a certain sense free himself from his body." I never wanted to become a priest to suppress my body, nor to serve the establishment of the church. I believed that Christ taught us to follow the inner voice of God rather than religious authorities. With hindsight, this belief meant I was on a path that would take me outside the Catholic institution. I did not realise this at the time. I felt and hoped the Church could be reformed from within. I was sure there was a place in the Church for me.

My first major act as a priest was to officiate at the wedding of the sister of a friend, Kevin O'Connor, in Dublin in 1967. He invited me to arrive in time for the festivities beforehand. I sat with his friends on the backs of seats upstairs on the buses, singing with the passengers a hundred lyrics. We burst into the hen party where I laughed and frolicked with Catholic women who saw me as somewhat safe target for flirting. And family members took me to show me what they called the scandal of Irish Catholicism. I was shown rows of double storied houses, one per priest, eight houses for the eight priests of the parish; while the married son with his wife shared a curtain-divided bedroom with in Kevin's parents, such was the housing shortage. They told me they had to drive to Northern Ireland to get contraceptives. This was not news to me. But it helped me see where I wished to go—and it wasn't into this type of parish.

My first pilgrimage as a priest was to Kildare, an Irish sanctuary once sacred to the Goddess Brighid. When the people became Christian, they called her the foster mother of Christ and sung of a threesome of Christ, Mary and Bridget. She has more holy sites named after her than St Patrick. For me the true way was beyond any classification of faiths. The God, the Goddess, our ancestral knowledge of the sacred, speaks to us across history. It is our sacred inheritance no matter if Pagan or Christian.

Now I was ordained, I knew that I could be put into a parish to work on maintaining its institutions. I felt I needed time to think, to see how best I could use this consecration as a knight, a priest, of God's people. I felt I was not meant to be a professional parish minder. I suspected I would not survive long in such gentlemen's clubs. I fled every offer of a place in a parish. I knew there was other priestly work that I could do. I wanted to work for social justice so I pleaded intellectual talent and persuaded my Order to send me to university to study social problems.

I then deftly sidestepped an offer of a place at Oxford, where I would have been accommodated among clerics in the privileged comfort of a Dominican hall, in the Order of St Thomas Aquinas, while reading Modern Greats. Instead I took a place at the more secular London University to read Sociology. This course was taught between the highly reputed London School of Economics and Bedford College, the former women's College of London University. I would specialise in industrial sociology and white-collar crime, hoping these would help me as a worker-priest when I needed to take on the powerful.

I was relieved to have survived the seminary. I had achieved my goal and was ordained. I felt I had less need now to placate superiors. I could now do my best to live the Gospels.

I was surprised to find that the sin that Catholics mostly wanted to confess was masturbation, not greed, not hurting or hating others. I told those who confessed this that masturbation was not serious and not sinful. But I was out on a limb in so advising. Pope Paul VI would write in 1975 that the masturbator forgoes the love of God and commits a mortal sin when he deliberately wastes male seed. He thus equated masturbation with murder. I did not know the God of which he spoke. I could not see the difference between wasting semen and wasting other body fluids such as saliva. I learnt later his ideas originated from a medieval science that thought sperm made up of tiny embryos.

Yet I got much pleasure from working as a Catholic priest. I enjoyed using my skill in ritual to make for those around me the celebrations of the sacred moments of life as special and empowering as I could.

The Claretians did their best to ensure I had fitting accommodation while at university. They found me a room in a West End parish, at St. James just off Oxford Street. It had a luxurious presbytery of polished stairs and panelled walls where women, encased as Nuns, scurried about like mice. They tried to be invisible as they polished the banisters, made my bed, cooked my food, and serviced me as a member of the priestly elite.

The evening meal at St. James was an elegant occasion. The parish priest presided over the table. He was a Monsignor, a rank below a bishop, and a highly civilised man. Fine wines were served while a squeaky little lift delivered rare meats, rich sauces, delicately cooked vegetables and delicious deserts from the nuns in their basement kitchen. Here for the first and last time, I experienced the very refined chauvinism of an exquisite gentlemen's club. After dinner the monsignor ritually flourished a vast red handkerchief, took snuff, and then invited us to his room where we sipped brandy and relaxed in vast armchairs to listen to Mozart.

I have never had the opportunity to explore the world of the elite female clubs or even luxurious convents, so I cannot reflect on how they might use male servants. But I am sure there are scarcely any equivalents. Our priestly luxury demanded maintenance by an underclass. This consisted of celibate women dedicated to servicing men reverenced because they held sacred powers that were inaccessible to women. We were essentially very fat camels quite unfit to get through not just the eye of a needle but even the door of a poor person's home.

My luxury came with minimal charge. In return I had to assist with on Sundays with the Sacraments in priestly finery descended from Roman Empire days, now decorated with Flemish lace. I heard confessions for an hour on Saturdays in a small dark wooden box. I never heard of a serious crime but did hear a thousand inconsequential scruples. I preached for fifteen minutes on Sundays and celebrated the Holy Mass for half an hour on weekday mornings in our neo-gothic church.

The Holy Mass celebrated there was a distant echo of what it was in early days. We believed that God himself was really present in Holy Communion. I had no problems with this for I experienced God as present in all his strength and wisdom everywhere. But I had problems with the soulless cobwebs in which the church's lawyer-theologians had enshrouded this sacred family meal.

I told in sermons of how there was once a friend, a God, who so loved the beings he created that he came to visit them as one of them. He ate meals with the people he dearly loved—as we do with our friends. He was willing to give himself to us totally. He thus said with utter seriousness that the bread he was giving them was not just grain but his very flesh and the wine not just grape juice but his very blood.

For me these words embodied a humanity-wide tradition of the sacred meal. I believed the living power of God was really and truly present in our material world, in the bread and in the wine and in each one of us. But Church lawyers had to coat this poetry of life in jargon. Pedantically they said the bread was no longer bread, even though it seemed to be bread, but flesh carefully disguised so as to fool any scientific analysis. To make sure it did not seem like bread, they had conspired with the ecclesiastical cooks to make sure it was pallid, tasteless and white—in other words, as far from Godlike as was possible.

So, feeling like this, what was I doing, preparing a meal dressed up in Roman Empire leftover clothing inside a sacred perimeter, separated from and elevated above other Christians, blessing tasteless bread on a table that no one else could reach? I was gradually coming to believe that this was not what any God worth his salt would have had in mind for me when he accepted my dedication of myself as his priest.[94]

Away from the confines of the parish, I celebrated the Sacred Meal as the family meal—with real bread, with friends at the table, with no marks of priestly rank. I sought to join all together in the consecration of the bread and wine so they might experience their own priesthood. I left it to the dry ecclesiastical God to work out just who among us had the power to make it really happen.

The income provided for me by the Order was even more embarrassing than the accommodation. It was Holy Mass offerings collected by Claretian missionaries in Latin America. I would be sent fifty or even a hundred offerings at a time. I could keep one offering per Mass if I remembered for a moment these nameless third-world benefactors while celebrating the Mass. This was a common way for Catholic priests to earn their income.

It should be remembered that this was the Britain of the late 1960s, when ideas were popular of social change and even revolution. I could not live in such a style and be one with the students or with radical priests such as the American Jesuit Dan Berrigan, who spilt blood on American weapons in protest against the Vietnam War. This lifestyle was a total contradiction to my ideals.

Thus I plotted my next move down the social order on a path where down was up. I somehow succeeded in persuading my superiors that I would be better off staying in an ordinary student's hall of residence, in a standard student's room at Tennyson Hall, in a square near Baker's Street Tube Station, where meals were unromantically served in a plain basement room and no nuns made my bed.

You might be wondering what was happening at this time with my gender identification problem? The feeling that I should be living a woman still haunted me as a perplexing fantasy that I could not understand and could not talk about. But the tension was lifting off me in other ways for at the age of twenty-six I at last had women friends.

Nothing sexual happened between us. I was just pleased to know women with whom I could joke and chat. This was an enormous relief and liberation. But I was distracted at this time from internal preoccupations by a multitude of happenings. I had long lived inside institutions and was now learning to survive and grow in an ordinary setting.

The prestige of the priesthood still occasionally served me well. I received headlines in a national Catholic newspaper because of my opposition to the Vietnam War. I thought it part of the job of a priest to make plain that the massive high-tech slaughter of a people was the very antithesis of Christian teaching. I found it impossible to pardon the distortion of Christ's teaching that allows churchmen to bless such endeavours. Yet I knew their rationale. I had been told it was a war waged against godless communists who persecuted and murdered Catholics. But as far as I could discover, the Vietnam War was started by the French who wanted to force Vietnam into becoming again their colony and, when the French were defeated, continued by the Americans to impose by force a government friendly to the economic interests of the West.

The very fact that my opposition made headlines showed how scandalously rare it was for a Catholic priest to oppose this barbarous war or to even raise the question of whether Christians should support it. I was summoned to our order's British headquarters in the parish at Hayes in Middlesex where Mary, Mother of God, ruled supreme behind the altar in a vast canvas painted by the Annigoni who had previously painted Queen Elizabeth II.

My boss, my former Novice Master, Father Angel, asked me to justify coming out in public against this war. I answered; "For the same reasons that you came out against Franco." He had been exiled because of his opposition to Franco. His Basque eyes broke into a grin. I walked out free of reproof.

I had learnt something of the need to be courageous from Fr. Dan Berrigan, who took many risks to publicly demonstrate his opposition to war. Today, when I re-read his books, they seem unduly couched in academic language—but I too have moved on. At that time I lived in a world more like that to his.

In his writing there was hard passion, unwillingness to compromise, a clear insight into our world and a call to action. He wrote in his book oddly entitled: *Consequence, Truth and,* "The opposite of love is not hatred; it is indifference. When we have learned indifference, when we are really skilled and determined at the business of ignoring others, of putting our own well being, our own opinions, first…we may be quite certain that at that point, life has become hell. We need be no more thoroughly damned."[95]

I tried to avoid pious Catholic circles for I felt uncomfortable with the status I had achieved because a Bishop had ordained me. In these circles people agreed with me simply because I was a priest. I knew that any dispute would be buried and re-surface behind my back. I knew this deference was partly derived from old custom. England has long been a society of elites and hat doffing. The institution seemed to want me to serve in a stately dignified way that kept me apart from the laity. This seemed to contradict the inner calling that had made me decide to train for the priesthood.

The Claretians now saw me as a potential source of revenue as a priest and sent me to work in parishes between the university terms. The priests I met were rarely house trained but had women coming in to clean and look after them. Their celibacy was comfortable, women made sure of this. But not all parishes were like this. One vacation I went to a parish in SW Wales run by the Franciscan priest who had officiated at my parents' wedding—and found no luxury there.

During my time in this Milford Haven parish, when not needed, I cycled the wild cliffed coastline and discovered, to my delight, an ancient hermitage built into a cleft in sheer sea-cliffs by my Celtic forefathers. There was much about this that appealed to my spirit. But I was not ready for it, for I felt my priestly life should centre on working with the poor in cities, fighting against social injustice. I then underestimated the importance of meditation, of working with nature, of influencing mundane events by strengthening people's dreams, the poetry of their ethics, the balance of their lives.

At Student Christian Movement conferences I met students from Northern Ireland and learnt of their commitment to the new 1960s non-violent movement for equality between Catholics and Protestants. Here I met Keith Kimber, an Anglican student for the priesthood, a troubadour with the guitar, who became a great and lifelong friend. With him, I prayed in Anglican churches and took communion with them. For me the churches have mostly been kept divided by bureaucracies that took comfort in the status quo.

Eventually my change of residence to Tennyson Hall, the student residence, was not enough for my sense of commitment. I had come to London to study wealth and poverty and I did not intend to do it just from textbooks. I soon found out about the Simon Community in Maldon Road in Kentish Town, a run-down area of north London,

This was a community inspired by anarchists, including Christians who did not believe in institutions. It was based in two down-at-heel terrace houses. Here were welcome people of the road, meths drinkers, drug addicts, and "no-hopers". We ate soup and bread, sitting on the arms of faded armchairs and on wonky chairs as heroin addicts mainlined maintenance doses, and then spurted blood from syringes into waste paper baskets. Volunteers collected vanloads of outdated food from supermarkets and bakers. The community was partly made up of volunteers, some full time, others part-time. All alike, guests of the road and full time volunteers, ate the same food, dressed in the same cast-offs, shared the same accommodation and were paid the same. The ideal was Christian in that it followed Christ's precept to love others as one loved God, without reserve and without undue worry about tomorrow. I knew however this was not a peculiarly Christian ideal.

If the guests from the road wanted, they could go to a farm near Canterbury to dry out or simply to relax. An old donated ambulance was used. A volunteer who kept a pet baby crocodile in a fish tank loved to race it down to the farm, siren screaming,

I became an organiser of a nightly soup run to the places where people slept out around London. This was the only time I smoked. Sharing a cigarette became a ritual of companionship on old bombsites, behind advertising hoardings or by warm air-grates beneath office blocks. I puffed, tried not to breathe in for that would make me choke (perhaps a consequence of my childhood asthma), to the great amusement of my companions. I did not do a great deal. The full time volunteers did much more.

Again my ill-deserved unwanted status came to the fore. People saw in me that the Catholic Church could have a human face. I thought the church institution had little part in what I was doing. My work was entirely my own initiative. I was sure that my idea of what it was to be a priest and a Christian would sooner or later get me into real trouble, for I knew the authorities would one day insist on my contributing to the strengthening of their institution.

The Simon Community put to use my talents as a sociologist by asking me to organise a survey of the ruined houses and yards of East London so they had information to use in raising funds. I met with truly poor and desperate people behind hoardings and in wrecked buildings. These included labourers, carpenters, priests, lawyers, and other professionals. All had fled from, or been deserted by, their former peers.

At university I was elected to a staff committee as a representative of the Sociology students. I found junior academics would ask me to bring up their own complaints. I was perceived as somewhat immune to professorial pressure, not subject to their fear of damaging their careers.

Authorities noted this. A Sociology Professor snarled as he passed me in the corridor: "It is obvious that you are not thinking of making a profession out of sociology." He was quite right. I had no interest in a career in which I put orthodoxy first solely in order to gain an income. But I learnt much from these studies. My work on white-collar crime helped me better understand corporate workings. My industrial democracy helped me better understand how to make the workplace more human.

But many of my lecturers were dedicated to Parsonian economics, head counting and the market. I saw this stress as insidiously undermining any principled approach. I now think it helped give birth to Thatcherism—the reorganising of society on the presumption that people are motivated better by competition, profit and greed than by the common good. This was to my mind one of the great heresies of our age and the root cause of much misery. It underestimated grossly the public spirit many possessed, thus crassly insulting them.

But there was another school of thought in the Sociology department. From this I learnt of Karl Marx and Max Weber. I was not overly impressed by the belief that class analysis could explain our world. I was more intrigued by the Webian theories of how bureaucracy and elites work to regulate and sometimes stifle. It was easy to see how Britain was ruled by an elite sharing common interests, common school ties and University backgrounds, for people find it easier to deal with others who share their background—even if mediocre and self-centred.

Goffman's description of "total institutions" that fully absorb their members helped me better to understand the church's institutions. I saw the same patterns used in armies, in prisons, in hospitals and in religious orders. Obedience was a most effective instrument of efficiency—at first sight. It all depended on what was one's aim—the perpetuation of the institution or the passing on of a truth that empowered people.

At that time I was riding on a floodtide of change. Paris was torn apart in 1968 by an idealistic uprising that threatened the French government. The London School of Economic was locked up, forbidden to us students, as we too demanded change. I thought we had every reason to do so. Much of the teaching of under-graduates was mediocre. The staff seemed much more concerned with advising governments, consulting businesses and working on research with the help of post-graduates, than with teaching us. Many lectures were poorly prepared and a waste of time.

It was a major disappointment for me, even if the LSE did have a fine library and some good lecturers, such as Robin Blackburn. It had not lived up for me to its reputation as a centre of biting social analysis, the whole reason why I chose to go there.

Fortunately my course was part taught at Bedford College. Here undergraduate teaching was of a higher standard and the setting much more amenable. It was based in Regent's Park, half surrounded by a lake, a gentle site in the centre of London, chosen originally as particularly suited to a women's college although now admitting men. Since my time there, Thatcher's government has sold it off to private foundations and American colleges who gave a premium price for such a setting.

We gave refuge at Bedford to the locked-out students of LSE. As ideas for change were debated, the Administration at Bedford opened a dialogue with us. We won changes to teaching methods, assessment and to the administration of the college that had been refused at LSE. Many of our changes lifted the academic standard—and probably made life harder for us!

After this I was encouraged to run for President by the socialists and communists, as well as leading members of the college administration, an unusual support basis for a Catholic priest. I lost by just eight votes. But perhaps it was as well. It would have taken up a year of my life and other things were in store for me.

I was still learning what it meant to be a priest. In France worker-priests were being ordered back to parish life by bishops under pressure from employers. Some of these priests refused to desert their brothers and sisters in the work places—and consequently found themselves threatened with excommunication from the church.

I looked for any priests that could teach me how to live a life truly dedicated to the poor. I was delighted when I met at LSE a Father Mario Borrelli who lived on Naples's streets with street urchins. I later hitchhiked to Naples and stayed a month with him, but disappointingly it was in a quiet marbled cloister rather than a street-squat.

I felt much more inspired when I attended a gathering of shop stewards in Sheffield to discuss worker-democracy. They wanted business enterprises to become co-operative efforts between workers and investors. It strengthened my belief that real social change would only be achieved outside the timid world of academia. With the uprising then happening in Paris, the atmosphere was charged, optimistic, and near revolutionary. We dreamt real social change. The people I met produced research and analysis that mocked university elitism. They believed that if workers had a real say in factories, they would be both better places to work and more productive. They were opposed by those who believed in the efficiency of dictatorial systems and the market place. I felt market-place ideology was not suitable for cattle, let alone for humans. At that time I was optimistic that the shop stewards might bring about real change.

As for the Church institutions, I was gradually edging closer to some of the ideas expressed by Thomas Paine who wrote in his 1795 book *The Age of Reason*: "I hope for happiness beyond this life…I do not believe in the Creed…professed by any church I know. My own mind is my own church…[Islamic, Christian and Jewish religious institutions are] human inventions set up to terrify and enslave mankind and to monopolise power and profits. Every national church and religion has established itself by pretending some special mission from God communicated to certain individuals as if the way to God was not open to any man alive…the Word of God is the Creation we behold." I thought the original purpose of religious institutions was not to "terrify and enslave" but agreed that Churches had tried to monopolise God—and had used coercion and terror to this end.

How then could I remain for these years in the Catholic ministry? It was because I saw its potential for good. I saw the charities it inspired. I had met its anarchists, its worker-priests and its liberation theologians that were trying to survive within it and reform it. The church had been part of my world since childhood. I wanted to help drive out its money-changers and to help make it the sacred institution it should have been. I seemed well positioned to help do this. But my naiveté in these matters was not to last much longer.

A special woman

My reputation as a priest had one enormous personal consequence. A worker in the Simon Community, whom I had admired for her dedication, became interested in me as a radical priest. She said I gave her hope that she could find a truly Christian place within the church. We found we shared many ideals. I gave her an open invitation to visit me if she needed to get away. After some months she took up my invitation when feeling utterly burnt out. Her name was Jackie (not her real name—but what I will call her here). She told me she was an ex-social worker who had found it impossible to treat people as "cases" and who had thus come to live full time with the Simon Community, because with them "clients" and "workers" were not separated by clothes, food or housing. She had great mad ideas about Christ. She thought he had wanted us to identify with the poor, be poor, be with them, and fight for justice. We became soulmates and our friendship changed my life.

Idealistic and deeply ignorant of myself, I believed that true love demanded self-surrender. This was what the Christian mystics had told me. I thus believed if I truly loved Jackie I would not reserve anything from her. This was an intellectual decision for I was little motivated sexually. I loved her; therefore I should give her all I could. I thought that divine providence had brought us together to work together, serve God together, sleep together, be together, and dream together. I thought that God was gently telling me that this was no contradiction to my dedication to him—despite my vow of celibacy.

For her part, she found me rather dead sexually. I can remember her sitting on the bed, blouse undone, looking quixotically at me for I was not reacting. I tried to do the right thing, to treat her gently, make her feel good, make her know I valued what she offered me. She was very tolerant as I stumbled between naiveté and ignorance. She put down my awkwardness and lack of drive to the influence on me of the Catholic Church. At that time, this was for me a plausible theory. When I told her of my very private fantasy about being a girl, I said what I then believed, that this was an entirely private illusion that could be kept in its place.

She introduced me to the Catholic Worker movement in the States, where anarchistic Christians ran open houses and looked after the poor without preaching at them. Its members were activists and pacifists. They took part in radical actions to show they did not agree with killing. They refused to pay that part of their taxes that went to the Pentagon. They did not take up posts within the Church—and are still today part of an inspiring movement of Christian anarchists.

Jackie and I also literally sat at the feet of R.D.Laing, the psychiatrist, listening spellbound as he related case history after case history and with brilliant analysis showed how people must be treated in the context of their closest friends and family. We went with her parents to Paris, staying apart from them idyllically on Isle de Sainte Louis in the heart of Paris. We saw the revolutionary slogans of the defeated left and ate snails. She then returned to Australia, stopping en route in a left-wing kibbutz in Israel. When back in Melbourne, she helped open a house of hospitality similar to those of the Catholic Worker movement.

I deeply missed her companionship. I had never before met a person with whom I shared so much. But, since she feared endangering my life as a priest she did not pursue me. I was not so concerned so started to pour out my soul in letters to her.

That summer, after she had left, as I was eager to escape from suburban England and the parish life that otherwise awaited me; I found myself a summer job in a Catholic parish in America. It was in Bedford Stuyvescent in Brooklyn, in the centre of the largest of the American ghettos.

Wide open to new ideas, I soaked in New York where I was delighted to find it easy to meet people who supported Castro and other critics of official policies. I also went to the Catholic Worker hostel on the Lower East Side to meet its workers and impoverished guests.

In Bedford Stuyvescent I found the streets full of kids, hanging out, bouncing basket balls, roller skating, who laughed at my accent and said in American monotones, "Gee, Mister, you don't talk, you sing!" I sought out soulmates and met priests that worked with the poor. They lived in rat-infested apartments in Brownsville, the worst part of the ghetto. Here emigrants from the Caribbean lived in housing deserted by the Afro-Americans. Burnt-out and partly demolished houses made it resemble a cityscape of wartime.

One of these priests showed me a primary school that had police with sniper rifles upon its roof. He explained that the parents and students of this school wanted African studies taught since their ancestors came from Africa. Why should White kids learn European history and they not learn African? The black children then came to school in mock leopard skins and with spears. The frightened white teachers went out on strike. Now the school was guarded with sniper rifles for fear of black primary school kids and their parents.

I came across a demonstration of women with children in prams protesting about welfare payments. They were flying balloons and holding posters. A man on the outskirts of the demonstration was handing out leaflets. I asked for one since I wanted to know about the protest. But his leaflet told me he was an off-duty policeman demanding the right to carry guns off-duty. It said, look at this protest; see what we are up against. I looked at the children, the prams, the women joking between themselves, and was horrified at his blind fear and anger.

Wanting to learn all I could, I walked into the poster-filled headquarters of the Black Panther Movement to discuss with them the gun culture of the USA. I could not get away from the parish so could not take the buses organised to take protestors to Chicago. Thus I missed the riots at the Democratic Congress. This was a tumultuous time in the US.

Finally, in order to learn why so many Latin American immigrants were coming to live in the worst parts of New York, I flew to Puerto Rico. At first I wandered the Spanish built streets of San Juan and saw nothing of poverty. Then, from the highest point in the town, I saw the shacks of the barrios between the fortified walls and the sea. I explored the barrios. Its narrow streets were mean and dirty. Pigs hunted along the sea edge. But it still seemed more pleasant than the slums of New York.

My position as a Claretian priest made it easier for me to afford this trip. I became a guest in a hospitable Claretian parish in a good part of town. Small green tree frogs chirruped outside my window and a seahorse swam past my nose the moment I put my face underwater in the Caribbean. These were the more pleasant memories.

From there I went to Santo Domingo, the capital of the Dominican Republic. Here poverty was immediately more evident. Here I found little boys touting for their sisters. There was a girl selling herself for every yard of pavement. Many were country kids saving to get to the golden city in the sky, the ghettos of New York. I went up into the hills to see the land they were deserting. An American Peace Corp. worker took me around. He showed me rich fertile lands, telling me that large American corporations had driven the people from their land to use it for cash crops to fill Western shops. Perhaps this was the reason why the Caribbean people were filling the streets of New York?

I would have gone on to Cuba, to contrast what was happening there, but the United States blockade stopped me. But I had learnt much about the terrible consequences of economies organised to serve unbridled greed.

About a year later, in response to the pleas in my letters, Jackie returned from Australia. I was cautious but felt little guilt in seeking out her company. We went to the mountains of the Lake District to find a space to be alone. One day we climbed to a pool between waterfalls half way down a mountainside. Swimming in it, we found we could overlook the clouds from its rocky edge then flip back and laugh under a cascade called Milky Gill that ran from heaven to delight.

Late one night, outside a pub, we saw a shadowy mountain nearby blocking out the stars. We decided to watch dawn from its summit. It was a long steep scramble between rocky crags marked by red sheep eyes in the torchlight. It was windy and cold on Helvellyn's summit, sheltering behind an umbrella. When the sun rose through the clouds, it was an anticlimax. We then went down into a valley to come out next to a white farmhouse. A farmer in wooden clogs was coming in from milking his cows. I asked if we could get a drink of milk.

He called out his wife, an ample woman in aprons, almost a fairy story farmwife. She invited us into her kitchen to sit before a warm hearth. Shepherds' crooks decorated the walls. She gave us fresh scones, cream and tea. It felt like a fantasy for it was the fulfilment of a dream I had while walking down the mountain. It was as though with Jackie I had stepped through into another world.

We went also to the rocky Caldey Island off the Southwest coast of Wales, where monks lived an austere life in the midst of wild beauty. They served us generous meals while fasting themselves. They told us we were free to attend their sung office but did not thrust religion at us. We walked along cliff tops, picking our way through the nests of unfrightened birds while on the rocks below a monk fished with a massive rod. At the centre of the island was an ancient Celtic chapel with a stone steeple worn into a rounded phallic shape, as Jackie quickly noted.

While we were there, a fellow guest had to stay much longer than intended because of a twisted ankle. When he went to say goodbye, he apologised to the guest master, saying that he did not have enough to leave a suitable donation for his extended accommodation but would send more when he got home. The guest master replied; "Please do not. We have more money than you. Here is something to help you on your way."

We hitchhiked to the Netherlands with friends studying for the Catholic priesthood to visit a Fr. Harry Haas, who had written books on spirituality. He introduced us to his close friend Eileen. Jackie and I stayed at the seminary, discussed our relationship, learnt Sri Lankan cooking and made warm friends with the students.

I was not as comfortable when we stayed for a while with Joan Wells, a wonderful Catholic wise-woman friend who also had a warm friendship with a priest. They had decided to keep their relationship platonic because church life was so important for them. Her different choice made it awkward for us. I remember telling her that celibacy came into Christianity from paganism. She kept an open house frequently visited by seminarians in the evenings and worked during the day in London hospitals with the dying. She told us of how she had taken her son in a last desperate hope to the Marian shrine of Lourdes in southern France. He was dangerously ill with a decaying bone disease spreading up his arm towards his backbone. Medical efforts had failed and death was the likely outcome.

The morning after they arrived, she dressed the wound on her son's arm, picking out decaying bone, cleaning the pus. She then told him to stay quietly in their room while she made a quick early morning visit to the cave where the Virgin Mary was said to have appeared to the young woman, Bernadette. She prayed in the grotto to Mary and then returned to the hotel.

On her return, she was horrified to hear her son shouting. She feared that he had disturbed the other guests. But when she entered their room, he was moving his wounded arm up and down—something impossible beforehand. The bandage was still marked with pus—but it was dry. When she removed the bandage, the skin was clean underneath. She called this a miracle. For me it came from her joining her will and being with a person she saw as Mary, Mother of All, and with all the energy and strength of a sacred creation and the divinity that infuses it.

When we left Joan's house, we went to live in Brixton in a tenement block in a fairly wild part of London. My brother Kevin came to stay and friends from the Simon community. I officially had a small single flat and Jackie a large communal flat.

We first thought to marry at Easter but I had difficulties with my parents even before mentioning Jackie to them. They saw me as moving away from their religious practices. But it was tobacco that first cracked for me the blissful cohesion of our family. My mother told me she had discovered that a member of our family was secretly smoking, despite having made promises to stop. This meant she said that the family could not stay together. She saw smoking as damaging God's tabernacle, the body. The argument blew over but not without me seriously questioning the values that governed our family. But it also highlit a gift I had from my mother—a belief in the body as holy, as a dwelling place of God—and not as corrupted and shameful. I thus was spared a doctrine that caused anguish to other Christians.

When I told the religious order of my intention to get married, I said I believed it was God's will and that we could do much good together. Needless-to-say my order did not appreciate this. They had spent many years training me and now saw it as a waste of funds. No use reassuring them that I still intended to do God's bidding. What upset my Provincial Superior even more was that I had no intention of asking the Pope for permission to marry. I thought our love for each other a divine gift—and that the Pope consequently could not tell me to refuse it. My Provincial Superior offered me money to help me settle into a new life—but only if I asked the Pope for a dispensation. I told him I would refuse money offered on such terms, and did. (I later learnt they were obliged in church law to help me resettle into lay life.) I maintained I had a vocation to be both a priest and married. The tense negotiations and the demands of my final-year exams made me ask Jackie if we could delay our plans and marry as soon as my Finals were over. She agreed—but was worried the delay was really because my parents had an undue influence over me.

I knew my marriage to Jackie would create a deep rift in my family. I intended to go to Australia with her so that would make an even greater divide. I had a brother Bernard that I had never really got to know since he was so many years younger. I wanted an opportunity to get to know him while I could. We met and talked and planned to hitchhike to the Lake District to climb mountains together, as soon as I had finished a month of working in a power station to get some first-hand experience of factory life and training in being a worker-priest. But we nearly did not get away.

In my final week of work at the power station I fell ill with glandular fever, had a temperature of 107 and was taken to hospital by ambulance. My mouth furred up with a revolting mess but I was determined to get my time with Bernard if I possibly could. Five days later, my fever willed down, I discharged myself from hospital and headed with him to the mountains. I felt weak but walked and walked until a few days later while transversing a ridge I felt suddenly the weight of the illness leave me.

Another day, in deep cloud, we set out to climb a pass below Scafell Pike, England's tallest peak. This would take us below its cliffs to the next valley where there was a hostel. The fog was thick, the path nearly invisible. It was marked by cairns, but since we could not see from one cairn to the next, the only way to move on was by one of us moving forward to the limit of visibility and shouting if another cairn were visible. We succeeded in doing this for some time—then suddenly the fog lifted. We then found to our surprise and horror that we were high on the cliffs with our intended path a thousand feet below. From here we had to cross the summit if we were to complete our journey before nightfall. Grey wet boulders loomed ghostlike around us as we reached the top. Then came the tentative exploration of pathways in the mists, looking for the one that would take us safely down to the hostel. The first led into cloud seas that we feared masked cliffs. Eventually by blind instinct or chance we found the right cairns. We did not know if we were safe until we reached the base of the clouds and saw the hostel far below.

This climb seemed a metaphor for my journey through the Church. I had not known better than to climb its mountain to its barren peak. I did not seem to have a choice. Once there I found a beauty that was quite apart from the world below, in which the real dangers were hidden, where instincts were my only guide, where the wrong path would lead to a sudden fall into a very different world of death. But to stay there would mean stagnation and starvation. From this summit there was only one way forward for me, down.

Wednesday

Discovering the Sexual God

I find it strange looking back to that distant time when I left the clerical caste of the church. It is as if I am recalling a previous lifetime. I can scarcely imagine how I could really be that same person. Yet I can remember worrying at the time if my getting married were selfish, thinking that it would mean throwing away a hard-won status that could have been used for good.

But I never saw Jackie as a temptation to desert my Lover God. On the contrary, I saw her love and presence as a divine gift. My vow of celibacy meant for the Church that I avoid dissipating my dedicated energy with marriage and sexual liaisons. It held that I was married already—to God. But I thought I was meant to accept my God's gift of human love. If bigamy, it were blessed. She would teach me of life, love and children. So, I delighted in her and thanked God for her. I felt that, if I trusted Him in this, I would still find my destined way to serve Him in the priesthood.

I now see my liberation required the demolition of my patriarchal status with all the fears that boosted it. The Church of course did not agree. It thought I had fallen to a deceit of the devil. Sadly my parents felt much the same. This much saddened me—but I felt I had chosen right.

I experienced my 'fall' as if were off a stony pinnacle of pride and stolen power into a very different land. I have no conceit that my path was for all. It was simply my path, my calling. I knew other priests in similar circumstances who had decided to stay on in order to try to reform the church.

I found the place I had "fallen" down to inordinately rich and complex, a virtual rain forest of possibilities where instincts seemed to be the only guide. There was much to learn. I may have believed sex to be a celebration of life, a divine gift—but my knowledge of it was entirely a matter of intellect without a shred of experience to back it.

Jackie had brought me dreams that my religious order could not have given me. They were of marriage as a blessed partnership and of communities with children at their heart. But one of the first lessons she had for me was on sexuality. She found my lack of it perplexing. She thought, she later owned, that the Catholic Church had made me sexually inhibited. She set out to educate me so we could better share the delights of creation—and so one day, when visiting me in my student room, she stripped down to her bra!

This really threw me! I thought, "What on earth shall I do?" My reaction was not from prudery. I thought human love and sexuality divinely ordained and wonderful in theory. But in practice—how should I react? I loved Jackie. But I wondered because I did not feel any passion. I was almost stupidly angelic in my sexuality. There was no co-ordination between soul and body. I believed that since I loved her I should be free in self-giving, that this was the divine way. My ambition was, to make her happy. I wanted to give myself to her. But it seemed that there was no fuel in my sexual engine.

Over the ensuing days among the many arts she revealed to me was that of masturbation. I laugh now at my incredible chastity at the age of twenty-eight, a chastity that was no virtue. What virtue could it be when vowed by an asexual? With hindsight, I think my female brain had little idea of how to handle the male aspects of my body.

Masturbation and Male Sexuality

I remember an earlier day when I was still at the seminary and about twenty-three years old. I was walking through the ornate study hall at Highcliffe Castle in my long black cassock and sash when the prefect (the priest in charge of students' welfare) came towards me looking very worried. He was staring below my belt. He hummed and ha'ard and then said that I should keep my hand out of my pocket. He suggested it could give the false impression that I was masturbating. I was simply amazed by his suggestion. The truth of it was that it had never occurred to me that sexual pleasure was waiting at my fingertips. I had never thought to experiment with masturbation. I was seemingly very pre-puberty. Given I now enjoy sex—it amazes me that I could ever have been such a Peter Pan. (Although I later learnt that the god Pan was not so innocent.)

So Jackie had quite a task. She did not know quite how hard it would be, although I was a willing student. She taught me the arts of loving, how to gentle her, how to be with her. It was so new to me. Her body felt so surprisingly different from mine, soft, strange, other. I felt enveloped in her love. I wanted to give myself to her without reserve and so was very willing to learn how this could be.

So she with vastly greater expertise and experience taught me much that was new to me—the way that tension and pleasure mounted in the groin, the sudden explosion and the strange peace that came once it was over. A male salute to life that I could give, a blessing, a shower of seed. There was a wonder in this for me, a strange marvel—and an odd jarring feeling at the back of my brain that this was most out of keeping with my inner secret reality. It was somehow an alien experience, a pleasure from another world. I wondered that it were possible at all.

Jackie and I had left in the world of dreams my strange fantasy that I should be a girl. I thought I could maintain my male identity so chose to enter a world of male sexuality. I had much to explore and learn. Any odd feelings we put down to my living so long among celibates.

At least I did not share the arrogance of Aristotle who argued, in an age when the Goddess Mother was still celebrated, that the male seed was more important than the mother in the creation of human life, seeing the woman as merely the field planted with semen, not the giver of half the chromosomes. Not sharing his conceit, I could not share the similar view of Churchmen that believed that wasting seed was almost the same as killing human life. Pope Paul VI had endorsed this, as I have mentioned, when he declared masturbation to be a mortal sin akin to murder just seven years after Jackie gave me my first lesson in male sexuality.[96]

It was not that the Church saw the male seed as holy. Although it carried life and was male, they still saw it as somewhat 'Yuck'. The Church Fathers argued that Christ could not possibly have entered a womb "contaminated" with semen—so the Holy Spirit must have made her pregnant without employing a penis. This belief still exists inside the Catholic Church. In 1987 Pope John Paul II declared Mary had "preserved her virginity intact"—meaning with an unbroken hymen despite giving birth.[97] In that same year, a female theologian, Uta Ranke-Heineman, lost her license to teach within the Catholic Church for suggesting that Mary might not have been a biological virgin.

But many early Christians had rejected the stories of Christ's miraculous conception, both because they did not share the "contamination" theory of human semen and because they saw the Holy Spirit as female. The rediscovered *Gospel according to Philip* read: "Some said, 'Mary conceived by the Holy Spirit.' They are in error. They do not know what they are saying. When did a woman ever conceive by a woman?"

The Catholic Church condemned masturbation by saying that God provided the pleasure of sex solely for the procreation of life. To engage in sex only for pleasure was a misuse of the body that would lead us down the path through which sin and evil entered this world. This argument might seem stretched to you, but when I worked as a Christian priest, masturbation was the "sin" that most worried Catholic men.

But it was worse in previous eras. In 19th century England doctors wired foreskins together to stop boys masturbating—and girls did not escape. I have told how some had their clitorises cauterised "with a white hot iron" in order to stop them masturbating.[98]

The Wonder of Sexuality

But these sick practices and doctrines were far from the minds of Jackie and I in our romancing. Instead there was a wonder, a delight, a circus of love, of touch, of laughter, of talk, of learning about each other. I learnt that the phallus has a purpose apart from aiming water and being a handle—it could make women happy and me still happier. The intense pleasure it gave made me hope my transgendered fantasy would pass. I lifted with her happiness. Jackie wanted a child. I had never thought I would have the chance to help create a child. For me it was a wonder that I could do this.

Looking back, reflecting, an element was missing in my lovemaking that perhaps is experienced by most men. I don't think I saw Jackie quite as men normally see women. Jackie was for me the sister and the teacher, the sharer of life and dreams—as well as a lover. She gave me great richness and taught me much about myself. It was wonderful to give her joy. But increasingly I found we seemed to share a similar sexuality. She was not perhaps as "other" to me as women normally are to men.

I learnt much about malekind from loving her. I found the penis, although not then attractive to me, is capable of much delicacy. It is of a man yet moves independently of his will. It stands between the couple, a bridging organ, that can be controlled and enjoyed by either partner, that can give ecstasy to one, both or neither. No wonder the Hindus exalted it as an emblem of divine creative power. It took me a long time to realise this. I thought it was just males who exalted it. Now I know it as the organ that both genders control.

Saint Augustine and his Penis

This was so different to how the "Fathers" of the Church regarded their male parts. I found to my surprise that their attitude towards women reflected how they saw their penises! One of the greatest of them, St Augustine, believed the pursuit of sanctity meant gaining complete control over his body. He thought the human body, along with nature as a whole, was so corrupted through the Fall of Adam and Eve that it had to be subdued and conquered.

The Pagan Stoics had taught Augustine that perfection lay in this rational mastery. He thus worked hard to gain control over his body—but found that there was one organ that he could not conquer. He saw the involuntary movements of his penis as disobedience. Eventually he worked out why this was so. He theorised that God had given man a disobedient organ to remind him that the "original sin" was disobedience. Later others took his theories still further. They asked; if God took away from men control over the movement of the penis, how could a woman make it lift simply by walking by? They looked for an answer to the same Adam and Eve myth. They thought it could only be demonic witchcraft. She was enchanting him, casting a spell through the power of the Serpent.

Augustine wrote these thoughts in his book *On Marriage and Concupiscence.* "When the first man transgressed the law of God, he began to have another law in his members which was repugnant to the law of his mind, and he felt the evil of his own disobedience when he experienced in the disobedience of his flesh, a most righteous retribution recoiling on himself…When it must come to man's great function of the procreation of children, the members which were expressly created for this purpose will not obey the direction of the will, but lust has to be waited for to set these members in motion, as if it had legal right over them, and sometimes it refuses to act when the mind wills, while often it acts against its will! Must not this bring the blush of shame over the freedom of the human will, that by its contempt of God, its own Commander, it has lost all proper command for itself over its own members? Now, wherein could be found a more fitting demonstration of the just depravation of human nature by reason of its disobedience, than in the disobedience of those parts?"[99]

These are not just the writings of a sexually disturbed man. They are critical to understanding of much of Western history. The eminent 20th century theologian Hans Kung noted that "Augustine shaped Western Theology and piety more than any other theologian—he became the spiritual father of the medieval paradigm." Augustine's work played a great part in the burning of thousands of women as witches as well as in the continuing Catholic anguish over contraception.

Augustine also wrote the crucial scriptural interpretations and texts on which the Catholic Church later based its ban on contraception. He denounced all sexual pleasure, saying: "This lust, then, is not in itself the good of the nuptial institution; but it is obscenity in sinful men, a necessity in procreant parents, the fire of lascivious indulgences, the shame of nuptial pleasures". It was for him only to be tolerated when it was directed to the continuance of the species. "It is impermissible and shameful to have intercourse with one's wife while preventing the conception of children."[100] In the 20th Century Pope Pius XI would quote Augustine then charitably add that God would pursue "with the highest degree of hatred" all who practised contraception.[101]

Augustine was furious that effigies of this disobedient and "unseemly member" was celebrated in pagan Roman rites. "The rites of Liber were celebrated with such unrestrained turpitude, that the private parts of a man were worshipped in his honour. Nor was this abomination transacted in secret that some regard at least might be paid to modesty, but was openly and wantonly displayed. For during the festival of Liber this obscene member, placed on a car, was carried with great honour, first over the crossroads in the country, and then into the city. In the town of Lavinium a whole month was devoted to Liber, during which time everyone gave themselves up to the most dissolute conversation until that member had been carried through the forum and brought to rest in its own place; on which unseemly member it was necessary that the most honourable matron should place a wreath in the presence of all the people".[102]

Some Christians would castrate themselves rather than have their penises disobey. Thus the Christian writer Origen who died in 254CE wrote that he followed the example of other Christians when he castrated himself at the age of eighteen.[103] This was not peculiarly an early Christian concept. In India the Jains taught that men could beneficially achieve the withering of the male organs through meditation.

The belief that the male sex drive was an obstacle to perfection gave pious Christian men dreadful guilt complexes—which many blamed on women. Tertullian expressed this in an open letter to women: "the grace and beauty you naturally enjoy must be obliterated by concealment and negligence…[Your beauty] is to be feared, because of the injury and violence it inflicts on the men who admire you." St. Augustine likewise wrote in a letter: "What is the difference whether it is in a wife or mother, it is still Eve the temptress that we must beware of in any woman."[104]

I clearly did not share Augustine and Tertullian's experiences. I was not upset because I could not control the movements of the penis. I experienced it as an independent entity that I could observe, feel but not dominate. Instead of worrying about its independence, I was more concerned about how to use it to give pleasure. I was also concerned at how it could be wrongly used by men, turned into an organ of domination, of hurt and exploitation—although I had not yet experienced what it was to be its victim.

Sacrifice and Male Sex

I leant in loving Jackie that giving seed was a sacrifice (A word of Latin origin meaning sacred deed). The giving of sperm left me strengthless, empty yet full, in suspense, quiet, when the work of fertility passed to another. It was a giving that was a receiving of Jackie 's welcome, a bonding,—perhaps a new life. I died and rose as the wheel turned. (This experience of emptiness, of weakness beside a woman, might be secretly frightening to a chauvinistic man.)

An ancient British story told of what happened when the magician Merlin, the advisor to King Arthur, fell in love with Vivienne. He agreed both to give her his magical secrets and to be held captive by her if she allowed him to stay with her. True love captures us and makes us willing to share our power. Merlin found he was complete when with her and wanted nothing more. I also felt that I must share all that was mine to give.

I later discovered that this male experience of surrender and exhaustion in lovemaking was indeed too much for some of the ancients. The Grecian and Roman pagan Stoics concluded that sex was not desirable for men because it weakened them. They thus recommended men to abstain from acts of intercourse unless they intended procreation, saying that sexual joy was not a sufficient reason for such a weakening. The Stoics exalted "virtue"—meaning by this a virile masculine strength. (Vir is the Latin for a man). They also thought women were not as exhausted by sex as were men—so they presumed sex not as damaging to women as to men. Such views led Pliny the Elder, the pagan naturalist who died in an eruption of Vesuvius in 79CE, to praise the elephant because it had such a mastery of its sexuality that it only mated once every two years![105]

The School of Stoics dominated much of the Grecian world between 300BCE and 350CE and became important in Rome. They put the control of sexuality at the centre of morality. The stoic Seneca wrote to his mother Helvia around 50CE: "If you reflect that sexual pleasure has been given to man not for enjoyment but for the procreation of his race, then, if lust has not touched you with its poisoned breath, that other desire will also pass you by without touching you."[106] His disciple Musconius went further and argued that all sexual acts not intended to procreate a child are immoral.[107] It was not that he was anti-woman. He argued unlike Aristotle that men and women were equal in nature and in virtue—and that women deserved equal education opportunities.[108]

Another major Pagan influence on Christianity came from Plotinus, a second century Greek philosopher (205-270C). He wrote in *The Enneads* that God or "the All" was "so great that all its parts are infinite. Name any place, and it is already there. It has not deserted its creation for a place apart; it is always present to those with strength to touch it." [6.9.7] From God came a living universe. "This universe is a single living being embracing all living beings within it, and possessing a single Soul that permeates all its parts to the degree of their participation in it." But again dualism crept in; matter "is the substrate which underlies figures, forms, shapes, measures and limits...a mere shadow in relation to real Being, the very essence of evil, if such is possible." [1.8.2]

Thus the Soul must separate herself from matter. "Sense-perception belongs to the sleeping soul, the part of the soul immersed in body; and the true awakening is a rising up, not with the body, but from the body. To rise up to very truth is altogether to depart from bodies. Corporeality is contrary to soul and essentially opposed to soul". [3.6.6.]. This doctrine led followers to advocate a harsh asceticism to purge the soul. He was particularly influential in the schools of Christian ascetics that preceded the monasteries.

His meditation method was similar to that taught to me when I was a Novice. He wrote, "Our thought cannot grasp the One as long as any other image remains active in the soul. To this end, you must set free your soul from all outward things and turn wholly within yourself, with no more leaning to what lies outside, and lay your mind bare of ideal forms, as before of the objects of sense, and forget even yourself." [6.9.7] I had found this very difficult. It interfered with what I had gained as a child—a very natural relationship with God that did not worry about the differences between us.

Male and Female Aspects of Divinity

Plotinus also held in common with many ancient pagan thinkers that ultimately the deity is beyond gender. He saw male and female energy as united in the Godhead through a divine trinity. The male Nous, Word or Mind, and the female Psyche or Spirit emanated from the ultimate God to form this trinity—but later chauvinists stripped from this its gender balance, for they believed with Aristotle that the male was superior to the female. They thus believed that it was impossible for "inferior" female energy to be present in a perfect Sacred Trinity. This was far less balanced than the Trinity believed in by Egyptians and by many Gnostics of a Mother, Father and Child.

My own instinct is that soul and matter flow from and are sustained by the divine creative energy, and are interwoven, two aspects of the same. The universe is a seamless robe. There can thus be no matter without soul, no matter that is not alive—and no matter without the presence of the divine. Souls are the spirits of life within creation and are not unique to humans. When gendered, as are human souls, they are daughters and sons of the divine spirit that sustains creation. They are separate consciousnesses, male and female, destined to find fulfilment wedded together in the unity that exists in the depths of their beings. Within us we are each a sacred family. When we join our male and female aspects we create a new fertile energy, the child. Thus in a fashion we are all are part of a Holy Trinity of balanced creative energy and we all live at the heart of a Holy and Living Cosmos. (The question of evil is examined in "Saturday".)

But if our souls and bodies are so intrinsically linked, what happens to the soul when its body dies? Many instinctively and hopefully believe that we live on after death, but can a soul that is so intimately woven with matter survive without matter? A Christian view is that the human soul can survive alone but is not completely perfected until it is re-united with its body on the Last Day. But I see it differently. I will be very glad if my spirit never leaves this created world when my body dies, but lives on within it, one'd with the divine creating energy that sustains our world, helping in a small way in this work.

As for gender and divinity, gender is an aspect of life that we apply by analogy to our visualisations of divine energy, knowing that the source of gender must be present within the divine energy because it exists in us. An English mystic, Blessed Julian of Norwich, went further in 1400, writing:

I it am; the might and goodness of the Fatherhood.
I it am; the wisdom and kindness of the Motherhood.
I it am; the light and grace of blessed Love.
I it am; the Trinity.
I it am; the Unity.
I it am; the high sovereign goodness of all manner of things.
I it am; that which makes you love.
I it am; that makes you to long
For the endless fullness of all true desires

Her words echoed much that was in my heart. I felt they came out of the pool of human mysticism that underlies most religions. This understanding is reflected in our science. When life first started upon this planet, a virgin creation reigned. The first life did not need genders to reproduce—and many species still retain this property. But a split occurred. From that time many species took on two genders, as if two species in one. This split was functional—but, as Plato said, it left us with a yearning to become one again. Male and female we now are. Virgin parent we once were.

The creation of genders gave us reason for a milliard love songs as well as a pattern for the other union, of the human with the divine, of ultimate sex as heaven. This sexual joy in unity is both a mystery and a teaching. It tells us how we can be fulfilled in knowing our Lover Deity—in ecstasy, in orgasm and in completion.

As for homosexual love, its existence surely teaches us that the yearning to unite with the other is deeper than gender. Homosexual love reveals that love is at its heart a unity of beings.

Thus homosexuality has deep lessons to teach us. It is that gender is not of such a fundamental importance as is our wish to bond soul with soul, person with person. We should first love then give as best our love, spirit and body allow. Love, not gender, is of the first importance.

Jackie and I in the 1960s discovered a Lebanese poet, Kahlil Gibran, as did many of the more romantic of our contemporaries. He wrote in *The Prophet*,

> When love beckons to you, follow him,
> Though his ways are hard and steep.
> And when his wings enfold you yield to him,
> Though the sword hidden among his pinions may wound you.
> And when he speaks to you believe in him,
> Though his voice may shatter your dreams as the north wind lays waste
> the garden
> For even as love crowns you so shall he crucify you.
> Even as he is for your growth so is he for your pruning.
> Even as he ascends to your height and caresses your tenderest branches
> that quiver in the sun,
> So shall he descend to your roots and shake them in their clinging to the
> earth…
> Life gives naught but itself and takes naught but from itself.
> Love possesses not nor would it be possessed;
> For love is sufficient unto love.
> When you love you should not say, "God is in my heart," but rather,
> "I am in the heart of God."
> And think not you can direct the course of love, for love, if it finds you
> worthy, directs your course…
> But if you love and must needs have desires, let these be your desires;
> To melt and be like a running brook that sings its melody to the night.

Gibran wrote with an ancient Middle-Eastern understanding that human love unites us with the very spirit of the Divine; that when we love we are "in the heart of God." This concept is as old as the human spirit.

Early Christian documents recorded similar thoughts concerning marriage. They spoke of it as a symbol of the oneness between Christ and His people. "Husbands love your wives, as Christ loved the church and gave himself up for her...Even so husbands should love their wives as their own bodies. He who loves his wife loves himself...For this reason a man shall leave his father and mother and be joined to his wife and he two shall become one flesh."[109] Just as God and his people became one, women and men became one. This text also embodied the ancient concept of God having to die to give us life, just as the wheat must die that we might live—a mystery the Greeks celebrated in the Eleusian Mysteries.

Marriage in Early Christianity

But, "one flesh"? The anti-flesh and anti-women faction of the early church must have been deaf to this biblical verse. They could not easily reconcile it with their belief that our flesh was corrupted by the Fall—and so they concentrated their attention on other biblical texts.

They twisted Paul's possible chauvinism making it much worse. Epistles unfavourable to women, composed long after Paul's death, were quoted as if written by him (and still are). Those still thought to be by him were misinterpreted. "Wives be subject to your husband",[110] is quoted, ignoring the adjacent clause, "be subject to each other." Some quoted Paul's first letter to the Corinthians, 7/25, that said, "do not marry". But Paul in the same chapter says this is not a teaching of Jesus. "Now concerning the unmarried, I have no command of the Lord."[111] Paul's personal opinion was that it was better to avoid marrying since he thought the world about to end. But if one was already married, he recommended: "Do not refuse each other, except perhaps by agreement for a season so that you may devote yourselves to prayer, but then come together again." There was no hint here that he considered sexual relations as harmful.

St Augustine misinterpreted a saying of Jesus about the need for couples to stay together. The apostles had protested to Jesus against this recommendation, saying it was better not to marry if one could not divorce. Jesus then conceded "not all men can receive this," adding "I say this by way of concession". His concession allowed divorce, but Augustine took it to mean that it was better not to marry.

St Jerome went ever further. In translating the Bible he deliberately doctored the text to make it advocate celibacy—when the original text advocated marriage. He removed from Tobias a verse that read "it is not good for a man to be alone"[112] St. Jerome set himself diametrically against St Paul by teaching that sex in marriage is dishonourable. He wrote, "If we abstain from coitus, we honour our wives; if we do not abstain,—well what is the opposite of honour but insult?"[113] It is worrying to think that it was this Jerome whom Pope Damascus asked in 382CE to revise the Gospels and who went on to revise the rest of the Christian Bible.

St. Jerome was given the sole responsibility for revising the translations into Latin of the books that Eusebius of Caesarea had selected for what we now call the *New Testament*. His Vulgate version remained the authoritative text in the Western Christian world until modern times.[114] He spoke of this work in a preface addressed to Pope Damascus: "You asked me to revise the Old Latin version and, as it were, to sit in judgement on the corpus of the Scriptures which are now scattered throughout the whole world, and in as much as they differ from each other, you would have me decide which of them agreed with the Greek original...for there are almost as many texts as there are copies." The Eastern Christian Churches never fully accepted Jerome's version and there still remain differences between East and West as to what books should make up the New Testament.

The Fathers of the Church said marriage is a dangerous activity that is regrettably necessary if the human race is to continue. Ambrose, the teacher of Augustine, praised marriage for its usefulness—but said "virginity is the one thing that keeps us from the beasts."

Nevertheless, some women welcomed celibacy as it enabled them to escape male demands. (Other factors could play a part in this decision. In 1999 a survey among young adult American women found that a large percentage experienced intercourse as painful). Thousands of women and men made the choice of celibacy in the first centuries of Christianity—joining ascetic communities in the deserts of Palestine, Syria and Egypt. Some of these copied the rigorous discipline of earlier flesh-mortifying and dualistic Pagan communities.

It was not just the Catholics among the Christians that were influenced by a dualism that separated spirit from matter. Some Gnostic texts, such as *The Acts of John* (not found at Nag Hammadi but known of earlier), questioned whether Jesus really had a natural body.[115] This text was bitterly attacked by the Catholics.[116] But other Gnostic texts found at Nag Hammadi such as the *Treatise on Resurrection* maintained that Jesus had a natural human body.

When St. Augustine became a Christian at the age of twenty-nine he deserted the woman with whom he had lived for twelve years and by whom he had a child. He put his views on women into his book *De Genesisi ad Litteram* written around 415CE, saying that there must have been sex in the Garden of Eden, for what else were woman created for, what else were they good for? "I don't see what sort of help woman was created to provide man with, if one excludes the purpose of procreation. If woman is not given to man for help in bearing children, for what help could she be? To till the earth together? If help were needed for that, man would have been a better help for man. The same goes for comfort in solitude."

The influence of Augustine sadly reached through nearly a thousand years to influence Thomas Aquinas, who taught that marriage was the least of the sacraments, and then on hundreds more years to Martin Luther and Calvin who carried Augustine's views into the Protestant churches. Luther wrote, "No matter what praise is given to marriage, I will not concede it to nature that it is no sin…How foul and horrible a thing sin is, for lust is the only thing that cannot be cured by any remedy! Not even by marriage, which was expressly ordained for this infirmity of our nature."[117] He also wrote: "A woman is never truly her own master. God formed her body to belong to a man, to have and to rear children."

But I think they had wandered far from the teachings of Jesus, who never suggested that sex was only for the generation of children or that marriage was regrettable. Instead he celebrated weddings by providing miraculous wine. The apostles likewise saw no shame in travelling with their wives. They lived in a society that glorified the family. This was far from what Augustine and Luther were to teach in Christ's name.

Since my mother ruled in my family home, it was not until I came to study Catholic theology that I found to my disgust that famous Christian teachers spoke of women as inferior to men. I was astounded when I learnt that they justified this dreadful doctrine with pseudo-scientific theories seemingly devised both to make women accept such a status as natural and to excuse males from feeling guilty about suppressing their sisters' rights.

Such "scientific" theories have continued to modern times. Freud held that women were psychically inferior to men. He wrote in his *An Outline of Psychoanalysis*: "A female child has, of course, no need to fear the loss of a penis. She must however react to the fact of not having received one. From the very first she envies boys its possession; her whole development may be said to take place under the colour of envy for the penis. She…makes efforts to compensate for her defect—efforts that may lead in the end to a normal feminine attitude. If during the phallic phase, she attempts to get pleasure like a boy by the manual stimulation of her genitals, it often happens that she fails to obtain sufficient gratification and extends her judgement of inferiority from her stunted penis to her whole self."[118]

But in nature the male is not always necessary. Many species manage reproduction without males. In other cases the male has a much shorter life than the female—such as with the Australian phasogales. This is a squirrel-like creature I have watched gamble in high eucalyptus forest in the Yarra valley of SE Australia. Their males are born in spring, make love in the autumn and then die. The females live for another year or more because of their greater responsibilities for the continuance of the species.

Male Superiority

I could not simply blame early Christianity for suppressing my sisters' rights. Some 300 years before Christ's birth the Pagan Aristotle had taught that the female body was an imperfect version of the male. He called them defective men.[119] He maintained that men as the "active principle" in nature are superior to women who are merely the "passive principle". His view was controversial, for he lived in a time when Goddesses were still honoured, but he had allies. Plutarch wrote: "Woman is a real devil, an enemy of the peace, a source of provocation." Still further back, some two hundred years before Aristotle, Greek dramas were presenting the theory that women were physically inferior to men.

The famous writer of tragedies, Aeschylus (525-456BCE) had Apollo say: "The mother is no parent of that which is called her child, but only nurse of the new-planted seed that grows." Thus the Goddess Pallas Athena could be born directly from the head of Zeus. "There can be a father without any mother. There she stands, the living witness, daughter of the Olympian Zeus, she who was never fostered in the darkness of the womb."[120]

Aeschylus knew this was a "modern" view. A Fury in the Oresteia drama protested strenuously against this dethroning of the mother: "Gods of the younger generation, you have ridden down the laws of elder time, torn them from my hands". The scholar Riane Eisler commented that Athena, by declaring for the Father, had symbolically sealed the fate of womankind.[121]

The male God had thus claimed the birthing power possessed by earlier Goddesses. He had become the Virgin God—able to create of himself without need for a partner. The medieval academic and mystic, Meister Ekhardt would speak of God's natural place being on the birthing table. Those who thought the female inferior to the male maintained that God remained male while giving birth. They did not say he was a she or to talk of a Goddess—as perhaps they should have done logically. Their belief in the superiority of the male also blocked them from thinking the Deity might be androgyne or hermaphrodite.

Aeschylus had embodied in his plays a rationalisation for a process that began hundreds of years earlier—perhaps during the development of large-scale agricultural societies. The Book of Genesis enshrines a theology that justified the clearing of "wilderness". It held that the Deity had set humans over nature and that it was thus proper for nature to be suppressed and controlled for the sole benefit of humans. Such concepts were alien to hunter-gatherer societies.

When I worked with Aboriginal nations in Northern Australia, I found children animatedly discussing seeing fields when on trips to other parts of Australia. They found land with just one crop very strange, for they were taught how to use every naturally occurring species and thus knew how to use far more species than the farmers. They had a sacred place and ritual to honour every food source. They saw themselves as custodians of the land, rather than its masters. In their cultures both men and women had sacred places and natural food sources to watch over and protect. They thus could not easily engage in large-scale farming practices. Clearing the land for a single crop seemed to the children I met like having a supermarket that only sold one product. It also destroyed the sacred places that honoured the plants and animals that gave us their lives. Aborigines believed that if they did not do their duty of honouring their sacred places, sing their sacred songs, dance their sacred dances, then the fertility of the earth itself would be affected. An Aboriginal woman explained, "We make the country good...for fruit. So it will grow up well, so that we make it green, so that we hold the Law forever." This was sometimes called "lifting up the land."[122]

This duty of looking after the spiritual welfare of the land was shared by both men and women. In Central Australia where gender roles are traditionally quite separate, the men would refuse to speak for the women and the women would not speak for the men. This led to difficulties when white government officials presumed that they could get a single person, (they nearly always expected this to be a man) to speak for the entire community.[123]

A major change in philosophy and religion must have accompanied the move to replace forests with fields to found the agricultural empires. It seems that some then applied the model of the seed planted in the field to their understanding of their own fertility, seeing men as planting the seed in females. This led to women being treated as fields. Men fenced them in so that they would know whose seed was responsible for which child. This viewpoint was endorsed by the Koran; "Women are given to you as fields. Go therein and sow your seed."[124]

Similar developments are documented in Celtic legends and history.[125] In the earliest Ulster stories, Samhain (now known as Halloween) was an after-harvest festival that celebrated all the gifts of Macha, Ulster's Mother Goddess, including the "mast', the nuts of beech, oak, chestnut and other trees. When a male warrior culture became dominant, seemingly in the Iron Age, the warriors brought to this feast their harvest of amputated heads—calling these "the mast of Macha". They said life came from the head and from blood spilt in battle, rather than from forest and the womb. They slept with amputated heads held between their thighs as if crudely simulating childbirth.

In the East, Buddhism was male-dominated, holding that women were reincarnated at a lower level than men. Buddha when dying said to Ananda: "Women are full of passion, Ananda; women are envious, Ananda. Women are stupid, Ananda. That is the reason, Ananda, that is the cause, why women have no place in public assemblies, do not carry on business and do not earn their living in any profession."[126]

But none of these ancient beliefs were so scornful of womankind as were the "Fathers" of the Church. So what caused these "Fathers" to become so extremist in their views, so vehement on women and sexuality? Why did Christ's own practice of a woman-friendly ministry change so quickly among his followers into a woman-belittling ministry? No one else can be held responsible for the "Father's" ugly attacks on women, on gays and on the transgendered. They were the authors of a major distortion of Christ's teaching which is still deep rooted in the churches and in Western society.

Perhaps part of the answer is that the "Fathers" felt they were engaged in a vital contest for control over a developing religion. Religion and power went together for them. They put more energy into attacking fellow Christians than into criticizing the Pagans who threw Christians to the lions. They wrote countless polemics against other Christians. They did not see themselves as spiritual teachers that helped people empower themselves but as authorised by God to tell them what to do. One of their first acts when their faction gained power was to have the books of pagan-friendly Gnostic Christians burnt and their meetings made illegal.

But this still does not explain why the Fathers came to write so critically of women. The answer to this in part lies in the change in the concept of "nature" from being sustaining and sacred to being scary and needing taming—a change that might well date back to the establishment of agricultural empires that cleared and "tamed" land.

The Fathers, along with other authorities in an increasingly male-dominated Mediterranean, perceived women as closer to nature than men and as governed by nature. The Fathers were deeply suspicious of nature. They thought it had become a domain of demons after the Sin in the Garden of Eden. The daemons, or nature spirits of the Greeds, had been transformed into devilish demons. They noted that God told man to master nature. They experienced women as a part of nature that refused to be mastered.

It was evident from women's periods, they maintained, that "corrupted nature" dominated the lives of women more than it did men. They preached that the devil's influence over women was evident from their reluctance to accept male domination—and that the salvation of women lay in persuading them to be "virtuous". The very word "virtue" suggested "male-like".

Extraordinarily, in modern times, Sigmund Freud accompanied his theories on the inferiority of women by teaching, as did the Fathers, that the individual "can only defend by some kind of turning away from…the dreaded external world" or even better, by "with the help…of science, going over to the attack against nature and subjecting her to the human will"[127]

The blood cult and male superiority

A pre-Christian creation myth justified the rise of the Patriarchies by saying humans did not come from a Mother Goddess but from the mingling of a male God's blood with the soil. The Bronze Age Babylonian myth of Marduk had him destroy his divine mother; "Then the lord paused to view her dead body, to see if he might divide the monster and do artful works. He split her like a shellfish into two parts, half of her he set up and called it sky."[128]—turning the rest into the earth. He then slaughtered a younger God who had loved his Mother/Consort and "out of his blood they fashioned mankind."[129]

The Fathers similarly fashioned the body of their church out of the blood of martyrs. The exaltation of martyrdom had helped Christians survive the horrors of several persecutions. The Emperor Nero scapegoated Christians for a fire that destroyed Rome, impaling them on stakes driven through the anus, then tarring them and setting them afire to light his parks and games. Other emperors upheld laws that condemned to death anyone who refused to acknowledge the emperor's "divinity", whether that person be a Christian, Jew or Pagan.

Tertullian became a Christian after watching such a massacre of Christians. He admitted he first enjoyed this—but said he came to admire those who could so triumph over pain. Several thousand Christians were thus killed. Irenaeus of Lyon saw fifty of his people killed after the Senate allowed provinces to cut entertainment costs by using Christians and prisoners it budgeted at one tenth of the price of a fifth-rate gladiator.

In such a climate Catholics found a way to transcend their fear by declaring that just as Christ conquered death through shedding his blood for them, so they would conquer by shedding their blood for him. They volunteered for death—sometimes with a determination that embarrassed Roman officials. Tertullian wrote: "the *sole* key to unlock paradise is your life's blood." Almost as if they were Celtic warriors, they held that the blood they shed was the seed of life. When some women joined the men in facing death—as also was the custom among the Celts whose women fought as warriors, they said they had transcended their female nature and triumphed by becoming men.

From all accounts many went to their deaths bravely—and women martyrs in trance and ecstasy took a significant role in inspiring the men. The group in Lyon found courage in the example of a young slave girl called Blandina. "Blandina was hung upon a post and exposed as bait for wild animals…she seemed to hang there in the form of a cross and by her fervent prayers she aroused intense enthusiasm in those who were undergoing their ordeal."[130] In Carthage around 203CE Perpetua took the lead. She kept a record of the dreams as she prepared for death. In one dream she became a male in order to achieve victory. "And I was stripped naked and became a man. And my supporters began to rub me with oil as if for a wrestling match." But when she was victorious, the fencing master greeted her as a "daughter." In her dreamworld she became both genders in victory.[131]

Her prison diary, completed by another, told of her belief in a "second baptism of blood." Her companion "Felicitas, [was] glad that she had safely given birth so that now she could fight the beasts, going from one blood bath to another, from the midwife to the gladiator, ready to wash after childbirth in a second baptism." When a leopard savaged a man and he was drenched in blood, this too was called: "a second baptism". The diary recorded that the crowd cried at this: "Well washed! Well washed!" The diarist commented: " For well washed indeed was one who had been bathed in this manner."

The leaders of the death-defying Christians organised their churches, as did other shedders of blood, along military lines. The laity were the foot soldiers. The Bishop of Rome was the General. As such he demanded absolute obedience from the laity to all the orders of his officers, even to lowly deacons. Just as the "divine" Emperor commanded the Roman army, the Bishop of Rome commanded Christ's army. Disobedience to any order from a cleric meant damnation. They put hierarchy above co-operation and obedience above consensus, while scornfully dismissing any of the "weaker" sex who thought to "trespass" into roles of power within this world of men.

The Catholics also poured scorn on the gnostic Christians—saying in effect. "If you are not eager to be killed, then you are not worthy of Christ." If they refused to enlist in their army-like church, they called them "pagans". They were furious that the gnostic Christians showed little solidarity with their martyrs. A leading Catholic, Justin, said darkly that he did not know if the Gnostics practised cannibalism and promiscuity but "we do know " they are "neither persecuted or put to death", suggesting that the Gnostics had done a deal with the pagan authorities.[132] Tertullian commented bitterly that the gnostic Christians were ignoring their God-sent opportunity for glory; "the heretics go about as usual."

The Gnostics in their turn were horrified at the joy Catholics showed at the deaths of fellow Christians, for they thought perfection was not so easily obtained by death. They taught it was rather to be sought through meditation and living lovingly in the community. They thus attacked the Catholic bishops and clergy as "waterless canals".[133]

It was the Gnostic Christians who first named the Father's "army" as the "Catholics" (Universalists) for demanding all Christians have identical festival dates, beliefs and rituals. Even Bishop Irenaeus of Lyon, a zealous campaigner against gnostic Christians, was surprised by the Pope's zeal in imposing Roman customs.[134] But the Emperor Constantine backed the absolute authority of the Bishop of Rome. He amazingly declared that anyone who disobeyed the Bishop of Rome was inspired by the devil!

Female Blood

The Catholic Christians did not extend their exultation of blood to that naturally shed by women. This was, they declared, an absolutely different affair, a product of a fallen nature, contaminating and dangerous. This became a major reason for barring women from ritual roles. Theodore of Balsamon stated, "They were ousted from their place in liturgy because of their monthly impurity."[135] The blood of childbirth was considered even more contaminating.

The Father of the Church Jerome (d420) wrote of intercourse during menstruation: "When a man has intercourse with his wife at this time, the children born from this union will be leprous and hydrocephalic; and the corrupted blood will cause the plague-ridden bodies of both sexes to be either too small or too large."[136] The Archbishop Caesarius of Arles (d. 542) likewise warned, "whoever has sex with his wife during her period will have children that are either leprous or epileptic or possessed by the devil".[137] In the 13th century the "Angelic Doctor", St Thomas Aquinas, taught it was a mortal sin to make love to a woman during her period—because her blood would harm male seed!

This supposed link between women, 'fallen' Nature and the devil would endanger the lives of European women for centuries.[138] It was a principal cause of the burning of women as witches.

There could not be a greater contrast with the attitude towards female blood shown by Australia's Aboriginal peoples. As before mentioned, at least one of their nations taught that when a woman stops bleeding and leaves the divine Rainbow Serpent, she is carrying the divine power of fertility, for it is in the days following this that she can conceive a child

The status of women fell so low that the Church Council of Mâcon in the Sixth Century reportedly seriously debated whether women had souls. The decision that a woman had a soul was only carried by a majority of one.[139]

In the 9th century Celtic Church the Christian phobia against female blood continued unabated. The Celi-De monks in Ireland taught that an excess of blood was the cause of sexual lust. This, they said, made women naturally the temptress, for menstruation clearly revealed that women had too much blood. But there was hope for women, the monks added. If the women starved themselves until their periods ceased, they could achieve perfection!

But to return to the rise of the Christian patriarchy; Tertullian eventually listened to those he had attacked. He left the Catholics, joined the Montanists and then attacked the very doctrine he had long maintained. He now said that wisdom comes from within and not from a bishop's dictate—and thus he was never made a Catholic Saint. The Montanists remarkably were particularly interested in finding a common ground between gnostic Christianity and the Gallae, among who were the transsexual priestesses who honoured the Goddess Cybele.

While the Christian community was increasingly split between the Catholics and Gnostics, more and more pagans were becoming Christian of one sort or the other. It was a fertile time for a new faith that had supportive communities and recruited from every level of society. The Emperor Julian, after converting to Paganism from Christianity following a vision, still maintained that Christian priests set a fine example for Pagan priests by being caring and sober. Many were also attracted by the story of how Christ had returned to life after three days in the tomb, for it seemed a real life enactment of a great pagan myth enshrined in popular initiation rituals. Middle Eastern Religions had for centuries told of a God who died and rose again to bring us life—and again these beliefs might have helped shape Christianity.

But the triumph of the Catholics also came from its disciplined clergy's willingness to be incorporated into the Empire's civil administration. This served Imperial authorities more than the ecstatic rites of many Pagan faiths. A male-dominated empire may have applauded the removing of women from sacred roles—and there were financial considerations too. Constantine found most useful the wealth he looted from thousand year old Pagan temples to rebuild Byzantium as Constantinople. Over the following years, mobs of Catholics sought out ancient Pagan temples and libraries as well as Jewish Synagogues to pillage and destroy.[140] St. Augustine did not oppose this. He advocated purifying with baptism the pagan spoils from destroyed " temples, idols, groves, etc.".[141]

As the Catholics took control over the Empire, the ascetic and chauvinistic attitudes of the Fathers became enshrined in society. Sexual desire was now to be purged from the clergy. Pope Siricius wrote to the Spanish bishop, Himerius of Tarragona, saying that, although a priest could be married, it was an obscene lust ("obscena cupiditas") and a crime for him to continue after ordination to have sexual relations with his wife. As for the attitude a priest should show towards his legal wife, Pope Gregory the Great wrote to Bishop Leo of Catana saying that priests should "love their wives as if they were sisters and beware of them as if they were enemies."[142]

Jackie would have been in great jeopardy if we had lived in those days. Pope Leo IX enslaved the wives of priests in his Lateran Palace.[143] In 1089 Pope Urban II declared that if a Sub-Deacon was unwilling to be separated from his wife, "the prince may enslave his wife"[144] and in England the famous Anselm, Archbishop of Canterbury, presided over a synod in London that made the wives of priests the property of the bishop.

No wonder the Church had excommunicated me for marrying. Rome had long seen marriage as unfit for consecrated hands. The rift between the Catholics and Greek Orthodox only became final when Cardinal Humbert, the head of a papal delegation to Byzantium, on July 16th 1054 damned and expelled the whole eastern half of the church because they accepted married priests. He reported with horror: "Young husbands, just now exhausted from carnal lust...serve at the altar. And immediately afterward they again embrace their wives with hands that have been hallowed by the immaculate Body of Christ. That is not the mark of a true faith but an invention of Satan."[145]

But Humbert knew that even in the West the battle to ban priests from sex was not yet won. Many Western priests were celebrating valid church weddings in the 11th Century, despite Pope Gregory VII (d 1085) telling Bishop Bernold that priestly marriage was "a crime of fornication" and ordering Catholics to boycott church services led by married priests under pain of excommunication. This caused outrage. Bishops refused to implement his ruling. They wrote reminding the Pope that Christ and the apostles were in favour of marriage and that the apostles were married.

In 1139 Rome finally declared invalid all marriages by Roman Catholic priests (Canon 10)—but this did not stop the practice. Over a hundred years later the Synod of Munster in 1280 forbade priests to attend the weddings or funerals of their children (Canon 2) and in the 14th century the wives of priests were denied church funerals.[146] But it was not a complete success for the anti-marriage lobby. A few small Eastern Churches in Communion with Rome (meaning, who recognise the supreme authority of the Pope and whose bishops and priests are recognised in return) resisted this pressure without being expelled from the Catholic Church. They still have married priests

The most influential of Catholic medieval theologians, St. Thomas Aquinas, a man I had to study in the original Latin, had worked out why women were inferior to men. His decision that only a boy was a perfectly formed human was based on his theory that only a boy could fully reflected the male seed from which he had grown, planted by his father in a womb. The birth of females he explained as due to a defect in the mother or in the environment on the day of conception. He stated; "the seed of the male tends to produce something like itself, perfect in masculinity, but the procreation of the female is the result either of the debility of the active power, of some unsuitability of the material, or of some change effected by external influences, like the south wind, for example, which is damp." Why would dampness help create a woman? He believed women's bodies contained too much water. This also explained apparently why they had softer skins and were so fickle. He held that for these reasons women were not suitable for the priesthood.

A hundred years earlier Hildegard of Bingen explained that girl children occur "if the man's seed is thin", not because of a defect in the mother.[147] Aquinas may have doctored this earlier theory to remove any mention of a male "weakness", but her theory was closer to modern science than that of Aquinas. In 2001 it was discovered that if the lighter semen are separated out and placed in the womb, girls are normally born, while if the heavier are used, boys are normally born.[148]

The Roman church, after losing its link with the Eastern Church over sexuality, then lost the northern half of Europe partly for the same reason. When Luther defied Rome by allowing marriage to the clergy, Archbishop Albrecht of Brandenburg wrote: " I know all my priests are living in concubinage. But what should I do to stop it? If I forbid them concubines they either want to have wives or to become Lutherans"[149] In the 21st century, the marriage of clergy in the Protestant and eastern churches is still seen by the Roman Church as a major obstacle to union. A still bigger obstacle is the presence of women in the priesthood of Anglican and Protestant churches. Sex is still the great divisive issue in Christianity.

For me, it is incredible that despite all this in-fighting, all this corruption of religion, that somehow among the debris were preserved much wisdom and some knowledge of Jesus as friendly to women. The evidence of modern archaeology and of pagan historians seems to confirm his existence, but cannot confirm he was the God-Man who demanded repentance. My own view is that he lived as the travelling preacher, healer and wise man, that he saw us all, male and female, as the Children of God, as all partaking in the divine, as sharing a Father in Heaven. He said both that he was the "son of God" and that others were "the children of God" He saw marriage as a time for celebration and provided wine. He protected women from the authorities.

I think that he had a sacred path to tread, a myth that he had to live for the sake of all—and that we too have paths we must tread, myths we must express and live for the sake of all. I think and hope that it is always this way; that the Wisdom we need is always there for those who have a need of it. I think this same wisdom can be found (with a bit of digging) in all religions and cultures. This basic religion is for me part of our collective unconsciousness and part of our instinctual being.

While training for the priesthood I had partly for myself the theological disputes over sex. My celibacy was for me a vow not to wed false Gods of money, worldly success and security, keeping true to the God I married. I never saw sex as bad in itself for it was part of a sacred nature. I wonder now why was I not more inhibited by the years of indoctrination? I do not know. I was perhaps protected by a certain naiveté and romanticism—along with a belief in a relationship with a Lover God who was not at all judgmental.

A Wedding

Shortly after my university finals, Jackie and I planned to celebrate our marriage in the large home of a Ceylonese architect friend. Our master of ceremonies would be a Catholic priest who led anti-nuclear weapons marches to Aldermaston. Many trainee priest friends were coming to our wedding. An Anglican priest wrote us songs, another friend would sing them. We had balloons with Snoopy pictures and greeted every guest, male or female, at the door with a bunch of flowers purchased in a dawn raid on Covent Garden market.

Before the celebration, we went to the registry office to officially but not sacredly wed. The sacred part would be that afternoon. We did not see ourselves as needing the state's approval, but told the state because we were taking on a social obligation by deciding to have children.

Jackie had found a silk yellow dress, long, glorious and simple, in a shop selling clothes from the East. Her parents came over from Australia and insisted on providing the food. They engaged a caterer that did functions for Princess Anne. We said we wanted something simple. Rice salad and salmon was the simplest they could dream up. We said the cake should only have one tier. A man in dark suit and waistcoat arrived an hour before the ceremony carrying a brief case. He carefully took from this the cake dressings and placed them on our single-tier cake. We asked if the waiters could be relaxed, mix in, be informal. We were told that their staff never fraternised! But on the day they were fine—and formal.

Father Simon Blake came to officiate in a blue sweater. He was a Dominican priest who held that nuclear bombs were fundamentally immoral—and did what he could to have them destroyed. A man in white in Rome would have excommunicated him—not for being anti-nuclear but for marrying us. The excommunication sanction was automatic—but ineffective, as the Pope did not know of his presence. Thus afterwards he could continue in the Catholic ministry. (Since Fr. Blake has died, I can now safely make this public.) Jackie and I were also excommunicated. It did not concern us. We had no belief in the Pope's power to exclude us from God's company.

I still can see Jackie coming down the staircase into the crowded lounge, wonderful in her dress, long hair dancing, eyes sparkling, the balloons and flowers everywhere. She came into a throng of wonderful people that had arrived to celebrate with us, the sharing of music, of song, and the solemn promises of marriage. I welcomed her; we stood before the priest and exchanged our vows—and the rest of it I only remember as a marvellously happy time.

Thus we entered deeper into the world of the sexual God. Locked in each other's arms, we were a refection on earth of the divine Trinity—one'd with each other and with God—a fitting place indeed for a priest—and priestess, for we saw ourselves as sharing in the sacred priesthood. My title of bridegroom went back 2000 years or more to the time when Bride was the name of a cherished Goddess of the British Isle (sometimes also known as Bree or Bridget.). Her emblem was a white mare. She rode the skies as the sun. Jackie was the Goddess and I her groom. That night she was also the ancient wild untamed and beautiful "Night-mare"—a word that has reversed it's meaning because of the Christian fear of sex.

A groom
To the Mare
The Sacred horse
Of the purest White
The Goddess
Consummated
Night groom,
With night mare
Scary, yes
Like first kisses.[150]

A Gibran poem on marriage gave us wise advice. "Let there be spaces in your togetherness, and let the winds of the heavens dance between you. Love one another but make not a bond of love. Let it rather be a moving sea between the shores of your souls…give your hearts but not into each other's keeping. For only the hand of Life can contain your hearts. And stand together yet not too near together, for the pillars of the temple stand apart, and the oak tree and the cypress grow not in each other's shadow."[151]

I felt I was still the knight, the priest, still bonded with my Divine Lover, still on the same path. I did not want to be part of a clerical elite and was glad I was no longer, but I hoped to share, to empower, to strengthen, thus to serve the priesthood of the whole community. I hoped and trusted that this would still be possible.

Pilgrimage to Australia

Now started a new adventure. Armed with rucksacks, Jackie and I set out some days later from Brixton in South London. At a bus stop in the centre of town, an old lady asked if we were going far. With glee we said "Only to Australia."

Jackie planned with friends to set up in Melbourne a "House of Hospitality" for the homeless people of the road. It would be something akin to the house for alcoholics and drug addicts where we had first met in Maldon Road in North London's Camden Town. This community was inspired by a Christian anarchism taught in the "Catholic Worker" movement by an inspiring American Christian who lived her own teaching, Dorothy Day. Unlike her, we were rejecting the institutional Church, but we were determined not to throw out the baby with the bathwater. We had found within its cavernous halls some marvellous individuals committed to a radical service of a God of love.

Jackie and I had decided to work together in this House of Hospitality. When we set off overland for Australia to begin this task, we owned 500 US dollars each—but it was 1970 when dollars went further. Our first stop was in Heerlen in The Netherlands where we had friends in a college that trained Catholic priests. Much to our surprise, the students and teachers asked us if we would ritually celebrate our marriage again so they could be part of it—and would we please do so by co-celebrating the Holy Mass? We were amazed, delighted and grateful at being asked to do such a wonderful thing.

Side by side Jackie and I presided behind the sacred altar on which was a chalice of wine and a plate of bread—all that is needed for the sacred meal. We felt bonded in the mystery, one flesh, one couple, joined in life and in the priesthood, one with the circle of participants. We knew that we were presiding as a couple put together by a divine blessing. We were celebrating life while one with God and all our ancestors and teachers. It went beyond the church in which we stood. We were celebrating with this food the bonding of Deity and Creation, the wedding of God and Universe. With the happiest of smiles we gladly celebrated—and this is a song I wrote later for these sacred feasts:

I, your Maker,
I, your Love,
Spirit of the sap that gives you life.
Here, is my bread.
Eat it,
Know it,
Live it
Become one with my bounty,
And know that I am one with the golden wheat
That blows in the wind
I am one with the grain broken by the mill
I am one with this bread that enters your mouth,
Come, take me, I am yours whole and entire
And take this cup of wine
The Holy Grail, the tinker's mug
Filled with the fermented blood of grapes
Drink this
And taste the blood of divinity
Know that I am the least of my grapes
Whole and entire
I am the one met in ecstasy

I am the cup, the grail, the mug
The source of life
Drink, Eat,
Love and be Merry.
And know that I am one with
You that I love,
All that I love,
The One
Who fulfils you.[152]

It had been something of a mystery to me how I would be able to use my priesthood now that I had been divested of patriarchal rank, but this pointed the way. I had simply to trust in the path given to me. I felt I had stripped off the first layer down towards the gold of life.

From Heerlen we set out for Australia via Asia, picking up medicines from a Swiss friend, then hitchhiking across the Alps by a minor lonely pass. In Yugoslavia a crazy Dutchman, rushing to catch up with a woman friend on a bus tour, drove us non-stop to Istanbul, killing a donkey as he sped on roads where animals and humans had priority. On arrival we explored markets, cafes—and found an ancient Christian church with a mosaic that showed a woman as a member of the Holy Trinity. I searched it out, as I wanted to see how Sophia was celebrated before she became desexed as the Holy Ghost. This memory now teaches me that I sought the sacred Female when I was but newly emerged from Church life—otherwise I might wonder if I were reshaping the past in the light of the present—something that can be done easily.

After Istanbul, we travelled by local buses and trains so that we would meet local people. The bus service was elegant. Cologne was poured into our hands before the journey began so we could clean and cool our faces; iced water sat in a fridge next to the driver, and everything was decorated in bright colours. We had decided to make first for Tarsus, St Paul's home city—basically because it was a city we had heard of and was on the

Mediterranean. But as we could not reach it in one day, we asked the driver to drop us when we reached the coastline. It was dark when we arrived. When we tried to put up the tent, we found the ground too hard for tent pegs. Eventually we slept under a tent hung between bushes next to a long low rocky ridge.

In the morning we were delighted to find that the ridge was a fallen Grecian column; the hard rock beneath was a pavement; the nearby rocky promontory a Crusader's castle built out of Grecian ruins. A rocky island off the coast hosted another castle. We washed in a half-submerged building, marvelling at the quietness of a scene that was once a place of culture and then of blood. In the West, charities run "crusades" yet in the Islamic world the word recalls the barbarity of a horde of religious fanatics inspired by a version of the blood baptism religion of the early Catholics—but this time the blood that took them to Heaven would hopefully belong to others.

But theirs was not the path of all contemporary Christians. In Southern France Cathar Christianity was embracing pacifism before becoming itself the target of a Crusade. Throughout Europe hundreds of men and women were dragging stones and scaffolding poles, chanting or in silence, building the great gothic cathedrals. These were mostly dedicated to Mary as a Mother of Peace. It was as if they were building a glorious stone forest in honour of a sacred woman to counter-balance the Crusader's "sacred" violence.

In Tarsus, since we had missed our train, the station manager pushed two waiting room benches together to make us a double bed then, wishing us a good night, locked us in till morning. I think Paul of Tarsus would have approved since he said marriage was sacred. Next morning a Turkish family shared food with us as our steam train climbed dramatic valleys. Others invited us to visit them in their mud walled and simply elegant homes.

In an Eastern Turkish town, very early one morning, we saw a group of Kurdish shepherds with cloth caps and crooks standing solemnly in a circle in the market place watching a lamb being born in their midst. Bullocks passed us pulling carts with solid wooden wheels—a design not changed for over 2000 years, a truly biblical scene. In the fields we watched the drivers of oxen stand on surfboard like boards as they went over heaps of grain to crush them. We had left a frantic Europe for another world where old crafts survived.

In Iran the Shah still ruled. We met in Teheran with westernised members of the government services who explained to us the plans to educate both girls and boys. From here we went south past the golden dome of Quom to Isfahan, the former capital of Persia. We arrived in the early hours, so slept in the central square while waiting for the dawn. As the first light stirred us, great mosques greeted us, like open portals to God, with wonderfully tiled and lettered half domes and pillars. Attracted by the smell of bread baking, we then went down side streets to find small shops with ovens made from open-topped earthenware vases set into bench-tops with a fire below. They expertly spun bread flat then slapped it onto heated inside surfaces so it could quickly bake.

We next crossed the mountains to the Caspian Sea where, for the last time in Asia, we used our tent. It felt so out of place, conspicuous and guaranteed to attract attention, that we did not use it again. We found that local hotels cost pence. Then we went to the holy city of Moshad, where we met girl tourists complaining about having to cover bare knees. Jackie willingly veiled her hair and covered her legs when we went to quietly watch the worshippers and to honour from afar the holy place within the city. As we passed through markets, drank coffee and chatted to locals, we heard and felt the first mutterings of the nationalistic and religious storm that would lead to the fall of the Shah and the rise of the Ayatollahs.

The men (for few if any Iranian women then used Moshad's coffee shops) expressed to us a softly uttered determination to keep up old Iranian sacred ways threatened by the westernisation that accompanied the Shah's regime. It seemed to us strangers that the freedom of women to expose hair and choose clothes were foreign concepts resisted out of national pride. It was understandable, but we felt uncomfortable. But personally, the only trouble we had in an Islamic country was as much against their cultural rules as against our own. It happened on the train crossing Pakistan. A husband to some of the travelling women invaded the supposedly all female carriage and harassed Jackie. I had thought her safe in that carriage. Afterwards very apologetic Muslims told us the treatment she had experienced was not in accordance with the teaching of the Prophet, that he had never wanted women to lose their rights to education and freedom. They explained that Mohammed had greatly honoured his own wife. The veiling of women was first intended as a mark of respect for the women of the Prophet's own family—not an instruction for all women.

The Koran, dictated by Mohammed to scribes while he was moved by visions, forbade the earlier practice of lamenting the birth of girl babies and killing them. It gave women legal rights of inheritance and divorce not possessed by most Christianised western women until a thousand years later (although Irish woman received this protection from the Pagan Seancchus Mor code before Islam appeared.). After Mohammed died, a chauvinistic elite of male teachers took over Islam, just as happened Christianity in its first centuries. The secluding of women in harems is a custom they adopted and developed from the practices of Christian Byzantium.[153] The custom of hiding female faces perhaps was more due to the prejudices of St Jerome than of Mohammed

We had reached Pakistan by crossing Afghanistan, fortunately before the recent wars began. A taxi with only first gear took seven Pakistani men and us grindingly and slowly into Afghanistan. We stopped for a meal at an ancient inn with high fortress walls, niches for oil lamps and rich carpets on which we sat cross-legged. After the ceremonial washing of hands, a feast was set before us in beaten bronze or copper bowls.

When we arrived at midnight in Herat, it seemed like a scene from a Dr Zhivago film. Stallions and mares in rich harness and plumes trotted or galloped past us pulling light carriages while we called at the high gates of ancient caravanserais to find one with room for our group. When we gained entry, we found within a large open courtyard with a well. On one side of this was a hall with high windows and minimal furniture. We slept in sheets or sleeping bags upon the floor, males and females in the same hall, as was the tradition.

We then travelled by local bus through Kandihar and Kabul, then down the Khyber Pass to Pakistan. Soon afterwards we were in India after a leisurely and wonderful seven weeks of travelling, costing about $13 a week each—very little even for 1970.

India felt strangely home-like for a country so very different. Perhaps this was so because we have in Europe a subconscious memory of India? Our European culture inherited much from India in the distant past. We decided to stay for as long as we could afford in India. In the end, we stayed three months.

We wanted to get to know the country, to empty ourselves as much as possible of our western baggage, so we decided to keep away from other Europeans or Americans. This included the hippy throng then heading for ashrams to study meditation. But this intention was sabotaged by a very small thing, an infected toe. This led me to ask for medical help from a house we chanced on in the foothills of the Himalayas. It had a notice on its door saying "Student Christian Movement"—a non-fundamentalist and radical organisation I had joined at university. They nursed me for a full week without charge and then dispatched us to an ashram they highly recommended. It was in Risikesh, where the river Ganges enters the mountains.

W e found it on the riverbank. I think it was called the Divine Light Ashram. It had attached to it both a general hospital and an eye hospital. When I was confined to my room with heat stroke, a monk with a trident painted on his forehead came to make sure I was all right and give me spiritual advice. We were also warned to keep our rooms shut lest monkeys raid them. One day I saw a cow walk along the top of the outer stonewall of the ashram in order to reach tree leaves. I was not surprised that they thought cows sacred. They seemed to be a different species to those I had known in Europe.

The Beatles made Risikesh famous when they came here to study under the Maharishi. We took a ferryboat to visit his ashram across the river. It had a very different atmosphere to our own. It had an air-conditioned meditation hut and a bath in a treetop "to help communing with nature", as we were told. It seemed sophisticated and westernised—but this was only an impression from a quick visit.

At our ashram we were invited to join in prayer in its traditional Hindu temple. A part of the ritual was the passing of a flaming lamp between all present. When it reached us, copying the others, we waved the flame towards us, asking that it purify us. At the end we were all given a little of the food dedicated to the Deity. It was the first time we had taken part in a non-Christian ritual and we much enjoyed the privilege. We questioned how different it really was from our own beliefs and practises. The flame was a symbol used in Christian Europe for the Spirit of Wisdom. (And for the Goddesses Macha and Bride in Pagan Eire) The communion was far tastier than the pallid wafer used for Christian communion but it carried the same meaning of uniting us to the Deity.

We found many others here who questioned the reality of the division between religions. Among them were Jesuits studying meditation—and a Christian Argentinean woman who took food to the hermits in the mountains. The Hindu monks regarded her as very saintly.

We spent three months in India. We travelled south by train, sleeping on luggage racks, amid clucking chickens and a thousand families, to reach Madras and the southern Temples. We were served "one yard" coffee poured from one cup to another held at arms length to aerate it. We went to Brahmin restaurants where we ate at separate one-person marble tables. Our food was put on carefully washed disposable banana leaves.

From Madras we decided to go to Bangalore. The train was scheduled to leave very early in the morning so we did what many other Indians do; we spent the night sleeping on the floor of a railway station's waiting room. Once on the train, we used the shower provided in each carriage. Then two elderly ladies started to chat to us. One asked us very politely where we would stay when we reached our destination? I replied " At an Indian hotel (i.e. a cheaper one than those for Europeans)."

A little while later, after some discussion between them, one of the women said. "You are strangers here and we feel like mothers towards you. We would like to look after you in Bangalore. Would you please consider coming to stay with me?

So we stayed for a few days in her home, where spices were ground for an hour, or so it seemed, before each meal. ("You eat them stale!" one woman exclaimed when I said we bought them ready ground and keep them for weeks in our kitchen cupboards.) We were then invited for dinner to the home of the other women. During this we were asked, "What have you not yet seen in India that you had wanted to see?"

"Elephants" I replied.

"What! You haven't seen our elephants. We will put that right."

A day later we found ourselves with them on a two-day bus journey. The first night we slept like them (but not as easily) on wooden benches in a school they knew in Mysore. Then, after admiring their fruit market, incredibly tidy, with many stalls specialising in just varieties of a single fruit, we travelled deep into the forested hills of the Western Ghats.

That afternoon we arrived at the small town where one of the women had worked as the hospital matron before she retired. She knew everyone. We became their guests in the club house, where Indians spoke in the stilted style of the Raj, served us brandy in full tumblers and explained how they circumvented Kerala government regulations that said they must give land to long-term labourers—as if they were sure we would approve of this evasion.

Next day a bus was diverted from its normal route to take us to a private government game reserve. On arrival we were put up by a ranger. A day later at dawn an elephant awaited us. The driver, the ranger, the two elderly ladies and we all climbed aboard and out we went into the jungle. For two hours we travelled beneath the trees in what felt like a wooden boat sailing through the tops of shrubs. The only time we saw the elephant underneath was when she occasionally used her trunk.

Eventually we reached a patch of very tall grass in which there were some large anthills. Then an anthill lifted a trunk and we realised we were in the midst of a herd of wild elephants. The ranger quickly assured us that we were safe from attack because we were on a female elephant. We travelled in great excitement and in considerable wonder for an hour with this herd. There were several baby elephants. When the adults eventually tired of our company, spreading their ears and throwing plants up into the air while staring at us, the ranger said it was time to go while slipping a blank cartridge into his shotgun.

On arrival back in the camp, a small hairy caterpillar fell from a tree and landed inside the neck of my shirt. The ranger looked at it, said it was poisonous and then rubbed his crew cut on my chest to draw the poison. The rash soon went. Thus I went out with wild elephants and was poisoned by a caterpillar.

We went on to stay with a Catholic Anglo-Indian family and spoke with them about their very European style of celebrating their faith. They said this was the proper way for them to do it—and that Hindus would not like them adopting Indian Hindu customs. Hindus had indeed protested when the Catholic monk Bede Griffiths set up an Indian style temple as his sacred place. Indians were proud of having a land that tolerated many religions—and did not see a need for them to converge.

Bede Griffiths however disagreed—for he sought the wisdom shared between Hinduism, Christianity and the mysticism of all paths. Jackie and I thus sought him out and found his ashram styled monastery had a sacred phallic symbol for its altar since "For the Hindu sex is essentially holy. It is a manifestation of the divine love."[154]

Hinduism enshrined a spiritual wisdom that he maintained exceeded that of the Greeks since the Hindu Gods had stayed strong when the Grecian Gods faded.[155] I have no notes of our conversation so I quote from his 1982 work. "The Christian cannot claim to have the monopoly of the truth. We are all pilgrims in search of truth, of reality, of final fulfilment."

"Even the Myth of Christ belongs still to the world of Signs and we have to go beyond the Myth to the Mystery itself."[156]

He saw the universe as having three levels of reality—physical, psychological and spiritual, each destined for unity with the divine consciousness. He said that it was "an illusion" that the physical world exists apart from consciousness, as was also held by Descartes. For this radical monk, the physical world was permeated by consciousness.

From South India we travelled north to work among the poorest with the followers of an even more legendary figure, Mother Teresa of Calcutta.

Conception and the Male

But the day before our train reached Calcutta, we first stopped to visit a famed Orissa temple shaped as chariot of glistening white stone, and covered with carvings of embracing couples. It was a dream of erotic love set in a small community of fishermen.

After marvelling at its glorious celebration of sexuality, Jackie and I settled for the night on the sandy shore by fishing boats. I will never forget that night. The power of the Goddess of that temple, of its thousand stone couples and of the seas of India seemed to be with us. It could well have been that night that our first daughter was conceived.

That night the asexual me vanished in the delights of male sexuality. I lost myself in the deep pool that was my lover. I surrendered and was drowned. I gave myself as deeply as I was capable (ignoring considerable pain from skinless knees on sand!). I rested, waited until the tide of male hormones lifted me again to descend again deep into a sea that lay between us, a sea of creation. I played the fiddle; the tension of the bow thrilled me. I caressed her, loved her, lifted again, swam and exploded. I was in wonder.

I was later thrilled that my confusion (and sore knees) had not stopped me. The dream of being a girl that night seemed irrelevant. I loved Jackie and I gave to her as fully as my body permitted. I ignored my confusion. I enjoyed what God had given me, a sharing in this male rite. Sometimes after the emptying, I wanted to yield; sleep—but this I felt would not fair to Jackie for she never seemed to need to sleep. So I would again lift, close eyes, go with the tide, enjoy the tide, on our beach be the tide, be the lover, love the seeding. When we could, we slowed it, allowing a spring of romancing, a summer of feasting and an autumn of giving. Then we both enjoyed a winter's sleep before the re-awakening. There were many such years in that night.

And thus I gave to the creation of a child. I learnt a typical male fruiting was a sudden harvest explosion. The whole cycle might last but 20 minutes. This explosion may be a good metaphor for the "big bang' theory but any act that lasts seconds and creates a teaspoon of seed is a shallow claim to human parenting. It cannot make the father the equal of the mother. I think fathers are made over years by nurturing and protecting children.

Patriarchy only happens when the protector mistakes his role and becomes over-zealous, believing he knows what a woman wants better than she. He needs to be one with the androgynous Father who does not neglect the gentler anima within. Then there will be a giving and a receiving that will create a small Garden of Eden of new life.

The prevailing Western concept of God as a power outside the earth gives men a dreadful model for their creativity. It inspires men to see themselves as powers apart from nature, able to subject nature to their will and change it. And this in turn leads to the most unfortunate and sad examples of male parenting.

The God of the Patriarchy is capable of being hard and merciless, as the Old Testament reveals. He is divorced from Nature, living in a world of Supernature created by intellect alone. He has lost his anima, his gentleness and his soul—evidently not a good role- model for men.

Nor can men find good role models in many pagan Gods—for many of their myths were composed in an age when men ruled women. In the Irish epic, "The Tain", the hero Cuchulainn rejected the offered support of a warrior woman, forgetting it was a woman called Scathlach who taught him his fighting skills, He insultingly said: "It wasn't for a woman's backside that I took on this ordeal." He then had to face the shape-shifting magical skills of a Goddess in battle for she was the Goddess Morrigan. He won by using the skills taught him by another women, but Morrigan tricks him afterwards into curing her wounds.

Many old tales about Gods were composed to justify men taking women's rights. Irish myths are full of accounts of Goddesses that have been tamed—and even raped. The Goddess Tlachtga was pack raped—and then died giving birth to male warriors. The Goddesses of Sovereignty sunk to become the wives or sisters of Gods. In one story Macha is demoted to being the wife of Nemed. She is subsequently powerless to prevent the slaughter she has foreseen. As part of the Trinity of the Morrigan, she was of even lower status as a daughter of the son of the god Neid, rather than his consort. This demotion went with the lower social status of women. Much later on, the fall of the Kildare Abbess in 1132 was marked in an horrid ancient fashion by her being raped by a soldier to render her unfit for office.

As a woman, I would experience some of this violence and fear. In 1979 in a cave in the mountains of Crete I was forced to flee the advances of the cave's guardian for fear he would rape me. The cave was said to be the one where Gaia hid Zeus as a boy after his mother Rhea put him into Gaia's care. Zeus then seemingly forgot that he had been born of woman and protected by woman. When he emerged from this cave, he came to represent a male power than had no need of women to give birth. It was a cruel irony that I too would experience male arrogance in this same place.

But when Jackie and I went to India, I was still on the male pedestal and so in social life I remained superior in power to females. When men chose to treat me as the authority rather than Jackie, as they often did, I felt very awkward. Their prejudices seemed to bind me. I feared their rejection so did not express my reservations as freely as I should.

At that time I took monogamy for granted—and still prefer it, but for St Augustine monogamy was an unnecessary limitation to the power of men. He believed that in some circumstances men could properly take several wives. He wrote that if a nation needed children, "I rather approve using the fertility of many women for an unselfish purpose than the flesh of a single woman for her own sake...for in the latter case we are dealing with the satisfaction of a lust aimed at earthly pleasure."[157]

But for the women of the ancient hunter-gatherer societies of the Amazon River valley and in similar societies elsewhere, things were very different.[158] At least eighteen Amazonian tribes in the 1990s believed that a child could have many fathers. A woman who wanted to have a child might select one man to give her child strong limbs, another to give the child quick wits, another to give the child a gentle heart and another to give her child great sex—and then she sleeps with all of them. The degree of fatherhood a male possessed depended on how often she slept with him. If she had a regular partner, that person becomes the primary father.

When the child was born, she told all her lovers that they had shared in the making of her child. They surrounded her. "Look the child has my eyes!" "Look the child has my nose!" "Look the child has my hair?" "Look the child has my laugh!" And they all happily protect the mother and her child—and protect the children they also share in fathering for other mothers.

Some of our scientists today think she is wrong because only one sperm fertilised her egg. But if they told her this, she would probably think them stupid and say: "Can't they see that fatherhood is much more, much much more, than any sperm?"

"Their fatherhood is expressed in love and in protection, in nourishment and in caring." They loved her didn't they, as she conceived this child? Their love has flowed into her egg, their spirit has joined with her, become one with her in creating this child.

She might add: "The child can only have one mother so why limit a child to one father—when many make it so much richer?"

But—if a real "man" was present, he might protest against losing his right to own a child. I imagine he might say: "I want a child I can own, that I can discipline, that I can train, that I can boast of—that carries ME into the next generation. Where I live we don't look with favour on women sleeping around. What man with self-respect could do so? No, I will support my wife, clothe her, and give her station and respect if, and only if, she sleeps only with me. How else can I know if a child is mine?"

To this I would protest: "But, you are treating her as if you owned her. How can you own another person?"

And being a reasonable man he might answer: "Of course, I agree, I do not own her. But marriage is a contract we both entered freely. She bears my children. I look after her. We keep our love-making for each other."

The Amazon woman might then ask him in some perplexity: "But don't you think if would be nicer if you could share your love-making and your child-making with many others? Why limit something so very good?"

"He is right," says stern voice from a dark corner. Then into the light came a priest, "Marriage reflects the unity between God and the Church. Christ taught marriage is as indissoluble as the union between the church and God. It therefore can be only between one man and one woman. Sex is given to us solely for the procreation of children and seed spent uselessly is sinfully wasted"

A passing woman on the arm of her lover could then protest, "I don't believe in religion—but I do believe in loving one person and in being faithful to that one person."

And laughter then would come from the woman of the Amazon. "So, what is wrong with the woman weaving with her thighs many men into one? Does not your god love many?"

"Two shall become one flesh" quotes the priest, with satisfaction. His bible gives him surety.

The Amazon woman stood up. She had done enough teaching for now—but before she went she said: "Would it not be more wonderful to give several fathers to one child, for four or five lovers to become one flesh, if families can intertwine?"

And she looked with pride at her child, a symbol of the unity of her clan.

And there are many truths that weave into one, many ways of expressing the wonder of creative love. Many ways that are not on any map. Today some scientists argue that she is right, that a child can be influenced by lovemaking during gestation—that the initial fertilisation is not the only way for males to influence the unborn child.

But enough of this reflection on the meaning of life. I was telling of making love on an Indian beach by an erotic temple. Next morning, we travelled on to a very different world. We went to stay with a priest and community working alongside Mother Teresa in the slums of Calcutta. They found us a private room with a double bed in a room within a children's home. The children lived in a great room in a separate house, a laughing melee of eager faces happy to eat plain flat bread spread with what they saw as the great treat of condensed milk provided by Western aid agencies. Washing up dishes was done with sand—a way that I now use when camping. Sand removes grease far more cheaply and effectively than detergent. Jackie in her sari helped feed babies brought to the home every morning. I helped with removing the propaganda-covered sacks from the American grain given as humanitarian aid. This was necessary, as otherwise the volunteers would be accused by Naxalites, local revolutionaries, of trying to buy support for America.

When we left two weeks later, we had been in India for three months. It was now time to complete our journey to Australia. From here we flew to Burma and visited a wonderful golden pagoda in Rangoon where people prayed holding flowers between their hands. The royal pagodas of Bangkok that we next visited were much less impressive for they felt corrupted by a hunger for money, with American dollars requested for even looking after shoes. We were then near to the war in Vietnam.

In Malaysia a flood covered the railway track so we travelled the last hundred miles or so by a remarkably cheap taxi to the skyscrapers of

Singapore. After this modern city, it was a relief to discover that Indonesia remained a home for a rich ancient Asian culture. Java and Bali were delights of rich street theatre and music—a society where TV did not force people to stay indoors. Thence we travelled via Portuguese Timor, where street markets were greatly impoverished, to Darwin in Australia where we arrived with about one hundred left of the thousand dollars we possessed between us when we left England some six months earlier.

A Pregnant Down-Under

My first memories of Australia include a Darwin hotel's notice banning men who were not wearing socks and shoes—a direction mostly aimed at excluding Aborigines although it also excluded me. I had not worn socks for many months. My other memory was of a single man raising and saluting the Australian flag in a rather singular display of nationalism. But the best of all events was receiving a letter in Darwin from a friend asking if we would like a large room in a house she rented near the centre of Melbourne. We felt we had arrived—but were dismayed to find out we still had over 2000 miles to go to reach Melbourne. We hitched lifts on road-trains down the endless "Track" to Alice Springs where we borrowed money to travel on by the *Ghan* train to Adelaide. A courteous attendant took us to our private railway cabin with a fold-away toilet mounted as if it were a wall safe.

Melbourne was somewhat of a let-down after such a wonderful long trip. Its grid of skyscrapers seemed soulless. When we reached Jackie's parents' home they gave us what they described as a "typical Australian meal". I imagined this would be a large steak but it was a pie containing a meat-flavoured liquid that oozed over the entire plate.

It was scarcely a month later that, on March 1st 1971, Jackie learnt that she was indeed pregnant. Our gynaecologist, who was supposed to be Melbourne's best and whose services were gained for us by Jackie's parents, told us the baby was due on September 8th. This meant that she was conceived in our last weeks in India.

The diary I kept at the time recorded; "What we've suspected since Thailand is true. We've brought in a secret immigrant from India! September 8th is the tenth anniversary of my First Religious Profession and Mary O'Christ's birthday in the Church's calendar. Anyway we are fab. Happy. We buy beer and go to celebrate with Chris and Jan, buy cake and go afterwards to celebrate with Mary, Val and Brian and Co. We make immediately good friends at their old house in Fitzroy where they are living with six blokes of the road. " (My maths was poor. It was actually my twelfth anniversary.) This was the "house of hospitality" that Jackie returned to Australia to help with.

The friends of Jackie involved in this venture were Mary, her partner Val, a former Catholic priest, and his brother Brian. They now all lived together in a house that was open to the homeless people of the road.

The next day we went to see the friend who had written to us in Darwin offering us a room. My diary records "we go around to visit Leslie Whyte and her kid Emily. They show us a large room in their beaut house in the heart of N Fitzroy for 5 dollars and 25 cents a week. Jackie was a bit hesitant especially because of the lack of a private kitchen but there's a lot to be said for communal kitchens. Anyway it's an incredible Godsend…but Jackie's mother is a bit upset about our plans to live in a "slum"" It was in fact a beautiful large clean house opposite a park and a tramway which would get us into town in 10 minutes—but Jackie 's parents had worked hard to escape from the inner suburbs at a time when these were run down and dilapidated".

I wrote to my parents to tell them about our expected child, hoping that the news of their first grandchild would overcome their anger at my marriage. My diary recorded "their first letter since they heard we were married. We had told them that we were expecting a baby. They addressed their reply to Miss Craig!—Said we could telegram them if we decided to get our wedding put right with the church—otherwise they wouldn't read our letters. Mum said she had hoped—but this proved I had really fallen! (We must have made love!) Alas! God take care of them and bring us together. I can do no more it seems." We both found this very distressing.

We soon set up home in Alfred Crescent with Lesley and Emily—and a short time later by the new man in her life, Peter; followed soon after by a concert cellist. The house had seven rooms and a large living area so there was plenty of room for friends to stay. A constant stream of people briefly rented the two or three rooms we still had spare. The total house rent was only $21 a week, even then minuscule. The lodgers quickly became friends, as we tended to cook and eat together. Eddy Ryan, a blind activist and teacher, came to stay, as did Justin Moloney, the Race Relations officer of the Australian Union of Students and many other active creative people. There was a sandpit in the back and the house faced a park of European trees, for Melbourne's cities were planted with such trees—thus starving out native parrots and humming birds.

Jackie's friends' house of hospitality was a rented large stone house in King William Street that they shared with alcoholics and other street men and women. This was the kind of committed Catholicism that I deeply loved. They really saw the poor as sacred. They were also constantly engaged in non-violent protests against the Vietnam War. I was happy and privileged to have a place among them. I thought it was a sign that God is always with his people even if the church establishments desert him.

A few weeks after moving into Alfred Crescent, on April 3rd 1971, I was at a demonstration against the Vietnam War when I saw a large policeman savagely beating a protester. Not knowing what else to do, I called out asking for his number. He swung around without hesitation and knocked me to the ground. He then seized me in a throat lock and, when I reached down to pick up my glasses, another policeman coshed my imprisoned head then deliberately stood on my glasses. I was subsequently arrested and taken to hospital with concussion. As it happened it was a Catholic hospital. I remember young Catholic medics were thrilled to discover that I was a Catholic priest, for they had heard rumours of priests such as Dan Berrigan, a Jesuit in the States who carried out anti-war rituals such as pouring a bottle of his blood over the nose of nuclear missiles, as I have mentioned. Like him I was now an underground priest. There may have been little room for us within a politically conservative church but I still saw myself as committed to the priesthood and still celebrated the holy meal that was the Mass.

Our political work went alongside our preparation for childbirth. On May 6th Jackie felt the baby move for the first time, just a slight flutter, and, on May 29th, while she was leafleting against the Vietnam war, she called me so I could feel for the first time the movement of our child.

Our friends Val Noone and Mary Doyle sometimes held political soirées to which a wide group of people came from the churches, the unions and many other organisations, or none, to generate ideas, argue, resolve and publish. They were for me a rich source of friends and a community that welcomed me. These meetings helped generate a magazine called "Retrieval". I was soon working with Val and others as a co-editor of this anti-war magazine. It set itself the task of summarising and distributing a vast amount of information on struggles for human rights or the environment, not just the Vietnam War. We also covered the Aboriginal struggle for justice within Australia.

This work soon led me into trouble. I summarised an article from *The Bulletin of Concerned Asian Scholars* that documented how American and Australian academics were recruited to help both the US and Australia with their war effort in SE Asia. One person mentioned was a Professor Geddes of Sydney University's anthropological faculty. He responded with heavy threats, saying it was libellous to allege that he was "helping the war effort" and that he had been working for civilian agencies when he set up the Tribal Research Centre in Chang Mai.

I went to a university library to find out what else he had written and there found the papers he delivered to US military funded gatherings in which he said he was working for quite different organisations than those he mentioned to us. These were all linked to the US military and intelligence establishments. I spoke on this at Sydney University and the Professor grew silent.

On June 30th 1971, the members of our household marched with banners into the centre of Melbourne. Next day the major evening newspaper, The Herald, covered its front page with a photo of 90,000 marchers and their posters packed into the city square. I discovered to my surprise that the paper had blanked my poster. It had said, "McMahon proves his virility in Vietnam."—McMahon being then Australia's Prime Minister.

A few days later, on 13th July, my diary recorded: " Can feel the arms and legs and back of our baby in Jackie 's womb—as hard slender limbs inside her." Next day I went to the Diocesan Priests Conference. My diary read: "I am the only married priest there. We got through a resolution next day recommending working in small groups with married worker priests—the only bit of radicalism in any resolution." Next month Jackie and I attended a talk by the radical German Catholic Theologian, Hans Kung, on Christ as a revolutionary. A few weeks later, I found myself accepted by La Trobe University to do a Master's thesis on the influence of military models of organisation on the institutions of the Roman Catholic Church. I was now supporting our family-to-be by teaching social studies to working-class students at the Royal Melbourne Institute of Technology.

But I felt something of an outsider in the Retrieval circle—a feeling to which I was no stranger. I felt these meetings and "Retrieval" had become very much Val and Mary's thing. This was not surprising. I had only just arrived in Australia. I had to find my own way of contributing. I set up a library of alternative magazines and information sources in our front room. Some of the information in these magazines we recycled into a news service.

Another "house of hospitality" started up among our friends. This included Val Noone's brother Brian; an innocent looking blonde, Barbara Russell; Michael Cardin, who loved to camp it up, and Bill the Pole, a friend made on the streets. This became a sister house to our own. We worked on shared projects. All our households were in Fitzroy, an inner suburban area of tree-lined streets, detached and terraced houses of brick and volcanic bluestone, with verandas and balconies dressed in wrought iron, all built in Melbourne's early days

On the 30th July 1971 most of the members of these households were arrested for giving out leaflets saying, "Don't register for National Service." I was ill at home but took on the task of printing the leaflets. We argued in this leaflet "if one considers a law to be immoral, it is immoral to obey it—and to say this publicly should not be illegal."

But the police refused to arrest one member of our household who gave out these leaflets. Eddie Ryan had been blinded and seriously disfigured in an explosion in a quarry. When he realised that everyone around him was being arrested but not him (perhaps because the police feared he was a wounded veteran), he asked someone to lead him to a policeman whom he then leafleted demanding his civic right to be arrested. He was later absolutely and rightly furious when the government dropped the charges against him, saying that the antiwar movement was manipulating a disabled man.

Among our friends were a group of four draft "dodgers" who lived in hiding from the police, constantly planning surprise appearances at rallies to keep up pressure on the government. The wives and girl friends of these resisters lived a hellish life. They were constantly followed by the police, phoned and threatened. One of these was Fran Newell who worked as the National Director of a third world education group called International Development Action, I.D.A., funded by Australian aid agencies. She had received death threats over the phone. As I remember it, a protester fell from the window of a police station onto a fire hydrant. Fran later was phoned and asked would she like this to happen to her? We therefore offered to protect her, saying she could use as her office our front room third world resource centre. She took up our offer.

From then on the police sat outside in cars watching our front door in the belief that Fran was permanently resident with us. They hoped she would lead them to her husband, Michael Hamil-Greene. But our home had a very convenient nest of lanes at its back with several exits off back roads. Fran used them to enter every morning undetected by the police.

Birth of a Child

So this was the household into which we were to bring our first child. We were happy about it being a place t so full of creativity. Lesley's young daughter Emily eagerly awaited another child's arrival. The sandpit at the back was ready. But the date the gynaecologist gave us as the likely time for our child's arrival, September 8th, passed without any sign of the baby wanting to be born. On September 22nd my diary records: " Today Jackie went to the Gyno and he said he'll 'bring on' our baby tomorrow. Jackie came home in tears as he was so uncommunicative, snobbish and without a trace of real interest in her as a person."

But a child is about to be born so we partied. We put the suitcase and dri-tots in the boot of the car, went to celebrate with a dinner—and then dropped Jackie off at St Vincent's Catholic hospital. We were told nothing would happen till next day. When I returned to the hospital at 9 am, Jackie was already in the delivery room, high and happy on a pethodin trip. An hour later her waters were artificially broken and then started a slow process. My diary records: "Her contractions are coming every two minutes by 1pm, by 5.30 p.m. her contractions are every 4 minutes and getting painful. She is vomiting and getting really bad back ache."

"I sit on the only chair available, a broken stool. I had to keep it upright by hooking my foot under the bed. The nurse's attempt to make me wait at home had failed. I offered to massage Jackie 's painful back but she did not want to be touched. At 10 p.m. a nurse said that there are signs the baby will come in an hour's time, but at 11 p.m. Jackie was put to sleep. Three and a half hours later a nurse gave me a proper chair.

"Near dawn, at 5.30 a.m. a sister showed me how to massage the base of Jackie's spine, pushing hard and rhythmically whenever a contraction came. She said this took away most of her pain. I wished I had been able to do this earlier. Just over an hour later, at 6.45 a.m., Jackie suddenly exclaimed, "I am pushing". A nurse heard her and quickly looked. The vagina is open and the nurse says, "Yes, the baby is coming"

"Jackie 's face lit up. She rolled over onto her back. Now the nurses were racing around and asking her not to push too hard, as the doctor needs time to get here. The oxygen cup and suction tube was put in the baby's cot. The instrument trolley was got ready. The four and a half feet long light above the table was switched on.

"At the contractions, the whole skin below the pelvis begins to lift. The head of our child, instead of vanishing back inside between pushes, is now constantly in view. I was standing beside Jackie holding her hand and now I lifted up her head and shoulders so she can see the top of her baby's head. Then there was an ear and then a forehead and then a face, a beautiful serene face—very still as if in deep yoga, or contemplation, rising up out of Jackie."

"A doctor we do not know arrives. He slips the whole of his hands into the vagina to lift the child and Jackie murmurs, "Umm, that felt good". The doctor chuckles and says, "That's a new one." He took our child by the shoulders and lifted one relaxed short arm out and then another, then the whole child slides easily out, arms and legs flopping in all directions— very relaxed and Indian-rubber-like. He said: " Well you've got a girl."

"As he moved to cut the cord 'our' baby girl flexed her leg. She moved one of her feet, her first movement outside the womb. She then opened her mouth a little to breathe, her chest moved—then she opened her eyes. The whites of her eyes were not visible. Two very dark pupils peeped from her narrowly open lids (she looked a bit Chinese). The doctor gave her to the nurse who carried her over to the small cot. As she arrived at the cot she gave a soft cry, "eheuer"—'all systems go' apparently. Jackie looked at her with a dazed, happy and contented look, and so did I. And then as an afterthought Jackie sat up and asked to see the placenta.

"Then came a surprise. The baby weighted only 5lbs and 10.5 oz. This surprised the doctor, as did her thick covering of grease and her need to go into a humidicrib because she had so little flesh on her limbs. These facts did not fit in with her being an overdue child. Rather it suggested that she was premature. This would explain why she was so reluctant to be born. It seemed that our expensive top gynaecologist got it badly wrong when he insisted that the child was overdue and must be induced. (An opinion not shared by our family doctor) In any case he was not there for the birth. He said he had to go off to a conference since our daughter took so long to be born, leaving us to the care of a strange doctor. We were so sorry that our child was forced to be born early. I was angry that Jackie was made to suffer so much unnecessarily. We were powerless in the hands of this male specialist in the female art of birthing."

The day after our daughter's birth, I was stopped for speeding by the cops. I protested. "I've just had a baby daughter born." The cop, tall, in dark goggles, looked at me. He said, "I know you. You live in the grey house in Alfred Crescent". He let me go. He was one of the police who parked opposite us, watching our house.

We named our daughter Kara Susan. Kara because "we like K sounds and one night about two weeks ago the name Kara came out of the blue to me and we both thought it a pretty name for our child, if we were to have a girl."

My diary continued: "Since then I found out it is Danish for Catherine. We like St Catherine of Sienna so she becomes our child's patron saint. She was a women who learnt from visions as well as study, and who spoke out fearlessly to the Pope while living a hospitable and poor life."(And suffered from anorexia, as I later learnt). Catherine herself wrote, "Christ has chosen me a weak woman to confound the pride of the strong"[159] and that " I have decided that the men who are wise in their own conceits should be made ashamed by seeing that weak and frail women, whom they account as things vile and abject, understand the mysteries of God, not by human study, but only by infused grace."[160] She was thus in the gnostic tradition in finding wisdom within her rather than accepting it from authorities.

I also noted at the time: "Kara is also similar to the Italian for Dear Little One (Carina) and that is appropriate right now. Catherine too means pure—and that is good as long as it is not used in a puritanical sense."

"'Susan' became her second name because we thought it gave her a more ordinary name to use if she so chose. It is pretty too. It was also chosen because a friend of ours, John Davidson, had nick-named her while she was still in the womb 'Susi' (Smash US Imperialism)." But I added, "She will probably react against us and turn out a die-hard reactionary conservative."

Thus a holy being entered our world, capable of doing her own dreaming, her own shaping. A being who we could only protect, nourish, teach the lesser things of life, and make it as easy as we could for her to find her own path.

No nonsense about "original sin" entered our minds. We knew her as the possessor of an 'original blessing'. We knew she had no "original sin." Oh, how words have got twisted! An earlier meaning of the word "demon" was an "indwelling spirit or soul" put into a child by its mother. Sick men had turned this into a devil. They said that only through their ritual of baptism could a child's spirit be worthy of heaven. Augustine of Hippo had pioneered this doctrine. He had diabolically declared; "Infants, when unbaptised, are in the Power of the Devil.[161]

This truly evil doctrine led in medieval days to churchmen forbidding the burying of a pregnant woman in consecrated ground until the unbaptised dammed embryo or foetus was first removed from her by a post-mortem caesarean. But at that time, such thoughts could not have been further from our minds. We were instead trembling with wonder at the marvels of this daughter, totally falling in love with her and under her own spell.

It was St. Augustine of Hippo, not Jesus, who originated the doctrine of Original Sin that had shaped the guilt complexes of the Christian world for over a thousand years.[162]

Thank God Augustine did not have it completely his own way. Around the year 390 Pelagius, a famous British monk (called Morgan at home), publicly challenged Augustine by stating that children came into the world blessed and not as sinners, that we are born loved by God, with all the divine gifts we need. He said infant baptism was a consecration of a child, not a rite to remove the stain of sin. He denounced Augustine for cruelly teaching that God sent to hell unbaptised infants.

Pelagius accused Augustine of basing his theory, not on the teachings of Christ, but on the dualism of his former religion, Manichaeanism. Augustine furiously denied this, explaining that whereas the Manichaeans taught that nature was evil, he himself taught that nature was originally good but had been made evil through the sin of the first humans. (If he had held that nature itself was evil, he could not explain how Jesus both had a human body and was untainted.).[163]

The resulting controversy rocked the Christian world. Augustine insisted that that heaven could never be the unbaptised child's fate. Pelagius insisted that we could not inherit a sinful state. Sin had to be a free decision. Two Church Councils supported Pelagius. Augustine's party only won at the last moment when they persuaded the Imperial Emperor to banish Pelagius and his supporters. Many bishops had to be banished before what became known as the "Pelagian Heresy" was officially suppressed—but the ideas of Pelagius never died for most parents instinctively knew their children are blessed from the moment they first see them.

By Christmas 1971 Kara was working her own magic on my parents. They wrote wishing us all a very happy and blessed Christmas, despite all their earlier threats to disown our children if we did not seek the Church's dispensation for our marriage. As Christmas is a summer festival in Australia, we then went away camping with Kara in the wilds of the Grampian Mountains in western Victoria. This is a region of peaks and cliffs, waterfalls and forest rich in wildlife. "We pace an emu that is effortlessly running along a road at 25mph." I was deafened by the violent screech of white cockatoos and watched kangaroos box in the evening light. Echidnas, spiny anteaters, shuffled through our camp. We saw Aboriginal cave paintings of fish and hands. We camped under 380 foot high mountain ash trees in tree fern graced valleys. I began to fall in love with this country of brilliant light and silvery grey trees.

When camping and at home I continued to see myself as a priest. Jackie and I frequently celebrated the sacred meal, remembering God's gift to us of food and life. But I missed having a wider group of soul friends with which to celebrate the gift of life. I noted in my diary that on Maundy Thursday I went to the local church and was "appalled" by the lack of lay participation. It was for me "completely dead". It seemed that the Church had nothing more to give me

But there was one ritual Jackie and I were very keen to celebrate publicly. We picked Easter Sunday in 1972, the 2nd of April, to welcome the arrival of Kara with our community of friends. (It was also about this same day that we conceived our next child.)

The Welcoming was to be in our front room. It was festooned with balloons, flowers and streamers. Ample food was piled on tables. About fifty people came. There were men of the road from the open house in King William Street, Bill the Pole, Tassie (who loved Kara much and who always had presents for her) and amiable Paddy. There was Trish McGrath with a violin. She had also played at our wedding; Brian Noone came with a guitar and Justin Moloney with a didgeridoo. There was Peter, the secretary of the draft resisters' union, Lesley, Peter and Emily, Graham and Rhonda Marshall, teachers who brought much food. Several Catholic priests came, some single, some married, some inside and some outside the official church. There was Eddie, Lesley and her mate Peter, Rowan Ireland, my tutor from La Trobe University, Mary Doyle and Val Noone of the open house, Charlie Davis, a former potato digger, and too many others to mention them all here.

Jackie and I printed copies of the ritual we composed at the DMZ (De-Militarised Zone), a radical education centre. I've dug it up. It went like this.

Kara thanks you for coming to celebrate her birth and for giving her such a big family of uncles and aunts. To welcome her we'll begin by singing

I can see a new day,
A new day soon to be
When storm clouds are all past
And the sun shines on a world that is free.
I can see a new world,
A new world coming fast,
When all men are brothers
And hatred forgotten at last.
I can see a new man,
A new man standing tall,
With his head high and his heart proud
And afraid of nothing at all.

The first verse was then repeated.

Charlie Davis, the spud-digger, had volunteered to lead the rest of the ritual. He then said to us

"God has entrusted Kara particularly into your care

Will you love Kara, serve her and cherish her, whenever she needs you?

R/ We will.

Will you respect her—allow her freedom to be herself—a new and different person?

R/ We will.

Not force her into your own patterns?

R/ We will not.

But share with her all you find beautiful and good.

R/ We will.

And listen to her, sharing with her whatever she finds good.

R/ We will.

Trust her and put her into God's hands?
R/We will.
ALL. And we in our turn, will respect, love and cherish
Kara, and share with her all that we find beautiful and true."

And then we all feasted and played music.

I saw parenting as having little to do with the initial creative act. That takes seconds for a male, nine months for the female—but for both parents it takes years to effect. It is not the child the parent creates, for the child will create itself. They create a safe place for the child to grow, to experiment, to make mistakes, to find herself or himself. The mother and the father donate the initial materials of life, bringing together the iron and flint. The spark that comes flies free is not of the iron or flint but of itself. From that point on both the mother and the father are creating a nurturing world. The mother provides her womb while the father may work with the woman and with others perhaps, for this can be a social act, to create an external womb, a nest, to gather the child into once it tumbles from the womb. Neither parent owns the child. All they own is the nest that they create.

Our group home at 21 Alfred Crescent had a rich life of its own. It was a rabbit warren of people and an enormously exciting and exhausting place. But we eventually found it was not good for little Kara to live among a kaleidoscope of human feet. Some were too busy in their own lives to relate seriously to her. They tended to speak over her head and to forget that she was underneath. But that was not true of all. Lesley, her daughter Emily and Lesley's friend Peter had much time for her. Everyone loved this quiet child that lay there closely observing before she decided to do anything. But I was happy that Jackie was expecting another child. We had decided to have a second child soon so that Kara would have a companion near to her own age.

We were determined not to be possessive parents. This was partly the result of the hammering my parents gave me to try to bring me back to their idea of the true and good way. She was a real battler, my Mother. She left no screw unturned in her efforts to reclaim me. One of her letters said that I had taken Christ down from the cross and put Jackie up instead

Sometimes it seemed to me that my Mother was mellowing and would make a grandparent yet—such as when we received the very welcomed letter from her at the Christmas soon after Kara's birth. But such lulls in the parental storm did not last long. It was a very tough time. I came to dread my mother's letters. I wrote back earnestly, lovingly, without recrimination, hoping against hope to end this cruel division between us. But my Mother continued to try to save my soul. It seemed that to her I was guilty of bigamy and that my real wife was the Church.

Mother Teresa comes to save me

The king hit was when I stumbled to the door at seven thirty one morning to find two short nuns standing there. "Good Morning", said the older one with the sunburnt wrinkled face. "I am Mother Teresa from Calcutta. I have come in the name of your mother. Please think of me as your mother."

I gaped. She was Mother Teresa of Calcutta, the living saint. Why on earth was she here, at our door??? Wild speculation went through my mind. She might have come because we worked briefly with their order in Calcutta. Or maybe she had come because we had signed a petition saying their convent should be allowed to stay in our locality, saying it did not attract undesirables, since such "undesirables" were already here. But her words about my Mother did not fit these theories. And, thinking of her as my mother also just did not fit. Not that my Mother isn't a living saint; she had just seemed recently more like a living menace.

"Come in." I eventually managed to say. I escorted the two black ones down the corridor and sat them at the kitchen table.

"Would you want a cup of tea?"

"No thank you," Mother Teresa said, her hands folded before her. "Our rule does not permit us to take refreshments on visits."

I abandoned them briefly to give Jackie the startling news. She bounded from bed. I threw on more respectable clothes, grabbed baby Kara and went back to the kitchen. I dumped Kara in her lap—not dreaming she could be thinking that Kara was the forbidden fruit of a broken priestly vow.

Mother Teresa explained that when my Mother heard she was going to Australia for an Eucharistic Conference, she had written to her, asking her to try to persuade me to do the right thing by the Church and Christ.

Well, Jackie and I spent the next two hours explaining to Mother Teresa at our kitchen table that we felt we had a vocation to be together that did not contradict my commitment to the priesthood. I assured her that we had followed our conscience and been honest with the church. Meanwhile we were dying for our morning tea. We did not feel able to make ourselves tea while they were not drinking.

Well, eventually it seemed they understood that we had married in good conscience. They gave Kara back and we processed out to the front garden to say goodbye. But on the way to the garden gate, Mother Teresa turned and said, "I am very sorry but I must say that you are sinning in pride." I stopped, and gasped in astonishment. "How am I?" She replied; "You have set your own opinion against that of Holy Mother the Church".

And then, leaving us stunned; they diminished, in every sense, down the street. I thought of the Catholic teaching on the freedom of the conscience. Clearly she did not share it. I joked for years that I had kept the chair she sat on so I could sell splinters from it as relics when she was made a saint!

The Archbishop's Secretary, a tall gentle priest, also turned up on our doorstop to try to save me. He was quite apologetic. It was clear that my mother did not believe in doing things by halves! But as far as I was concerned, Jackie and I were married before humankind and before God and we were very blessed in this. I had no intention of deserting my family and doing penance in a monastery, as happened to other priests who went back into the church's fold.

A dichotomy ran through official Catholic theology. It taught both that the conscience was truly free and that we must accept truth from authority. But now I felt I had moved away from such dilemmas. The tree of my life was growing branches that seemed entirely natural and predictable when they appeared, but which could never have been foreseen.

Lessons from Chaos

As for my work life, I had thought to look for trade union jobs, but tertiary teaching jobs were easier to find with my academic record. But I decided first to study how to teach, since I had long thought it strange that academic teachers were presumed not to need teacher training. There were no courses in tertiary teaching so I had to study secondary. I thus enrolled at a Technical Teachers College in a course in teaching English and Social Studies. This involved spending half of each week teaching in a school and the rest of the week at the college.

But to my dismay, I immediately discovered that I had no skill in being authoritative. My philosophical and theological studies, and my instincts, had made me a critic of authoritarian structures. But now I had to learn how to control large numbers of children. When I first tried to take a class, showers of sandwiches and papers interrupted my efforts. They enjoyed their quick and accurate assessment that they had power over me. Consequently they were delighted to find that I was equally ineffective in punishing them.

Because of this near riot, the head of my department ordered me to give out textbooks immediately classes started and to keep my students' noses firmly in these books. When she later found that I was starting classes by asking students what topics were their favourites, she ordered me back into textbooks. I soon decided this was not a school where I could learn to teach, so I secured a transfer on the grounds of personal incompatibility with the department head.

The next school was far better, but inevitably my efforts become controversial. It all started quite innocently—as it always did. Our teachers' union was planning a strike so I discussed strikes in my social studies class with fourteen to fifteen year-old students. I explained why strikes happen, saying that they should only be called for very serious reasons. One student asked if students had a union. I gave him the address of a secondary students union. I then spent the next few days away from this school, studying at the college.

When I next returned to the school, an excited crowd of my most able students met me in the corridor. They told me they had joined their union and were on strike! Perplexed and startled, I asked them over what issue? They told me: "compulsory school uniforms". I then saw over their heads the conservatively suited Headmaster and Deputy Head standing at the end of the corridor and glaring at me standing among the ringleaders. Clearly they thought I had instigated the strike. Later that day my cleverest student won the right to call off the strike over the school loudspeaker system. The students were happy, excited, felt empowered. Just what I wanted for them. But my own future at the school began to be in doubt.

My department head began to take a very personal interest in my tuition. He invited me to sit in on his classes. When he heard a boy whisper, he would immediately bark "Silence" and then turn to me to see if I had understood why he did this. I said silencing the child surely depended on the purpose of the whisper and on whether other children were disturbed. This exasperated him.

One of the boys in my class then came to visit me at home. I was not there but a friend who taught in Catholic missions in Niugini welcomed him and lent him Jerry Rubin's book "Do It", the inspiration of the 1960s

Yippee movement in the US. I did not know of his visit when, a few days later, I received an urgent summons from the Head. When I arrived at his office the boy was already there with his parents, all waiting mystified to discover why they had been summoned. The Head then produced this book, said he had confiscated it from the boy and apologised to the parents for their child obtaining this book from my home. The parents looked at the book and said, to the Head's dismay, that they had utterly no objection to their son reading it. I survived.

Then a tutor came out from the college to watch me teach. By this stage I had quieted all the rebellious students by finding ways to engage their attention without need for punishment. They were working in small groups on their chosen projects. An open book on my desk contained my comments on their work, one page per student. I marked according to effort, not talent. Students would come up to check how they and their friends were doing, and discuss each other's marks. Quiet talking pervaded the room but much work was done. The tutor gave me his assessment. It began "This is no mere lip service to the ideals of teaching..." but when I left the classroom with this in my hand, a furious department head confronted me. He had been watching my class through the window. He ordered me never to teach like this again. A few days later he ordered me to report to the Education Department.

Thanks to the intervention of the union, my next school was one that prided itself on innovation. I was given the wildest thirteen to fourteen year-olds—and a class of students in their final year. Again there was chaos while they got to know me, but after a while the students were waiting for me in the school car part before school to talk over their projects and to try to get out of other classes into mine.

I gave my senior class the task of writing a paper on what made a worker happy at work. They were encouraged to draw on the experiences of older friends and family members. We visited factories that might soon be employing them. They saw this as so relevant that they produced thesis-length reports. The Department Head was impressed and asked me to team-teach with him next year all the final year students. But my fate was already sealed. I was sacked by the Education Department on the afternoon of the last day of the school year—a timing that made it hard for the union to protect me. This decision was not reversed despite a petition from nearly all the teachers at my school. There were consequently graduation day protests by my fellow students. The reason given to sack me was that I had not demonstrated that I was able to teach conventionally. My problem was that I was absolutely no good at being a male authority figure and not much good at protecting my career. On their criteria, they were right in sacking me. If being a teacher meant being able to be authoritarian, I did not have what it took.

But I had got what I wanted from this year. I had learnt something of how to teach. I had previously decided that I would move on to teaching adults—and an opportunity to do so now grew out of the fertile soil of our shared home and sister households.

Fran Hamil-Greene was still using our front-room as her office while we protected her from police harassment—but when a new Prime Minister, Gough Whitlam, abolished the draft, she decided the time had come for a change. She resigned as National Director of IDA and I was appointed to succeed her. This meant organising national "third-world" education projects for the aid agencies. This meant that I could work from home and much more easily share in the raising of our daughter. This pleased me very much.

The birth of our second child

Meanwhile our second child was growing within Jackie. She was born, easily and naturally, on the 5th of January 1973. This time no gynaecologist was there to guide us. We had decided against a home birth as this was difficult to organise and Jackie thought a hospital safer. We arrived at the hospital at 8.30pm. The second stage of childbirth, the pushing, started just over an hour later and by 10.15 p.m. Cathy was born in a marvellously easy fashion.

She came out remarkably active. She pushed and cried at the same time. She wasn't covered with the white cream that her sister had as a premature baby. She was a normal red-pink colour and had light auburn hair. She opened her eyes almost immediately. She weighted 6 pounds 5 ounces. Jackie, Kara and I brought her home on the 13th.

Her name also came out of our love of the sound K. She was not given a name so much as a sound, a K with a gentle ending, a "Cathy". We thought Catherine of Sienna could also be her exemplar although we knew that children inevitably shape the meaning of their name to suit. Two weeks after her birth, I started work with IDA. A few days later, on January 27th, I saw her sister Kara taking her first few careful steps after a thoughtful fifteen month study of the art of walking.

As soon as we could, we went off on a wonderful celebratory camping holiday in Tasmania. We saw Tasmanian devils, poteroos, bandicoots and many more creatures. We had to think out a welcoming ceremony for Cathy. It would not be the same as that for Kara for her's had been, in large part, our public dedication to a certain way of bringing up children and thus needed no repeating.

We had also changed. I was now further from the ritual-centred life of a Catholic priest, and missed more than ever a community with which I could share my beliefs. Cathy would have a very different thanking ritual. She was to be given a ritual devised for her when she was four years of age. We would bless our red-haired transparent-skinned Celtic-looking child in the waters of a running, bubbling stream on a Welsh hillside. We called on God, and on the spirits of the Celtic ancestors that Jackie and I shared, to bless her, inspire her, enrich her, help her be creative and live in tune with Nature.

Cathy was a very different child to her sister. She would look at things, grasp them, and throw them away. Kara would look at them for longer until she seemed to have absorbed their very essence. Cathy did not hesitate about walking. She tried it before she was ready, not minding the falls. By about November 1973 Cathy was walking at ten months of age.

Our lives wound around those of friends rather than of relatives. I was not comfortable with my more conventionally minded in-laws, although they were most considerate and generous. I did however feel at home with Jackie 's sister, and with her Dad's sister, Auntie Eve. I was deeply grateful to them, as I otherwise felt quite relation-less in Australia.

I was very aware of the political atrocities that continued to surround us. Nixon was re-elected President of the United States despite his use of criminals to retain power. His downfall seemed more likely to happen because of Watergate than the murderous bombing he inflicted on Indochina. So I co-wrote and published with a friend, John Davidson, a leaflet on Nixon that documented the people involved in Watergate, the arms merchants, FBI agents, former Mafia lawyers, the paymaster for the Bay of Pigs invasion and the links to the Teamsters Union and the Mafia. This leaflet came out a month after Cathy's birth.

Over the next months Nixon continued to bomb the hell out of Vietnam. Two months later, in April 1973, we joined with a Roman Catholic youth group, the Catholic Workers Movement (YCW), to organise an all-night vigil in Melbourne's City Square to publicise the plight of political prisoners in South Vietnam. We built out of wooden car-crates mock-ups of President Thieu's infamous "tiger cage" prisons. The terrible war in Vietnam overshadowed us. We were horrified at how that land was blanketed with death. In its war to "save" Vietnam, the US was killing its inhabitants as if they were germs.

We held a Service for Peace outside the War Museum in Canberra. It was organised by Jan Madigan, a National President of the YCW, and Peter Calliman, the National Chaplain of the YCW, with myself. Jan and I presided over the peace ritual. Later Jan and Peter asked me to serve as the priest for their wedding in January 1974, a wonderful invitation. They knew that at my heart I was still in the priesthood, no matter how the church regarded me.

The year of Cathy's birth was hectic. Brian Noone of our sister house wrote a leaflet on Australia's economic links with apartheid South Africa that I helped publish as national director of IDA. We also researched the role played by Australia in Fiji. This resulted in the distribution of five thousand copies of a booklet called *Fiji, a Developing Australian Colony* and in a tour by Fijian speakers. This caused the Fijian government to ask the Australian government for an Intelligence Report on me.

The First Australians

Then Justin Moloney, the Race Relations Officer of the Australian Union of Students, asked if we had a spare room in our commodious house for an Aboriginal activist, Cheryl Buchanon, who was coming from Queensland to campaign for her people. Her arrival dramatically changed the focus of my work. We learnt from her what life was like on Aboriginal reserves. She challenged us to focus on the treatment of Aborigines as a "third world" problem.

As we began to work together, her friends came to stay. This included an Aboriginal "Country and Western" band and political refugees from the north. We came back from a trip away to find about 20-30 Aborigines had moved into our home, all sleeping in one room! Aboriginal militant Bobby McLeod was among them. He was famous for walking with a revolver into the Department of Aboriginal Affairs in Canberra to demand justice for his people. The climate of ideas and spirituality in the house changed. I found Cheryl's wise grandmother appearing in my dreams.

The first month of their stay was exhilarating and exhausting. We learnt much but we grew concerned, as the children seemed to be disturbed by such a crowd. We also became increasingly annoyed with Bobby McLeod saying housework was women's work.

One day we heard that Paulo Freire was coming to Australia to speak to a church gathering. We knew of him as the author of *Pedagogy of the*

Oppressed and as a man who had worked to free the minds and spirits of the downtrodden in Latin America. He had been invited to talk to church people, but the Aboriginal people of the household decided that they should have the first call on the talents of such a man. After some pressuring, the Churches agreed to lend him to us for an afternoon. He came and met mostly Aborigines. He told them that their way to liberation was to join with the working class to fight a common battle. Bobby McLeod disagreed. He said this tactic would make them just black currants in a white cake.

It was not always easy being such a disparate community. I remember getting highly annoyed when we came into the kitchen and found our Aboriginal friends cooking and not including us. I exploded. "We always include you when we cook. How can you exclude us? Thought you said Aborigines believed in sharing!" I stormed off. Half an hour later Bobby came to see me. "You are right. We should be sharing. We are not used to Whites wanting to eat with us."

Gender troubles

But I was growing tenser for another reason. Under the surface of our hectic life, my gender problems were increasing. I was finding it harder to take on the male sexual role. I would cry secretly after making love. I was scared to mention my pent up feelings to Jackie. The pressures were showing in the strain between us and in the reoccurrence of asthma.

My diary records that around Easter 1973, just three months after Cathy's birth, I confessed to Jackie that always acting as male was increasingly difficult for me. I found this confession humiliating, for I had absorbed the Stoic and Augustinian teaching that our reason should control our instincts. I wrote in my diary: " during the past year (1973), Jackie and I have come to terms with each other, especially with my being transsexual—so at last I don't feel scared to record it in the diary. " This self-admission was an enormous step for me. But I was still hoping that some private cross-dressing might be all I needed to relieve my pain. I hoped to remove the tension by pretending occasionally that I lived as a woman.

My diary continued: "Although I told Jackie, I loved dressing up in female clothes before we married—and neither of us made much of it. To me it was merely my Achilles heel. It was an Easter, when we were at Jackie 's parents, staying in the bungalow at the back, that I brought myself to confess to her that I desperately needed to relax by being free to wear female clothes with her. I'd been scared to mention my pent-up feelings, fearing the consequences of relaxing my self-control, fearing to upset Jackie, not being sure of how she would take it…I felt I had a duty to fulfil my male role for her sake as well as for the children's sake. But the pressure of feeling had become just too much. I had been increasingly tense. But Jackie 's reaction was marvellous. First she assured me that this was no danger to us as a family, then she put her poncho coat on me."

She had put her woman's coat on me to show she accepted this aspect of me. It made me feel better. I kept this very secret. Men in our culture learn to see female clothes on a male as symbolising either fun or a humiliating weakness, so I had violently mixed emotions. I fought shame at giving in to these desires. I feared ridicule. Yet there seemed no choice. I had dreams, escapist fantasies, where I was forcibly made to wear female clothes, forcibly made to live as a woman. Thank God those fantasies are now redundant and have long since ceased.

In 1974, I went to Niugini to reconnoitre a new IDA educational project. This involved travelling in a light plane over the wildest of chasms and over the beehive huts of remote villages in the Highlands where I met beautiful people in full tribal regalia. But the turmoil inside me made this a nightmare trip for me. I was terribly afraid of losing the care of our young children, if I acknowledge the rights of my body and mind to live in the gender they seemed to be assigning me. I was scared this would wreck the dream shared so intensely by Jackie and I.

On the way back, I stopped at the home of Jan Madigan in Brisbane, and managed to relax when she lent me some female clothes to wear in her home. In those days my female friends helped keep me functioning with their acceptance of me. My wish to live as a woman seemed a crazy obsession, yet it would not go away.

But soon all cross-dressing compromises failed for me. The clothes were a comfort, but they were not reality. I was tired of being a male in the eyes of the public. I loved Jackie—but not as a husband should. I buried my feelings again and again for fear of losing my family. I could understand if Jackie should want to leave me, but I did not want to lose her. Even more, I could not bear losing the children. They were only one and two years old and seemed unaware of the crisis in our family.

Our big house did not last much longer. One day our landlady came and apologised, saying her family wanted her to sell the house. Lesley Whyte and her daughter Emily were the first to leave. They went to live in Tasmania on a farmlet with Peter, her lover. We went to a much smaller wooden house in Dunstan Avenue a mile or two to the north in Brunswick. Its veranda was spider web shrouded. It had stained glass windows and many kinds of fruit trees. Our Aboriginal friends followed us to this new house. The IDA office moved into our backroom. But we noted that the children showed signs of disliking the invasion of their space by more strangers. My diary said they were "real scared of strangers".

We had earlier looked at buying a house, but only half-heartedly. We set our maximum at $16,000 (for that was over twenty years ago), so when a house in fashionable Gore Street came up, with bluestone walls, large front and back gardens and kitchen, four bedrooms, for $17,000, we rejected it. The plea of the estate agent who pointed out that we would only have to repay the mortgage at a rate of $25 a week met tempted but finally deaf ears.

I rued this decision for years as life became tougher, and as the price of houses in that street went up by twenty times within fifteen years. But we had elected to remain in rented houses. The principal reason for our decision was that Jackie told me owning a house would oppress and depress her. We instead put our deposit money towards going back to England.

We had agreed to come out to Australia just for three years and that time had passed.

It was good that our new home was not so large. It kept down the number of guests and gave us more opportunity to relax with our children, our chooks, our kittens and our trees. We also often went away camping by ourselves in the bush. We explored nearly all the back roads of Victoria. I have always needed wilderness.

It also gave us time to talk out my gender identity crisis. We both took professional advice. Eventually Jackie assured me that come what may; I would not lose the children. We would continue to bring them up together. This amazing assurance freed me. For the first time I felt free to seek a remedy to my gender problems. I went to the one doctor I could find in Melbourne who "specialised" in transsexuals. I told him that one of my problems was that I knew no one else like me. I simply did not understand what had happened to me, and would appreciate recommendations of relevant reading matter. But he refused to recommend any reading. He said; "Reading on this subject would spoil our assessment of you."

Much more seriously, he also refused to treat me unless I left my children. He said that if I changed my gender role while still living with them, I might spoil their gender typing! He did not see the insanity of his insistence that I first desert my children before he assess whether or not I should live as a woman. Surely such an act would prove that I was not a female? I did not see that doctor again. Instead I researched and assiduously read, trying to understand myself, ordering books from America or from Blackwell's, a bookshop in Oxford that sent books wrapped as if to resist monsoons. It was from these textbooks that I first discovered how transexuality had a proud history among the shamans of indigenous nations.

I had to seek help elsewhere. I found a clinic that specialised in sexual problems. It assigned me to a psychiatrist who had never met anyone like me before. My assessment was then a stop and go affair, for I still did not fully accept or know myself. Despite Jackie 's brave words, I feared we would not survive together if she no longer had a male in her life, or at least the apology for a male that I felt myself to be. Late in 1974 I decided that cross-dressing would probably suffice. I wanted this to be so and was determined to make it so—and stopped going to the clinic.

During these years of maledom, a persistent dream dogged my sleep. In this I was visiting a large college that was training priests. I thought somewhere in this building I must have my own room and so set out to find it. This always proved extremely difficult. It seemed my room was hidden high up in the attics, in a warren of staircases and corridors. I was to have this same dream persistently—until I resolved my gender crisis.

Fighting alongside Aborigines

Meanwhile I was continuing to run educational projects on Third World issues. We persuaded the Aid Agencies to sponsor a *White Colonialism in Australia Project*. Our idea was to publish a case study that revealed how government, church missions and private enterprise had treated Aborigines. We thought this would show it was a true Third World issue. Our team was now joined by members of our sister houses. These included Barbara Russell and Mike Parsons.

But before we could put this project into operation, we had to make sure we were not repeating the mistakes of others. We would seek Aboriginal approval beforehand, and ask them to help us find communities that would want us to work with them.

An Aboriginal friend in Canberra, Harry Penrith (who later took the name of Birnum Birnum) arranged for us a meeting with a group of Aborigines from around Australia. They really put us through the hoop. "What wages are you going to make out of studying us?" "Have you ever had contact with ASIO (the Australian FBI)?" "How can we know to trust you?" "Will this study further your academic careers?"

At the end of the grilling, one of the Aborigines present, Mick Miller from Cairns, said he knew of a community that had been crying out for outside support. He thought what this community had experienced would make it ideal for our purposes. Thus we met the Mapoon people of Cape York. The police had burnt down their settlement just eleven years earlier. The State Government had given their hunting lands of virgin forest to mining companies that planned to strip hundreds of square miles for bauxite clay, the raw material of aluminium.

But this project then took unexpected directions; reshaped by the people we had set out to study. We found the Mapoon people had other priorities to our own. Our publication to educate white Australians had to take back stage. The Mapoon people wanted to re-occupy their land so they could care for it and its sacred places. This became our own priority.

The Mapoon people have lived for thousands of years on the Western coast of the Cape York Peninsula. They remained in possession of their lands until fairly recently. They had fought off the colonisers in many a skirmish, including the Dutch in 1606. While still unconquered in the late 19th century, they had their lands made part of the largest continuous strip of Aboriginal Reserves in Eastern Australia. On these coastal reserve lands also lived the people of Weipa, 50 miles south of Mapoon, and Aurukun, 100 miles south.

I learnt that the Government had decided in 1963 to evict the Mapoon community, leaving the land empty for the miners. When the community refused to go, the police were sent in. They arrested the community, put them in irons and burnt their settlement to the ground, including their homes, church and store. They were then taken to Bamaga 100 miles north where they were told they must learn to live like the white folk.

We raised funds and were very excited and happy when in 1974 the Mapoon people set out in a caravan of old trucks, a bus, vehicles of all kinds, past the vast red earth mines, up under the open forest trees to Mapoon to reoccupy their ancestral land—a move the authorities opposed.

When I went to Mapoon after the Aborigines returned, it was wonderful to see that the forest, rivers and inlets were still in much the same condition as they had been for thousands of years. It was a spacious

monsoonal forest, rich in plants, kangaroo, possum, goanna—and crocodile. The coastal inlets were home to large and tasty barramundi fish.
Coral sealed the coast. The Weipa bauxite mine was still was some 40
miles away. The reason that it was not closer was that the miners had a
thousand square miles of virgin monsoonal forest, all former Aboriginal
Reserve lands, to strip for bauxite. The company involved was Comalco,
then half owned and managed by CRA, a subsidiary of RTZ of London.
(It is now wholly owned by RTZ through CRA) When I last saw the
Mapoon community, they had planted flourishing gardens, rebuilt houses
and were catching large barramundi. I believe they are still there today.

The people of Mapoon, many of the Tjuntgundji tribe, told us how
they fed the elderly. "Now about the emu. You must have grey hairs or you
will not get any to eat. If any of the young fellows find a nest with eggs
they cannot eat them. They must go and report their find to the old people."[164] Such easily digested foods were reserved for the elderly. All food
sources were under the care of elders who were responsible for ensuring
they were not over-exploited. Harry Toeboy of Mapoon told us: "the yams
have bosses who look after them. There is a man or woman who has to
look after them."

Elders always controlled the hunts. Harry Toeboy was in charge of the
hunt at Pine River as his father was before him. They used fire to drive
game into traps. He told us; 'When the time comes to burn, they get messengers and send them to different tribes…They carve on these message
sticks how many moons until they meet…they count by how many days
before full moon or no moon. When they all get together, the boss of the
land gives them the time to begin burning…you would be surprised by
how much they catch that day. They never waste. They can keep meat for
nearly a week underground. They heat it up when needed. When the last
bit is eaten they say goodbye and travel back to their own territory."
Likewise when the yams are ready to dig, "Everyone dances and claps."
What yams they cannot eat they bury again.

The bauxite mine is now so vast that it stretches from horizon to horizon as one flies in. Some say it is the only mine that can be seen from space. When I was there, the company was not restoring the original forest after mining but putting in exotic timber trees. They paid no royalties to the Aborigines whose lands and lives they had devastated. The Weipa Aborigines had to find petrol money to get to hunting grounds that were once at their door. Many were utterly demoralised.

Once the Mapoon people had returned, we set out to complete and publish a three-volume case study of Mapoon. The first volume recorded their story in their own words. The revenues from this book went to supporting their community. The second volume drew on official records. It included much of the correspondence between the government, mission and mining company. The third volume documented the impact these same companies had on Aboriginal lands elsewhere, as well in the Amazon and around the world.

I attended the Annual General Meetings of CRA (RTZ) to protest against the taking of these tribal lands. This had the consequence that major companies got to know me when I was still working in my male role. When I did change gender roles, their knowledge of my background would prove dangerous to me.

Rejecting Maledom

By October 1974 Cathy and Kara seemed to have recovered from the stress of the last days of the communal house of Alfred Crescent and we were mightily relieved. But while the Mapoon project was getting under way, the gender issue again emerged. It just would not go away. Every time it returned it felt seemed stronger. I was finding it harder and harder to bury it—although at the same time I wanted to believe that my wish to live as a woman was nonsense that I could safely ignore.

I did however wonder what would happen if I went onto female hormones. I hoped I would not lose my drive and sink into a languorous castrati soup. Behind this thought lay church teachings that women were the passive principle, male the active. But my inner soul laughed at this male prejudice. I reminded myself of Jeanne d'Arc, Boudeccea and many a female warrior.

I loved Jackie and wanted to make her happy as a woman, but I again started to cry after we made love. A dark suspicion emerged within me that making love as a male was very wrong for me and I should cease doing it. Jackie wondered if I was still suffering from sexual repression from my religious order days. I feared it was something much more primordial. I wrote:

Rejecting Maledom
In the pain of making love
Its pleasure taken while
My soul was elsewhere.
A fantasy it seems
Becoming obsessive.
Humiliating not to be able
To repress.

Jackie puts this down
To Catholic Church repression
But loving as a male
Serves only as a catalyst for change.

Attempts at therapy
Makes it stronger
Clothes are hollow
It is not the trappings
Therapy fails to arrest
What is this?

A gift?
Whence go I?

I sometimes wore in public a gender-neutral caftan. With Jackie's support, I was cross-dressed in private in our room, seeking any answer short of changing my gender identity, any answer that seemed safer for our family. But I was encouraged by the acceptance I found with the members of our sister households, especially with gay outrageous Mike Cardin and outgoing Barbara Russell who was our field officer on the Mapoon project. They made me feel relaxed, not crazy. I wrote "I stopped keeping the subject of my sexual identity taboo" but that was only between close friends. Otherwise in my work I did not talk about this issue. In writing this book I am only now answering a challenge made by Mike Cardin to me over twenty years ago. He said it would only be if people were open that others can learn and society change.

It soon became evident, much to my regret, that I was in the grip of a crisis that could never be resolved through cross-dressing. By now my external male being was but a shadow of my reality. I lived—but not where others saw me. My inner self thought the clothes an irrelevancy. I became increasingly convinced that I might have to change my social reality to match a female inner self, if I were ever to hope to end the tensions now tearing at me. The alternative was to grimly strive to master and suppress. This second choice was then my preferred option, if it were the only way for us to stay together as a family. But I did not know how feasible that would be; for it seemed that I had no control over the changes that were happening in me. It was as if my attempt to become a normal sexually active male had back-fired on me, that it had triggered my psyche and my body to move as rapidly as possible in the opposite direction. We were both now having to cope by taking tranquillisers. We had come together with a strong sense of being fated to be together, of having a sacred work to do together. Was all this about to fall apart? I did not know what the future might bring. It was a dark time.

Thursday

The Maiden Aspect of the Goddess

St Augustine sought to control by will power every movement of his body, but I ultimately had no wish to be a Canute opposing a tide rising to reclaim her own. My body was its own domain and my instincts conspired with it. They seemed to urge me to desert what society had told me, blindfold my reason, trust and leap. With hindsight this awful choice taught me one of the most important lessons of my life. It was to trust my instincts.

I had been delighted to discover that "transexuality" or "hermaphroditism" was associated with the priesthood and with shamanism in ancient cultures. It was good to know my instincts had a sacred history. It helped me resolve my crisis. Slowly I gained courage.

But I was a very newborn creature emerging into the female world. I recorded in my diary in early March 1974 my first very nervous excursion: "Going out for the first time by myself as a woman was like walking through a looking glass…I was wolf whistled and chatted up—I certainly did pass." My hair was long and chestnut brown. It blew in the wind, as I had always wanted. My taste in clothes was simple and classical. I had started to enjoy clothes as never before. One of my favourite dresses was black, long sleeved with a v-shaped neckline, but I cannot remember what

I wore that day. I certainly wore eye makeup. Life was immediately retextured, totally different, exciting, and good. I was at last accepted in everyday life for myself. It seemed to legitimatise that time as a teenager when I secretly dressed as a girl. I was beginning to understand my childhood and why it was so plagued by asthma. Everything was falling into place.

But my tentative experiments also opened my eyes to the realities of female life. The first time I walked home alone as a woman, I experienced vulnerability in a way I never had before. Maybe my makeup was a little overdone that day? Maybe I moved wrong? But on Nicholson Street in Melbourne two car drivers stopped to ask me the way. They chatted me up and a truck driver gave me the wolf whistle. I soon deserted the main street to walk via back streets and was not troubled further. I may have been pleased at being accepted as female but I found it disconcerting to suddenly be treated as if a commodity on display.

It was important for me to find some counselling, for I had no family or tribal elders with knowledge of such matters. I did not think myself "ill" but as "different" from most others. But many doctors had presumed that I, and others like me, was "ill". We were defined as suffering from "Gender Identity Disorder (GID)", a disorder only resolved through helping the body match the gender of the brain, thus creating "order". Once this was resolved, once one had changed gender roles, then the doctors hoped the patient was cured of GID and no longer a "transsexual".

I went back to see my psychiatrist. She later told Jackie and I that we would be "playing games" if we did not accept that I had a female gender identity. She told Jackie that I was not a transvestite but rather a person who had been landed somehow with a female gender identity. She told us that I had to recognise that I was female at the deepest psychological level and that I had to re-order my life to accept this as my reality.

Jackie also consulted an old and dear Jungian psychologist who asked to see me too. He actively encouraged us to stay together, saying it was evident that we still loved each other. He also told her my female gender identity was constitutional and could not be changed. My diary of June

1975 recorded after a rough few days, we "went away together. It took us just one and a half days to realise that we both just wanted to stay with each other; that we both just wanted each other to be free. We had a really free time together; a new getting to know each other." Jackie again reassured me that I could jump the gender barrier without fear of breaking up our family. Whatever I decided, we would continue to bring up the children together. This freed me. I was deeply grateful to her for this. For the fear she too was taking on. For us both it was a leap into the unknown.

Despite all the supportive advice, all the holidays together, I remained fearful that if I started to take oestrogen, the physical and mental changes in me might shatter our family and my own life. I knew it would mean burying my male reality for good. Yet it seemed like an inevitable step, as if I had no choice. The turmoil of that time gave Jackie and I enormous pain. We both needed tranquillisers. I frequently thought that I just could not go through with it. If Jackie had said I would lose the children, I would have tried not to change until it killed me. It was like the turmoil in my adolescence when I oscillated from wanting to be a girl to despising myself for thinking of it; but now there were two small children to consider so there was very much more to worry about. But Jackie assured me again and again that we would stay together as a family whatever I decided. She said that I had to be myself. I still worried that it would be too hard for her. She insisted that it was my own personal decision and I had to make it fearlessly.

Hormones and Gender-role Transition

On the 1st August 1975 I took my first oestrogen pill fearfully and excitedly. It was the culmination of so much. It turned out to be mysteriously alchemic. It was probably the biggest decision of my life. I felt the pills looked too small to be so significant and powerful. They should have been sparkling and spinning. It was much later that I realised the date's significance. August 1st, Lughnasadh or Lughnash (pronounced as 'loonasah'), one of the four great festivals of the ancient Celtic year, when thanks was given for the harvest's gift to us of life through its death, part of the great wheel of life. This was sometimes traditionally celebrated by "a solemn cutting of the first of the corn of which an offering would be made to the deity by bringing it up to a high place and burying it."[165] This celebration is today mythically portrayed as the death of a Corn King. So I had made the crucial act that would kill the male social me on the day when the King died to bring life. All this seems to have been utterly and somewhat weirdly appropriate.

I had learnt about hormones from a self-help group in England called the Transsexual Action Organisation (TAO). It was run by two people travelling in opposite directions, male to female, female to male. Layla was its secretary. They answered my letters with practical advice about gender and transition. Their advice always seemed a step ahead of my needs. I thought it sometimes beyond my needs. But their instincts were right. They were able to predict what would be happening next for me because they and their friends had been there first. Most of all, they told me about the safest and best hormones.

As my doctor had no knowledge of what hormones were best, she accepted their advice, perhaps after checking independently. She ordered for me Premarin, a natural oestrogen. I was to take 1.25mg 3 times a day, the same dosage as Layla was taking. It was a hormone extracted from the urine of pregnant mares. Nowadays I think of this as highly appropriate. The white mare was a symbol of the Goddess among my Irish and British ancestors. She still runs the chalk hills of England with her image carved giant-sized into the turf.

Mare's urine was a very ancient medicine seemingly once made by witches. In the first century BCE the poet Ovid wrote from Tomis, a Black Sea Grecian colony near to the Scythians who had a reputation for honouring gender-changers. "She's a witch, mutters magical cantrips, can make rivers run uphill, knows the best aphrodisiacs—when to use herbal brews or the whirring bull-roarer, how to extract that stuff from the mare on heat."[166] He also wrote in his poem *On Women's Facial Treatments*: "Put no faith in herbals and potions, adjure the deadly stuff distilled by a mare in heat."

Thus I was midwived by a wise craft (for what else is good psychotherapy), using the urine of the fertile mare. I had to help create my own body, surely a divine work? I was not content to be just a female soul or mind. I wanted a body that could give me my full natural sexuality. There are those who believe that nature can be cropped and chopped, but deplore as unnatural the desire of the transsexual to change the shape of her or his body, calling it a mutilation. But when done in conformity with the soul, it is a wondrous alchemic act. It clothes the soul, a sleeping beauty, in the body destined for her. It awakens her new body with a kiss of love.

The immediate effect of taking the hormones was that I became vastly more relaxed. Inside I was exultant. At last I felt that the dichotomy had ended between my body and my mind. For the very first time in my life I felt whole, and good. My soul was at home in my body. I was one. Both Jackie and I came off tranquillisers. Some weeks later she told me that it was obviously the best thing that had happened to me, that I was like a cat with a pail of cream and she much preferred the new relaxed me. I truly felt much less uptight. Only now did I fully realise just what I had been forcing myself to do in "pretending" to be a male. Now that I knew this, I had much less need to prove myself.

There was one jarring shock. Three weeks later my psychiatrist had second thoughts. She wrote to say that she was going to stop prescribing me hormones for she was concerned about its impact on our family. Jackie went to see her to assure her that we were all right and after this the treatment continued.

We knew our young children (then one and two years old) needed above all else to experience our love for them as constant and honest. We thought this could best be done if we tried to stay together as they grew up and to answer their future questions honestly. We would explain to them that there are many kinds of people in our rich world, including those with bodies that have both male and female aspects and who were brought up in the wrong gender. This would lead to many an entertaining discussion that started: "Jani, when you were a girl inside but living as a boy, did you…" Our young children seemed to regard this as an undisturbing but interesting fact of life.

I recorded in my diary: "I have now been taking oestrogen for some five weeks. The effects have been remarkable. Jackie has said that I've become much more relaxed, not scared of emotion, human even. We are getting on far better with each other, freer together. I have become a far better person, easier to live with, less on the defensive. Judging by these factors, it seems I should keep on taking it. We are not going to worry about the future, just grow into it."

"The physical effects so far are:

Three days after starting with hormones, the right nipple itched all day.

Four days after the left nipple did the same—then at six days both breasts itched.

By three weeks, a general softening of the skin became noticeable, on the back especially.

By four weeks, dresses start to fit me better in front because of my changing contours (although the change is subtle).

By five weeks, although my figure change so far is not noticeable if I am wearing loose clothes, my face is noticeably fuller.

"In all the changes have been astonishingly rapid. I may well have to cut the dosage to a maintenance dose (for last three days took pills just twice daily. One of the doctors [well used to dealing with transsexuals} remarked with surprise on this and said he wished they had tested my chromosomes. They might explain my unusually easy and dramatic change."

It seemed to me that somewhere in my brain, in a room controlling cell replacement and shaping, a controller had sat up with astonished surprise when sensors in front of her recorded the arrival of much more oestrogen than she had been accustomed to see, and had exclaimed: "About bloody time! We've been waiting for this since she was twelve." She had then promptly dumped into the rubbish bin the tattered blueprints on her desk and pulled from underneath a set of fairly unused female blueprints, dusted them off enthusiastically, and set to work to adjust all the mechanisms within my body that were accessible to her. It seemed this was easier for her because in subtle ways my body was already prepared for oestrogen's arrival.

My diary recorded more of my thoughts and observations some months later: "In my early thirties I have begun to go through a second puberty, this time as a girl. My light body hair vanished, as my breasts became magically sensitive. Down deep at the base of the brain a key hormonal switching station has taken note of the female hormones now in my blood and pulled the mainline lever. Now every new cell in my body is a female cell. My body now belongs with my mind. The changes, although commencing immediately, still take time to complete. For months I could pass either way if I wore loose clothing. But I felt very much more at home in a dress; although I feel less need to 'dress up' in a skirt as I no longer have a need to pretend I have a female body. The element of conflict seemed to have gone. But I still feel it's all rather mysterious science fiction. It's very good to be at home with my body!"

I also observed "Kara and Cathy both accept it very well. Sometimes I join my new name with my old. We think it is easier for them when young to accept transexuality. We hope we can protect them from too much confusion by teaching them about transexuality openly."

The most surprising elements for me were both the totality of the change and the utterly unexpected sexual awakening. Every part of my body became wonderfully erotically sensitive, as at long last I began to become alive sexually. Suddenly I started to notice men as attractive! I presume this was much the same as it is for most girls at puberty. Bit by bit my path was unfolding. I could not yet see where I was going, but I rejoiced in waking up, rejoiced in the wonderful sensual kiss of the God that had awoken me. My skin was at last alive all over. (I cannot speak for men, as I never was fully one, but my experience is that men's skin is only sensitive erotically in limited areas—while a woman's skin is erotic everywhere.)

I most unexpectedly also found myself surfing the lunar cycles with monthly lows that were always followed by a magical lift. These were at first disconcerting. I had to adjust to being a lunar animal, to being part of the earth's tides. (However I did not bleed, for the internal female organs atrophied before birth.)

I found being a female with a male was entirely different to anything I had previously experienced, as new to me as for any pubescent girl. I must confess I enjoyed feeling protected and cared for. My whole body tingled when a man in a caring gesture puts his arm behind me. It perhaps meant more at first to me than it would to most women for it also signified something I had long craved, acceptance as a woman.

Not all changes were welcome. I also found myself much more vulnerable to strangely predatory males—a beast that was as alien to me as to any woman. I thought I would have understood them better, but eventually concluded I had never been truly within their skin. Trustworthy males were usually not around when I would have liked protection—and wanting protection was also a very new thing. I had absolutely no intention of welcoming vulnerability in order to have men protect me.

I might have been born with a female brain, but I certainly had not been socialised to accept the female lot. I had no intention of taking a junior role to men, but I had an awful lot to learn. I had to quickly learn how to keep men at bay. I found to my sudden alarm that steady eye contact with males was seen as a come-on signal. Yet such steady contact was natural to me. I had to learn eye control. I learnt that females control their gaze while males in our society are free to simply look.

At first I tried to keep my eyes from meeting those of men. This felt strange—like accepting a lower status, but I did not know how to safely flirt. As my body was still physically in-between, flirting was particularly dangerous for me. But I was determined to learn how as a woman I could look males straight in the eye, laugh, flirt, enjoy life, and still keep them at a distance. I knew women who could do this. The flamenco dancers of Spain served as a role model. I saw them as expressing dignity and strength. But I was not yet sure enough of myself to follow their example. I simply had to learn how to avoid entanglements. My socialisation process was as hilarious as was Eliza Dolitttle's in Pygmalion. I needed the survival skills I would have learnt as a teen-age girl. Meanwhile I was delighting in the birth of my new body as it appeared with all the speed of a roller coaster.

In 1975 it was not just my body that changed. I also had my passport changed and the name on my sociology degree. These were the easier things to achieve. All they required was a letter from my doctor. The letter she gave me said that in her opinion I was "psychologically hermaphrodite", born with a female brain and male genitals. But the Jesuit Lateran University in Rome refused to change the name on my Masters in Theology certificate on the grounds that the name on it was correct at the time I took that degree. I think they did not want me to use it as the basis for a new career! My driving license I retook as a woman so as to save hassles, and promptly failed it.

I wrote some weeks later in my diary, after we had moved from the large communal house: "I have stopped being paranoid at home and most friends now knew me as a transsexual. This quieter house gave me the opportunity to work myself out that had been lacking at Alfred Crescent. Most people who have to go through this experience are advised by doctors to start a new life somewhere else where no one knows them. I had no intention of doing this. My life was too full. The Mapoon project was in full stream. [This was our project on Australian racism and Aborigines] I had too many friends I valued. I had long personal talks to my friends and colleagues. The nearly inevitable result was that I became closer to them. Women friends reacted by lending me clothes, helping me be who I felt I should be. Male friends were sometimes more awkward."

My diary continued: "The attitude of nearly all friends has been tremendous and free. For example, take Justin. He was a good mate.

When I first told him at his house, he found it easy. He said he had seen the female in me. We then decided to go down the pub together to talk about the meaning of life, as we were accustomed. I saw no reason why we should not do this as a man and woman. Our first trip to the pub after my transition went fine, but I could see his startled reaction in his eyes."

While it was easy in his house, it was a different matter at the pub. "Being with a woman in a pub demanded a whole set of different reactions and behaviour that he was not used to associate with being with me. Like suddenly, awkwardly grabbing at doors to hold them open. Moving a chair out for me. It was more confusing for him than me. I was just being myself and laughing at him."

I found much fun in the sexual frisson now at play in relationships with men. But I soon found that some men thought it OK to rub up against me in order to satisfy their sexuality. Their phallic drive was quite new to this naive new kid on the block. I was perplexed at their behaviour, at their thinking. This taught me how different they had always been to me. I did not like being patronised and finding that, if I protested, I would be seen as unstable and emotional. It was disturbing to find myself suddenly so handicapped by gender. No matter how "feminist" a person is, it is a major eye-opener to experience at first hand the continuing male chauvinism.

I detested being put down. I could not stand being patronised. It made me angry. I was not socialised to accept this, not socialised into being a "girlie". I had not been trained to be subservient. I had no great need to please men and did not see my fulfilment as a relationship with one of them.

There were now many attempts to socialise me as a woman. I had to appear conventionally a female when I saw my doctors. This was an experience I shared with most "male to female" transsexuals. I am not sure what happens with people travelling the opposite direction. If one wants to get through the system, get hormones and perhaps an operation, one is put under great pressure to confirm to the male-imposed stereotype for femalehood, because otherwise doctors might reject you as not sufficiently "female". It is mostly male doctors that do this assessment. God help those candidates who are judged too "masculine"! Transsexuals during this period feel especially vulnerable when in the street. They are scared they will not "pass" as women, and this pressure also leads to conformity. (These "medical' criteria have relaxed since unisex ways of dressing became commonly adopted.

I enjoyed using make-up in these early "pubescent" years. I discovered war paint was fun and should be used by all—but freely, without coercion. (I would stop using much makeup when I tired of its mandatory use.) I took pleasure in a newfound freedom of clothes. In winter I relished the way my skin was now a much better protection from cold than it had been earlier. I no longer needed so many layers of clothing. I mostly wore skirts since it is always exciting to wear what has been previously forbidden

Above all, I loved the feeling of coming home, of being reborn, of finding my sexuality. I had walked a lonely path on the borders of my femalehood for many years. It was as if, after years of stumbling over a high moor in rain and strong winds, I had suddenly discovered a hidden green valley inhabited by sisters who welcomed me home. From this haven, the time when I lived as a male rapidly became like a distant memory of a previous lifetime. I now find it very strange that I once lived so alien a life.

A Same Sex Marriage

Jackie and I were most surprised when we discovered we were happy living together in effectively a same sex marriage, another problem for the church! I do not know how Jackie adjusted—or how much pain she went through to keep us together as a family. For me, the change of gender role proved much less of a problem to our family than I had thought possible. We loved each other. We expressed this love. We slept together as two women. We were also both attracted to men and exchanged notes on them. Outside our relationship she remained heterosexual. There were perhaps certain compromises here. Jackie and I were still able to have delightful times together sexually, but I believe this was more due to our spiritual and emotional bond than to her innate desires. I had to learn to listen closely to her, so I could discover when she wanted to be alone, or to seek male company.

So I came to another step on my path downwards from a peak of prestigious status. I had left the clerical elite. I now lost the privileges of malehood and probably wrecked my job prospects. I feared ridicule, embarrassment and lost credibility—not just because I would be seen as a woman, but because I would be seen as a freakish woman. I knew that I also faced other risks. I faced legal discrimination and, if by chance arrested, as a pre-operation transsexual I would be put in a male prison to face nearly certain sexual harassment and rape. This was not a distant threat. Within months of this change, I would take part in an armed Aboriginal occupation of a major mining camp.

As for my vocation to the priesthood, I felt I had dedicated myself to the priesthood forever. I had not deserted this commitment. I had accepted the call from the Lover God within. I had been consecrated to the priesthood. Now, I would be the priestess I had always been within. I was travelling far from when men called me Father.

As for ritual work, since Jackie was very keen that we avoid publicity, this became limited to saying Mass privately in our family. Yet it remained important for us. We saw this sacrament as the sacred meal that symbolised our bond to our Creator, to each other and to the earth. Celebrating this as a woman gave it a new richness for me. I saw it as a very female act of nourishing. It symbolised how Divinity was wholly present in Nature, sustaining it with food in which the Deity was wholly present. Through this we magically and symbolically celebrated the presence of the sacred in the mundane.

On Priestesses

When the Vatican decreed in 1994 on May 30th "there must be no more discussion of women priests", they presumed they had not yet ordained any. It did not know that my Lover-God and I had ducked under their guard.

The Church of England laudably permits the ordination of women, but oddly calls these "female priests" rather than "priestesses". This suggests that their role is to be female men;—or that they are to work in the priesthood in precisely the same way as men. I suspect that the title "priestess" is now so associated by default with pre-Christian religions that the churches fear the use of this title would unleash a female pagan energy into the churches.

I was now travelling in the reverse direction to that prescribed by Church Fathers such as St. Jerome who wrote: "as long as woman is for birth and children, she is different from man as body is from soul. But when she wishes to serve Christ more than the world then she will cease to be a woman and will be called a man (vir)."[167] Another Father, St. Ambrose, made transsexuals of female believers: "she who believes progresses to perfect manhood, to the measure of the adulthood of Christ. She then dispenses with the name of her sex, the seductiveness of youth, the garrulousness of old age."[168] This was not a view always adhered to for St. Joan of Arc was arrested for wearing male garb![169]

There had not been priestesses in Christianity since the Roman Church declared against Gnostic Christians, in the Apostolic Constitutions of around 380CE, "to take priestesses from among the women is an error of pagan godlessness."[170] The Synod of Laodicia of the same century went further by declaring, "Women are not allowed to approach the altar". In 1994 Pope John Paul II issued the following edict:

"'I declare that the Church has no authority whatsoever to confer priestly Ordination on women and that this judgement is to be definitively held by all the Church's faithful."

From the Vatican, on 22 May, the Solemnity of Pentecost, in the year 1994, the sixteenth of my Pontificate, Joannes Paulus Pp. II

Yet we know there were priestesses among the early Christians, not only from the Roman Church's edict in 380CE banishing this practice, but also from its attack on women who took priestly roles among the Gnostic Christians. In the 3rd Century Bishop Irenaeus of Lyon attacked the Gnostic Christian Marcus for teaching women to preside at the Eucharist. "He bids them consecrate these [chalices] in his presence."

Bishop Irenaeus also attacked Marcus for encouraging women to prophesise. In words that revealed his chauvinism, he accused Marcus of going to "his deluded victim" and saying to her, "'Open thy mouth, speak whatsoever occurs to thee, and thou shalt prophesy'. She then, vainly puffed up and elated by these words, and greatly excited in soul by the expectation that it is herself who is to prophesy, her heart beating violently, reaches the requisite pitch of audacity, and idly as well as impudently utters some nonsense as it happens to occur to her, such as might be expected from one heated by an empty spirit." He also protested that Marcus told women: "Adorn thyself as a bride who is expecting her bridegroom, that thou mayest be what I am, and I what thou art. Establish the germ of light in thy nuptial chamber." Yet this was the language of the Biblical Song of Songs. It described the celebration of the mystic marriage between the soul and God. Irenaeus misinterpreted his words when he suggested that Marcus sought a sexual advantage.

The Bishop explained Marcus's reputation for accurate prophecy in words that the Church would use over a thousand years later in witch-trials to justify killing those who had a sacred role or ability not sanctioned by the Church. 'It appears that this man possesses a demon as his familiar spirit, by means of whom he seems able to prophesy." The Bishop further alleged that Marcus was 'deep in the black arts of magic'. He was outraged when Gnostics in turn called him "unspiritual" and "ecclesiastic" and said that they did not need to obey his narrow rules in order to know God;[171] as would also be said centuries later to the Inquisition by Marguette Porete of the Beguine women's movement. The Church would never succeed in suppressing those who found their wisdom within.

The Church and Hermaphrodites

The Fathers of the Catholic Church particularly loathed the hermaphrodite (transsexual) priestess of pagan faiths. Augustine called the Goddess of Rome, Cybele a 'demon' and a 'monster' whose: "priesthood are 'castrated perverts' 'foully unmanned and corrupted'.[172] "These effeminates, no later than yesterday, were going through the streets and places of Carthage with anointed hair, whitened faces, relaxed bodies and feminine gait...The Great Mother [the Goddess Cybele] has surpassed all her sons, not in greatness of deity, but of crime...This Great Mother of the Gods has brought mutilated men into Roman temples."[173] Tertullian went still further: "I do not call a cup poisoned which has received the last of a dying man; I give that name to one that has been infected by the breath of a fricix, a high priest of Cybele...I ask if you would not refuse it as you would such a person's kisses."[174]

Their revulsion was not at castration but at the taking on of a female identity. The eunuch who saw himself as a man was accepted and honoured. They quoted Isaiah: "Thus says YAHWEH: 'To the eunuchs who keep my Sabbaths, who choose the things that please me and hold fast my covenant, I will give in my house and within my walls a monument and a name better than sons and daughters; I will give them an everlasting name which shall not be cut off.'"[175] Eunuchs were used in choirs in Catholic churches right up until the 20th Century. They were thus more honoured than were women who were for many centuries banned from singing in these churches.

Jesus seemed to have little problem with eunuchs of any kind. "For there are eunuchs who have been so from birth, and there are eunuchs who have been made eunuchs by men, and there are eunuchs who have made themselves eunuchs for the sake of the reign of heaven. He who is able to receive this let him receive it."[176]

Josephus, an influential Jewish historian of the first Century after Christ, believed that every sperm ejaculated contained an entire child. He wrote: "Shun eunuchs and flee all dealings with those who have deprived themselves of their virility...expel them even as infanticides who withal have destroyed the means of procreation." He thus went beyond Deuteronomy's ruling against the physically imperfect male entering the Temple: "He whose testicles are crushed or whose male member is cut off shall not enter the assembly of the Lord."[177] The "eunuchs" denounced were probably transsexuals for he continued: "For plainly it is by reason of the femininity of their soul that they have changed the sex of their body"

The attitude of Church Fathers towards those who deserted the male gender was a direct consequence of their fear of womankind. The disobedient phallus was explained by saying that women were given power over it through the Fall. But what when the woman who gave them an erection turned out to be transgendered? Such a person would be thrice evil; through rejecting the divine gift of malehood, through deception and through utilising women's sexual magic.

This compounded fear is still present. This was illustrated in 1998 by the case of a transsexual woman returned by US Immigration to Nicaragua. When she arrived, the local customs officials saw a pretty woman. But when they learnt of her background, they became angry at her "deception", anger increased by their guilt at being attracted by her. They took her to a separate building, stripped her; multiple raped and tortured her. I feared I was in a similar danger on one occasion when Indonesian Immigration officials frisked me. My body was then totally hermaphrodite in appearance, female everywhere except between my legs. I was terrified but managed to stare down the official who felt me there. She suddenly backed away. I was not always so lucky. Later I would be nearly killed by an assault committed by a man who refused to accept me as a woman.

But I had to accept this risk if I were to resolve my gender problem, for I was confined to living in a prejudiced and sexist society. I did not justify my path by referring to the Biblical texts concerning eunuchs. I did not even note them, for I had no wish to be a male eunuch.

I have told how there were many ways to effect gender transition in other cultures. (See "Monday"). Sometimes elders would interpret the dreams of suitable youths to see if he or she was called to the path of the other gender and was potential material for training as a shaman, teacher and healer of the people. The act of changing was seen as a powerful rite of empowerment and of self-shaping. In the early 1970s, at the time of my own change, I combined my conviction that I had been called to a sacred role with my new knowledge of the Shamanic path. I asked myself, "Did my gender path mean that I was called to an ancient path of my own people. Was I born to have this role?"

I knew in my heart that I was. I now proudly bonded with that Zulu youth who dreamt and changed; I was that Siberian youth changing; I was the American Indian who stood in the ritual circle and changed gender roles; but above all, I knew I was part of my own people's dreaming in the British Isles. It did not matter that I did not know what happened here before; for it was now happening in my life and thus part of my people's life.

The elders of our people, like the shamans of other nations, would have known much about the uses of plants, and possibly knew how to use oestrogen rich plants to transform bodies. But when I began this transition, these matters were not well understood, and transsexuals were under attack from various schools of gender theorists who loved to practice their speculations on us.

Bigotry and Gender Theorists

In the 1980s I was shocked to find *The Transsexual Empire* by Janice Raymond, a woman paranoid about transsexuals, was used as a textbook at an Australian university. Raymond saw transsexuals as a male conspiracy to penetrate the lesbian-feminist movement (ignoring those who travelled from female to male roles). She imperiously told transsexuals not to try to adopt female stereotypes, but stay in roles they were assigned at birth. She apologised for sounding cruel and unaccepting. She was being unaccepting. I found her insulting. I still find her theory insulting. I do not think anyone could see my life as unduly conforming to any kind of stereotype. The same goes for most of my transsexual friends. She was ignorant of the biological basis of transexuality and of gender. Her theories did not accommodate the thousands of the "intersexed" assigned at birth to a gender by surgical convenience. Sadly she had a major influence on the thealogian Mary Daly, who quoted approvingly from Raymond everytime she mentioned transsexuals in her book *Gyn/Econlogy*.

A group of radical women working on a printing press in a communal Melbourne house, my home in 1979, who wore overalls as uniforms, expressed disapproval whenever they observed me wearing skirts. I must admit that it took time before the novelty of wearing such clothes wore off. I enjoyed experimenting and trying out make-up. I preferred clothes that identified me as a woman Nowadays my self-confidence is much higher and I wear mostly today's unisex gear. If they now met me, I think they would approve; but I still claim the right to dress up!

But I was much more dismayed by the attack on transsexuals launched by the feminist Germaine Greer. In a full-page internationally syndicated article she described with biting scorn a person she said was ugly and dressed in appalling taste, who came at the launch for her book *The Female Eunuch* to congratulate her on what she had done for "us" women. Greer cruelly said this was no woman but a parody and fool.[178]. I had thought Greer would have been consistent in her stance that clothes do not make the person and much more enlightened on the biological basis for transexuality and intersexuality.

In 1999 she returned to her attack on transsexuals. This time she dreamt up a particularly nasty argument. An ABC interviewer asked her, in an interview about her latest book, "Can I quote what you said though on page 74? 'When a man decides to spend his life impersonating his mother like Norman Bates in *Psycho* it's as if he murders her and gets away with it.' That's a pretty damning assessment of what it is to be a transsexual?"

Greer responded:

"Well, if that's what happening. You see transsexuals typify their mothers as the enemy. This is the family that wouldn't admit that inside this male body was a female. I think it is very strange."

This was a flippant and ignorant comment. It clearly seemed clever to her to typify and demonise transsexuals as if they were mother-fixated clones of Norman Bates. I have never met a transsexual who saw her mother as the enemy. Instead I have met many who enjoyed support from their mothers during their difficult and often traumatic transition.

Greer ignored those who change in the other direction from living as a woman to living as a man since they did not fit her ill-conceived theory. It was not as if she had not had the opportunity to learn about transsexuals. In the mid-1990s she had launched a cruel attack on a "transsexual" woman appointed as bursar to the all-female Exeter College at Oxford University at which Greer was a Fellow.

The applicant did more than obtain the Bursar's job, she also organised at Exeter College an international conference on transexuality in 1998 attended by female-to-male and male-to-female transsexuals and professionals who assisted their transition. I was among the many speakers. The many doctors present gave papers describing how transsexual children had their gender wrongly specified at birth. But unfortunately Greer put her trust in the infallibility of other doctors, mostly males who issued birth certificates! On March 16th 1999 I heard her on television again complaining about these "males" who invaded her female space.

Another display of ignorant bitchiness was an article by a Guardian columnist, Julie Burchill, published on 20th January 2001. She wrote; "Transsexualism is, basically, just another, more drastic twist on the male menopause, which in turn is just another excuse for men to do as they please." She imagined men who had idly decided in late middle age to have a go at femalehood; then called her creation "transsexuals"! She clearly had not a clue about the medical background to transexuality. Like Greer she seemingly did not know of those who travelled from girlhood to malehood or of the children who had to change. If she did know of them, she ignored them, for they did not fit her dreamed-up theory. She ignored the trauma and the facts to write an easy article that on the surface was feminist.

Another but sadder mistake was made by the author Randy Connor in his book *Blossom of Bone*, a finely documented account of the sacred roles given to transsexuals in ancient cultures. I learnt much from his book, but boringly found I had to mentally change pronouns throughout. He presumed people like me were homosexual males like him. He thus claimed for gay males the many sacred roles that were given historically to transsexual women.

In his introduction he thoughtfully said that he would leave it to lesbians to document their own sacred roles. I wish he had given the same courtesy to transsexuals. He evidently believed that I was homosexual when I slept with a man. It did not matter to him if my partners perceived me as a female, if I perceived myself as such, and if my partner and I saw us as heterosexual, as did our friends. Connor presumed he knew us better then we knew ourselves. I thus felt colonised by him, taken over.

His mistake was also that of the early Catholics. The Catholic Emperor Theodosiumon decreed on 6th August 390CE, shortly after the suppression of the cult of Cybele and her transsexual priestesses: "all those who shamefully debase their bodies by submitting them like women to the desire of another man and in giving themselves to strange sexual relations shall be made to expiate such crimes in the avenging flames in view of all the people."[179] The crime deserving death in the Emperor's eyes was changing from a male sexual role to that of a female. He, like Connor, would have defined me as homosexual. But that was not how I saw life or how I still experience it.

I presume that my transsexual priestess sisters of past millennia would have experienced sex with males as heterosexuals, even if they had not yet had any operation; for that was my experience after I gained the oestrogen that I so much needed. They would have known of plants rich in female hormones that could supply them with the hormones their bodies and minds missed and craved.

Monica Sjoo and Barbara Mor in their epic book: *The Great Cosmic Mother: Rediscovering the religion of the Earth* claimed shamanism for the bisexual rather than hermaphrodite. They wrote, "The Mother was deprived of her ancient bisexual nature. As shamanism and bisexuality always go together this means the disappearance of the shamanic techniques."[180] I have seen no records that link shamanism to bisexuality. But I have seen many that link shamanism with hermaphroditism or transsexuality. I am bisexual—but feel this has little to do with my shamanism and all to do with my preference in sexual partners. These authors wrote of the hermaphrodite Goddess under another name—and ignored the hermaphrodites that served her.[181] Instead they talked of "eunuch priests" who lived "like women."

I do not want to get too medical here, for I am dealing more with magic and self-perception. But it is hard to have one's self-perception challenged by the few who cannot accept that having a female brain matters. I remember when a woman told me I had to be a man, since I had no womb and had experienced male sexuality. She told me her brain was her womb. For her a woman simply could not have experienced what I had experienced.

Yes, it is hard for people in our society to see how this could be so. It was very hard for me to understand it myself. I knew as a child I had an instinctive belief that I belonged in the female space. If Jackie had not entered my life, I may never have known what male sex could be like. If I had then changed gender identities, I would never have known this. But because it happened the way it did, my life was enriched, and I learnt much more about gender. The lesson my unusual experiences have taught me is that gender identity has much more to do with the gender shaping of our brains rather than the genitals or socialisation. No other theory seems to explain what I have experienced, unless it is the Aboriginal theory that gender resides in our soul.

It is not true that if one is born without a womb, one cannot be a woman. Of course a woman with a womb might find it hard to understand what it is like to be to be a woman who has never had a womb—and vice versa. My lack of a womb of course greatly affects my experience of life within the gender with which I identify. It must limit me in many ways, as infertility limits other women.

But those who have to find their true gender through a long journey, as do those assigned to the wrong gender at birth, can be enriched by having a unique experience of life in both gender roles and by having to trust instincts and dreams. We are forced biologically to find our wisdom within ourselves. It is this experience that we have to offer society.

Hormones may have made dramatic changes to my body but it still was not female shaped in every aspect. It was now like to that depicted in the oldest wooden carving of a human so far found in the British Isle. This was a figure with female breasts and a penis, carved in ash wood and found under a track near Glastonbury, perhaps a figure of imagination, perhaps depicting the body of one who took oestrogen rich herbs or mare's urine extract. At that time, when I had sexual encounters with men I told them that all below the waist was off limits while all above was definitely fine! In this fashion I had some of the most marvellously gentle and loving encounters with both Aboriginal and White males. Before my transition I had no sexual interest in men so all this was entirely new to me. But more later on these encounters.

On Androgyny and Having a Gender.

Some friends challenged me when I had just started my transition, suggesting it would be preferable for me to adopt an androgynous gender identity. They recommended that I should not seek any particular gender but instead seize the high ground of neutrality. This made me scream. It was a nice theory. But I was not a neutral person. I identified as a female and fought to have this accepted. I saw nothing wrong with a bipolar gendered society for humans, for this is natural for us, unlike for amoeba. The two genders are fun. They are how we are made. I relish the balance of energies and frisson between us, well, most of the time. The same goes for the "third gender" theorists, the academics that argue that there are more than two genders, that genders are purely a cultural construction. They ignore our biology. They are mostly people who have never walked between the genders.

But the superficial ramblings of theorists who wanted me to fit their schemes made no difference to me in practice. I was happy to be at last at home, mind and soul, brain and body.

It may be a long time since St Thomas Aquinas taught that the female body is naturally inferior to the male; but it is not so long since Charles Darwin taught that men evolved to be superior: "Thus man has ultimately become superior to woman. It is indeed fortunate that the law of equal transmission of characters to both sexes prevails with mammals; otherwise it is probable that man would have become as superior in mental endowment to women, as the peacock is in ornamental plumage to the peahen."[182]

A more recent theory contrarily stated that the human female form has been shaped by unique evolutionary changes not shared with any other species. It posited that evolutionary needs caused women to develop a menstrual cycle that gave her sexual capability at all times, not merely when she was fertile. Her sexual potential was further uniquely enhanced by the development of the clitoris, breasts and frontal sex.[183] Males underwent sexual evolutionary changes of much less consequence since they still made love the way of other male animals.

In that case, the authorities of the Catholic Church seem not to have noticed this dramatic change in female bodies! They prescribed that women should have sex only to conceive; much as if they were still governed by the oestrous cycle of other animals. But I note that other female animals can have sex simply from pleasure; at least this is what I observe when certain dogs visit my energetic Border collie bitch. She seems ready at most times. I have noted also that she seems to be bisexual.

"Unnatural Sex" in Nature.

Unfortunately scientists long ignored the occurrence of variant gender sexual relations within a very wide range of species, declaring, almost with the fervour of the Catholic Church, that animal sex is only to pass on genes. They presumed that in the world of tooth, claw and beak the sexuality of animals is regulated purely by procreation requirements. But Bruce Bagemihl, the author of a recent work, *Animal Homosexuality and Natural Diversity*,[184] documented, as I have mentioned, homosexual and transgender behaviour among at least 450 species of mammals and birds.

"Biology must reconsider functional explanations based on evolution by natural selection," Bagemihl wrote, "and it must recognise the inherent multiplicity of all life forms." It is "part of a larger complex tapestry, a web of seemingly incongruous forces, that interact to produce the flow of life."

He described as the *law of biodiversity* that the vitality of a biological system increases when it contains more diversity. As diversity expands, so do stability and resilience. Viewed this way, homosexuality and transgender behaviour are expressions of the natural exuberance of a healthy biological system, and help to maintain its stability.

By December 1975 I had passed through the initial stages of my transition to living as a woman but only at home and with close friends. Outside this small arena it was an increasingly dangerous time for me. It would not have been so dangerous if I had taken the usual advice of doctors to break with old associates and go to a strange town where I could establish a new identity. The danger was increased by the risky nature of the work I took on before my transition to the female role. I was deeply involved in civil rights work with Aborigines in Northern Queensland. I had no intention of stopping this work. I would rather be proud and open.

The fight to save a forest and a people from Shell

My work brought me to the attention of company directors and the media for it was unusual for whites to be working so closely with Aborigines on such issues. The corporations I investigated for Aborigines noted my gender-role change and were in a position to try to use their knowledge to discredit me. To their credit, they did not attempt to do this, at least for several years, but I felt vulnerable to such attacks. Jackie and I were at one on this. The work had to come first. We trusted in providence to protect us, but with a degree of fear.

In December 1975 I was asked to speak at a major Aboriginal Land Rights Conference in Cairns where we were launching the "Mapoon" book that I had co-authored and edited. I had been on female hormones for four months by then and was androgynous in appearance. I was also calling myself Jan, short for Janine. Jan had not been my first choice of female names, but Jackie had wanted a more neutral name.

One night at this conference a dance was organised—and a man invited me onto the floor. I was very awkward. I did not know where to put my hands. It was my first dance with a man. He must have thought me dead ignorant. But I loved dancing. I later learnt that some of the Aboriginal women were watching me. Later that night, one of them tried to check my sex while I was asleep. She exclaimed at finding my pubescent breasts. She and her companions laughed at my confusion and wanted to know more. I explained that I was "half and half" and then fled before they decided to investigate further. I spent the rest of the night sleeping under a car parked on the drive. I felt naive, ignorant and vulnerable. Barbara Miller, my co-worker, was later called on to do much explaining.

When I told the elders with whom I was working , they were serious and courteous. They accepted what I had to say and thanked me for telling them. The only other transsexual I then knew was an Aboriginal woman on a Reserve not far from the conference. She was reportedly very well accepted. The men who had helped organise the conference, men such as Mick Miller and Clarrie Grogan, had little difficulty with my change. Mick simply accepted it. Clarrie, a former boxer, took me on a drive up the mountain so he could have the chance to ask me more about it. He was charming, intrigued and very accepting

But I was up in Cairns on serious political work. Mick and the other organisers wanted me to be the first speaker at the conference. I discussed this with Aboriginal people who travelled with me from Melbourne to Cairns. We agreed that a white person should not be the first speaker at an Aboriginal conference. On arrival I said this to Mick and, although he disagreed, he re-scheduled my talk. I now think I should have gone along with the local organisers. I later learnt that I had been wanted as the first speaker so the delegates would immediately get to know the full scope of mining plans for their tribal lands. I had unique knowledge of what was planned. But what they wanted did happen, albeit with some confusion. Before my rescheduled talk, the delegates from the Wik nation at Aurukun discovered the extent of my knowledge. They promptly absented themselves from the scheduled talks to meet with me. I spread out for them maps showing how Shell planned to take over 1,905 sq. kilometres (736 sq., miles) of their tribal lands. I explained that Shell planned to strip off its forest to remove a billion tonnes of aluminium-rich bauxite clay. I told the Elders where Shell planned to put a port, roads and processing plant.

They were shocked. This was land where they buried their dead, where they hunted, gathered and which they honoured with rituals. They had cared for this land for millennia. They asked me to come back with them to tell their community. They had space for me in their hired plane (in the wet season planes are the main means of transport), as they would be sending a delegate south to raise support from trade unions. Urgent action was needed as the Government was preparing the legislation that would give their ancestral lands to Shell. If this happened, Shell would have the right to build on tribal lands a mining town, to run the town, to mine the coral reefs for calcium, to fell the trees and strip-mine the clays for bauxite, to build and run a harbour and to decide where Aborigines could hunt or run cattle. The Aborigines would be offered no royalties, but, as I would learn, money would not have satisfied these elders. They regarded their ancestral lands as priceless.

The Aboriginal delegates at the conference immediately formed the North Queensland Land Council to fight for their rights . The Whitlam government had set up similar bodies in the Federally administered Northern Territory—but Queensland had refused to permit the Federal Government to set up Aboriginal Land Councils in its state. This Aboriginal initiative would set off a chain reaction across Australia and eventually led to the setting up of a National Federation of Land Councils. For over a decade I worked within this movement, helping it with research and raising funds.

Before I boarded the plane, I had my first serious disagreement with both Cheryl Buchanon, the friend who had first involved me in her Aboriginal people's fight, and with Lionel Fogarty, her partner and a militant Aboriginal poet. They asked me to give up my seat so an Aborigine could go. I replied that the elders had invited me because they needed my specialised knowledge. While I could see that my knowledge was partly due to the privileges of being born White, I did have this knowledge, and it was only right that I used and shared it. The argument saddened me. I owed Cheryl much. She had welcomed me as a sister when I transitioned, saying that I would better understand them now I was now myself a member of a minority.

I thus flew with the Elders and Delegates over seemingly endless primal forest until we reached Aurukun on the other side of Cape York. It looked tiny from the air, an airstrip, dirt roads and corrugated tin roofs, a speck in a wilderness. It lay about half way down the eastern side of the Gulf of Carpentaria in the far Northeast of Australia.

Soon after my arrival, I told what I knew at a community meeting, under the frangipani trees. There was stillness about my audience, an intensity, a pain—and a sense of defiance. When I explained that Shell was an Anglo-Dutch company, a man said: "My Grandfather and father-in-law defeated the Dutch. We will do it again!" (The relatives mentioned indicate kin groups rather than individuals.)

Later, with his family sitting on the ground around him, he explained to me how they defeated the Dutch. A Dutch ship had called at Mapoon, one hundred miles to the north. He laughed as he told how the people there "had thrown spears hoping to hit the bullets!" The ship then arrived at Aurukun. "They asked us if they could put up a village. We said yes. They put up huts. We helped them put in a well, cut a path through the mangrove swamp. But then they started to take our women and to make us work and work and work for them. Then they got their guns. Maybe they were going to shoot ducks but we thought they were going to shoot us. One of us chopped one of them on the back of the neck, then we got our canoes and came down to their boats and set fire to them with our firesticks. We can take you there, Jani, eight Dutchmen buried there."

When I later checked the records of the Dutch East Indies Company, I found that a Dutch vessel had mapped precisely the coastline that lay between Mapoon and Aurukun. The Captain's log recorded that after trouble with natives he had decided to return to New Batavia (Indonesia). He omitted to say that he had set up a village in Australia. The year was 1606. I had just learnt of the first European settlement in Australia. They told it to me as if it had happened a few years ago. I think I was the first person to write down this oral history

Men and women took an equal part at the Aurukun meeting, and in most of the subsequent fights for the land. A young woman, Gladys, was particularly outspoken. She has since become a leading campaigner for her people. When I mapped the tribal lands affected by the mining plans. I found that every part of their land had its elder to speak for it, sometimes a man, sometimes a woman. It seemed that men and women worked equally as guardians of the land.

Frank Yungaporta, my "uncle" at the settlement, was adamant when we discussed the mining proposal. "I say that there will be no mining here and that's that." (In Aboriginal communities even a stranger can be given uncles and aunts, rights and responsibilities. The traditional "skin" system gives the newcomer people who are responsible for her welfare, people she can marry, people she cannot marry, people she has duties towards, thus integrating her into the community.)

The elder Geraldine Kawangka stated: "Give the answer back that we are Aurukun people. Do not let the mining company in to destroy Aurukun for it is a beautiful place." Albert Chevalthun, whose ancestral land lay to the north outside the Shell lease—but which Comalco had already seized for Britain's RTZ, said; "Comalco never asked for this land. This is our forefather's land…we cannot give away our land. It is not well for the country to be destroyed and given away. We are trying to save this land for our children to help them stand firm and strong…No, we don't want the money. We don't want the jobs. We don't want the companies to take our land. All our children look very healthy here. They don't just live on store tucker. We have our own food out in the bush. If our country is destroyed, there will be no hunting places left just like Weipa. No, we don't want any mining. I speak on behalf of all my peoples land." Mabel Pamulkun, another Elder, added in almost Judaic terms: "From generation to generation it will be our land. God has given it to us."[185]

After the meeting I had time to look around the community and to make a fool of myself when I saw a man painting a didgeridoo. I asked him how he made the hole down the middle. Keeping his face absolutely straight he said: "You get a mob of termites then march them up and march them down again." We laughed and talked. He told me only a few tribes had didgeridoos. Click sticks are much more commonly used.

I also played a favourite game with the children. I walked into the bush with them and said; "Now that bush there. That is a useless one. We can throw that one away." "No, Jan, no, no" would come the chorus. Then they would tell me just how they used that plant for food or medicine. The mode of preparation might be quite complicated and include leaching out toxins. But I never could find a plant that a twelve year old child had not a use for it. This was their traditional literacy.

That afternoon, while I was with the children, a Queensland State government minister visited the settlement and said that there would be no mining unless the community agreed. This seemed like a victory, but that night, while I was having supper with the Chairman, we heard on the radio that the minister had announced in the state capital, Brisbane, a thousand miles away, that the Aurukun people had agreed and the mine would go ahead. This barefaced lie shocked us. That night the elders decided that they had to do something dramatic quickly to make their opposition known. They decided that in the morning they would drive to the mining camp to evict the miners. This was meant to be a seen as a show of force, so they decided to bring their weapons.

Shell's Mining Camp Seized

Next morning the male elders came with their rifles, spears and shotguns. Even the Aboriginal State police came. We then drove together up the track to Shell's prospecting camp some two hours away. I was the only white person present. Whenever we came to a tree marked by the miners, the elders stopped to remove the painted bark and burn it. When we drew near to the camp, they dropped me off saying they would return for me after they had introduced themselves to the miners (they knew my white face would have the miners presume I was a leader). But just five minutes later they were back. They had discovered, to their surprise, that the miners had already fled, abandoning their vehicles on the airstrip.

They had presumably been warned by radio that armed Aborigines were on the way.

We broke into Shell's radio hut in the deserted settlement so we could let the press know we had captured the mining camp. It was national front-page headlines. Nothing had happened like this before. We also wanted to sabotage the abandoned earth moving machines. It was just as well that we did not know how to do so effectively. If we had destroyed over a quarter of a million pounds worth of machinery, I could have been jailed in a man's prison with all the attendant risks for a person with a feminised body. But it turned out that we had no need to sabotage the machinery to make our point.

We also radioed Aboriginal organisations so they could organise help. We thought we might need lawyers to protect us, and were delighted when we learnt that by coincidence Aboriginal lawyers were already on the way and would arrive that same day. When we returned to Aurukun, we found Paul Coe and Kevin Smith had arrived from the Sydney Aboriginal Legal Service. Later that day, Eric Koo-oila and other elders came to ask what I thought of Coe's suggestion that they send a delegation to see the British Queen. They thought that as I was British I would be able to advise on the effectiveness of such an action. I told them I thought it based on an exaggerated idea of the Queen's importance. Delegations came to see her all the time without attracting much media. I suggested that a different kind of campaign was needed to marshal public opinion .

The Elders asked me to put my view to the community. Their way of making decisions was through full community discussions. I did not like to do what they had asked. I feared with some reason that this would alienate me from Aboriginal lawyers that I respected. But I did as requested. The community listened, and decided that they would not go to see the Queen.

I felt that their story of how they defeated the Dutch would be certain to gain public attention, if only a delegation could be got to Holland. We looked for ways to achieve this. We were then editing *The Mapoon Books*, our three-volume study of oppression at Mapoon, so we put in a section about Aurukun and helped organise a separate campaign for Aurukun.

These events answered for me a question that had concerned me earlier. Female hormones had not made me docile or hurt my creativity. If anything I was stronger, more self-assured and more the warrior.

I do not think I was given any special status among Aborigines because of my gender change, although I received nothing but respect. I simply presented myself as a woman, was accepted as such and was taken to the women's sacred places as only a woman could be. I am not sure if Australian Aborigines ever gave shamanic status to people who made a gender-transition. It is likely that they did, going by the customs of similar societies. I simply found I got on well with Elders. Usually we looked into each other's eyes, laughed and that was that. This especially happened when I was with "Dreamers"; the elders honoured for their deep knowledge of their land and of the Dreamtime within them.

Perhaps some Aboriginal tribes had customs like to those of the Mojave Indians. I know Aborigines regarded American Indians as a sister people. Among the Mojave, a boy-child of ten or eleven who wanted to change to live as a woman would be taken out of his tent by two women who then danced in front of him. The youth would copy their dance. The women then gave the youth a dress and painted the youth's face as a token of acceptance. From then on that person took a female name, lived totally as a female and was a female in the eyes of the people. Girl-children could be equally solemnly be made men. Afterwards such children could pick a partner of either sex.

The First Encounter with a Surgeon

I knew that was my next step in transition. In our society surgery rather than hormonal changes marked the point when officialdom protected us from such risks as being put into a male jail. I thought it wrong. The hormonal changes and the adoption of a female lifestyle were the vital factors, not the surgery, but our society saw the lack of a penis as the vital factor.

So I went to the only establishment in Melbourne where transsexuals could obtain approval for surgery, ironically to a psychiatrist attached to the Roman Catholic hospital. He was arrogant and judgmental. I wanted to better understand myself so asked him to recommend books on trans-sexualism. I was astonished, as I have mentioned, when he refused to do so. saying; "I prefer you do not read up the subject. It would make you harder to assess."

He then asked me about my relations with my children. When I told him that Jackie and I were joint custodians, he said: "I will not treat you while you are living at home and caring for your children. Your gender transition might upset their gender identity and confuse them."

I was astonished at this, made my goodbyes and left. I never went back to see him. There was no way that I would "prove" to him that I was a sat-isfactory candidate for womanhood by abandoning my children. It would take me another seven years to find a hospital that would accept me with-out demanding that I abandon my children. It meant that from 1975 until 1981 I lived with a very hermaphroditic body. As I was both very politically active during this time and sexually active as a woman, it meant I had to run a great risk of exposure, of male violence and perhaps of rape.

But the hormones helped so greatly that I questioned whether I would have wanted surgery if I had been born to people who would have accepted me as a woman without requiring surgery. I was managing quite well as a female hermaphrodite, or so I thought. I was reasonably attrac-tive as a woman. The hormones had made my genitals almost child-like with a deep dark line where a cleavage would have developed if I had been born girl-formed. But as far as the medical profession went, my transition was incomplete and it was advised that I went for surgery. I knew this was the safer option. I was also told that my sexual life would be much better afterwards!

I had no doubt that getting the hormone balance right was vastly more important to me than having this operation. The hormones made me feel right inside. They had changed very many of the aspects that discomforted me. My body had now rebuilt itself with female bricks. I was now utterly at home with my moods, my rhythms, and my way of moving, and even my place in society. It was not that I enjoyed men discriminating against me; it was that I was comfortable with my sisters.

My gender crisis was at its root a crisis of self-acceptance in an unaccepting society. Ultimately I learnt that self-acceptance was even more important than hormones or surgery. My self-acceptance meant for me that I was now claiming with pride my birthright of living as a female person whose body had male aspects that could be amended if I so chose.

As Christmas 1975 drew near, the time came for our normal ritual visit to Jackie's parents. She hated anything that made them feel uncomfortable so begged me at the last moment to go as a male. I hated the pretence and could hardly stomach it. Jackie said if her Dad knew what was happening with me, she was nearly certain he would pressure her to leave me. I thus reluctantly entered this charade, dressed as a male for the last time—and it was a nightmare. My mind and body screamed at this temporary reversal. Since my last visit to see them I had been five months on hormones. Male clothes could not hide the resulting changes. Jill later explained to them that it was the effect of a medicine I took for a mysterious disease. My diary recorded: "She is still worried about her parents discovering that I am living as a woman. Everyone else now knows about me being Jan; even her Dad's sister, Auntie Eve, who had been a wonderful surrogate grandmother for me. But Jackie and her sister feared that telling their father might kill him. They also feared he might see Jackie as the victim, be enormously distressed and do all he could to rescue her."

We had intended to stay three years in Australia but had stayed five, finding life much richer there than expected. I loved life in Australia although I was missing my own land, family and old friends. But now Jackie told me she wanted to return to live in Europe, as it would be away from the more conventional influences of Australian society. She also felt it would be easier for her parents if she told them by post of my change. She felt that it would be easier for them to accept. They were also less likely to feel she needed rescuing.

When we returned from this traumatic visit to her parents, we celebrated Christmas with our Aboriginal friends Cheryl and Lionel who had come to stay with us, as they had many times before. Cheryl was expecting a baby by Lionel. The argument over Aurukun had not created a barrier between us. It was also Lionel's 18th birthday and it turned out to be a good and tearful occasion. Lionel said he had never had such a good Christmas.

But in January, just before we were to go to Tasmania for a family holiday, our relationship with Cheryl and Lionel collapsed. The first sign of this was when they said a bark painting from Aurukun hung on one of our walls was a sacred "life and death" painting and, if I did not return it, they would lose their baby. This shocked us—but we soon discovered that there was also another purpose to this. They insisted that I must not be open with the Aurukun people and tell them why I was returning it. I was simply to say that it belonged to Aurukun.

I had found this small bark painting in the Aboriginal-run store at Aurukun. It was not expensive. When I asked the artist about it, he was delighted that I was interested. I was aware at that time of controversy aver sacred objects purchased by Whites, so asked the artist if it had any sacred meaning? He replied: "None at all. `I painted it so I could sell it. Do you like it?" Surrounded by his family and friends, he explained the painting in detail. All the community now knew I was buying it. They were delighted I like it. They treated it like a present from them to me. And this is what it had become.

I now feared that they might be insulted if I obeyed these instructions and returned it without saying why. So I phoned the North Queensland Land Council and explained my dilemma. They said, "If you send it back without explaining what has happened, it will cause deep hurt. It will be seen as an insult." But Cheryl and Lionel were clearly very agitated. They came from communities far removed from Aurukun and of a different language group. Perhaps the images in the painting had a different meaning for their people? Since they were only staying a few days more, I decided to put it away out of sight until they left.

But they searched the house when we were out, found it and were furious. When we returned, Lionel hit me repeatedly with his fist while holding a meat cleaver over my head with his other hand. It was very scary. I was frightened he might kill me. But he was convinced the painting endangered their unborn child. Cheryl was adamant that she would miscarry if the painting stayed. And I believed her. Her belief made it dangerous to her. I decided to send it back to Aurukun but with a letter that explained the full circumstances."

But soon a senior white haired Aboriginal elder, Harry Penrith, who later changed his name to Birnum Birnum, came to see us. He was sleeping on our couch when we woke up. He knew our backdoor was always open. He came because of what had happened between Cheryl, Lionel and myself. He explained that this had only happened because we were the safest and closest outlets for the youngsters' frustration. They knew we would not go to the police. Harry begged us to understand why it had happened. I did understand. I had seen Lionel cheer on coloured men when they attacked white women in television films. I knew something of his bitterness but had not expected to be his target. Harry emphasised that his people still wanted us to work with them. He had a particular task in mind. We were going back to Europe. Would we raise support for them in Europe? They greatly needed international support. We promised to do what we could. But we sadly never saw Cheryl and Lionel again although we tried to send them a present for their baby.

There were far too many divisions between people who needed to fight united. Paul Coe, the Aboriginal lawyer who came to Aurukun, savagely attacked both Cheryl and myself, at a conference of the Australian Union of Students for advising the Aurukun people against the visit to the Queen.

We then finally escaped for the longed for holiday in the ancient forests of Tasmania. It was our first together as two women with children. It was confusing, and it made us chuckle, when a seaman carried my bags up onto the boat, leaving the much smaller Jackie struggling with her's. We were also allotted a luxury cabin for an economy price which all added to the fun of the voyage. We were very glad to get away. The primeval Tasmanian forest was wonderful and richly healing. It contained wildlife that had become hard to see on the Australian mainland. There were tiny kangaroos known as poteroos (pot-sized roos), Tasmanian devils—and weird plants above the snowline that looked like transplants from a Jurassic world.

But this trip made me even more aware of how vulnerable women can feel all their adult lives. When carloads of males drove past and saw two women camping in the bush, they wolf whistled, offered beers, and approached us looking for sex, disregarding the presence of children. I simply did not know how to handle this. I hid whenever possible. My figure was rapidly developing.

Under the influence of a tiny amount of oestrogen, not much more than the amount in the birth-control pill, my body had found its set of female blueprints. This included a remarkable change in hair distribution and breasts that some of my female friends envied. I was soon to be a D cup. I remember one day turning too quickly to go through a doorway and hitting my breasts painfully on the frame. I had to learn to move differently, to adjust to a different balance; all stuff that girls easily and naturally learn in their early teens. The tides that now ran through me meant that I was vastly more susceptible to emotion. I would get depressed regularly. Tears would spring easily. And I learnt that next day, or the day after, my mood would naturally lift if only I endured. I learnt to accept that tides had become just as part of me as of the ocean.

Although I shared through this gender journey something of the path of the shaman, they would also have received years of training from elders and I had none. They were trained in the Siberian tribes to travel in the spirit realms, to heal, to balance, to teach, divinate and prophesy. My own people may once have had the equivalent, but if so, I had heard little talk of it.

In Australia far from my own lands, I knew none among my own people who identified as a shaman. I was instead a guest in Aboriginal lands and learning from their elders. In my writings I documented how traditional Aboriginal spirituality was under assault from Christian missionaries who labelled it as an evil sorcery. The theft of Aboriginal lands orphaned the people and caused demoralisation and drinking, but I met many Aborigines fighting against these evils. I saw how they succeeded in strengthening their people's pride. I remembered how English children at school had labelled me as a child of a no-good drunkard Irish race. As their guest, I put everything into helping them protect their heritage.

I was now outside the Christian community and often felt alone. When I visited churches, I felt myself an alien in a once familiar world. But the inner relationship with the Lover-God remained. I still felt bonded to Him and to the Mother Earth. When Aboriginal people spoke of the land and the need to protect her, my spirit seemed to sing with theirs. The priestly element I most missed was the opportunity to use my skill in ritual and sacred drama to celebrate with others the sacred side of life. I celebrated ritually only in our immediate family or by myself.

One Christian ritual we preserved was the construction of the Christmas Crib. We would go deep into the bush, collecting moss, logs, bark, rocks and ferns, from which we would create in a corner of the living-room an elaborate wild landscape that had at its centre a stable sheltering a mother and child. It was a great pleasure to make it as beautiful as we could. It was an island of nature and hope within our home. Another lesser rite of fun was constructing the birthday cake. I was challenged each time to produce a still more exotic landscape out of cake, colourings and icing. It could be anything from a volcano, pirate island or fairy grotto. Unveiling the cake was a major part of any birthday celebration.

After we returned from Tasmania, Jackie and I worked hard to complete the Mapoon books. Jackie did much of the layout work. I did the editing and co-wrote them with a small team of friends. The first was edited from the words of the Aboriginal people and entitled *The Mapoon Story by the Mapoon people* The following extract was told by an elder, Mrs Jean Jimmy of the Tjungundji people. It revealed how her people made sure a prospective husband had a proper attitude towards the prospective bride.

"When the chief man of their tribe sees a young man has a moustache and hair on his chest, they talk to the parents about his promised girl. It is now time their son takes his girl on their walk-about. The man and his girl must be away for three months. The man picks up his spears and woomeras, and his girl gets her basket and yam stick, and both of them leave their tribes to be alone. When they reach the first water, tribal law says her husband-to-be cannot drink first. His girl must drink first. After she had her drink, she passes her urine into the water before he drinks it.

"(Then) he must find a lagoon so his girl can have a swim. When they find this, they camp there. They both gather wood. He then gets out his wood [fire-sticks] and makes their fire. If he didn't get any meat or fish on the way, he must kill something before nightfall. When he comes back, he must cook the meat but he cannot eat. It must be given first to his girl and he eats after her. This much must be repeated each day, also their swimming in the lagoon.

"But at the first moon, the girl watches and when she gets her moon sickness, she gets up and sticks a spear above her head while they are both asleep with a fire between them. When he sees the spear he moves away…until she is well again. They both eat pangi (water lily root), kangaroo, fresh water turtle, sugar-bag (honey), fish and other foods that Nature has created for them to eat.

"All this is a test given to the man to see if he will be a trustful man under the three moons…They then can get married. They both kneel on the ground with their hands on their laps. A woomera is held above their heads…the husband then takes the girl to live with him and his tribe."

All revenues from this book went to the people to help them resettle their land. The second book drew on anthropologists, historians and others. It was called *The Mapoon Story according to the Invaders*. Mike Parsons contributed anthropological background and Barbara Miller, our field researcher, innocent looking in her long blonde hair, contributed a vast amount of documentation when she persuaded the Presbyterians who ran the missions at Mapoon, Weipa and Aurukun, to allow us to copy their mission files.

We thus obtained first-name correspondence between missionaries, mining company executives and members of the Queensland Government. It provided material for a devastating indictment of church and government for breaking promises made to Aboriginal people and abandoning them under pressure from the mining company Comalco.

The last of our trilogy was entitled *The Cape York Aluminium Companies and the Native Peoples* In this we examined the operations of these aluminium companies internationally. We examined the impact of their operations on the lands of other indigenous peoples such as those of the Amazon where there were also giant aluminium mines—and those at Aurukun. Everywhere we found the same dispossession and impoverishment of indigenous peoples.

By July 1976 the Mapoon books were published with surprisingly good press. A leading Australian historian, Humphrey McQueen, called them "the finest study to appear during the Whitlam era", referring to a Labour Prime Minister famed for his stimulus to the arts and to social change. But I was not able to promote them myself. I had to leave that to others, for I had promised to protect my partner Jackie and thus our family from my gender-role change becoming a media story. She was very afraid that her parents would discover from the press about our books that I was now living as a woman. I would love to have campaigned with our books, to help make sure they were used effectively. I would rather have been the proud woman who dealt with everything face-to-face rather than flee the country. But Jackie was certain that leaving now would help us stay together as a family. It made me feel somewhat better that we had been set another task; that of raising overseas support for the Aboriginal fight for justice.

Pilgrims to St. Francis

Thus midway through 1976, as the books came out, we set out as Jackie and Jan, Kara, 4, and Cathy, 3, for Europe. Since we had also decided to use this trip to explore our European spiritual heritage, we left the plane in Rome so we could to visit places associated with St. Francis of Assisi and St Catherine of Sienna, the namesake of the children. Francis was a troubadour of nature, a very non-materialistic man of the 13th Century. He had inspired us though his verse and life. We went first to Gubbio, a small medieval town on a mountainside, where according to legend; Francis made friends with a wolf. We purchased here a plate depicting a ragged Francis with a wolf standing against him in affection. This took pride of place above our dining table for the rest of our time together.

We acquired a minibus in which we could sleep. This took us on to Assisi, the hometown of St Francis. He taught that there was no need for expensive churches, that all we need as sacred space are simple buildings or the open sky, but we found the Church had erected over his tomb an ornate basilica covered in frescos, exactly the kind of building he deplored. By its entrance we found a large Franciscan friar collecting donations. Inside we found ourselves in a gloriously painted void. The church felt dead. I could feel no spirit, and when I descended into its vaults to see the shrine, I felt suddenly sick. It was as if a corpse lay there that was not Francis. I quickly left a building that had become for me ominous and dark. I felt the church had sought to imprison his spirit. (I felt there was a certain grim appropriateness when an earthquake later damaged this church.)

Jackie and I then sat with the children in the square, wondering if there was anywhere in Assisi where we could find the spirit of Francis. We went to the simpler shrine to his friend St. Clare. That felt much better. We then looked at a small history of St. Francis, and found he had sought refuge in a wood on top of nearby hills. There we found a pine forest with a needle-soft floor and the small caves that gave Francis and his friends shelter. Immediately our spirits lifted. We opened the car windows, drank in the air and said hello to Francis. We walked into his forest and visited a modest little chapel with a custodian who radiated welcome. We danced through the forest with the children. We read his song in praise of Brother Sun, Sister Moon, Brother Wind and Sister Water. For him all nature was his family and was sacred, as was his body. He once stripped naked in a church pulpit so to better speak of the glories of the human body. He would have been certified mentally unfit if he had done this today.

We had found what we came to seek; a person we could learn from, a man who combined love of nature with Christianity, even if his Christianity seemed to bear little relation to that of the institutional church. By now I was beginning to integrate Aboriginal concepts with what I had learnt from my people's inheritance. From Aborigines I had learnt that we are not the owners but the guardians and protectors of the earth; that we speak for the earth and thus must listen to her. This seemed also to be close to Francis' understanding.

I knew we are not really that different from the rocks, trees and birds around us. We are intrinsically one with them. From a galactic viewpoint, we are indistinguishable from our planet. We are a sprinkling of dust upon its surface. But, from a microbe's viewpoint, each one of us is a walking planet. There are more creatures living on and in us than there are humans on this planet. Every one of us is thus a self-conscious world just as I think Gaia, the earth, is a self-conscious planet. Then again, the tiny multi-coloured quark, the building block of atoms, would insist quite correctly that we are also walking, talking and dreaming galaxies. And, as we evolved from quarks, they could rightly claim to be our ancestors. Likewise the photon, darting about, not sure if it is energy or matter; that too is our relative. We are the living, moving, self aware, spirits of the rocks and atoms. We are one of their tongues. In us they are self-conscious. They are not our sisters but our very selves. We perhaps evolved so they could express their innate awareness. They changed part of themselves into us. "Remember man that thou art dust" is not a humbling saying. It records our very triumph.

This does not mean that we cannot use rock as building blocks for our cities, or probe the mysteries of chemicals. It means that, as we do this, we must remember we are dealing with our own body. It behoves us to treat the beings of which we sing and speak with enormous respect. I think many know this is so as children and forget it in later life.

When I studied for the priesthood, I was greatly influenced by a more scientific mystic, Teilhard de Chardin. He was a Jesuit palaeontologist who, in his book *The Phenomenon of Man*, wove the theory of evolution into theology. He saw us as fulfilling our Creator's plan, fulfilling our destiny, by weaving around the earth a "noosphere" or knowledge sphere ("noos" is also the root of gnostic.) This he saw as the latest stage of evolution. He predicted before the arrival of the Internet that we were destined to link ourselves together worldwide. Our radio, television and electronic communications, were for him part of our evolution. They were the evolving nerves of a conscious world. The earth was thus to realise its destiny as an intelligent planet. As such, it would know its Creator in a richer way. This brought Chardin close to St. Francis.

It was years later that I learnt how revolutionary had been the movement of which St. Francis was a part. The Papacy during his lifetime felt threatened by a torrent of social and spiritual radicalism. Everywhere there were Christians preaching that following Christ meant driving moneychangers from the churches, sharing property and celebrating life with simplicity. It seemed to be a renaissance of aspects of Gnosticism. But it was evident that the affluent Papacy did not share this view of Christ's teaching.

Pope Innocent III met in 1209 with the twenty-six years old Francis with the intent of using this charismatic youth to help stem the tide of change. This hope was based on knowing that Francis believed in Papal authority. The plan seems to have been to appear to adopt the non-materialistic ideals of the movement then sweeping Europe while taking steps to ensure it did not threaten the Church's rich elite and their possessions. This strategy was in great part successful. Francis's closest followers became members of an order vowed to obey the Pope. Many who joined his order would desert his simplicity within decades of his death, but the wider movement of which Francis was part continued throughout Europe.

The Inquisition

Thus it came about early in the 14th Century that the Inquisitor Bernardo Gui was sent to investigate the lay followers of Francis in his "Third Order" in France and Catatonia. Many of these were known as Waldensians. Gui reported in his *Inquisitor's Manual*: "Many of both sexes were judged heretical and burnt from the year 1317", and they died "saying they defend the gospel truth, the life of Christ and evangelical and apostolic poverty". He was outraged that they put their vows to God before their duty to obey the Church. He noted with astonishment that they would refuse an order from the Pope to relax their poverty by giving themselves a wine cellar! He reported their commitment was to an inner voice, called sometimes the Holy Spirit, rather than to the Pope. He said they deserved to die for this. He recommended testing suspects by asking: "If there were only one woman left in the world and she did not wish to marry, should she, to preserve the human race, obey an order from the Pope to marry?"

I was proud that my parents belonged to this same Third Order. As a youth I found the example of Francis inspiring. Idealistic concepts of radical social reform excited me, thus I had read Thomas More's 16th Century *Utopia* when I was fifteen. A statue of Francis had an honoured place in our home, as did a copy of his *Canticle to all Creatures*. My father would be buried in the robe of this order. But my parents did not question Papal authority; nor would my parents have been aware of this early Franciscan history.

Gui reported that the Waldensians were related to the Beguine. I was then amazed to discover the Beguine were a many thousand-strong movement of women that was both long lasting and Europe-wide. It was one of the first targets of the Inquisition. I learnt that the independent minded women of the Beguine formed themselves into all-female settlements with up to 2000 members and from which men were excluded. These might make up sections of cities and be protected by their own walls. In them laywomen studied a wide range of subjects, from warfare to healing to cloth making. These women wrote the oldest documents that we still have in Low German, Flemish and French. Their movement lasted centuries and predated the universities, which were set up for men only, dominated by the church and used Latin. The Beguine spiritual leaders challenged these universities and even the spiritual usefulness of the institutional Church. The more I learnt about them, the more I wondered why such an important body had escaped the attention of my school history syllabus and even my theology Master's course? I will write much more about them in a later chapter. (See Saturday)

Gui reported that a Beguine or Waldensian could be recognised by their habit of greeting each other with the words: "Blessed be Jesus Christ". He instructed that anyone who greeted thus should be arrested!

He noted they could also be detected by their habit of not joining hands while praying. He said they were to be arrested because they had dared to deny his authority came from God. Even more seriously, he claimed that they said the church persecuting them was not the true church but the "Great Whore of Babylon". He noted darkly: "They say they are laity and simple folk, but in reality they are astute, cunning and crafty." He was angry that they would not betray anyone to him. Finally he noted with astonishment that they even dared to collect the ashes of those he burnt and venerate them as relics of martyrs! Eventually the Church would accuse the Waldensian women of being witches who rode on broomsticks.

There was a long record of dissent against Papal authority in Southern France that went back over 600 years to the time of Marcus and the Gnostic Christians. A hundred years before Gui tackled the Waldensians; Pope Innocent III launched in 1209 an armed crusade against the Cathars of southern France (also known as Albigensians). This was partly because they were pacifists and refused to take part in his crusades against Islam, but the main reason was that they had refused to recognise the divine nature of the Pope's authority. When the Cathar City of Beziers was sacked, the soldiers were told to kill everyone as "God will know his own." The Cathars were eventually decimated after twenty years of warfare waged against them by the Catholic great and pious.

This was also the region where the troubadour movement flourished, that celebrated to the Church's disquiet the sacred Woman, the Grail and noble values of chivalry. Eleanor of Aquitaine was known as the Queen of the Troubadours. She later became the mother of Richard the Lionheart. She was the first Queen of France and married Henry 2nd of England.

The Cathars had a strict version of Christianity. Norman Cohn, a modern historian of religion, said the Cathars were non-Christians but this did not seem to be so when I examined their rituals.[186]

Their adult baptism is described in their *Lyons Ritual.*

"An Elder said to the Postulant,

'God bless you and make you a good Christian and bring you to the good end.'

Elder

'Do you give yourself to God and the Gospel?'

Postulant: 'Yes'.

Elder:

'Do you promise that henceforth you will eat neither meat nor eggs, nor cheese, nor fat, and that you live only from water and wood [i.e. vegetables and fish]; that you will not lie, that you will not swear, that you will not kill, that you will not abandon your body to any form of luxury, that you will never go alone when it is possible to have a companion, that you will never sleep without breeches and shirt and that you will never abandon your faith for fear of water, fire or any other manner of death?'"

Hildegard of Bingen in a letter of around 1165 criticised the Cathars for regarding the body with disdain and not as holy, but concluded that, since they were images of God, these heretics should be banished, not killed.[187] She thus did not support the Church's slaughter of them. She also severely criticised the Church's clergy, prophesising that the people "will chase you and carry off your riches because you have not been attentive to your priestly office in its time. And they will say about you: 'We reject the Church with its adulterers, its abductors, its people filled with evil.' And in doing so they will wish to render service to God, for they say the Church is polluted by you."[188]

The Christian Communists

The Church never completely succeeded in suppressing a similar challenge in central Europe. Cosmas of Prague, Bohemia's earliest known historian, (c. 1045-1125) wrote of local customs that might well have come from pre-Christian days: "Marriages were held in common. In the manner of beasts they mated for a single night. No one knew the meaning of saying 'mine' but as those who live in the monastic life they referred to all goods as 'ours' in word, heart and in deed. None of their quarters were bolted and the doors were not closed in the face of the poor. Among them exists none who are...destitute." (This was not the only local challenge to the Church. A recent study revealed that the ancient Shamanic Craft was still practised among the communities of central Europe.[189])

In the 1400s the Taborites and Adamites of Bohemia believed in a similar religious socialism. They distributed goods according to need, but kept the means of production in private hands. In 1420 they declared: "Henceforth, at Hradiste and Tabor there is nothing which is mine or thine. Rather, all things in the community shall be held in common for all time. No one is permitted to hold private property. The one who does commits sins mortally...No longer shall there be a reigning king or a ruling lord for there shall be servitude no longer. All taxes shall cease and no one shall compel another to subjection. All shall be equal as brothers and sisters."

The Adamites believed in communal marriages and gender equality. They were lead by a man and a woman. Their practice of communal marriage died out among their followers in the late Middle Ages, but their practise of the communal ownership of goods was continued by the Hussites and by the Unitas Fratum movement among the Czechs. Goods were "neither mine nor thine" but for the common good. They held this was in the earliest Christian tradition. When their movement spread into Poland and Switzerland in the 16th Century, their members were attacked as "witches". Any unauthorised spiritual movement in this period was likely to have its adherents damned as witches; especially if they held their own rituals and were critics of the Church.

These traditions were hard to suppress. They continued to my own time. They inspired the people who inspired my wish, when working in the Catholic Church, to be a "worker-priest", committed to the poor and to sharing goods in common. Perhaps anyone with foresight could have seen that some day I would find myself outside the Church? The Waldensians, as the Cathars before them and the Hussites after them, were in the tradition of the more ascetic of the Gnostic Christians who flourished in Southern France in the dying days of the Roman Empire. Women were not universally barred from the ministry in these medieval spiritual movements but might serve as prophetesses or preachers.

The Inquisition was created to suppress these movements and investigate the related female-dominated Beguine movement. Later it was aimed at other religious "dissidents". It became particularly aimed at women who allegedly practised sexual magic. This would lead to the largest recorded peacetime slaughter in Europe. As witches and heretics they died horrific deaths at the hands of states and churches, both Protestant and Catholic. Both as a dissident who had followed her own conscience rather than the rulings of the church and as a Republican brought up as an Irish rebel, I felt a natural sympathy with these dissidents.

Inquiries into Witchcraft

I wanted to understand my roots, including the forces and spiritual ideas that shaped the society in which I lived. As a newborn woman who had lived in the heart of the Church, I was interested in the fate of women at the hands of the Church. Had the Church made up the witchcraft practices it had damned or had some of the persecuted really shared a widespread "witch" religious practice? Were other religious practises suppressed that should have been tolerated or preserved? I knew that Aboriginal elders had an animistic religion and practised magic, and that some of them were labelled by missionaries as "witches". Was this also true of my own ancestors? I was now on a shamanic path, albeit very much as a "maid" who was but starting, so wondered if some condemned in Europe as witches were the shamans of my people?

I had been delighted when I found shamanism described by academic researchers as "techniques of ecstasy"[190] for I knew my own practice as ecstatic. This made me wonder if I had instinctively found the shamanic path my elders would have set me on in earlier times? Great scientists recognise true theories by sensing their beauty, so I wondered, could the experience of an ecstatic bond with the Deity (or Deities) be a test for true religion?

Some theorists, such as Michael Hamer, said shamanism was not a religion. I could not understand this. Shamanism was based on an ecstatic relationship between the shaman and spirits or deities. For me my religion is such a relationship and from it grew religious actions, rituals, prayers and meditations. It is a religion that does not need a temple, book or clergy—or so I thought.

My knowledge of the modern European Craft reached beyond instinct when I chanced on people who called themselves witches on returning to live in Europe. I will describe this experience in my final chapter, *Sunday* but I will say here that I discovered that modern western witchcraft is an ethical mystical practice based on traditions with a very long history. But was witchcraft always thus, or did it once deserve its labelling as a danger-ous and harmful practice? Was its modern form a new development?

I am ever curious and ever a researcher. When I looked for evidence that my people had shamans I chanced across the work by Professor Eva Pocs entitled *Between the Living and Dead*. She concluded, after research-ing over 2,000 Central European witchtrials held between the 14th and 17th centuries, as well as associated oral history, that her earlier thesis that shamanistic practices preceded European witchcraft was inaccurate. She wrote, "I was forced to the conclusion that shamanism and witchcraft were coexisting or even tightly interwoven systems"[191] "that assumed each other and were built on each other"[192] and that both included mediatory techniques. "Contacting the supernatural [the spirit world] through trance techniques in order to accomplish community tasks was common among mediators connected with the system of witchcraft."[193]

My exploration of old ways did not mean that I had ceased to value all the reported teachings of Jesus. Some of these had shaped much of my life. However I was selective. The Gospels also contained texts that said little to me, such as the talk of sinners and of devils, or of women staying silent in Church, but these seemed to me to be on the periphery of the main mes-sage or later additions.

But questions over Biblical texts did not distract me from developing my relationship with God, using all that I had, mind, imagination and spirit. I had an image of this man and god I loved. He personified much that was rich and beautiful. As a child I usually called him Jesus, but he was essentially a person rather than a name. I had a relationship with him that was and is entirely personal. From him I learnt I was a Daughter of God, just as he was a Son of God. I saw myself as his happy colleague and lover. I travelled with him from the land of the religious hierarchy into the wilderness, not to be tempted, but to learn.

In my early years, my hermaphroditism[194] and my vocation to the priest-hood had seemed to be in direct opposition, I had to bury one to have the other. But now I started to see a pattern set into my life. It seemed that I might have landed on my feet in a predestined way. But to move forward I had to learn a different language, or rather re-learn a language that had started to come with childhood but had been overlain with Church.

I had learnt in the 1970s that shamans practised "magic". I did not share the Church's implicit dualism whereby saints did miracles with God's aid and others did magic with Satan's help. I experienced a natural world imbued with a "divine" energy that was there for all to use. Using this energy is "magic". Modern witches, such as Starhawk, defined magic alchemically as "the art of turning negatives into positives, of spinning straw into gold". Dion Fortune called it "the art and science of changing consciousness according to the Will." Underlying their practise was the belief that natural human mental or spiritual talents can effect real change in ourselves or in the world around us when used with confidence and skill. I also discovered that that we could work magically in conjunction with others in the natural world, whether they are Deities, spirits or humans. (I give examples later.)

There are many magical traditions in the West, but Norman Cohn in *Europe's Inner Demons* spoke of two main types, "High Magic" and "Low Magic". He said the "High Magic" of the 12th-15th centuries received its label because it was practiced by members of the Christian literate elite. He described how these magicians prepared with prayers, fasting and sexual abstinence for rituals designed to summon demons and to trap them into doing the magician's will. They saw themselves as Christians taming devils and would not hesitate to invoke the aid of Christ or the Holy Trinity. They sometimes tried to entice the demon into their trap with a pact or sacrifice. I have since learnt of more favourable descriptions or other versions of this magic. It seems that some in conquering "demons" were in fact seeking to conquer the faults within themselves by using magic.[195] One version in Renaissance times drew much from re-discovered Pagan Hermetic written sources.

But "Low Magic" was very different. It was more the old tradition of the countryside. It was based on a pagan animism that saw nature as alive and filled with spirits. It relied more on instincts and less on books. It seems to underlie much of modern Western Paganism as well as the modern Christian "creation spirituality". It was also more akin to the practices of Australian Aborigines who drew for their magic on the strength of the earth.

I felt Aboriginal magic belonged to the beginning of all religion, to its maiden time, and, for me personally, to my maiden time when I was first exploring life as a woman. What I learnt from Aborigines would help me later when I worked with those who drew on my people's oldest traditions. Some of these said they were witches. This did not deter me. I was aware how the Church had damned witches, but I knew that sometimes it is the truth that is tarred as dangerous.

Aboriginal Magic

The years I worked with Aborigines coincided with my first years of living as a woman. It was thus a very special time for me. As my work with them extended over years, I became more and more immersed in the magic that lived in their land. I worked, stayed and travelled with Aborigines both before our journey as a family to Europe and after we returned some three years later. I learnt, not by joining in Aboriginal rituals or being initiated by them, but by simply being with them, travelling with them through thousands of miles of bush, forest and desert, eating together, sharing in their fight for their land. This taught me to be sensitive to the energies within the vast ancient landscape of Australia. It was not my continent by birthright but it was part of the earth that birthed me. I fell in love with Australia's vast wilderness as I got to know her better

A brilliant anthropologist, Diane Bell, has written extensively on Aboriginal women's magic. When we met in Alice Springs in the 1970s she was in the midst of her research and enjoying life with her two children in an Aboriginal community north of Alice. She seemed to get on exceptionally well with Aboriginal people. She also did well academically. She was appointed around 1999 Professor of Anthropology in Washington DC. In her work she told how Aboriginal women elders instructed her for years and took her, painted with ochre patterns from head to toe, with the "mothers" into many rituals. Before her work, Aboriginal women's magic was scarcely understood outside their communities.

She described one of its most common forms as "love magic." In the language of the Warrabri people in Central Australia this was "yilpinji" and practised by both genders although she wrote of the female practise, as it was more accessible to her. "Yilpinji is achieved through a creative integration of myth, song, gesture and design against a background of country. The circle, the quintessential female symbol, finds expression in the body designs, the rolling hands gesture and patterns traced out by the dancing feet...Ownership of myth and the rights to perform certain rituals provide the power base for the women's claims....In yilpinji the women [describe their social world and] attempt to shape their world."[196] For example, if a woman who wants rid of a husband because he is playing around, she may ask her group to perform yilpinji to help make him leave her. Yilpinji, love magic, is invariably based in the empowering link with land possessed by everyone in Aboriginal culture

Aboriginal women also work healing magic. This they might do by gifting the sick person with something that carries the healer's own energy. This could be a gift of blood, secretions from under the arms or tears from the eyes.[197] I learnt of the importance of "sweat from under the arm" from an Aboriginal elder in Mapoon in North Queensland. He told me he was most upset by the police burning clothes containing his sweat "from under the arm" when they burnt down his house. This loss more affected him than that of his house.

Senior healers, known as ngankayi, had the ability to remove foreign bodies from the sick person's body. (Western medicine calls its foreign bodies germs or bacteria). The ngankayi used ritual and magical tools to draw the foreign element from the victim with a holistic approach that encouraged the sick person to take part in the healing. There was also magic used for revenge. In central Australia the victim of an assault might keep a sample of blood from the aggressor to use it later in a magical attack. Aboriginal people believe that they live in a world full of Ancestral Dreamtime energy that could be used by the adept for good or hurtful purposes.

Diane Bell described the care and reverence with which women approached all their rituals. The senior women grease then paint the naked bodies of the participating women with ochre patterns that show their link with their country. They do this while singing gently and harmoniously of the Dreamtime. During rituals the women might hold up the sacred boards and dance with them. These were marked with sacred signs denoting their links to their country. Beforehand energy was sung into the boards until the paint itself was said to "shine". Their bodies, their dances, their chants and their boards, tell of their totem links to creatures such as the dingo as well as to their much loved country. The red ochre they use represented the power of life and blood. Through their rites they reaffirm their bond with their sacred land and their responsibility for it.

Once the ritual is over, the energy of the Dreaming is sung back into the ground, the signs of dancing feet erased and dirt thrown on the ground where the sacred boards have laid to nullify and ground the energy. The sacred boards are then rubbed on the women's bodies to remove the sacred signs and re-absorb the energy. They see this grounding as extremely important. Men and women had separate sacred rituals as well as shared rituals. The major themes and purposes of women's rituals are love, land and health.

Aboriginal women could decide to live independently of men in the women's camp or jilimi. This was located out of sight of other camps. Aboriginal men would never walk in sight of it. The women built for their camp a long snake-like building. It had on its northern side a large clearing known as the "ring place" or "business ground". Here Aboriginal women conducted rituals, displayed their sacred boards telling the stories of their Dreaming, and sometimes slept, especially when ill or in trouble. The ring place was also traditionally the place where female offenders were put on trial and disputes resolved by ritual means. The storehouse for sacred objects backed onto its eastern side. On the far side of this, to the east, it opened onto a bough shelter where the women made or repaired ritual objects, or simply chatted and rested while monitoring all activity around the jilimi. If any women approached the ritual ground, she had to stop and wait until she was signed through.

The elder women taught in the jilimi the Dreaming to the younger women and arranged ritual events. Women might go out with their children to gather and hunt from here, as from the other camps. As they moved through the country they would sing of the travels of the creating Ancestors and teach their children about the land and its Dreaming. All food gathered was first distributed among the women and children before any were given to the men.

Diane Bell noted that eminent male anthropologists, with no access to the senior women living in the jilimi, often had no understanding of the important place of women in rituals, and of the vital role they played in the principal male celebration, that of the ritualised rebirth through circumcision of the young men. This ritual could not be performed without the women participating. They could even bring it to a halt if they felt that the men were not performing it correctly.

Diane told how after many seasons of instruction she found herself "red ochred from top to toe and propelled into ritual action I had only previously observed from afar."[198] She was present at twenty or so male initiations and, over time, she took "all the major female roles". In being painted with red ochre, Diane had become part of an extremely long tradition.

But the Europeans are also an ancient people, even if we have forgotten much. We once also used red ochre for sacred purposes. Archaeologists found in central Europe statues of women covered in red ochre from the Palaeolithic period. These are some 18,000 to 20,000 years old. Ochred buried corpses were also found.[199] Red ochre traces were found on an image of a sleeping woman made of brown clay around 3,700BCE. This was found in the Thypogeum temple in Malta. Spirals were painted in ochre on walls.

Carl Jung, the psychiatrist, would not have been surprised by this commonness of ritual significance. He wrote that every human contains: "the mighty deposit of ancestral experience accumulated over millions of years...to which each century adds an infinitesimally small amount of variation and differentiation."[200] I believe that we access this not just by dreams but also by instinct.

A. K. Radcliffe-Brown, the first to hold a Chair of Anthropology in Australia, did not know of the business of the jilimi. He instead interpreted Aboriginal society according to the dualistic theories of Emile Durkheim. Not knowing of the secret ceremonies that celebrate a girl's menarche and only of the men's rituals, he saw initiated Aboriginal men as representing the sacred realm and Aboriginal women as representing the non-initiated profane world. Many anthropologists followed him in dismissing the women's spiritual work as just "magic". They thought their "magic" was without power because unconnected to the Dreaming! They said Aboriginal women had no religion.

A consequence of these theories was that Aboriginal women were unable in the 1980s to obtain the same protection for their sacred sites as was available to the men. Thus, when I went to visit the managing director of a mining company to tell him his geologists had trespassed on an Aboriginal women's Dreaming site to explore its diamond content, he immediately pulled from his bookcase a supposedly authoritative report that said Aboriginal women have no Dreaming sites. He suggested that I was being hoodwinked. Thus this very important women's Sacred Site was not protected legally. The women have since lost this to the Argyle diamond mine, which now extracts from it and the land around it some 40% of the world's gem diamonds. No serious compensation was paid and no royalties; although the elders said no money could ever compensate for its destruction. This women-only sacred site was dedicated to the barramundi, the Australian equivalent to the "salmon of wisdom" in my Celtic people's myths.

Around 1982 I had a magical time at Uluru in Central Australia, which Whites called Ayers Rock. On my arrival the local storekeeper offered to introduce me to the Elders. He took me across a patch of scrub to where the senior men were sitting in a circle on the ground under a desert tree. "Jani, this is the Chairman," he said pointing him out: "He will look after you." I later learnt this was a mistake. As a male he saw the males as the proper people for me to meet.

I walked towards these elders but stopped and sat when I reached the distance from them that desert etiquette dictates. It is a rule of privacy. I estimate it as the length of a reasonable front garden. An Elder then called out and asked my business. I explained and he invited me to come closer. I moved in half way. He then said that the women had been waiting for me. To my surprise I then heard a woman's voice calling: "Sister, over here." She was calling from a distant tree where a circle of women was sitting. No one knew I was coming so I was most surprised.

They waved, made space and warmly welcomed me. We talked, eyes sparkling. Then one said. "We have something to show you." They had me climb with them into the back of a truck parked nearby with its engine idling expectantly. We then drove towards the long red-grey cliffed monolith that dominated their horizon like an enormous hunch-backed caterpillar.

They kept clear of a small fenced-off area at the base of the rock. I later learnt that this had been fenced because Aboriginal men used it for sacred purposes. They invited me to walk single file with them up a path towards a cave that was partially concealed behind bushes. One woman started chanting to greet the spirits of the place. Another turned to me and said with a grin: "See that cave? It looks just like a vagina, doesn't it?" And with laughter we all drew near and sat down by its entrance. Here they regaled me with the stories of creation in this most appropriate place, stories many millennia old. It felt as if I was with the ancient tribe of Israel hearing its creation stories. As I listened, it seemed that Aboriginal women's magic was tied to a Dreaming that some would say went back much further than that of Israel.

They told me that this vaginal cave was sacred to women and could not be knowingly approached by men. But I saw no fence protecting the women's sanctuary; no warning like to those that had protected the male site. Tourists could freely enter and were doing so to other nearby women's caves. I saw white men, cameras in hand, ignorantly exploring them.

The women explained that their men had been able to secure Government protection for their sacred place because their Aboriginal Law allowed a man to tell a man where his sacred places were, and the men could thus tell male government officials of its location. But the women had lacked this opportunity; for the government had not thought to appoint a woman officer they could tell. They did not see me as bound by their restrictions. I could tell both men and women. Thus they wanted me to tell the world where were the sites that the women of Uluru wanted to be protected.

They then took me to two deep pools under these high golden cliffs. One was sacred to the Rainbow Serpent who slept within its depths. They showed me the snake-like markings it left on the cliff when it entered or left the pool. Such permanent waterholes are very precious to a desert people, but even more so here where they are linked through the Serpent stories to the creating and renewing energy of water and earth. Finally they took me into their birthing cave and showed me with much laughter, how to sit astride a most precious thing, a large central sloping rock which served them as their birthing chair.

They finally told me that I was to write of all these things, for they were relying on me to make public that the women of Uluru had sacred places as well as men. I felt extremely privileged. It had been utterly a day of wonder for me. I had also learnt how the women and men of the Central Australian tribes have two Sacred codes of Law, one for men and one for women. Both are of equal status and compatible. Both had their separate parliaments. Only when an elder had grey hair could she or he know secrets of other gender's Law.

In SE Australia, traditional society is differently organised. Men and women sit together on the same councils. This lent to some hilarity when Aborigines met for the first meeting of the National Federation of Land Councils in Alice Springs. Aboriginal women friends told me how the locals had presumed to organise separate meetings for each gender. The southern women refused. The Central men said: "We have always met separately since the Dreamtime." The Southern women replied: "We have met together since the Dreamtime."

This caused an immediate meeting of Elders at the end of which they decided that men and women would sit together to discuss the Law for the first time in the Centre for possibly thousands of years. But the Central Australian men remained uncomfortable. In the first meetings one by one some would leave "to have a smoke". My women friends regaled me with stories of the patrols they mounted to track down the men to persuade them to return!

A day after my visit to Uluru, an Aboriginal man took me in his utility truck past the smoothly eroded phallic shaped rocks of the Olgas, a range of hills west of Uluru. As we passed, he directed me to avert my eyes. The other women with me also put up a hand to shield their eyes. These rocks are sacred to males.

I had a sense that the sexual and sacred implications of caves and of tall slim rocks were a subject of much enjoyment and not a little fun among the local tribes of the Arunta and the Pitjantjatjara. The traditions were both respected and enjoyed. Sex was clearly fun and pervading the landscape. These were not a prudish people. Were our ancestors much the same? Did they laugh at the sexual implications of tall slim standing stones and fat squat diamond shaped standing stones? I hope so. Certainly the British Pagans of today note and much enjoy the implications at such facing stones in the Avebury stone avenue.

One day I was walking with Aboriginal women along a path on a beautiful wild part of the coast of S.E. Australia when they told me to stop and wait until the men had gone on ahead. Then they quietly told me that we were in an ancient women's sacred place. I asked did they want it protected and fenced, as had the women at Uluru? They said no, too many whites around here. If it were fenced off with signs saying this place is sacred to women, it would be disgustingly vandalised and the place desecrated. I sadly agreed.

But in the centre of Australia the women won their battle. As I had promised, I made public their need to get their sacred places protected. They probably also roped in other white women At Uluru today most of the women's sacred area is fenced off. The base of Uluru is recognised as mostly women's territory.

Tourists still climb the rock totally unaware of the sacred lands that lie below, and despite Aboriginal protests at this desecration. Uluru was returned to Aboriginal ownership, but only on condition that within five minutes of regaining their title, the Aborigines assigned rights back so their land could be used by the government as a tourist park.

Sadly a uranium mine was also part of the price charged Aborigines for recognising their ancient title to Uluru. In the 1970s the campaign for Aboriginal land rights gained support from the Australian environmental movement because Aborigines were refusing to allow uranium mining. I took part in the consequent massive demonstrations in Australian cities but was utterly dismayed when suddenly the environmental movement withdrew its support after the Government announced that it had won Aboriginal agreement to uranium mining. It turned out later that the government had deceived the public. It had secured the consent of only three or four Aborigines out of the thirty-two or more whose consent was needed and only won the consent of these few by threatening that, if they did not agree, the Aboriginal nations would not have any land rights at all, including to Uluru.

For me that day I spent with the women at Uluru was the most enormous of privileges, a day that I will never forget. Uluru makes Australia very special, for how many nations have at its heart a woman's sacred place enshrining the story of creation?

The whole of Australia is a cobweb of Dreaming Tracks woven in a shared mythology of the several hundred Aboriginal nations. These weave together many people of diverse languages, cultural customs and different skin and hair colour. These tracks are rich in energy for the Creating Ancestors, both male and female, once walked them while forming the land. Today the great creation sagas are re-enacted and renewed by the Sacred Boards that travel the same routes with their accompanying songs and dances, passed on from one community to another. The totemic animals, reptiles and birds also helped create these Dreaming Tracks. All these Tracks, all the Totems, all Aborigines, have their songs, dances, painted Sacred Boards and chants.

These tracks are not seen as confined to Australia. Some Aborigines said they sensed the dreaming tracks of North America when they first travelled there to meet the American Indians. In Britain some sense energy tracks that they dryly call "ley lines" and possibly straighten. Could it be that they are sensing a natural worldwide pattern of creative energy?

One day in the Kimberleys I showed a photo of Uluru to a group of elders. I naively asked if they knew it as it lay a thousand miles away. They laughed at this. One of them pointed at a distant hill. "Jani", he said, "our dreaming track (he named it for a totem) starts behind that hill and goes straight down there. We all know that place." I had exactly the same experience when I showed the same photo to elders in Darwin. They too had a Dreaming Track nearby that went to Uluru. I have since found out that there are Dreaming Tracks linking Uluru with Sydney Harbour and the site of Melbourne. These were not just ritual paths but also travelling and trading routes. An axe found in the Kimberleys was made from volcanic glass found near Melbourne. It had travelled over 3000 miles up the

Dreaming tracks. Tasmanian tracks had regular rest huts and water supplies for travellers.

Aborigines and Witches

As for Aborigines and "witchcraft", many Aborigines first heard of this word from missionaries who translated it into their language as "a worker of evil magic". Thus those who held fast to the Old Ways denied their spiritual work had anything to do with this horrid word. This was also true of other indigenous peoples. Some of the Sami, who traditionally herd reindeer in northern Scandinavia, honour their shamans while thinking witches evil.

The anthropologist Professor Robert Tomkinson, in a study of the Jigalong Aboriginal community of Western Australia, entitled: *The Jigalong Mob: Aboriginal victors of a desert campaign* (1974), told how Aboriginal people kept their religion intact despite the missionaries' efforts to suppress it. He reported, "the missionaries view the Aborigines as the children of the devil and the antithesis of Christian virtues". A 1901 Report to the Heathen Missions Committee of the Presbyterian Church in Queensland stated of their Mapoon Mission: "Where formerly Satan ruled supreme and kept his prisoners captive in sin, cruelty and superstition, the voice of prayer and song is being heard."

But I found in the 1970s that many Aborigines at Mapoon still prized what they sometimes called the "old ways". I found the same true in the 1980s in a remote Catholic mission run by Benedictine monks at Kalumburu in the far north of the Kimberleys. I was there researching a program on Aboriginal spirituality for the BBC's "Everyman" series, but more about this later.

Mission staff worried about how hard it was to convert "witch doctors". A Presbyterian missionary wrote about two witch doctors living at Mapoon in the 1930s: "Awari, or better known as old William, is a witch doctor and rainmaker. The other is Namatu…Namatu's bearing is digni-fied…he takes a leading part in the midnight councils and is held in esteem by all. Under these circumstances it seems strange that although he has been greatly influenced by the preaching of the Gospel…he has never openly confessed Christ."[201]

Bell reported that missionaries at Philip Creek in Central Australia labelled women doing traditional "love magic" or yilpinji as "witches". Some Aboriginal men took advantage of this labelling to try to diminish the influence of the women while quietly continuing to do yilpinji them-selves.[202] Much the same may have happened in 18th Century England when male "Cunning Folk" found clients by suggesting they needed pro-tection from female witches".[203] Likewise in Africa, male witch doctors offered to protect clients against the evil magic of women. Yet, on closer inspection both men and women believed in and shared similar magic.

When I looked at the traditions I inherited as a Catholic child, I found "magic" was not done just by the heathen, but also by the "saints" who worked as healers and reportedly did miracles. Their endorsement by the Church did not change this. The source of their power was said to be their inner union with God and their love for others. It did not come from a Church edict. If they had power, I think it must have come from their union with a natural God joined with their own strength of mind or spirit. There is an extensive literature on their miracles, and on similar work by holy men and women in other religions.

This subject is bedevilled by translations. For example, I read that a worker of evil magic in Classical Rome was called a "witch". Yet the word witch is of Anglo-Saxon origin and thus unknown in Roman Empire times. The Anglo-Saxon word was probably "wicce", meaning a female "shaper" or "weaver" (as also in "wickerwork"), perhaps used for a strong woman who magically wove and mended, or shaped reality with her magic.

"Wicca" was the word for a male witch. Others say the word "witch" came from "wit" and meant a wise person, although this is truer of the word "wizard". Some scholars link together witches and shamans.[204] The word "sorcerer" is from the Latin word "sortiarus", meaning "diviner" or "lot-caster". Druid meant of the sacred oak and a worker of magic. Thus none of these names originally bore any hint of evil.

Aboriginal "converted" communities rarely change all their beliefs but pick and mix what they most like. Missionaries also adapted their message to gain more converts. This process among Aborigines has led to religions unlike any preached to them. This also happened among my own people. The converted Angle-Saxon and German nations retained so many pagan beliefs that their "Christianity" was transformed. In Germany and Ireland Gods and Goddesses were renamed as saints. Relics of saints substituted for pagan sacred objects in the working of magic. Augustine of Hippo used a special form of words to re-dedicate pagan objects as Christian. Christ became among 6th century Germans the supreme warlord who magically guaranteed victory, strengthening a militarisation of Christianity.

When I worked as a Christian priest, when I joined myself with my Lover God, did I ever work magic? I now think I sometimes did, although I would never then have called it magic. I did not only pray. I did not beg a God to do all the work. I felt him in me. We worked together. I used different words. It was inner energy. But my work on this level was purely instinctive. I received no training in working thus. If anything, my training hindered it. As priests we were told we could occasion miracles, such as turning bread and wine into the blood and flesh of Christ. But this did not happen because we were one with God. We simply said the words. God did the rest. We were told we were too weak and sinful to do more. We were not co-workers, more obstacles that God's energy swept past.

Pagan-Christian Magic

There is much evidence that after Europeans became Christians they continued to use their healing or fertility spells and even to honour their traditional Goddess by adding "Saint" to her name. They also used their old spells, adding invocations to the Christian God. (Since our knowledge of these mostly comes from Christian monastic records, it may have been pious informants or monks that first added Christian elements.) The traditional cures or "spells" were often holistic, seeking to cure, not just the body, but also the soul, by engaging the will of the patient in the work of healing. They combined herbs, sound medical and psychological knowledge with chants and rituals.

The Church had its own kind of magic based on a supposed link between the natural and supernatural world. "Relics" were supposed to have imbued the sanctity of a holy person, perhaps simply by being touched by his or her body. The pious often believed that touching such an object brought blessings from the supernatural world. The Church used relics to "Christianise" former pagan sanctuaries. Pope Gregory I instructed missionaries in England in 601CE; "The idols are to be destroyed but the temples themselves are to be aspersed with holy water, altars set up in them and relics deposited there."[205]

The following is an example of a complex merging of my people's traditions. It is an Anglo-Saxon field blessing from around 1000CE.[206] A field was to be blessed to increase its fertility. Four sods were taken from it at night and soaked in oil, honey, yeast, holy water and the milk of every female animal that was to be kept in it. A fertility invocation was then said, half in Latin and half in Anglo Saxon. The sods were then kept in a church while they were soaked in more good energy by having four Masses said over them. The sods were then returned to the field and a prayer said to the East, the Christian direction.

The next step was for the farmer to obtain unknown seed from beggars, paying them generously. He then put on his plough incense, fennel, sacred soap, salt and finally these seeds. Over this he said an old blessing, including the words:

Erce, Erce, Erce, earth's mother,

> May the all-ruler grant you, the eternal lord,
> Fields growing and flourishing,
> Propagating and strengthening,
> Tall shafts, bright crops,
> And broad barley crops
> And white wheat crops
> And all the earth's crops…
> Be well Earth, mother of men!
> May you be growing in God's embrace,
> With food filled for the needs of men.

Magical practices received a boost in the 14th century when an influx of mostly pagan "gypsies" arrived in Europe out of the East. Some came via Egypt and thus the misnomer of "gypsy". The influence of the Roma (a name they call themselves) in medieval Europe is often underestimated. Roma talents in divination or spell craft were much in demand. A Romany word for Wise Woman "Shuvihani" once had much the same meaning as "Witch". She knew the rites and rituals for such occasions as weddings and baby blessings as well as of spells and herbs.

Indigenous European Witchcraft and Shamanism

The Roma arrived in a Europe in which an indigenous witchcraft still survived. A strong shamanic tradition of witchcraft was still present in Central Europe between the 15th and 17th centuries—and possibly after this period.[207] Eva Pocs found a widespread uniformity in witchcraft testimony over several countries and centuries. She concluded that the witchtrial evidence about the Sabbats or witch gatherings was "undisputedly" not invented by the prosecution unlike the evidence about the devil—he was only mentioned after torture. She suggested that

Central European witchtrials perhaps were less influenced by devil-centred Church imagery than those of Western Europe.

In the shamanic tradition recorded in statements to these trials, people passed to and from the Otherworld in trance, dreams and visions, foretold the future, rode with the Wild Hunt and communed with the dead. Pocs saw no sign of these practices ceasing at the end of the period she studied.

The meetings of witches were described as "merriments", a word that seems to fit comfortably with having an ecstatic path and a lover-god. (The word "sabbat" came, I am told, from anti-Jewish prosecutors.) In medieval records, these gatherings were happy occasions, where there might be dance and music, where great flags of silk or fine embroidery were flown, where the witches believed they met with fairies or nature spirits and learnt of herbal cures and the art of healing. Mircea Eliade documented how the ancient European belief in faery societies went together with a belief in witches' gatherings and were expressed in rituals.[208] Communication with the spirits was through visions and sometimes the rituals.[209] Some gatherings may have been real meetings, but many were individual journeys undertaken through trance and ecstasy.

The following is a witchtrial account of a trance journey. Midaly Antal "lay dead for eight days while she was taken to God in the Otherworld. Once there she was among great joy and hospitality and had a delightful time. However she returned because God sent her to remedy and heal."[210] Eva Pocs reported: 'the most important role that can be detected from the witchtrials was that of the healer."[211] She estimated that among the half or more of the accused who were healers, some were "charismatic healers who maintained a ritual connection with a supernatural fairy world". She noted that these were also to be found in 20th century Ireland.[212]

As for accounts of witches engaged in 'black magic', Pocs concluded that the accusations brought against magic-workers were "generally positive magic being interpreted as maleficium [evil-doing]."[213] Other cases grew out of the imagination or ill will of the accuser.

Carlo Ginzburg also documented the shamanic aspects of witchtrial testimonies. Many of the accused spoke of "flying", which he saw as a typical shamanic explanation of spirit or trance journeys to the Otherworld.[214] Pocs noted that some said that they flew as eagles or were carried by the wind to the Witches' meetings. Margaret Murray noted in witchtrial records before the 16th century, the accused travelled to these meetings by normal means. Pocs suggested that perhaps after the 16th century real meetings became more difficult, or perhaps the concepts of witchhunters were intruding.

Pocs found that the accounts given of witch practices and beliefs were very similar in Britain and the continent, despite torture not being quite as hideously applied in England as on the continent. Although many of the accused were hapless victims, many were also young, strong, good looking and proud, not the hags of popular mythology, and certainly not helpless old women. Some were well educated. The Jesuit Friedrich von Spee recorded that the victims of the trials included many of the literate elite. Many of the victims spoke in shamanic terms that would be better understood when ethnographers had recorded the words of shamans in remote areas of Russia and northern Scandinavia, where the oldest forms of Eurasian religion survived. The accused spoke, as did these shamans, of spirit journeys that took them across the land and into underworlds, of flying, dancing and ecstasy. This was not a language taught by the Church.

Catholic authorities thought the resistance to torture shown by women accused was so extraordinary that it must be due to help from the Devil or from other witches. (It has been suggested by some witchcraft authorities such as Doreen Valiente that herbalists may have provided painkilling preparations.) The Catholic Encyclopaedia, in its entry on Witchcraft trials, said the most surprising element was that many women who had not been tortured still maintained that they were witches even when on the scaffold. They did not beg for mercy or "repent" but declared that they treasured their spiritual experiences in the Craft

Von Spee wrote of the German trials he witnessed, "many died under enormous tortures, some are crippled for life, many are so torn that when they are beheaded the executioner does not dare to bare their shoulders and expose them to the people. Some have to be hurried to the place of execution lest they die by the way."[215]

It seems that the study of witchtrials reveals far more than the misogynist hang-ups of men and invented evidence. The testimony of the accused cannot be entirely discarded as the products of wishful thinking, as some historians have suggested. It may well be many testimonies reflect a widespread country-based animistic spirituality and an instinctive shamanism. By "instinctive shamanism" I mean a relationship with the spirit world gained from following instincts and visions. Among the Arctic tribes, shamanism was always understood as a talent discovered within oneself, with the help of tutors perhaps, but not learnt from any book.

Witches and the Goddess

My European ancestors may thus have had a witchcraft inheritance, but how long did they retain a Goddess heritage? Church sources report that between the 9th and 13th Century a "vast" number of European women were involved in a pagan cult within the "Christianised" nations that involved magic and the worship of Diana, a Goddess of witches. The mention of Diana suggests that it was thought to be a cult that had continued from pre-Christian times.

As for the stories of the flying witch, these Goddesses and their followers were often said to fly, which again may reflect shamanic practices and descriptions of trance and spirit journeys. These flights were associated traditionally with blessing the countryside and not with evil magic. The Goddesses were Queens of Nature, and were accompanied with their own "wild hunt" of animals, birds, spirits of the dead and living women. This was not a scary hunt but one welcomed all over Europe with gifts of food and drink left out by households who desired them to visit to bring a blessing. The dead who took part were honoured ancestors. It was "wild' because wild creatures participated and because of its merry energy.

These beliefs are recorded in several documents, but most famously in a Church report entitled *Canon Episcopi*, dating from around 900CE. It was incorporated into Church Law around 1140 and repeatedly issued in various forms until 1310, so presumably in the 14th Century the Diana cult continued. It stated: "It is also not to be omitted that some wicked women, perverted by the Devil, seduced by illusions and phantasms of demons, believe and profess themselves in the hours of the night to ride upon certain beasts with Diana, the goddess of pagans, and with an innumerable multitude of women; that they in the silence of the dead of the night traverse great spaces of earth; that they obey the commands as of their mistress and are summoned to her service on certain nights. But I wish it were they alone who perished in their faithlessness and did not draw many with them into the destruction of infidelity. For an innumerable multitude, deceived by this false opinion, believe this to be true, and so believing, wander from the right faith and are involved in the error of the pagans when they think that there is anything of divinity or power except the one God."[216]

The Bishop of Verona complained in the 9th century that a third of the world were worshipping the Goddess Herodias·[217] John of Salisbury around 1150 stated that she was still being honoured in France at joyful gatherings: "they assert that a certain woman who shines by night, or Herodias,…summons gatherings and assemblies that attend various banquets. The figure receives all kinds of homage from her servants…"[218]

There were other ancient and pervasive European legends of Goddesses who travelled the sky at night, blessing the earth, accompanied by a procession of the departed, wild creatures and women. In Germany this blessing journey was lead by the Mother Goddess Holda. Her winter travels brought fruitfulness to the land and to the families she visited. Babies were said to come from her. Food and drink were left out at night as a ritual gift to these visiting spirits. The Goddess (St) Brighid was similarly honoured in Ireland. It was widely believed that on her feast day, Imbulc (February 2nd), she visited virtuous households and blessed them while they slept.[219]

Woods and groves were associated with this practice. A 13th century bishop of Paris, Guillaume d'Auvergne, "heard of spirits who on certain nights take on the likeness of girls and women in shining robes, frequent woods and groves and visit and enrich homes led by Lady Abudia or Satia, if food and drink is left out for them."[220] In Sicily such stories were believed in the 20th Century, according to Norman Cohn. He reported that they still told of "ladies of the night" who entered well-ordered houses through keyholes or cracks in the door. These were guardian spirits, not destroyers.[221]

Why did these stories mostly involve women? Miranda Green, an eminent writer on ancient Celtic Culture, in her book *Celtic Goddesses* stated: "the presence of humans was required by the spirit world to undertake a particular task...It may be that women were, like animals, perceived as appropriate mediators between worlds, maybe because they were deemed especially close to the natural world."[222]

Cohn concluded his study: "from all this there emerges a coherent picture of a traditional folk-belief. Its origins seem to lie in a pre-Christian, pagan world-view. It is certainly very ancient; and, despite certain variations of detail, it has remained constant in its main features over a period of at least a thousand years and over a great part of Western Europe. It is concerned with beneficent, protective spirits, who are thought of above all as female, and who are sometimes associated with the souls of the dead." He added: "And this age-old folk belief can be brought into relation with equally ancient beliefs about witches. In both cases, we find that women are believed, and sometimes even believe themselves, to travel at night in a supernatural manner, endowed with supernatural powers by supernatural patrons."

It seemed to me that these traditions had somehow helped shape the spirit of modern witchcraft. Recent books on the Craft reflect this Goddess magic, but few say from where it is inherited. Perhaps it emerged from such hidden corners of passed-on wisdom, or perhaps from a deeper inheritance, emerging from our unconsciousness?

The legend of "Father Christmas" took over from these old myths. It is now a man, not a woman, who travels the skies accompanied by reindeer, rewarding good families, gaining entry into their homes by coming down chimneys and for whom cakes and drink are left out. The witch is still said to fly the sky but now few know the traditional purpose of her journey.

It was suggested by Cohn that the image of the flying blessing woman was tainted in medieval times by being, perhaps deliberately, confused with that of the Strix of Roman times. This was a hideous bird or harpy-like creature. Pliny the Elder and Ovid said it flew at night and lived on humans. Ovid said it ate babies, but could be warded off if a wand of whitethorn were placed by the window and it were offered a young pig's entrails. Petronius claimed the strix could rob a man of his virility by eating him from inside. There may have been overtones in this of a Dark Goddess, similar to the Indian Kali, the mother goddess who ruled over death.

The Romans also had stories of "witches" who shape-shifted into the form of birds. Pocs reported that these were still present in medieval Europe. She saw such stories as describing a shamanic Craft that "flew" in trance, shape-shifted and worked with the dead. Shape-shifting was a common feature in witch, druid and shaman traditions across Europe. Ovid said the witch hag Dipsas knew the magic of herbs, could destroy the chastity of the young, conjure up the dead and fly in the form of a bird. Apuleius in *The Golden Ass* spoke of the witch Pamphile, who with a magical drink of laurel and dill, turned herself into a bird and was always after young men. Women who practised sorcery and could fly were called by Festus "strigae".

It seems that these stories of strix and strigae merged in the Dark Ages. The earliest surviving Germanic legal code, the 6th Century *Lex Salico*, stated, "if a stria shall devour a man, and it shall be proved against her", she should (only) be fined. The code also set a fine for a false accusation. The 634CE Lombard Law, the last of the Germanic codes, stated: "let no one presume to kill a foreign serving maid or female slave as a strega, for it is not possible, nor ought it to be at all believed by Christian minds, that a woman can eat a living man up from within." Cohn believed the medieval persecutors of witches drew from these confused legends when they depicted the night flying woman as of evil character, as the eater of children and bringer of misfortune.

The Inquisition accused Waldensian women of using a flying ointment donated by the devil to grease the sticks on which they allegedly rode to meetings on high in the French and Italian Alps. According to Eliade, mountaintops symbolise the centre of the world in shamanic traditions. Shamans frequently "flew" to this centre. (As for flying ointment, I have a sample of a hallucinogenic ointment made according to an ancient recipe by a German student of such matters.)

I would not however argue that a darker magic did not exist. Humans are quite capable of using their skills, telepathy, whatever, to try to hurt others. I have read of, but never witnessed, magical acts of vengeance in Aboriginal society. There is clear evidence that such magic was practised in Egypt in the first centuries of our era by the Coptic Christians, in medieval days by pious Christians as well as by village witches who might make a wax image of a person in order to send them illnesses or blessings.[223]

Old grimoires of unpleasant spells in Hebrew, Aramaic and Arabic were recently discovered in the "used paper store-room" or "Genizah" of the medieval synagogue in Cairo. University of Michigan researchers reported, "numerous medieval manuscripts in Greek, Latin, Arabic, and many other languages discovered here...attest to the vitality of such recipe-books throughout the Middle Ages."[224] This is a mild example of malicious magic from such a book.

Take bran of first quality and sandalwood and vinegar of the sharpest sort

And mould cakes. And write his name upon them, and so
hide them,
Saying into the light the name of Hekate and:' Take away
his sleep from so-and-so' and he will be sleepless and worried.

This spell invoked a pagan Goddess but Coptic Christians and Jews
used this kind of magic and had "demonised" her. These spells were typically made by men. They inscribed "binding" spells onto lead tablets to
make women love them. Their spells presumed humans could order spiritual beings to obey them. They thus imperiously ordered a deity, angel or
demon, or perhaps the spirit of someone who had committed suicide, to
do their will.

Demonic Medieval Magic

But medieval Christian High Magic apparently went further, as I mentioned earlier. It wanted to enslave demons permanently. Many of its practitioners believed demon taming a suitable task for a pious Christian.
They argued that, since Jesus cast out demons, it was proper for Christians
to seek mastery over demons. They could not enslave good spirits or
angels as they belonged to God, but demons were OK. High Magic was
Exorcism Plus. They believed that to simply expel demons would be to
waste of a wonderful source of power.

Their practise could also be interpreted in a Jungian manner. The
demons mastered could be seen as our imperfections and bad habits.
Perhaps some practitioners did so interpret it, but many were reportedly
fascinated by the possibility of forcing a real demon to serve them through
invoking the name of the Holy Trinity. In 1267 Roger Bacon complained
about the numbers of Grimoires available on the techniques of demon
raising and high magic.

These men prepared for their demon-taming rituals rigorously. In their Grimoires they told of magical tools that were to be fumigated and consecrated while psalms were recited. According to Norman Cohn, these often included a sword, staff, white handled and black handled knives. When all was ready, they would try to summon a demon and trap it inside a glass jar or the jewel of a ring while invoking the power of Christ or the Holy Trinity. They claimed that this put the power of the demon at their disposal.

These rituals could involve a pact offered to the demon or a sacrifice to it. Michael Scot, the tutor of the child who was Emperor Frederic II, wrote for him a personal grimoire known as the *Liber Introductorius* early in the 14th Century. This primer gave the names by which demons could be summoned. It advised that sacrifice should be made to a demon before it was enslaved and imprisoned in a ring or bottle. It suggested this sacrifice could be human flesh taken from a corpse!

Although clergy tried their hands at High Magic, it gained powerful opponents within the Catholic Church. Thomas Aquinas believed it could work but taught that this was likely to lead to the demon gaining mastery over the magician. Aquinas charged that the practice involved apostasy, since the practitioner made a pact with the demon in order to secure its aid. In 1233 Pope Gregory IX ordered punishment for "Luciferians" accused of worshipping Lucifer. In 1258 Pope Alexander ordered the Inquisition to punish the sorcery that involved consulting demon. (This Pope also authorised the Inquisition to torture suspects.)

In 1307 the French Emperor Philip the Fair used the controversy over high magic against the powerful and rich Order of Knights Templars. Early in the morning of the 13th October he had the unsuspecting Knights arrested throughout France. Philip's ambition was to become both the supreme head of a new Order and the Emperor of the West. Some suggest that the Knights were linked to the more gnostic inclined Christians in South France. I have not researched this. But I think the major motives for their suppression was the Emperor's avarice and wish for personal power. On 22nd July of the previous year Philip had arrested

Jews throughout his kingdom, seized their assets and expelled them. He had proclaimed this as a great victory for the church, just as he described his action against the Knights Templar.

The Knights were then under the protection of the Pope, so Philip tried to discredit them by saying they worshiped the devil in the form of a stature, and of a black cat, and of engaging in ritualistic sexual orgies. When Pope Boniface VIII refused to endorse his actions, Philip threatened the Pope himself with charges of heretical devil worship. It seems he then arranged for the Pope to be kidnapped and put on trial.

The Pope was rescued but died shortly afterwards. So Philip put him on trial posthumously in 1310. Thus a dead Pope became one of the very first to be tried for high magic! The charge was that he had three demons, one of which he had trapped inside his ring. A monk testified that he saw the Pope engage in a Voodoo like ritual: "he saw how the Lord Benedict went out into a garden adjoining the palace, drew a circle with a sword, placed himself in the middle of the circle, sat down and pulled out a rooster and a fire in an earthen jar." He then saw the Lord Benedict "kill the cock and throw its blood on the fire" while reading from a book and conjuring up demons.[225]

Philip the Fair charged in 1308 Guichard, Bishop of Troyes, of using demonic witchcraft against Queen Joan. The Bishop allegedly employed a Dominican Friar to summon a demon, which instructed him on how to attack the Queen. He was to make a wax doll, baptise it in the Queen's name, prick it with pins and throw it in the fire.[226] The Emperor also produced twenty-seven witnesses who vowed that the bishop was the son of an incubus (a devil) who had slept with his mother. The bishop allegedly kept a demon trapped in a glass flask and another in the point of his cowl.

In 1317 Pope John XXII had the bishop of Cahors arrested for allegedly trying to kill him by poison and "maleficium" or evil magic. The Pope interrogated the bishop then had him tortured, scourged and burned at the stake with his ashes thrown in the Rhone. Other cases involved leading Italian and French families and clergy.[227] In 1320 it was reported to the Pope that ritual magic was being practised at his own court in Avignon. He then empowered the Inquisition to charge all practitioners of ritual magic as heretics.

A leading Anglo-Norman family was charged with high magic in Kilkenny in Ireland in 1324-5.[228] The accused included Lady Alice Kyteler, the banker William Outlaw and the cleric Robert of Bristol. The charge was using demons raised through sorcery to gain wealth. Alice was also accused of learning from demons how to make love potions, to have organised a heretical sect that sacrificed cocks to demons and to have slept with a demon called "Robin, Son of Art". A major motive for the action against her was probably the belief of her stepchildren that her riches should have been theirs. Evidence against her was forced from a maidservant who was then burnt to death. Lady Alice herself was rescued by relatives and taken to England.[229]

Trials of alleged high magic magicians were comparatively rare. In 1374, the Inquisitor of France wrote to Pope Gregory XI complaining that many clerics and others were invoking demons; but his jurisdiction over clerics was contested whenever he tried to proceed against them. He said most of men who practiced high magic seemed immune from prosecution.

Before the 13th Century most punishments for witchcraft were for isolated cases of "maleficium", or the working of harmful magic. Punishments were levied for the alleged doing of harm, rather than for simply doing magic. But from the 13th Century things began to change dramatically. Over the next 400 years a countless number of women were to be killed as witches accused of doing all kinds of magic, even healing spells.

Somehow acts of common or low magic became confused with acts of high magic involving pacts with demons. Cohn concluded in his book *Europe's Inner Demons* that the campaign "against ritual magic helped to produce the fantastic stereotype of the witch." He noted a pact with a demon, a feature of high magic, became after the 12th Century the main charge against alleged witches, despite low magic having no place for a pact with the devil. It could be that church scholars and Christian judges, taught to look for the hand of the devil, well acquainted with "high" magic, framed their charges against witches in the magical terms with which they were acquainted. Cohn gave examples of how women of low social status had their "confessions" formulated in court in the terms of ritual magic. But Cohn's theory does not explain why charges against high magic magicians were relatively rare and why charges of working with devils were nearly entirely levelled against women who had no association with high magic.

Professor Eva Pocs noted that: "in the first century of the hunts there was no mention of the devil at all in the narratives about the witches sabbat" and that the judges asking, "When did you pledge yourself?" alluded to commitments to witchcraft groups, not pacts with the devil.[230]

But there was another quite separate reason for specifically linking women, the devil and witchcraft. It lay in the teachings of the great Christian "Angelic Doctor", St. Thomas Aquinas, who taught in 13th century both that women were naturally inferior to men and that all true Catholics must believe that there are female witches who practice a demon-assisted sexual magic.[231]

Witchcraft and Male Paranoia

Behind the persecution of women as witches lay an ancient male paranoia that fed on the belief that women could work a magic that could not be controlled by men or Church. It was expressly and repeatedly said that women could use magic to thwart male sexual prowess. Some 400 years after St. Augustine taught that penises were made disobedient to remind men of the Fall, Archbishop Hinemar of Rheims in 860CE ordered women not to use magic to make men impotent.[232] In the 13th Century, another four hundred years on, church gatherings condemned sorceresses "who put spells on married people so they cannot engage in conjugal relations." These included the synods of Salisbury in 1217, of Valencia in 1255 and of Besel in 1434.[233]

These repeated prohibitions must also have had an affect on women. It would have strengthened their belief in the existence of a magic that could be used, if they dared, to impede male sexual prowess. Women were then so under attack from male theologians and preachers that they might have sought all the weapons they could get! And even without this motivation, we know from Aboriginal customs and other cultures that there has long been a belief in the ability of women (and men to a lesser degree) to use "love magic." It could serve them well as a psychological weapon and as a protection from forced sex.

In 1484 Pope Innocent XIII, who was then well known for giving his illegitimate children splendid Vatican weddings, so feared the influence of magical women over his sexual prowess that he appointed as Inquisitors two German Dominicans, Jakov Sprenger, and Heinrich Kramer. The Pope said he took this step because of reports that in the dioceses of Cologne, Mainz, Trier and Salzburg many women and some men were engaging in sorcery "to make the conjugal act impossible."

Church authorities theorised that witches and devils were able to control human sexuality because it was the most corrupted part of human nature, quoting in support the early Fathers of the Church. Saint Bonaventure (died 1274), a Franciscan theologian, taught "because the sexual act has been corrupted (though original sin) and has become, so to speak, stinking, and because human beings are for the most part too lustful, the devil has so much power and authority over them." He justified this by quoting the biblical book *Tobit* that Jerome had doctored to make it pro-celibacy.

The Inquisitor Sprenger was deeply devoted to the Virgin Mary, a woman and mother he believed to never have known carnal pleasure. He founded the Confraternity of the Most Holy Rosary in her honour. He was highly influenced by the earlier Dominican, St Thomas Aquinas, who ruled that Satan had control over human sexuality particularly because "of the loathsome nature of the act of generation, and because through it original sin is transmitted to all men."[234]

It is worthwhile reading Sprenger and Kramer's book *Malleus Maleficorum* (*Hammer of Evil Doers,* mistranslated popularly as *Hammer of the Witches*). It is a good way of learning from "the horse's mouth" just what was behind much of the persecution of witches. There were many similar books. Women must have greatly suffered from hearing constant sermons about their inferiority to men, their blame for the Fall and their peculiar susceptibility to temptation.

Sprenger and Kramer demanded the death sentence for all witches who caused impotence. Their views about masturbation also outdid the current anti-abortion extremists. They saw both the masturbator and the abortionist as committing murder. Masturbation murdered by not putting the children (the semen) into "the ordained vessel", the vagina. They justified this by quoting St Thomas Aquinas. They went on to rule that all acts of masturbation deserved the death sentence.

They used mock science to justify saying women were inferior to men, declaring: "there was a defect in the formation of the first woman, since she was formed from a bent rib, that is a rib of the breast, which is bent as it were in the contrary direction to a man. And since through this defect she is an imperfect animal, she always deceives.... All witchcraft comes from carnal lust, which in women is insatiable" Their book went through nineteen editions and was a text used for witch-trials.

They justified their views with extensive quotes from the Fathers of the Church. It was as if these had lived only a few years earlier, rather than a thousand years before. The Fathers' theory that women were more susceptible to temptation was used to explain the alliance women made with the devil in order to gain power over the penis. Surprisingly Ronald Hutton, who wrote much of value on the pagan history of the British Isle, exonerated the early Church from all blame. He wrote: "Certainly the early Church cannot be held responsible for the mass burnings of heretics which commenced seven centuries after its installation in power or the great witch hunt that commenced eleven centuries later."[235] He overlooked that those responsible often relied on the misogynist authorities of the early church.

Women were said to be practising witchcraft when they "charmed" men and inclined "the minds of men to inordinate passion"[236] (Thus if a man raped a woman, he could claim she was to blame because she had "enchanted" him.) We still use the words the witch-hunters used when we speak of the power of a beautiful woman. A glamorous woman is casting an illusion or "glamour". A beautiful woman is said to "enchant", "charm" and "bewitch" us. These words relate to the natural magic of sexuality, but in the medieval period Churchmen said that it was not her beauty that attracted, but her use of diabolical magic. They thus never needed to acknowledge any woman as more talented or spiritual than they. If a woman seemed superior, she must be literally bewitching them.[237]

The authors of *Malleus Mallificorum* said they were very grateful they were not women. They thankfully prayed: "Blessed be the Highest who has so far preserved the male sex from so great an evil." These authors acknowledged that women had a particular natural talent for using the powers of nature in their magic. They agreed that witches could do wondrous things without supernatural help for "the most extraordinary and miraculous events came to pass by the workings of the powers of nature."[238] They stated witches cannot operate "except through the medium of the natural powers"[239] but added that, as women were weak, they could only do major acts of magic by putting themselves under the command of (male) devils.

They thus saw a pact with the devil as an essential part of witchcraft. This attitude was modified in more recent Catholic teachings. The *Catholic Encyclopaedia On-line* defined witchcraft magic as "the production of effects beyond the natural power of man by agencies other than the Divine." This 1999 definition still relied on the existence of a supernatural world separate from nature, a distinction not accepted by modern "witches" who see magic as entirely based on nature.

But, as we have seen, the separation of Catholic Christians from "nature" goes back to the early days of the Church when it even made nature spirits into demons. A work of great influence was the *Book of the Watchers*. This was written during the Maccabean War in late Old Testament times. It is full of stories about fallen angels. One of these tells how some angels violated the divine order by mating with human women, generating all manner of evil giants and demonic spirits.[240] This book could well have helped inspire the stories of witches mating with demons.

Incinerating Female Healers and Midwives

The authors of the *Malleus Maleficorum* particularly targeted midwives. A question that excited them was why "the witch-midwives exceed all other witches in deeds of shame".[241] If a baby was stillborn or aborted, they said the midwife present might have killed the child to steal its soul. This they based on Augustine's teaching that unbaptised babies belong to the devil. They also accused midwives of dedicating children to the devil. These charges led to the deaths of many midwives by "incineration", the word used by these authors.

In the High Renaissance period, even alleviating birth pains brought midwives into conflict with a Church that preached that women had a duty to suffer pain in childbirth as a punishment for tempting Adam. In Cologne nearly all the city's midwives were killed as witches between 1627-30. The Jesuit priest Spee wrote of these witch trials: "Thus I have to confess that in various places I accompanied a good many witches to their death, women whose innocence I have just as little doubt about even now as I expended every effort and enormous diligence to discover the truth…but I could find nothing but blamelessness everywhere"[242]

The Inquisition gave the "Medical Doctors" trained by the universities and sanctioned by the Church, the power of life or death over female healers and midwives. If any woman was accused of 'healing' before a witchcraft tribunal, the presumption was that she had cured through witchcraft. But to be doubly sure, the authors of *Malleus Mallificorum* said that the question should be put to a "Qualified Medical Doctor". If he said she had cured through witchcraft, then she would die.[243] As women were not allowed to study in the universities, there were no "qualified" female doctors. This then presented an easy way for a doctor to get rid of female rivals. Churchmen were concerned about the prestige won by women through herbal knowledge and healing work. Some believed that cures should only be sought by drawing on the power of the Church's relics, chants, prayers and holy water.

As I have mentioned, Eva Pocs noted that about half of the accused were professional healers who prescribed herbs and other remedies and used healing blessings or rituals.[244] The image we have today of the "witch" boiling ingredients in her cauldron is that of the medieval woman healer as well as of the cook. The cauldron of the healer was celebrated in many a chant of the bards and druids. It was called the "cauldron of regeneration" and "of inspiration". These women and men possessed knowledge accumulated from the keen study of nature over many generations. Among the drugs they discovered were ergot used to relieve pain, belladonna to regulate contractions and prevent miscarriages, and digitalis for heart complaints. Derivatives of these still play a major role in modern medicine.

Sprenger and Kramer, as you might guess, ignored any female medical achievements and instead put a blind trust in male doctors. They recommended using them for cures for witch-induced impotency. "Although some of their remedies seem to be vain and superstitious cantrips and charms [for] everybody must be trusted in his profession."[245] The operative word here is "his". No such trust was extended to female midwives and healers, unless one was a bishop and thus presumably capable of resisting a witch's magic. They noted that a bishop could gain a dispensation to allow him to go to a witch to have removed an illness inflicted by another witch, and that witches offering to do such magic were so common that they could be found "every German mile or two" along the highways.

Sprenger and Kramer quoted a ruling of St Thomas Aquinas supporting the belief in the existence of witches with power over human conception. Aquinas stated this was an inspired Catholic doctrine so certain that denying it would be a heresy! A provincial synod held in Lombardy in 1579, under the authority of a man later 'sainted', Charles Borromeo, imposed penalties against sorcery that impeded conjugal intercourse. The Synod of Naumur in 1662 renewed such laws "because we know that every day marriages are thrown into confusion by enchantment."[246]

The Roma or Gypsies brought to Western Europe their traditional medical knowledge when they arrived between the 14th-15th centuries. These Pagan nomads were of North Indian origin and well known for practising magic. They reportedly still have "love knot" spells. A version of this was to tie knots in a cloth while concentrating on the person one wanted to bond with, then wearing it for a day before giving it to this person as a love present. Young girls would make clay beads in which they would mix their first menstrual blood. This was a charm against pregnancy. They kept them safe until when they wanted to get pregnant. They would then take them to a stream, toss them in and wish for pregnancy as the beads slowly dissolved. All such charms were aids to human will. It is not hard to imagine versions of these same spells designed to protect a woman from marriage or pregnancy.

Montaigne wrote in the 16th Century of knot magic: "people are no longer talking about anything else."[247] The Jesuit Professor of Physics in Palermo explained: "No other kind of magic is more widespread and feared nowadays. In some places married couples no longer dare to be married publicly in church before the pastor and witnesses but they do it at home the day before and then go to church on the following day."[248] The Church officially allowed marriages to be dissolved because of magical spells that stopped consummation.

But there may have been something behind this apart from the fear of women. I strongly suspect that some women may well have used magic, or the fear of magic, to impede forced weddings and frustrate male sexual power. But the cruel result of these unbridled male fears was that even during the Renaissance thousands of women burnt while Shakespeare wrote and Michelangelo carved.

Hutton concluded in his own study; "that it is now obvious that the main force in driving the persecution was pressure from the common people who genuinely feared and hated witches". I would query this, but if true, he did not explore why this fear was so strong and violent.[249]

Although more died by sentences imposed by state or community courts than by ecclesiastical courts, it was the preaching of the Churches that incited the civil slaughter and the lynching. (With the exception of the Basque region of Spain where an Inquisitor stood out against the persecution of witches.) The killings were whipped up and reinforced both by the doctrinaire chauvinism of clergy and by the Churches attempts to monopolise spiritual authority. During the period of the Reformation this persecution was worse whenever and wherever the Churches felt most insecure.

Thus over a period of several hundred years pious men had used a myth to explain away their own neurosis and hang-ups. It justified them blaming, torturing and killing many women and some men, including healers, mystics, practitioners of magic and those who held onto old pagan religious belief. This the pious men did in the name of religion and of all that is holy.

Yet I think the persecutors were right in a sense when they said women are closely linked with nature and have some power over both conception and male sexuality. The persecutors admitted this female power was based on natural powers. But they added it was sometimes aided by the devil. These misogynists then damned women for exercising their power. I saw this natural power as a blessing and a strength women could take pride in. Thus I liked what I had found when I at last sat among my sisters in my destined place, as perhaps a fresh-eyed, wild and uncommon element in a female world.

But none of this made it easier to bring up children. I will now tell of the adventures, frustrations and difficulties of trying to bring up my much-loved children as a most unusual parent.

Friday

The Mother Aspect of the Goddess

My parenting was always full of apparent contradictions. I was a female father, whom my children knew only as a woman although I had created the seed that fathered them. This may have made life difficult, but I know that if I had transitioned earlier or not met Jackie, I may never have had children, nor had the delight of watching my daughters grow. It was our two wonderful girls that made me a parent. They helped forge me, sometimes with pleasure, sometimes with real pain. They taught me about the reality of being part of life's cycle. This book is dedicated to them.

As they grew up I saw how differently they treated males and knew that they had missed the fun and benefit of having a father in their lives. I knew what I would like to have had in my life. A Dad I could relate to as a girl. A Dad that I could have had fun with. A Dad I could have experimented with as the safe male in my life. If I had wanted this, then how much did my daughters want it?

I could only offer them something different, someone different, a parent born between the tides, a person nonetheless that loved them deeply. We were for them two parents that gave them a safe loving place to live. We enjoyed sharing our lives, despite all the pain experienced. This chapter is the story of how we tried to keep our promise to share with the children all we had while leaving them free to grow.

When we returned from Australia to England in 1976, we were tired but still shared the ideals that brought us together. We had only got this far because we loved each other and saw what we shared as very precious. We were determined to preserve our family, to continue to live together. Jackie and I also remained physically close despite all the changes. We remained lovers, finding other ways to give each other pleasure. I was bisexual, but I think Jackie was only so in the context of our relationship.

I both loved her and put her on a pedestal as my father did my mother. I was enormously grateful for her agreement that we could bring up the children together. I idealised her and probably did not see her realistically. I still think of her as a wonderfully talented and generous person. It took years before I learnt of how she had both loved and hated me. Loved me for what I gave, hated me for trapping her in a life that she had not planned.

There were aspects to our relationship that I did not understand until much later. I did not realise that our family relationship had trapped me in role behaviour that was formed by Jackie's needs and cultural expectations. I thus did many things that were expected of a father—but then again I too was in part shaped by socialisation.

The basic human attributes of masculine and feminine are naturally and usually connected to the reproductive functions of the genders. Males are usually predestined to want to be fathers, females to be mothers. We enjoy being gendered. Perhaps a gift that transsexuals have for society is that of helping to break the mould that always associates certain reproductive organs with certain parental roles. Science is leading the same way. Today fathers need not physically father. Mothers need not physically bear their children. Transsexuals thus have a symbolic value. They can stand for the power of individuals to define their lives, to value spirit over genitals; although like others, they enjoy being gendered in the gender of their spirits.

Gender does not determine sexual partners. This is wholly another matter. Jackie and I found we continued to enjoy going to bed together, at least on many occasions. We wanted to make each other happy and to share bringing up our children. These two wishes kept us together for many years.

When I started to write this chapter, I was not sure how to proceed, so I asked for inspiration. I then looked up and saw a heron flying past with heavy majestic wings assuaging the air on its way to feed its children. This gave me the thought that the beauty of nature's constant cycle of children was a sufficient reason for a chapter entirely centred on the beauty that grows rich and deep from the spilling of one's children out into the world. This process took up a major part of my life and enriched me. So here is my story of bringing up our children, as a woman who is Dad. This is not their story, for that is for their own telling.

I have told how we came to visit Francis's groves above Assisi. From here we went to the Renaissance city of Sienna, where once lived St. Catherine of Sienna, the namesake of both of our children. We named them after her because she was a strong-willed, mystically inclined woman, not past lecturing the Pope when she felt he had need of it. We went to visit her home with the children. Her *A Treatise of Divine Love* told of the mystic wedding, when God " shall be one with me and I with him". This she sought thorough love and through elevating over her own wishes what she saw as God's wishes. It was only later I learnt that an anorexic need to conquer her body drove her anxiety and penances, and that she gave to the church authorities much of the job of defining what was God's will for her.

Kara and Cathy saw Italian "flag-dancing" in medieval style processions in Gubbio. So, in honour of "their city" and their saint, these two small children danced in the great central square of Sienna with large splendid flags. Then we sat on steps in the square to eat a coiled-up snake-like cake. The children loved this place but my own feelings were more ambiguous. I knew that I was now further outside the institutional church than Catherine ever went. I could not see where my path was taking me.

Our family pilgrimage ended when the gearbox of our newly purchased minibus failed. We could find no one to fix it in the time we had. We spoke no Italian and the promised car papers had not come. We bought train tickets to England and abandoned the minibus in the streets of Turin with the keys in its lock.

A debonair brother of mine met us when we arrived in Folkestone, the town where he and I grew up. Kevin told me he had always wanted a `"big sister"! I had not realised he was so good looking. Cathy and Kara were so happy to arrive in what they had learnt was their ancestral country that they danced naked on the sandy beach.

Another old friend, Keith Kimber, now an Anglican priest in Bristol, welcomed us as dear long lost friends. He found us a house opposite his in a street filled with lively children of West Indian parents. By good fortune, a few months later, I obtained an international scholarship from a Geneva-based Church organisation to support me for three years while I set up support groups for Aborigines and other indigenous minorities. I had the resources; all I needed now was the people. But everything seemed to be falling into place.

However, Kevin was the only one of my childhood family to welcome me at first. My brother Tony told me that my gender change was too hard for him to adjust to quickly so he felt it best that we did not meet. It took us over a year to be reconciled (and we are now the best of friends). My brother Bernard was much younger than I, so I had not got to know him as we grew up and thus found him harder to approach. The life of my sister Maryanne was still very much centred on our parents' home and her decision I felt, perhaps unfairly, would be theirs.

I wrote to my parents to tell them the hard news that I was now Janine. My Mother's answer seemed to lack comprehension. She seemed unable to believe her dreams for me were not my dreams. I wrote again and again. She could not see that I was not her dream. She could not accept me, her iconoclast of dreams.

But later I came to see that in a sense she was instinctively right. She was so adamant because she saw my gender-role change as a barrier to the priesthood that she saw as my destiny. It would eventually be no barrier but she could not see this.

In the June of 1977, after a year had passed without my parents inviting me to visit, I decided that I should simply go and see them. I went to their flat by the sea near Brighton, taking a great bunch of flowers. I thought that if they saw me, they would better understand how natural it was for me to live as a woman. But it was predictably impossible. I remember sitting on the sofa very ill at ease as my mother and my sister tried to convert me back to male ways. I was offered a man's jacket. No harsh words were spoken but it ended with my father putting me, wet-eyed, out of the house giving me back the flowers I had brought them. He said he wanted to protect my mother from getting upset at my stubbornness.

This rejection was partly expected. I was more surprised and hurt by the rejection I suffered from others of my family. I knew it did not need to be like this. I knew of many whose gender-role transition was supported by their parents. These rejections reinforced in me a primal fear of rejection that went back to my childhood. I still bear the scars. I am still terrified by rejection, even while I try to overcome this fear by writing this book.

Jackie's fear that the news of my transition would kill her Dad proved thankfully baseless. He responded to her letter with great sympathy. He wrote that since the genders are so alike, it was surprising that there were not more like me. He asked, was there anything they could do to help us as a family? This was so refreshing after the attitude of my own family, that I wondered why we had fled Australia to such a harder world. But I understood why Jackie feared to tell him. Her parents lived in a world that she had rejected as her living place but which still drew her through blood ties and a sense of family obligation. I think she felt she needed to leave Australia to create a space where she would have more freedom to be herself and with me. Even if we had not left when we did, we would probably have returned later. I wanted to see my ancestral lands again and to be reconciled with my family.

Soon after arrival we travelled to Wales for a family holiday, where, in a tumbling mountain stream, we dipped our youngest child, red-headed, transparent skinned Cathy, with her strong Celtic looks, to unite her with the energy of her ancestral earth, to bless her and thank God for her. This was her own welcome rite; quite different from the party we gave Kara with its blessings from street people. As I have said, the difference between these rites was more to do with our changing lives and ideas than the difference between our children. Cathy's young skin however definitely did not like the Australian sun. She seemed to belong in these hills. At Christmas we rented a Welsh cottage so that they could experience their first snowy winter. They frolicked, snowballed and made snow angels

Kara started primary school in Bristol but she was very shy; unlike Cathy who was a confident social mixer at her nursery school. Jackie took on most of the care for them as my work to establish an Aboriginal support group network took me away from three to five days a week. I organised support groups for Aboriginal Land Councils in Geneva, Frankfurt, Bonn, Copenhagen, London, Amsterdam and Heerlen. I hoped my work would help put pressure on Australia to grant justice to its Aboriginal peoples.

I did not find it easy to start raising support for Australian Aborigines. I was first invited to speak on the plight of Australian Aborigines at a Welsh university. Three people turned up, yet over a hundred came to a meeting on the evils of apartheid. I went to the *New Internationalist*, a leading third world magazine. I told them how Australian Aborigines lived on average thirty years less than Whites, that British companies were still dispossessing tribes leaving their people without compensation and impoverished. I argued that colonised minorities worldwide shared the same fate. I met with a disinterested reception. I was asked how many Aborigines were there in Australia. I said around a quarter of a million. The man then yawned and said the *New Internationalist* had to deal with problems on a worldwide basis that affected millions. They had no space for such a local problem. Since then the magazine has had a change of heart. But this is how it was in 1976.

Few outside Australia then knew of the Aboriginal situation. We needed a book to educate people—and the charity War on Want gave us funding for it. I also found a partner, Roger Moody, an editor of Peace News. Roger also did youth work and cared for his elder brother, Peter, who had Down's Syndrome. When their mother died, Roger had taken over care for him. Their home in North London became my London base. It was a "licensed" squat, a house scheduled for eventual demolition that was temporarily lent to a housing association. It was also a crazy creative house of brilliant piano music where Roger worked miracles from broken instruments, and lived in a riot of children because of his youth work. The basement kitchen was always in confusion. A damp air of dissolution hung on the condemned walls. Documents clustered like colonies of bats in every available place. Fascinating people shared the house, and overall hung the brilliant concerned intellect of Roger, steadfast in working for many an endangered race and careless of a need for more than sustenance for himself.

Avebury Circle and an Aboriginal Elder

As I had to commute between London and Bristol, I took advantage of this to spend time with a very special sacred place that lay between these cities, the Stone Circles of Avebury. I trod the ancient avenue of standing stones to seek a better understanding of my heritage. I always felt at home there. I sung greetings to its stones. When an Aboriginal Elder, Mrs. Hyllus Maris, came from Melbourne, I took her to this spiritual centre. She lay her hands on one of the megaliths, stood quietly contemplating, then turned to me, her face radiant, and said: "Why did no one tell me that you have places like this in your country?" She was delighted to discover that we also were an ancient people.

Hyllus named our nascent Aboriginal support group, BARAC, the name of one of the famous elders of her people. BARAC also stood for the

Black Australia Research and Action Centre. I have found a poem of hers. This is part of it.

> I am a child of the Dreamtime people,
> Part of this land like the gnarled gum tree,
> I am the river softly singing,
> Chanting our Songs on the way to the sea,
> My spirit is the dust devils,
> Mirages that dance on the plains,
> I'm the snow, the wind and the falling rain,
> I'm part of the rocks and the red desert earth,
> Red as the blood that flows in my veins.[250]

Then unexpectedly, in August 1977, Jackie asked if she and the children could leave our Bristol house and come up to live in the two rooms available in Roger and Peter's home, a dishevelled house scheduled for demolition. Our Bristol home had only been rented to us for a year but we had been offered as alternative accommodation the nearby gigantic top floor flat of the Anglican Vicarage of St. Paul's. Jackie rejected this, even though it would have been much more comfortable, because she was uneasy about moving into the more settled routines of an Anglican parish and not happy with me being only with the children for three to four days a week. She feared they were becoming more bourgeois, more consumer-centred. I was reluctant to give up a place that had resonance of priesthood but I had my work in London and it would be good to spend more time together.

I was concerned that the London house would be too difficult, too crowded and too chaotic, but it was wonderful to be together and I loved Jackie the more for coming to live in this crazy poverty. It was in line with the principles we shared when we first met. It was as if we could transcend anything. We seemed to be getting on well as two women and as lovers, sharing ideals, spirituality and children while washed by a sea of visitors. And our two girls loved this slum house

The children's school was right behind our home. My diary recorded that "Kara at last comes out of herself at school and does very well. Cathy in town is less sure of herself…but is losing very quickly her consumerism". We had many wonderful visitors, many volunteers to do work on behalf of Aborigines. Roger also brought with him to this work his links to tribal peoples around the world.

Roger and Peter wrote a delightful book together called *Half Left: The Challenge of growing up "not quite normal"* which received a brilliant review in the Times Literary Supplement. Peter was not at all stereotyped as a person with Down's Syndrome for he had not been institutionalised. He modelled himself on his brother by organising his own careful research projects, not into issues of social justice but into horror movies. I remember being woken up by screams and rushing into Peter's room, only to be met by a sheepish smile. He was reading aloud a horror tale and had inserted sound effects. He identified with people seen by us as "monsters". Peter became close to me but closer to my partner Jackie. A score of years later Peter would still ask after her. They would both come out to visit us after we returned to Australia.

In this ramshackle house we had one large room and a smaller room for the children. The large room was our bedroom, sitting room and study. It was in this room that I wrote the book on the Aboriginal struggle for justice that War on Want was funding. It was to be called *From Massacres to Mining*. We planned to launch during a speaking tour of Europe by Aborigines.

In Copenhagen, our principal supporter was Professor Helge Kleiven, a professor of Eskimology, who founded an International Workgroup on Indigenous Affairs to document oppression and raise money for international gatherings of tribal people. He was the gentlest of men, with an old fashioned courtesy. But at one gathering, a young American Indian vented his frustration by denouncing "white" people "like Professor Kleiven" who made a good living from writing on their plight. The Professor sharply responded that his grandmother was a Sami and that his people had for millennia worked with the reindeer herds of the north. They still held onto ancient European shamanic traditions. The Indian made his mistake because the Sami are white skinned and blue eyed. But all of us who retain a spiritual bond with our ancestral lands have an indigenous inheritance, although most have forgotten this.

In Germany we gained help from the Society for Endangered Peoples. They invited me to address their conference and I was overwhelmed by their response and eagerness to help. They arranged to translate my book *From Massacres to Mining* into German. I also remember with some amusement how a leading member of their organisation thought me most female, simply because I had sat at his feet patiently listening to him. Yes, I had found it strangely easy to slip into a "female" role of being support- ive to men, to appear "female" by being non-assertive. I fear I found it tempting sometimes to give away responsibilities, to let men make deci- sions for me. I never had this option before. I experimented with it. I wanted the men to treat me as female, to like me as female. It was beguil- ing but only a rare experimental indulgence. Normally I was not this patient, this accommodating, this weak.

In the Netherlands it was a very different bunch of people that gave support. They were mostly old friends from before I married, with whom Jackie and I had co-celebrated our wedding mass on our way to Australia. They were not dismayed by my change of gender roles. They translated the Mapoon books into Dutch. The Aborigines that subsequently visited told me they felt more at home with them than anywhere else in Europe.

In London, Survival International and the Anti-Slavery Society gave us support as we founded our own organisation, which later became known as CIMRA, Colonialism and Indigenous Minorities Research Action. We had a penchant for academically accurate but verbose names. Everything we did was in consultation with the North Queensland Land Council and with other Aboriginal land councils.

While all this was happening, the children forced me to my most cre- ative efforts. I continued what was now a family tradition, making up and telling a fresh "Kathy" story every night. Kathy was a kid who ran the

"Children's Emergency Service." A distant aunt had given her a wardrobe that could turn itself into a Doctor Who-style "tardis". When it heard on the ether a cry of help, it woke Kathy by banging its door. She then grumpily, dragged on her dressing grown, climbed into the wardrobe, and went to rescue whatever adult, gnome or other creature was in distress. She had a friend and helper in these adventures that lived in a swamp behind the mirror in her wardrobe, Dino the Dinosaur. It stretched my imagination to the limit inventing on the spur of the moment a new adventure every night. I could not repeat an adventure; Kara and Cathy would not permit it. I think they still remember the stories today.

Proving One's Femininity

Also, quietly, in the backwaters of my life, away from my political work, I proceeded along the gender role reassignment path I had set for myself. (I do not say I changed gender, for I believe I always was female in the shape of my brain.) By 1977, after two years of taking hormones, these had done their work of adapting my body, but still some surgery was needed, or so I decided at the time although a nagging doubt dogged me as to its absolute necessity. The hormones seemed to have done their job fine—but it was socially dangerous for me to have such an archetypically hermaphrodite body and definitely very awkward sexually. At that time the only place in England that was willing to surgically reassign transsexuals was Charing Cross Hospital in London. The procedure there was that I should see for half an hour every month a certain elderly and eccentric psychologist, a Doctor John Randel. If after a year he felt that I was succeeding in living as a woman, he would recommend me for surgery.

The sessions with him were always shallow and somewhat strange but fortunately I was not going to him for help in untangling myself. They were simply for him to vet me. The first such meeting in February 1977 was what my diary called "a terrible grilling, deliberately provocative". I think his idea was that if I continued to see him after this, I would be demonstrating that my "condition" was not superficial. However I felt his criteria were superficial. In order to prove myself "female" during my visits to him, I had to put on my most careful and ladylike behaviour in a most old fashioned way.

In a sense, I was fulfilling the expected "patient's" dance for I wanted access to the mysteriously alchemic hormone pills. If I were to be prescribed these, then I was expected after a year or two to proceed to surgery. I recognised that surgery would make my life far safer. I lived with the fear that if I were arrested, I could be thrown into a male prison and raped. But I also knew that surgery would presumably allow me to have intercourse as a woman. This was an unknown territory that was somewhat fearfully desired. But while I was living with Jackie it was scarcely a problem. It was a potential problem only.

A hospital requisite for surgery was that Jackie and I got divorced. It seemed that doctors feared being sued by deprived spouses! We found that if we declared we had separate bedrooms for a long period of time, this was sufficient in English law to get a divorce on the basis of separation. So we filed for divorce and for joint custody of the children. Jackie and I were one on this. We had simply told the state when we married. We now simply told the state we were separating. It was not at all traumatic.

There was however one aspect of the procedure that scared us. We could not prevent our divorce being listed on the daily chart of the business of a court. As my name was now legally Janine, we would be listed as a divorce between two women and this we knew could invite the intrusion of nosy tabloids. But in the event, in 1978 the case was listed under our initials and no publicity was generated. English law was somewhat insane on this. The authorities issued me a passport as a woman, would mostly treat me as the woman I said I was and refer to me by a female name, but they would not allow me to marry as a woman, declaring that I legally remained the sex the doctors announced at birth. This was particularly odd when one thinks of how some children are surgically assigned to a gender prior to the issuing of birth certificates. In 2001, the only countries in Europe that refused to amend birth certificates were the UK, Eire, Andorra and Albania.

While all this was happening we had very children-centred Christmas seasons, taking full advantage of London. We went to three pantomimes one year. When we met with Peter Pan at a stage door, "the kids were jumping up and down with excitement". The Royal in Stratford, a wonderful East End traditional multi-tiered theatre, was a great delight, as the characters would race from balcony to balcony in a confusion of confusions.

In the harsher prosaic everyday world, we edited in our single room, with permission from its original producers, a shortened version of an early film called "Ningla-a-Na" on the Aboriginal struggle so we could use it to support the Aboriginal speaking tour. We took from it the story of the embassy tent that was erected opposite the Australian Parliament to bear witness to the nationhood of the Aboriginal people and to the indignities suffered by them.

RTZ and Aborigines

We did our best to put pressure on the major British mining company, RTZ, which controlled CRA, the biggest mining company in Australia. They effectively ran the Weipa mine where Aboriginal people were herded into a small reserve so that the company could more easily profit from Aboriginal land. It was ripping out hundreds of miles of the aluminium rich red clay from beneath a vast ancient forest that Aborigines still hunt-gathered. It contained many of their sacred sites. We raised funds to bring representatives of the local Aborigines to the UK for a speaking tour planned for mid 1978.

But first, in March that year, Jackie took the children back to Australia for a three-week holiday. She wanted to assure her parents that we were well. She told me that she was really optimistic that things would work out with her parents. With hindsight I think it likely that she was also starting to find a bit too much for her the pressure and crowding in our slum home.

I think it was while she was away that I saw the surgeon Mr Davies at Charing Cross. I had passed successfully the psychological assessment and had been recommended to him for the operation. He was a dried up looking character with no hint of sympathy about him. He came in, sat himself down and without taking more than a glance at me, told me to explain how my transsexualism developed.

I was most surprised by this. I thought he was to see me purely on physical matters relating to the surgery. Why was he re-assessing my psychological suitability? I wondered if he distrusted the psychiatrist. He wanted to know "how early it started being manifest" and the story of my life. He was particularly interested in my present relations with the children. Having established that I had married and was divorced, he asked if I had children. When I said yes, he asked who had custody. I said it was joint. He then promptly ended the interview, saying he would not operate on anyone that still looked after their children for it spoiled the children's sexual stereotyping.

I then learnt from the psychiatrist that there was hope that the surgeon's decision would be reversed, if I agreed to come in for a psychiatric consultation that would take just 10 minutes every two months for another year or more. He recommended that I be patient. But I knew that there was no way I was going to prove I was a worthy candidate for an operation by pretending to abandon my children. What woman would agree to such terms!

Anyhow, that put a stop to any immediate surgical plans, I did not have the money to look for private treatment. And there was no way that I would desert my children. No surgery with children so no surgery. I thought I was getting on fine as a woman without this operation. I simply had to make sure I avoided any occasion when intercourse was a likely outcome!

I wondered, would I have wanted surgery in a different society that did not require this operation before accepting me as fully female? I think I would have survived fine without an operation, as long as I could freely live as a woman, be recognised as a woman and have access to the oestrogen my body could not make. This supply would not have been a problem—many societies knew oestrogen-rich plants such as black cohosh with its slender stem and three pointed leaves. These hormones were especially important to me in the early days of transition. Today I find my body seems to balance itself. I am prescribed merely what an average woman has as an HRT[251] dose after menopause.

But at that time, I felt the surgeon had made my decision for me. Rather than continue with this hospital team, I would proudly but privately live with my hermaphrodite body. "Privately" because I could not easily reveal to lovers my wondrous body, with our society being as it is. I would not have sex with men who thought me male. My gender identity as female was essential to my lovemaking. What if a man had fallen for me who saw me as a woman despite knowing all about my body? At that time this seemed an impossible option. I simply focused on our family and my relationship with Jackie, despite being aware that I was constantly in danger. Without an operation, I was susceptible to being assaulted by those men who were affronted by me "pretending" to be a woman, as some of them would see it.

Today, over twenty years later, more in tune with my life, I would be happy to be the proud hermaphrodite; as long as I was not seen as gender neutral or as having both gender identities; as long as I was seen as a woman with a different body. I now understand why ancient cultures called their hermaphrodite Goddess "she" and did not use a gender-neutral pronoun. I know from experience how it is that one can be female without being female shaped. Without my experience of life, I might have thought this impossible.

In May 1978 our group CIMRA, with the support of War on Want, Survival International and Greenpeace, protested at the Annual General Meeting of RTZ in London against the action of its Australian subsidiary CRA in "targeting" Aboriginal Reserves. CRA had commissioned an internal report listing as "targets" in order of priority all the most important Aboriginal Reserves. The Aboriginal elder Birnum Birnum leaked this to us. He was then an Aboriginal employee of CRA. We used it to good effect.

The Chairman of RTZ, Sir Mark Turner, responded by saying that he would ask Lord Shackleton, the Deputy Chairman of RTZ, to investigate these allegations on his forthcoming trip to Australia. We had excellent press. The campaign was now truly launched. It is now a campaign that has lasted more than twenty years, serving the needs of nearly a hundred indigenous minorities around the world.

I also wanted a film made that would bring these issues to television screens around the world. We had seen a powerful documentary on apartheid made by a producer called Chris Curling. We felt it would be great if a similar documentary could be made to support Australian Aborigines. So I went to see Chris. I found he now worked for a current affairs program called "World In Action" produced for ITV by Granada Television. The film I planned was made and called *Strangers in their own land*. Over 200 million people have now seen it worldwide. Unfortunately it was banned in Australia due to legal action by the mining company, more about this later.

Shortly after this we received a notice that the tatty terrace in which we lived was to be demolished in order to extend the playground of our children's school. The adults among us thought this a good idea. The houses were slums and every bit deserved their death sentence. But the children saw them as a magic playground of much more value than the school playground.

It took the council over a year to get around to knocking them down. We knew they had a duty to rehouse us so stayed on. The council began demolishing the furthest end of our terrace. For a long hot and dusty summer we waited while the rumbles from the constant manoeuvring of bulldozers took chunks of plaster off our walls and filled our home with dust. The rats and mice sought refuge with us. When we asked if we could move out temporarily to stay with my brother outside London, we were told: "No, if you move out, even to go on holiday, the Council will no longer feel obliged to rehouse you." We stayed with the rats. It was not long until the neighbouring houses were completely demolished with the exception of parts immediately to each side of us. These were left so that our house would not fall down. It now looked like a ruined castle blasted by an invading army.

My daughter Cathy told me that she remembers this wrecked home as one of the finest of her childhood. She particularly remembered the front yard as a happy place. It was scarcely a yard wide. It was extended by the use of an abandoned tray top lorry parked in front. This became the stage used for plays and story-telling by neighbouring kids of mostly African or West Indian ancestry that were our children's closest local friends. The roof of the old bomb shelter in the back yard became their dancing place. An elaborate treehouse appeared in a backyard tree.

Although Jackie had wanted to come to London, the hardships of living here exceeded her expectations. Our relationship was growing strained. She told me she wanted to sleep with a mutual friend because she needed a man. She assured me this was not a danger to our family staying together, unless I made it so. I had long thought Jackie heroic in agreeing to stay with me. I knew she had given up much. Because of this, I fought against feeling upset at her request. I was in fact scared and insecure, but I loved her and wanted her free and happy. I walked her to her lover's flat through the rough streets of our neighbourhood to show her that I respected her freedom, leaving her when near his door.

Jackie afterwards told me that this relationship had not had as good chemistry as she had hoped. She had left him unsatisfied. He remained my friend although naturally sheepish about all this. Jackie now seemed happy with me, although I have since learnt that she had very conflicting feelings. This sometimes showed in disputes but I remember these as unusual and quickly resolved. I now wonder if my acceptance of her liaison trapped her into living with me at a time when she might well have wanted an excuse to leave me. She may also have felt she had trapped herself by agreeing that we would bring up the children together.

Life improved when the council rehoused us as we requested with Roger and Peter. Soon after this the time came for the Aboriginal speaking tour of Europe. We had raised funds for three Aboriginal spokespersons. Jacob Wolmby came from Aurukun, Mrs Joyce Hall JP from Mapoon and Weipa, and Mick Miller, Chairman of the Land Council, from Cairns. They accomplished an incredibly packed agenda with some eighty meetings in five countries in five weeks. Joyce Hall moved people to tears when she spoke about her land on television. Mick Miller was precise and strong, Jacob Wolmby accomplished great things in the Netherlands when Shell agreed before television cameras not to mine their several hundred square mile mining lease on his people's tribal lands without their consent.

About one hundred journalists attended our press conference in London. The delegation then led the press to the nearby offices of RTZ where they presented a very surprised company spokesman with an invitation to meet with them and with some dirt, as a symbol of the land taken from them in Australia. When Lord Shackleton earlier went to Australia to investigate the treatment of Aborigines by the Comalco bauxite mine, he had ignored a public invitation to meet with the North Queensland Land Council. The Land Council now forced RTZ to agree to this meeting.

Lord Shackleton and the Aborigines

It took place several days later in a RTZ boardroom. Both sides were allowed to bring their own neutral witness. We brought the chairman of the Antislavery Society. RTZ brought the Private Chaplain to the Queen, the Dean of Windsor. Two representatives of Comalco were flown in from Australia for this meeting. Roger and I came in with the Aboriginal delegation.

Mick Miller informed the meeting that the Land Council had been asked by the Weipa Aborigines to request the company to open negotiations with them, for the company had never seriously discussed loyalties, compensation or land ownership issues with the traditional owners of the land they mined. Joyce Hall then spoke of the suffering Comalco brought her people.

But the two and a half hours of discussions were fruitless. Shackleton admitted the housing at Weipa was very poor but nothing else. We tried to face him with the dilemma of moral versus legal rights. He surprisingly claimed that moral issues were not RTZ's concern but for the civil authorities. He said that, if Australian law permitted, it was totally proper for their subsidiary Comalco to take and mine a thousand square miles of land that had been traditionally owned by Aborigines and which had been protected as their reserve.

The value of the meeting was primarily that it forced RTZ to take Aboriginal objections more seriously. It felt somewhat amazing that we had succeeded in getting RTZ to meet with us so prominently and seriously. It provided some public education and served as a media focus for the beginning of a long campaign. In 2000, some 23 years later, Roger Moody with extraordinary dedication was still helping organise protests by investors at RTZ's AGMs over how RTZ treats Aborigines. And he was still organising support for indigenous groups around the world who were faced with devastation due to transnational mining projects. The organisation he helped found to continue this work is known as PaRTiZans.

But with Shell in Holland we had much better fortune. We went to see them after our London meeting with RTZ. The Aboriginal delegation gained good media coverage in Holland by telling how the Aurukun people defeated the Dutch in 1606. Shell then agreed to a televised boardroom meeting with the Aboriginal delegation. At this, to our surprise and delight, the managing director of Shell's mining arm, Billiton, gave the delegation a written promise not to mine without their consent on the 536 square miles of Aboriginal ancestral lands it had in its mining lease at Aurukun. The Wik nation, the people of Aurukun, thus retained a wide swathe of ancestral lands covered in virgin forest that they still hunt/gathered and which contain many sacred places. This was a wonderful victory.

On a very personal level I was given a very important and delightful lesson. Joyce Hall, the Aboriginal delegate and elder from Mapoon, a guardian of the female mysteries, had something to teach me about my own sexuality. One day when we were on tour in Germany, she encouraged me to sleep with a younger German man who was showing interest in me, making sure we had some privacy. He was younger than me, awkward, and shy, and I was so focused on the tour that I had not realised quite how much he was attracted by me.

I was so focused on keeping our family together, that I had never thought much about my sexual needs even when Jackie had her own lover. I was also nervous about making love. I had changed physically nearly everywhere in my body. My body was now sexually alert everywhere, softer, craving gentling, but, I had not yet had any operation. I consequently avoided sexual encounters, not knowing how to cope with my hermaphrodite body.

The night with this shy young German turned out marvellous. We were unsure and careful with each other. I told him about my own gender background and it made no difference. That night proved that there were gentle ways of making love that did not involve intercourse. He pleasured me, thrilled me, all that night. My body woke up delighted. But sadly, the affair did not last and it was my own fault. He wrote to me after I returned to England but I could not see how my life with Jackie and the children allowed me room for a lover. I did not answer his letter.

At that time it was hard to keep Jackie together. She was often depressed. But when I told her about my brief affair, her reaction was marvellous, putting into shadow all my hesitations and fears on her own 'affair'. She seemed freer on this than me. She said she was just happy for me and did not feel at all threatened (at least as far as she showed). Jackie's brave words may also have come because she wanted me to be freer of our family so that she too could feel able to look forward to a freer life.

The Elder, Joyce Hall, was also expert at other kinds of guidance. After one meeting in London she told us she would be able to guide the driver back to the house where she was staying. She did so by pointing out trees. "Go up to that tree over there, the tall scraggly one, turn right, then down to that fat little tree, see the one, down there, turn left there…" and so on until she brought us unerringly back to her temporary home. Thus she navigated around London as she would at home.

After the Aboriginal tour was over we thought we could relax. But it was not long before something terrible happened. Police raided our family home at dawn on the 21st November 1978, targeting Roger seemingly because he had written an article in "Peace News" that tackled a sacred cow of the moral brigade. He had pointed out that "paedophilia" as a word simply meant in its Grecian origins "love of children", that love was not wrong, what was wrong was exploiting children. This enraged some hunters of paedophiles. They misunderstood his distinction between love and exploitation. Every effort was made by the police to find evidence that Roger had abused children. This they did through traumatic interviews with every child he might have met. The parents concerned were sure he was innocent. We could think of few people who would be less likely to abuse a child.

Jackie's concern was broader than what might happen to Roger and to the brother for whom he cared. She was afraid that if my parents learnt of this legal action, they might use it to have our children made wards of court. My mother had campaigned so hard for me to remain on the one true path, that I thought it not entirely impossible for her to do this, if she convinced herself it was for the children's sake. But despite Jackie's belief that my mother was a danger, I had no proof that she would do any such thing.

Still I agreed to see a lawyer to discuss what my parents could do if they had a mind to. He told us that if my parents were to allege that our children were in moral danger, the children would be automatically and immediately made wards of the court. He advised us that my parents would not need to have any evidence to achieve this. It did not matter that our children were happy with us, that they were happy at school and progressing well. Just the complaint from a grandparent sufficed. And with our unusual family structure and the allegations against Roger they had enough.

Our lawyer further advised that, if my parents did undertake such an action, our children could remain wards of state for years, even if my parents did nothing more than this. Indeed with good reports from the children's school and no critical reports from social workers it would be hard for them to do more. But this would mean we would have to take legal action ourselves to clear our family's name and to have the court orders lifted. This scared us. Such a legal case could expose us to tabloid newspaper exploitation and, above all else, it would mean that we would not be able to go back to Australia with the children while they were wards of court. The very thought of this possibility left Jackie paranoid. She was increasingly seeing Australia as a much more safe territory. Yet we both believed we could not desert Roger by fleeing back to Australia. We decided to stay until after his trial.

My mother has since said that she never thought to do such a thing. But Jackie's fears were real. The lawyer had confirmed that my parents had the ability to cause us much trouble. Jackie was very scared. Without me realising it, she was growing away from me, seemingly blaming me in a way for the difficulties of our life together. She told me later that it was at this time that she started to grow cold to me.

Her depression grew so deep that I agreed that she could take the children back to Australia immediately after Roger's trial. She would not need even to pack. I told her I would do this immediately she had gone. My work commitments meant that I would have to stay for six weeks after Roger's trial. I would then put our luggage on a ship and follow her by air. In any case I needed to return soon if I wished to keep permanent residency rights in Australia. The law was that I would forfeit these rights if I did not return within three years, and two and a half had passed.

Then there was another shock. We had come to rely on my brother Kevin and his wife who had particularly become a friend and confidante for Jackie. But on a visit to them in Kent, they told us with set sad faces, drawn and miserable, that they had been forced to make a choice between my parents and us. They had been told that if they carried on seeing us, their children would lose them as grandparents. They decided that they could not do this to their children, so sadly wanted us to no longer come and visit them. It was a terrible shock. I cried bitterly all night. Jackie was calmer, but she later told me that this was one of the last straws. She had depended on Heather's support as I did on Kev's. It left deep scars, but did not last. Over the next few months, Kevin and Heather came to retreat from this. They too were very unhappy at their decision. In fact we did meet up again about six weeks later. But it did confirm us in our fears that my parents would try anything to gain power over us.

But for me Australia did not look like a paradise, despite our fears in England. Around this time Jane and Paula, the children of Jackie's brother Jeff, visited England. They were two girls that I used to get on well with in Australia. Jackie went to meet them but I could not do so. Jeff had requested that they did not meet me because of my gender change. This messed up their visit for all of us. But I still hoped things would work out in Australia. After all, Jill's Dad had offered to give any support he could give to help Jackie and I as a family.

Soon a major element in this web of fear unravelled. After the prosecutors presented their "evidence" against Roger at the Old Bailey, the judge told them that they should never have brought the case. He dismissed all charges against Roger before the defence case was even presented. It was a wonderful party afterwards, an enormous breath of relief. We had gone through hell for nothing.

Nevertheless, Jackie still wanted to leave. She was exhausted and still feared my parents. She booked on the first flight available and I took her and the children to Heathrow Airport. It was tears all around and mutual assurances. "It won't be long. We will see you soon". I watched Jackie walking off down the corridor with the two small girls, seven and eight, holding her hands. I can still see them now, their backs getting smaller and smaller until I could see them no longer. They flew off and I went back home. The house felt incredibly empty without them. I started packing and looked forward to joining them in Australia.

The Death of my Father

Then next day, before their plane had arrived in Australia, a phone call came from my Mother. She begged me. "Please come down, Dad has had a stroke and is dying." It was a total shock for he had not been ill and was only in his early sixties. My mother's request forced me into confusion. She also asked, "Please come down as a man for your father's sake". This was something I could no longer do physically with any conviction let along psychologically. I hesitated. I feared I was being manipulated. If I went down as a woman, and Dad died, I could be blamed for this. If I went down dressed as a man, and Dad recovered, I would be a nervous wreck. I feared that it was not my presence that was wanted but my compliance. Nonetheless I desperately wanted to be there.

But within a short time, Mother phoned again to say Dad had recovered consciousness. He seemed much better so the urgency seemed less. I had the chance to talk over what I should do with my brother Kevin. We agreed on a course of action. I phoned Mother and said that I feared my presence would make things worse, that it might cause problems for Dad, raising old issues that he would find it hard to deal with while so ill.

But then Dad had a relapse and slipped into a partial coma. Mother did not expect Dad to recover. Now she pleaded for me to come down. She wanted all the children there. I wanted to be there. Mother phoned again and I agreed to go, saying I would wear slacks and a sweater as a compromise.

It was extremely ironic. For the first time it did not matter that I was a woman. It was at last more important that I was one of the family. He was in a Southampton hospital in a single room. I soon learnt that there was little hope for his recovery. Mother told him I was there. He just managed to open his eyes to look at me once or twice. He was beyond speech or expression. A squeeze of hands was all that was possible but I was enormously grateful for this.

The next morning I spent on watch with him. We had no idea how long he would survive. I was happy to have this time alone with him for it gave me a sad chance to tell him all the things I had longed to tell him for so long. I told him how much I loved him, how I had missed him. I told him that nothing that had happened made me less his child, I sang to him softly. I did not know for sure if he heard me but I hoped and believed he did even if at a nearly unconscious level.

Then in the afternoon, after mother and my sister Maryanne had taken over the watch, his colour suddenly changed and a few breaths later he died. I went back to the hospital but did not go in to see him again. I had never got to know him properly. I still think of him with affection, see his sandy hair, poise and laughing eyes, as I knew him as a child. I am very sorry I never knew him as a daughter. I mourned him deeply.

The parish priest who knew my whole story from my mother was beautiful. He referred to me as her daughter when speaking to my mother. I did her shopping and took her and Maryanne out to dinner the night Dad died. Suddenly Mother started to see me as the same child she had always had, not a monster, not the figment of her imagination. It was strange, a meeting with my Dad of sorts and then a much longed for reconciliation with my Mother. She discovered, I think to her surprise, that I was not the Danny La Rue she feared and that I was socially acceptable as a woman. Although I continued to wear sweaters and slacks, she found if she referred to me as a male socially, it simply confused everyone. Those who did not know me thought my mother must be talking of someone else or that they had misheard her. Those who did know me were as embarrassed as I was.

The only difficulty was at Dad's funeral. Many relatives turned up that had only recently learnt of my transition. They were very uncomfortable, did not understand, their eyes mostly seemed condemning.

Otherwise mother and I had an amazingly relaxed time. All the terrors of many years seemed to melt away. She said she too felt freer. I wondered if I had misunderstood her earlier. She still made mistakes with pronouns when talking about me but would apologise if she embarrassed me in public. It was terrible that it had to be the death of my Dad that brought us together.

It made me wonder if I had really ever understood my parents. When Dad wrote, many years before, saying Mother was right in trying to stop him smoking, I had seen him as dominated by Mother. But, if that had been so, why now did Dad's dying free Mother?

I then immediately turned my attention to packing and moving back to Australia. I was eager to see our daughters again. Jackie would not have yet received my letter telling them of what had happened, for my Dad died as they were arriving in Australia. Ironically as she fled, my Dad's death had removed the danger from which she fled. It was similar to what drove us to England three years earlier. We then fled because Jill feared hurting her own Dad and then found out immediately that our flight was probably unnecessary. Jackie's fears were real for she was deeply torn by them. But if she had waited one more day, she would not have fled. She would not have felt able to leave while I was dealing with my Dad's illness and death and then we would have been able to leave together. I would still have gone to Australia, not just because Jackie wished to return there but because my three-year grant for work on Aboriginal rights had come to its end and I needed to return to retain my rights of residence.

But then something else happened that was awful and devastating. Something unimaginable. A letter came from Jackie, written before she knew of what had happened with my father, saying she thought I should not follow her and the children to Australia. She said it gently. She felt she was dragging me to Australia, that my talents for international work would be wasted in Australia.

But her gentleness did not disguise for a moment the bite of what she said. She had decided to break the relationship between us. I suddenly realised that my view of the backs of our children walking away down the airport corridor might be the last that I saw of them for many years. Effectively, without my consent, without even discussing the possibility,

Jackie, the woman that I loved, my equal legal partner in caring for the children, had practically abducted them to Australia.

A great cry of anguish went up from me. I was nearly out of my mind. I had presumed that we would be soon united. I found the idea that I might well have seen Kara and Cathy and Jackie for the last time unimaginably horrific. I wondered how pre-planned this had been. I howled in disbelief. I wept and cried. I drove out of London, through the woods and trees that I loved, crying. Great for my figure. I lost a stone and a half in seven weeks. It took me weeks to get over the initial shock. I cried and cried. (Hiding all this from Mum. I did not want her involvement.)

I wrote Jackie a desperate letter. Not reproving her, but telling her that my international work was of tiny importance to me compared with caring for our children…something that I knew that she well knew.

I told her too that I loved her, but that if she needed an independent life I would respect this. She and I could live apart but, I begged, please don't put up a barrier that would keep me from our children. I reminded her that I couldn't stay in England because I would lose my residency rights in Australia. I told her about my father. Letters to and from Australia are cruel. I had to wait two weeks for the response.

When it came, she was begging for forgiveness and telling me to come. She had not realised quite how devastating her plan would be for me. Yes, I was welcome to come back to Australia. Of course I could see the children and be with them. They needed me.

I very happily took her letter at its face value. I would go back to Australia. But I knew in my heart that my relationship with Jackie would never be the same. The element of trust was undermined. I knew that she had not made this decision lightly. She must have been hiding much from me. Still I knew there was truth in what she said. I knew that she did feel guilty about taking me from my work as she had some three years earlier. She did not want to damage my work again.

But I also knew, felt again in my gut, that if it had been that simple, she would have told me to my face. I knew but did not want to know that she had not told me of her plan for two further, still unspoken, reasons. One was that her plans were illegal. I had rights as a parent and the children also had legal rights to have me as a caring parent. But parenting for me was something quite apart from human laws. I would not use the law and Jackie knew this. The other reason, and a more realistic reason, was that she knew that, if she told me to my face, she would not be able to persuade me to abandon my role in looking after the children.

I knew that once more my gift with words had persuaded her to have me back, as it had when I had originally wooed her by letters to Australia. I did not like this but she had invited me to return and I was much relieved. So I packed up our belongings in thirteen tea chests and sent them off, nearly sending off my passport too. I recovered this at the last moment from the warehouse. If I had lost this, I might well have not been able to return in time to retain my residence rights in Australia.

Roger and I organised one final CIMRA protest, bringing up issues about the rights of Aborigines at RTZ's Annual General Meeting. Two Aborigines then turned up in London, Gary Foley and Bruce McGuinness; two well-known Melbourne based activists. They came to my going away party. I was very glad to see them and we had many a drink together. They asked me for contacts in Europe with friendly groups. I shared with them those I had made to help the Aboriginal Land Councils.

The North Queensland Land Council was then working with others to set up a Federation of Land Councils. This would co-ordinate nationally the campaign for recognition of Aboriginal land rights. Its officers had asked me to find funding for an Embassy in Europe, to be set up under the authority of this Federation . I had found funding for an initial three-year period and now had to report back in Australia to the land councils involved.

But I first needed time to think, to relax, to recover, to digest and understand what had happened to us as a family, so I decided to make my way slowly back to Australia. I found an air ticket that allowed me to stop for some days in countries en route. In mid-June 1979, on a rainy day, I set off with much trepidation for the airport.

Returning to Australia

'I had tentatively worked out what to do on my return. I anticipated much pain. I was now unsure how Jackie was really feeling. I did not know what would be the future of our family but thought that the wise course would be for me to find separate living quarters and, if possible, to spend extended weekends with Jackie and the children.

My first stopover was in the Greek islands. I headed first for the island of Patmos just off the Turkish coast, as it was associated with the Evangelist John, my favourite gospel writer. He was the most mystically inclined.

Patmos has at its heart a hill crowned with a town. My energy was mad. I hired a motorbike and with my scarf trailing I accelerated past men sitting in front of cafes, luring, laughing, then heading off to safety. I was reckless in my flirting. As I moved from island to island, I found 2.5 days the average safe period for me to spend on each. I kept clear of any deep involvement. In Crete I travelled through a valley of windmills to find the cave where Zeus lived as a child, only to flee from the advances of the guardian of the cave, who wanted to lay me within it. I was both not having this and scared he would discover too much. I feared that men might react violently if they found I was still pre-op., hermaphrodite in body, but I still enjoyed myself.

The most magical moment came on a Sunday in Heraklion, my last day in Crete, when I heard the haunting music of the balalaika coming from a side lane. I investigated and found a seaman (or so his boots, cap and sweater seemed to say) dancing in slow concentration in the lane between two cafes. His arms were stretched, fingers clicking. It was enchanting and fascinating. One of the cafes had men sitting at its outside tables. I sat at a table on the other side of the narrow lane and ordered calamari and their pine flavoured wine, Retzina. The captain continued to dance. I applauded. Between dances, men bought him drinks and snacks. So, when he paused again, I lifted my bottle and offered him a drink.

Immediately he dragged me to my feet and for the remainder of a wonderful day we danced together in this lane and in the brief interludes enjoyed treats and drinks bought for us. It was like the scene on a quayside when Melina Mercouri danced with a seaman in the film "Never on Sunday." It was my favourite image of Greece. How I lived it that day in Heraklion!

Eventually I had to leave to catch my boat. The men asked me to stay. They told me they would fly me to wherever I had to go tomorrow so I would not lose any time. I declined. Again the necessary caution. But the magic of that wonderful afternoon has stayed with me.

My next stop was Cairo. Still the mad energy continued. My recklessness was not purged. I was still grieving the possible loss of my family and the death of my father. My way of mourning was that of the wild wake. I walked the dusty sand-worn streets. I chatted in cafes in the backstreets. I smoked hashish pipes, sitting on a bench in a narrow lane lit by oil lamps that ran between high ochred walls crowned with overhanging balconies of darkened wood. I marvelled at proud Nubian women walking barefaced, tall and graceful, amid the heavily veiled Arab women. I explored the dusty, lofty and wonderful mosques and wondered at the staggering beauty of the brilliantly painted marvels of Egypt's past in their national museum.

I also fell for the talk of the headwaiter in a revolving restaurant high above an island in the Nile, in sight of smog-shrouded pyramids. He offered to take me to his village by the pyramids and show me traditional family life and the pyramids. I accepted but was astonished when he did not drive me to a village but into a high walled compound containing a cottage. No one else was present except another man, a friend of his. The garden was sealed with high wooden gates. I was offered a drink on the veranda of the cottage and then shown the rear room. It contained an enormous double bed He looked at me. I reacted with absolute icy dignity but underneath was very scared. "You tricked me. Get me out of here, back to Cairo." I glared, savage, and started to march towards the closed gate.

The two men argued between themselves in Arabic but they drove me back to Cairo untouched. It was not only rape I risked. In my experience, men were more likely to see me as a fitting target of their violence if they knew I was a pre-op transsexual.

I later made my way to a pyramid, going up a long sloping narrow passage into a central chamber, a room formed from colossal blocks, solid, heavy, cubic. I became aware that I was at the centre of a structure pressing in on me with enormous weight. I found myself alone with its caretaker. I don't know what I was giving off. Obviously something sexual, although I found him unattractive. I soon found myself backing away from his approach in what seemed like a claustrophobic nightmare. I found the small entrance, and fled down the long sloping passage, to tumble out into the blazed, bleached desert where a gaudily decorated camel awaited me like a figure from Sesame Street. I rode her from the pyramid to the Sphinx, my head wrapped in scarves, the ends flying in the wind. A crazy woman that even the camel driver wanted ridiculously to seduce. Perhaps it was because a wild and alone woman was a rarity in this society, but it wasn't easy for me.

It was just as well that I was not staying many days. I was soon back on the plane. My next stop was in India. I decided here to simply pick one small city and stay there rather than travel the country. I flew from Delhi to Jaipur, the famed pink walled city of Rajastan.

Oh, this was not easy either. That first night my hotel proprietor came to my palatial bedroom, begging me to let him stay on in the room even after I had rejected his advances. It seemed that he had a wager that he would lose if he were booted out! Eventually in frustration at not being able to make him leave, I crumpled into a ball and cried him out. Next day I was again crying, while sitting on the lawn near the railway station. I knew the next place that I had to go was Australia and I dreaded what would happen. I was in despair.

A gentle man came up to me, a professor, asked what was wrong and took me to a cafe. Over tea I spilled out to this stranger the whole story about my life and my fear that I would lose my children. To my surprise he seemed to regard me as a highly magical person, a privileged person. He set me up in another hotel from where one day I watched a wedding procession approach. There were elephants and highly decorated horses in plumed headdresses. I went down to the roadside to watch it pass. An elephant driver, seeing my spell bound face, had his elephant kneel down for me. I then rode with him in splendour on a tapestry-bedecked elephant through the streets. This time of travelling seemed unreal to me. I felt ever more vulnerable, ever more alien.

I explored the bedrooms of ancient palaces with tiny mirrors set into their ceilings to make them seem starlit. I visited reception rooms cooled by waterfalls. I laughed sadly at the long tailed monkeys in the gardens and watched from my hotel room the camel and bullock carts winding through a turbulence of bicycles and mopeds. The Indians seemed aware of my brittleness. I attracted more attention than I needed.

The professor offered to fund my operation. I refused this. I had no wish to become so indebted to any man. He also told me he wanted to become my lover and on this score too I was cautious. He wrote to me after I returned to Australia, offering to send me saris. But by the time I received this letter, I was trying to rebuild our family life. It seemed his letter came from another world. How could I explain my feelings by letter to someone of so different a culture? I could not find space in my life to construct a separate reality.

And thus I arrived back in Australia, my wild, near-suicidal grief spent. I received a great welcome from Kara and Cathy and a happy welcome from Jackie. I was also immediately offered a job by an Aboriginal Rights organisation. But Jackie and I had much to work on, much pain. I decided that I could not live with Jackie in her current home, her parent's spare mansion on the cliffs overlooking Melbourne's bay. I needed the company of others.

Instead I found myself a room in a collective household near to my new workplace, sharing space with the radical Walker Press. The people here were marvellous. I spent four days a week there and the rest of the week with Jackie and the children. I was happy with this arrangement and thought it wise.

I also discovered at a centre attached to Monash University in Melbourne a reputedly excellent medical team caring for transsexuals. It was the same team that was pioneering in vitro fertilisation of otherwise infertile women. When I went to see them, I found that my looking after the children was no obstacle to my treatment. They took me on, said they would need to assess me for themselves, but if after a year all had gone well, then they would schedule me for an operation.

Diamonds and Danger

But before I could do much else, I had to fulfil a commitment to travel to the Aboriginal Land Councils in Australia's far north, giving them details about the funders in Europe that would support an embassy. I travelled with a woman friend I had made at Walker Press.

We flew 3000 miles across Australia to Perth in Western Australia where I met Robert Bropho, an Aboriginal spokesman and Elder responsible for the traditional care of the land on which Perth now stood. His people lived in poverty on Perth's outskirts. He agreed to drive us to the Kimberley Aboriginal communities, over a thousand miles to the north, and to introduce us to communities along the route. When we first met, I noted his deep eyes, his brow ridges and thought how ancient was his face. I went silent and tried to tune myself in to his ways, to even use telepathy. He told me weeks afterwards that this was what made him decide that he could work with me.

I still remember the wonder of that journey in a friend's battered car. Brilliant flowers rioted across the land until it grew too dry. The dirt road's edge was then lined in bull dust, a fine powder created by traffic and piled deep. At night we slept under the stars. At dawn Robert would make us billy tea.

One stop was at a Catholic mission to Aborigines. When we arrived, a priest was saying an outdoors Mass, at which my friend snorted in derision because she had seen how the missions had destroyed Aboriginal traditional culture. Robert got very angry. He said that if we did not respect the sacred traditions of our own people, how could he expect us to respect his?

In the rich mining region of the Pilbara, where hills are made of solid iron and its waterholes are of enormous fame among Aborigines as the sites of sacred legends, we met the people of Jigalong, a former Christian mission. Here Protestant missionaries did all they could to convert the people from a Pagan religion they labelled as Satanic and had failed. Robert also took us to a sacred place that was legally protected, but for archaeologists not for Aborigines. The carved rocks were still there but surrounded by railway sidings. Robert said it had been murdered. Aboriginal sacred places only live in the heart of sacred landscapes.

The Aborigines at Jigalong lived in shanties; low shelters made of the debris of white society. There were a couple of wrecked geodesic domes, a failed trendy housing scheme. The other Aboriginal shelters seemed randomly situated. But I have since learnt that many traditional Aborigines will site their camps according to the footprint of their totem animal or bird. So if one was an eagle and looked down, one would see a camp sited on every claw or pad.

`The Jigalong people adhered strictly to their own belief system. They had recently founded a settlement deep in the desert, so they could bring up their children well away from the influence of white society and from the devastating influence of pubs, for their people reportedly do not have the enzymes to cope with alcohol like whites.

A nearby (just a hundred or so miles away) Aboriginal community at Strelley had made money by small-scale mining and purchased a cattle station. Here they ran a bicultural school, teaching their children both in their language and English, a near revolutionary innovation in the

Australia of that time. They too had built a second settlement deep in the desert far from any white settlement or pub, by a sacred water pool.

This community, known as the "Strelley Mob", used strikes and walk-outs after the Second World War in a fight against the exploitation of their people on cattle stations that had taken over their ancestral lands without their consent. An Aboriginal Elder told me that the Whites made them look after the cattle. "If we escaped, they would bring us back, put us in irons, brand us like cattle, burn our feet. It was real slavery in those times, up until the 1950s."[252]

When we arrived at the office of the Kimberley Land Council in Derby we were surprised to find a delegation from the North Queensland Land Council arriving simultaneously, having driven thousands of miles from the east coast of Australia, despite badly damaging the front of their car by hitting a large red kangaroo.

I was delighted, surprised and secretly flattered when they told me that they had decided to hold this first joint land council meeting while I was in the Kimberleys so they could discuss together the information I brought with me. They wanted to know the details of the funding I had secured for their European embassy and for other plans. But they gave me an unpleasant task. When they leant from my funders that Gary Foley had appeared at their European offices, using contacts I gave him at my going away party, allegedly claiming to represent the land councils in Europe, they instructed me to tell the funders that he did not represent them. This caused me much trouble later with Gary, a powerful man in the cities. Another event that gave me trouble was the incredulous anger of a white lawyer at my presence at meetings to which he was not invited. It was as if he possessed the local Aborigines and I was an interloper.

We spent much time at this meeting discussing the rush by diamond exploration companies into the Kimberleys. They asked me to explain just what diamond mining would entail. I told them that diamonds were brought to the surface by ancient volcanoes. Mining them meant digging vast pits into the pipes of the volcanoes and also scraping up over many

square miles all the surface clays, sands and rocks to separate out the diamonds removed by erosion from the extinct volcanoes. My account so
shocked them that they asked me to repeat my explanation at a second
joint land council meeting held under shady trees in a dry riverbed at
Fitzroy Crossing, the heart of the diamond exploration region. Present at
this were elders from Noonkanbah Station, who had just given CRA
(owned by RTZ of London) permission to explore for diamonds as long as
they did not trespass on sacred sites or burial grounds.

My way of explanation was simple. We were all sitting on the ground. I
took a handful of sand, picked out one grain saying that was a diamond. I
kept this and put the rest into a separate heap saying that the mining company would consider the rest rubbish to be piled up out of the way. Soon
the heap of "rubbish" would be higher than the nearby hills, as had happened at many mines. I also pointed out the nearby rocky hills that I knew
were the cores of potentially diamond rich extinct volcanoes.

They knew of volcanoes through the memories of their people. An
elder sung me a song about them. It celebrated their memories of the last
volcanoes to erupt in Australia very many thousands of years ago. The
South Australian geology department had verified that a traditional
ancient Aboriginal song listed eruptions in their correct order. The
Aborigines also knew and valued diamonds before whites came to their
land. The first diamonds discovered by Whites in Australia were in the
shamanic pouches of a murdered Aborigine. The most beautiful of the
larger diamonds contained rainbows and were thus considered very special
by Aborigines since the Rainbow Serpent was their name for the great
Creating Spirit. Sometimes their shamans or spiritual healers used crystal
stones in their healing rituals. I knew that many had carried quartz crystals, evidently some had carried diamonds.

I told the Aboriginal gathering that mining companies dug up the roots
of diamond-rich volcanoes down to a mile or more in Africa, where
hundreds of square miles of land once owned by tribes have become

"forbidden zones" because they contain diamonds. I showed pictures of African diamond mines taken from mining company Annual Reports.

This deeply disturbed the Noonkanbah Aborigines at the Fitzroy Crossing gathering. They wondered if they had been misled into giving permission for diamond exploration. They asked me to come to Noonkanbah to explain what I knew to all their community. This was a great privilege. Noonkanbah was the first cattle station to be secured by Aborigines in this vast region and at a song and dance festival there they had decided to form the Kimberley Land Council.

The elder who looked after me at Noonkanbah was Nipper Tabagee. His eyes were wounded by trachoma, his clothes dusty and old, but he was a man known as a "Dreamer", the highest of all Aboriginal titles. A Dreamer was a person who knew their ancient wisdom, who could travel deep inside to explore the ancient ways. He was respected throughout Aboriginal society. But he did not put himself on a pedestal. When we met we laughed in each other's eyes. It was like meeting a favourite uncle that I had known since a child. I was much honoured by him taking me around and explaining to me what had happened to his people.

He took me to an ancient volcanic hill, Djada, scarcely higher than a tree, which had been claimed by a mining company. He climbed up to a cave in its side and showed me human bones inside it. He told me "These were shot by the police when I was this high." He indicated about three feet high. These were victims of one of the last punitive raids sent out against the tribes around 1938.

This cave, he told me, once housed their most sacred carved boards. Such boards represented the creative energy of the Ancestors or spirits that had formed the land. A mining company had smashed some of these boards and taken the others to their Melbourne office. The Noonkanbah people had fortunately managed to retrieve these and now had them safely secured elsewhere.

The result of these deliberations was that the elders reluctantly decided to withdraw their consent to diamond exploration on the grounds that they had not been sufficiently informed. Tabagee then asked me to tell their lawyer of their decision. I suggested that the lawyer might not accept my word for he already considered me an interloper. They then drove with me in a dust filled car without a windscreen down the few hundred miles of dirt roads that led to the lawyer's office, leaving me the colour of the earth when they went in to tell him of their decision. They then made sure the media knew. Next day their eviction of CRA was national headlines.

And immediately a reaction came from Perth lawyers who worked officially on "behalf of Aborigines". They decided to come up to see if this eviction was really the Noonkanbah people's decision and, if so, whether they could be persuaded to change their minds. Jimmy Biendurry, the Chairman of the Kimberley Land Council, asked me if I could stay until these lawyers arrived in two weeks time. If I could, he would use the time to get me to as many as possible Aboriginal communities so that they had the information they needed about mining. I agreed.

But I then found myself under attack from the very white people whom I thought would be supportive, those working with Aboriginal communities. It turned out that some whites had planned to use the previous Aboriginal decision to allow diamond exploration to push for the Noonkanbah community to receive additional funding as a "reasonable" community. I soon found myself isolated from most local white people

A Desert Lover

I also had one of my most wonderful sexual encounters. One night when making camp in the outback with a softly spoken, intelligent, good looking Aboriginal man, I put my sleeping bag on the opposite side of the vehicle to his, Then there came a gentle call. "Jani, do you really want to sleep by yourself?"

I did not need to think long. I would have loved to sleep with him but had not thought it possible. I was still very much hermaphrodite in body shape. So I came around to his side of the vehicle and in the moonlight I explained to him why I was being so diffident. I explained how I had changed, how above the waist my body was as I wanted it, but not below. Then ensued the most delightful of nights. He respected my wishes but I still shivered with ecstasy. My skin, breasts, face, arms, all was much loved—and so was he.

With hindsight, I wonder at why I made such a rule. It seems I was as embarrassed as any girl with a deformity, as I then thought of my shrivelled organs. Given time and perhaps guidance, I might have come to terms with it. But then it represented part of my past that I had rejected. It represented a part of me that I had not managed to integrate. I did not hate this part of me; I simply could not use it sexually.

A few days later I suffered what then seemed like a serious rape attempt on me. I was the last to go to bed one night when staying with two other women, not in an Aboriginal camp but in a town. My room was deep inside the house. My bed a mattress on the floor. I swaddled myself in a sheet, lay on the bed and wondered if I should have shut off the noisy air conditioner that kept me cool.

Then suddenly I felt a hand go across my mouth. It was pitch dark. I heard no sound, no voice. I was helpless. I had swaddled myself in the sheet and thus could not free an arm quickly. The fact that he was trying to keep me quiet told me what I should do. I twisted my head aside and screamed and screamed and screamed.

Much to my surprise neither of the other women in the house came. But the man did no more. He withdrew his hand leaving only darkness. I still had not seen any of him. I hoped he was appalled by the noise I had made and had gone lest he be discovered. I stopped screaming, twisted to the foot of the bed. Listened. The darkness was fearful. The silence continued.

Finally I crept as quietly as possible to the door and switched on the light. He had gone. I went for my friends and found that my friend in the next room had thought that I was being murdered and in the dark could not find out how to reach me. She had opened her wardrobe door instead of the room door. The other woman was sleeping in a hammock on the veranda. She simply thought she was having a nightmare. It was frightening to find out how easy it was to get attacked even with friends close by.

We armed ourselves with kitchen knives and hammers but found no one in or around the house. One of us fetched an Aboriginal friend who lived around the corner. It was the man who secretly had made love to me a week earlier. She did not know this. He said he found tracks outside and it was an Aborigine who attacked me. He mounted guard for the rest of the night. I did not regain my voice for days. Secretly I wondered if I had been wrong, if in fact it had been he who had crept silently into my room and who had tried to stop me exclaiming with surprise before saying anything himself.

I was over this by the time the Perth lawyers came up to Noonkanbah. They told them that a mining company would give them jobs in any mining town it built. Tabagee then asked me to repeat what I had told the community earlier. I presented what I knew of the mining industry, including that so far no mining company had given Aborigines much more than menial work. During the following discussion in Aboriginal language, Nipper Tabagee interpreted for me. No one interpreted for the lawyers and the Aborigines maintained their decision to ban mining.

Afterwards the angry lawyers asked me to have a meeting with them. They took me well away from the Aborigines and then let loose at me. Who did I think I was, coming up here and interfering? "Did I intend to take over as their legal advisor? Should we resign?" I was astonished and appalled. I told them I was no lawyer and I hoped they would support the Aborigines in their decisions. They then warned me. "We know where you are going next. You are going to Oombulgurri. You better watch it when you get there!" And with this mysterious threat, they left.

I had indeed intended to go to Oombulgurri. The Land Council had told me that this community on the far eastern side of the Kimberleys was deeply disturbed by the diamond exploration companies that were trespassing on their ancestral lands and had recently expelled a company owned by De Beers of South Africa. Despite the lawyers' threats, I accepted the invitation of this community to come and see them to share what I knew of diamond mining. One of their elders accompanied me but I was warned before I set out that they had heard rumours that the government was very angry with me.

Later that day, when I was sitting in the shade of a banyan tree at Oombulgurri talking about diamond mining to the senior elders, I received a radio message from a friend in Melbourne some 3,400 miles away. It was that the Federal Government had ordered the police in by helicopter to arrest me. This was so extraordinary, so unprecedented, so ridiculous a use of force, that I was amazed. Clearly someone in the Government saw me as very dangerous yet all I was doing was giving factual well-documented information to Aborigines so they could be better informed when making their own decisions

I did not wait for the helicopter. I instead asked the community boat to return me to the nearby town of Wyndham. The boat was smaller than the crocodiles that played around the boat and lazed on the nearby banks. That night I was staying with the district nurse in Wyndham when the police came around and arrested me, and a woman friend travelling with me. We were only detained some hours. I learnt later that the police had to be ordered to do this. They could not understand why the government saw me as dangerous.

As for the crime for which I had been arrested, it was for not obeying a newly promulgated regulation. The state government had been so angry with the Oombulgurri Aborigines for expelling De Beers, thus blocking "progress", that it had changed the law simply by issuing a new regulation. This said that Aborigines had no right to invite anyone to visit them on Aboriginal reserve lands or to stop anyone coming onto their reserve. In future, visits could only be authorised by the state government. My crime was that I had not followed this new regulation. Apparently after being invited by the community, I should have flown over two thousand miles to Perth to apply for a permit and then wait some months for their decision. I was the first person prosecuted in this region for this crime.

On my return to Melbourne, I restarted the process of trying to mend the scars in our family life. I did not try to return full time to caring for the children. We had agreed on my return to Australia that I would spend three days a week with the children but it was not long before Jackie asked me to permanently return. She said the children were missing me too much and that she herself hated having no adult company. I was not sure about the wisdom of this. The wounds were still raw but how could I refuse? If the children needed me to live full time with them, I could not say no even though it took me from a very relaxed shared household where I was gaining many new friends.

I returned without saying much about my doubts. I felt I should return for the sake of us as a family and to see if we could rebuild things, even though I was not keen on being a nuclear family. I enjoyed community households, but we could only afford to rent a small house. We found a small cottage in an inner suburb just before Christmas in 1979. As for Jackie's family, one aunt and a sister were still happy to meet with me, but I was told by Jackie that her parents refused. But despite all my fears, life together again started very well. We were again a lesbian couple and for a while it was as if nothing had happened between us.

Meanwhile the Aboriginal Land Councils set up their national Federation, thus fulfilling the plans discussed at the Kimberley meeting. I was appointed its mining advisor. I was also to teach about mining the staff of "The Aboriginal Mining Information Centre". I agreed that once this was done, I would resign; for what was wanted was a wholly Aboriginal staffed organisation.

My problems were mostly with white men. I found at parties that many I fancied were not happy to simply flirt. They soon wanted to have sex with me. It was not so easy to put them off. I was often shocked by their single mindedness. Even if I wanted to, it was not always the right time. Also I did not want to tell casual acquaintances that my vagina was non-existent and I was not the slightest bit interested in anal sex. But if I put them off, they became irritated with my frustrating them and a pest.

As a newly sexually awake woman, I was surprised and appalled by the numbers of times this happened. Had I not understood males at all when I lived among them? Many seemed to be incredibly penis centred. When I said it was not a good time for sex, some still asked if there was a place where they could put "it". This treating me as a sexual relief machine disgusted me. Why did they not simply go off and masturbate? If they really pushed me, I could suggest a lot of other appropriate places where they could put "it"—such as in a sawmill!

It was as if I were a field they thought they had a right to plough. I wanted not to be rude, not to hurt their egos, but there was no way I would give way to their demands. For me it was utterly demeaning and insulting.

A final salute to Maledom.

But Jackie and I, Kara and Cathy, had many good months in our ship-like house on top of a Northcote hill. We often went exploring the bush outside Melbourne together. We spent as much time as we could in the wild. My Aboriginal work was centred on an office at the foot of our hill. Then in late 1980, while I was helping with a vigil-protest, collecting money by a mock drilling rig set up in the heart of Melbourne in support of the Aborigines at Noonkanbah, Jackie brought me the message that a local hospital had accepted me for the operation. It was seven years since I transitioned. My elder daughter was now nine, my younger eight.

By a remarkable "coincidence" my operation was scheduled by the hospital for May 1st 1981, the Beltane festival when my pagan ancestors in Britain and Ireland celebrated life, fresh green spring growth and sexuality, and my Christian medieval ancestors celebrated much the same with maypole dances. I now think this was a highly appropriate day to come into the full use of my own sexuality.

By now I was utterly relaxed about having the operation. I felt it was hardly sex or gender changing, for my brain and other aspects of me had been female since birth. Immediately before the operation, I made a quick trip to the male toilet and I gave my penis one final exercise, seeing how high up the wall I could piss in a final irreverent salute to the male world.

In Honour of the Unwanted Penis

Now there is a clear need to sing a song to my penis
Before it gives its life that I might better live.
It too is part of the divine creation
Much to be celebrated.
But for me, its transformation
Was the magic that I welcomed.

I will sing of the four-inch fellow who lived in my groin.
Well, that was his average size.
When he wasn't growing or shrinking.
But for him it was perhaps unfortunate
That he found himself living with a female spirit.
But did that make him a failure, a mistake?

Some similarly minded transgendered friends
Reckon he was a disaster, an illness, a cancer,
The sooner cut off the better.
But that is not fair to him

There is nothing else like a penis in human kind.
He has a mind of his own.
He will strut up and down as he pleases.
Most males reckon that he is something special.

They celebrate his presence with high ritual.
So they should. He deserves an accolade.

But females know that he is not whole
Until he is contained within them.
They know his weaknesses.
They know he often lacks stamina
And must be conserved
Until the time comes for the grand climax.

The Last Rite I gave him
Was to go to the bathroom
Just before the operation
So he could spray as high as he could
Up the urinal wall.
It was a salute like that given by fireboats to ocean liners.

Thus my penis welcomed the birth of my more female body.
It sacrificed its sensitive skin to give me a vagina.
Its glans became my clit.
I am grateful to it and honour it.[253]

I wanted to get rid of the "no-go" territory with my male lovers, to be utterly at home with my reformed body, testing it, enjoying it. I wondered what it would be like to be able to fully relax and enjoy every bit of my body. I had been warned that this was a serious operation that could go wrong but when I took the pre-op drug that would make me unconscious I was not just relaxed but also a bit excited.

I had been approved for this operation by a medical team based at Monash University. It had subjected me to supervision for a year by a psychotherapist, a psychologist and by Professor Williams, who headed the team, to see how I managed living as a woman, despite my having already spent six years doing just this before I met with them. Effectively I had to be "certified" a woman!

It was an odd kind of psychotherapy for people like myself. I came to this clinic, as did many others, because I already knew myself, had diagnosed myself and chosen my own treatment. The year of waiting was to make sure we had made the right decision. This meant that the members of the medical team were being examiners more than providing therapy. This was a great shame. It deprived us of therapy that we might really have appreciated. We often found we could not confess any doubts without endangering our own treatment. Yet intelligent people would be constantly questioning themselves while going through this process.

To give a personal example: I had successfully lived so long as a woman that I sometimes questioned my need for this somewhat risky operation. I mentioned this to my psychotherapist on just one occasion. She immediately questioned her assessment of me as a transsexual and decided I must be sent to yet another psychotherapist for a confirmatory assessment. My frankness had put into danger my approval for the operation and seemingly their view of my femininity. That was the last time I mentioned any doubts. This was a great disappointment for me. I would have enjoyed having the luxury of a proper relationship with my psychotherapist in which I could relax, be open, without fearing being judged.

I had a bigger problem with the psychologist on this team. I was very cynical about many of his tests. I was not a naive subject, for I had studied something of psychology as part of my training for the priesthood and Jackie was also a trained psychological social worker. But he presumed that I was naive. Thus, when I was given the inkblot test and asked what I could see in a series of seemingly random black and white smudges, I could not take it very seriously. I told him I imagined all sorts of sexual connotations, of pistons going in and out! He did not smile but took copious notes. He also seemed surprised that I was interested in stories about war and human rights. Military matters were seemingly inappropriate for a woman's psyche. Later, in hospital for the operation, a nurse told me that my whole file was in the nurses' station and she had read that I had "failed" my psychological assessment! He had decided that I would be better off as a man! I took this up later with him for I was angry and did not want him to make similar mistakes with other patients. Luckily I had passed all other assessments.

Surgical Re-assignment

But despite these difficulties, I had now finally reached the operation table. For the next few hours I was in the hands of an excellent female surgeon. When I woke up it was to a happy painfree daze. Soon I was besieged by a group of curious nurses. One of them asked me: "Please may we have a look?" I was curious too. They lifted the bandages and took a quick peep. I looked too. A long slit, shaved. The nurses grinned when I asked if it looked all right. They assured me that I was now nothing other than totally female in shape. I happily drifted back to sleep.

Later I found that my new clit was totally erotic. The only thing lacking was a vagina of great depth. The surgeon told me that I had unfortunately provided her with too short a penis to wall the new vagina for a depth of more than 2 or 3 inches. I was not sure whether I had always had such a short penis. As a child I had never examined that of others. It could be that the hormones had made it shrink. Perhaps it was a combination of both factors.

Everyone's body is a bit different. I was lucky that my body was very happy to take on a female shape. It acted as if it was a purely natural task that it only needed a little help from a surgeon or hormones. A consultant my medical team sent me to for an independent assessment said he was very surprised by the degree of my change. He said he had never seen such good-sized breasts on a transsexual! Unwanted body hair had simply vanished. I also had remarkably obedient hair cells on my face.

I had found the operation really easy emotionally. This was another argument in itself for my transexuality. True males would have run away screaming at any threat to their genitals. I certainly did not feel castrated. On the contrary, I was now more myself and felt empowered. It was now obvious to me, as never before, those male organs had simply not belonged here, in my house. I was very much at peace with my post-op body and much more relaxed. I also felt safer.

I did not see this operation as making me a woman. The Castrati singers that were the glory of Italian Catholic Church choirs up until the 19th Century saw themselves as male. I knew that I was a woman beforehand and had been since birth. Surgery does not give one a gender. It is plain daft that this operation is required in the UK before a person is allowed to correct a wrong gender assignment. I fear that some of today's male surgeons get a sexual kick out of creating beautiful women—and may reject candidates they think will not make pretty women. I suspect there is a very high rate of suicides among those rejected.

As for me, this is my opinion:

I am not female because a doctor certified me so

I am not female because a doctor made me so

I am not female because I am castrated

I am not female because I am conditioned

I am not female because I am attractive to men

I am not female because I am able to give birth

I am not female because I bleed monthly

I am not female because my clitoris is less than 0.7cms long

I am not female because I have breasts.

There are many women that break one or more of these criteria and are still women. No, being female is something utterly dark and deep, something that happened when we were within the safe sanctuaries of our mother's wombs. It is there that we are given our gender wired brain, there that the true foundations are laid of our richly gendered lives.

Vaginal sex was in theory made possible for me by this magical operation. I could now in theory make love freely, spontaneously, simply and gloriously, without having first to make a deeply personal speech or explanation.

And within two weeks of the operation, a diamond prospector was in my bed! He had originally come to see me because he knew I had been researching the diamond secrets of the Australian outback. He then became fascinated with me. A few days later he turned up with two large steaks and a bottle of wine. I was amazed. Jackie had to instruct me that an old fashioned Australian male custom was not simply to bring alcohol but also meat. Within days, although still sore, we were together. It was a purely sexual fling and nothing to do with love. But I thanked the Gods for sending me so quickly a lover that could help consecrate, integrate, my reshaped body. I was in pain but exultant.

However having a lover was difficult for me when Jackie and I were living together, even though she had frequently told me she wanted me to have lovers just as she had in London. I did not feel free to do this within our family home. I needed some privacy. I suggested to Jackie that I rent a house a few doors away to give us more space. I was then astonished when Jackie greeted this idea by launching a blistering attack. She asked how could I dare to even think of moving out when she had been done so much to support me through my operation? She accused me of wanting to desert her and the children. She had been amazingly good at looking after me when I came home from the hospital. I had no wish to make her feel rejected. I loved her. My priority was still to maintain a relationship that allowed us to completely share our caring for the children.

So once again my efforts to secure a little more independence collapsed. It turned out to be only a fleeting affaire with Graham anyway, so soon Jackie and I were back to living together in the manner that seemed to be the pattern of our lives. But Jackie was preparing for greater freedom. In the January of the next year, 1982, she had her tubes tied.

As for my first experience of vaginal sex: well there had been a certain wildness in it, a joy in being ploughed. But I had physically hurt. My vagina was small and raw. I also wondered at the cruel fate that had created AIDS to bring an end to the 1960s age of sexual freedom on the pill before I could enjoy it. If I had been free earlier, I thought I would have enjoyed sex as much as any infertile woman could.

But when Jackie and I made love, there was much more gentleness, much more of tuning in to each other, much more of the shuddering delight of bringing each other slowly on to orgasm. Humans that are bisexual perhaps are the most fortunate. Maybe, if conditioning did not have its play, many more would be bisexual. A wise Australian friend of mine once said that she fell in love then noted the gender of her partner.

Investigative Journalism

There is a male myth that their "balls" give men their courage and drive their creativity. For me the operation was no hindrance to energy or creativity. It rather unleashed it. In August I had my first article published as a journalist. It ran over three pages in a Saturday broadsheet and was nationally syndicated throughout Australia and advertised on television.

Not long after this, Aboriginal elders were launching my book: *Massacres to Mining: the colonisation of Aboriginal Australia.* They put the book into a traditional carved wooden bowl over earth from the four corners of Australia, adorned it with dingo fur and emu feathers, and went to the offices of the major mining companies to present it to them with a request that they read it.

This book launch was covered on all major television news programmes, the more so because of the stupidity of RTZ's CRA subsidiary. They incredibly locked the door to their skyscraper in order to bar the delegation of four Aborigines and myself, much as if we wanted to give them not a book but a dangerous virus that would infect the entire building. They did this in the presence of TV crews, then compounded their PR disaster by giving out a press release warning the broadcasters that I was much too dangerous to be reported since legal action was still being undertaken against a film of mine. This only gave us more publicity. I remember that the PM programme gave a long and very unfavourable report on the company's action.

The film in question was the *World in Action* documentary entitled *Strangers in their own land.* I had initiated this while in England. It described the treatment of Aborigines at Weipa whose ancestral lands were given by the Queensland state government to CRA to strip-mine. This company now held a thousand square mile bauxite-mining lease over land that was previously Eastern Australia's largest Aboriginal Reserve. It was destroying virgin forest that was still hunt-gathered and still had many sacred places that were cared for by the Elders.

This film had been seen around the world before it came to Australia. But when the ABC televised it in Australia, they were sued by the mining company. Justice Blackburn ruled in the company's favour principally because of Aboriginal statements broadcast in the film. I remember that he did not like an allegation that CRA's subsidiary Comalco had "stolen" Aboriginal land. The judge said this was libellous, for it was not the company that had taken the Aboriginal land but the Government who gave it to the company when asked for it.

He also found libellous the allegation by Joyce Hall, the elder we took to Europe, that the company had "treated them like a pack of dogs." He did not mention Joyce's undisputed evidence in court that the company had bulldozed her people's traditional Aboriginal cemetery, burning corpses with the trees.

The local Aboriginal custom was to place the bodies of their dead on platforms between trees until they had dried out. Mrs Jean Jimmy, a Mapoon elder, explained to us that the bodies were burnt once dried. They then "carry the ash until a certain time, using the moon as their calendar…the ash has to go to a sacred ground." What Comalco had bulldozed were the platforms containing the bodies of the recent dead. The judge's only comment on this atrocity was that Joyce had been over-emotional in describing this sacrilege and libellous in alleging that the company had treated Aborigines like dogs. In fact she was quite accurate. Australian law was that Aborigines had the same land-ownership rights to tribal lands as had the animals on that land.

What I had also found particularly alarming, arrogant and revealing in the evidence was the company's presentation of its carefully devised "three generational" program of assimilation. They said that since the local Aboriginal culture did not have an appropriate work ethic for a modern industrial culture, the company had employed experts from Monash University to remedy this by modifying the Aboriginal culture through a kindergarten program. They did not say if they told the Aboriginal parents of what they planned for their children. They hoped to modify the local Aboriginal culture, so that the local Aborigines would no longer think it fine to simply work to get the funds needed for current needs before leaving to visit hunting grounds and carry out seasonal rituals.

I was now in the full flight of my new journalistic career. My investigative articles were prominently published. I also championed the small-scale miners against the majors. One article was particularly successful. It revealed that CRA had plans to pump cyanides into 700 kilometres of underground rivers in northern Victoria to extract gold from their waters. As farmers depended on wells sunk into these rivers for all their water, the article stirred up all kinds of community groups and the scheme was abandoned by CRA.

I kept up my film work. I set up and researched a film produced for the BBC Everyman religious documentary series. It described the Aboriginal spiritual relationship to the earth and how this was threatened by indiscriminate mining. It was during my research for this film, that Aboriginal women took me to their sacred places around Uluru, the massive rock that whites call Ayers Rock.

While I was away, in the relative freedom this gave her, around June of 1982 Jackie began another affair. This was ironically, and strangely, with another Catholic priest. She told me she had fallen in love with him "head over heels."

I was happy for her but was threatened subconsciously for it gave me nightmares. In one dream a bomb had caught on scaffolding and was hanging suspended over us like a sword of Damocles. Later in the same dream I realised that the bomb was also suspended over the nave of a church in which a priest was levitating up towards the bomb, lying back at a 45-degree angle as he rose, but failing to reach it. These dreams captured my insecurity and fears. I was scared of what this relationship would bring. It was the first time Jackie has fallen in love with anyone else since we first knew each other. But it had a surprising consequence.

My diary recorded: "Last Sunday I moved to a bed in my office in case Jackie wanted to use the double bed in the other room. She came back late. I kept to my room and from down the corridor I could hear her laugh, sigh and pant with her lover. It is the first time this has happened within earshot of me. I had the strangest feelings. I felt both lonely and jealous, but as soon as he had left, Jackie came to see me and then I was glad to see how happy she was. Jackie and I afterwards were closer together, even sexually, than we had been for a while. It was so good to see the old Jackie back and see her looking younger and more confident. I'm glad she's found a man to love her. She's needed this for so long. I've known for a long time that I cannot satisfy all her sexual needs. She tells me she thinks she's found someone she can be herself with who will never be a threat to us as a family. He is a lovely man and the kids do like him."

Another major change in Jackie was her decision to use an investment given to her by her parents towards buying a house. Up until now she had been adamant that owning a house would burden her spirit. My diary recorded: "For years and years Jackie has opposed us buying a house (stopping us back in 1972, the only other time we really looked), saying she knew it would oppress her spirit and dominate her. Yet now she felt the time had come—and that it now won't dominate her! We had much need now for stability after the constant moving and after having to move into smaller and smaller houses as the rents went up. We should be able to find a house that would enable us again to be hospitable."

When we did find a place to buy, my diary recorded: "Today we bought our first house, a lovely wooden house on one level surrounded by trees and with seven rooms full of light. Cathy and Kara are thrilled. I am pleased and a bit apprehensive, especially about the re-stumping and draining we have to do." My diary added; "My journalistic earnings provided the vital deposit but Jackie's mother, I think, provided the rest of the funds." The day we signed the contract for the house was the first of the Australian spring, September 1st, 1982.

I felt sure in my bones that this house was really for her and not for me; that our relationship was doomed despite my remaining in love with her. She told me she wanted the house to be a place where she could bring her parents—when I was absent. I was then still naive about our relationship. I still enormously admired her, even though I knew that she was separating herself from me.

Knowing this, I decided I would show my love for her and the children by leaving her the gift of the most beautiful and well-sorted home possible. I thus spent much time working on the house, making it a fine nest for our family, making sure its foundations were sound, drained, planting many trees, helping to give it a fine new kitchen in the very centre of the house. My diary continued: "I did most of the practical work on fixing up the house, researching and finding contractors, learning much, for Jackie is working full time. I have set aside my writing for a while. I work so hard on the house because I think I must have something to give to Jackie and the kids." While I was doing this work, inside I was crying. I knew that I was no longer a permanent part of our home. (Jackie or her parents had stipulated that the title was to be only in her name.) But we were still sharing a wonder at the continuing beauty of life.

My diary continued: "But for now I am here. I have to grow into the house, get used to it. I've better working space than ever before but I do not know if it suits me spiritually. I've done my best writing under terrible conditions. Poverty suits! But no doubt Divine Providence has brought us here and there's got to be good reason for it. Certainly it is doing Jackie's spirit good. She's suffered terribly from the conditions we've had to live in during the past few years and from insecurity.

"This house has been dominating me but I expect, once all the basic things are done, I too will be free (and so it seems)…I feel that the house is particularly Jackie's, not just because it's in her name as most of the money was hers, but because it meets a great need of hers for space, for a place where she can happily bring her friends and even her parents (apart from the problem of my presence) because it isn't ugly and has room aplenty to entertain." By mid-November most of the work had been done on the house. We had a house warming party with some fifty to sixty guests and had a few weeks later a New Years Eve party with a similar number of guests.

My journalistic work resumed and helped maintain my confidence. "I had felt accepted as myself among the Aborigines, I was building my own reality, I was now writing features for the major local broadsheet, *The Age*, and researching television documentaries for the BBC's Everyman programme, but with Jackie, an old reality clung on. And I was aware of her other world that rejected me…or rather that she excluded me from (my in-laws). I was never sure whether it was her or them (that excluded me)."

Jackie took our children to meet with her relatives but I was not to meet them. I wondered if this was because I was a scandal to them but this seemed unlikely, given the open, friendly and accepting letter her father had sent us when we first told them of my transition. I would have felt very awkward at our initial meeting but this might have been overcome. But I now knew that this exclusion was at least as much her decision as theirs.

My eyes were opened to my naiveté and Jackie's wish to isolate me from her family when she instructed me that I was not to see her Aunt Eve again. This elderly aunt, her Dad's sister, lived nearby and I found her very open and friendly. I loved calling on her. I did this for years. We got on very well. Our friendship partially made up for leaving my own relatives in England. But now Jackie said she found this too embarrassing, even though she rarely went to visit her aunt. I did what Jackie wished although

I thought her wrong to so insist. I was thus isolated from all her relatives. I missed Auntie Eve much.

Our alienation from each other was a slow process. We still had many very good times together. We went camping frequently, rejoicing in the beauty and symmetry of wilderness. We spun tales together; we wove magical things. But sometimes a dark shadow seemed to hang over her. She would get depressed and then angry and hurtful. The children would see me crying. Everyone was upset. I knew that I could only find healing when away from the house. I needed to be under trees in wild places. Then the tears would vanish as the beauty of nature distracted and called me.

The darkest day for me was when we went back to Europe for a brief visit and took a holiday in Italy. We went by boat into Venice and it was as beautiful and magical as ever. The children played in the great squares and rode in gondolas. It was at first a happy time. I don't know what went wrong when we went on to Umbra but a cloud came down. At the end of one awful day when we were in a heavily built grim hotel in a fortressed town, Jackie's anger at me became incandescent, smouldering, dark. There was no way that I could escape noticing the hateful hurt. It seemed to be produced by the conflicts tearing at her, for soon afterwards it seemed that we were again the best of friends.

But a distraction came. My career took another twist at the instigation of Aborigines. Jerry Bostock, an Aboriginal poet, came to visit from nowhere and gave me wonderful encouragement. He said I should get more into television and make films about his people's fight for justice. He gave me practical help. We decided to go first for a film about the diamond industry, Aborigines and human rights. He also suggested people who could teach me the ropes of this industry. It was thus that I met David and Vivien.

Soon we had set up a company called "Investigative Media Productions" and were seeking funding for a television documentary series on the world diamond trade. David and Vivien were also very keen to work with Robert Bropho, the Aboriginal spokesman who had taken me up to the Kimberleys. It all seemed marvellous.

A year later, on January 24th 1983, a surgeon operated on me again in order to make my vagina of a more adequate depth by taking a skin graft from my inside thigh. I had become somewhat depressed at having a vagina of inadequate depth. I'd had a sexual fiasco with the diamond prospector Graham back in 1981 and on three other unsatisfactory one night stands. This second operation was much more painful than the first and kept me a month in hospital, twice as long as for the first. It left constricting scar tissue so it was not completely successful.

I was still there on Ash Wednesday when the hospital began to smell like a bush fire. I could see from the ward the smoke of fires. They surrounded Melbourne and totally obscured the horizon. Heavy red dust and smoke enveloped the hospital. A week earlier a drought had caused dust storms that totally obscured the sun and now firestorms were racing through the bush nearby, incredibly raw, violent and devouring. The ashes fell around the hospital. Melbourne was besieged. A friend who was building a home on a forested hill east of the city took refuge in a protected house in the nearby town. When she went back, the only thing that had survived were her oven-proofed Pyrex glass dishes. She would keep them on her mantelpiece for they had been melted into wonderfully warped shapes. The temperature in the firestorms had been over a thousand degrees centigrade. Seventy-two people died and about 2000 homes were destroyed. Seven towns were practically burnt to the ground, especially along the magnificent Otway coast.

But six months later the eucalyptus trees turned into blackened pillars of charcoal were putting out tiny baby branches as they started to regain their glory. Australian trees have long survived fires.

Musing in hospital I felt utterly uninterested in further one-night stands. Now I had the physical possibility of sexual union, it seems something much too special to waste. Lying on my back gave me time to think and pray. I wrote: "Now I'm physically open, it is the time for becoming much more spiritually open and less self-centred."

When I returned home from hospital in February, I found Jackie so exhausted that her speech was slurred. I suggested that she should go and stay at her sister Jenny's to get a complete break, for a week or two. My diary recorded: 'Her face lights up. Her speech comes back to normal." I loved having the chance to look after Kara and Cathy by myself. It was something that I had long wanted. I noted: "Kara is maturing beautifully. Cathy is in her difficult tenth year (it was hard for Kara too). She is no longer a little child but in pre-puberty...By the time Jackie returned, both children were volunteering to do more and more household tasks and Jackie, impressed, said she now would have to go away more often." We had different styles of household management. But Jackie had only given herself a four-day break. She probably did not realise it, but her sense of duty was so strong that it was hard for me to find opportunities to take full responsibility. I tried to get more opportunities.

After her break, I took my own much-needed post-surgery break. I went to Mt. Buffalo Chalet high in the Australian Alps and immediately had a brief affair. It did not continue afterwards. I found that it was only when I was away that it was possible to make such new male friends. This was true also for Jackie. She had met her priest friend while I was away in the Kimberleys.

Some three months later I shot my first film with funds raised from Overseas Aid Agencies. We then used the rushes to raise the money for editing. I co-produced it with the West Australian Aboriginal elder, Robert Bropho. It was called "Munda Nyuringu" and gave an Aboriginal insight into the colonisation of the Goldfields of Western Australia. While making it, we were attacked in the West Australian Parliament for "manipulating" Aboriginal people to make this film, yet every voice in the film was Aboriginal and the local Aborigines approved the film before it was released.

After making this film, I took the children to Bali and helped Jackie get away to have a holiday by herself on Brampton Island on the coral coastline of Queensland. I later took Cathy to Europe and New York when our film was exhibited in European film festivals. On returning to Australia, I received a wonderful welcome back from Jackie and the family. I had been away seven weeks and felt very optimistic.

Then three days later George came to stay. Jackie had met him on Brampton Island. The first night after he arrived, she booked into a motel with him but next day told me that he wanted to stay at our home, so he came and stayed for ten days. I was not as comfortable with this as I had hoped. I felt as if a stranger in my own home. I now wonder at my acceptance of this. At that time I idealistically wanted to be totally self-giving to a woman that I loved, but of course it was not easy.

Jackie then decided, since the children and I were uncomfortable with his presence, to ask him not to stay over Christmas. I felt strangely guilty about this. I hated booting out anyone over Christmas. But with much relief we then had a wonderful family Christmas. Then on Boxing Day George phoned to say that he had decided to move semi-permanently to Melbourne and by the first weekend of 1985 Jackie and he were back together, although this time only for a few days.

Jackie and I then went away with the children for a peaceful week camping by a mountain river in the rainforest on the West Tyers River in western Victoria, an area of temperate rain forest rich in ferns and wildlife. We talked about our relationship and I felt much reassured. She told me that her relationship with George would not displace me from my place in the family. In the ensuing weeks Jackie and he spent an occasional night together but slowly that relationship ended. Jackie told me she found him boring and that it had been more a meeting of bodies than of minds.

What do the children say?

Around this time the children started at a secondary school they much enjoyed. One of the hard decisions we had to make as parents was what to advise the children to say when they were asked who were their parents, or who I was. Jackie was keen that they kept quiet about my real identity. She said this would expose them to being teased or us to tabloid newspaper curiosity.

In their pre-school days this presented them with few problems, or so it seemed. They grew up knowing that I had fathered them and then changed my gender role, as had others before me. They knew I still loved and cared for them. They said I was their second Mum, but for simplicity sake, Jackie and I had them call us both by our first names.

My own instinct was to be open to those who asked, who were friends or I judged appropriate. That was how I acted with my own friends. If it had only affected me, then I would have been still more open. I could understood why other "transsexuals" sought privacy but I thought, and still think, that my chosen role demands of me that I walk openly on the risky public lands where I can be hurt, but where I can also teach and find understanding. I felt myself a coward when I backed away from acknowledging the many gifts that enriched my life.

I also knew that if no "transsexuals" were open, then society would not change and become more understanding. I had admired Jan Morris, a transsexual woman who wrote her story in the book "Conundrum". Aunt Eve had told me that she understood me much better because she had seen Jan Morris on television talking about her own transition. She said that Jan had come across as a very fine woman.

But Jackie was a very private person. She left me in no doubt that any publicity would make it impossible for us to stay together as a family. It would bring to an end our dream of bringing up the children as partners, even as two women who were still lovers, for our physical affection for each other continued for many years despite these changes.

The other fear Jackie had was that our children might be cruelly teased at school if our family became a subject of press gossip. We believed if my ordination as a priest became known, given my public profile in Aboriginal affairs and as a journalist, there was no way we could prevent the tabloids making us household names and faces. Thus Jackie suggested, and I reluctantly agreed, that I should keep my previous work private. I felt that I was only hiding this from the public eye temporarily. But this was still a terrible contradiction. The priesthood was central to my life and had been so since my youth. It still was. My instinct was that it demanded of me openness and a trust in providence. It now sadly seemed that I must not be open lest I put at risk our family. Nevertheless this seemed to be the right decision for that time.

I also agreed to a subterfuge to help us survive as a family. Our children would say when asked about their family: "We have two Mums, Jackie and Jan." But when pressed by teachers or classmates, they were to say that I was really their aunt. It was probably presumed at their school that we were lesbian lovers, which was close enough to the truth. The school were told Jackie and I were joint legal custodians of the children. What they made of this, I do not know.

There were occasional minor problems. At one primary school dance, a woman asked me: "Is she your daughter?" and was answered simultaneously by Jackie, standing behind me, and by myself, with a "Yes" much to the questioner's perplexity! But the subterfuge normally worked.

The BBC and the Missionary

I have no doubt that rumours did circulate. This was evidenced when I researched a film for the BBC's and ABC's "Everyman" religious series. I went to a Catholic mission in far North Western Australia called Kalumburu in 1982. I had heard rumoured before arriving that this Benedictine mission had stopped the World Council of Churches' team investigating Australian racism from visiting their mission by putting flaming oil drums on the airstrip. I thought they might stop me coming too, so I simply hired a light plane and flew in, walked up the avenue of palm trees and knocked on their door.

The missionary who opened it was astonished to find a journalist. He muttered something about "permits" but I looked as innocent and naive as I could contrive and told him truthfully that I was working for the religious affairs departments of the BBC and ABC I added that I was putting together a programme about Aborigines, had heard much about Kalumburu and wanted very much to meet the missionaries of so historical a mission. He hesitated, then opened the door. I was in. I am sure being a woman helped.

For the next two hours I sat on the veranda while the missionaries plied me with their home made wine and beer and told me tales about the mission. Eventually the conversation came around to Aboriginal spirituality. I asked them; "Do the Aborigines still have initiations?" "Oh no" came the answer. "They are Christians now and have put all that sort of thing behind them." I then asked about something I had heard about down south from relatives of Kalumburu Aborigines. "Didn't one of the carved sacred boards come up here recently?" These are boards that symbolise the creative energy of the Ancestors and of the land. They traditionally travel along the ancient Dreaming Tracks from community to community, accompanied by dances and by songs, recreating the journeys and energies of the creating Ancestors. The missionary I asked quickly admitted: "Yes, one did come up here. The Aborigines here were highly embarrassed when this pagan thing arrived and asked us if we could help by quickly sending it away by plane. We flew it off to some other community."

My preparation for this visit had included reading a book by a Kalumburu missionary. This reported two similar incidents in 1947 when Aboriginal elders brought in Sacred Boards: "They went completely wild. It was disgraceful to discover that…the guardians of the boards, which were not a symbol of Aboriginal culture but symbols of a most degrading practice, were Christians from the mission. The boards were destroyed before their eyes." In 1950 when boards arrived again: "That such boards have semi-religious significance is open to question, what cannot be denied is the degrading influence which this practice has on our

Christians and on the work of the mission. It cannot be denied either that such practices have contributed to the destruction of their race."[254]

At the end of the conversation, I asked if I might speak with the Aborigines. The missionaries said "Of course!" and told me the way to the huts on the opposite hill. The Aborigines were suspicious of me when I reached them. They had seen me talking to the missionaries for hours and drinking wine. The elders had banned alcohol from this Aboriginal settlement. But they were astonished when I told them that I was carrying greetings from their relatives. "How do you know them?" they asked. "I work with the Kimberley Land Council" I told them and continued; "The missionaries told me that you no longer initiate?" This provoked a sudden and furious denial. "That is not true. We bring up all the young men properly". I grinned to show that I was on side and said: "They told me that you got them to fly the sacred carved board away?" They laughed; "The Board had next to travel [along the Dreaming Track] to another community and we thought, why walk? We persuaded the missionaries to take it for us!"

I wrote up what I learnt here for *The Age*. Melbourne's premier newspaper, as the Everyman producer had decided not to go to Kalumburu. But I was astonished when the missionaries soon discovered that this female reporter had twelve years earlier worked a Catholic priest on the other side of the world. They consequently banned the Everyman team from visiting them. I was totally amazed that stories about me were reaching even the remotest corners of Australia.

On another occasion, a journalist from *The Age* interviewed me over dinner about a new book of mine about Aborigines then switched off his tape recorder and asked: "How did Aborigines take your change of name?" I was dismayed, but not totally surprised. I wrote for that paper and, although everyone there treated me well and professionally, I had wondered if rumours had reached them. When I explained that Jackie and I had decided to avoid publicity in order to protect our children from teasing, he agreed not to write about this aspect of my life.

Our shared decision for good or ill was that what was most important for our children was that we both stayed together to love and care for them and that they were protected from teasing.

Although it was supposed by many that Jackie and I were simply lesbians, we could not simply leave the story at that. We had also to explain to the curious why we both had the same last name and why there was a family resemblance between the children and us both. Thus our decision that the children if pressed were to say that I was the sister of their father.

I did not understand what a strain this deception would put on our children. My younger daughter in her early adulthood once said to me with some anger: "Do you know what it was like to spend all those years having to lie about you? I wanted sometimes to boast about you, but could not." It seemed she thought she was told to lie simply to protect me from embarrassment.

I knew, but she did not, that she would have been able to be honest about me if protecting me had been the main consideration. I did not need protecting. If my own reputation had been the only consideration, I would have gritted my teeth and gone for openness.

But I think she understood that protecting them was the main consideration. When eventually a newspaper exposed my gender background while I was working as a producer for the BBC's flagship program Panorama, she phoned me up from Australia in some indignation, to say: "Jani, I wanted to tell you that you don't need to protect me any longer. You can be open now. Go and fight them" Her statement freed me. It helped me realise it was time to write this book.

I am still glad for the wonder and privilege of sharing in their growing up. Kara was always the quieter one, but not so quiet that both of them did not become "Goths", thus standing out from most of their fellow students with their black clothes and whitened faces. I had feared that they might react against my radicalism and become reactionary but totally independently of me they became founding members of an organisation in Melbourne called something like "Young People Against Nuclear Arms." I was surprised and delighted by this.

When I brought Cathy last to Europe, she arrived with a beautiful butterfly painted on half of her face. Later in autumn it changed to a golden leaf. My mother looked a bit askance over Cathy's choice of clothes and was delighted when I told her that I had stopped by a clothes shop at Cathy's request.

"Oh, you got Cathy some more clothes. Excellent! What did you get her?" my mother asked.

My response of "A bowler hat" left my mother laughing.

Kara delighted me when she began to write short stories. They revealed that this person who at home was quiet and retiring, had a very keenly observant eye and sense of humour. I was surprised by the insights they revealed. Like my mother before me, she had a talent for writing. In the short story category, she was much better than me. I treasured all the writings she shared with me. She gave me a most precious gift of a folder filled with her short stories. They were brilliant, keenly observant and humorous. Now I thought, at last I know what you are thinking when you quietly watch from the side! As I write this on the other side of the world I miss her deeply, all the more so because of later events that ripped us apart.

Jackie and I never stinted on the children's artistic development, buying paints, brushes and other art gear whenever it was wanted. We wanted above all to keep their imagination alive, fresh and creative. This was, we thought, one of the finest things we could do for them.

I think imagination is our most God-like faculty. Creation was not completed with one big bang. We are still engaged on the same work. We defended our children from school uniformity, not just by taking them out frequently into wilderness so that nature would feed them, not only by putting them in a school with a reputation for creativity, but also by the liberal supply of artistic materials. Kara was a prolific and fine writer but Cathy particularly took to art. Her sculptures, drawings and paintings came to fill much of our family home. Today she is managing her own gallery. Kara also drew well. The artistic talent and vision of both girls helped make our family home beautiful. Jackie too was talented as a painter. As for me, my art form is mostly spinning words.

My writing career was progressing. I now had another book project. Melbourne was about to celebrate its 150th Anniversary by turfing its main street and having a party. The celebration showed no consciousness of the disaster Melbourne's founding was to the local Aborigines. For every sheep station established on Melbourne's outskirts, settlers' diaries revealed an average of fifty Aborigines killed, sometimes by putting strychnine into bread and giving it to families. Aboriginal skulls were nailed over farm doors in order to scare Aborigines away.

I discovered that the famous Tasmanian Aboriginal woman, Truganini, rightfully famous for her beauty and wrongly reported to be the last of her still existing people, was a leading member of an armed group that fought against the British invaders who set up Melbourne. I came across the diaries of the military officer who lead expeditions against them. It seemed this would be a worthy story for a book.

I soon learnt that the story that all Aborigines were nomadic was a lie framed to hide what happened. Before Melbourne existed, there was in the hills nearby an Aboriginal spiritual centre where men and women lived who specialised in teaching dancing, music and spiritual skills, and who were supported by gifts of food from their students. There was also nearby a major fish farm with canals joining rivers. Elaborately woven dams and fish traps supported a settled Aboriginal population. Some of their houses had stonewalls. The first Europeans to arrive reported finding houses with roofs so strongly made that they could support the weight of a horse. What the locals had to say about these strange newcomers riding over their roofs was not recorded. In East Gippsland the Aborigines reported seeing centaurs when they first saw a man on a horse.

Some Aboriginal elders feared that the invading whites were ghosts. The local Aboriginal culture taught that the spirits of dead went to islands off the coast and that ghosts were white. So when white people arrived on "floating islands", some thought these were the dead returning. (The Aboriginal word for whites in Victoria is still "num, meaning, "ghost.") But the new arrivals found Australia so utterly alien that they brought with them their own foods and seeds and avoided eating local vegetables. A white Melbourne woman immigrant was thought strange for growing local yams. Most found Aborigines very scary. The invading migrants had been bred on stories of cannibals and black witchdoctors.

I was fortunate for this writing project to be lent a mudbrick cottage in the upper valley of the Yarra River by which Melbourne was built. It was 1986, some seven years after my traumatic return to Australia and five years after my final operation. It was again evident that Jackie was torn between wanting to be independent of me and wanting me around. This cottage gave us both a break.

It was a privilege to live in this wilderness. One evening while working on a computer I saw the hammock on the veranda start swinging. I was amazed. There was no wind. Then a head emerged from the centre of the hammock. It had a wide flat mouth, two eyes, and low forehead. It clearly belonged to a very short body.

Then suddenly it leapt and fluttered to the ground. It was an owl, a tawny frogmouth (so called because of its wide mouth). It hopped into the house and sat on the coffee table watching me. It was a marvellous visit. It came back several times to see me. I was also given a young wallaby to look after. A car had killed its mother. It would stand by the sink and watch everything I did, as long as I left the kitchen door open so it could escape if needed. I once shut this door, and immediately had a panicked wallaby leaping from surface to surface, from armchair to tabletop to floor to chair, with its long tail sweeping everything down.

But this writer's cottage was only briefly available to me. I had a sweet affair with a local man, but it only lasted for a couple of days and I did not bring him home. Tensions mounted when I had to work from our family home. Our usual way of dealing with this was to go away into the wilderness together as often as possible. We found our own peace in the rain forest, or the red river gum forest of the northern Victorian valleys, or in the high mountain ash of the hills. The greatest tensions were usually when Jackie's lovers came to our family home. I wanted her to be happy and she me. She told me that she would not allow these men to separate us. I said the same of my lovers. My own very brief affairs, although much delighted in by me, were always when I was away from home. There was no way that I would let them destroy the most precious thing in my life, my family.

Years went past on this basis, with us living together, sleeping together, but having some outside adventures with men. But by 1986, five years after we moved into our new home, when we had been together for some seventeen years, things were getting much more difficult. Sometimes cruel things were said. These often had me in tears, confused, not knowing what was happening or how best to react. The children were very upset by this and sometimes they asked Jackie: "Why are you trying to drive Jani out". I perhaps wrongly let the children see my grief. I needed any help I could get. I desperately hoped their words to Jackie would make her realise how important I was to them and thus keep us together. But I was even more miserable about this for I feared I was using children who I should be protecting. This demeaned me.

My diary recorded that sometimes I was almost out of my mind for grief. I would get into the car but would just "sit, thinking I must leave but not knowing where to go." I was always, however, rescued by the children or Jackie coming out, telling me I was in no fit state to drive and asking me to come in. This too made me miserable. I felt this was no way to live. It certainly did not make me feel proud.

Or so I saw it at the time. Perhaps one reason why I fought so hard to keep my place was because I feared the consequences of rejection. I had experienced rejection by my birth family. I had faced social rejection. But this was not a major factor. I had tried previously to find space outside the family home only to have Jackie and the children ask me back. I had anticipated this separation but that did not make it welcome. I did not want to leave the children before they chose to fly. I loved being with them.

I now did not want to be reborn into a single life even though it meant I could be more open, be myself, and find myself. I feared the space beyond the family walls, even though it might be a fertile rich place. Thus the Goddess had a hard delivery, birthing me to the wider family. I went kicking all the way. Yet the children were in mid-teens and would soon fly. I knew it was easy to construct a sandcastle as a parent and decorate it beautifully, only to have the incoming tide wash it away.

I was not at all sure about my wisdom in staying on. These times were awful. I am sorry for my role in any hurt. But these dark episodes were like thunderclouds. They would be followed by sunny times. We would renew our pledges to each other; rejoice in the sacredness of life. But my instincts were right. Jackie's affairs would finally bring an end to our relationship. It happened in a way that felt appropriate and part of our destiny.

In 1986 Jackie came home with an amazing story from the local university where she was studying. She found in the bar a friend, Dan, from over twenty years ago. I knew of him as an old flame of hers that had married another. Jackie some years earlier had even taken me to a certain pub because she had previously gone to it with him. She had now found him sitting in the bar, nursing a beer, trying to drown his sorrows, for his marriage had just fallen into pieces.

Jackie was excited and happy as she told me about meeting up with him again. There seemed to be an amazing pattern to this. I felt I could not deny fate. I was very happy for her. And when Dan came to visit, I found him a lovely guy, the kind of person I would also welcome as a friend. He seemed a sensitive visitor to our family home. He was careful to avoid staying without consulting me.

A few months later, in the September of 1986, I went with Kara for a much needed and wonderful holiday in New Zealand. I had promised her this trip at the time when I took Cathy to England. It was her choice of holidays. One of the first things we did, at her request, was to visit a very special place, the Greenpeace ship, the Rainbow Warrior, as it lay beside a quay in Christchurch. It was badly damaged by a French bomb that had killed a crew member; sabotaged to stop it going to the French nuclear tests. By it was a replacement ship, a larger vessel with a crated helicopter, being prepared for an Antarctic trip.

Two crew members, Davy and Graham Woodhead, showed us over the vessel. In the engine room a minibus-sized hole marked the site of the bomb explosion. Metal pieces had been driven through steel decks, the whole ship twisted. The quarters of the crewman who died were sealed. Kara greatly respected this legendary vessel and took time to sketch it.

She then navigated superbly as we drove south down North Island. We took a side trip by boat along an underground river to see glow-worms form another milky way, and then went via a Maori village swathed in the smoke of hot springs to Wellington to catch a boat to the South Island. We crossed mountains to see glaciers where wild winds smashed our car door, then past a maze that she solved in forty-four minutes (I took forty-eight) over a snowclad pass where the Kea parrots ate the rubber window surrounds of our hired car. Other delights included a steaming outdoor Jacuzzi bath, with a wonderful moonlit view of snowclad mountains. We shot river rapids on jet boats that did wheelies on water and went by helicopter to high snowfields where Kara danced on the virgin snow. All in all it was a marvellously exhausting and enjoyable holiday. The memories of this are poignant for it was to be some of the last days I would spend with this much loved and cherished daughter.

The end of us as a live-together family came soon afterwards when Jackie told me she wanted to leave to live with Dan in his flat. At first this seemed like a good way to resolve the tensions. I told her that I understood, that I would be very happy to look after Kara and Cathy (who were then fourteen and sixteen years old). I assured her that she would always be welcome to come back at any time; she would always have a place in the house and she would never need to feel that she had cut herself off from us.

Jackie was pleased that her going to live with Dan did not upset me. But she then dramatically changed her mind, presumably after discussing the idea with Dan, and maybe with her family. She now told me she wanted to stay on in the house with Dan and so I must go instead. I thought she had changed her mind so she could better care for the children. I wanted to give her space to be happy with him, so I very reluctantly agreed. I found myself a flat nearby where the children could come to see me and stay.

I was then mystified when Jackie insisted on giving me back the deposit that I had paid on the family house. I had not asked for this and had not expected it. I simply was not interested in money but in making sure Jackie and the children had a good family home.

But I was even more surprised when six months later Jackie moved out of the family house into a flat with Dan, leaving the girls, then about fifteen and sixteen, living on their own or with their boy friends as they so chose. Jackie assured me she would call in daily to make sure that they were all right. I was shocked and perplexed. Had she known she would move out when she insisted on me moving out? Had she persuaded me to leave by hiding her own plans? Why did she now insist she did not want me to return to care for our teenage daughters when she had chosen not to live with them? I worried, thinking that the girls were too young for this to be a wise decision.

It was some time before I realised that she may have insisted both on me leaving and on giving me back my deposit on the family home because she wanted to be sure that I had no legal claim on it. Perhaps she was so advised by Dan or her family. I could have argued, given the work I did on the house, that I had a far greater claim on it than simply my deposit. But I did not argue this. I did not even see what was being done. I now think myself naïve—but this is ever the fault of lovers.

I only came to understand what had happened some six years later, when Cathy and her partner Tree, by then the sole occupants of this commodious family house, decided to offer me a room of my own, a "granny room", to use when I was in Australia. When Jackie heard of this, she immediately vetoed it, telling me she could not permit it as the owner of the house for "I may want some day to move back into it."

I was stunned. Why was her possible future need more important to her than my being able to stay occasionally with my daughter? It seemed to violate all the values we had held dear. I was not even given the option of agreeing to move out when she wanted to move in. She has not moved back in the following years. Cathy is very important to me and I would have loved to have a home in my daughter's home to use when I was in the country. It would have given me somewhere to leave my most precious possessions. It would have given me a chance to stay with my grandchild when one eventually arrived. It would have made me feel vastly more accepted and much more a part of the family.

But the shock of this veto made me realise how much I had been blinkered by love. I knew of no other way of loving than of being trusting. I knew this left me vulnerable. I felt I was now the pariah, expelled. With no place. With no rights. An utterly unexpected fate. When I left Australia to make a film on human rights and the diamond trade, I no longer had the possibility of returning to share the home of my daughters.

But I still loved Jackie and the idea that she could have put a financial consideration before my relationship with our children was not one that then would have crossed my mind. I then simply could not understand her actions. It is only know with hindsight that I am less naïve.

A further decision she took was to keep secret from me the address to which she moved to live with Dan. She instructed the children to make sure of this. She said this was because Dan wanted his home to be a sanctuary where he could be alone and relax. I accepted his need, but wondered at being treated in such a fashion. Again the children were to know a place from which I was banned, as had happened with their Australian grandparents. I wondered if the reason for this was really because she needed a place where my words, my gift of the gab, could not reach her, where she was sealed off from me. I was not even to have a phone number.

It all seemed so strange coming from someone with whom I had shared so much and with whom I still shared responsibility for the children. But then I knew her reality was not my reality. We can never really be in another's space.

When I thought I might have been naïve, blinded by my love for Jackie, this drove me into an underworld where I must confess I found myself dealing with my self-righteousness and pride. I thought healing impossible. I wanted justice. I sought openness, feeling it would justify me. But, stepping back, I saw my pen in such a mood could cause more hurt. I needed purging. It ultimately did not matter that I was hurt. We were all hurt. My own healing had to come from within me. Was I really so naïve? I foresaw the coming separation. I had earlier walked Jackie to her lovers because I believed that love is self-effacing, self-forgetting. I had to let the fires die down, walk on the ashes, transform them.

Leaving Home

But to my surprise moving out proved to be a liberation that I had not sought, but which I much needed. I found that a male friend, strangely like to my father with red hair and good looks, was interested in me. While I lived with Jackie this had not been obvious to me, and indeed he may well have wondered if I were lesbian. But now I began a wonderful affair and thanked God for my unexpected freedom. This was my first real affair as a woman. I slipped into it as if born to it. I loved being with him. I felt I was now finding, at last, my own identity.

I realised now that when I was living with Jackie, the old me had been kept alive, if only barely. I had not been free but caught in a role, a somewhat male role, the role that Jackie did not do. I had not felt free to follow my instincts. This I had not resented, I merely saw it as a necessary compromise.

Cathy had now a regular boy friend, a lovely man with a great sensitivity for plants and nature. Kara was with a boy friend named Joe, the ex-flame of her closest girl friend, a prodigy who entered university at 14. It seemed that he was a counter-point to her intellectually, and that she found him much fun. I wrote at the time: "They are both blooming with love. It is great to see them so happy."

I also learnt what it was to be loved as a woman from a tracker who lived alone in the deserts of the Nullarbor Plain. It was but a one-night stand, but it was wild and rich. It also helped me understand males in a way I could not before. I met him near the border between West Australia and South Australia and asked him to take me into the interior to find an ancient ceremonial place of which Daisy Bates had written.[255] He was a magnificently wild lover. I felt ploughed, seeded, made fertile. It was a wonder finding my own way to being sexually alive.

Then at last after many delays my diamond series was fully funded. It was an expensive and ambitious project. I had raised from the US, from the UK and from Australia, a production budget of $1.2 million, quite a step up when my previous film had cost around $70.000. It was to be shot in five continents and meant going away longer than I ever had previously. I remember as if it were yesterday saying goodbye to Cathy and Kara. They were standing by the door, happy and glowing. They told me not to worry about them, that it was great that I trusted them. Yes, they had grown up and would show me that they were. They would call on Jackie if they needed help. With love we separated and looked forward to seeing each other again.

But alas, it was not so easy. One of my Australian funders got cold feet at the thought of taking on a major cartel and made moves to withdraw pledged funds. I was in London trying to sort this out for weeks. I made regular phone calls to my daughters. I noted that Kara on the phone seemed more self-confident. It was a good conversation. About two weeks later I phoned her again, and this time it was devastating.

Kara's boyfriend Joe answered my call, He promptly told me he was talking in her stead. He said they had decided that I was not to talk again to her until she decided to talk to me! I was stunned. It was so utterly unexpected. Kara and I had had no fight, not even a disagreement. Joe then added that Kara wanted me to know that it was nothing to do with my gender change and that the holiday in New Zealand had been wonderful. To my shocked and puzzled inquiry, he said they had made this decision because I was "too possessive". I was even more amazed. Leaving her alone with her lover and her sister was scarcely the act of a possessive parent. I had always taken care not to be possessive. Even now I try to respect her wishes despite missing her most terribly.

I then did not know what to say. But a few days later I decided to write to Kara. I wanted to know if Joe was speaking on her behalf. I told her that as far as I was concerned, she was now seventeen and grown up. If she wanted to fly free, not to be in touch with me, that was her right. But if she did, I wanted her to know that I loved her very much, that I would always keep a place for her in my heart and that she should never fear returning. I would always be there for her if she needed me.

About ten days later I phoned home to speak to Cathy but Kara's boyfriend was the first to pick up the phone. He angrily told me I was a "monster". He had told me not to try to contact Kara and my letter had made her cry for two days! This was all so utterly unimaginable. When I left Australia there was no sign that this would happen. I had chatted with Joe and had only friendly contacts with him. My only criticism had been when they did not emerge from bed to see me when I came to visit. Not long after these terrible phone calls, my film crisis deepened due to a funder's panic and I had to return to Australia to sort it out. This gave me the chance to discover what had happened with Kara and Joe.

I received a wonderful welcome back from my younger daughter Cathy and her boyfriend Tree. But the situation was extremely awkward. Both girls were still living in the family home with their boyfriends. I was probably much too timid. I hate family fights. I could not easily visit Cathy with Joe demanding that I keep away from the house. A few days later, when I phoned Cathy, Joe again took the phone. He told me not to phone the house even to talk to Cathy. "You know very well that every time you phone up, it puts great strain on Kara."

Later that same day I managed to let Cathy know of this demand. She was upset, doubly. She had just discovered that Joe also had not passed on a message about a friend who had over-dosed. I only know what happened that night by report. But apparently Jackie came in to try to sort out matters. The end result was that Jackie helped Kara and Joe move out to another address—another that she told me I was not to have!

Thus my eldest daughter followed the precedent set by Jackie. She remained in touch with both daughters but I was increasingly isolated. I wondered what I had done to deserve this. I felt I must have done something. Of course I had not been a perfect parent, but I loved them all very dearly.

What was this about my path that demanded that I be so burnt? Why this pain? It is now well over a decade since these events and Kara has not contacted me since. She did not even open the presents I sent her that first Christmas. When I last asked Jackie to see if Kara would talk to me again, Jackie responded that she could not as "Kara cries whenever I mention you."

I discovered soon that it was not only our relationship that was damaged. Also damaged was the relationship between these once so close sisters and with other friends. I felt these were at least as serious, and perhaps more serious, than her break with me. I was glad to later learn from Jackie that Kara now has new friends and is happy. But I live in hope that one day she will speak to me again, that we will be reconciled. It is still hard to write of this gulf between us, of the hurt and pain. I still mourn her. I too cannot think of her still without crying. I still wonder if my gender change is at the root of the division between us although Joe assured me it was not. If not, what is it? What have I done? Have I been awful to her? Was it the pain of our family breakdown? Was it—but what is the use of asking these questions? I know that I had good relations with her when we went to New Zealand not long before the break, I love and value her and worry over her.

I hope and pray that one day we will be together again. I wondered if Kara might have felt undervalued because her sister gained praise by being outstandingly outgoing and hospitable while she was much more retiring. But this does not make sense as a cause of division. Jackie and I both did this and only I am excluded. I know that Kara needs to be private, to create her own space. She was like me in her creativity and love for writing. Perhaps this also meant she had extra need for her own space.

I asked my God, "Where, oh where, is this stripping to end? Why are you taking so much from me? Why are you making me love children that reject me? Was it that I fought too hard to stay with them? Hurt them in so fighting? Did I not trust your providence enough?"

We live in a society that presumes gender roles depend on genitals. In such a system I have no place. I did not sleep with a man to create our children. In such a rigid system, what relationship do I have with grand-children? What relationship do daughters tell sons they have to me? In other times and places the social system was more flexible. In such societies there are places for grandparents, god-mothers, aunts, magical aunts, spinners of good night stories, second mothers, second lovers, for a wealth of relationships spun out of the depths of the human heart that reflect all the magic of the many kinds of humans.

Children know who you are and are happy with you if you truly love and care for them. They need no theory. You can tell them they have a second mother. They can accept it and are happy, as I found with our children. The trouble only comes when they find the world outside the family is far more judgmental, narrow and rigid.

Women and men do not only create with wombs and seed. This is the least way. We are in our essence a whirling storm of creation, with every particle of our bodies constantly changing, coming and leaving. We create, as do the deities, with the womb of our imagination. The work of creation is never done, and we share in it. God's normal posture is on the birthing chair or bed, according to the mystic Meister Ekhardt.

After this trauma, I went in August 1991 to seek some healing from wild sacred places with a good friend, Hannah. We travelled through the Barmah Forest that is still revered by Aborigines. This great forest of eucalyptus stood the Murray Rivers floodwaters with moss-splattered rocks and grey shimmering bark. I made fire Aboriginal-style by using the dry underbark.

From here we went deep into the mulga desert with its slender trees, stiff saltbush and willowy peppercorn trees. We reached the ancient wind plastered sand dunes of Lake Mungo, where once communities of Neanderthal and Homo Sapiens lived side by side, two races of ancestors that helped create us. I watched caterpillars taking advantage of the constant winds to roll themselves across the sands. There were also eagles, kangaroos—and dreams.

I dreamt that I was with Jackie and another younger but adult person that was probably Cathy but could have been Kara. We went to Roger's home in London where my daughter was assigned a first-floor front room. I was assigned the back room of Roger's brother Peter. It was in its usual state with pictures roughly stuck onto walls and talc upon the floor. Jackie went upstairs to her assigned room. I was jealous, picturing her in a bedroom with en-suite bathroom. But I overcome my jealousy and accepted my room. I then went up the stairs to find Jackie, only to find she has been taken unexpectedly through a newly created corridor into the house next door to find her room. I set off after her—but could not find her. I then woke up and watched with Hannah a spectacular dawn.

After this I walked from our camp through seemingly endless glades that enticed me deep into them, a trance-inducing place that I knew could kill me if I did not take care to note the crooked branch, the twisted bush, the markings on the ground. The plains I crossed were not of grass but fine round leafed plants, thinly layered on clay pan in glade after glade; the product of recent rain. When I found fresh kangaroo paw marks, I tracked them, head down then was startled to find I had walked into a herd of equally startled kangaroos. I felt strangely at home in this wilderness despite my lack of knowledge. Here were the spirits that I was coming to know.

In my second remembered dream in the bush, I was with my brother Tony on the roof of a double-decker London bus taking him to college. The bus then stopped. I then realised that I had not got on the bus that my daughter had told me to take. I fumbled the change, dropping coins. When we reached the college, Tony left, leaving me stranded. He did not need me. I felt helpless. My interpretation of this was that my family was to be other people, not members of my blood family. I was stumbling over the old names but ready to meet new.

Soon after this, Hannah and I entered a range of desert hills bisected by the large Chambers Gorge. Early in the morning, fishing in a pool near our camp, I saw the heron I had been given by an Aborigine as a totem to help me with my investigative journalism—for it, like me, wades in mud to find its catch. It was, I think, called a boobok. Its body looks like that of an owl for it folds and hides its long neck in its feathers when upon the ground. But when it strikes, and when in flight, its long slender neck is displayed.

After watching the heron for a while, I went for a dawn walk before the day turned hot, and discovered nearby a small canyon, a narrow dry valley with smooth rocky walls. As I walked up its narrow course, I noted a circle carved into the rocks. Then, as I turned a corner, the creek bed opened to form a wide circular arena of flat sand. It had cliffs on two sides and a stepped dry waterfall that provided amphitheatre-like seating. It had the feel of a sacred place where many rituals had been celebrated. Then I noted the taller of the cliff faces. It was covered with carvings. There were lines, circles, S-shapes and spirals. At first I thought this must be primitive drawing then suddenly realised that they were the symbols of a language.

Later I learnt that these were some 23,000 years old and still read by local Aboriginal Elders. They were the writings of a race that Whites said had no writing. I found that cultural prejudice had labelled these symbols as simply "primitive drawing", purely because "everyone knows Aborigines do not have writing." They were reportedly over twice as old as the ancient Egyptian and Middle Eastern hieroglyphics.

Such wonders and such dreams helped assuage the pain of separation. Soon after this, my film demanded my attention and once more I had to leave Australia, leaving behind me the vivid raw pain of three women that I much loved, Kara, Cathy and Jackie. The journey tore at me. In the plane I felt their pain, but, however much I wanted to remove it from them, the bitter and humbling lesson was that this was not work for me but for them. I was powerless and tearful. I hoped instead, and prayed, that the time will come for healing. I reflected that we were all on our separate journeys. It is the way of all life. I wished them from the bottom of my heart fair winds, many encounters with beauty, many friends and much support.

I had no choice but to continue on my path. Whatever I wanted, I was now being freed of old bonds. My trust had to be in my Creatrix as she re-birthed me. She was there for me from the beginning. She was there when I was a child, when I was ordained, and now she was there for me in all her strength and terror as a parent creating me, forging me so that I might be what she always meant me to be. I had to accept this pain and turn it to good. Perhaps I needed to be torn free? But I wish that I could have been sent a different path. I find awful the hurt that came after we split up, for until then the children and I had seemed so firmly bonded.

This is my story of our family, apart from a little more in the next chapter. There are of course other aspects. Jackie has her own song, her own path to follow. Despite my pain at learning how she saw me and how hard she found her path, I remember the beauty we shared and what I learnt from her. For the splendours of what we shared I owe her and our children gratitude. Cathy and I are still good friends and perhaps by the time you come to read this book, Kara and I will be friends. I want this very much.

I had longed for both of my children to grow up, I had longed to have them as equals, and I longed to have them as companions on the journey of life. But that has not proved to be my fate, at least for now.

Perhaps we have not finished the task of growing up, none of us four adults. Is pain meant to so divide us? I very much doubt it. There is much healing needed. It is a great task but not one that can be done before all are ready and willing. I love Kara; I respected her wishes to be away from me but I now fear we do not know each other. I hope one day we will find each other again. I would now like to cast a spell of love, to wrap a spider web lightly over the wounds, so they heal with the softest touch of love.

My children of course have their own stories. I cannot tell what it was like for them to have such a parent as myself. That is for them to tell if they so choose. I now also have a grandchild from Cathy and Tree, a magical boy. And thus the cycle continues.

Two Pillars in the Temple,
Crucible and Metal.
Parent and Child.
Who rules?
Both.
Who is born?
Both.
Who is superseded?
Both.
Who comes from the fire?
Crone and Adult.
And a new Child[256]

Saturday

The Warrior Aspect of the Goddess

There is a myth that women are not naturally warriors, that a society dominated by women would not be warlike, that warfare is naturally a domain of men. This gave me great problems.

Some of my friends were influenced by Maria Gimbutas, an archaeologist who confounded the male-dominated world of archaeology by claiming that the many ancient female images found in Central European excavations were evidence that a non-Patriarchical age once existed. She noted; "its people did not produce lethal weapons or build forts in inaccessible places" and had "Goddess" images. She deduced that it was a society: "matrifocal and probably matrilineal, agricultural and sedentary, egalitarian and peaceful." An example of this earlier respect for women were the three aspects of womanhood depicted in carvings at Anatolia's Çatal Hüyük ancient site (7,000-5,000BCE). These were of the maid, the mother giving birth and the old woman or crone. But she said this glorious age in Europe ended violently with the arrival of the Kargan marauders with warfare, military technology and patriarchy.[257]

But I think there should have been another aspect of womanhood, that of warrior (and thus the title of this chapter). The Kargan clearly were once not as patriarchal as Gimbutas portrayed them, if indeed they ever were, nor were warlike skills foreign to their women. Tombs of warrior Kargan women dating from around 5,000BCE can be found near the Caucasus Mountains. Their frozen bodies had wonderfully elaborate horse or deer tattoos. They had the bowed legs of horsewomen. From the grave-contents it seems they carried arms and worked as both warriors and priestesses.[258]

But there is some evidence that Europe was both less patriarchal and less war-like before the Iron Age. The great palaces of Crete and the temples of Malta suggest their high culture had no need to be protected by ramparts. They were also cultures in which women played an important economic role.

Elizabeth Barber in her excellent book *Women's Work*[259] demonstrated that the work of women in weaving, orchard managing and household controlling played a major part with the men taking on tasks that did not lend themselves to child rearing, such as mining and sailing. She believed that Homer (writing around 900BCE) reflected the past glory of these lands when he had Helen of Troy spinning threads with a golden spindle and weaving fine cloths. Women made precious cloths for ritual, and recorded stories and legends with woven patterns and pictures. Barber using linguistic analysis revealed the names of Athens and of Athena, its weaving and spinning goddess, came from an earlier Balkan pre-Indo-European people known for its cloth-making. The weaving of cloth was associated with the "weaving" of spiritual healing and of magic—thus the original Germanic meaning of the word 'witch", or "wicce", was that of a shaper and weaver—and thus the depiction of many a Goddess as a spinner of thread.

The people who lived in what is now Hungary had looms for weaving fine linen some 6000 years ago at the same time as the Egyptians. The Gravettian Eastern European culture of some 20,000 years ago had string skirts like to that worn by the Goddess Hera when she set out to seduce Zeus wearing her "belt of many tassels". Such skirts with front and back aprons remain present symbolically in the folk costumes of Eastern Europe, as Barber observed.

But the theory that womankind and warrior did not go together gave me much trouble when doctors assessed me to see if I were psychologically female. A male psychologist seemingly believed that warlike fantasies were inappropriate for a woman. I had from childhood a secret female identity and a secret warrior self. I often played in dugouts or climbed into trenches guarding the Channel coast, while imagining myself fighting invaders as a warrior girl or sometimes as a boy who had been captured and turned into a girl by fiendish scientists. If I could not have been both a woman and a warrior, I would have had to invent a new gender.

I also wanted from childhood to work in the priesthood. This combination of callings sometimes puzzled me. I did not understand how I could both dream of war and of the priesthood, of destroying evil empires and of being the openhearted healing spiritual leader? Surely these aims were contradictory? When I decided to go into the priesthood, it had been the Jesuits that I selected for they were said to be the front-line army of God. When I was ordained a priest, I saw the ritual as also my consecration as a knight. Could this warrior instinct come out of a relationship with a loving deity? Or was it a relic of my male conditioning?

Non-patriarchical societies and violence

I wondered if Gimbutas's theory that non-patriarchal nations lived in greater harmony was true of non-patriarchal Aboriginal society. They also did not construct fortifications. But the myths of Aboriginal society spoke of battles. The Aboriginal women at Uluru told me ancient Dreamtime stories that seemed akin to those of the ancient Irish about the war between the Tuatha ni Danu and the Formanians. They pointed out to me holes in the Uluru rocks where spears struck during these mythical battles. Other elders told me of ancient hostility between Aboriginal nations.

Misunderstandings must have been commonplace in a continent of over 200 languages.

In an Aboriginal settlement in central Australia the anthropologist Diane Bell was armed by the women with "fighting sticks" and instructed in their use in 1977 after drunken men harassed her. She also reported; "In Aboriginal society women of importance are capable, not dependent. In this context my driving and mechanical skills were duly admired, as was my sewing ability, although my reluctance to handle rifles was sometimes mentioned as a weakness."[260]

The young men and women of the Warrabri nation of Central Australia learnt to use weapons to defend themselves Some Aboriginal nations have Dreamtime stories of how once women controlled fire and men stole it from them so perhaps equality always had to be fought for by both genders.

Historically an Aboriginal woman's weapons seem to have been more the magical and psychological rather than the sword and spear. Central Australian men feared to hurt a woman since she could take ritual action to achieve justice or revenge. The spiritual power of an Aboriginal woman was said to be considerable and entitled her to much respect. They believed it came out of her bond with her country. She was seen as sharing the enduring strength of her land.[261]

She would undertake magical action only after much serious discussion with other women and weighing of circumstances. Men told Bell that women's rituals were invariably successful unlike their own. But men generally did not resent this female power, for they saw themselves as needing strong women to strengthen their own spiritual bond to the land. Bell wrote of the gender-balanced negotiations she observed during ritual preparations: "the women needed men within their ritual groups, the men needed the [women's] knowledge to back their claims to rights in the country."[262]

Similar stories about women using magic abound in Irish or Celtic mythology. Thus, when the mythical Ulster hero Cu Chulainn came under attack by 'the three skinny handed daughters of Cailidin", he needed the magic of other women to help him withstand them. The magic of women became demonised in a later age of Patriarchy partly because magic was a traditional female weapon. Church authorities argued that women were dangerous because of their strong bond with both nature and magic. This might help explain the centuries of witch-hunts. Perhaps women need these weapons still but more about this later.

Aborigines did not use only magical weapons, as the British found when they invaded their lands. Their spears were flung, and are still, with the use of an arm extension called a *woomera*. This makes spears literally hum in near-level flight. They were trained to hit a spear in flight with a spear and to deflect a fast-thrown spear with a short stubby shield when it was only a foot away from hitting them. They also had various different kinds of bone-breaking throwing sticks. Aboriginal resistance meant garrisoned forts had to be built along the trail from Melbourne to Sydney. The Aboriginal campaigns of armed resistance were co-ordinated over hundreds of square miles. Martial law was declared in Tasmania and in parts of Eastern Australia before the tribes was crushed. Treaties with them were declared illegal! Although they faced western technology and were greatly weakened by imported plagues, armed struggles continued to occur until the 1930s in the far north.[263]

When I sat as a child on the edge of the English Channel cliffs speculating how I might defend my country if it were to be invaded, it was not, I think, an idle warlike fancy but rather an understanding that I should defend the land that bore me. Perhaps it was part of the ancient spirituality of these islands. We honoured Goddesses of Sovereignty who spoke for the land and nurtured it, and these in turn were served by a court of Round-Table warriors and kings. The armed Britannia on our coins is perhaps but a faint image of this ancient sense.

Hildegard, Wise Woman.

In the 12th century the mystic Hildegard of Bingen, 1098-1179, was well aware that the Earth must be defended. She wrote in words that seem today prophetic:

> Now in the people that were meant to be green
> There will be no more life of any kind.
> There is only shrivelled barrenness
> The winds are burdened by the utterly awful stink of evil selfish deeds.
> Thunderstorms menace.
> The air belches out the filthy uncleanness of the peoples.
> The earth should not be injured!
> The earth must not be destroyed!

Hildegard alarmed a Church uncomfortable with strong women, especially those who honoured nature. She ran an unusual "convent" in which the women wore crowns as symbols of their sovereignty. She wrote from her stronghold authoritative books on medicine and nature that pre-dated the foundation of the universities. This warrior woman saw her religion in female terms and used her pen as a weapon. She wrote of the earth as our mother. One of her poems went as follows:

> Holy persons draw to themselves all that is earthly.
> The earth is at the same time mother.
> She is mother of all that is natural
> Mother of all that is human.
> She is the mother of all,
> For contained in her
> Are the seeds of all.[264]

She seemingly saw the Goddess in her visions: "Thus I seemed to see a girl of unsurpassing radiant beauty, with such a dazzling brightness streaming from her face that I could not behold her fully. She wore a cloak whiter than snow, brighter than stars; her shoes were of pure gold. In her right hand she held the sun and moon and caressed them lovingly. On her breast she had an ivory tablet on which appeared in shades of sapphire the image of a man. And all creation called this girl Sovereign Lady. The girl began to speak to the image on her breast 'I was with you in the beginning, in the dawn of all that is holy. I bore you from the womb before the start of day' and I heard a voice saying to me: 'the girl whom you behold is Love, she has her dwelling in eternity.'"

Ronald Hutton credited her as one of the first users of the pentagram as a religious symbol, although others say it was used in ancient Middle Eastern faiths. She used the five-pointed star as a symbol for humanity, for we have five senses, five fingers and five limbs (including the head). In modern times this symbol is used for Paganism. This raised the question for me of how we define such women as Hildergard, and even define "Paganism"? It affected how I defined my own beliefs.

There was much in her writing I found inspiring. She lived within a Church dominated world and identified as a Christian; albeit as her own kind of Christian, much as I had myself. Church authorities suspected that she was not really a Christian. They harassed and even excommunicated her. I too was excommunicated. She honoured the female in nature and saw it as sacred, and met the criteria for membership in today's European Pagan Federation![265] Clearly labels can mislead.

I hoped a study of Hildegard's time would help me better understand the great witch-hunts that scarred Europe for the next few centuries. In her time the troubadours celebrated, in popular tales and song, the sacred role of women and the hunt for the Holy Grail. The tales of the Knights of the Round Table symbolised the commitment of the true warrior to this higher struggle. The object of the quest, the Grail, sometimes symbolised a woman who represented Divinity. Significantly the Church establishment played a very minor part in this popular mythology.

Pre-Christian Celtic elements infused the popular stories of the period and spoke of lands ruled by women. Thus the great bard Taliesin said: "That is the place where nine sisters exercise a kindly rule over those who come to them from our land. The one who is first among them has greater skill in healing, as her beauty surpasses that of her sisters. Her name is Morgen and she has learned the uses of all plants in curing the ills of the body. She knows too, the art of changing her shape, of flying through the air."[266] This was also a time when the Welsh were inviting to their Eisteddfods bards from Scotland, Brittany and Ireland.[267] The old Celtic culture and spirituality were very much alive.

It was not only war that flowed between Europe and the Arab world. The troubadour movement learnt from Islamic Sufi mysticism. Ibn al-Arabia, 1165-1240, saw a vision of the Goddess Sophia in a young woman when he was ritually walking around the Kabah on a pilgrimage to Mecca. He wrote that her beauty was a reflection of divine beauty. She was "the object of his quest, the virgin most pure." He declared in his book *The Mecca Revelations* that "love was the faith I hold", and that love made one all religions, including the Pagan: "his heart is capable of every form, a cloister for the monk, a fane for idols, pasture for gazelles, the votary's Kabah" (Sufi spirituality also influenced the modern revival of a ritual witchcraft.[268])

At that time in Grenada Jews, Christians and Muslims were peacefully co-existing and influencing each other's development. In search of their wisdom I went on pilgrimage in 1990 to Grenada in Southern Spain, where religions now terribly divided once shared so very much. I wandered through superbly decorated and ghost-filled palaces and sat by their fountains. I found only a whisper of a past that was smashed by the Catholic fundamentalism that united Spain. I then went across the windmilled plain of Don Quixote to visit the walled city of Avila, the former home of a great mystic who inspired me, St Teresa. Much to my surprise I discovered before its' cathedral a great statue of the Green Man, the ancient symbol of the Deity living in Nature. But elegant Avila otherwise left me feeling empty. I went instead to find the spirit of mystics in the nearby Sierra Mountains where I climbed high on foot to spend the night with eagles and red-eyed sheep.

In the 11th century the revival of the Jewish Qabbalah mystical school in Grenada gave a renewed emphasis to the female aspect of the Divine. The book *The Bahir* (c1200) identified the female Jewish figure of Shekinah in the Qabbalah with the Goddess Sophia of the Gnostics. It held that we had become alienated from her and that she must be re-discovered if we are to regain wholeness. The Qabbalah has had much influence in modern western Paganism. With every step on these pilgrimages, I was finding the roots of a mystical and nature-honouring tradition deep within my people's European history.[269]

The Beguine Women's movement and the Inquisition

While the great cathedrals of this period were under construction, the Inquisitor Gui attacked the Beguine movement of women, (as I have previously mentioned in "Thursday"). This influential movement of thousands of women started in the 12th Century and was strongest in Belgium, Germany, Holland and France. Their communities were self-governing and self-supporting, with members engaged in skilled and manual labour, working as blacksmiths, bricklayers, brewers and surgeons. Some communities were 2000 strong. They saw themselves as Christian, engaged in communal rituals and developed a mystical spirituality that was very much their own, even to the point of some saying they were not part of the same church as the bishops. The bishops in turn condemned many as heretics, naming their heresy significantly as that of the "Free Spirit".

These women wrote exultantly of the spirit of love. Their spirituality was based on a personal relationship with the Deity rather than with religious authorities, and was reminiscent of the Gnostic. They were part of a movement inspired by, and inspiring, the troubadours who were then celebrating at many a noble woman's court the depths of human love and sexuality as well as ancient stories of Merlin and King Arthur.

Its foundation was an amazing self-empowerment by women that lasted throughout the Middle Ages. It gave women an alternative to a male-dominated society, a space away from men to develop their own skills and to help each other acquire qualifications. In their settlements women could own their own homes or share communal accommodation.

They were not Church-run institutions (although from the 14th Century many communities had their freedom curtailed by the Church). They vowed to share goods communally and to minimalise consumption. They were free to marry but, if they did, they must leave, as their communities did not admit men. They did not all live in communities. Some were travellers. This particularly worried the authorities, for it meant their ideas became widely spread. The Mendicant Orders of Dominicans and Franciscans suspected them as rivals.

The Beguine taught a mysticism which united them to God and which empowered them. They had brother communities of men living by the same principles known as Beghards, but there were far fewer of them.

Some "Beguinages' still exist in Belgium. One is in the city of Bruges. A lace-making elderly woman living there was recently asked what her Beguinage was originally and replied "Oh, I think they were hostels for reformed prostitutes"! This reminded me of how Mary Magdalene, a leading figure among the Apostles with clearly a very close relationship to Jesus, was later presumed to be the "reformed prostitute" mentioned elsewhere in the Gospels. It was easier for the Church to depict her as a repentant sinner rather than as the strong woman who rallied the apostles after the Crucifixion. The Beguine suffered the same fate.

But at the same time as the Beguine communities were expanding, St Thomas Aquinas was teaching at the newly established University of Paris from which women were banned. His influential tomes justified the rule of men, linked witches to the devil and were to be much quoted by witch hunters. Although the Vatican later honoured him as the "Angelic Doctor", he was a fanatic hater of sexuality and belittler of women. A Catholic theologian recently listed the words Aquinas used for "sex". They were "filthiness", "staining", disgusting", "shamefulness", "disgrace", "degeneration", "sickness", "corruption of integrity" and a reason for "aversion" and "loathing". Aquinas also said the lack of chastity resulted in the "feminisation of the human heart".[270]

Aquinas and the other scholastics did not go unchallenged by the Beguine women despite them being targeted by the Inquisition. The Beguine Hadewijch of Antwerp was forced to leave her small Beguine community around 1260 for fear of the Inquisition. She was a scholar familiar with the Fathers of the Church and Ptolemaic astronomy. Although fluent in Latin, she wrote the first prose to be published in the Dutch language, and for this she was the more suspect in the eyes of the Inquisition. Her poems and letters all reflected a strong vibrant mysticism and showed a love for God interwoven with love for nature. Her poems were written in the traditional troubadour style and sometimes sung as love songs.

She challenged the exaltation of reason (perhaps a criticism of the dry debating style of Aquinas whose chains of logical deductions were sometimes based on very dubious premises.) She wrote: "Love despises reason and all that lies within. For whatever belongs to reason stands against the blessed state of love. For reason cannot take anything away from love or bring anything to love, for love's true reason is a flood that rises forever and knows no peace."

She personified love as female and divine. " Love does not yield to saints or men or angels, heaven or earth; she enfolds the divine in her nature. To love she calls the hearts that love, in a voice that is loud and untiring. This voice has great power and tells of things more terrible than thunder."

In 1274 the Second Church Council of Lyons moved against the Beguine. It declared all religious communities founded without the permission of the Pope were forthwith to be closed, but the Beguine had political support, especially in France, and so survived.

Thus they were still strong twenty years later when the French Beguine Marguerite Porete began to teach. She was a traveller who moved from settlement to settlement while writing the exhilarating book *The Mirror of Simple Souls* between 1296 and 1306, in the high summer of Aquinas's Scholasticism. It was in the "love poem" style of the troubadours and a direct challenge to the Church and its theologians. It declared that the hierarchical and worldly "little church" of Popes and Bishops must give way before the "greater church" of the Spirit.

She sang: 'Theologians and other clerks, you won't understand this book, however bright your wits, if you do not meet it humbly. Only in this way will Love and Faith help you surmount Reason, for they are the mistresses of Reason's house." She regretted that; "Desire, Will and Fear take away from them the understanding, the outflowing and the union of the highest Light of the ardour of Love Divine."

She taught that the soul that was united in love with God did not need works of penitence. They are replaced by what we do naturally when living in a state of love. "Virtues, I take leave of you for ever more. I'll have a freer heart for that, more joyful too. Your service is too unremitting; indeed I know I have quit your tyrannies now I am at peace."[271] She boldly declared that the powerful institutions of the Church were also not needed if we love God. She wrote in vernacular French while Thomas Aquinas wrote in Latin, making her seem, like the other Beguine women, all the more dangerous to the authorities.

When she was brought before the Inquisitor of Lorraine, she defied him, saying he had no authority over her, as she did not belong to his Church. He represented, she bravely said, only the worldly "little church" while she belonged to the great church of the spirit. When he condemned her as a heretic, he noted as outrageous her teaching that, when united to God one "could and should grant to nature all that it desires". The Inquisitor must have thought, "Doesn't she know that nature is corrupt?"

The Church's use of the new universities to reinforce its power is illustrated by how the Inquisitor, William of Paris, asked twenty-one of the masters of Paris University's Faculty of Theology to sit in judgement on Porete in 1310. William was at the same time managing the Emperor's campaign against the Knights Templars. Later, in 1429-31, the same Faculty would be consulted during the trial of Jeanne d'Arc as a witch.

The Church burnt Porete's book publicly in Valenciennes. She was condemned to death in May 1310 when she refused to repudiate her book, and was burnt at the stake in Paris on June 1st 1310. Her reputation was such and her appearance so dignified and gracious, that the spectators were in tears. After her death her book did not vanish despite the Church uniquely condemning it on three separate occasions. It was secretly copied, translated and smuggled throughout Europe. The readers knew that they could be killed as heretics if found to have it in their possession. Despite this, a complete copy was found enclosed within the personal writings of Blessed Julian of Norwich, a British mystic. This copy is now in the British Library.

Porete's death sentence had been promulgated only days before fifty-four Knights Templar were burnt to death in a field in Paris on orders from the Emperor of France, Philip IV ("The Fair"). Her death may have been linked to theirs, for one of the main witnesses against her was key to Philip's action against the Templars.[272] The Emperor had earlier supported the Beguine, despite them being targeted by the Inquisition in Germany. He had even helped set up a large Beguine community in Paris, but the women in this community were partially enclosed and subject to his authority, unlike Marguerite. He had also been friendly towards the Knights Templar right up to his move against them. He may have supported her execution because he wanted to gain support for his move against the Templars from the powerful Franciscan and Dominican Orders who were vehemently against the Beguine. It may also have been because she defied the established church that Philip claimed to have protected when he moved against the Templars and the Jews.

The year after Marguerite Porete's death, the Catholic Church attacked the Beguine movement at the 1311 Council of Vienna. It ordered the imprisonment of the Beguine within the walls of their communities, saying they will need a bishop's permission to leave them. It called their theology "madness".

In its decree *Ad Nostrum* it condemned "an abominable sect of malignant men known as beghards and faithless women known as beguines" for a "heresy" called "Free Spirit" that held that people could achieve a union with God that put them beyond the laws of the Church. This condemnation resulted in "what was tantamount to a 100 year war' against the Beguine and Beghards in Germany, ending with the Council of Constance in 1417."[273]

Civil authorities also tried to destroy the Beguine communities by heavily taxing them. (The word "beg" might well come from them, since many communities were plunged into poverty.) The church had to deal with organised Beguine women in Germany, Switzerland, France, Belgium and Holland. The Church damned as Beguine the communities in Southern France and Catalonia that were also known as Waldensians. (As mentioned earlier, the Church also accused female Waldensians of being witches that flew on broomsticks.)

Porete was not the only 13th century female "mystic" targeted by the Inquisition. Earlier another Beguine, Mechtild of Magdeburg 1207-1282, came under attack for mystical work written in Low German. Her influence spread across Europe. Dante is said to have borrowed from her writing for his rendition of Bernard's prayer to the Virgin. Chaucer later translated this to use it in his *Second Nun's Tale*. She attacked as "goats" and "Pharisees" the corrupt members of the clergy. She was fiercely critical of the hatred of the body shown by pious ascetics. "Do not disdain your body, for the soul is just as safe in its body as in the kingdom of heaven".[274]

Mechtild had a lesson for me, for I was afraid that if I were open about the gift I had been given at birth, that of walking between the genders, of being rejected. She wrote:

> The truly wise person
> Kneels at the feet of all creatures
> And is not afraid to endure
> The mockery of others[275]

Another Beguine mystic, Hadewijch from Brabant, escaped being tried as a heretic by the Inquisition only by leaving her community and living in isolation from where she advised by post. Her writings are the earliest works we have in Low German. She died around 1260 but her letters were only discovered in 1983. She, like Porete, wrote in the style of the troubadours, called minnesingers (love singers) in Germany. She did not disdain the body and its sensuality. She spoke sensuously about the union between the divine and human:

> So neither knows themselves apart
> But they possess and rejoice in each other
> Mouth in mouth
> Heart in heart
> Body in body
> Soul in soul and sweet divine nature
> Flows through them both
> And both are one through themselves and always.

She wrote of deity as female and as her "Love". For example: "I showed my pain to Love and begged her pity". She was very happy with her nature. She "sinks deep in herself utterly satisfied with her nature, she fully rejoices in herself". She thus was very different to Aquinas. She said the ecstasy of divine love couldn't be understood "save by those who have been thrown, into the abyss of love's mighty nature, and those who belong there, and they believe in love more than they understand her."

Aquinas' successor in the Chair of Theology at the University of Paris was Meister Ekhardt, 1260-1328. He was a very different man from Aquinas, more influenced by Plato than by Aristotle, and very much in the mystic and gnostic tradition. He was said to be strikingly alike to Porete.[276] He held that we grew spiritually by "birthing" God within us. His love for nature was evident: "Here all blades of grass, wood and stone, all things are One. This is the deepest depth."[277] He also declared, in courageous opposition to the demonising of witches; "Evil is opposed to being, therefore the devil does not exist." Some of his students quoted early Gnostic works that were later lost and not rediscovered until the 20th century. He died while his works were under investigation by the Inquisition, the one mercy showed him was that he was allowed to die naturally rather than be executed.

The women enclosed in Church convents held to the mystic marriage tradition. They saw themselves as wedded to God. This became the basis of their initiation rituals or vow-taking. This also applied to some solitaries. A well-connected woman of the 14th century, Blessed Julian of Norwich, lived as a hermit in a room attached to a church in Norwich, then the second largest city in England. (She also possessed, as before mentioned, a secret copy of the Church-condemned Porete's work.). She did not write like Porete of a "little" church but for the "even-Christians", meaning those not influenced by rank. She like Porete wrote about the presence of God in nature, saying Divine love is present in and maintains Creation.

"And after this I saw God in a point…He showed me a little thing, the size of a hazelnut lying in my palm, or so it seemed to me, and it was as round as a ball…. It is all that is made…it lasts and ever shall be, for God loves it. So have all things being by the love of God…the Maker, the Keeper, the Lover."

She acknowledged both male and female aspects of the Divinity, much as had the Gnostics. "The almighty truth of the Trinity is our Father, for he makes us and keeps us in him. And the deep wisdom of the Trinity is our Mother in whom we are all enclosed". She had no time for the ascetic anti-sensuality of the Fathers but taught: "Our sensuality is grounded in nature…In our sensuality, God is."

She concluded that the search for God should lead us to the mystic marriage. She thus taught a mystery that was also enshrined in the Greek and Egyptian pagan mystery religions. She said in this marriage we are "one'd" with divinity and know ourselves as ultimately divine. "Till I am substantially one'd to him, I may never have full rest, nor full bliss…God is nearer to us than our own soul for he is the ground in which our soul stands." "God does not love us any less than He loves Christ". She has God say: "I am the ground of your seeking. First it is my will that you have it and I make you will it".

She was a great scholar who translated Biblical texts from the early Greek and Hebrew versions, unlike the contemporary translator John Wycliffe who translated the Bible from Jerome's later and less accurate Latin Vulgate. But her very female imagery was a danger to her. She described how in a vision she became pregnant with God's Word, just as Mary was pregnant with Jesus. Her close advisor and protector Cardinal Adam Easton had her delete this, saying that Marguerite Porete had been burned at the stake partly for using that same imagery. Birgitta, a contemporary Swedish mystic and mother of eight children, used the same imagery, saying that her book was moving within her like a child in the womb. After Easton died, Julian reinserted in her manuscript her pregnant imagery.

There was thus a pan-European weaving of powerful mystics in the 13-14th century. These were women that had inspired me since I was seventeen. Catherine of Sienna, the namesake of my daughters, quoted from Julian in her 1378 book *Dialogo*. These women were all influenced by the Beguine mystics Mechtild of Magdeburg and Marguerite Porete. They organised the secret Europe-wide "Friends of God" movement that included Meister Ekhardt and other mystics . This group sent a mission to the Pope to plead for peace and accurately prophesied that the Pope would die the following year. It continued underground up until the 17th Century and involved the descendants in exile of Thomas More, an executed English Chancellor who also reportedly had a copy of the condemned mystical book of the Maid of Kent.

Some of the Friends of God died at the hands of the authorities. Julian of Norwich, attacked for daring as a woman to translate the Bible, was forced to delete from her books some of her biblical translations. If she had been condemned for disobedience, she could have been hung, drawn and quartered. In 1407 Archbishop Arundel forbade women and laymen from teaching theology, seized vernacular bibles, burnt John Wycliffe's books before St Paul's Cathedral and, in the Arundel Constitution, decreed a licence from a bishop was needed if one wanted to quote the Bible! Julian had to revise her book "Showing of Love" in 1413, when she was seventy, to get it past Arundel's censorship. She probably died around 1416.

It was a highly dangerous time to write of spiritual experiences not sanctioned by authority, the more so if your writings directly challenged the authorities. The Holy Maid of Kent, Elizabeth Barton, was executed at Tyburn because she had criticised the monarch in her mystical book, *Revelations*. Several died simply because they owned a copy of this book. St Birgitta of Sweden was critical of her monarch and had to go into exile in Italy. These were not inconsequential mystics but literate women of great influence feared by kings. Their manuscripts were hidden in Antwerp, in Lisbon and in Paris. In Spain the Inquisition imprisoned the mystical writer St John of the Cross, who had described his mystical experience as a love affair. I read him when I was seventeen, as a Novice in the Claretian Order. I loved his work. We sang with the same music.

The women of Italy gave the Church a shock in the 13th Century when a Princess Blazcma of Milan became Guglielma the Prophetess and set up with other women an alternative female-led hierarchy. She said that the

Holy Ghost was female, in the old tradition of Sophia, and that in the coming "Age of the Holy Spirit" all the cardinals and the Pope would be women. The priestess Maifreda was designated as the coming Popess. These women presided secretly over a solemn Mass in the company of a selected six men and six women at Easter in 1300. They also preached and forgave sins. Pope Boniface arrested several of them and had them "incinerated".

In Southern France in 1335, where the first mass witch-trials commenced, the Church particularly targeted a woman leader. Na Prous Bonnet, a prophetess. She had bravely said the Pope had forfeited his title by his corrupt killing and persecuting. She claimed that the Holy Spirit inspired her words.

The Medical Profession and the Church

When the Church and its 13th Century allies set up the new all male Universities, they were in part countering the female dominance of the medical profession as well as the all-female vernacular Beguine centres of study. In future only university-qualified men were to be allowed to practice medicine. Their medical courses focused not on current herbal knowledge but on 2nd century Latin texts as well as the rediscovered works of Aristotle. They were taught only in Latin, the Church's language.

Medical students were told that they should be accompanied by a priest when they went to see patients, and that they should deny medicine to patients who refused to go to Confession. Some preachers condemned attempts to heal the deaf and dumb, saying their disabilities were divinely ordained curses, quoting St. Augustine.[278]

The medicine taught at these universities for over 200 years was much inferior to that of the better women healers. Its cures were mostly based on superstition rather than experimentation. Thus they learnt to cure leprosy with the flesh of snakes caught in hot rocky places or to cure a toothache by writing a prayer on the sufferer's jaw. Bloodletting became a cure-all remedy. Their main textbook was the thousand-year-old works of Galen who prescribed medicines that required rare and costly imported ingredients. It was not witches but these doctors that prepared the potions of legend that had ingredients as unicorn horn, viper's flesh, powdered mummy, crabs' eyes, oil of earthworms and rhino horn. These "medicines" were sold for very high prices, enriching both apothecaries and doctors.

For many of the university-trained doctors, women healers with cheap local herb-based remedies were commercial rivals whose skills were to be disparaged and replaced. A woman healer, Jacoba Felicie, famed throughout Paris for her healing skills, went on trial in 1322 for daring to practice medicine without authority. Without Church endorsement, no matter how effective their remedy, women healers were liable to be accused of curing by witchcraft. Professor Eva Pocs found healers made up over half of those accused of witchcraft in the 2000 trials she studied.[279] In England a witch-hunter wrote: "It was a thousand times better for the land if all witches, but especially the blessing witch, might suffer death." A "witch" who did good was presumed a greater danger to the Church than the cursing" witch" for she was more likely to undermine the claims of the Church. Later, the new male medical profession petitioned the British Parliament against the "worthless and presumptuous women who usurped the profession", asking for "long imprisonment" for those concerned. This was despite mistresses of some noble English households treasuring lists of up to 500 useful herbs passed onto them by country healers.[280]

Hildergard back in the 11th century had published a work telling how to use medicinally some 200 local plants. For example: "If a pregnant woman is struggling mightily to give birth, then with fear and great skill let gentle herbs like fennel and ground ivy be boiled in water and strained. Let them be placed upon her thighs and back and be tied there with a linen cloth, so that her pain and closure will be more gently and easily relieved…. They will induce her womb to open."[281]

When the Black Death struck in 1348, killing within months a third of Europe's population, the new schools of male doctors blamed it on a conjunction of Saturn, Jupiter and Mars.[282] In 1496 the doctors had not learnt much more when syphilis arrived. Mercury was then adopted from alchemy as a toxic substance that could kill the infection, but it often also killed the patient.

In Ireland the Druidic tradition continued into the Middle Ages in medical schools with textbooks written in Irish. These schools were famed across Europe from the 8th century. In 1648 Baron Van Helmont, a famous physician, reported Irish Doctors "obtain their medical knowledge chiefly from books belonging to particular families left them by their ancestors, in which are written down the symptoms of the several diseases with the remedies annexed; which remedies are in the vernacular."[283] The English closed these Irish schools in 1615. The British Library holds a wealth of Irish medical texts dating from the 14th to 16th centuries. Some of these are based on older texts. Few are available in translation.

University medicine was not reformed until Paracelsus in the 15th Century angrily denounced the excessive profits made by selling expensive preparations with rare imported components. He said that Nature had provided cures near to the need; that local plants could do much better than imports and that nature looked after us by making plants indicate their medical function by their appearance. He wrote of the herb St John's Wort: "it puts to shame all recipes and doctors. They may yell as much as they wish. They will only break their teeth." Where did he himself get his own knowledge of medicine? One day he dramatically burnt his text on pharmaceuticals rather than take credit for it, saying he "had learnt from the Sorceress all he knew". He recommended to his students: "A physician…should learn of old women, Egyptians (as Gypsies were then called) and such like people, for they have greater experience in such matters than all the Academicians."[284] But despite his great reputation, women healers were still not brought into the schools as teachers.

The local healers documented by Pocs might prescribe steaming or other healing procedures, or heal by the laying on of hands. In one case, a woman asked, when confronted by a child she had allegedly hurt, "who would wish to hurt such an innocent?" and cured her by twice stroking her head.[285]

The Papacy in this period thus believed it had conspiring against it Beguine women, Waldensians and Cathars, male and female mystics, witches, healers and some major theologians—a great league of people who mostly saw nature as sacred rather than as the domain of evil spirits. This was by no means an alliance of illiterates or of people without political connections.

Powerful Women and the Witchtrials

Recent historians have tended to see women condemned to death as witches as the hapless victims of witchtrials. It is presumed that they did nothing to protect themselves. This is both chauvinistic and insulting to women. They would have had to be remarkably stupid not to notice their danger. Women at risk as healers or midwives must have taken counter-measures. Also, it was not a period when women were politically passive. The medieval campaign against "witches" began in a period of exceptional female enterprise. Laywomen had access to learning via the religious houses and from their own institutions. The Inquisition did not pick on women as hapless victims but as women organising or working in a way that it felt threatened the patriarchy.

Most were not persecuted because they were engaged in demon entrapping high magic (as Norman Cohen alleged in *Europe's Inner Demons*). If high magic surfaced in the charges, it usually was because the authorities were inventing reasons to kill them. They were killed principally because they were seen, rightly or wrongly, as a threat to the ideology of the ruling male elite.

It was not just a medievally created persecution. Learned women were killed as witches from early in the Christian centuries. The death as an alleged witch of Hypatia of Alexandria, a famous woman philosopher,

mathematician and inventor, took place in the 5th century. She headed
the Alexandrian Platonic School and invented apparatus for water distill-
ing and measuring the density of liquids. Her charisma and eloquence
were widely revered. She had many leading citizens among her students.
One of the few sayings of hers to survive was that "all formal dogmatic
religions are fallacious." This must have angered the Catholics. The local
Catholic bishop, Cyril, began to plot against her. (He was also notorious
for organising attacks on Alexandria's Jewish synagogues.) Around
415C.E. stories were circulated saying she was a "witch". She was then
attacked by a Christian mob, dragged into a church and stripped naked.
Her flesh was peeled off with oyster shells or tiles and her mangled body
burnt. No one was ever punished.

During the so-called Dark Ages, from the Sixth to the Eleventh
Century, when there were still Pagan states in Europe, the official Church
line was simply a straight out denial of the efficacy of pagan magic, prayers
or rituals. It was taught that only Christian prayers and rituals worked. It
was a heresy to believe that the spells or prayers of witches worked.
Nevertheless some women died as "witches" in this period in nations
already Christianised. Others, spiritual healers or shamans, may have died
as "witches" at the hands of invading Christian armies. But going against a
persecution of women in this period were the efforts by missionaries to
obtain the support of Pagan women. In Ireland this was done by denouncing the slavery of women in the kitchen and their use in low military
ranks. The seventh century St Adamnan condemned Irishmen for flog-
ging their wives into battle.[286]

But once the rulers of Western Europe were officially "converted", the
Church changed its tune. It was presumed that the subjects followed their
rulers into the Church. If not, then they had a duty to do so. The Church
thus claimed jurisdiction over them. The Bishop of Rome held the mantle
of the Roman Empire and ruled the rulers. Its Bishops lived in palaces and
held secular power. Heresy now became a crime equivalent to treason.

Those who kept up Pagan practices were now declared by church lawyers to be "fallen Christians" punishable by the Church. Henceforth "witches" would be killed not as Pagans but as Christian "heretics". In 1220 Emperor Frederick II made burning to death the penalty for heresy. In 1231, just as the Beguine reached their full strength, the Papacy authorised church courts to "incinerate" dissidents and set up the Inquisition.

Under the heading of "witches" went the village wise-woman, healers, herbalists, spiritual guides, female Waldensians and many others named in hysterical or malevolent accusations, and others the authorities simply wanted to remove. The efficacy of their healing or other work was ascribed to the Devil, the imagined supernatural opponent of the Church. It was widely believed that the witches were part of a pan-European "heretical" cult with Pagan antecedents.

As I examined the history of this period, I was also querying the nature of my own beliefs. Did I belong more truly to the Christian, the older Animistic or the modern Pagan community? Who were my spiritual ancestors? What label was more appropriate for me? I was now outside the official Church but I knew I had been enriched by the works of mystics I found preserved in Church libraries. I found much of their poetry magical. I loved their spirit of defiance, their pride and strength. I sided with them against the persecuting Church. I asked myself was I one with the Christians who followed them or was I more radically with the Pagans? Or—was it necessary to choose?

Did the witch-hunts target Pagans?

In "Thursday" I told how those who witnessed the medieval witch trials with horror also noted a prevailing paganism in those persecuted. Many victims spoke with pride of their witchcraft gatherings and merry celebrations, even when on the scaffold. Pocs reported that she found convincing evidence of an ancient Europe-wide shamanic tradition in her extensive study of testimony given at witchtrials.

I found some were explicitly killed as Pagans, for "heidenjachten" (heathen-hunts) were organised against the Roma or Gypsies in Holland and cavalry hunts against them in Saxony. A 1646 Bern City ordinance gave to all the right to hunt and kill "heiden" (heathens—taken as meaning mostly "Gypsies"). In 1665 they were deported from Edinburgh to be slaves in the West Indies.[287] They were hunted in Denmark until 1835.[288]

The Baltic States were the last to be Christianised in Europe, so in Finland legal action was undertaken more against the evil use of magic rather than all magic. But in Western and Central Europe, where Christianity was longer established, the Church killed sometimes as witches, but always as "heretical Christians" those it perceived as spiritual rivals, Malleus Maleficorum defined witches as heretics who were "forsaking the catholic faith". The same assumption pervaded State laws and was required legally for the Church to have jurisdiction. (Thus Porete challenged the jurisdiction of the court that tried her by saying she belonged to a different Church.)

Yet today some historians prominent within the modern Pagan community have accepted the definition of those accused by these infamous courts as "Christian heretics", ignored the "heathen hunts" against the Roma and insisted that these was no evidence that there were *any* Pagans among those accused.[289] On the other side, radical Catholic scholars, such as Dr Hans Kung, the Director of a major German University faculty at Tubingen and a man whose theological vision gave him enemies in Rome, found evidence of a strong Pagan element among those targeted. It was the opposite of what I expected. It seemed the more Pagan a historian was, the more they denied any community of belief between themselves and the people condemned for witchcraft.

The answer probably is that the labels Christian and Pagan do not belong to the supporter clubs of rival football teams. There is much historical evidence that people mixed and matched and were both Pagan and Christian to varying degrees. Many of those accused seemed to believe: "If it works, use it." The early Gnostic Christians did this. Aborigines do it today. Giordano Bruno did so naively. He tried to convert the Pope to a religious system that combined Christian elements with those of Pagan Egypt. He burnt at the stake on February 17th, 1600. (He was a famed mathematician and astronomer who developed ahead of Galileo a concept of an infinite universe with many worlds.[290])

The literate who rebelled against the Medieval Church expressed their beliefs in the terms with which they were most accustomed. Some said they were part of a "greater church" as did Porete; that they were honouring a Female Divine Holy Spirit as did the followers of Guglielma; that the voice within them was that of Holy Spirit, as did the Cathar women. The Church made little difference between them and the less well educated. They were all labelled as heretics, often also as "witches", and were sent to the stake, axe or noose.

Some had studied magic and the techniques of ecstasy, as is shown in surviving grimoires or personal magical "recipe-books" as well as trial records. Some spoke of having learnt magic from their grandmothers or other elders.

Hans Kung concluded: "it is beyond dispute that there would have been no trials of witches without a popular superstition which had a pagan stamp"[291] that was "an underground, uncontrollable popular culture" and "the background to this is the archaic anxiety about magical knowledge and practice which was so widespread among the people…[plus] a patriarchal anxiety about solitary women and their often real knowledge of contraception and medicine."[292] Trevor-Roper, an important Catholic historian, concluded, "some of the coarser elements were directly derived from German Paganism"[293]. The result was, Kung stated, "the greatest mass killings in Europe outside of wartime."[294]

The accused may well not believed in a Church who condemned them. Some, influenced by the popular dualism of that time, may have called their rival to the Church's God "the devil", but Pocs found in the 2000 cases she studied that the devil was only mentioned in evidence extracted after torture, but law court officials presumed that if people did not respect the Church's authority, it was the devil they worshipped. Some of the accused may have named a different God. Jeanne d'Arc spoke of the Christian God and the voices that spoke to her under a tree. Her final adherence was to her inner voices.

The Horror of the Witchhunts

Some historians from the modern Pagan community have minimised the impact of these centuries of "peacetime" massacre, perhaps as an over-reaction to the large claims made by the witch-hunter Springer and others. In consequence they have not given due weight to the traumas inflicted and the communities devastated. They mostly argued about the number killed and Hutton even asked why the fuss when so many more men were killed in wars: "The number of people put to death for the alleged crime was miniscule compared with those executed on other criminal charges or killed in battle during the centuries involved. The distinction was that the overwhelming majority of the dead in the other two categories were male."[295] This was a very different stance to that of such respected Catholic historians as Trevor-Roper who acknowledged the massacres of witches as a holocaust.

The Reformation increased the fervour of the witch-hunters. Calvin preached that "the Bible says there are witches and they must be slain". After the Reformation, Catholics targeted their witchhunts on Protestant areas, the Protestants on Catholic areas. In Denmark, saying Catholic prayers was declared an act of witchcraft. The persecution in Germany greatly accelerated after the publication of *Malleus Maleficorum*. By 1630, according to the Jesuit Friedrich von Spee who bravely met many of the accused: "in Germany especially, the smoke from the stake is every-where."[296] Trevor-Roper wrote that after 1630 "lawyers, judges, clergy themselves, join old women at the stake." Terror haunted the countryside and towns in France, Germany, Switzerland, England and Scotland. Calm periods in any locality could suddenly be broken by a spate of killings as the persecution died down or flared up with all the frightening irregularities of a bush fire.

It is impossible to total just how many were arrested, terrorised, tortured and killed; to total the seared memories of relatives and friends; to number those who lived with a deep fear, imbued over generations of executions, that they too might be accused and killed. In a few villages practically every woman was killed. Enormous numbers must have been traumatised. Their cumulative experiences must surely have seared the collective memory of Europe's women. As for the numbers killed, records are very poor. Recent estimates from conservative academic sources give tentative figures mostly ranging from near to 100,000 up to 240,000. The Cornell University's Witchcraft Studies Centre estimated that there were 160,000. Vivienne Crowley estimated 130,000 to 200,000. Ron Hutton went far below these figures with an "educated guess" of 40,000.

The following are a few examples extracted from a very large number of executions reported. In 1430 over two hundred were burnt in the Valais and some one hundred and sixty-seven in l'Isere- as well as Jeanne d'Arc in 1431. In 1437 one hundred and fifty were killed in Briancon. Ten years later Margery Jordemaine was burnt in London at Smithfield, one of the few burnt in England where the noose was the preferred way. She was burnt because she was accused of using witchcraft against the King. In 1524 over one thousand were reported in an old account as burnt in Como alone. In Germany in 1589, one hundred and thirty-three were burnt on one day in Quedlinburg and in that same year forty-eight were also burnt in Wurttenburg. Between 1590 and 1600 ten were burnt every day in Brunswick. In 1598 twenty-four were burnt in Aberdeen. In 1603 two hundred and five were burnt at the Abbey of Fulda in Germany. In 1645 twenty died in Norfolk. In 1647 witch killings started in what is now the United States. In 1658 eighteen were burnt on Castle Hill in Edinburgh.

In 1659 the Bishop of Galloway allowed a woman from Irongrey to be put into a tarred barrel that was set on fire and thrown into a Scottish river. One of the last of the mass burnings of witches occurred in Bradenburg in 1786. Isolated killings in Europe continued after this at the hands of mobs. Thus died Alice Russell in Great Paxton in England in 1808.

Women comprised from 75% to 80% of those who died in this slaughter of people accused of using pagan or diabolic magic. Thousands of killings are likely not to be in the surviving records. Very inadequate or no records were kept of the numbers subjected to torture yet not killed and of those imprisoned. To gain an idea what it must have been like for hundreds of years, we have only to think of the trauma that would be suffered today in any village if just one of its inhabitants were tortured, burnt or hung. No one has assembled all accounts. Few historians have seriously considered the impact on European culture and on the psyche of women of this half a millennia of persecution.

Yet these "burning times" are not yet over. I am appalled that people are still being killed as witches in Africa and other parts of the world. Thus a Syrian died condemned as a witch in 1998 in Saudi Arabia. Many black women accused of being witches still die every year in South Africa…The list below shows the killings have not stopped. It documents the killings of African witches for about 14 months of 1997 and 1998 using reports from news agency and newspapers.

> March 20, 1997—Meningitis kills 542 in Ghana; witch-hunts started and a mob killed three middle-aged women in the village of Yoggu, accusing them of spreading the disease through witchcraft. *Reuters*
>
> April 1997—Swami pastor and wife hacked to death by members of rival church. The victims were accused of killing the rival church's choirmaster with witchcraft. *Independent Newspapers*
>
> May 13, 1997—A cat was beaten and kicked to death at FNB stadium during a competition because the cat's presence was

considered a bad omen and a symbol of witchcraft. *Independent Newspapers*

September 1, 1997—A family of four was killed while sleeping with AK-47 assault rifles, south of Durban. The victims were killed because the wife had been accused of using witchcraft. *Independent Newspapers*

October 27, 1997—Ghana's human rights Organisation called for a halt to the dehumanising treatment of women accused of witch-craft. Women in the Northern, Upper East and Upper West regions accused of witchcraft were being lynched or banished to "witch camps". There were four such camps located at Gambaga, Kukuo, Kpatinga and Nagani. There were 123 women at the Gambaga camp, 450 at Kukuo, 42 at Kpatinga and 193 at Nagani plus 13 men accused of being wizards. The ages of the "inmates" were between 35—90 years old. *Africa News Service*

January 8, 1998—In Durban, Northern Zululand, five people were burned to death accused of witchcraft. Two women and three men were the victims and evidence suggests that a considerable amount of people carried-out the attack. *Independent Newspapers*

January 13, 1998—A 79-year old farmer in the Volta region of Ghana requested compensation (equal to $23,000) from the chief and elders of his village for banishing him on accusations of witch-craft. The human rights commission was pursuing the matter, they have sent a letter of inquiry to the chief, and have received no response as of yet. *Africa News Service*

January 27, 1998—In Northern Ghana, masked vigilantes clubbed and stoned two women aged 55 & 60 to death for allegedly practising witchcraft. *Reuters*

January 28, 1998—Police shelter "witch" and her two children after her village accused her of witchcraft in Hlogotlou in the Northern Province. *Independent Newspapers*

February 16, 1998—In Tanzania's Mwanza and Shinyanga regions, an alarming number of elderly women were being killed for witchcraft. Major General James Lubanga, the Mwanza regional commissioner said that the problem of witchcraft is common and behind every misfortune they believe somebody is involved. *Africa News Service*

March 6, 1998—A human skull and a puff adder (snake) were found on a Principal's desk in the Dete district. A witch doctor claimed that these were acts of witchcraft designed to kill the school headmaster. *Independent Newspapers*

April 3, 1998—a 50-year old man shot a security guard on Pritchard Street, central Johannesburg. The killer believed that the guard used witchcraft on his daughter. *Independent Newspapers*

May 7, 1998—A man who murdered his aunt is jailed for 11 years in Umtata. Hloniphile Mdludlu, 52, told Eastern Cape Judge Cecil Somyalo that after his uncle died he consulted a sangoma (witch finder) in Gauteng who told him that his aunt, Nodimile Mdludlu, 70 was bewitching members of his family. *Independent Newspapers*

May 16, 1998—Last year, police in the Northern Province investigated over 150 murders of suspected witches. The problem became so serious that a village was set aside by the police as a "witch sanctuary". The village is named Helena and is about 60 kilometres from Pietersburg. *Independent Newspapers*

How do we deal with the catalogue of evil, what is the origin of evil? How can we maintain that the world is sacred and we are created in love when such evils occur? What of other awful mass killings, such as those in Cambodia, in Rwanda, in Nazi Germany?

What of the genocidal massacres that occurred when the British arrived in the lands of the Aboriginal nations of Australia? In 1795 the newly arrived British military were sent out with instructions "in the hope of inspiring terror, to erect gibbets in different places whereupon the bodies of all they might kill were to be hung."[297] In 1816 it was made illegal for Aborigines to approach Sydney in groups larger than six. Any larger unarmed group could be shot.

After a massacre by police Rev. Thelkeid reported: "forty-five heads were collected and boiled down for the sake of the skulls. My informant, a magistrate, saw the heads packed ready for exportation…to accompany the commanding officer on his voyage to England."[298] In 1829 martial law was declared in Tasmania. In 1840 it was made illegal to sell guns to Aborigines. Around 1845 swivel guns were installed on sheep stations. Yet it took over 60 years for the armed resistance of the southern tribes to be broken. In the north and centre massacres and armed resistance continued until the end of the 1930s.

The last Australian massacres are within living memory. The Aboriginal Elder Tabagee showed me in 1979 the bones of family members killed by a police party when "I was this high". He indicated waist high. What should be done in their memory? How do we honour them? I would like to see monuments put up in the memory of those Aborigines who died fighting for their land. They have at least as much right to be honoured in Australia as those who fought in two World Wars. It is a national shame that they are not.

False Gods

The 20th Century mystic and Benedictine, Thomas Merton, expressed the anger of the mystic who sees the sacred earth in danger in *Emblems of a Season of Fury*. He took the Christian teaching that God became flesh to mean that God was one with the object of his love; not just with Christ, but with the universe.

Thus when a mining company covets the minerals on an Aboriginal tribe's land and elevates their hunger for profits above the rights and needs of the tribe, then they are making of profits an idol. When a man puts keeping his job above doing anything about a dangerous product his company makes, then he is making an idol out of his job. But when we see creation as sacred and fight to protect her, see our neighbours as sacred and fight to protect them, then we are not committing idolatry but worshipping the true God.

Merton wrote sadly of the Idolaters.

"They are those who have lose their real self and their passion for truth. Some are those who cannot bear the weight of being women or men. They have given their womanhood or manhood to the corporation or to a political idol. They and our race alike suffer from their wrecking of their potential. For me they had a place to fill that they have left empty, a destiny that they not fulfilled. The earth may well suffer more from what they have not done than from what they have done."

> Please do not look only at the dark side in private life
> These are kind men
> They are only obeying orders…
> You have the sympathy of millions
> As a tribute to your sorrow we resolve
> To spend more money on nuclear weapons.
> There is always a bright side.
> If this were only a movie a boat would be available.
> Have you ever seen our movies—they end happily…
> You would not want the authorities to neglect duty.
> How do you like the image of the free world?
> Sorry you cannot stay.
> This is the first and last time we will see you in our papers.
> When you are back home remember us
> We will be having a good time.

He saw nuclear armed military forces as serving one of the most frightening of idols. They have in their custody the ultimate gift, the eggs of nuclear death. These they protect although they should be destroyed. They hold in their power the lives of all we know and love. Their temptation is to worship these eggs as an ultimate symbol of power, the ultimate antibiotic.

Merton pointed out that abortion is condemned while churchmen bless wars. He reminded us of what happened when the first atomic bombs were exploded. Over the radio went the religiously encoded message that the bomb Tinian had been successful. It was "visible effects greater than Trinity...Proceeding to Papacy."[299] Then the military governor of the Prefecture of Hiroshima issued a proclamation to the people without hands, without feet, with their faces destroyed, with their intestines hanging out: "We must not rest a single day in our war effort...We must bear in mind that the annihilation of the stubborn enemy is our road to revenge." Then a bomb was dropped on Nagasaki although Hiroshima was still burning. The American message came: "The Original Child...is now born..."

The poet Lee Carroll Piper wrote:

Many are called
But most are frozen
In corporate or
Collective cold,
These are the stalled,
Who chose not to be chosen
Except to be bought or sold.[300]

The evils that we must fight are being birthed today in the gloom of lives lived under the shadow of human fabricated idols. These bring about different weddings of the human spirit. Not the sacred marriage to our holy earth, to the creating energy that sustains us, but I believe

The false weddings are:
To social norms

To social class
To race or faith
To skin or nationality
These are the idols.
And they bring emptiness
And leave room open
For the empty God
That seeks power and is jealous,
That makes us feel insignificant,
Unimportant,
Who robs us of our birthright,
Our innate knowledge of what is good and beautiful;
Of the gifts of a divine lover,
Of our home.
We thus in ignorance create our spirit's prison.

Gaia Protects Herself

The world is not so different from us. I see her, Gaia, as a living sentient planet that strives to protect herself from evils. In her birthing chambers she dreams into life the helpers she needs. The children she is creating will know each other, strengthen and support each other. I see her as the mistress of Creation, as the One who Dreams, whose creations live, dance, sing and love, and sometimes sadly hate and thus create a separate home, their prison.

We are born to fight to protect her. This warrior thread wove through my time of parenting. I knew it meant working to protect the earth and my fellow creatures. I felt the Earth did not make us in an idle moment or out of a blind evolutionary process, but for a purpose. This purpose is to be found within us, not in any book.

Working with Aboriginal Warriors

I learnt more about the magic of the Australian land when I went back to the Kimberleys a year after the police were ordered in by helicopter to arrest me. On this return trip I was smuggled by the Aboriginal people of Halls Creek into the Argyle diamond mining lease.. They took me past closed-circuit cameras, security guards and gates, because they wanted me to interpret for them the mining works and to see their rich land filled with food; plants, animals and fish. They wanted me to try to protect it with newspaper articles or by making films. I thus wrote for the papers but I did not succeed. The miners have now destroyed the women's ancient Barramundi Dreaming Place.

But what I did not write about was the magic I experienced when I travelled this ocean of bush, this vast expanse of wildlife, with the Elders or by myself. The strangest, most wonderful thing happened when I drove away from the Argyle diamond lease and the women's ritual site. It is the sort of thing that seems impossible but it really did happen. The track I followed wound through light slender trees. Then when I turned a corner, to my astonishment I found the track bordered on both sides by owls sitting on the ground. There were many, all lined up along the roadside. Their necks turned a full 180 degrees as I drove past slowly. I was in enormous awe. It was as if they had come to farewell me. It was as if I had been given a Guard of Honour! I have no easy explanation. It was the most extraordinary encounter. I thank the owls for it.

Nature did not always treat me so solemnly. One day when I visited a meticulously clean bathroom in a nearby Aboriginal settlement and sat on the virginally clean toilet, something suddenly smacked into my bottom. I leapt up, turned and looked. There, in the toilet, looking up at me, was a large green frog! It had evidently just swum in and then tried to get out quickly before I dumped on it!

In the Kimberleys I felt at home with Aborigines but was suspected by many local whites that saw me as a "southern stirrer". Those who worked professionally with Aborigines tended to think of Aborigines as their exclusive "clients". As for white government officials, I found in many a racist tendency to presume that "our Aborigines" would not cause trouble, and to look for any white faces that might "lead" Aborigines to protest.

My research for the Everyman program also took me to Alice Springs. Robert Bropho, a spokesman for the Aboriginal nation on whose land stands Perth, was keen that I consider making a film with the Aborigines of central Western Australia. He thus drove from Perth to Alice, a distance of about 1,500 miles, to collect me and take me into the West Australian Central Desert Reserve.

I decided this time I would not take the risk of being arrested for entering a West Australian Aboriginal Reserve without a government permit. I surely now had good establishment credentials as I was being employed, not by Aborigines, but by the Religious Affairs Departments of the BBC and ABC. They had offered to obtain my entry permit for me. I knew that tourists obtained these permits over the phone on the day of their request so I anticipated no difficulty.

But the ABC producer learnt to her astonishment that it would take at least three months to process any request for a permit for me. Apparently my application uniquely had to go to a government committee that met in two months time and then, if they approved me, they would seek the opinion of the Aboriginal people I proposed to visit. Only after this would the application be laid before the State Minister of Aboriginal Affairs and his decision would be utterly at his discretion. The fact that a noted Aboriginal leader had invited me was totally irrelevant, or more likely a handicap.

I was fortunate to find a way around this effective banning. A friendly Alice Springs Aboriginal Affairs officer phoned up the relevant West Australian department and I overheard his conversation. "Yes, she does have a Pommie accent. Yes she does definitely work for the BBC." Eventually he put down the phone and grinned. "You have a permit, on the grounds that there are two of you. One of whom was in the

Kimberleys last year, and another that works for the BBC, both with coincidentally the same name."

I also had to apply for permission from the Aboriginal Pitjantjatjara Land Council to cross their lands, for the state of South Australia, unlike Western Australia, had returned land rights to traditional owners. This proved easy to obtain. No government officials had to be asked. Next morning the land council asked the communities over a two-way radio if I could come. Every Aboriginal camp had a radio connected to a car battery. It is the new bush telegraph and ideal for a culture that was traditionally oral. Instantly came back the response from what seemed like a dozen camps. There were no private rituals happening. I would be a welcome visitor.

Next day Robert Bropho arrived to take me to Western Australia along the Gunbarrel Highway, a thousand mile long dirt road across the heart of Australia, a track whose endless vistas I found beautiful and entrancing. I have seen this road from an airliner at full cruising height. It was a thin line stretching from horizon to horizon. They say that it crosses desert, but at ground level it passes through delicate small trees, sharp grasses and shrubs, all with but a small space of sand between them. Everywhere there were raucous parrots. The more so as this region just had a rare rain. The lion of this bush is the dingo, a wonderful wild dog with a golden mane that I saw lying on rocky outcrops as if the lord of all around.

Robert's car was old and battered. When a brake went, the faulty part was simply discarded. Aboriginal mechanics seemed able to do magic with wrecks. The road was eroded and poor. We drove sometimes through large shallow lakes guided by one of us sitting on the car's bonnet.

After a long journey, a cloud of dust heralded a West Australian officer coming to meet me on the invisible border. Deep in the desert he surreally proceeded almost to erect a customs station, demanding my permit before I went any further. I fortunately had my West Australian permit telexed to me before setting out so he was unable to stop me. No tourists were ever asked for this permit. But government officials no doubt did not want me to write about the 7-foot cubes of metal sheets that I saw later that day.

The government were provided these as housing fit for Aboriginal families in a region of blazing sun and freezing nights.

After receiving my report, the Everyman team decided to focus their film on how the Aboriginal spiritual relationship with the land was affected by the Argyle diamond mine. But the producers did not appreciate the importance of the dust-covered old man who met us at Derby airport, nor the honour done to them by his presence. He was Nipper Tabagee, a "Dreamer", and a most important and honoured elder among the Aboriginal people.

His presence opened Aboriginal doors. The production team needed to have him on side. Protestant fundamentalist missionaries had been active in the region with the result that Aborigines asked me if it was true that the ABC's producer had 666 tattooed on his arm. They had been told that the devil was staying at the pub and suspected the producer was this devil. The level of paranoia was such that the woman helping us with translations demanded that she be given the film from my camera when I took a photo of her house from down the street. She worked for an American bible translation society about which Survival International had written a most scathing report entitled: "Is God an American?" The accusation was that while translating the Bible for remote communities they naively facilitated the entry of American big business into tribal lands. I found the same society was active in Aurukun when we were fighting Shell.

One day the BBC producer asked me to negotiate filming access to a male initiation ritual. I refused on the grounds that this was inappropriate for me to do as a woman. I feared that asking for this could damage my credibility among Aborigines. My refusal caused the producer to angrily ask me for who was I working, the Aborigines or the BBC?

The Everyman team then negotiated access to a preliminary ritual before a boy's initiation. They gained this with a promise to send the community a copy of the film before it was broadcast for checking by elders. But they did not keep this promise. This resulted in a film that the Elders sadly told me could not be used by their people since it included a few seconds of ritual dancing private to men.

I mentioned earlier how to my astonishment I found that rumours about my previous incarnation as a Catholic priest had reached the remotest of Catholic Missions, that of Kalumburu. This Mission reported this to the Everyman team, much to the producers' astonishment. This was after I had finished my work for them and had returned home. A producer later angrily asked me if this were true? He said if it were, I should have told them beforehand. I said this was none of their business, reminding him that they had said my research was among the best they had ever seen for an Everyman program He did not know it, but he had me phoned just before my operation. I had by then lived for seven years as a woman.

Shortly after I came out of hospital, I was asked by Aboriginal friends to produce a film for them. When I protested that I had never produced before, only researched, I was simply told: "You are clever, you can learn!" I agreed to do this, on condition that I had an Aboriginal co-producer working on the same salary as myself and that the Aboriginal communities involved had the right to finally approve the film. I did not want to make the same mistake as had Everyman.

I returned to Perth to discuss this project with my friend, Aboriginal elder and spokesman, Robert Bropho. He agreed to work as co-producer and co-director. We decided it would tell the story of the last Australian gold rush from an Aboriginal perspective. The prospectors had killed many Aborigines, leaving their descendants living in destitution by some of Australia's richest mines.

Robert consulted elders living by the Kalgoorlie gold mines. They spent weeks discussing what kind of film they wanted. Then I received a letter saying: "Our film will be called "Munda Nyuringu: [which means] they have taken the land, they believe it is theirs, they won't give it back." My reaction was both pleasure that they wanted this film and "Help!" for I had no idea how to correctly pronounce "Munda Nyuringu". These words were from the Wongi dialect of the still widely spoken Pitjantjatjara language of South Central Australia.

The Elders made another very serious decision. They had previously told only fables meant for uninitiated children when speaking to white people on spiritual matters, as the deeper stories were only for initiates. Many Whites thus thought Aboriginal spiritual beliefs were simple and childlike. They heard of what the lizards did, or what the kangaroo and emu got up to, but did not hear the deeper stories that explained the meaning behind the fables.

The elders realised that this had given rise to false ideas about their religion, so, knowing our film's final cut would be sent to them for approval, they had decided the time had come to let white people further into their ancient faith. They would tell the White community in our film how two Creating Ancestors or Gods formed the land that underlay Kalgoorlie, rather than about the deeds of two lizards.

They took us out into the wasteland that is now Kalgoorlie's "Golden Mile", filled by waste tips and mine heads above vast pits, and told us how two Creating Ancestors had sung and formed this land. They pointed to where red ochre could still be seen amid scrap metal. "You see that red earth there? That is where the Gods painted themselves." They showed us the hill surrounded by gold mines where the Ancestors' song once rang out, forming the landscape. This reminded me somewhat of my own Celtic people's stories of Ancestors who created wells and rivers and mountains. In Wales the ancient legends spoke of a wild boar that formed the land, much as did two lizards in an Aboriginal children's tale.

An Aboriginal woman showed me some small golden nuggets and told me their bright colour symbolised traditionally the yolk of the emu's egg, full of richness and fertility. For her gold was a beautiful rock that should be celebrated by song and dance, not melted down to hide in safes! A senior elder told us, near the statue that celebrated the white "discoverer" of Kalgoorlie's gold: "Paddy Hannon did not discover this place. Why we used to have a tall pole here. People danced around it. People came from far away to this place to dance, from right up to where is now Darwin (some 1000 miles north)." The area had been famed for its golden beauty throughout Aboriginal Australia.

I found the diary of a local gold prospector, a Robert Menzies. He found a rich deposit north of Kalgoorlie and recorded, "I leapt off my camel. I ground my heels into piles of nuggets. The ground was saturated with the metal! In two hours I had gathered up 250,000 pounds worth of the metal." He told how the resulting gold rush resulted in thirty-six public houses being set up within six weeks "in this place that had only known the pad of the blackfellow's feet."

He also told how Aborigines tried to free a captive. "I set charges around my camp and made up some hand grenades. Spears began to fly. I pressed the detonator. Dirt, shrubs and blacks went up into the air. I threw a few hand grenades then went out to survey this 10-minute battlefield. Eight dead natives, blood trails all over the place." He did not say why he held a captive, but a common method used by European "explorers" to find water in the desert was to capture an Aborigine and feed him salt until he was forced to reveal where the wells were situated. Menzies became the Major of the new mining town. He named it after himself, named the other councillors, and became a Fellow of the Royal Geographical Society.

After this many local Aborigines were taken in chains to Australia's Alcatraz, the prison island of Rottenest near Perth where hundreds died. A different fate awaited children with mixed blood. They were taken to distant boarding schools since it was believed that their mixed blood meant they were more intelligent and could be "assimilated" into white ways. We interviewed a woman of fifty who cried as she told how her mother had tried to hide her from the police who wanted to take her away. "She tried to darken my skin with boot polish but it all washed off. She tried to put soot on me but that came off too. We had to run and hide whenever the police came." The local Aborigines were now living in tin shacks on the only land they were allowed, the common land on the edge of Menzies.

An Aboriginal elder told us "We cannot go out into the lands we once hunted. We are driven off at gun point." He also told me of mythological creatures that lived among the stars.

Not far from Menzies lies a place known by Aborigines as "Yeelirrie". When Whites took this land, they asked those they dispossessed for the local place name and gave it to their cattle station. They were not told what the name meant. When a mining company found on this same cattle station a surface deposit of uranium, they also called their mine prospect "Yeelirrie".

"Yeelirrie" meant, in the local language, "the place of death" An ancient Aboriginal myth recorded that a dangerous spirit was imprisoned here and that the people must not dig this land lest the spirit escape and destroy the earth. When we went to film there, we took a Geiger counter. It went off its dial when we were still some fifty feet from the central exploratory pit, filled with water from which kangaroos were drinking. We hastily backed off.

We heard an appalling story in nearby Kalgoorlie from an Aboriginal woman who had survived a nuclear bomb. The government only appointed two officers to patrol the remote desert boundaries of a vast nuclear testing range set up by the UK on tribal lands in the 1950s; even though Aboriginal people hunt-gathered and had sacred sites on this land. Thus some Aborigines were still there when the bombs exploded. She said her family were under the desert pines when planes went overhead and then a vast black cloud rolled over them. "We walked out of there, but I was the only one that lived." Local health officers estimated that about 350 died from nuclear explosions. Many others were blinded or otherwise injured. We added the story of this nuclear attack to our film.

Local state officials tried to intimidate our interviewees. When this failed, we were attacked in the State Parliament for "attempting to manipulate" Aborigines. We filmed inside the gold mines. We recorded the atrocious living conditions, the shanties, and the wall-less "houses" that the Federal Government built for them in a valley hidden by mining dumps, out of sight of the white residents of Kalgoorlie.

Our film made on a shoestring budget was shown on the ABC and was chosen unanimously by the judges to win a "Best Documentary Nomination" from the Australian Film Institute. I was more impressed by how many Aboriginal people drove in from the desert to watch it and saw it in Freemantle Gaol. It became clear that it was their film, their victory and their story. It was road-showed in Aboriginal camps, by the side of desert tracks and at Aboriginal demonstrations.

It would have never have been so honoured if Robert Bropho had not driven it, and me, to make it as excellent as possible. He taught me to go for the finest quality. He asked questions like "Who is Australia's finest cartoonist?" When I replied "Bruce Petty ", Robert insisted we immediately drove to his home some 400 miles away. Petty then agreed to make for free a wonderful series of cartoons.

I was privileged to work alongside Robert. What kept him going, he said, was the need to do all possible "for the sake of the children of tomorrow." The film contained the spirit of this leader who had grown up on his much loved land amid the debris of white society. The film was also influenced by my spirit, that of a woman who had from her Northern Irish mother a bonding and a mourning for lands stolen by colonisers. Robert liked my sense of history for it matched his.

Robert taught me to trust my instincts in filmmaking. When the professional editor we hired shaped our film differently from our script, I at first deferred to his expertise. But Robert did not let this continue. He looked at the copy I sent him and phoned to say he was coming to put it right. I then tightly directed the editor and worked all night while Robert drove the 3500 miles from Perth to Melbourne. When he arrived, he was surprised and pleased to see the corrected film. The only complaints were from my younger daughter whose bedroom was adjacent to the Steenbeck 16mm film-editing desk. It drove her crazy as I spent nights endlessly repeating phases until they matched the pictures accurately.

Robert spoke of the greed of modern society like an Old Testament prophet. I first tended to defer to him but eventually learnt when I should not. Eventually our few disagreements vanished, he said, "like dirty water washed away under the bridge".

It was odd that I had to learn this, given my background. Why should I, brought up as a "male", have to learn not to defer? I had not been conditioned to be submissive to men. But it was not so simple. When I began to live as a woman, it was easy to slip naturally into what seemed to be my destined place on the gender map. I wanted very much to be accepted. Thus I found myself uneasily placating men's egos in order to get them to do what I wanted. I did not know how to deal with males who presumed authority; who presumed to adopt the air of expertise even in areas where I was better qualified; who did not try to empower the women with whom they worked or treat them as equals; who no longer gave my opinion the weight given to the thoughts of males.

Just the same, I also found wonderful men with whom I could work, among them the editor and deputy editor of *The Age,* one of Australia's foremost newspapers. They were much surprised when I appeared in their office to sell them my first article for it was 3,000 words long. After checking me out, they published the entire article over 3 pages. It was about the discovery of the world's largest diamond deposit at Argyle in NW Australia, and the fight by De Beers to get control. The piece was nationally syndicated, advertised on television and put in for awards by the paper. It was cheeky of me to put in such a major article as my first, but I had learnt that cheekiness makes it much easier to get what I wanted! Since then I have had published many front-page news stories and major features on human rights, health or environmental matters. As I had an electric typewriter, The Age arranged for me to use a sub-editor's office. None of the journalists' desks had electric sockets when I started in 1982.

I made sure my first article was as effective as possible by briefing beforehand the deputy leader of the Labour party, Paul Keating (who later became Prime Minister). His questions resulted in Prime Minister Malcolm Fraser querying the wisdom of selling diamonds to an apartheid-linked cartel. This opposition gravely concerned De Beers. It could put their price-fixing cartel in danger.

Sometimes poor whites got in touch with me, even small-scale miners, for I had gained a reputation as a defender of the underdog. This led me to discover that CRA (owned by the UK's RTZ) planned to pump cyanide into seven hundred kilometres of underground rivers in SE Australia to dissolve out the gold they contained. These rivers were the major water resources for the farmers of the region. This was the only time that just one of my articles succeeded in reversing a development.

Other stories came to me by seeming chance. One day when we were driving back from dining at a Vietnamese restaurant, the cars in front stopped suddenly in the middle of Hoddle Street, a major Melbourne road. A few moments later two police cars raced up from behind. One swerved outside us and the other went across the grass into a nearby park and between the trees. Gunshots rang out.

We had nearly driven into an ambush. Drivers in front of us had been shot dead. I then reported from the "front-line" what became known as the Hoddle St. Massacre while police in pyjamas ran with guns between trees. It was like a scene from a movie. The dead lying in the street seemed like models. It was utterly unreal—it felt as if at any moment a film producer would shout; "Cut" and everyone would get up. I learnt later a young man rejected by a military school had set up a sniping post in bushes by one of Melbourne's busiest intersections. It was nearly an hour before he was captured.

The nature of evil

Atrocities are fed into the newspapers at an ever-increasing rate. In today's world the nature of evil is often confusing. Christians have explained evil as disobedience to laws in a Maker's Manual known through supernatural Revelation. These laws seemingly regulate our sexual life much more than they do our aggression. Christian spokesmen thus condemned President Clinton much more for his sexual behaviour than for bombing a vital pharmaceutical factory in Sudan. Some Christians saw themselves as besieged by devils that tempted them to disobey this Rulebook. On one side was the Good God with squadrons of angels. On the other was Lucifer with a host of demons.

This was alike to the theories of Philo, a Pagan philosopher who lived around the time of Christ (25BCE to 50 CE). He held that God created the immortal part of man while Satan created the mortal part, from whence evil could come. Some early Christians believed in a soon-to-come final battle or Armageddon when the evil spirits would be defeated. Similar views are held today among some American fundamentalist sects.

But the mystics did not share these views. They believed that a Rulebook could never replace the inner voice of God. Some Christian mystics questioned the very existence of evil demons. They said these could not be created or sustained by a good God. The Pagan philosopher Plotinus maintained much the same.

Many believed in a God that created both good and evil. This was described in Old Testament texts that taught a monotheistic God had created all, even "disaster".

I am Yahweh, and there is no other
I form the light and I create the darkness,
I make well-being and I create disaster,
I, Yahweh, do all these things.[301]

But the mystics held their God did not create evil or disaster. Instead they said evil was a negative thing that could be created by a human. Porete defined evil as "nought" or non-being, the absence of life. Humans created evil by "noughting" their potential for good and for love.

Maester Ekhardt, 1260-1328 held, as I have mentioned, that "Evil is opposed to being, therefore the devil does not exist and the sinner, the 'son of the devil', is nothing." Blessed Julian of Norwich also denied that devils existed, and denied that nature was evil. For them there was no evil power.

They saw God as Perfect Goodness, as the only Creator and as incapable of creating anything that was not good. Evil therefore was simply "nought". These views radically challenged the contemporary demonising practices and theories of the witchtrials.

Some Pagans and Gnostic Christians saw evil as a product of a lesser God, who was an emanation from the Ineffable Godhead as Plato had suggested. Such lesser Gods could create imperfect beings just as what we create is usually imperfect. This theory seemingly resolved the issue that perplexed monotheists who wanted to reconcile Jesus' teaching on the loving nature of God with an Old Testament record of a jealous God who incited massacres. The latter became for them a much inferior God, a demiurge ("half-God"). The Gnostic Christian book *The Testimony of Truth* taught that this lesser jealous God had plotted to subject women (Eve) to men (Adam) and had punished the first humans for eating from the tree of knowledge because he wanted humans to stay ignorant. Its authors saw this lesser God as sharing humanity's responsibility for the presence of evil.

The Gnostics believed human nature retained a divine spark that would illuminate and transform those who gained "gnosis" or wisdom. This view was opposed by St. Augustine who maintained human nature was so corrupted by the "Fall" that not even a divine spark remained. Instead Christ had to restore to it everything good.

As for the serpent in Genesis, many Gnostics viewed it as holy. They said it was "wiser than all the animals in Paradise." The serpent instructs Adam and Eve that they are of high and holy origin and not slaves of the demiurge in the Gnostic book, *The Hypostasis of the Archons.*
Some Gnostics saw the Adam and Eve creation myth as having a psychological interpretation. The demiurge symbolised a powerful evil inclination in us that is lower and less important than the human potential for good. The psychiatrist Carl Jung interpreted the demiurge as symbolising the destructive creative urge within us, an urge that I often had to suppress as a despairing escapist futility.

But I needed no demiurge for my theology of evil. I saw evil as created by other humans. I thought humans quite capable of evil actions. It was a consequence of us being both imperfect and free. I was not worried about how to reconcile the presence of evil with a loving God for I knew how humans could both be loved and be atrocious. The God I knew was both large enough to be a creator of a free being and small enough to know me and to wish to work with me, not a dictator or a universal doctor. It is our job as humans to fight against the evil humans make.

Blood tainted diamonds

A year after my gender "re-assignment" operation, I returned to hospital for a skin graft. While recovering from this, I thought about what I had learnt while investigating the diamond mining companies. I knew they were guilty of human rights violations around the world. I wondered how I could help bring this to an end. I knew I could not do the research needed by relying on money from newspaper articles. Only a television series would give me this. I thus wrote up and sent to television networks a proposal for an investigative television series on diamonds to be shot around the world.

When the ABC took up my project and sent me on an initial overseas research trip, I met John Kelly in Washington DC, a well-known television investigative researcher, the unsung hero of many a major investigation presented by others. John and I got on very well. He too was a campaigning journalist. His focus was on the CIA and FBI. I gained my own contacts in the intelligence world. It was exciting but somewhat scary to listen to their tales of murder, subversion and of official deceit at the highest levels of political power.

I soon found myself writing front-page newspaper stories. I set my cap at the White House, at its Iranian and Iraqi operations, at alleged treasonous activities of George Bush and Ronald Reagan before they came to power. I investigated the story that George Bush and the Republican Party undermined President Carter by making undercover deals with the Iranians to prevent the President gaining the release of American hostages held in Teheran. The plan was to make Carter look like a wimp and it apparently succeeded. The hostages were not released until the very day of Reagan's inauguration as President. NATO weapons then flooded into Iran as they allegedly received their reward. I tracked down the agents involved and this story ran at two full pages length in a major newspaper.[302] It was entitled *Armsgate*, created an international storm and was copied widely.

I had first proposed this story to a leading American investigative program *Frontline*. They were at first sceptical, wondering how a foreign journalist could uncover a story that was so American before most American journalists. But my research convinced them. A leading Frontline executive then phoned to say they would do my story but would not employ me to do it, as the story was so American. Instead they would use an American journalist. This apologetic phone call lasted over an hour as he tried to assuage my anger. He said that at least I would know that my work was respected and taken seriously!

Robbed of the film, I then wrote the Armsgate story and released it before the Frontline program appeared, so that at least among journalists I would have the credit for publishing first the story. When I came to see the program, it was as I had written, and it did create a storm. A Congressional Investigation was ordered to look into its allegations but nothing then happened. So I went to Washington to meet with the Congressional Investigative Officers They were quite frank. They told me the names of the Senators who had restricted and then stopped their investigation in mid-stream.

Some months later I met Ari Ben Menashe, a former Israeli Intelligence officer, secreted in a flat overlooking Sydney Harbour writing his memoirs. He told me he was present at the pre-election meetings between

Republicans and the Iranians. His role was to supply the Israeli expertise needed to deliver the arms supplies to Iran.

Ben Menashe agreed to give me his secret testimony to the Congressional Investigation. A meeting was set up in his flat high in a tower block. Incredibly, just at the moment when he was handing me the papers, a "window cleaner" on an outside cradle leaned forward so keenly that he fell through the open window into the room! Ari also gave me arms sales documents that helped me expose in the Evening Standard a newspaper editor as an arms merchant.

I was greatly enjoying myself as a woman warrior. I liked the thrill of setting the power of my pen against the diamond cartel and the White House. Even Ari laughed at my arrogance. But the BBC in England backed me, as did the ABC and one of Australia's finest newspapers. With such support I naively thought I would be safe. I had lessons to learn.

I was also at that time focussed on keeping our family together. While the children were young I never went away for long on projects. There was too much to do at home and too much joy in watching our daughters grow up. This was before the events that tore us apart.

The Hunt for Daisy Bates

When the children were sixteen and seventeen, their age gave me the freedom to plan a longer trip. My diamond film series was an expensive project so took time to organise. More than one broadcaster was needed to fund it. So I asked the ABC if there were a project that I could do in the meantime and they gave me one on Daisy Bates. They asked me to research her for a proposed documentary.

She spent many decades in the deserts with Aborigines in the first half of the 20th century. She lived with the Nullarbor tribes while they watched a railway spin a serpent-like line across Australia. Her autobiography also fascinated one of the greatest stars of Hollywood, Katherine

Hepburn, who decided she wanted to play Daisy Bates. Hepburn thus commissioned two Canberra academics to research Daisy's life for a proposed feature film.

This could have been a truly marvellous film, as Hepburn had instinctively known. Daisy had even looked like her. But the academics succeeded in putting her off. They told me as if they expected me to be outraged: "Did you know Daisy Bates was a bigamist? She lied to the authorities in order to remarry!" They also said some Aborigines did not like Daisy because she had tried to stop Aborigines marrying Whites. I thought these were flimsy reasons for recommending against this film, but I needed to find out more.

I discovered that Daisy, born into a large impoverished Irish family, made a terrible blunder on arriving in Queensland. She fell for a man called Bates who deserted her two months later to go to South Africa. He never returned. (His death as the result of a court martial was later the subject of a feature film.) Daisy had to return her ring, as he had not paid for it. A divorce was then impossible so it seemed that she would be condemned never to marry again. Well she was an ingenious woman who had no intention of remaining Bate's victim. She embarked on another ship, landed in New South Wales and declared to the authorities that she was only now arriving in Australia and was a single woman. She then married a drover and travelled around cooking for cattle hands (cowboys in US parlance).

But despite having a son by this drover, this life-style did not satisfy her so she deserted them and returned to England. When she next appeared in Australia she had acquired yet another identity in one of the few careers then open to a woman. She was now a lady in corsets and a journalist, who had met the Queen and who was to report on Aboriginal affairs for *The Times*. She apparently told its editor that it was not true that Aborigines were being mistreated and undertook to establish the true state of play. But a Catholic missionary on her boat insisted she was quite wrong. He invited her to visit his mission to interview the Aborigines.

Daisy's diary of her consequent journeys through the Outback revealed her great sense of humour. She laughed when Aborigines mimicked her tying her corsets. She told how Aborigines mocked a missionary by pretending to hold Catholic religious services. She found Aborigines were badly treated but, above all else, she became fascinated by Aboriginal culture. She spent time in every Aboriginal camp she found. She taught herself some forty Aboriginal languages and took copious notes. I found some eighty boxes of her writings on Aboriginal subjects in the Australian National Museum. She established a reputation for academic scholarship despite never having been to university. The West Australian government commissioned her to write the first definitive ethnographic study of the State's Aborigines. This entailed her travelling by stagecoach and train from one Aboriginal camp to another. Robert Bropho told me his mother remembered her visit and had nothing but good memories of her.

She then became the first woman invited to join an "Oxbridge" (Oxford and Cambridge) University Expedition, organised because they were intrigued by her discoveries. But this was a disaster for her. It's leader, Radcliffe-Brown, assured her that he could get her book published in England. She trusted him and so gave up plans to travel back with government funding to get it published. It was consequently never published. When she recovered her manuscript, it was covered in Radcliffe-Brown's chauvinistic comments. But years later she had something of a vengeance. They were both invited to speak to a scientific congress. At the end of his talk she went to the podium as if to give her own paper. But all she did was to publicly thank him for presenting her research so well.

With no book published, she found it impossible to secure properly paid work with Aborigines, unlike Radcliffe-Brown who became Professor of Anthropology at Sydney University. When she applied for positions in the Outback, she was told such work was too hard for a lady. The only work she could find with Aborigines was mediating with tribes whose lands were wanted for a train line from Adelaide to Perth. For this she would be paid a pittance.

I decided to follow in her footsteps as recorded in her diary. The ABC gave me a train ticket west from Sydney to Perth and a four-wheel-drive vehicle to drive back east from Perth to Adelaide. I planned to trace her steps across the Nullarbor desert. On the way west I persuaded the transcontinental express to stop in the desert so I could visit her monument. As I walked into the shrub, festooned with cameras, scores of heads leaned out of the train to watch me. When I returned, the train conductor told me that a couple in my carriage knew Daisy Bates.

It was one of those extraordinary coincidences. This was their first trip on this train in ten years. They were thrilled I was interested in Daisy. The husband told me he had been responsible for delivering supplies to Daisy. She would come to the line surrounded by armed warriors who loved and protected her. They carried a chair for her to sit on, as she was elderly, while supplies were being checked. When Daisy came to town, she stayed with his family. They remembered her as unpretentious and much fun.

The drive back from Perth took me over 3000 kilometres of desert tracks from sheep station to sheep station to Aboriginal settlement. Whenever possible, I phoned ahead so people would know where to find me if I broke down. I did not have a two-way radio, but was told I should set fire to the spare tire to create a smoke signal if I needed help. One day, after visiting a family in a sheep station built of surplus railway sleepers, I found in all directions the horizon was absolutely flat. Not a tree, not a rock, broke its curved line. I spun, looking at the circle around me, realising as never before that I lived on a planetary ball; that clearly had not shaved as low saltbush shrub evenly covered its surface. It was an elating experience of space and wonder. If I had been any good at cartwheels, the desert would have seen an amazing sight.

The plain is known as the "Nullarbor" from the Latin for "no trees" but later that same day I came across a small solitary tree covered in cobwebs—and soft white fruit. They were delicious, something like a lychee but without any hard covering. I marked it on a map, as it was a very rare specimen, but so far I have not had the chance to do anything about it.

A desert tracker helped me trace Daisy's journey near the West Australia boundary. We climbed down great cliffs that faced the Antarctic Ocean on steps carved by Aborigines. These took us to the flint beds they mined. The cliff top was covered in flint-knapping shards. The tracker called the flints dropped along desert tracks "Aboriginal visiting cards", for, since the flint beds were deeply buried, any surface flint had to have been dropped by a human. One day I climbed down into a great pothole that local historians said Aborigines were scared to enter, but it was more likely that they did not want to enter ill prepared. They may have needed the consent of the appropriate elders and perhaps ritual preparation. I found an underground tunnel the size of a London tube line. It took me down to the flint beds. Inspecting them I stepped into a lake of water so pure that I could not see it before disturbing it. Such a place would be considered of extraordinary richness by a desert people.

I searched to see if the site of a boro ring survived where she had witnessed Aboriginal rituals. The local Aborigines had been removed so we could not ask them. I travelled with the only local guide I could find, a man on a half ruined cattle station. We went along the edge of the tree line in the desert until we found a sunken circular depression with cleared stone ledges serving as natural seats around it. On one side there were bushes and behind these the cast-off "water roots" that Aborigines cut and carried. They were not from local trees. My guide showed me the signs of a local burial. I was much affected by this place and very sorry that there was no one left locally to ask about it. I meditated and tried to sense what was in this place to which I` had seemingly been drawn.

I then found on one side of the ring, a low cave nearly hidden by flat rocks. I was drawn to peep inside. Much to my astonishment I saw inside the face of an Aboriginal woman, lying on the earth peacefully as if asleep. I looked again and again and again, and there she lay, as if the mother of the earth, uncorrupted, whole. I felt it had to be an hallucination—but every time I looked she seemed very real. But next day she had utterly vanished. If it were a delusion, it was the strangest and most convincing that I have ever experienced. To this day, she symbolises for me the Mother that lies within the earth. I can still see her face and feel privileged to have met her.

A common element between Celtic and Aboriginal spirituality is the use of stones to mark out ritual areas. Warlpiri men and women marked out ritual sites with stones, arranging them sometimes to show the direction from which totemic animals or Ancestors had travelled. These rituals were still being carried out in the 1970s and no doubt are still happening.[303]

A few days later, some hundreds of miles from this boro ring, I found the Nullarbor Aborigines who knew Daisy. After her death they had been forcibly moved to the Yalata mission because their tribal lands were wanted for testing British atomic bombs. It became known as the Maralinga testing range—and many Aborigines were killed and crippled by radiation while the tests proceeded. They returned to the least polluted part of their lands some thirty years later in the 1980s. They then built themselves a settlement some two days journey into the desert, far from pubs and white ways, where they could teach their young their culture while caring for their land and sacred places. They also employed a white teacher to help the children learn English. They gave this very special settlement a name that was in English "Oak Valley".

I had previously written to the elder spokesman at Oak Valley to ask if I might visit but had received no answer. I could guess why. I knew that a party of young boys with their kinsfolk were travelling here for initiation from the centre of Australia, from near Uluru. No one knew quite when they would finish this long trek, but when they arrived, my presence would not be appropriate.

When I learnt on arrival at Yalata that the initiation party had not yet arrived, I offered to carry in my car as many as possible to Oak Valley. The local elders immediately approved my trip. My vehicle was filled with a happy overflowing crowd who regarded my arrival as providential. On the way I was taken to the traditional red ochre mining ground. We stayed overnight nearby. The women lit their campfire some fifty feet from the men's and invited me to join them. When we had eaten, the women moved the ashes of their fire aside, dug me a hip hollow and offered me the warm sand to sleep on. This was their traditional desert hospitality.

Next evening we reached Oak Valley. The track passed through widely separated Aboriginal family camps, each with its own windbreak but with no houses. Protection from wind, not rain, was needed here. As we arrived, a four-wheel-drive approached and one of the elders told me, "That man there. He is the man you wrote to. You should speak to him."

I leapt out and ran across to him. His eyes lit up as if he recognised me. He opened the door to his car. I smiled at him, knelt by him. He said; "So you are the woman who wrote to me! I was looking at your letter only yesterday. I did not know how to reply. The young men are coming down. But they are not here and you are here. This is very good. I will show you where you will camp. It will be near my camp."

I did my best to copy the nearby families in building my windbreak and in preparing a small fire. That evening the elder sat by my campfire and introduced me to the other elders. I offered to share my food. He accepted. I asked him if he had known Daisy Bates. He replied: "Why yes. I used to play in and around her tent when I was a boy."

"What was Daisy like? " I asked.

"She was just like you! She shared her food, talked like you. Are you coming to be another Daisy?"

I was startled by his suggestion and secretly somewhat flattered. I told him, "No, I am not, at least not now." I wondered afterwards could I do this? One side of me would love it but other elders had suggested that there was work for me to do back among my own people in my own land. I felt instinctively that they were right.

We spoke that night of many things. He told me how Daisy in her old age wore pistols, and used them to threaten police when they mistreated members of the community. She was so revered that the police would desist and not arrest her. He told me that Daisy travelled with them on their sacred "walk about" to the special places and ritual sites. Later he took me for a two-day journey to her old camp where I found her cooking pots and wind break still intact.

I knew from Daisy's writing that Aboriginal men allowed her to touch their sacred objects. I was surprised at this, for I did not know then that men and women could show each other their sacred boards and that the women sometimes danced with the male boards.[304]

The Elder Spokesman said that Daisy only made one mistake. She was so keen to protect Aboriginal culture that she was outspoken against Aborigines sleeping with white people and having their children. This gave her a poor reputation among mixed blood Aborigines. One day she also persuaded her community to burn mattresses they were given, saying that these would make them too soft to resist the influence of the white people

When she went to the cities she tirelessly campaigned for the central region of Australia to be given back to Aborigines to manage. She always wore elegant old-fashioned dresses, perhaps in the hope that this would help her maintain some influence in society and prevent people saying she had "gone native". She also contrived to stay in upper class women's clubs when in town, despite being nearly penniless. She impressed but never received any significant funds. None of her enormously detailed academic work was published in her lifetime. When some professors of anthropology came to visit, she asked for help in finding research funds, but their response was simply to search their pockets. She was so indignant that she threw the coins back at them. When her health finally deteriorated, she had to be physically forced by an ambulance crew to leave the Aboriginal camps.

It was ironical that this was to be my last journey with Aborigines, at least for the next thirteen years. I could have learnt a great deal more from them but I also knew I might always feel I was a guest in another's land. I had more to discover about myself, much more to learn about my own land, and, with the diamond project, I had a bit between my teeth. I wanted to pursue the cartel that had taken Aboriginal lands. I was a huntress who was not yet ready to be a desert wise woman.

Yet I had come to love this Australian land, this vast ocean of rock and ancient plants, with its elegant white trunked silver leafed trees. I had learnt to see the magic in it, the poetry and the myths, to wonder in its creation. It had taught me of our common inheritance. I had learnt that we of the West were also of ancient blood, that our human minds have ancient wiring, inherited wisdom and paths of instinct that could lead us to our common inheritance of wisdom. When I bonded with elders in a sparkle of eyes, we recognised this as a bond between us.

There is much we can learn from the Aboriginal nations. Few books written by Aborigines are currently available outside Australia, leaving open the way to inadequate books and poorly researched films. I was once sent a book of New Age spirituality in which the author began by telling of a trip to Australia. She told how she went to an Aboriginal community, explained to them the technical wonders of a transistor radio and offered onc as a gift. The elders thanked her for her explanation but declined her gift, saying they had no need of it. She concluded by marvelling at how Aborigines kept themselves untainted by western technology. What she did not know was that they already understood radio technology. They were just too polite to say. They ran a very successful radio station, started the first Australian pirate TV station and obtained the Northern Territory's commercial TV license. An oral culture much values oral technologies.

One of the best-known books about Aborigines outside Australia is *Mutant Message Down Under.* Many believed its stories but, according to Australian newspapers, it allegedly was fictitious and much criticised by Aborigines When a well-known German filmmaker, Werner Herzog, decided to make a film about Aborigines, he called it, if my memory is right, *Where the green ants dream.* I had mentioned this Dreaming in a book of mine that was translated into German. Green ants live in nests in trees but he depicted them as living in magnetically orientated termite hills. But much more seriously, he depicted Aborigines as receiving planes as compensation and sitting in them on the ground contentedly and foolishly.

But enough of comments on other literary works and films: my work for Aborigines caused me to be more the critic of the Australian mining industry, partly because I loved rocks and geology, partly because of the injustices involved. I knew Aborigines were still losing sacred lands to corporate greed. Most of the major Australian mining houses were controlled from outside Australia, so my colleagues and friends felt the campaign for justice should be taken overseas. We had done this successfully with Shell. I now wanted to do it with De Beers.

In 1991, after three years intensive work, I finally succeeded in raising the $1.2 million needed to produce a television series on human rights and the diamond industry. I had commitments from the BBC, from American Television (WGBH) and from the ABC. We decided it should be made from a London base. It would be the most international and expensive television investigation ever shot.

Just before leaving, I went for a quick visit to the Barrier Reef. I had been frightened away from swimming as a primary school child and had since lacked confidence to swim out of my depth. I had an idea I could do so if I were to wear scuba gear, so wanted to experiment. During the long boat trip out to the reef from Cairns we were told that a shark might visit while we were under water but not to be alarmed. It was fed by the boat crew and would be non-aggressive. The instructor told us: "If it turns up, treat it as if it were a big dog."

Well, I gritted my teeth and tumbled backwards as instructed into what I saw as sinister blue water. It was one of the scariest things I had done. We then swam with our instructor deep into the reef. It was much noisier than expected. The bubbles from the mask sounded like a coughing engine. But as the fish swarmed around, I forgot the noise with fascination. A moray eel comically waved at me from a hole like an ugly glove puppet. Then the shark turned up. It was vast, graceful, a racehorse of the sea. It was a large reef shark with white tipped fin. It curved closely around me. I remembered the instructor's words so reached out and stroked its rough skin as I would a dog. The shark regarded me impassively as it turned back to have another look at me. We looked each other in the eye. I was amazed by its beauty and strength and was both nervous and excited. There was no point in thinking of escape—only in enjoying the thrill of the encounter. It was only afterwards that I found out that everyone else had fled.

The Little People

The film took time to get underway even after I arrived in England to make it. This gave me the opportunity to explore my heritage in Northern Ireland. I went to Falls Road in Belfast, as that was where my mother's father came from. I was surprised to find a seemingly typical northern British street with terraces and small shops. The only difference was spectacular graffiti, a grimly and fearfully fortified police station inside a box of metal sheeting, and a social security office shrouded in anti-rocket netting. It was a sad visit, a spectator's sampling of fear and ordinariness.

I went on to the wild hills of Donegal to stay in a friend's croft. Nearby I found by a farm gate a painted sign saying "Rowing Boat for Hire to visit Castle." I could see no sign of water, let alone of a castle. The farm was apparently surrounded by flat moorland. But when I curiously knocked at the door, the farmer did not break out into laughter and tell me "You've been had" but led me behind the barn into a small gully. This took us down by a twisting path until we suddenly came out onto a sandy beach on a large concealed lake. A boat lay on the beach. Well, there was water but I could see no castle. The farmer instructed me. "Row out to the second island, then look to the left." Feeling somewhat foolish, I did just this. After about fifty yards I found a hidden bay containing an island crowned with the walls of an ancient fort. A plaque on it told me that it was as old as the pyramids. I climbed stairs in its courtyard and walked around the circular ramparts enjoying the song of larks overhead and the surrounding wilderness, but then found a small square opening containing a staircase leading down

The only way I could descend was by sitting on the top step and sliding down while leaning backwards. At the foot of the stairs, I found a corridor with a solid well-built stone floor and roof. But I had to walk on my knees. I could not imagine that the original inhabitants built this corridor so tiny unless they too were small. Astonished I realised that, if they fitted this corridor, they could not have been much taller than four feet. It seemed that the little people were really here!

I went also to the Hebrides, another part of my people's traditional lands On Hogmanays I walked from farm to farm with a flask of whisky to do the ritual "First Footing". More whisky and snacks were always waiting Sea otters sometimes barred my way; surprised that anyone would walk in hurricane force winds in which hailstones travelled like bullets. One day, after a couple of 'first footings", I had to walk home from island to island for forty yards with the water within an inch of the top of my Wellington boots. "Hebrides" means the Islands of Bride, Bride being a Goddess whose fame, like Scottish whisky, went across Europe. Likewise Ireland itself is named for the Goddess Eriu as Eire.[305]

Warrior women

In other breaks during film production, I went to the Loire to visit the places associated with St Jeanne d'Arc. I wanted to learn more of a warrior woman who spoke with God or spirits under trees, fought in male clothes, was inspired as a mystic and condemned as a witch. I went with Kate, a woman I secretly loved, for I had started to discover my bisexuality. I don't think I ever told her. We visited ruined castles and chateaux by the lazy winding Loire. We went on to Bosnia where we received marvellous hospitality from a Muslim family in soon-to-be devastated Mostar.

In my search for women warriors, I had also researched the Amazons, discovering that, at a time when Grecian men ruled their women folk, the Amazon women controlled their own lives north of the Black Sea. Many had fled from Grecian men It was not that the Amazon women lorded it over men. They lived without men, except when children were wanted.

It seems that many women have had a need to separate themselves off from men to develop skills and talents and perhaps to be themselves. The Beguine women did this, so did Aborigines with their single women's camps and so did these Amazons. They gained their warlike reputation when they launched attacks on the lands of Greece and Asia Minor. They were given credit for founding important cities such as Ephesus, Smyma, Cyme and Myrine. Monuments and tombs are ascribed to them on the plains and mountains around Thermodon. They were besieging Troy when Achilles killed their queen, Penthesilea, and then fell in love with her dying face. It was not recorded if the Amazons came to free their Grecian sisters; if so, they did not succeed

Aristotle and Plato told what Greek men expected of women. Aristotle noted that a good Greek woman was submissive to her husband and should be trained by him as was appropriate to one of an inferior nature. Plato regretted that it was not possible to turn cowardly soldiers into docile women.[306] Perhaps it was not surprising that Greek historians recorded that the Amazon society was the result of a rebellion of women who joined with other rebellious women from the cities of the Thacians and Euboeans

Some said the Amazons also had a homeland north of Greece in the land of Kosovo, recently a land of hideous atrocities and of NATO bombing. The Amazon custom of women warriors may have continued here in a fashion. Local women led guerrilla bands against Hitler's forces. Some of these women had a special status, lived as men and did not marry. Rene Cremaux in the book *Third Gender* documented twenty such women warriors.

When I went with Kate to Bosnia, our Mostar host took us to an ancient graveyard with tomb carvings of running horses and beardless small-chinned warriors carrying swords and shields who could be women; although this is far from certain. He told me these were of a people who lived there long ago.

But by all accounts the principal land of the Amazons lay northeast of the Black Sea near the Caucasus Mountains. Greek authors reported that the Amazons were a self-sufficient society without men, in which women ploughed fields, looked after cattle and, particularly, trained horses.

Modern archaeology has started to confirm these early histories. Nicola Di Cosmo of Harvard observed: "Perhaps the Amazons have a basis in historical fact after all. It's certainly interesting to note that Herodotus's ethnographic descriptions of this [Kargan] region have now been largely confirmed by archaeology. It's a fascinating question, whether he was right about the Amazons as well."[307]

The Amazons apparently consecrated themselves to Cybele, the Mother Goddess of Nature, whose rites included ecstatic dancing and music. Cybele's priestesses had among them those who had changed gender roles. I do not know if transsexual women were welcomed among the Amazons but, given this tradition, this was entirely possible. Indeed Walter Tyrell, a classical scholar, has found evidence that "eunuchs" joined in the Amazonian rituals.[308]

For procreation the Amazons had an agreement with neighbouring men. They met once a year at a spring festival on a mountain between their territories. The Amazons would lie in the dark with men they selected at random. The boys born from these encounters were returned to their fathers, according to Strabo.

The Amazons had to become warriors to defend their lands, their women's society and perhaps to extend their territories if they were to remain politically independent. They hunted on horseback, making their shields, helmets and clothes from the skins of animals. They used a wide range of weapons including the bow and arrow, the sagaris and especially the javelin. It was said that they would cut off their right breast if it interfered with the throwing of the javelin. I know from bitter personal experience that the left breast can get in the way of the string of a powerful bow (you should have seen the bruises!) but I do not quite understand how the right breast could impede a javelin throw?

Greek writers also reported that the warrior elite of the Scythian nomads, living north of the Black Sea near to the Amazons, included "the most impotent of men" due to spending so much time in trousers and on horseback. They added: "the great majority among the Scythians became impotent, do woman's work, live like women and converse accordingly....They put on women's clothes, holding that they have lost their manhood...and suffered from "the female sickness". It was said that some were blessed with this condition by the Goddess in order to make them prophets and diviners.

Around the time that I was exploring my cultural roots, archaeologists were discovering that women warriors once also lived to the east of the Caucasus. Between 1992 and 1995, a team led by Jeanine Davis-Kimball, director of the Californian Center for the Study of Eurasian Nomads, excavated a site of Neolithic kurgans (burial mounds) near Pokrovka.

The skeletons uncovered were of women that were on average five foot six high. Next to one young female was a quiver containing forty bronze-tipped arrows. Her skeleton had bowed leg bones, possibly from a lifetime spent in the saddle. Wonderful tattoos of horses or stags decorated her arms and shoulders. Male warriors were found also buried nearby. It seems that gender roles were fluid among these people of the steppes. These armed prosperous women belonged to the Kurgans, the same people that Gimbutas thought brought to an end a gentle age of women and introduced patriarchy when they swept into Europe, with a first wave between 4500-4300 BCE and a second wave between 3000-2800 BCE.

Lotte Motz argued against Gimbutas in *The Faces of the Goddess* (Oxford, 1997) that images of men and animals are as prolific as goddess imagery in early European cultures. "There clearly was no introduction of warrior gods and warrior values, no imposition of a patriarchal system, and no humiliation of the Goddess." Others argued that some of the images Gimbutas interpreted as female were of hermaphrodites, as is the oldest human image yet found in the British Isle. This is a figure with penis and breasts carved in ashwood, as before mentioned. Such figures may represent a primal Deity with both genders.

Davis-Kimball found evidence of powerful female warriors and priestesses, "all over the place" in the museums of central Asia, unearthed in the Takla Makan desert by Chinese archaeologists and dated to around 2000 BCE. These finds were similar to those of Pokrovka. Both included cultic spoons and mirrors and spiral tattoos on faces, arms and hands. This older Eurasian culture may have influenced the later nomads. There is thus ample archaeological evidence that women once occupied powerful positions as priestesses and warriors in ancient Eurasian cultures

The Warrior Women of the British Isles

In the British Isles and in Ireland before the Iron Age, it seems there was a society in which women and men worked together as equals with safeguards and pledges. According to ancient legends, the kings of Ulster had to pledge to look after the women's rights. Specifically they promised that women receive ample supplies of cloth dyes and medical supplies, and that midwives would be provided so that no women need die in childbirth. If they broke these pledges they could apparently be deposed.

In the early days of agriculture in these islands, it seems that the prevalent divine image was of the Mother who fed and watered her people with her crops and springs. In Ulster this Goddess was known as Macha. She warmed the earth making it fertile, bringing the people their food. Armagh is named after Macha's hills. ("Ard Macha"). An image of Macha is still preserved in its cathedral. Macha was born on land lying between the tides "as the daughter of the Strange Son of Ocean".[309] This reflected an ancient concept that the creating energy possessed the energy of both of the sea and of the land, as of both the male and female.

There is no doubt that a strong female warrior tradition once existed in the British Isles. This might have developed, as Gimbutas suggested, when invaders threatened traditional societies or even as a counterbalance to the development of male dominated and aggressive Iron Age cultures. The great Irish saga known as *The Tain*[310] had women as leaders in battle. A woman, Scathach the Shadowy One, who lived in Alba (Britain), trained the great warrior Cuchulainn in the arts of warfare. She taught him to outfight all male warriors. When he was sent against her enemy, the warrior woman Aife, he could only win by trickery, not by force of arms. Warrior Queens included Melb, Cartamundu and Boudeccea.[311]

The old stories also seem to show that women had failed to hold their own in the Iron Age in the face of male aggression sanctioned by a male-dominated religious culture. There are many Irish myths of demoted Goddesses. In one the Goddess Tlachtga was pack-raped by the three sons of a man she had visited in order to learn his magic—and she then died giving birth to male warriors. Macha herself was demoted into being the daughter of the son of the god Neid. The Irish legend *The Pangs of the Men of Ulster* came from this period. Macha was no longer the unchallenged Mother of Life, the Goddess of Sovereignty. She was a Goddess with the social status of a wife of a boastful man who had agreed foolishly to a challenge from a king. The king wanted her, who represented womankind, the Old Ways, and whose symbol was the horse, to race against his chariot.

The king knew that she was heavy with child and thus hoped to defeat her. He refused to honour her request to giver her time, despite being asked in the name of the Mother. He was determined to defeat her and this seemed a good opportunity. But she raced against his chariot, defeated it, and then gave birth to twins. Afterwards she cursed the men of Ulster for bringing shame on the Mother. They were to feel the pangs of childbirth "for five days and four nights in their times of greatest difficulty...for nine generations any Ulsterman in these pangs had no more strength than a woman on the bed of labour."[312] Men had challenged women so it seemed appropriate for them to share in women's troubles!

Celtic society then evolved a head collection culture, perhaps because the head had replaced the womb as the mythical source of life. (As it had with the Greeks.) The Celtic warriors sometimes slept with the severed heads of enemies between their thighs, perhaps in a crude imitation of a woman in childbirth.[312] They may have hoped this gave them the power of the mothers.

Women had to fight in the wars of the Iron Age, when hill forts were built in fear throughout the land. Thus they needed the help of Warrior Goddesses. Macha was then cast into this role. The warrior men started to call the harvested heads of enemies "the mast" or food of Macha. This Macha was probably better known in Britain as Morgan.

When a still more powerful protector was needed, they began to honour "The Morrigan"; into which Macha was subsumed as part of a powerful Trinity of Goddesses with her two sisters, Badb and Morrigan. The Morrigan protected the wounded, conveyed the dead to the next world and confused the enemy. She was depicted as the Sacred Cow whose milk was an antidote to the poison put on weapons. She offered to help the hero Cuchalain in his battles and, when he disdainfully rejected the help of a woman, she contested with him by shape shifting. She did not use the weapons of which the Gods were so proud but instead used her wits, her knowledge of men, her bond with the land and the magical powers this gave her. Men feared her. They thus demonised her. She was turned into the three hags that inspired the depiction of witches in Shakespeare's Macbeth.

But perhaps Irish culture had become more gender-balanced when a less militant image of the Goddess became popular. This was Bride or Bridget, popular throughout the British Isles as well as in Ireland. As the Triple Goddess of inspiration, healing and smithwork she was a role model for independent women. In Christian times she became called St. Bridget, the leader of the Irish women at a time when St. Patrick became the leader of the men. To this day, there are many more springs, bays and Churches dedicated to her than there are to St. Patrick. (A poem on the changing images of my people's Goddesses is at the end of this chapter.)

In short, women and warrior energy, fighting Goddesses and healing Goddesses, priestess and warrior, are utterly reconcilable concepts of very ancient history. Women may have used different tools, might have had different aims, but both women and men felt a need to fight to protect children, the home and the greater home, the earth herself. The old stories say women tended to use magic in this work while men used swords and spears.

The power and strength of women and their magic was said to reside in their link to nature (and thus, as we have seen, they became targets for a Church that saw nature as corrupted). When Aboriginal women lost access to a certain sacred place, they were said to be no longer able to send people up "in a puff of smoke". They retained contact with other sacred lands and were said to be still capable of sending lingering illnesses and even death.[314] The Aboriginal author Kevin Gilbert, who was one of my most valued friends, said Aboriginal Elders had the power of shape shifting and astral travel. Aboriginal male and female shamans would go into trances, during which they were said to meet spirits, cure patients and fly to the spirit world.

Gender Balance in Aboriginal Society

Diane Bell reported in her book *Daughters of the Dreaming* that Aboriginal society was gender balanced: "Under the Law, men and women have distinctive roles to play but each has access to certain checks and balances which ensure that neither sex can enjoy an unrivalled supremacy over the other. Underlying male and female practice is a common purpose and a shared belief in the Dreamtime experience; both have sacred boards, both know songs and paint designs that encode the knowledge of the dreaming."[315]

Men and women sometimes shared rituals. Bell told of how grateful men were for being shown a women's dance. They promptly return the favour by painting up their own boards and bodies and showing the women one of their own dances. Through these dances they exchanged ritual knowledge of the country and its' Dreaming. It was painted on their bodies and their boards, and spelt out by the patterns made by their pounding feet. The women picked up the male boards and danced with them while the men called out approvingly "they are your dreamings now".[316] But Bell noted that something was always held back and kept for people of the same gender.

What Diane Bell observed, and I have noted too, was that women and men were equally responsible for the sacred sites—and could exchange responsibilities. One Aboriginal woman told her; "As my father could not go into the Waake country, from when I was a young girl I kept on doing the *yawulyu,* the looking after of the country." Her sisters also did this with her. Her father could not do it because Whites had massacred his relatives there within his lifetime. He was barred by the rituals of grief[317] from visiting the site of this atrocity, but their Dreaming needed to be maintained, their country had to be looked after, so his daughters did it for him.

Sacred sites are not passed on in European style inheritance. Bell witnessed Warrabri women, rich in dreaming sites but poor in health, handing over sites to a healthier group of women who lived along the same dreaming track but had far fewer sites. The "giving away" ritual involved passing over ritual objects and teaching the basic elements of the songs belonging to these sites. The new custodians then embellished the songs to demonstrate their new rights.[318]

Panorama, the BBC and the Sun newspaper

But enough about what I learnt looking for my warrior antecedents and the magic used by women. Back to the story of my own battles. The diamond film took a year more than it should to get underway when Australian government funders retracted on a written pledge. This perplexed me, for I had met their official criteria for funding of raising one third of my budget abroad. I had raised two thirds. I wondered if these men, drawn from the private banking world, feared the consequences of taking on the diamond cartel? But I could not contest the actions of these funders without running the risk of losing my funding from other sources. While this was being solved, I had to find something else to do.

I discovered that President Gorbachov had offered the West the help of the KGB. My research gained me an invitation to a Moscow meeting between the KGB and "lay" Western experts that I suspected were undercover Western spies. When I questioned them, they volunteered that there was only one among them, a member of GCHQ, the UK government's telecommunications snooping operation. I had to agree not to identify him. I did however take a photograph of him in Red Square. He had a handkerchief covering his balding patch and an English guidebook in his hand as he photographed the Kremlin. He seemed the very epitome of the quintessential British spy.

When I told Panorama of this invitation, the BBC promptly hired me as a producer and sent me to Moscow. The first interview I had with a KGB general was stilted and useless. The interminable delays for translation robbed it of spontaneity. The next KGB general was somewhat spunky so I set up his interview differently. I told my translator not to translate his responses. I sat close enough to him (but off camera) for our legs to touch. I sparkled at him and he sparkled back. My questions were quick. I acted as if I understood his responses in Russian, firing back questions that kept up the pace. When the session was later translated, I found that he had admitted that a hot line had been agreed at this meeting between the KGB and MI6 and that all participants would be reporting back to their governments. When I repeated his words to the British delegates, they gave themselves away by exclaiming; "He should not have told you that."

I then secured for the BBC the exclusive television rights to a joint training exercise between Russian and Western Intelligence. This included the mock hijacking of an airliner carrying Russian diplomats. Panorama loved it. BBC reporters based in Moscow would give reports of the incident as if it were a real event. But unfortunately for us and for Gorbachov, he was overthrown before this exercise happened.

On my return to London, I came under an unexpected attack. I received a phone call from an Aboriginal friend in Australia, Gerry Bostock, to warn me that the *Sun*, a British tabloid, had asked its journalists in Australia to hunt up my gender past. I was stunned and horrified. It was some twenty years since I transitioned. I had got on with life as a woman. Everyone accepted me as such. Why was I being challenged in Britain where I was hardly known? I didn't think it was the intelligence agencies. I feared a deliberate leak to the media from the diamond companies. I wondered if it could be an attempt to discredit me. At that stage, if the BBC had dropped me, the diamond film would never have happened.

I was forced to warn the BBC of the coming exposure and thus to tell them of my personal background. My Commissioning Editor at the BBC said it made no difference to them. It did however cause amused smiles at Panorama, especially when the Sun ran a Page Three story headlined "It's Manorama". It was full of invented detail. They did not get to see me, for I sat on the 4th floor roof of my London flat hidden by a chimney stack until their journalists had left, so they described me wrongly as a blonde—perhaps because they wrapped the story around the picture of a blonde Page Three Girl. The best thing that came out of this was a phone call from my younger daughter, Cathy. She had seen the story in Australia and was outraged. She told me that as she was now grown up, I no longer had any need to protect her. She told me I could go for them, be proud, be open if I need be.

The BBC and the diamond film

I noticed afterwards a difference in how the BBC treated me. When I completed raising the needed funds for my diamond series, I received a letter from the film director I had hired, telling me that the BBC wanted me to agree to be only the nominal producer of my film—but to hide the fact that my title was nominal in order to make sure my film retained its Australian funding. I was to stay in Australia while they made the film in London. This was a sly device that could have discredited me in Australia. I flew back to London and insisted on my contractual right to produce my own film. One of my British staff later apologised to me, telling me that they had mistakenly decided to "quarantine" me!

So the diamond film started with me at the helm. I was the producer and the senior journalist on the shoots in the US and India. These came in on schedule and on budget but the opposition from the diamond cartel made life difficult. On Fifth Avenue a major diamond merchant, William Goldberg, who previously had agreed to give an interview, told me when I turned up with the crew: "I think I am the wrong man for you." I asked him if he had received a phone call. He said, "Yes, I was told that you worked with Black Australians and made life difficult for diamond mining companies."

I could only plead guilty to this, but he decided to co-operate after I suggested that as a Jew he should understand why Aborigines wanted to protect their sacred lands. But Tiffany's refused to speak to us, despite our backing by a major US television channel and the BBC. In India we luckily had diamond merchants agree to interviews before they received phone calls. We then found the merchants very evasive so with some bravado I would turn up unexpectedly in their officers with the film crew. They were not able to refuse us to our face. We knew some of our interviewees resented the power of De Beers, but they also had a very real fear of losing their supplies of diamonds and thus their businesses if they offended De Beers. I later learnt that Goldberg allegedly had to threaten to expose publicly the threats to his own supplies in order to get them restored.

But in India my main problem was not the cartel. It was the director I had hired. One day he told me to start interviewing—and seconds later the camera assistant sitting by me started to talk to the camera operator. This distracted me and was near the mike so I asked him to be quiet. A furious director that night fiercely scolded me, telling me that addressing the crew was his sole prerogative. Another time when he was indisposed, he gave me the crew to work with. Afterwards, when I inadvertently spoke of "my crew", he angrily demanded that I never again say this. It was "his" crew. I thus learnt I must do the woman's act every day to soothe his wounded ego so that the shoot could continue on schedule and on budget.

As we shot the film, we discovered the hidden side of the diamond industry. We found in Surat an ant-hive of workshops where over half a million Indians, some as young as eight, recruited from poor farming families, cut 80% of the world's romantic gem diamonds. They had no protection from the diamond dust that blackened the walls around them. They sat with bare legs beside fast spinning cutting wheels in what India classifies as one of its more hazardous industries. They got just a 10c US for cutting a diamond and 20c for polishing it. Many were trapped in what the United Nations indicted as a form of slavery.

We also learnt of armed operations by De Beers's agents in West Africa that allegedly ambushed and killed Africans who independently traded diamonds. We interviewed those involved. We also traced how the diamond trade helped develop apartheid and had supported Hitler, in the view of Allied Intelligence.

But Nicky Oppenheimer, heading the cartel's operations in London, wrote plaintively in letters about me, asking why the BBC would work with someone like me who was "obsessed" with their company. He refused to give us access to De Beers' operations while I remained at the film's helm. It seemed he seriously feared what I might uncover. They did not want the image of the romantic diamond damaged by it being seen as the product of child labour and apartheid. This was the truth of it. It was what I intended. But this powerful opposition seemingly unnerved the director I had hired but could not sack without the BBC's permission. He started to do De Beers' work for them by working to have me removed from the film.

A Halloween gift

In the midst of this battle, I threw a Halloween party on my boat in London. At least that evening we would relax. I knew Halloween as an old Celtic festival, Samhain, when the old stories said the veil was thinnest between the worlds of spirits and humans. Thus it became the Christian festivals of All Souls and All Saints. The party went well, the only unexpected incident the arrival of a guest with three strangers he had met in a local pub. He said they had heard of me and wanted to meet me. He asked: "Do you mind if they come on board? They have drinks with them". I had about thirty guests on the boat and saw no harm in a few more. The party continued. It was one of the best I ever held on my boat, a 41ft. American motor yacht bought to give myself a London home.

It was only at midnight, the witching hour, that I became uneasy. All my guests had left by then except two of these strangers. Then suddenly one accused me of not being a woman and started to sexually attack me. I slapped his face. He then rained on my face a furious torrent of punches. Every blow drew blood through the skin. My nose and cheekbone were broken. Blood was everywhere. I fell down the stairs but from its foot I managed to hit the emergency button on my ship-to-shore radio. I yelled at its open microphone. When the marina security responded over the loudspeaker, the assailants fled.

Next day much to my horror I was again ambushed; this time non-violently by lawyers acting for the film's insurers. They demanded to my battered face that I immediately cease producing and give my film to a British producer named by the BBC. They made no allegations that I had mismanaged the film (even when my lawyer later asked them for reasons). My contract stipulated that I could not be removed unless such reasons were given and, even then, I had to be given time to remedy the complaint. Our accountant had praised my management skills. All the shoots I managed had come in on budget. I told them that I could not agree to their demands, even if I were willing, for my Australian government funders stipulated the film had an Australian producer[319]. I wondered about the seeming coincidence of the assault and this sudden demand, but perhaps I was being paranoid? But there again, this demand was definitely not the normal way of doing business. I then learnt that the producer the BBC wanted to place in charge was the person who had told me earlier that they had wanted to "quarantine" me. He was a long-term friend of the film's director—and of our BBC Commissioning Editor.

I went back to Australia to seek support from the government funders who had stipulated the film remain Australian. I went to the women who worked for the Australian film funding agencies, expecting their support, but I found that they were so engaged with their careers, that their overt friendliness had no reality. For me they were reduced to being suits. I was clearly seen as a danger, not as a sister needing aid to combat injustice. I decided that they did not want to upset the BBC, a heavy investor in the industry.

When I first started living among the female ranks, I was thrilled by the easy sense of co-operation, trust and sharing prevalent among the women with whom I worked. For a while I could have shared the vision of Gimbutas that matriarchy would naturally be highly civilised. But I had now discovered another female world, in which women painted themselves with a more inhuman competitive spirit than ruled the lives of men. This was despite their male colleagues still demanding of them that they soothed the male ego, serviced their need for comfort and be an attractive decor.

While I recuperated I continued to try to resolve the problems with the BBC. Eventually I took them to arbitration. The BBC then attempted an out-of-court settlement. But while hearings were pending, the BBC quietly restarted production on my film without informing me. I protested to the head of the BBC, John Birt, that my company held the copyright and contracts. His office replied that they would not answer my points as I was about to be taken over!

I had physical pains that had persisted from the time of the beating. I thought these a product of stress. An acupuncturist friend attempted to treat them. I then went for what was expected to be an afternoon's stay in a clinic to have scar vaginal tissue removed. It was Friday, the 29th April 1993. The night before this minor operation I had a strange dream. I was standing by a van in a bleak industrial landscape when a car stopped by a nearby gate. The men who got out had the sombre air of undertakers. I thought they were coming to discuss with me the death of a near one. They took me to the back of my van and spoke to me of the need to give myself space and time, to accept what would be a loss. I was perplexed. I did not know of anyone who had died or who was near death.

A week after this operation I was in deep trouble. It had gone wrong and I had been admitted into the Royal Women's Hospital with necrosis of vaginal skin and a chronic infection. Two days later they discovered that the pain that had bothered me was no psychosomatic illness but a deep vein thrombosis. A surge of blood clots was migrating up towards my heart. They immobilised me and pumped me full of blood thinners. The Registrar gave me an emergency alarm, telling me to keep in my hand and use it if I felt myself going unconscious. He told me I would be critically ill for the next two weeks. When I had to use this alarm a day later, I witnessed in a haze the rush of a medical team to save me. Luckily I recovered without need for an emergency operation.

But despite the dangerous state of my health, the BBC and the Australian Film Finance Corporation employed a Barrister who immediately put pressure on me to drop my right to arbitration and give them my film. A lawyer presented their papers to me the day after I learnt that I was critically ill. They would not allow me any extra time—saying `I had to make a decision within two days or fight them in court. I at first threw their papers across the ward. But I very soon realised that my body could not take the stress of a continuing fight, no matter how willing my spirit or how unjust their action. I now knew this stress really might kill me.

I realised that if I refused to give way, the BBC would kill my film, and the reasons why I was making it were bigger than my ego. The BBC offered me a guarantee in writing that they would complete the film to my script—and provide me within seven days with the film's research materials so I could write a book on the diamond industry. I felt with my health as it was, I might not be able to survive this pressure. A day later I signed, giving up my right to an arbitration hearing and to compensation—so I could concentrate on recovering my health.

I was relieved to win this commitment. It meant that the film series would still document the human rights atrocities in the diamond industry. But once I had signed, the BBC ignored my letters and not one of the promised research documents reached me. I was to spend a further two months in hospital. For much of this time I stayed on oxygen, as my lungs were fouled with blood clots.

Pain and Rebirth

I now needed time to think, to understand what had happened to me. Within hours of learning my life was in danger, I also learnt that it was not seemingly sufficient to my God that I was so ill, or that I had given up my precious film, for everything else seemed to go wrong simultaneously that could possibly hurt me.

I had always absolutely presumed that my friends and family would come to see me if I were in danger of death. My daughters and former partner lived in the same town as the hospital so travel was not a problem. I contacted Cathy, then eight months pregnant with her first child, and asked her to tell Kara and Jackie—but, very upset, she told me it was impossible for her to ask Kara.

One of the lessons I then learnt as never before, was that my daughters had now much pain in their lives and that I could do very little to alleviate it. Kara, my eldest daughter, had been out of touch with me for over five years. I missed her very much but had not sought her out because I did not want to make her feel that I did not respect her wishes. But she would surely want to know that I was critically ill. I explained to the hospital social worker the family circumstances and asked her to find Kara at her university and tell her what had happened. I was thrilled when the social worker came back to tell me Kara was coming straight in to see me. I thought at least my illness meant that the gulf would be bridged between us. But when she came in, she took one shocked and seemingly angry look at me then went out quickly, reportedly saying to a nurse that she had left home years ago.

I was horrified, dismayed, mystified, until I learnt from a pale social worker that she had made a dreadful error. She had not said "Jan" as instructed, but "Mum" when speaking to Kara. She had presumed that she would know which of her Mums was in hospital. My eldest daughter must have rushed into hospital expecting to see Jackie and then thought I had deceived her. Shortly after this Jackie phoned to say she was on the way to see me and would bring Cathy. This was wonderful. I asked if she would also make sure Kara was all right. I told her of the mistake made by the social worker. Jackie said she would but did not turn up. I later learnt from her that she had decided not to believe me, not to bring Cathy into hospital and not to come in herself, leaving me very much alone.

Flat on my back, on oxygen in hospital, it was hard for me to understand why I was being shown so little love. Even if I had not been careful with instructions to the social worker, I would have thought some forgiveness would was in order when the mistake was by someone on the balance between life and death, let alone by an ex-partner and parent with whom they had shared so much of beauty. But their actions left me with a clear choice I could either drown in my pain or use it as fertiliser. It was evident that the members of my family were in deep pain. I was forced to learn that I could not always resolve the pain of others. I had to focus on my own path. It would do no good feeling guilty, wondering what I had done wrong and if I could put it right, when I could not even talk to them. I could do no more than put them in love into the hands of God.

One friend did come to see me that first critical week She was my landlady and also a director of my film production company. We had enjoyed marvellous times together in the outback. I thought we were still friends but now she sat next to my oxygen supply absolutely wooden faced, demanding that I consent to the BBC's demands. With hindsight, I think she was scared my fight with the BBC could hurt her financially. I later learnt that, while I was in hospital, she signed away our film rights to the BBC. I thus lost the ability to protest that the film was improperly removed from my company while I was critically ill. Two months later, when I left hospital, she asked me to immediately leave my rooms, leaving me homeless.

But in hospital, thrown back totally on my own resources, the extraordinary thing was that I was not miserable. I lay there marvelling at how so many things could go wrong "co-incidentally" and simultaneously. It was as if every crisis that I had had ever experienced had been piled up then multiplied ten times. Just one of these by itself could have devastated me. All of them together meant I kept smiling. I felt there were too many co-incidences for it to have been accidental. I might have been deluding myself, but I did not think so. I thought I could see through the divine stratagem. It was aimed at getting a message through to me.

I promptly told my Lover God: "There was no need to kick me so hard. This is over-kill. I've got the message." It did not seem necessary to withdraw from me all my loves, my cherished daughters, the much loved six-year-old film project, all my emotional dependencies, in order to force me to give my life utterly and completely to God. Or was it?

I found I had to die to my family. I learnt that I could not build my self-identity on being the parent of my children. My pride in them could not be the foundation of my self-confidence. This helped me find the only strength I really owned, my inner strength. This did not mean that I did not cry in the hospital when I saw how other families came to visit, loved and supported their sick. I had been so proud of our family and of my relationship with Jackie, of the bonds of love that we had formed, or so I thought. Was it that I had failed, was a no-good parent? Was it that I deserved such rejection? Many such questions came but they could not take me anywhere useful. They could solve no problems.

I knew that I loved my children and was proud of them, and I knew that I had done all I could to stay with them until I was not allowed to do so any longer. I knew I had to trust this instinct. I knew that I had not been possessive. They were part of my heart. The words of Gibran inspired me. He said children are arrows shot into the sky and the parent was no more than the steady bow. I was horrified that my children now were so very hurt, that my former lover was so hurt, that the principles that guided us as a family of giving hospitality, being generous in loving, sharing with strangers, now did not extend to loving me. I longed to see them, to give them my love, to do what I could to heal wounds, before I possibly died. It was extraordinarily hard to be rejected by people so close to me. It was hard to keep my pride when the family who had been my pride and joy now mostly rejected me; that is apart from Cathy who lifted me high when she finally turned up in hospital with an enormous bunch of flowers just six weeks before she gave birth.

Thus I did not collapse in tears. Instead I found myself to my surprise, laughing at my Lover God. I was sure His hand was in this. Looking back, my reaction seemed illogical. Why did I not blame my God for my misery? How could I see in these events the hand of a divine Lover? I can only explain this in terms of the relationship between us. Stripped of family and friends, of work and of health, naked, as I had never been before, I felt that I had all I needed within me and within my relationship with this divine Lover. I went in love to him, and was held in ecstasy for days on end

It was my time of rebirth. I instinctively knew the time had come for me to change from being the professional woman journalist warrior who had kept private the magic of her life in order to be accepted and "effective". I knew I did not want on my tombstone "She died to reform the diamond cartel". No, I wanted on it the poetry of my life, that I was a woman gifted to walk between the gender worlds with a wicked sense of humour and a love for life, who had two daughters, who loved the earth and saw in it the face of her Lover, perhaps even that she was a mystic or a witch! Kids would love to find a witch's tomb! This is what I wanted for my epitaph—among other things.

If I had died at that time, I would never have celebrated and shared the precious gifts I had hidden. I knew that these had not been given to me just for my enjoyment. I knew I was not alone in such reluctance. Hildegard kept quiet about her visions for fear of rejection until she was past 40. She said this continued until: "I was forced by great pressure of pains to reveal what I had seen and heard."[320]

I was well aware that all my campaigning as a warrior could not put right more than the tiniest fragment of the things that needed to be rectified. I knew that my campaigns for the impoverished, for the damaged, could be endless. I knew that it is the prophet's, the mystic's and the poet's message that gets passed on from generation to generation; that it is their inspiration that can do most to help create a beautiful world.

I now knew that my naive campaigns against the powerful, although important, should take second place to sharing and learning the poetry of life. I now told my Lover God that I would openly re-dedicate myself to the priesthood, bring it to the fore and live as both a warrior and priestess since that seemed to be what he wanted of me. I promised this, but had little idea how it could be brought about. I simply had to wait and think and pray.

When a nun on her charitable rounds came to visit me in hospital I started to tell her of my resolution and my rich life. I can remember the look on her face. She was resolute and calm, as if dealing with a lunatic.

On the seventh day after I was told I might soon die, when I was still critical, the nurses at my request put a cable across the ward's floor so I could use my laptop computer. Thus I started to write this book, taking on my fears, determined to share unashamed. I wanted it to be my legacy for my daughters and for my greater family. When I left hospital I continued with writing it but found that I was not yet ready for the task. I had much more to learn. My hospital time was but germination. The wild weed had to grow stronger. I still had to conquer my fear of the vulnerability that openness would surely bring. There was still disunity within me. A voice within nagged me. I knew I needed to run with the wild creatures, to fly with owls and lope with foxes, to seek wisdom in unity with nature. I had faith that I would grow strong enough to do this.

My greatest fear was that of rejection. I liked being accepted as a woman. I enjoyed being a woman. I was at home as a woman. I was scared that if I were more open, then people would reject me, saying that I was not really a woman but a freak. If I were open about being an ordained catholic priest, I could easily find myself a commodity in the pages of tabloids and thus even more a freak. I was ambitious for success as an influential journalist. I greatly feared openness would wreck this ambition and instead marginalise me.

I was worried about exposing my spirituality. My mysticism was, I knew, naive, childish, trusting and precious to me. It was at the very root of my being. I did not want to expose it lest I be hurt by it being ridiculed. How could I then maintain my credibility in a media manned by cynics? Yes, despite all my bravery in taking on diamond cartels, the White House and the intelligence agencies, when it came down to it, I really was a scared and nervous cat!

So this tabby cat that was a lioness that was a tabby, needed all the courage she could muster for very different kind of fight. But I knew in theory that every fear I conquered would make me that much stronger. I also came to understand that if I could write about what was most precious to me, I would gain self-knowledge and find my way to freedom.

It was good that this critical time came after I had learnt of the ancient shamanic path that might be my destiny. Shamanism is a path in which one travels between the spirit and the material worlds in ritual and trance and uses this skill to serve the community. I knew that my experience of life in both gender worlds was seen in old cultures as good training for shamans. There was also another route called the shamanic wound, a passage undertaken by those who had experienced over weeks the danger of death. I thought this was teaching me the time had come to reach beyond gender, to centre on a love in which my very skeleton was painfully taken to pieces and reassembled to accommodate a larger heart.

On one of my last days in hospital, when I phoned my younger daughter she told me she had good news. I replied: "What? Your contractions have started?" Her reply came: "No, I am at home with a baby boy." She had given birth to a red head, like herself and like my father. She had experienced a very easy delivery. Thus from near death, I left hospital to celebrate a birth.

But once out of hospital, I found that the hard part was only just starting. Melbourne was now a nightmare for me, an emotional minefield. My Australian family seemed to be riven with more pain than I could imagine. I was still in trauma from my illness. I could not cope with the hurt around me. Every so often another blood clot dissolved in my lungs, giving me a sudden and scary chest pain.

I had one minor success. I managed to persuade my former lover and partner, Jackie, to spend time with me in a coffeehouse after I came out of hospital to talk about what was happening with our family. She told me she had nearly refused to have this meeting but was glad that she had. She did not explain her fear. It was then that she told me why she had not visited me in hospital. It had been because she thought I had used the social worker to deceive our eldest daughter into visiting me.

I previously told how she had vetoed an offer made to me by our younger daughter Cathy of a room to use on visits to Australia. If she had not, I may have been there now, and may have had the chance to restore relations with Kara. I probably would have continued my work with Aborigines and the Australian media. But I would not have learnt more about my own country and its spirituality. I would not have learnt what it was to be stripped so naked. Thus Providence may have had a hand when my former partner and co-parent made it so very hard for me to come back into my daughters' lives.

But I still wanted these old wounds healed. This meeting with her in the coffeehouse was important for me. It helped me to better understand the depth of her pains and fears.

But what I needed most was time to recover. With no home in Australia, I fled to my sixty-year-old boat lying on the river Thames. I fled praying that healing would come to the people that once had made me so very welcome, that I loved but could not help. And as I left, I failed to notice that my Permanent Resident Visa for Australia had expired while I was in hospital. It needed a stamp every five or so years. It would have been granted automatically, if I had asked for it before leaving. I thus lost my right to live in Australia. Whether I liked it or not, my life was being changed very radically.

It was not easy back on my moorings. While I was away, my gender background had somehow become common knowledge around the marina. My attackers had known of my background, so I guess they must have spread the word. Either that or some friends had been indiscreet. Perhaps it was a bit of both. The day after my bashing, I had taken my black and blue face into the South London pub where my assailants learnt about my party to tell them what I felt about their customers. Afterwards some heavy-duty men swore to me that they would in future protect me, with guns if necessary!

So I was utterly incredulous when a friend told me that this pub had banned me because of my gender background! When I asked the pub manager why, he said, "People like you cause trouble." I replied in shock "But I have never caused any trouble here." He responded: "No, you haven't caused any, but your presence could make others violent". My women friends and I then mounted a campaign to force the pub to drop this ban. They bought me drinks, and asked; "Why don't you allow Jani to buy her own drinks". Eventually the pub dropped the ban and later changed management. Now I find a welcome in this pub although I rarely go there.

I may have decided in hospital to be publicly open about my gender background, but I had to have a friend literally hold my hand when I sent my first email to strangers about my gender background! I had more traumas to overcome than I had realised. I think it took me some three years to recover from the beating, a truly humbling period of time. I thought that I would be better in months.

The local hospital gave me counselling support but this was directed to resolving why I had what I called "my crushed paper bag syndrome"! This was a feeling that the right side of my face was crushed like a screwed up paper bag. My face looked entirely normal so this was treated as a psychological problem. It was not until a year later that a cranial osteopath told me that since all the blows to my face had been on its left side, the right side had suffered compaction injury. I find this kind of thing much too common. Women's complaints are often wrongly presumed due to emotional or psychological problems.

I found signing on for social security benefits unusually embarrassing. The office clerks when they found my records on their computer, gulped, and asked me to look at the screen. "Was that you?" they asked. They had discovered records of me from the 1960s when I was in my previous incarnation as a Catholic priest. I had to face down their amazement and explain. But even after I explained that I had changed my name legally over 20 years ago, they still put on their computers that my female name was merely an "alias".

It took me about four years before I got back into my stride as a journalist and film maker and started again writing front page pieces for major papers such as *The Independent* and *The Independent on Sunday*. I now had a new focus for much of my writing. As usually happened, this came to me rather than was chosen by me. My brother Tony phoned one day to say there was a woman in his village whose son had fallen seriously ill after his MMR vaccination. Could I look into it and see if I could get something done by using my media skills? This led me eventually into co-producing an investigative documentary for Channel 4 on another vaccination problem linked to many thousands of cancers. I had at last remounted the media horse from which I had been thrown, and this time it was an utter relief to find trustworthy television colleagues.

Transworld, the owners of Doubleday, then contracted me internationally for a book on the world diamond industry. They sent me their reader's comments. They were that my manuscript was "accomplished, important, sensational and a hot property correctly handled."

My diamond film was now televised. Its first showing was on American television and a friend sent me a clipping about it from the New York Times. I was then horrified to discover that my credit as producer had vanished. My voice was in the film, my interviews were used and it had followed my contracted script—for all of which work I was denied credit. Instead the producer's credit was given to the British researcher I hired who had once wanted to "quarantine me". I immediately protested to my Australian funders that this was illegal under the terms of our funding, for my film had to have an Australian producer. The General Secretary of BECTU, a powerful media union, lent his weight to my protests to the BBC. When the film was subsequently shown on BBC2 at peak times on two consecutive Sundays, I found my name had suddenly prominently re-appeared and the name of the British producer had vanished. Later the name of this British producer was also dropped from WGBH's published record of my film, but oddly in favour of my insurance agent for she happened to be Australian!

I later learnt more about how this had happened. I was shown a letter to the BBC from lawyers acting for De Beers complaining because my name was still on my film! They claimed that the BBC had promised De Beers my removal. A BBC lawyer then told me that, if I helped the BBC defend the film, he would have my full credits restored. He wanted me back to help defend the film, he said, since I had researched and written the film.

But he later told me that he could not credit me as Producer because he had now learnt that the BBC had promised De Beers not to give me this credit! This was despite him having no doubt that I had in fact been its producer. He offered to find some other similar credit for me

Since then allegedly the BBC has refused to sell my film to other television stations despite contracting with my company to market it. I was told this had happened under pressure from De Beers. Apparently South African and Namibian television channels were stopped from purchasing it. WGBH, the producer of Frontline, has also refused to sell video copies to the public. The ABC also withdrew it at the last moment. Effectively these companies are now protecting De Beers, suppressing the film without need for a court ruling against it.

Banned from diamond mines

But I was delighted that I was about to have a book published by Doubleday that would tell the full story about the diamond trade. Transworld, the owners of Doubleday, were so keen on it that they facilitated my research trip to South Africa, giving me the use of a luxury flat on the slopes of Table Mountain.

By extraordinarily good chance, when I arrived in Johannesburg and contacted the Mining Union there, it was hosting a gathering of the shop stewards from De Beers diamond mines in order to show them my film, without knowing that I would be coming to South Africa. They invited me to speak to them—and then to visit their mines. But when De Beers heard of my presence, it issued against me the first ban it had made since Nelson Mandela came to power. But I got into their mines nonetheless—and my film about De Beers was secretly shown inside their mines.

I did not stay more than a few days in the luxury publisher's flat Transworld had loaned me. I soon moved into the townships with the workers. They were elated that a white woman would do this. I was taken into the most horrific diamond mines. I learnt that De Beers was disclaiming responsibility for its increasing numbers of sub-contracted workers despite them living in hovels on De Beers mine properties. They were employed without the safety gear given to the directly contracted workers. Their wages were less than a third of the minimum union rate, not enough to support their families, even at subsistence rates.

I went also to De Beers's mines where diamonds were extracted out of asbestos rock with consequent highly toxic dust problems. De Beers dealt this by giving the miners what they called "nose-bags", a piece of cloth tied to the ears. A shop steward alleged they got just one a year yet the bags were black with dust within 20 minutes. The ventilation inside the mines allegedly broke down frequently. I went into the De Beers controlled "Forbidden Zones" along the coastline of South Africa and Namibia where company law prevailed over hundreds of square miles. I saw the ships that sucked diamonds from the seabed. I learnt how Namibia was being robbed of hundreds of millions of dollars worth of undeclared diamonds.

I was invited to be the keynote speaker at the first Post-Apartheid Conference of Diamond Mineworkers for Southern Africa. I took to this conference US State Department documents I obtained that revealed that a major client of De Beers, a former companion of Jackie Onassis now advising the President of Namibia, was in the 1950s linked to a coup against the democratically elected President Nkrumah. He had recruited many of his senior staff from high in US Intelligence including the CIA Chief who helped assassinate the elected president of the Congo. Lumumba, and put into power the corrupt dictator Mobutu. I made this public at a press conference with the two most powerful men in the Namibian Trade Union movement sitting on either side of me. Afterwards, back at my hotel, an American government agent warned me that my words were being reported to Washington.

I was then invited to show my diamond film in Yellowknife, in the diamond rich Canadian Arctic. This came about because De Beers made threats to stop my film being shown by a local environmental group. This became headline news locally. They defiantly put the film on in the largest cinema in town, flew me in from London and I had to answer questions for days afterwards. I felt flattered when they said that only Karen Silkwood had a similar impact. I also flew by a plane that landed on a frozen lake to take me to the hunting villages of the Dene Indians where I advised their elders on the diamond mines planned for the rutting grounds of a 340,000 strong caribou herd that their people had hunted for over 7000 years.

All I learnt on these trips went into the final version of my diamond manuscript. Transworld designed my book cover; advertised it brilliantly in their Hardback Catalogue as appearing under their Doubleday imprint; told me two major newspapers were competing for serialisation rights and their Reader had reported my text was "sensational, accomplished and important." Then, the last moment, Transworld left me a recorded message on my phone and then sent me a confirmatory fax to say they were cancelling it because of opposition from "rich and powerful people". Although "we might win any ensuring case", they feared the cost of defending it. This left me aghast and wondering just who had seen that catalogue and put such pressure on them.

Again I was being silenced. This caused me to think about my work. The diamond book was a distraction from the sacred work that nagged me, this book that you are now reading. Yet it was also important. I tried several other publishers in London but it seemed that all now thought it dangerous.

Even when I was invited to cross the Atlantic to testify at the US Congress on human rights and the diamond trade in March 2001, I still found it difficult to find publishers. But my work was getting known, basically because I had put it up on the Internet.[321]

While I hated being silenced, I cannot pretend my work for others was utterly altruistic. I am a warrior. I get pleasure from the battle. I have enjoyed fighting as a woman against those who endanger the earth, exploit workers or spread disease. I enjoyed setting my cap against major corporations, and even against the activities of the White House. I am proud that my media work helped instigate Congressional Inquiries and angry that these turned into cover-ups. I relished getting into diamond mines from which De Beers had banned me. I loved uncovering secret intelligence operations when working with the BBC or writing for The Age.

But looking back on my years as a warrior, I find I often fought by identifying with the mass of oppressed, the tribe, the community, the nation, rather than with the individual. I was not so good on the individual level, for I hid my own pain; I was the warrior but not the priestess, not the healer, not the crone, and thus a quarter of what I was meant to be.

I know I hid myself to protect my children. I hid myself to protect causes. I hid to protect my professional status and, underneath, despite all my bravado, I was scared of authority, scared even of social workers, scared of rejection, ridiculously vulnerable. It was at this time that I wrote the following parable.

The story of the cowardly lioness

I know a lioness, sulking deep in a dark cave that has been terribly wounded, betrayed by a friend to a demon. The betrayal hurt more than the wound—which is healing but she scarcely knows it, so deep is the hurt in her heart. She knows her friend wished her dead. This is incomprehensible to her.

Yet she can see the mouth of the cave and, in the radiant sunshine, a deep pool of cool water set in a grove of shady trees not a hundred yards away.

She has been in the cave a very long time. She is getting terribly thirsty but fears that the demon is waiting to pounce on her as soon as she comes out into the sunlight. She slithers on her stomach towards the light, looks out at the pool of water, hears the murmur of the stream that feeds it, but in dreadful fear does not venture out into the light.

Lying there she invents excuses. If she writes a brilliant book on *The skills of hunting*, others outside in the light might come to the cave to see her and might protect her, so she can safely emerge and go to book launching parties, and drink. The book will take nine months till it comes out. Maybe she can drink the dew on the moss and lichens and survive till then. This is dubious. Still she is tough; she is a lioness after all. She writes and writes but desperation and thirst weakens her. The completion of the book becomes an obsession…and she weakens.

She thinks, this book is not bringing me in any income, and will not for two years, so I should try right now to sell some articles. I should use this haven as a "writing opportunity". She sets to work again, feverishly scratching her stories on rocks and phoning them through to editors (it is a cave with a phone fortunately)…but as she does so she gets thirstier and thirstier and more desperate. The tasks she set herself seem more and more impossible…. She starts to think she may die in the cave…she works still more feverishly.

She does get some satisfaction. Some of her articles get published, some do well, and most are remembered. Hundreds of thousands read them…but she is still practically as lonely as ever as her readers presume she must be so sane, so well provided for, so healthy to be writing like that and few ever contact her…. she stays in her cave.

She is right about the demon. It does lurk by the entrance, sent there by the fears of others that dread her entrance into the world of the light. But the demon does not lurk in the light. It lurks in the half-light just inside the entrance to the cave. It too dreads the light but with reason…it knows its one chance to destroy the lioness will come in that half light.

The Lioness does have a Lover—out in the light…a Lover that has long been able to send her thoughts to her Lioness, ever since she was a cub playing and rolling in the light.

As the Lioness lies in the gloom, a persistent vision lures her towards the light. "Have courage," the voice mutters in her ear "Don't be a scared little puss."

"But my scars," mutters the Lioness.

"They are nothing. Look, they are healed."

"Don't feel like it," says Lioness, scratching them open.

"You need to drink, come and immerse yourself. It's sparkling, life giving. You will die without it."

"I know, I know. As soon as I am ready." The Lioness picks up her manuscript, sent back to her by an equally cowardly publisher for the hundredth time.

Once this is off to the publisher and at the printers, and then I will come out.

There 's a peal of laughter close to her ear.

"You are so daft! Why not write it while lazing in the sun by the pool. There is fresh food waiting for you as well as water. You would write better in the sunlight."

"I am not sure of that," mutters the lion slinking backwards into a crevice…. "It is dangerous out there…there's some muddy water somewhere back here, it will keep me going and I will finish it.

Out there I might be distracted by pleasure, and really, writing gives me pleasure and enables me to escape mentally from the cave."

Again the laughter came. "You daft lioness" said the Lover. "You only have to make one leap, and I will protect you."

"You will protect me?"

"Yes, what good are lovers if they do not care for those they love?"

"Well if you are sure."

The sparkle in the eyes of the Lover filled the cave with a storm of fireflies.

"Well, if you don't mind protecting me."

"Come."

"I will come."

It was at this point that the Lioness became aware that there were others there. She looked wide-eyed and saw others had come to help her.

"Wait a minute," she protested. "I am not out yet…don't come in here, it is mucky!"

"But you are coming, let us get you ready. Let us get to know you."

"But, I have not groomed myself, I have scars."

"We want to know the lioness that is about to leave the cave"
"You too are daft", she told them, and with no more ado,
She leapt into the light. The demon was so surprised by this that he grasped at empty air then tumbled after her into the light, and faded into a harmless fog.

The Goddess Fires of Ireland

I wrote this as I learnt of the old traditions of my ancestors in Ulster. Macha is their ancient name for the Goddess who blesses and gives fertility to the land. Armagh means 'the heights of Macha'. The poem draws from the " Tain" and other early Celtic sources.

Macha, Once it was written of you in Ulster
That you were Grian Branchure—"the Sun of Womenfolk".
Your spirit lived in hills and moors,
Our rugged headlands, sweeping shores;
Ard Machae or Macha's Height;
The old name of Armagh.
Every feast we would thank you
For the harvest that fed us,
For the mast that fed our sacred pigs.
While you ran our skies,
As a brilliant White Mare Sun Goddess
Few Stallions would dare mount.
Then came the savage men, eager to replace you,
Who could not tolerate a Goddess they could not tame,
Who would not respect a mother's pains.
Whose king at a Samhain gathering,
Challenged you to outrun his horses,

Thinking you, near childbirth, would be but slow.
Thus he set out to overthrow the mother.
We share your pain as you were forced to plead:
"Help me, for a mother bore each one of you.
Give me King but a short delay until I am delivered."
He would not delay for he cruelly thought he had the Mother defeated,
And so you cried: "My name and the name of that which I shall bear
Shall forever cleave to this place of Assembly.
For I am Macha, daughter of "The Strange Son of Ocean."
And with that she raced the king's horses
And in victory lay down to birth her twins.
And then she cursed the men of Ulster:
"From this hour the ignominy that you have inflicted on me
Will rebound to the shame of each one of you.
When a time of oppression falls upon you,
Each one of you will be overcome with weakness,
As the weakness of a woman in childbirth,
And this will remain upon you for five days and four nights,
To the ninth generation it will be so."
And the cursed men did not respect the mother of all life,
They tried instead to curse her by saying
She was but the goddess of their wars.
On sweet Samhain, where Macha's gifts of harvest were once celebrated,
When she was thanked for the mast that fed the pigs,
These savage men brought to this feast the heads of enemies,
Calling these "the mast of Macha",
In savage mockery of her harvest.
They claimed that life came not from the womb but from the head.
By taking heads, they boasted, they had captured the source of life.
Thus they denied the wombs that bore them.
But when the time came for Ulster to be oppressed,
When foreign princes rode their northern necks.

Then Macha with her sisters as the dreaded Morrigan
Fought to stop the men from fighting
While protecting her sacred land
With all the power of the threefold spiral.
But men listened less to Macha and her sisters,
And the mother goddess had less sway,
So other forms the Threefold took;
Suited for the songs of her Bard and Druid,
Of Exalted Bridget they did sing,
Fading the ancient image of the Crow,
They spoke of her inspiring Arwen breath,
Of her as Mistress of poets, of smithery and of healing
So they reshaped the triple Goddess for an Ireland of high art,
While with her ancient strength, spreading throughout Europe,
She inspired the Brigantes to fight the power of Rome.
And thus as Brigit she stemmed the power of Patrick
As he in the name of a newly fathered Trinity,
Strove to defeat her dragon snakes
Knowing her as the serpent mistress of high magic.
Named for bree-saigit or fiery arrow,
Goddess of the fires tended by priestesses
In the fire sanctuary that become Kildare
For Cill Dare, the Oaken Church.
But the women in savage wars had hunted and were hunted
By men that prized their heads above all others,
That feared them despite all the songs of Druid and of Bard,
And thus the mothers listened when a Christian man,
Sweet-talking Saint Adamnan,
Promised freedom to all women of the Western World
And said that Brigit was the friend of Christ
And that as Saint Brigit she would be honoured for all time.

Thus we know that they are honouring the Mother still,
Even if some now credit her magic to a Father
We know that Candlemas
Is a memory of our fiery Goddess Brigit,
So, on this day, on ancient Imbulc
We invoke the Goddess of Fire
Our Crow, our Cow.
Our Brigit, Our Morrigan. Our Macha.
Come Oh Never Forgotten Goddess.
Come Oh Fiery Sun,
Giver of heat and of health
Chantress of our Sacred Earth.
Midwife of Emmanuel
Breathe your life into the earth,
In Winter's Dark, we call You,
Come, Oh Mare!
From the Night bring Day.

Sunday

The Aspect of the Crone

On learning to be a whole.

"When Adam and Eve split,
Then death entered the world,
When Adam and Eve become One,
Then death will leave the world"[322]

I had finally reached my cronehood, a time when supposedly a woman reaches full maturity, relies more on acquired wisdom than on physical strength, when she balances all the energies of life and passes on her acquired wisdom. Some task! For me this meant it was time to share what I had learnt of the mystery that united genders, as well as of what I most loved and most fulfilled me; the experience of union with the Lover-God, of being one with a Nature that is alive and intelligent and of the ecstasy this brought.

It was time to unite what I had learnt of religion and of magic, to find the under-sphere that united them. Why should such labels as Christian, Pagan, Jew, Islam, Hindu and Buddhist separate us into seemingly rival

461

football teams or even armies when at the centre of all traditions was a common secret, a common relationship and a common treasure?

I wanted to put my priesthood back into the centre of my life, uniting it with my warrior journalism, but this was easier thought than done. My imagination would roll over helpless with laughter at the thought of what would happen if I knocked on the door of Westminster Cathedral to ask to be let back in. The Cardinal would have been indignant or thought I was kidding. No way he would have a vacancy for a priestess! Yet the Catholic teaching was that I was still in the priesthood; that my ordination was a personal act between God and myself that the Church was powerless to undo.

I attended a few services of Anglicans and charismatic Christians who had women priests. But I thought the work I must do would not fit their job description. I did not want to do priestly work because I needed a job or wanted to serve an institution. I was instead seeking to fulfil a mission, a dream and perhaps a destiny.

Instinctually I knew there had to be another way. What if I simply forgot my preconceptions, forgot my guilt at not following a priestly vocation, forgot my conceits about being called to a priestly job, and simply followed instincts?

When I did try asking my instincts a different path appeared. It was of a track through heather and small trees above a wild coastline. I saw myself climbing up this track wearing a small rucksack and quietly singing thanks for the beauty surrounding me. When I stopped to camp, a boulder became an altar as I thanked my divine Lover and the spirits for wine and bread and for their presence. If I were meant to share with others such small rituals, then surely they would come?

My instincts took me to my ancestral lands on the western coasts of the British Isles. The life I was envisioning for myself was that of the Celtic women and men who consecrated their lives to God, and no doubt also to the Goddess in pre-patriarchal days. They set up their hermitages in the wildest coves or caves. They saw the face of divinity in nature. Their path had long inspired me, but I put aside this for years as a mere daydream. I thought I should live in the cities where I could work against social injustice. I thought it escapist to choose to live in the wild.

But despite such musings, for the next few years London was be my home as I painfully slowly recovered from the assault and consequent illness. My shelter was the womb-like interior of a boat called Baltimore, a 1937 "Elco" built in Rhode Island but now lying on the River Thames, of cedar, a wood used by American Indians for its sweet purifying scent, and of oak, a tree that Druids saw as representing the strength of God.

Magic Circles

But I had much to learn while living in this haven. It was now the 1990s, the age of the Internet had started—and so, for the first time, I found it easy to locate people who shared my gender history. I even found some inspired by the Gallae transsexual priestesses that served the Goddess Cybele in the days of the Roman Empire. So my journey into old European traditions began contradictorily with my flying out to America to visit them.

It was an intense experience, partly because I had a wonderful sexual encounter with one of them. Our lovemaking seemed strangely beyond gender. It was utterly exciting and transporting, enhanced by all we shared. I loved her hands, hips, and life sense. It was as if we could fertilise our very souls. Over the next days I learnt much from her. She was proud to be a priestess who had walked between the genders

I did not want it to be only a holiday romance but she was deeply committed to the other members of this Arizonian group. The attraction between us seemed mutual and so I set out to woo her. When we talked on the veranda a rainbow appeared. I laughingly pointed it out and said, "Look, there is a good omen! We are meant to be together." She still resisted. Then came a humming bird, hovering between the branches of a dead tree. "Look, at that", I said, "surely that is another omen?" When she still resisted, I asked her what further sign did she need? "Would some lightning do?" The sky was then clear blue. There was no wind but within twenty minutes a sudden storm broke with thunder and lightning. I could not but laugh at this co-incidence. But our relationship was not to continue. It was her decision. She was too much part of that place. I still remember her with love. She taught me that we all have extraordinary gifts to give each other.

One night in Arizona we decided to have a Circle; that is to hold a ritual in a circular space consecrated for the occasion. Circles have long been used for rituals. Aborigines in Australia used a "ring place" or Boro Ring and in the UK there are of course stone circles. I had used such places for private meditation and prayer, but not before in a Wiccan, or modern witchcraft, way. Beforehand we singly went for a bath to purify and prepare ourselves. One of the group called out as I went, "Talk to your Lover". I am not quite sure what was meant but alone in the bath, I called on my divine Lover and the thought came of what I was to do.

We started by invoking the elements to ask them to help and protect us. The circle was then defined by drawing its perimeter. Next my Priestess-Lover had the Goddess "drawn down" into her, so she became Her embodiment.

I was then asked if I had anything I wished to do. It was then that I utterly and completely rededicate myself to my priesthood, as a priestess of the God and Goddess, as a lover who had a divine lover, as the person who had consecrated herself to the priesthood forever as a child. This was a transfiguring moment. Suddenly my priesthood was very real again. I had not thought it would happen like this. It was utterly unexpected.

A few days later I was walking alone through sequira cactus trees and prickly pears in an Arizonian valley when, in the sands by a stream, I found the pawprints of a mountain lion or puma, making this for me a place of wonder and some fear. This 'near meeting' felt most special. I saw the lioness as an archetype of female power. Cybele's chariot was pulled by lionesses. I was one who was rebuilding her pride.

I also spent a few days with transsexual witches in the Californian redwoods where we celebrated the blessings of life amid these warm-barked trees. It was from them that I learnt to add the aspect of Warrior to the more widely used three divine aspects of womanhood, Crone, Maid and Mother.

When I had to leave, my Arizonian lover gave me one last present. It was an ankh, an Egyptian sacred symbol like to a cross with a loop above it. This small thing turned out to be an unexpected blessing. It led me to others who would teach me. A woman noted it when I was at a bisexual woman's meeting in London. She showed me her own when she introduced herself. Over coffee I learnt she was part of a magical circle that met in Catford, not far from where my boat was moored, and she warmly invited me to meet the others in her group to see if we could work together.

These contacts with people who called themselves witches or workers of magic was strangely appropriate. I had learnt to look for God among the poor and outcastes. I was now seemingly finding the Deity among those who identified with the rejects of the Church. I found I had much to learn from these new friends. My first meeting with the Catford group was a delight. After years of working with Aborigines, it was wonderful to discover among my own people some with whom I shared the same sense of magic. The group was mostly made up of young people who were extraordinarily dedicated, dancing with the energy of the earth and immersed in learning from our ancient mystical and magical traditions. I was happy to learn from them. I felt, tasted, it fitted the great pattern and so I decided that this was for me good and appropriate. It felt like coming home. In their rituals I recognised much that reflected the insights of mystics, the Pagan Egyptians and the Gnostic Christians.

I found to my surprise the modern Craft practiced the Gnostic belief that all initiates were in the priesthood, men and women alike. All were encouraged to learn the arts of ritual making. These they composed from intuition and by drawing on the ancient traditions of Western mysticism and magic, learning mostly by example rather than from books. Their rites did not require the approval of congresses of bishops, nor of other groups. Ritual writing was a sacred tool accessible to all. Strangely, I had found a spiritual home where I might never have thought of looking.

I also learnt that modern Witches called their sacred rites and magic "work" just as Aborigines called theirs "business". Both meant they were working alongside the ancestors, spirits or deities to achieve an end, not "praying" for someone else to do it. They used their focused natural spiritual or mental energy in this work of "magic".

As for the rumours that witchcraft was a form of devil worship, few I met seemed to believe in a devil. Our rituals were centred on honouring Nature, the Creating Deities and nature spirits under varying names or aspects. We were taught that if we used magic to harm others, this would hurt us much more than it hurt them.

Our rituals were happy and often intense. The central focus was on raising collective energy for healing and other good purposes from our bond with the Earth, its spirits and the Deities. We worked as a circle of equals. The more experienced did not put on airs but taught others by example and answering questions. We had no mediators, no pretension. Our group used no titles although the couple that founded it were much respected for their magical experience. I marvelled at the focused attention with which the members created circles that felt truly magical, spiritual and safe.

When I had worked with Aborigines, I felt my path had been a private song sung in another's space, although I felt welcomed by their Ancestors as a child of the common earth. In Australia, as a guest who knew her birthplace, I had talked with the spirits, dreamt my dreams, while helping protect the earth that gave birth to the Aboriginal nations. It was thus a thrill to discover a nature spirituality alive in Europe that appeared to be fanning new flames from old sparks. In the rituals I recognised the old inherited elements. These modern witches saw nature as sacred and to be honoured and protected, much as did the Aborigines, and as did our distant ancestors, at least in my belief.

A New or Old European Paganism?

Yet, outside our group (which did not worry about such things) I found among modern Pagans a debate over whether they were part of the flowering of a new religion or of an old religion that never died. I did not see Paganism as a religion that was "truer" than other religions, but as a sacred tradition and way of working that could be expressed in the vocabulary of many cultures, many faiths. My instinct was that our quiet rituals and blessings in the countryside were part of a very ancient intuitive religion that arose from human nature and human destiny. Our core beliefs seemed to be shared by mystics of many religions. My version of this path was animistic, a truly old path. Did it matter if it were labelled as "Pagan"? I thought the label of little importance. Did it matter if it were a new religion or an old? Yes, I thought, for it felt as if part of my birthright. Its belief in Nature as Sacred and as infused with Divinity had surely never died?

For many decades in the 20th century, British Pagans had honoured Margaret Murray for giving their path a relatively recent historical antecedent. They too felt what they were doing was old—and welcomed academic support. Murray, a noted Egyptologist, claimed that a coven-based witchcraft honouring an antlered Pan-like God survived in Europe until the 17th century. She expounded this theory in books such as *The God of the Witches* (1933). She noted horned images of deity were apparently used by some Palaeolithic hunters, quoting an interpretation of a drawing on a French cavern wall,[323] were later used in Egypt and Bronze Age Europe and were recorded in witchtrial evidence in the 16th century. She was not the first to argue that ancient Pagan beliefs continued into Renaissance times. Jacobs Grimm held in his *Deutsche Mythologie*

(Gottingen 1835) that witch beliefs were lingering relics of a systematic pre-Christian Teutonic religion.

The Craft she found described in witchtrial evidence seemed to share something of the chauvinism of the period. It was centred on the honouring of a male horned God with its rites guarded and controlled by a "Man in Black". Murray did not claim that this 15th to 17th century witchcult was identical with that of a pre-historic past, but only that aspects of it might be truly old. She did not look for links to ancient shamanism. This was not surprising, as shamanism was then little understood. She also did not consider other Pagan traditions to see if they had survived in Europe into modern times, such as those of the Hermetic Gnostics and of the wise woman or solitary witch.

After her books appeared there was a revival of witchcraft in Europe, but it was in a form quite unlike the cult she described, for it honoured Goddesses as well as Gods and had priestesses as well as priests. I wondered if there was any evidence that this more gender-balanced practice had recent historical antecedents? Some evidence perhaps lay in the discoveries of a BBC Chronicle team in 1977. It found in British Pennine valleys people who did not identify as "witches" but had a strong belief in a Mother Goddess and a male horned God who led the Wild Hunt—but much more about this later.[324]

Murray's work was heavily criticised by Ronald Hutton, a Professor of History at Bristol University whom I had met at Pagan gatherings at which he was a celebrity and speaker. People at these expressed pleasure at having such an outstanding historian among their members. I find his work valuably assembled a wealth of historical material but I was much less sure about some of his conclusions. (As I noted in the previous chapter, he seriously under-valued the impact of the witch persecutions in Europe.)

In his 1991 book *The Pagan Religions of the British Isles* he based much of his thesis that these pagan religions died out centuries ago on the "demolition" of the Murray thesis by other historians. He claimed they had proved beyond doubt that she had deliberately omitted crucial witch-trial evidence that would have discredited her main sources. He insisted that their critique destroyed her thesis that a coven-based Pagan witchcraft existed up to the 17th Century. He concluded that Pagan religions died out in the 1100s only to be re-established again in modern times. He was seemingly winning the debate. It was increasingly the Pagan party line that Wiccans (a modern form of coven based witchcraft) had effectively created a religion with no antecedents in the medieval period.

But I found myself questioning his seeming presumption that if Murray were discredited, it followed that no kind of Pagan religion survived. He could have simply said that Murray had not established the historical antecedents of a 16th Century coven-based cult. He might have legitimately noted that she did not know of 17th century French groups that honoured a Goddess[325] or of possible surviving witchcraft groups in Anglesey, the evidence for both he gave elsewhere.[326] But he instead maintained more sweepingly that no pagan religion survived.

While he presented evidence for folk and magical practices surviving from pagan to modern time, he disdainfully dismissed these as "trivialities such as [at] the occasional [sacred] well or tree"[327]. But I wondered if these practices dismissed so sweepingly might instead be evidence that a nature religion survived that needed no institutional framework? I had for years regarded as part of my own religion the meditations or spiritual work I did by such a spring or tree.

Was it that we defined religion differently? His above-mentioned book did not help. In it he expressly refused to define "religion". I then went to the Oxford Dictionary to verify its popular sense. It gave several alternate definitions. These were a belief in God or Gods, the honouring of these in worship or "a system of faith and worship". Religions did not need to have hierarchical structures or institutions as Hutton had seemingly presumed. There was also nothing to prevent a religion from including elements from other religions.

In 1999 he wrote a further work, *The Triumph of the Moon: A history of Pagan Modern Witchcraft*, to answer questions he said he had previously left open. This evidently included defining "religion". He adopted a definition proposed by a relatively obscure writer, Sir Edward Taylor, who in 1871 defined "religion" as a belief in the existence of spiritual beings with which humans had a need to form relationships.[328] But despite adopting a definition of religion that allowed a relationship with nature spirits to be a religion, and admitting that people still related to nature spirits, Hutton still maintained that no pagan religion survived in Western Europe.

He then defined "Pagan", casting doubt on whether its modern definition as a religion of nature had a firm foundation in antiquity. He cited late Roman Empire Catholics who called those who would not enlist in the Catholic "army" or church "pagans". That was more likely to have been an insult. He quoted another who had it mean "the rooted or old religion" of a "pagus", the Latin for a country locality. I had no great dispute with the latter but Hutton then added that since it was a local religion, it could not include a belief in universal spirit beings. But countryfolk still speak of a universal Mother Nature, albeit in a vague but loving way. Aborigines speak of the All-Father or All-Mother. It seemed to me that he had not established that a definition of paganism as the old local religion excluded the honouring of universal Deities, or that it was not a religion of nature in the modern sense.

Perhaps his difficulty lay in the way he separated "Christian" from "Pagan" practices? If a vicar in a Derbyshire parish blessed a sacred well, keeping up a very ancient custom, is he being Pagan or Christian? Perhaps the honest answer is that he is being both, that his system of belief is not entirely inherited from Israel but incorporates local Pagan elements. But Hutton said that for it not to be Christian, "It is necessary to demonstrate that certain things, although now existing within a Christian structure, kept alive a memory of, and a reverence for, the old deities. Otherwise they were part of Christianity."[329] I would suggest that honouring a well is not part of the Christian Revelation but a belief of a far older origin. As for "a reverence for the old deities", it may continue out of reverence for the Sacred Earth and Mother Nature, probably the oldest of our deities.

Hutton told how Christian authorities condemned as Pagan the practice of venerating the Deity or spirit symbolised by sacred springs. Wulfstan, Archbishop of York condemned this practice repeatedly around 1001. In the 13th century the bishops of Wells, Hereford, Exeter and Worcester all condemned this practice.[330] After this time no more condemnations were issued and such springs continued to be ritual sites until today. Hutton concluded surprisingly that either "the old religions were effectively dead by the mid-eleventh century"—"or the Christian establishment chose to call off the attack on them around that time." He then said that this "second option seems very unlikely" and with this presumption dismissed the possibility of Christianity coming to terms with aspects of the old nature religion, and of the continuing rite being Pagan in a Christian garb.[331]

The answer is, I think, that religions have always mixed and matched. If we believe in a personal relationship with a Sacred Deity or Deities living among us, then its practice takes us beyond sets of doctrines or hierarchies. Labels can only limit. Nothing prohibits sharing. My spiritual brothers and sisters are those who share such a relationship with divinity and a belief in nature as sacred—no matter what label they apply to themselves. The very argument that pits Pagan against Christian, religion against religion, takes away the common sacred core.

Eliade held that, while shamanism has its most defined forms in certain ancient pagan societies, it could and did coexist with other forms of magic and religion.[332] Associate Professor Eva Pocs concluded, after researching two thousand 16th to 18th century Hungarian witchtrials, that the witchcraft of that period was shaped by a surviving pagan shamanism. This was within a country that was officially Christian. It is thus a mistake to presume that Pagan systems of belief cannot co-exist alongside other beliefs. For me it suffices that some local healers, farmers, mystics, dreamers, spellworkers or others had always believed in the sacredness of nature and honoured her. It did not matter what they called this work. For me, this is our innate religion and part of the very reason for our existence.

Doreen Valiente (died 1999) was proud to call herself a witch and Pagan. She wrote many books on the Craft and worked with Gerald Gardner to develop the rituals of the modern Craft or Wicca. In two lectures she gave in her final year of life, I heard her say that she had come to believe that the Craft originated from ancient shamanism. She spoke of how witches worked with animals as familiars, suggesting this was similar to the use of "power animals" or totems among ancient indigenous societies. She believed that medieval stories of "flying" witches were akin to the Sami accounts of shamans "flying" to the spirit realm. Such "flying", she said, could be brought about by mediation practices, trance techniques or the use of drugs such as the significantly named magic mushroom.

But since Hutton had set his cap against a continuing Pagan religion, he castigated Doreen Valiente, Vivienne Crowley and other leading Pagan authors for quoting Margaret Murray's thesis while making only "fleeting" reference to the criticisms of her,[333] while he himself did little more than baldly allege that these criticisms had "demolished" the Murray thesis.[334]

When I asked Hutton for the evidence for his critique of Murray, he referred me to *Religion and the Decline of Magic* by Keith Thomas and to Norman Cohn's *Europe's Inner Demons*, praising both highly. Hutton summarised Cohn when he alleged that Murray "ignored or misquoted evidence that indicated that the actions attributed to alleged witches were physically impossible. Or she rationalised it by suggesting, for example, that an illusion of flying was created by drugs". Hutton did not present Cohn's evidence but told us it was correct. He concluded that this "cast doubt on the truth of anything else claimed in these confessions." Thus he dismissed the testimony gathered by Murray for a medieval witchcraft that honoured a Pan-like God—and likewise dismissed as discreditable the witchtrial victims she quoted.

Prudence Jones and Nigel Pennick in *A history of Pagan Europe* similarly relied on Cohn to dismiss Murray. They re-phrased his allegation, saying she omitted from accounts of witch-trial testimony "fantastic details such as shape shifting, flying through the air, making rideable horses out of straw and so on".

I checked Cohn to discover the texts that Murray allegedly omitted. I then checked Murray's work to see if Cohn were accurate. To my utter astonishment, I found that far from omitting these texts, she had in fact considered all but one of them in detail. It seems Hutton, Jones and Pennick had hurried to condemn her on another's word without checking on his accuracy.

I had come across a reference to the authors Hutton recommended in a work by the highly reputable scholar Karen Armstrong. She wrote; "To deny, as male scholars like Norman Cohn or Keith Thomas have both done recently, that the Witch Craze bore any special malevolence to women is to ignore a substantial amount of evidence in the principal writers on witchcraft at the time of the craze."[335]

I think it might be valuable to go through the allegations against Murray in some detail because they have been used in recent years to discredit many who said their magical Craft was part of an ancient tradition.

Cohn alleged Murray omitted the following testimony deliberately to make her source more credible. "I was in the Downie-hills and got from the Queen of Fairie more than I could eat. The Queen of Fairie is bravely clothed in white linen." But Murray quoted it at length.[336] She also told how Aberdeen witches honoured the "Queen of Elfin".[337] In folk belief "downie Hills" or "fairy mounds" were the Otherworld homes of the "Little Folk". These were in fact ancestral sacred places or burial mounds. The fairies, or nature spirits, were said to be lead by Queens or Goddesses. At least one, Bride, traditionally wore white. Pocs described many cases of "fairy witches" who had honoured such spirits in central and southern Europe. The accused was describing a meeting with the Goddess as a feast that completely filled—a rather beautiful metaphor.

Cohn also quoted as damning the following alleged omission; "All the coven did fly like cats, jackdaws, hares and rooks…rode on a horse that we would make of a straw or a beanstalk" and that a witch allegedly turned herself into a horse. But Murray again dealt at length with such testimony, quoting many cases.[338] Again this did not go to the witness's discredit, since there was an ancient folk-belief in the magically adept's ability to shape-shift enshrined in our earliest Celtic literature. It could relate to dreams or experiences in trance. Magical straw horses were common symbols and are found in the ancient German grimoire quoted below. Pocs reported that the accused frequently claimed to fly to witch gatherings and that "flying" was a symbolic expression of a journey to the other world in medieval witchcraft and in shamanism.

Cohn quoted another quite terrible testimony as allegedly a Murray omission. It was that one of the accused dug up the corpse of a baby to eat its flesh. Again Cohn does Murray a great injustice. She wrote about it at length.[339] I cannot say it did not happen, but there is little other evidence of cannibalism. It should be remembered that cannibalism accusations were also falsely aimed at early Christians and Jews.

Cohn also alleged she omitted: "The Devil was with them in the shape of a great horse and they decided on the sinking of a ship." This was allegedly an attempt to kill a king who had grievously tortured and killed witches. `Also, "the devil would be like a heifer, a bull, a deer, a roe or a dog...and he would hold up his tail while we kissed his arse." But Murray did not omit the strange aspects of this story. The truth was very much the opposite. She in fact included other aspects that could have been seen as even more discrediting.[340] Pocs in her study of two thousand Hungarian witchtrials gave many examples of "weather magic" (but reported no cannibalism). She noted that the devil was only mentioned in evidence produced after torture. "Kissing his arse" might have been a wryly humorous response to being asked if they worshipped the devil. She found examples of the ancient belief in shape shifting (as also found in the Welsh legend of Taliesin), and in the ability of humans to do magic for harmful purposes.

Cohn also alleged that Murray omitted; "they [went] through at a little hole like bees and took the substance of the ale", saying that if Murray had not done this, it would have been obvious her source was lying. I could not find this particular quotation in Murray but the above was a harsh judgement by Cohn. "Small holes" represented in shamanic accounts entries to the Otherworld. Cohn had clearly forgotten that he had himself cited as authentic the ancient belief that the followers of the Goddess might enter houses through small holes to take food and drink left out for them and to leave blessings.

Feasting was commonly mentioned in descriptions of witches' gatherings, as reported by Murray,[341] Pocs and others. Pocs told how much witchtrial testimony concerned journeys undertaken to feast and dance at "merriments". These were said to be bright glittering occasions of great beauty. The Goddess or the "Lady of the Forest" might appear at them.[342] Sometimes a splendid flag was flown, often made of silk.[343] Women condemned as witches spoke of their happy memories of such gatherings.

Cohn's research on Murray was thus remarkably flimsy and inaccurate and in no way deserved the ringing endorsement Hutton had given it as "meticulous and formidable".[344] If Murray's quoted testimonies cannot be so easily discredited, then we owe it to her witnesses to take their testimony more seriously.

The other critic of Margaret Murray quoted by Hutton was Keith Thomas in *Religion and the Decline of Magic*. Thomas quoted Murray as saying: "the only explanation of the numbers of witches who were legally tried and put to death in Western Europe is that we are dealing with a religion which was spread over the whole continent." He dismissed this by saying: "the absence of any organisation, co-operation, continuity or common ritual among witches makes it impossible to speak with Margaret Murray of a 'witchcraft' let alone of the 'old religion.'"[345] However Pocs and other researchers have since shown that there was on the contrary a remarkable continuity of witchcraft belief and practice across Europe. Pocs specifically said her research findings in Eastern Europe matched what Murray found in Scotland.

Thomas presumed, as had Hutton, that a "religion" could not exist unless it was more tightly organised than demanded by the dictionary definition of "religion". Thomas also maintained, as would Hutton, that; the "accused witches had no demonstrable links with a pagan past."

However Thomas' worldview was very different from that held at the time of the witch-trials. I can even quote here Normal Cohn. "The early church already regarded all magical practices as manifestations of paganism…" Thus for the Church authorities it did not matter if the witch's magic were beneficial or couched in Christian terms. It still remained essentially Pagan. Pocs expressly mentioned the "taltos" put on trial, saying these were the equivalent of the pre-Christian shaman. She concluded; "the belief systems of European shamanism and witchcraft developed as twin siblings from common parentage and were closely bound to each other. This is how we see things in the light of both German and Slav documentation."[346]

Carlo Ginsburg, described by Hutton as a "brilliant" historian, in *Ecstasies: Deciphering the Witches' Sabba*th linked the witchtrial stories of witches' sabbats or gatherings back to ancient shamanic traditions. Pocs had likewise linked accounts of gatherings to ancient shamanism.

Further light was cast by a recent study of a medieval grimoire in *"Forbidden Rites: A Necromancer's Manual of the 15th Century.*[347] This contains directions for creating such illusions as "flying horses", like the flying straw horses mentioned by Murray. Kieckhefer commented that these illusion spells "done for entertainment" sadly "became sources of Boschian nightmares of the witch-trials."

This grimoire is typical of many surviving from this period. Other spells in it are psychological, intended to have an impact on the thoughts or imaginations of others, and divinatory, using a mirror, crystal or a polished fingernail! They asked spirits for information but did not seek to command them. The book detailed several ways of setting up magical circles in order to protect and focus energy. Exorcisms were also of interest as they were to the Church.

It seems that that such practices influenced the "spellcraft" of the modern Craft, for people such as Doreen Valiente and Gerald Gardner were assiduous students of "natural magic". For them it was an essential study for a Craft that both venerated and worked with nature. This is not to say that Christians did not study spellcraft. They renamed it as "miracle working" and "prayer-power". Many Christians saw the face of God in nature. I knew this because I had been one of them.

This does not mean that Wiccan circles have an initiatory lineage back into the distant past nor is this a necessity. Self-initiation is widely recognised, including by such authorities as Doreen Valiente. Many often drew on book learning as well as on instinctual knowledge and experiments with magic and meditation techniques. I feel this has long been the way in this non-authoritarian tradition.

There were many signs of a surviving Paganism in Europe throughout the Middle Ages and into modern times. Hutton quoted how in 1589 the effigy of a pagan god with its priest was brought to London from Wales where apparently the god had many followers. Both priest and effigy were burnt at the stake. In 1677 the French Catholic Church found it necessary to forbid the honouring of pagan gods and, most interestingly, the holding of lunar festivals, a ritual said to be associated with women.[348] The church authorities condemned: "those believing that because women worship the moon, they can draw the hearts of men towards the Pagans." A book published in Paris in 1677 listed woodland huts that served as Pagan sanctuaries and water springs serving as "sites of sacrifice."[349] In Brittany some elder women kept shrines where they taught "the rites of Venus" to young women. This included reportedly instruction in shamanistic practices. In 1656 the Dingwall Presbytery in Scotland denounced the local "heathenish" practice of sacrificing bulls to the God Mourie and of pouring milk on certain hills.[350] Sir A. Mitchell reported that Mourie was still respected two hundred and four years later in 1860.

In the Pennine valleys of central England, as I have mentioned, a Pagan religiosity or religion survived at least until the 1970s. David Clarke with Andy Roberts in their BBC program-related book, *Twilight of the Celtic Gods*, quoted a Pennine man, Blandford, as saying, "I come from a very old tradition if the learning passed down through the families is to be believed, my maternal grandmother was responsible for passing on the teachings....I was slowly eased into the fundamental belief of our tradition, that the land is sacred. And to that end we thought of ourselves as stewards, guardians of the areas where our family dwelt, many ordinary countryfolk knew of our knowledge of plants and animals and certain members of our family would help them…this just seemed to be accepted and expected.

"We revere, and stand in awe of, the powers that create and sustain us and the world…To us being alive and part of the body of the mother was worship for us. The powers that we held in awe were locked inside the landscape, inherent in the power of the weather and manifest in the changing of the seasons and in the end they in turn ran through us. It was nothing complicated, nothing supernatural, and to me at least, the way people are supposed to live…The fells were seen as places of the goddess and the high moors, rocky scars and peaks such as the Beacon were the places of the male power. The core of the old faith was the constant coming together of these two, whether it be in the creation of human or animal life"

Blandford did not call himself a witch. He wrote: "I've never met a witch and from what I've heard about them I am not sure I want to. I know some old books on the Dales refer to some local characters as being witches…but they were not witches; if anything the label 'wise woman' or 'wise man' was more strictly true." But I think he had quite a different concept of "witches" from my own. Members of the Craft I have come to know and love could have testified much the same as he. Names such as witch, wise woman and saint may describe the same person as seen through the eyes of different people.

Ronald Hutton in *The Triumph of the Moon* described the many "cunning folk" in Wales, Southern England and the Midlands.[351] It seemed they inherited much from the "high magic" of the Middle Ages. Their work often centred on exorcising demons. Folklorists believed their Welsh name "dyn hysbys" or Cornish equivalent "peller" meant "expeller" of demons. The dominance of high magic in their practice was reflected in the definition of magic made by Sir James Frazer—"practices designed to bring spiritual or supernatural forces under the control of human agents."[352] They might attempt this in the name of Christ or the Holy Trinity. Some used rituals such as the Lesser Key of Solomon passed on by medieval magicians.

Were cunning folk Christian or Pagan? Hutton concluded that they were mostly Christian. But when I checked with a person who works today with similar energies, she said; "We use the words that convey the meaning of sacred and divinity to our client. Thus with a Christian I might speak of Christ. This does not affect the magic I am doing. It is beyond words. It is not specifically Christian. It is deeper."

To the "high magic" of controlling demons, cunning folk joined elements of the traditional "low magic" of the countryside. They healed, used herbs, love-charms, lifted or imposed curses and told fortunes, but in so doing were careful to say they were not "witches" to protect themselves and their trade. They claimed to do "white" magic and alleged that it was "witches" that did "black" magic. They agreed with the courts that witches were women who worked with demons. James "Cunning" Murrell proudly said he was "the Devil's master" since he specialised in countering the demonic spells of "witches"[353] for 2s.6d a time.[354]

On the island of Mons (Anglesey) there were secretive "circles" in the first part of the 20th century as verified by Ron Hutton.[355] The members called themselves part of the "Old Religion". They met at ancient megaliths and sacred lakes, casting into the waters sacred leaves and other offerings. In their rites they used carved stone heads as symbols of the Gods. These were presided over by elected women leaders whom some locals called "witches".

Much of Britain is still rich with sacred wells at which token gifts are left. I recently visited the Welsh "Virtuous Well" at Trellick, south of Monmouth and west of the river Wye. It is signposted and has a small walled court with niches for offerings. The thorn trees overhanging it are festooned with offerings in the form of ribbons, lace and rags, some old, some new. There were similar practices elsewhere. The BBC Chronicle team reported how in 1977 in certain Pennine valleys Beltane (May 1st) fires were lit and flowers put by springs. Traditional stone heads were also carved and buried. These signified an invocation of protective spirits or deities.

The magical group I joined on my return to England drew its practices from a wide range of sources. I recognised elements that had an ancient pedigree. I later found major elements of our rituals described in Renaissance works. I noted that our rites showed no sign of being influenced by the writings of Margaret Murray in form or content. Yet I soon discovered that the founders of our group had been initiated within and learnt some of their ritual and magical expertise from a tradition popularised by Gerald Gardner. He was a man who much admired Murray and had asked her to write an Introduction to his 1950s book *Witchcraft Today*. She contributed an academic note that said that he had discovered, "there are many peoples, whether in the Far East or in Great Britain, who still perform acts of worship to the Almighty Giver of Life according to ancient ritual." She took no credit for this discovery.

The birth of the modern Craft

The work of Gerald Gardner and his group had a great influence, and I owe it much. In the mid-20th century they wove together some of the ritual craft inherited by the secret societies reportedly with material passed on by families with a witchcraft tradition.[356] Their rites emphasised the sacredness of nature and the Goddess. There was no reliance on a guru, authority or revelation. Today there are tens of thousands of initiates following in the tradition they established.

Gerald Gardner developed his ritual magic while working with a resourceful group at the Rosicrucian Theatre in the New Forest, as well as with friends in Freemasonry, Co-Masonry and in modern Druidry and magic. He also told of how he met with a traditional group of witches in the New Forest and was initiated by them in a house in Highcliffe village, and, as I have mentioned, once owned by the Highcliffe Castle Estate, the very castle in which I had lived and studied for the priesthood for many years. I was intrigued to learn that his work in English witchcraft began after he returned from decades of living among the indigenous peoples of S.E. Asia, for it gave us both a somewhat similar history.

He claimed he realised the historical nature of his initiation when he heard "wica" mentioned. It was an ancient word for witchcraft among the Anglo-Saxons, The 7th century Archbishop Theodore of Canterbury condemned "wiccaecraft". Alfred the Great condemned to death the followers of wica in the late 9th century. Of course, this does not prove that there was a continuous tradition of witchcraft in the British Isles from the 7th to the 20th century. Nor does it refer to earlier British practices. Pliny referred to the Druids as the "magi" of the Celts and wrote, "Today Britain is still spell-bound by magic, and performs its rites with so much ritual that she might almost be seen as the source for the Persian customs".[357] Druid could well be a Celtic word that covered what the Anglo-Saxons called wiccae.

While the "spellcraft" of the modern Craft seemed linked to some of the traditional magic of the countryside, its "ritualcraft" clearly owed much to a wealth of ritual knowledge refined over centuries. Gardner seemingly drew from the Renaissance grimoires known as *The Keys of Solomon* (such as his blessings for salt and water) and from the alchemic knowledge of magical societies such as Golden Dawn. Some said he drew sexual magic from his knowledge of Tantra gained during years in the East. He may have drawn from the Freemasons the use of a rope tow and a pointed weapon before First Degree initiation. Freemasons used a compass pointed at the chest, he used a sword or dagger, but perhaps he and they drew from common sources? Freemasonry had originated, after all, from the ritualistic Secret Societies of the Renaissance that in turn had drawn from older sources, such as mystic, gnostic, neo-platonic, alchemic and Greek initiatory mysteries. These in their turn may well have drawn from still older shamanic tribal wisdom. In my experience, the modern Craft is constantly weaving newly dreamed elements with those of an ancient ancestry.

In this renewed Craft, there was no Bible, no defined Creed, and no *Book of Shadows* that set up a pattern that could not be broken. It was simply a craft, a spiritual skill based on a reverence for nature and for the God and Goddess dwelling within nature. It celebrated the creativity of the human spirit and the sacredness of its inheritance.

For me,
The Craft is of the present
And of the past
Of the Gnostic past
Of the Mysteries past,
Of the Shamanic past
And the Druid past.
They are its roots
But not its branches
For they are lifted
To catch the future
That we cannot help but birth.

We would call the God or Goddess into a member of our circle, so that this person became a symbol for, or a voice for, the divine presence among us. This we might do with words that came spontaneously (after some training in ritual) but we might also use the *Charge of the Goddess* by Doreen Valiente. In part this reads:

"I who am the beauty of the green Earth and the white Moon among the stars, and the mystery of the waters and the desire of the heart of man, call unto thy soul, arise and come unto me, for I am the Soul of Nature who giveth life to the universe. From me all things proceed and unto me all things must return and before my face, beloved of gods and men, thine innermost divine self shall be enfolded in the rapture of the infinite. Let my worship be within the heart that rejoices, for behold all acts of love and pleasures are my rituals. And therefore let there be beauty and strength, power and compassion honour and humility, mirth and reverence within you. And thou who thinkest to seek for me, know thy seeking and yearning shall avail thee not, unless thou knowest the mystery that if that which thou seekest thou findest not within thee, thou wilt never find it without thee, for behold, I have been with thee from the beginning and I am that which is attained at the end of desire."

The ritual heart of the Craft

In our circles a male might invoke the Goddess within him or a female the God within her. Not all circles did this—but ours delighted in expressing the richness we possessed within us. We acknowledged that all have both gender polarities within them. I found that when I called the other energy, the male, the God, there was an excitement and a creative force within me that did not come when I invoked the Goddess. It was as if She did not complement me but was I; while He was other, powerful and completed me.

Hildergard of Bingen saw great meaning in the circle, describing, "Divinity is like a wheel, a circle, a whole." Human imagination and fun had its place. The Beguine Mechtild was told, "I God am your playmate! I will treat the child in you in wonderful ways."

Likewise there was laughter in our rituals. Once, instead of invoking the "Archangel of the South" to protect our circle, I said by mistake the "Archbishop of the South!" I had an immediate vision of a furious archbishop in full regalia, apoplexic with rage at being summoned to protect a Pagan circle and we all collapsed with laughter.

I had now learnt at last that I did not need the approval of a bishop or pope in order to practice openly my priesthood. Fundamentally it rested on the commitment I made to my Deity. I had now found people with whom I could be a priestess. The Craft thus re-empowered me by giving me a clearer understanding of my inner power.

My feeling of coming home was reinforced when I discovered the mystic marriage tradition was central to the initiations given within the modern Wiccan Craft. These initiations were not however necessary to the practice of witchcraft and many modern witches do not use them, especially those who work by themselves or who are in the older family traditions. But they are part of the regular practice of the Wiccan coven tradition. I find them to be teaching tools that create occasions of much mystery and magic. As a priestess, they are perhaps the most powerful aspect of my work.

The First Initiation has at its core a commitment between the Initiate, the Goddess and God that was alike a couple's engagement. The Third Initiation is the solemn celebration of the complete and utter bonding between the initiate and deity, akin to a wedding. Thus the ancient mystic marriage tradition was celebrated in a fashion quite unlike the asexual way it is still celebrated in Christian convents when a Nun consecrates herself to God. It had regained among us an exultant spirit, perhaps like that which infused the ancient initiatory Mysteries of Greece.

The Second Initiation is different in character from the other two. It is also alike to the Mysteries celebrated at Eleusis for over 2000 years, in which the initiates descended into the underworld, died to this world and were reborn. Plutarch wrote "to die is to be initiated." This may have been partly inspired by earlier shamanic rebirth rites—and it may have had great influence on the early development of Christianity—but more about this later.

The group I joined suited me, for it encompassed members of many different sexual or gender paths. We had straight heterosexual, gay, lesbian and bisexual members—and myself of many labels. We saw all forms of sexuality as sacred. We called ourselves the Rainbow Tree circle or coven in honour of our many coloured ways. It reminded me of the Tree of Celtic Wisdom and the Tree of the Qabbalah, the basis of the pathworking or mediation always included in our weekly circle.

Many Deities?

Some pagan beliefs made me stop and reconsider. One was polytheism, that there was more than one god or goddess. I had been brought up to believe in monotheism, that there could only be one God, although Christians perhaps cheated by saying their One was a Trinity of persons. (This was however not so unusual a concept. The Irish Goddesses Morrigan and Brighid were both Three in One and the Egyptians once had a similar triad of divinity.)

At first I thought perhaps the many pagan names for deities were simply aspects of the one ineffable Godhead. But then I thought of the wealth of spirits in our family home. My parents called them angels. If angels could create, would they resemble what the Greeks called lesser Gods? Why should the only creative beings be humans or members of a Trinity? The Christian concept of angels has changed over time. They were said to have bodies in the first Christian centuries. Some thought of them as much the same as Pagan guardian spirits. Late in the first millennium they were thought to be able to shapeshift into animal forms. But in the time of Thomas Aquinas they became refined to creatures of pure will and pure intellect without material content.

Some Gnostic Christians held with Plato and the pagan Greeks that creating spirits called demi-urges (lesser gods and goddesses) emanated from the ineffable supreme Godhead. Some of these Christians also honoured Pagan Goddesses. Catholic Church Fathers reported with horror that the Alexandrian Gnostic Christians carried the Goddess Persephone in procession to their church. She was a Goddess of Rebirth honoured in the Eleusian initiatory rite, called by Cicero the greatest ennobling experience available for humankind. The Fathers called this idolatry but other Christians seemingly saw this as a good way to honour the female aspects of the Deity—and apparently saw the Grecian Initiatory rituals as in tune with their Christianity.

In my pathworking and meditations I experience a Creating Energy whom I know as my Lover and Sustainer. As a Christian child I knew him as Christ. But, if I had to explain him, how else could I have fitted him into the Christian vocabulary? I have since realised that the name I used for him is unimportant and over-limiting. He is more than any name.

I nowadays have a warrior Goddess I call on when I have need. She comes quickly. To call her I raise my right hand and slap my palm against hers. I visualise her as having her upper arms and shoulders tattooed with deer and horses and as having facial piercings and dreadlocks. She is my warrior partner and we march into battle together. I see her as a manifestation of a particular aspect of Divinity but as nevertheless a person. Today I think of my Lover as one with a galaxy of loving and united Deities who share the work of Creation, who are essentially both one and many. My warrior goddess is also one of them.

Gender distinctions ultimately vanish. I call this Lover Energy either God and Goddess in this book but for me She can also be the Hermaphrodite, for She is me and I am Her and She is both inside and outside me and She has for me as many guises as there are crystals in a flake of snow.

An Aboriginal friend and writer, Kevin Gilbert, wrote that his people believed in the beginning; "the great Creative Essence of Life, the Creator, had filled the land with creative spirits and in a transmorphosis these spirits took on physical shapes and became the progenitors of the modern animals or earthworms we see today." These creative spirits his people knew as their Ancestors.

The Jewish and early Christian Gnostics had to find a way to reconcile a Loving God with a Jehovah who authorised racial pogroms and genocidal wars. They said Jehovah was clearly a lesser jealous God, a demi-urge, who turned a blessed garden into a vale of tears. But I thought there was an easier answer; that much of the Old Testament was written by Hebrew priests who were attempting to justify their people's misdeeds by claiming that they were done on God's orders.

For me, the living symmetry of creation demands and is balanced by a Creating Person, one or more, which also live in a wonderful balance and symmetry. I think it is pure arrogance to presume that we are intelligent and purposeful while the creating force is not. For me, this creating force could belong to one or a trinity or even a galaxy of divine persons. They could be emanating from one divine Godhead, or be of equal status, or even exist in a multitude of universes if some theories of modern mathematics are confirmed. Just as we are individuals who can love, the creating energy must also be able to love. My own experience in my cronehood is of divine persons who are big enough to be part of the making of a universe and small enough to want to relate to me.

Some say the history of our universe is the story of unconsciousness becoming conscious and self-aware. In this myth perhaps we are the brain-cells that help make the universe self-aware. Carl Jung in his later writings spoke of life as a process in which unconscious knowledge, accumulated over millions of years of evolution, becomes conscious in us through dreams and visions. I was enriched by such an internal process, but I think the hand of the architect so visible in our world is not that of an awakening giant who only now is becoming self-aware, nor that of an architect living apart from his creation.

For me the dynamism of our universe, within us and around us, has a purpose greater than achieving consciousness. We are a creation that needs love for its completion. We find our completion in knowing our creator as our lover. We are part of a creation that is uniting in love with its creator.

Lessons in modern Witchcraft. 1. Meditation and Imagination

A vital part of our weekly ritual was a quiet "path-working" period when we meditated. This provided a space where the Gods or Goddesses could talk to us. Many covens have this practice. Each pathworking commenced with one of us telling a short story in which we travel from the circle, through a gate and then perhaps a forest, to a place where a God or Goddess was waiting for us. After about twenty-thirty minutes of silence we would return to the circle. We would then bless cakes and wine and tell, while sharing this sacred food, what we had each experienced in the pathworking. When we had a particularly wonderful ritual, we might all have similar visions. It was as if our minds swam in a common pool.

We often used the meditative tool developed by Jewish mystics called the Tree of Life or Qabbalah. This depicts divine energy as flowing through spheres from the highest ineffable place to the earth and back again. This has long been used in magical circles. The person leading the pathworking took us through the same imaginary gate and forest but then to a place infused with the energy of a particular sphere or of the path from one sphere to another.

I had long practised meditation. But this was different for it trusted the imagination and encouraged its use. We did not fear it as a source of distraction. Rather it was for us a divine faculty that we could use to travel into other realms, with which we could be creative and with which we could dream stories that came from deep within. I now cannot imagine not trusting my imagination. It is the ship that has taken me into secret worlds. It is the faculty by which the heart and mind see together.

On of the greatest of modern Christian mystics, the monk Thomas Merton blamed the Christian religious institutions for abandoning imagination, symbolism, enchantment and the sacred. He wrote a poem on this called *The Lion*:

All classic shapes have vanished
From alien heavens
Where there are no fabled beasts
No
Friendly histories
And passion has no heraldry.
I have nothing left to
Translate
Into the figures of night
Or the pale geometry
Of the
Firebirds.
If I once had a wagon of lights to ride in,
The axle is
Broken
The horses are shot.

William Butler Yeats expressed a similar sentiment.

The woods of Arcady are dead
And over is their antique joy
Of old the world on dreaming fed.
Grey truth is now her painted toy.

But I thought that there was no need to be so sad. The world of imagination and magic was still alive. Arcady lived. The horses raced the sky. As we create with our imagination, we share in the divine creation. The act of creation was not something that only happened at the beginning. It is always happening. Creation is the sustaining energy of our earth. When we create a painting, a book, a poem, a machine, a building, then we are putting our energy into the divine creation. That is why it is good if acts of creation are infused with love.

For we can also create badly, poorly, with ill will or hatred, and when we do, our universe suffers. We can create demons that haunt us. But how can we complain? We do not want to lose our creativity for without it we are not truly human. Being human carries a terrible responsibility.

I do not think our world is doomed because of our mistakes. I see Nature as very capable of creating the children she needs. I see this happening. I also think that the Creatrix gives us parts to play in previously devised myths that help shape our lives and history and give us much delight, but more about this later.

Imagination is for me a wonderful transforming delightful faculty. It gave many tools to our early bards, poets, mystics and shamans. One of these was shape shifting. The Gaelic visionary bards and poets talked of experiencing life as salmon, hawks and stags. This arose because, bonded with nature, we are one with all that is, was and will be. We live in a cobweb in which all creatures are woven.

This oneness with nature was used for protection. The Scots did this through a chant called a "fith-fath" (pronounced "fee fawh") involving shape shifting. An example is:

A magic cloud I put on thee,
From dog, from cat,
From cow, from horse,
From man, from maid
And from this little child,
Till I return again.[358]

2. Familiar animals and Shape-shifting

The Celtic bard, druid or witch (The word "Druid" in its Irish root includes all magic users.) might ask other creatures for help, such as a hawk for insight or for sharp eyes to find the missing. They identified with other creatures and practiced seeing through their eyes. As for myself, I once sang:

> I am Dragonfly, and Lioness, but they are not I,
> I am Dragon and the White Horse running the Sky
> I am the Mare of Night, guardian of the gate.
> I am the Enchantress
> Weaving with the music
> Of Earth, Sea, Air and Fire.
> Making the cloth of the Universe.
> I am the Flame, the Wind and the Storm
> I am the glistening drop on a twig
> I am a Jewel of the People of the West.

Aboriginal clans have totemic creatures. An Aboriginal camping ground in Central Australia might look as if the family camps are pitched at random. But from above, as previously mentioned, you would see that the various camps are set on the pattern of the footprint of their totem; thus if their totem is the emu, there might be one camp on each claw. In Alice Springs an Aboriginal housing estate has been built on a totemic footprint pattern (despite opposition from the town council).

When the police shot dogs in an Aboriginal camp, saying it had too many dogs; elders told them their action had made children ill. They then learnt this clan had the dog as its totem and thus could not kill a dog without damaging its health. The elders invited a leading police officer to spend time with them learning about "dog dreaming". After this the police stopped threatening to kill dogs and instead provided veterinary services.

Animals evolved along with us. If we cannot speak to them, listen to them, then how will we ever cope with aliens from other planets? One modern theory of evolution has humans co-evolving with dogs. In this the dogs helped shape us, making us develop talents they needed while we dropped talents that dogs provided for us such as a keen nose and protective claws and teeth. When my dog licks me in the morning, enjoying the salt on my skin, even my skin seems to assist in this dog human bonding.

All the indigenous cultures seem to honour the essential link between humans and the rest of creation. The ancient cultures of the British Isles and Eire did so, just as did the Aboriginal. For me, if our bodies remember in our embryonic youth that we were fish millions of years ago by briefly growing gills; if our bodies remember in the womb that we were animals with tails by briefly growing tails then losing them; then the old Celtic wisdom that we retain memories of being these creatures is not so very strange.

We would also invoke the elements in our rituals. This practice is not unique to modern paganism. It is part of a common Pagan and Christian heritage. One of the rediscovered 1,800-year-old gnostic Christian texts, *The Gospel according to Philip*, describes the four elements of earth, water, air and light:

> Farming in the world requires the co-operation of four essential elements. A harvest is gathered into the barn only as a result of the natural action of water, earth, wind and light. God's farming likewise has four elements; faith, hope, love, and knowledge.
>
> Faith is our earth in which we take root. Hope is the water through which we are nourished. Love is the wind through which we grow. Knowledge, then, is the light through which we ripen...
>
> It is from water and fire that the soul and the spirit came into being. It is from water and fire and light that the son of the bridal chamber (came into being). The fire is the chrism; the light is the fire. I am not referring to that fire which has no form, but to the other fire whose form is white, which is bright and beautiful, and which gives beauty.

Most Craft circles today invoke fire instead of light but both are aspects of the sun. The text also revealed that the "bridal chamber", or mystic marriage, was as much part of the gnostic teachings of Christ as it was of the Hebrew Wisdom literature and the initiatory tradition of Greece.

I define the human Craft at its core as
Oneness with divinity,
Oneness between nature and divinity,
Oneness between nature and us
Thus a triple oneness, of human, nature and deity,
This is the source of all magic,
Love is not all that is, it is simple "is".

3. The tools of the Craft

The Craft uses tools as a focus on which we can centre our energy. In the Wiccan path these include such ceremonial tools as knives called athames, brooms and even jewelled swords. These are not in the least bit essential but have useful symbolism and have been around for a long time. Most of the Wiccan tools were described by Agrippa in a Renaissance book about magic.

The broomstick is an ordinary part of any household, and for some a symbol of female power. The wise woman might use it to keep her space clear, to keep out dirt and bad magic. It is a symbol for her power over the dirt of life. She may use it sometimes as a focus for her magical energy and thus to "fly". It is used today symbolically both to cleanse the space to be used for a sacred circle and also as a symbolic "fairy" gate into a new life. Thus handfasted couples may jump together over a broomstick to symbolise their entry into a new life together.

But in one pathworking or meditation, I found myself led by the stag, Herne, deep into a wood until we came across an open and somewhat muddy area. Here Herne nosed at a stick lying upon the ground and I was given to understand that this was my appropriate wand. Through it I would join myself to the power of the wood surrounding me. He then indicated a pool of water in a forked tree trunk. There was my water for blessing and scrying. Finally he pawed at the muddy earth. This was to be my Pentacle, my Earth, and the source of my magic. In this vision there was no tool to symbolise fire, perhaps because we bring into rituals our own energy or "fire"? Fire also can be symbolised simply with our hand, although I have also used a flint, a flame a metal knife or arrow. Since then, when working a ritual in a forest, I seek the piece of wood that will link me best with the energy of that forest. Likewise, when I invoke earth, I will kneel, kiss the earth and pick up a handful of earth or a particular rock to honour within the circle. Sometimes we pass the earth from one another welcoming it with kisses.

Some covens call themselves Gardnarian or Alexandrian after two men who had a great influence in expanding the modern Craft. A founder of my first magical group had trained and initiated in all the degrees of the Gardnarian tradition of the Craft, but then went his own way after a disagreement over magic. I was thus a little apprehensive when first invited to meetings of other covens, but to my delight I met with acceptance and found many with which I shared a common magic. It seemed that in the forest that is the Craft, many covens naturally grow in similar ways.

When Gardner practiced the Craft, it honoured women but had not rid itself of all aspects of the patriarchal society that surrounded it. Thus this version of the Craft was named after leading male practitioners rather than the women involved, such as Doreen Valiente who composed many of its most loved invocations. It was also called Wicca; a word ironically meaning "male witch", "wicce" being the word for female witch.

Not all covens shared the flexibility of the coven I first joined. Some had frozen rituals into one format that never changed. They would repeat their loved words and rituals, putting their energy into the same forms, charging these with their magic. This was reinforced when books were subsequently published with titles such as *The Witches Bible*. This perhaps was a change from the original intention and practice of the founders of

Wicca. I have been told they hoped their rituals would inspire others to create rituals.

I had quit a Christian priesthood tradition with a lineage going back the greater part of two millennia, so I was not too impressed when I heard of some Wiccans who boasted on a "lineage" going back thirty years to Gardner. I could understand and appreciate why they might wish to honour their teachers, but I could not see how such boasting would benefit the craft. I thought Gardner would have been horrified at this practice. The proudest lineage any witch can have is to Mother Earth.

In 1999 I visited a witch who traded gypsy ponies. He told me how Gerald Gardner initiated him into the Craft when he was but a teenager. He had an out-of-body experience when helping Gardner at the Museum of Witchcraft on the Isle of Man. When he recovered, he found Gardner was there for him, supporting and looking after him. Afterwards Gardner suggested that perhaps this experience meant that he needed what the Craft could give him. With his agreement, Gardner took him by the hands and led him through a simple rite of dedication as his First Degree initiation. This rite had none of the trappings of binding, blindfolding or of swords (as depicted in Hollywood movies and as done in many Wiccan covens). He then went through the other initiations with a priestess who worked with Gardner, but he never called himself a Gardnarian witch but simply a "muddy seated witch". He emphatically told me that Gardner did not want anyone to exactly copy him, rather to share with others and empower them

Another aspect of the emerging modern Craft was the teaching of the "threefold law." This is that if one does harmful magic, the harm will be returned to you threefold. This is sometimes taught in a way that motivates solely through fear of punishment, an ethic I had rejected as a child. Doreen Valiente stated that this was not an old law but was written in her time. It may however be good 'headology". It can deter people from doing harm. But a sounder basis for Craft ethics lies in the witch and mystic belief that we are one with all around us; thus, if we hurt others (including the plants and animals) then we are hurting someone bonded to us, part of our own family—and thus hurting ourselves.

4. Sexuality and Ecstasy

Another "in-between" aspect of the emerging Craft was the idea of some that the Third Degree initiation was best done between a priest and priestess, as it was a celebration of fertility. But fertility in nature is not limited to heterosexual means! Ask the trees! But all forms of this ritual, whether performed alone or with a partner of either gender, symbolise, celebrate and realise the union between the human and deity. This is the source of our spiritual fertility. It can be equally expressed by gay or straight love. Most covens today celebrate all aspects of love.

Although many ancient religions celebrated human sexuality, they sometimes sought a perfection they called "virginity". This was the very opposite of being non-creative. It did not involve the giving up of sex. They taught we must learn to be creative of ourselves like the ultimate Creatrix who did not need male seed to give birth. We do this by uniting two aspects of ourselves, the anima and animus, the female and the male, and becoming one. This was for them the virginal path of perfection.

The Catholic Benedictine monk Bede Griffiths wrote, after visiting Hindu shrines with carved female and male genital images; that Christians could learn from a religion that saw sexuality as divine. "For the Hindu, sex is essentially holy. It is a manifestation of the divine life and is to be worshipped like any other form of the divinity."[359] For me it was a shame that he had to go to the East to discover this when it was in our ancient European sacred inheritance, perhaps especially symbolised in our Sheila-na-gigs.

According to hostile Christian sources, the Eleusian Mysteries had at their heart a ritual coupling of the high priest and priestess. Bishop Asterius of Amaseia alleged that during 'the descent into darkness" there took place "'the venerated congress of the Heirophant and the Priestess, of him alone with her alone" and that the initiates regarded what was done "by the two in the darkness is their salvation."³⁶⁰ The bishop was repulsed by such alleged sacred celebration of human sexuality.

What really happened was sealed in secrecy, but the few published comments by participants talk of a sacred drama enacted in near darkness in which the Goddess of Spring was called from the underworld of winter. The initiates experienced symbolically death during the winter darkness, their own rebirth in spring, and their unity with the Deities through sacred food. The rite concluded with the rebirth of the divine son, seen symbolically as a head of wheat.

In India, as in the ancient book of the *Kama Sutra*, human sexuality in all its forms is celebrated as a sign of the union of the Goddess and the God, and as a way to grow closer to the Deities. Hildergard of Bingen wrote: "It is the power of eternity itself that has created physical union and decreed that two human beings should become physically one."

In the Craft a couple may privately and ritually celebrate a sexual union as a symbol of their bonding with the Deity. In the broader sense, it is a symbolic celebration of the union of divinity with humanity. The woman is the Goddess or the Sacred Earth. The man is the male God joining with the female Earth.

In the Renaissance, alchemists celebrated this same union as a process that might produce the "gold" of alchemic transformation, lifting the couple to divine ecstasy. At their climax, the lovers know for a moment what it is to be bonded into one being, to be beyond male and female, to be the Deity beyond gender, perhaps to know what it is to be the Sacred Hermaphrodite.

In the Alchemic text *The Crowne of Nature* the alchemic couple: are "wrapped in each other's arms in the bliss of connubial union, they merge and dissolve as they come to the goal of perfection. They that are two are made one, as though of one body."³⁶¹ An early alchemic school founded by "Maria the Jewess", wrote: "see the fulfilment of the art in the joining

together of the bride and the bridegroom and in their becoming one."[362]
Such old alchemic knowledge was passed on through Renaissance secret
societies to the groups that revived magical practices in the 19th century,
such as the Order of Templars of the Orient (OTO) and Golden Dawn,
and then to the modern Craft.

The Secret Societies and Alchemy

Did those who knew themselves in danger during the witchhunts try to
protect themselves? Reportedly they did—it would be strange if they did not.
Some of those killed as witches were accused of plotting to overthrow the
monarch. Montague Summers in his 1928 Foreword to his translation of
Malleus Maleficorum stated that Bodin, an infamous Protestant Lawyer and
French Assembly member, claimed that the witches "were, in fact, the active
members of a vast revolutionary body, a conspiracy against civilisation."

This is no doubt a paranoid overstatement, but it is hard to imagine
that people did not try to protect themselves. The suspects often included
independent people engaged in spiritual healing, midwifery or in magic,
who must have been very aware of their danger. They were by no means all
illiterate. Many were upper class with connections and political influence.
Some were condemned for challenging men who held authority. Many
would have escaped danger and need sheltering. Since the persecution was
Europe wide, so presumably was their self-support and resistance network.

During the Renaissance period, when many female witches were burnt
or hung, men who loved magic organised secret societies to minimalise
their danger. Some women joined these societies, Vivienne Crowley told
me, but their names are rarely found. These men wrote books on magic
but few were persecuted. They may have been protected by having friends
in the nobility. Their societies were inspired by early pagan gnostic literature, including the *Corpus Hermeticum*, or *Works of Hermes*, obtained in
1450 by the nobleman Cosimo de'Medici. Some invoked archangels to

protect their ritual space, as also did the first magic group I joined. Pico Della Mirandola helped to re-introduce the Jewish Qabbalah. We too used it. Their rites were sometimes known as High Ceremonial Magic. But we had no such pretence. We simply said we were doing magic.

The well-connected German Cornelius Agrippa published his extraordinary *De Occulta Philosophia* in 1531. It taught that magic was based on natural psychic gifts and not on demons. His drawings showed a magical circle protected by pentagrams at the quarters, much as many groups set up their circles today. We did so in my first circle. His book *On the Nobility and Superiority of Women* argued for gender equality and for women to be ordained to the priesthood. He held that women should be venerated by men for reflecting the beauty of God. He held that menstrual blood had a unique ability to rejuvenate and bestow wisdom. He was eventually banned from Germany but escaped the death that was the fate of others with vastly less magical knowledge.

The secret society known as the Family of Love had over a thousand members in 1580. Some societies mixed magic with aspects of Christianity and Paganism. Thus were formed the societies of the Rosicrucians, the Freemasons and the Illuminati. The alchemist John Dee was a member and despite this, although once imprisoned as a magician, became highly influential at court. His personal library was said to be better than that of the University of Oxford. As a mathematician, he made the first translation into English of Euclid. He was an advisor to Queen Elizabeth, suggested to her the most auspicious date for her coronation and was her secret envoy to European courts. At that time the French Court was experimenting with the Eleusian Greek Initiatory Mysteries. Some groups created or treasured Grimoires, such as the *Two Keys of Solomon*, which were later to influence Gerald Gardner.

There was never a time when magic and science were so united as during the Renaissance. Scientists such as Isaac Newton were deeply involved in alchemy and were members of magical societies. But that is not so today (with the notable exception of Jungian psychoanalysis). Our post-Rationalist world still suffers from a presumption that came in with rationalist ideology. This was that if we do not understand how something could work, it couldn't happen.

Yet many testify to phenomena not yet understood by science. A personal example: While walking along a wild part of the Welsh coastline, the thought came that a certain friend was about to phone me. I switched on my mobile phone and then thought, "It will ring within 20 seconds". I laughed at my own presumption. For fun I counted to 20, and it rang. In Bristol 150 miles away my friend had just come home. He had walked in the door and suddenly thought he must phone me. It was the first time he had tried to phone me that day and my phone had been switched off until that time. Such events are now a frequent part of my life, the more so since I started to attend to instincts more closely. For me there is no conflict between magic and science. Both work experimentally. Both are techniques for understanding the same natural world

The word "alchemy" may derive from Al Khymia, an old name for Egypt. It teaches that spiritual processes are reflected in nature and thus embraces both chemistry and mysticism. The poem *Hermaphrodite Child of Sun and Moon* depicted alchemy as a process whereby opposites are joined together, including male and female, to achieve the "gold" of spiritual perfection. The following is an extract:

Alchemy
Turns the swan into a
Salamander abruptly.
She feasts on heat
And lives in flames,
Blood-Red in colour,
Nourished by the glowing embers:
Those who bow to her rule,
(Like the Pelican
Who gives all to his young):

Will see the Salamander
Develop their Strength and Virtue,
But she only appears to those who
Understand seven stars:
She opens up the seven gates for us.

My species gives me a grey belly,
But I'm neither male nor female.
Rather, I have both genders.
My flesh and blood proves it.
My blood is male, my flesh female.
The power of both is spiritual.
I have both male and female organs.
So people call me a hermaphrodite.

My treasure is the Earth Element
Where there are minerals, metals, and such.
Yet I'm nothing that you may suppose.
I am One Substance by my nature.
In my metal form I am simultaneously
Hot and cold, wet and dry.
Just One Thing under the Sun
Its Possession is the secret of making Gold.
Its form is both male and female.
Its nature is both hot and cold.
Its nutrients pour out,
Its male part, solid,
Its female part, liquid.
Its unity makes it the beginning and the end.
Its state changes from male to female:
Dissolving, putrefying, purifying, coagulating,
Until the golden Child appears.

Its milk feeds the Child anew,
And lets you immediately repeat the Work,
Until everything flows and penetrates.
Then fine gold accumulates,
Its Spiritual Body turns acid.
Its Colours have to be made ready for the Work:
But be righteous and guard against sins,
And God will grant you this treasure:
Its colour will eventually turn red,
And then remember to thank the Lord.

The Jewish Qabbalah was reinterpreted in the light of alchemy. The pillars of Severity and Mercy support the Spheres. They became emblems of Freemasonry under the names of Jachin and Boaz. They were said to be the two pillars in front of Solomon's Temple. They signified the unity required for contemplation in their union in the temple. Between them the column of Harmony or Beauty balanced their energies. It was crowned with the highest Sphere, Kether, the first emanation from the Godhead.

Howard. Francis Thynne, 1543-1608, the Lancaster Herald, wrote of the Qabbalah as "the most profound knowledge" and of John Dee as "the learned Quabalist". The Society of the Rosie Cross (the Rosicrucians) may have influenced Shakespeare. His play *Midsummer's Nights Dream* started where a Rosicrucian play *The two Kinsmen* finished.

In 1598 the French historian, President de Thon, noted that Beumont, a man sentenced for magical practices: " held commerce with aerial and heavenly spirits" and confessed that "schools and professions of this noble art had been frequent in all parts of the world and still were in Spain, Toledo, Cardona, Grenada and other places; that they had also been very celebrated in Germany but here for the most part failed since Luther had sowed the seeds of his heresy...That in France and England it was still secretly preserved as it were by tradition in the families of certain gentlemen so only the initiated were admitted into the sacred rites." Beumont also claimed that John Dee had at Hallow E'en (Halloween) 1590 "entered the circle for necromantic spells".[363]

Freemasonry at first admitted a few women, but excluded them from early in the 18th century. The Rosicrucians were more gender balanced, but from their work it seemed to me that male interests and approaches dominated. I found it full of hierarchical ranks and to exalt reason over emotion. It had little of the sparkle and spirit of the Beguine women mystics. Gerald Gardner mixed with members of the Rosicrucian Theatre in the New Forest in the first days of what became the revival of the modern Craft. But I do not know what if any Rosicrucian influence there was in his work. The rituals we use today seem to breathe a freer and much more female friendly air.

Initiation and the Sacred Marriage

For me initiation essentially happens between the individual and the God and Goddess. The others in the Circle are best man, best woman, magical aides, givers and protectors of magical energy, facilitators, witnesses and friends, but not the chief players in this ritual. I will not speak here of how others do these rites in our private circles For us they are "copyright", private to those who compose the rituals and perform them. Our circles are safe spaces where we support each other, places for intimacy and trust. What I can share is what I myself have created.

My Third Degree Initiation, or "Great Rite" as it is known in the Craft, was utterly transforming, something I will never forget. Every such ritual is very personal. Its experience is different for every initiate.

It was a rite in which I became one with both the Goddess and the God. I did this without a sexual human partner, as others sometimes have, simply because I had none at the time and needed none. I chose in my rite to reach directly to my Lover God. This was my way, our way. In this bonding was the heart of my magic. It had been so since I was a child.

Now as an adult, verging on cronehood, I was ready to celebrate its mysteries as I had never before.

I had need for the gender bonding aspects of this ritual. I am a woman who needed the male for completion. I believed my spirit had been born single gendered despite being gifted a body that had features of both genders. For me, my self-identity was beyond explanation. I had come to accept it was as much part of me as was the colour of my eyes. A Jungian might say that in this ritual I was bonding my anima and animus aspects, but this would miss out all the mystery and much else. I was celebrating my long-standing bond with my dearest Lover God, once a secret passion, now an open passion and an empowering thrilling ecstasy.

The ritual preparation started at the Winter Solstice rite when I was asked to be one of those calling down the Sun-child so the Sun could be reborn. To my surprise, while doing this, something most unusual seemed to happen to me. There seemed to be within me a room filled with white light. Into this came a spiralling brilliant energy in the shape of the figure eight. I did not understand this for several days but remained aware of this presence within me. It felt if it were alien, apart from me. Then, suddenly I realised that this was another life. It was as if I were pregnant of this light form. Then I recognised the form. It was an infinity symbol. It was God himself. For the next few months I continued to be awed by His presence within me. Honouring His presence became the heart of my preparations for my initiation.

I had picked for it Imbulc, February 2nd, as it was the feast of the Mother Goddess Bride. Imbulc meant the arrival of the Ewe's milk, the first sign of spring. It also celebrated in Scotland the snake's awakening from hibernation. The snake was a symbol of everlasting life. Imbulc is also the day when our ancestors asked Bride as Sun Goddess to give them sacred fire to warm the spring. Her ancient fire festival has become translated into Christianity as Candlemas. From before all records a school of dedicated women in Kildare kept a ceremonial fire continuously burning in Her honour until agents of King Henry VIII extinguished it. A few years ago it was happily relit and is now tended by nuns who call her "St Bridget."

I was told me that I should write my own initiation ritual so that it celebrated my gender path. I took the old forms of the ritual, reworked these, and then had it agreed to by those who were at the heart of our Circle. It included a formal thanking of the God for sharing with me the male mysteries and a thanking of the Goddess for bringing me home to live among my sisters as a woman and priestess. I was closing this circle, acknowledging that both anima and animus had played a powerful role in me, celebrating the gift of experiencing life between both genders.

I would also honour my bisexuality. I would honour the bonding of woman to woman by pouring wine from one chalice into another. I then would celebrate the joining of male with female by dipping a consecrated hunting arrow into a chalice. I would then exchange wedding vows with the God and Goddess. Here is a part, just part, of my ritual:

After the purifying and setting up of the circle.
As water is poured into the Cup.
Brighid on this your Day…
We consecrate this Cup
So it may hold the Water of Life
And be a symbol of the Mother's Womb.
May this serve to keep Jani
In the company of the Mother.
R. / So may it be.

Over the Bow and Arrow. *(Used instead of an Athame or sacred knife, as Brighid's name is translated as "Bright Arrow" and because these were my sacred tools.) The Arrow and Bow were laid on top of the Chalice (not dipped into it) and then held up vertically.*
Brighid, on this your day,
We consecrate these instruments of power.

We imbue them with all our passion and our strength
We bind to them all the powers of Fire.
We bind to them all the powers of Love.
May they serve to keep us in the presence of the Sun God and Goddess.
R. / So may it be.

After the calling of the God and Goddess into her, Jani then says...
"I who am the beauty of the Green Earth and the silver moon among the stars and the mystery of waters and the desire of the heart of all, call upon you. Arise, come unto me.

"For I am the soul of nature, who gives life to the universe. From me all things proceed and all things must return. Before me let thine innermost divine self be enfolded in the rapture of the infinite. Let my worship be within the heart that rejoiceth; for behold all acts of love and of joy are my rituals. And therefore let there be beauty and strength, power and compassion, honour and humility, mirth and reverence within you. For behold, I am with you, within you. You need not look elsewhere.

"Tonight we celebrate the feast of the waxing light, The Child Sun grows stronger as the days grow longer. It is the time of initiation, when the seeds stir in their dark sleep.

(All then spiral dance for Brighid...chanting. weaving and kissing...
Fire of the heart, *Chorus with each line...*She shines for all...she burns for all...
Fire of the mind,
Fire of the Art,
Fire beyond time...
After nine spirals we stop...
Jani standing in front of the Altar takes up the Cup and the Arrow and turns towards the members of the Circle.
I thank you for being with me this day, I thank you for your energy and love, May you all be ever one with the Goddess and God. And in thanks
She takes up her cord and it is tied around her wrists saying

I give myself to the service of the Goddess and the God and bind me.

She places a ring on her wedding finger saying…

With this ring, I wed myself to the God and Goddess. I am they and they are I.

She sits on the edge of the Altar, arrow and rod crossed over her breasts, and is given two chalices of wine. She pours wine from one into the other.

As wine is to the cup, so too is love of woman to a woman. When joined they can bring blessed ecstasy and wisdom.

Jani lowers the point of the arrow into the cup and says.

As the blade is to the male, so is the cup to the female. When joined they can bring a completion, blessed fire and fertility.

I who was born a woman able to experience life in both genders.

Thank the Goddess and God for their gift…

I, a woman, knew the plough, the phallus and the heat of the giving of the seed. And give thanks for the great gift of living within the God.

I honour the God who shared with me his way of loving.

I give thanks to the God that made me his priest

So I might know his magic.

I thank too the Goddess who in due time came to reclaim me, to slip me back into a female body, to bring me home to be her priestess.

Jani takes the cup…

I choose the cup, the womb of life. I bring my female spirit to its true home.

Jani exchanges the cup for the arrow…

I choose also the arrow so that never more will I be closed to loving life.

She holds the arrow to her.

I thank the Goddess and God from bringing me to this your sacred priesthood as a sacred sacrifice, I offer you myself, whole, in heart, body and spirit."

More followed. Then in the meditation, I had an extraordinary experience. I was wearing a snake shaped bracelet as I had for some twenty years.

The snake symbolised for me the never-ending cycle of life as it did for Aborigines, Egyptians and many of the ancients.

Suddenly the snake seemed to wriggle, grow, turn into a great python, and plunge its head into my astonished mouth. The sexual implication was obvious. My reaction was somewhat amused. I muttered to myself "but I am not into oral sex!" But it did not stay in my mouth; it plunged on, deep inside me, getting to know my stomach, heart, all my organs.

It seemed that it was taking possession of me. I though wryly of how some Christians would interpret this. They might think the snake was the devil coming to take possession of me! But I knew this was wrong. The Serpent symbolised other things to me. It symbolised the power of God come into me.

I then found myself walking alongside with this giant python as it went down into a deep dark cavern. I wondered where it was taking me. It was large and powerful and felt very male. I enjoyed walking beside it, and then we came out into what seemed to be a temple. At the far end on a dais stood two beings and I realised that the snake had taken me to meet with the God and Goddess.

I stood before them and simply said; "I am here now. What is my work to be?"

Then suddenly I was in the birthing cave at Uluru, attended by Aboriginal women and giving birth to a son. My final vision was of myself sitting like Virgin Mary with a manchild in my lap, presenting him to the world. I was very surprised, intrigued, perplexed. The vision seemed to be an answer to my query about my role but I scarcely understood it. A similar statue was over the altar in the seminary where I trained to be a priest.

I puzzled over it. Why such a Marian image? Such a Christian icon? I had not thought of her as my model. Was there something deeper here than I had thought? How could my work be to show the world the divine child? Why was it a boy child?

But if I put the question to instincts and inner voices, the answer came that if I lived true, I must be a Mother who shows to all the teacher-child that she has birthed, the promise of new life, a new life that was a God, a God that would grow up and then die for the people, for the ancients a cycle that would be repeated again and again while the Mother sustained the continuity of the people and of the world. It seemed that I had to live a very ancient myth. I have never been one for consciously re-living myths. But perhaps I had no choice.

I researched and found this image had a long history. The Neolithic inhabitants of Crete had an image of a Deity with both genders, depicted as a woman with horns. In the subsequent Cretan Minoan period the gender energies separated and the image became that of a Mother Goddess with the God as born of her and still dependent on her, thus as a boy sitting in her lap.[364] Likewise as women we must create and honour our male aspect; a lesson especially for me since I had seemingly rejected this aspect.

When the members of our circle shared what we had individually experienced during this mediation or pathworking, we found that we had all seen snakes even though snakes had not been mentioned beforehand. One saw me as Medusa with my hair all snakes. We finally completed the ritual with a grounding exercise. Everyone painted me! I was covered in trees and serpents and flowers to the accompaniment of much laughter. It grounded me. It is always important when working magically to ground oneself afterwards, perhaps simply by placing one's hands on the ground and wiggling fingers into the grass. Otherwise this energy can become uncontrolled once we have stopped consciously directing it. Aboriginal elders also believe in the importance of grounding at the end of rituals.

The linking of serpents with the devil in Christian mythology perhaps came originally from a Jewish attack on the magical and spiritual symbolism of Egypt. Moses said: "He made the devil a serpent <for> those whom he has in his generation." Snake symbols were everywhere in Egypt. They symbolised in the shedding of their skin the renewal of the earth. There were two hieroglyphics for Goddess in Egyptian. One was an egg, the other a cobra. The Gnostic Christians pointed out the Bible's ambiguity on serpents, quoting snake-friendly texts such as; "It is written thus:…the rod in the hand of Moses became a serpent, It swallowed the serpents of the magicians." And "He made a serpent of bronze (and) hung it upon a pole…for the one who will gaze upon this bronze serpent, none will destroy him, and the one who will believe in this bronze serpent will be saved."[365] The symbol of medicine remains a snake wound around a staff. It stood for Asclepius, the Greek God of healing. In Thessaly 7000 years ago the enthroned goddess was shown holding a child and with snakes around her,[366] an image very similar to my vision.

For me all creatures are holy and thus I honour the serpent. It is an act of the greatest ignorance to demonise any creature. It leads to much cruelty. Snakes were held to be sacred by many races. Somewhere deep in the human psyche, there seems to be an archetype of a primitive snake. Some call this the Kundalini,[367] a power rising from our loins through our body to eventually breathe fire from the top of our skull. It is called the dragon energy of the earth.

My circle was much influenced by Egyptian magic. I often saw myself while meditating as a raven flying from the sacred chambers of pyramids to the sacred caves of Uluru in the centre of Australia, where lies the pool of water that serves as a home to the Rainbow Serpent. One day when I arrived, I saw myself as lying on the desert earth, merging with the earth, becoming the earth and giving birth to many creatures.

As for the wonder of my initiation experience, of seeing myself as pregnant with the Divine Child and giving birth to Him, I do not see being pregnant with God as the unique privilege of Mary, nor see being the Child of God the unique privilege of Jesus. It is not even a unique privilege of humans. It was and is the divine right of every particle of creation, of this universe and universes beyond. Every part of creation is pregnant with God and every particle is a child of God.

Every tree, every insect, every being, is giving birth to part of the divine plan. We are all part of the outcome. We are the Child born of the divine plan, we are both the child of Divinity and pregnant with Divinity. We are part of a symphony of beauty and ecstasy.

The ancient Greek Eleusian rite celebrated the birth of the divine child, depicted Him as an ear of wheat. His birth represented the renewed fertility of our sacred Earth. It was an initiation into a vision. Towards the end of the ritual, when sacred objects were revealed, there was an explosion of light and the proclamation, "the great goddess has borne a sacred child". At this point " a single ear of corn is held up." Finally, after the sacrifice of a bull, water was poured upon the earth with all present crying out to the heavens "Rain ", then to the earth "Conceive."

Aeschylus had Aphrodite say: "The pure Sky longs passionately to pierce the earth and seizes the Earth to win her in marriage. The rain falling from the Bridegroom Sky makes the Earth pregnant. The earth gives birth for mortals to pastures filled with flocks and corn, Demeter's gift. The fruitfulness of trees is brought to completion by the dew of their marriage. Of these things am I part cause."[368]

The experience of being pregnant with God is part of a mystical tradition thousands of years old and worldwide. Porete spoke in 12th Century France of being pregnant with God. She wrote: "He is fullness, and by this am I impregnated. This is the divine seed and Loyal Love." This was so female an understanding that the Church could not stomach it. It was given as a reason for burning her at the stake in 1310. Julian of Norwich wrote how she saw herself as pregnant with God's Word. For her "God" had both genders as had the Virgin Goddess of old. She wrote of the motherhood of God, in a manuscript now held at Westminster Abbey.

In the vision that accompanied my Initiation, I gave birth without the need for another parent. Again this is a concept from deep within. The primal creating energy gives birth of itself without the need of a partner. The Goddess Innana over 5000 years ago was called the "Virgin Mother of Earth and Heaven". According to the wisdom of ancient times, Virgin Mother was a title only possessed by divinity.

The *Apocalypse of Adam* is one of the most ancient and beautiful of the Gnostic texts and probably pre-Christian. It predicted that the One who is to come will be born of a Virgin and grow up in the wilderness. Here are some excerpts:

"And the sixth kingdom says that [the Virgin went...] down to the world below in order to gather flowers. She became pregnant from the desire of the flowers. She gave birth to him in that place. The angels of the flower garden nourished him. He received glory there, and power. And thus he came to the water.

"And the seventh kingdom says of him that he is a drop. It came from heaven to earth. Dragons brought him down to caves. He became a child. A spirit came upon him and brought him on high to the place where the drop had come forth. He received glory and power there. And thus he came to the water.

"And the eighth kingdom says of him that a cloud came upon the earth and enveloped a rock. He came from it. The angels who were above the cloud nourished him. He received glory and power there. And thus he came to the water.

"And the ninth kingdom says of him that one of the nine Muses separated herself. She came to a high mountain and spent time seated there, so that she desired herself alone in order to become male-female. She fulfilled her desire and became pregnant from her desire. He was born. The angels who were over the desire nourished him. And he received glory there, and power. And thus he came to the water."

The Magic of a Warrior

Nowadays I both work in a coven and in investigative journalism. After recovering from the assault, I went to investigate the human rights conditions in the diamond mines of Southern Africa. I will never forget the defiant dances the workers put on for me in the mining compounds. Nor will I forget addressing and answering questions in a meeting of seven hundred workers that lasted over three hours inside another diamond mine. Nor can I forget that many diamonds are found in asbestos rock and sit in thick asbestos dust within the mines, making the practically unprotected miners very susceptible to a crippling and deadly disease.

Nor will I forget the children I saw in India working in debt bondage, a form of slavery, cutting the world's diamonds in what India lists as a hazardous industry, in dingy workshops coated with black diamond dust. In the year 2001, the wages paid to them for cutting and polishing a diamond were cut from an average of US 40c to just 25c, giving them an income after deductions of just a dollar a day.

When I went to Northern Canada to speak about my diamond film, I was grateful to De Beers for trying to stop it being seen there, and to the environmentalists who then invited me to speak. It gave me the chance to hear the chimes of the ice crystals clashing when floes drift; to see the night skies sparkling with a milliard stars and washed with showers of rainbow colours; to experience an Dene dog sleigh ride over sparkling ice and to eat hundreds of the berries that are exposed when the snow melts to feed the awakening bears.

In 2001 it also gave me the chance to officially testify in the US Congress on the De Beers link to conflict diamonds and on human rights in Africa. I found this unsettling for it brought back the fears I faced for years while investigating the diamond cartel. Yet, such fears have to be faced. As I conclude this book I am still working on human rights issues relating to the diamond trade.[369]

While working on this most international of issues, I was also concentrating on the microscopic—on the world of the virus within us, writing about it as a medical journalist. This inner world is as rich as any rain forest. Its snakes and tigers are viruses and bacteria. While all live in harmony, all can happily co-exist and do within us but sometimes this harmony is disturbed.

I came to know Jackie Fletcher, her husband John and their son Robert, in a village where also lived my brother Tony who had introduced us. As Jackie minded Robert, she told me how he had first started having fits and showing signs of brain damage very soon after an MMR[370] injection. When she took him to the hospital, they told her that the relationship between the vaccination and the onset of illness could only be co-incidental. A little later she spoke to the other parent in the waiting room, to find to her surprise that she had been told the same. Jackie then organised a public meeting through a local health centre, and 150 people turned up. After this she met very many parents whose children had "co-incidentally" fallen gravely ill immediately after vaccination.

I researched and found many similar cases. I then phoned Professor Michael Stewart, the top vaccination expert at London University's School of Hygiene and Tropical Medicine, and told him of the reports of these parents. His response was totally unexpected and shocking. He said: "What else do you expect? You are injecting a living virus. Why do you think I head up a team of immunologists? We are trying to make the vaccines safer because we know the current ones are dangerous."

I was left wondering about the possible relationship between vaccination with living viruses and the recent great increase in autoimmune diseases in children and adults. Could they come from injected multi-doses of attenuated viruses? Most viruses have co-existed with humans for ages, just as other potentially dangerous creatures have co-existed with us for millennia in the wild. We do not exterminate the snakes in the jungle because they occasionally do damage. They are part of the balance of the wild. Many viruses may sometimes help us or make us ill. Thus adults who had measles as a child have a better immune system as adults, according to peer-reviewed Danish research, as well as give us lifetime immunity to measles, something no vaccine can currently give us.

I was soon writing front-page stories on the risks of vaccination for the British newspapers, *The Independent* and the *Independent on Sunday*. A year later I co-produced an investigative television documentary *Monkey Business* for Dispatches on Channel 4. This told how a monkey virus was injected into hundreds of millions of children after the polio vaccine became contaminated with it. At the time all the rodents injected with the vaccine got cancer. Twenty years later the monkey virus appeared in human cancers. Today it is found in a vast number of human cancers. According to leading scientists I met and interviewed, this virus turns off a key human gene known as p53 that stopped the multiplication of cells, thus removing one of our body's ways to prevent cancer.

This film was based on published peer-reviewed research . Channel 4 also sent us to attend an urgent meeting of international scientist at the US government's Institutes of Health in Washington D.C. It was reported at this that 33% of human bone cancers and over 85% of childhood brain tumours are contaminated with this monkey virus, known as Simian Virus 40 (SV40). In one experiment, every one of the female pregnant rodents given SV40 got breast cancer.

The reason why the vaccine became contaminated was purely because the drug companies chose to take an outrageous risk with our health. They continue to take this risk, yet the polio vaccine can be manufactured by far safer methods. The World Health Organisation (WHO) allowed three ways of making the polio vaccine. One was to grew the polio virus needed for the vaccine in cloned human tissue, the second to grew it in cloned monkey tissue, and the third approved way was to catch wild monkeys, kill them and grow the polio virus in their kidneys. WHO warned that this third way was the more dangerous, as it would be hard this way to remove monkey viruses from the vaccine culture. But it turned out to be a slightly cheaper way to make it. Thus all the polio vaccine for the UK is currently still produced in a factory/slaughter house in Belgium that consumes approximately 150 monkeys caught in the Caribbean every year. A similar system is used for the United States. The research around which we made our film made no difference—it was not refuted, just ignored. Perhaps the companies feared the cost of compensation? For me this is a campaign that has not ended.

I was again back in the saddle, this time for those affected by careless medicine. But now I did not hide my gender path or my work in the Craft from my colleagues. I had nearly conquered the fear that openness would damage my career. But maybe it was society that had changed? Maybe it really was now safer for me?

Nearly all the tests for SV40 in human cancers had been done outside the UK. In 1988 a Government spokesman in Parliament admitted to thousands of doses being contaminated with SV40. Since then no English laboratory had equipped itself to test for this virus. So Channel 4 insisted that we did not rely on the new American and European research presented at the conference we attended in Washington, but persuade British doctors and patients to allow us to test their biopsy cancer samples for SV40. Since there was no UK facility, we had to send the samples to an Italian medical lab. We tested about twenty and found the monkey virus. We were the first to do this work in England, a ridiculous and somewhat scary situation to be in as journalists. We found the virus in a mesothelioma cancer and in a bone cancer. The mesothelioma killed the patient before our film appeared.

Since we made our film, doctors found another monkey virus, SCMV, in the damaged brain cells of ME sufferers. This virus comes from the African Green Monkey, the very species used for today's polio vaccines, and the species that recently reared a 'wild human child" in Africa. This research is peer-reviewed and published but this virus is still not screened out of the vaccine. On the contrary, the US government has refused to allow a Professor's request to check government vaccine samples for SCMV on the grounds of "commercial secrecy"!

I found questioning government scientists on vaccination issues very much like investigating a church. They seemed to regard my questioning as a heresy. They repeatedly told me I should not make my findings public, for they might put parents off vaccination. It had almost become a holy practice. Parents who do not vaccinate are accused of neglect. They are put under great social pressure to conform. Vaccines may help us but official scientists have a sorry history of reassuring parents there is no risk when there really is a risk.

But while making this film on vaccines in 1997-8 I found I was still suffering from the assault of four years previous. Many blows had landed around my eyes. I now became painfully light sensitive. I saw three moons in the sky at night even when entirely sober. My doctors hazarded that the beating had cracked the lens of my good eye (the other is "lazy") and consequently cataract damage had accumulated. The surgeon took out this lens while I was looking through it and put in another. The colours I saw during this were amazing and scary. I was desperate not to move a muscle lest the surgeon slip. And while I was recovering from this operation, there came another call.

Eco-warriors and Magic

This time it was an email message from a Kentish witch called Motherwort. She told me of a local forest threatened with destruction. A company wanted to turn Lyminge Forest near Canterbury in southern England into a private park with nearly a thousand holiday houses and a car park for 2,700 vehicles designed to curve around a 4,000 year old officially protected burial mound. There had been a forest here for at least a thousand years. It was officially an Area of Outstanding Natural Beauty with over 140,000 visitors a year. Margaret Thatcher's government wanted to have it "privatised". I used to go to Lyminge as a child. I had to see what was happening.

What I found were camps of young people, styled by the press as "eco-warriors", living under beech, birch, oak and pine, without electricity, who had to carry water over half a mile to their camps. They were there with the support of local people determined not to let this forest be destroyed. It was on top of the North Downs, on an ancient track lined with sacred wells and tombs.

Newspapers had written with admiration of these protests, of the deep tricky tunnels and the scary tree houses built to make any development too costly, but they did not describe the magic that was afoot. To find this I had to go and join the protesters, live with them, humbly listening, sharing and laughing.

They soon made me one of their family. I found it easy to be open about being in the Craft. I was made more than welcome at Kyros, at Bastards, at Gone to Pot, at Fortress and the other camps. It seemed that they wanted the crones, the witches, and the priestesses who did not represent a patriarchal religion or any power pretence. This was not the English society that I remembered, but I was at home.

It was a delight being back in a forest that I first saw as a child. This was my land, my ancient people. As we sat at night around the fire, fetching water, putting on the billy, it felt strangely alike the Aboriginal camps I had experienced. I sensed a nod of approval from over my shoulder from the Aboriginal elders with whom I had worked. This was what they wanted Europeans to do: to learn of the Mother Earth who gave them birth, to learn to protect their Mother; to learn to listen to our ancestral dreaming and to learn that we are sister races. And thus another circle in my life began to close. I had gone from Folkestone near Lyminge where I had been ordained a priest, to Australia where I had worked to save forests and sacred places. It seemed that I had now returned to do the same on my own familiar land.

What I found was that these camps were a seedbed for magic, a place where young people remembered, where the Craft grew as it always had, deep among the trees, in the heather, in the moonlight. This was not the seedbed of the town, of the urban coven or grove, where sacred traditions were treasured amid suburbia. It was the seedbed of the protest camp, of those who leave the cities and their houses because they felt they were called to protect the wild.

As we shared and chanted around the fires, talked and did magic, I felt that this was how the Craft had always grown. I feel that I was meeting some of the new cunning men, wise women, who were forging their magic in poverty and sharing, learning their herbs and toadstools, becoming one with the spirits of our island. Their firepits, with their tarpaulin or wooden shelters, are now in many places around this land. They are the children whose instincts have been awoken by the mother, who know where they are needed

> We stand for the land
> For the right to protect the land
> For the right to dream the land
> For the right to know her
> And to teach the children about her.

For me the world is vibrant, alive and ready to teach those with open ears. We are woven into the patterns of the earth like the threads of a tapestry. I remember the night in Lyminge forest when a young woman said to me softly: "Jani, you will understand. When I am digging a tunnel I can hear the rocks singing to me."

"Faery gates" are places able to take us through into regions where other domains of existence become evident. They enable us to start to see a world with trees that sing, rocks that sing, of imps and elves and fairy folk. Our imagination teaches us not just with words, but with images, music, smells and touches. Living close to the Nature that birthed us and sustains us, we are close to the womb of life. Here we can find the ecstasy that is our birthright. It is a gift that comes from deep within.

And into this world of instinctive knowledge, we must inter-weave our history. There is much to be learnt. The Druids of old studied for some twenty years before they were ready to serve the people. There are treasure houses around us to be explored. But we need to stand barefoot upon earth before we start. The wise person keeps "well-earthed".

The tactics used by these warriors come out of a long learning of non-violent ways to achieve change. They knew that the people who wanted to possess the forest were only doing so in the expectation of profit. So, if they could make it too expensive for them to gain control, then the developers might lose interest.

Thus we dug tunnels in the sandy clay that coloured us bronze to create egg shaped chambers protected by steel doors. These were in different parts of the forest and well concealed. Others had fortress towers erected over them with protected access to the tunnels so the warriors could sleep above the shafts out of the reach of the bailiffs who might try to surprise them.

Concrete bunkers were dug with pipes set into their walls into which our arms could be padlocked to make our removal expensive. Other pipes were concreted in and concealed around firepits in case we were ambushed by bailiffs while eating our evening meal.

Those with a head for heights put tree houses high in the beech and pine, woven into a cobweb of walkways some one hundred feet above the ground. One young man had a drum filled with concrete and flints hoisted it up to his platform. If anyone tried to evict him, he would padlock his arm into this drum. A crucifix was suspended high over the main entrance to the wood. If there were an eviction, a daring protester would be chained to this as a symbol of the sacrifice we were making to save the woods.

The curse of our forest was that it is the nearest to the Channel Tunnel and thus was coveted by men who want to fence it and charge tourists for "The English Countryside Experience." But we believed it should not become private. It supported our ancestors. It contained the remains of their rarely found Celtic, Roman and early medieval woodland settlements covering a period of over 4,000 years. They had left behind pottery, tools, sunken ways and charcoal pits and their dead. When I found some Neolithic tools and located burial mounds already listed as ancient monuments, some protesters said softly "We knew it. We could sense them. We know they are here."

These ancient places are not the only thing precious in this forest. One night I saw a nightjar hurtle itself over a Bronze Age burial mound. Nightjars are a "red book" endangered species. We heard them every summer night, along with owls and nightingales.

The forest included many different kinds of woodland, shady beech with bluebells, patches of Douglas firs. Some areas have been coppiced for centuries. There were sweet chestnut groves, lily of the valley, heath and areas of baby Corsican pines, the latter the ill-thought gift of the Forestry Commission after a hurricane felled many trees. Fast growing silver birch now surrounded these imported pines. Four times more species grow in a broadleaf forest than under pines. The forestry commission told us that when we went, they would kill the broadleaves so that their pines might flourish. They asked why did we want to protect it when it was merely a "tree farm"?

We used every means that we could dream of to protect this forest. On our camp, we dug tunnels and did magic, joining with the energy of the wild wood, putting our wills entirely into the effort of shaping a future in which this forest would be safe. When it grew too dark to dig, when the nightingale sang in counterpoint to the mechanical sound of the nightjar and the hoot of the great owls, then we began to chant, joining hands, weaving, travelling deep within ourselves to use our inner energy, drawing more energy up from the ground.

Motherwort composed her own song to the small trees around our camp. She wrote: "Grow strong little trees, live long, outlive us, shelter the birds and our children's children." She also noted: "at night we went deeper and wilder. Jani is telling us about the dragon energy that she has woven through the wood, singing and dancing, invoking the primal power of the earth goddess, wakening her. We are humming, the night is with us, the trees surround us, the energy is high because we are so close to the wind and fire and stars. No need to imagine a magical space! This is one.

"We begin to hum, whispering "Come dragon, come dragon, come, come, come, we your daughters, we your sons", a deep drumming refrain, a tune springs up from nowhere and we are singing. The pulsing energy of Lyminge is thick with dragon energy, now the low pines are filled with circling mist.

"As we reach a crescendo we were shaking with the red energy of the earth, the dragon was present. We felt we would turn them back; we are too strong for them. John cried out "Look there is a dragon in the clouds!" we whooped and yelled. The clouds, lit by the moon, formed a dragon's head with a serpentine tail. We held each other looking at the sky. Someone started high kicking. We were doing the can-can, laughing and singing.

She concluded: "It was two in the morning, ordinary folk were in bed! But we were in love with Lyminge, dancing in the moonlight. The earth is strong! We are strong! We will win."

For me it was a marvellous night and its magic went afield. I had to leave the woods for a week in August to attend a gathering of witches for workshops and rituals. I did not want to leave. It seemed utterly the wrong moment. We believed the developers were about to move into the forest. We had good reason to think so. Bailiffs had been sworn in and police leave cancelled. But I was supposed to be giving talks at this gathering and had to go.

When I arrived at its secret location (secret in order to ensure the press did not bother us) I found there was to be an opening ritual in which about 120 witches would be in the Sacred Circle. I was worried about Lyminge Forest so I went beforehand into the surrounding wood to ask it to strengthen me and help send supportive energy to Lyminge. I found in it a piece of wood that could serve as a staff. I took it with me into the Great Circle. With it, I thought, came the trees.

I went to the presiding priestess and asked if I might request help for Lyminge. She agreed and offered me her finely carved staff. I declined it with thanks. My piece of wood was all I needed. I expected to be asked to just say a few words about Lyminge. But then, half way through the ritual, to my surprise the priestess turned towards me and said: "Jani, would you now go to the centre to raise energy for Lyminge." Gulp! I had never done anything like this with so many. The people in the circle were nearly all strangers to me. They came from covens all over Europe. They were likely to know a great deal more than I. They were mostly Gardnarian witches. I heard rumours that some were quite conservative. They would probably think me ignorant of the "proper" way of doing this

Gripping the local staff, I nervously went to the centre of the circle and after a few introductory words began the same chant we used in our forest camp, "Come dragon, come dragon, come, come, come; we your daughters, we your sons", Nothing happened. I crouched, gripping my staff, and with closed eyes concentrated on finding the energy. I felt my voice grew stronger, urgent, summoning. I added another line to the refrain. "Come Goddess, come God. Come, come, come; we your daughters, we your sons." It took time to catch. I squatted closer to the earth, willing it to send me the energy needed. Then, like a forest fire, the chant whirled up around the circle. I was now standing but still my eyes were shut. Soon the energy took over. It was like surfing a great wave. I soared with it but had to keep control for I had the responsibility of turning this into effective magic. I had to reach above this whirlwind of a chant to give a signal so that everyone would know when to simultaneously release and send the energy. I managed to shout a final "COME" while on tiptoe. We then knelt and grounded ourselves. Only then did I open my eyes to find myself surrounded by panting people. Afterwards a mother and child told me how they saw cracks in the earth that contained fire when they grounded themselves, to their great surprise. Energy had been sent. This too was part of the protecting of Lyminge.

This happened the same week as the eviction was supposed to happen. The forest was full of people digging tunnels, putting up walkways and being scared. Many of the young, and old, had never confronted authority before. It was very stressful. It was they who took the primary role in protecting the forest. We but added our support.

Motherwort wrote of what was happening back in the forest. "The local sheriff has been sworn in and the police are all on overtime, they're really coming. All the protesters are working through the night in preparation for the eviction. Within three days I learn how to make a lock-on, fortify a tunnel and get a bail address. As I work I sing and pray. I call on my heroes, the tribal peoples who lost their homeland and on the strength of the rocks beneath me, I feel her (the earth) and I feel us (my forest family), I know that we are strong. The trees feel scared, yet they are with us, they know somehow that we are on their side, and in small ways they help us. We can always find the path even in the dark, the woods open up for you."

But when I returned after the witchcamp, there was no longer such an emergency. The police and bailiffs had not come. We continued to put up defences but learnt later that the orders requiring the police to evict us had been cancelled around the time of our ritual. We had more time.

Our camp had on its powerless fridge, used as a rat-proof cupboard, the slogan "Possessions own you". Wiccan slogans decorated the shelter's roof. Some nights a senior Druid protester came to visit. We cooked, communally, shared books and lives. We treasured water, as it had to be carried nearly half a mile every morning. Our tunnel became deep with many rounded chambers and concrete lock-ons. A local woman in her seventies planned to "lock-on" with us.

Nearly every camp had tree houses and at least one tunnel. The Fortress had a palistrade that leant outwards. It was hung with tapestries painted with large scary spirit faces. The Underground Elephant camp had an elegant lacework above it of net sleeping platforms and, above them, tree houses. Scary Pine treehouse was nearly impenetrable, even to the protesters. With no television to possess us, at night we told stories, sang and meditated.

On one pathworking, in my imagination a slow worm took me around the forest in a very slow weaving and then down into a hole into the burial mound next to which I had earlier seen it. It showed me myself buried within. It did not surprise me. I grew up on the hills that surround these woods. I was at home here. It was a good place to meet ancestors. On the winter Solstice I pathworked at this ancient mound with a small group, In meditation I learned from a shadowy figure that I should not just look forward to the sun's return, but celebrate the rich darkness of this the longest night. This festival symbolised the dark but good energy that moves within the earth and between the stars.

We learnt on dark nights to let our feet find paths by their different feel. Sometimes our eyes were strangely useful too. We found dirt paths seemed to glow on moonless nights. Perhaps the compaction made them able to reflect starlight? One day I thought I could see the lights of cigarettes nearby. It was not cigarettes. I stood entranced while fairy lights seemed to dance around me to soft music. A hundred yards away some protestors were dancing. It seemed the local spirits were joining in. If it were my imagination, well then, I still enjoyed it!

There was still a risk the police could return. Motherwort wrote: "The witches on site were working overtime, we had to stop the developers coming in. We joined hands round the firepit and circled the energy. We had never worked together before, but we were closer than many covens. Facing your fears together means that you show each other who you really are very quickly, there's no time for bullshit."

Once the fear of immediate eviction started waning, when the police and bailiffs still did not come, we found we had to continue to guard the forest as the company started to play a waiting game. It had several more years before it must commence the development. It tried to out-wait us.

In order to get more people involved, part of Motherwort and my work in this forest became organising summer "witchcamps" to which we invited all who saw nature as special or holy and wanted to learn how best to protect her. These camps were five days long and so designed that no one was excluded for reasons of poverty. A cauldron of vegetarian food was provided every evening and other food as income provided. In the event, no one went hungry. We asked for donations of say £15 from those who could afford. Others could come free. It was a chance for people to share magic and rituals and to get to know about eco-protest. The principal instructor was always the wood itself.

The first year we did this, we invited Starhawk and her partner David to participate. She had written many books on magic and self-empowerment. She had also worked against nuclear power stations and to protect American forests. It was a delight and inspiration having her with us in the forest. She in turn went around photographing the fortifications. She said she had never seen such a determined effort to protect a forest.

She then invited Motherwort and I to attend her first British witch-camp some two weeks later at a centre near Glastonbury. We could not have afforded to attend if she had not invited us, waiving her own fees. This weeklong camp otherwise would have cost us over £300, with half of this going to pay for accommodation and food. The result was that it excluded the many local witches who knew the spirits of that land but had little money. When Starhawk took participants to the Glastonbury Tor, telling them to note the energy left by those who did magic there, I pointed out to her the rooftops of the local witches. I felt it was a pity they could not come. They might have introduced the local spirits of this place.

But then it would have been a different kind of witchcamp. Her camp schedules were carefully constructed and aimed at self-healing. For the first half-week even experienced participants had no input into planning the rituals. She ran these with her American co-teachers. When they allowed the participants to be ritually creative, there was a sudden and delightful flowering; as were unleashed the talents of some of the experienced European witches present. With our very different backgrounds, it was not surprising that there were differences in how we did magic. I particularly missed the close working with the spirits of the local place, and missed invoking the God's male energy. When I could participate, I drew Herne from the floor of the Circle into our midst. When the participants were sent to work with the spirits of plants in the tended gardens, I found myself looking wistfully at the wild woods guarding the slopes of the neighbouring hills. They seemed to be calling me and when I found a spare moment, I went to meet them.

Deep in a wood I found a stream issuing from a little cave. It was on the edge of a wide clearing shaded by two large trees with rope swings. I swung, and then turning, found a powerful face carved into a tree scar at head height. It was the face of a Crone, an old wise one, a God or Goddess perhaps, but certainly a guardian for this place. I had no idea how old this place was but it was certainly being used for rituals, or so I felt.

After enjoying this place, casting circles while swinging on ropes, laughing and thanking its guardian, I continued past witch hazel trees to find yet more sacred places. I felt that this was how Glastonbury used to be before it became a bustling town. I introduced to these places some that came to Starhawk's camp that did not mind doing rituals in the rain. This became my special contribution to this camp.

We need a web woven between witches and magical people, linked by love and craft, a web of increasing strength. I saw witchcraft as a skill and religious practice that belonged of all of us by its very nature, that could and should be available in all its fullness without consideration of income. Starhawk told me she would burn out if she did her many witchcamps for free. Everyone needs to find ways of supporting him or herself. These camps are part of her way.

Magic and Ecstasy

Magic as I know and love it differs from prayer. When people pray for help or forgiveness, they beg for the intercession of a superior supernatural being, or a saint existing in a supernatural world. They often see themselves as ultimately weak and unable to save themselves. But with magic, we attempt to use our natural powers to affect change, perhaps with the help of other natural entities.

Our power comes from our union with nature and the divine creating energy. Our knowledge of natural powers is experiential. When we observe inexplicable happenings, we know these are achieved by natural causes that we do not yet understand. The divine energy is part of nature, not of a supernatural world.

Ecstasy is at the heart of the shamanic practices of nations that still live close to nature. Eliade subtitles his classic work *Shamanism* as *The Archaic*

Techniques of Ecstasy. During my life I have experienced ecstasy in paths that have been called at different times the Mystical, the Christian, the Shamanic and the Craft. Whatever it was called, it has given me the same ecstasy.

The psychiatrist Karl Jung wrote that the alchemic path to human perfection entailed us all becoming the child of the divine mother. "To become what he really is, to fulfil the purpose for which his mother bore him, and after the peregrinations of a long life full of confusion and error, to become the filium regius, son of the supreme mother."[371] For me it is deeper. Our fulfilment is to become the Deity; one'd in the ecstasy of union, human and God.

The mystic Meister Ekhardt recognised this when he wrote:

> Oh wonder of wonders!
> When I think of the union of the soul with God!
> The divine love-spring surges over the soul, sweeping her out of herself into the unnamed being of her original source…
> In this exalted state she has lost her proper self and is flowing full-flood into the unity of the divine nature.
> Henceforth I shall not speak about the soul, for she has lost her name in the oneness the divine essence.
> There she is no more called soul: she is called infinite being.[372]

This spiritual path is one of ecstasy. A constant ecstasy is seen as behind all happenings, all realities. It is linked to the very nature of creation. We were created, I believe, to experience it as we come to know the intelligence and love at the heart of creation. Einstein, a scientific genius of the 20th Century, wrote:

"The most beautiful emotion we can experience is the mystical. It is the sower of all true art and science. He to whom this emotion is a stranger…is as good as dead. To know that what is impenetrable to us really exists, manifesting itself to us as the highest wisdom and the most radiant beauty, which our dull faculties can comprehend only in their most primitive forms. This knowledge, this feeling, is at the centre of all true religiousness. In this sense, and in this sense only, I belong to the ranks of devoutly religious men."[373]

He also wrote: "The most important function of art and science is to awaken the cosmic religious feeling and keep it alive." He thus disagreed with those who thought, "being scientific," meant abandoning their trust in their instincts, including in their innate religious feelings. They have disempowered themselves by losing confidence in their inner selves.

Children have sometimes asked: "Jani, are you a white witch or a black witch?" My usual answer is: "Neither. I am a green witch." Magic is for me ultimately green, for it comes from nature and is dependent on nature. It is thus for me a divine energy, and a blessed energy allied to the divine energy that underpins our world. It is of itself good but can be distorted. If we use it for evil, we are trying to turn the power of the earth against itself. I rarely come across the harmful use of magic, but this may be for the same reason that I rarely come across pornography on the Internet, I had not looked for it.

But I have read Egyptian and Coptic "love-spells" that I thoroughly disliked, dating back to the early centuries of Christianity. In these the magician, a Christian or Pagan male, might order Deities or Angels to force another to "love" a client. Sometimes he casts a "corner-spell" meant to protect the home of a client against all curses. The targeted person was often identified to the spirit by presenting it with a personal item, such as some of the victim's hair. The spell was sometimes inscribed on tablets of lead or pottery bowls and thus we have copies of it. If these had efficacy, then it came from the focus these objects gave to the human will, and the focus they gave to the fears of their intended victims if they got to know of their existence. But the existence of such harmful acts of magic no more means that magic itself is wrong than we could say that intercourse is wrong because sometimes it turns to rape.

For all that I loved my time among Aborigines, I knew some communities had male or female sorcerers who reportedly used a very harmful magic to enforce cultural rules or for vengeance. I never came knowingly in contact with them but anthropologists I trust have described their work. Diane Bell reported they still had much influence.[374] They might use bones and human fat, or hair or toenail clippings from planned victims. They were blamed for many deaths. But they also helped train spiritual healers and doctors". There were two sides to their magic, they took away health and restored health. Pocs reported that some medieval witches or shamans similarly were healers who could both curse and remove their curse.[375]

The Witchcraft Museum in Boscastle in Cornwall, founded by Cecil Williamson, where Gerald Gardner worked when it was on the Isle of Man, contains a wealth of West Country folk magic dolls, paintings and carvings. Some were found in house chimneys or attics where they had been put to protect a house. Some were used to focus healing or cursing magic. I felt uncomfortable there because for me there was too much of the cursing magic and not enough of the green or healing magic, and little about the mystic's path or ecstatic shamanic journeying skills or even the centuries of persecution. It did not reflect the positive magic of the Indonesian shaman or Aborigine done to maintain the balance and energy of creation.

On one occasion, when invited by a coven to a Beltane maypole dancing, I wondered what to take as a gift. As they were meeting in town, I decided to bring May blossom from one of my favourite places, Oxley Woods near Blackheath in London. Its ancient woodland was successfully protected by a protest, by the "eco-magic" of witches among the protestors, and, I believe by an European Union ruling, from being carved up for a major road.

I went to the wood also intending to work magic for some things I wanted in my life. But when I went among the trees, I knew the answer. There was absolutely no need for me to work for myself. My job was to join with the trees in creating the spring. I felt the energy of the sap rising around me, up the trunks into the fresh canopy of leaves. I joined with them and celebrated their reborn vitality. As a human I celebrated being part of nature, not separate from her, but a person created to play her own part in the great dance of life and love. As I danced through the trees, singing to them, caressing them, being the wild woman I love to be and should be, but am only shyly, when no one else is around, I instinctively trusted that there was no need to do magic for myself. When I later left the forest all the other things that I had wanted to resolve were wonderfully resolved.

Another tiny example: The weather looked dubious the day before some Craft Initiations in a hilltop wood. So I walked out onto the pontoon on which my boat and home was moored and, uniting myself to the strength of my sister elements, imagined myself so tall that my head was among the clouds. I chatted to the forces shaping the clouds, told them what we had planned to do and asked them, if it did not disrupt their plans too much, would they mind keeping rain from the clearing where we would be carrying out our ritual? Now it may well have been chance, but next day we spent some twelve hours in our wood and, although it poured all around us, it was dry there until half an hour after we left. Weather magic was something quite ordinary. It treats nature as alive. It is known to many cultures.

When we were working magically to protect Lyminge Forest, we had to think up spells that would not harm others. We joined together to attempt to send a delusion by telepathy. We sent to the police the delusion that there were more protesters in the forest than there were. We sent to the accountants of the company that wanted to "develop" our forest, images of leaves to make it harder for them to focus on the profits that would come from the development. We have no idea whether they were received. Whatever did happen, the forest has been preserved.

We were in an ancient tradition in so working. Here is an example from a very old Irish legend. "The children of Calilidin gathered shaggy sharp downy thistles and light-topped puff-balls and fluttering withered leaves of the wood, and made many armoured warriors of them; so that there was not a peak nor a hill around the valley which was not filled with hosts and battalions and troops, so that the hideous quick wild cries that the Children of Cailidin raised around it were heard even to the clouds of heaven and the walls of the firmament; so that the entire land was full of woundings and raids, of burnings and swift lamentations and of the bleating of trumpets and horses, through these magic arts of the Children of Calidin."[376] All this was simply a delusion sent to fool a foe.

This alliance between the realm of nature and us is as it should be. I am not suggesting that we can reshape nature. When we work magic, we are part of nature; Our magical strength increases the more our spirit is united with the spirit of Nature, or, to put in another way, is married to the sacred Earth or Deity.

This union is based on love and self-knowledge. Married to our God or Goddess, we are both nothing and extremely powerful. We are nothing for we have nothing that is purely our own. We are powerful in that we are transported by love beyond all restraints to be one with the Deity.

But magic may be not ecstatic. Sometimes we might need to protect ourselves. I believe that people who work with magic need to learn how to do this. I will sometimes do this symbolically by imagining a wolf lying curled up around my home! It reminds me of the power of my Lover and of Nature and to trust in them.

In the rituals I help shape, I provide room for inspiration and time to listen to the inner voice. The role of the priestess overseeing a ritual is like that of a conductor of an orchestra. She must not only carry the rite forward, she must sense the energy coming from each participant and weave all together so that the song or spell that results is as powerful as possible.

I also attended inter-faith camps organised by a dedicated and open-minded Christian, Michael de Warde, called "Meeting in the Presence". These were occasions for Christians and Pagans to share their insights. One day Michael invited me to the launch of a new book by an Anglican priest to be held in the presence of the Archbishop of Southwark at his Anglican Cathedral. It dealt with the presence of God in all and concluded by saying God saves all of us no matter what our religious affiliation. Although I accepted his good motives, I was somewhat uncomfortable for he seemed to say that his Anglican God saved us all.

When audience responses were requested, I said: "I was very happy to hear you talk about the immanence of the divine presence around us. This is what I also teach in my coven." I then hesitated, appalled that the word "coven" had so slipped out. It seemed to ring around the arches and everyone, including the archbishop, turned to stare at me.

Michael de Warde broke the ensuing silence by asking the speaker if his book was relevant to pagans. Much to my surprise the author responded by saying that he had no problems with most major religions but he had with Pagans for "I cannot see how their view that nature is sacred leaves any room for the redemption of nature."

It was my turn to be surprised. How could nature be tainted with sin? Amazed I said: "Do you mean that the wind, the tides, the moon, all need to be redeemed?" The priest acknowledged that this was so and at this point the Archbishop closed the brief debate. Afterwards many clergy thanked me for being present but this brief event again brought home to me that the critical divide was between those who see nature as holy and those who see her as corrupted.

Ancestral lands and their magic

With the Lyminge Forest of my childhood countryside hopefully saved, I was now free to respond to that nagging voice that kept on saying: "When are you coming to learn from your ancestors' lands on the wild west coasts?"

I had been brought up to acknowledge my Irish ancestors. Later I learnt that their lands included the west coast of Scotland and part of the west of Wales. The latter was the nearest and easiest to reach. It thus particularly felt like home. My younger daughter had her birth rite in one of its mountain streams. One of my names, Roberts, was at home among these hills as well as in Scotland (and among smugglers I was told) My other name, Farrell, came from Ulster, from my mother's father. I was also related to the McBrearties and McArthurs, the Western Scottish clans of my mother's mother.

Since the spirits of Wales seemed impossible to ignore, I fitted out my Lada station wagon so it could run my computer and packed into it a tent. I had no sooner done this, then the Goddess made it easier for me. A friend had a large ex military Land Rover that he had not used for two years. It had been a command vehicle for senior army staff and had under-floor gas heating, a toilet, fridge, cooker, a table that could seat six as well as a roof that lifted to give access to bunks.

If I were to travel like this, a dog would be a welcome companion, so I was thrilled when Sarah, a woman I spent much time with in Lyminge Forest, offered me one of her two dogs. Thus did Storm, a black Border collie bitch come to live with me. We instantly bonded. We knew each other from the forest camps. Her presence would make my travelling safer. All now was ready and we soon set out. I had everything I could possibly need in the Land Rover including my laptop computer, everything but a bath.

I decided to go first to the Prescilli mountains of South West Wales, for I knew our ancestors thought them so special that they brought from them by sea and land the enormously heavy blue stones erected at Stonehenge over 150 miles away.

Just after entering Wales, I stopped at an ancient sacred "Virtuous Well" with thorn trees by it festooned with new and old ribbons, each symbolising a prayer or spell. Nearby stood three standing stones. I then followed the Wye River along a wide and beautiful valley into the mountains. Near its head I found a monument to the death of the last Welsh prince to fight for his country's freedom, Prince Llywelyn ap Gruffuff, I washed my face with water from the well in which his severed head was washed. His Bard, Bleddyn Fardd, sung of him around 1280: "Man was killed for us, who ruled over all, Man who ruled Wales, boldly I'll name him, Manly Llywelyn, bravest of Walesmen, man not enamoured of too easy a way."[377] That night I slept nearby in a wild dark valley with a rushing torrent. I woke to find myself by a rocky pool overhung by small oaks with twisted trunks, dressed in bluish green lichens and mosses. They carried the last of autumn's russet leaves but were surrounded by the spring's first daffodils.

I had picked a cove near the Prescilli Mountains as my destination. When I saw its wild headlands lit by a sun setting over the Irish Sea, I found myself grinning with recognition. It was a perfect place. Next day, after the dog and I had explored the bay, a woman started chanting on the beach, clearly thinking she was alone. I came out to meet her. When she learnt what I was doing, she immediately said: "Well sometimes you must need a bath. My back door is always open. Please feel free to come any time whether I am at home or not." I grinned and thanked my God and Goddess for looking after me so well.

The cove was called Caebwr. It was watched over by the earthworks of an ancient small fort and had in a field half a mile back a three-legged cromlech, a massive boulder supported on three others, the remains of a burial mound. It was heavy, solid, reliable, a reminder that our ancestors had loved this land.

I used this cove as my base over the next few weeks. The Welsh made me feel very welcome. I had many a discussion about the land. Some whose first language was Welsh told me the ancient stories. The woman who had made her bath available told me her favourite place was an ancient oak wood in the mountains. She felt she had found there the place that was the heart of its magic. I wondered if I should go there but decided I should first explore this wild coast and then the still wilder mountains that had supplied Stonehenge.

I felt somewhat apprehensive that I might suffer from the stigma travellers were often accorded. I understood that local people who loved their wild places did not want to see them invaded and possessed by vehicles parked over a long period. Thus I never stayed in one place for very long.

This was no great hardship. I am an intensely curious creature and always have liked to see what was around the next corner. Only once did anyone at Caebwr make me feel at all unwelcome. This was when a man gave a courteous warning that local authorities would be sure to come and evict me. No one ever did.

He nonetheless made me feel uneasy. On reflection I thought that this was ridiculous when so many others had made me welcome. I clearly had a fear that needed conquering so I started a song about being a coward. I then picked up a stone, attached to it my fears and threw it into the flowing water. As I threw it I was reminded that I was one'd with the Goddess, a priestess loved by her and therefore a person who belonged in her wild places.

One of the first places I wanted to visit was the large bay nearby named after the pagan Goddesses varyingly called Bridget, Bree and Bride, to whom the first Christians gave the title of a Saint rather than try to demonise her. I arrived at her bay on a wild evening, deep mist coming off the sea, great waves breaking. I sung out a greeting to the Bay of Bridget:

> "Here I am, here I am, here I am,
> On Bridget's shore, by Bridget's sea.
> Wild and strong, wild and strong,
> Here I am, Here I am,
> Greetings from the shore.
> I've come at last, come at last. Here I am!"

Then I scrambled down to discover a well dedicated to another Saint called Non. A plaque told how this spring miraculously appeared when Non gave birth at this spot to St David, the patron saint of Wales. Visitors had thrown money into its water as a gift and prayer. A statue of the Mother of God, Mary, looked over the well—a confirmation of the traditional female status of sacred wells.

Near to the well overlooking the bay stood a ruined ancient building dedicated to Non and containing a simple old Celtic Cross. This is a symbol that goes back to pagan times. It unites a sacred circle, the wheel of life, with a cross representing the four quarters, the four elements and the four festivals, as well as for Christians the cross on which Jesus died.

I meditated on this ancient sign. It is good to use it in ritual as we did that other symbol of the elements, the five-pointed star of the Pentagram (spirit being added to the ancient four of earth, fire, air and water.) The Celtic Cross can be found everywhere in the land I love. For me it symbolises the sacred beliefs of all our ancestors, both Pagan and Christian.

Non's ruined chapel has standing stones guarding it on all sides. It had evidently been a holy place from long before Christian times. One stone has what are said to be the finger marks left by Non when she pushed against it while giving birth to David. If this story is so ancient that it is honoured with standing stones, then perhaps this myth about St David has a more ancient form. Could it be that the ancient myth is that here, on this cliff, the Goddess Non gave birth to Dyfed, the name of this part of Wales; that it was here that Dyfed had its birthplace? Was Non the Goddess of Sovereignty, the Mother giving birth to the king or high priest of the land? Was the spring her breast milk?

So I found myself chanting to a horse that was grazing around Non's Sanctuary;

> This is where. This is where,
> Non gave birth. Non gave birth,
> To the nation of Wales,
> To the nation of the Welsh.
> Sing oh horse. Sing oh horse,
> Non gave birth. Non gave birth,
> To the nation of these hills,
> To the nation of these hills.
> Sing my stones. Sing my stones.

> Her fingers you felt, her fingers you felt,
> As she gave birth to this Welsh Nation.

While walking east along the cliff top from this chapel I found carved into a great rock another Celtic cross. This one had in its centre the sun, with flames radiating out between the quarter marks. It did not have an arm extended beyond the circle, as in most Celtic Crosses. (Although that elongated form is used for the 5000-year-old great Celtic cross stone ritual site of Callendish in the Islands of Bride or "Hebrides".)

This carving was appropriate for a bay dedicated to Bride for the Sun was one of her symbols. The other form of her name Bridget came from the Celtic bree-saigit meaning "the bright arrow", the sun in the sky. Another of her symbols was the white horse that runs the sky.

A woman I met on this cliff top took pleasure in explaining to me other ancient myths about this land. She pointed past Non's Well and the interestingly named Chanter's Headland to an island, saying that is where the ancients slept when enchanted for over 20 years. She also pointed to where, in the Mabinogion epic, the giant boar ran ashore leaving a great cleft that now hosts a long narrow harbour. It was a marvel to me that the Welsh language had preserved such stories. It reminded me of the stories of creating Ancestors in the Aboriginal Dreaming sagas.

The following poem about Bride is from a book of Druidry. It tells of the lighting of nineteen candles in her honour. I will only here give some of its lines and a reference to the rest.

> The first candle lit is our sunrise birth; the flame of your house reaching Ceugant's bride.
> Your fifth is eternal life's spring that sings your name, in crystal gaze.
> Your sixth is the flame of your altar that never dies.
> Your tenth is a milk white cow with red ears, the earth Queen's nectar, sweet!
> Your fifteenth is the Kildare grove, with solid oak and crystal spring,

Your last is your first, the beginning of the turning sea, the ending of the
three in one,
The dancing sun in the heart of all! The candle that never dies."[378]

We celebrate the presence of the Goddess Bride when we marry,
although most do not know this! The words we use are ancient. In former
times the King of the land symbolically married a mare, her totem, signi-
fying in so doing his mystic marriage with Bride as the Goddess of
Sovereignty.

The ancient Celtic song below shows how the Celtic Christians melded
their love for Bride with their new faith. They called her the midwife or
"aid-woman" who helped Mary give birth to Christ. They asked her to be
the guardian of their new faith. They still needed her help. The following
is from the Carmina Cadelica, a collection somewhat edited in its translation from Celtic.

Mary fair and Bride;
As Anna bore Mary,
As Mary bore Christ,
As Eile bore John the Baptist without flaw in him,
Aid thou me in mine unbearing,
Aid me, O Bride!
As Christ was conceived of Mary
Full perfect on every hand,
Assist thou me, foster-mother,
The conception to bring from the bone;
And as thou didst aid the Virgin of joy,
Without gold, without corn, without kine,
Aid thou me, great is my sickness,
Aid me, O Bride

Over the next weeks I roamed the Prescilli Mountains in blizzard, high winds, rain and sun. I found by their highest crag, that once provided stone for Stonehenge, a ring of standing stones in the form of an upside down boat, with the side stones leaning inwards and a flat stone for the transom. I had not seen the like of this before. I wondered if they were set up to bless the boats that transported the stones across an open and stormy sea towards Stonehenge?

I found other ancient stone circles and single stones marked in the ancient script of Ogham. Many a Welsh field was blessed with standing stones. I also found that the custom of erecting them was still alive. I asked a farmer, whose property was called in Welsh the Druid's Spring, about the tall stone next to the farmhouse. He told me he had put it up because it seemed the right thing to do!

The old ways seemed very alive in Wales. When walkers asked me what I was doing and I told them I was writing about the old religion, they would ask if I were writing about the Druids. They were keenly interested. I did not detect any sense that they deplored Druidry as a pagan practice. It seemed that this ancient priesthood was still honoured in Wales—even regaining its strength since the Eisteddfods were re-established after only a brief period of suppression. Many a town had a new stone circle erected to host bardic events. I was surprised to find one in the ruins of the castle in Aberystwyth and another in the heart of the university town of Lampeter.

I also heard many stories about the ancient healing magic practised in the hills. When a cow fell ill, it was not always only the vet that was called. Sometimes, when the vet failed, they called a member of a family that knew the old ways. This person might use dance, chants and herbs. The survival of their language had clearly preserved the Welsh culture much more than political independence by itself could ever do. One family took me deep into woods to see a cliffed ravine containing a waterfall. They told me that behind this waterfall there was an entrance to the underworld celebrated in the Mabinogion. A passer-by then told us that this was said to be a place where ritual magic was still done. It was clearly a wonderful place for a rebirth initiation.

I also sought the burial mound of the great bard Taliesin above the sandbanks of Barmouth Estuary. Although several local villages were named after him, his traditional gravesite was without a signpost or a marker although on my detailed map. The local farmer also told me where to find it, up beyond his tractor on a nearby rise. Taliesin's grave mound had a stone lined cleft across its top, for all the world like a vulva, with an egg rock lying within. This was the grave of a druid who was said to be reborn when he tasted the three drops of inspiration from the cauldron of regeneration and wisdom.

The oak grove and Druidry

The very last place I explored in the Prescilli Mountains was the oak wood the chantress mentioned when I first arrived at Caebwr. My vehicle had a problem with its lights and I had to wait a day until a spare part arrived. My garage mechanic, a Welsh speaker, a dowser and magical man, told me that this same oak wood was his favourite place. He suggested I park by a path into it that night. I now had no excuse and so had to go to the wood.

I parked where I was told, on a high dirt track by a brackened hill crowned with rocky crags below the Prescilli Mountains. I then walked to the woods below the crags. I first came to a grove of small oaks richly carpeted in bright green moss spread over boulders trunks and branches. It seemed a rich and friendly place and so I lightly skipped into the grove and happily greeted the old trees. I feel rooted amid them, welcomed. Through my sandaled feet I could feel the torrents of life flowing in the earth.

Here, cradled under oaken branches, embedded in soft mosses, I felt to my surprise the oaks speak. It was a gentle welcome and enquiry. They seemed to ask, had I come to be initiated into Druidry? With surprise I listened. I had long wondered whether I had a place on the Druid path. I had been put off by stories of the bloody sacrifices of the past, by the male chauvinism in certain branches of modern Druidry, by feeling that they once were the established religion. I had felt that perhaps I was meant to be outside such established paths, the loner, the chantress, a dreaming daughter of earth.

Now I realised that it might not be a Druid Order that would make me a Druid and initiate me. That was not the way of this oak wood. Druids were its people[379] and the Oak chose them. The very word Druid meant "knowledge of the oak" and of magic. The Druids had been much maligned by their enemies, the Romans. But, no matter what happens to others, no matter what the Druid Orders did, it seemed it was the privilege of the Oaks to sometimes choose Druids. It is they who chose their dreamers, and sometimes their priestesses and priests. For them a druid was simply their person. I accepted their gift with joy. When I left it was as a Druid, as well as a Witch and priestess. I was laughing with pleasure as I thanked them for their great gift.

Later I would learn that ancient Irish Druidry had female druids known as a ban-drui (a "woman druid"). According to the ancient document Dinnsenchus, the Goddess Bridget was a ban-drui and a ban-fili (poetess). St Patrick hated them and called them pythonesses. (I now happily remember the great snake at my Initiation.) It seems these women druids were indistinguishable from the Irish witches called ban-tuatha or ban-saithe (fairy women).[380] The word for magic in Irish is druidecht, which simply means "Druidry". No wonder that I had been confused as to whether to call myself a Druid or a Witch![381]

Leaving this glade, waving it goodbye, I went deeper into the ancient wild mossy rocky woods. It felt so very rich; full of old knowledge. I wandered enchanted until it was late. I was about to turn back when I found a small valley within the woods. It held a clear pool fed by a spring and beyond it, to my surprise, stood a tall standing stone. Next to the pool was a flat rock. Immediately the idea came that this was a dousing pool. I sat on the flat rock in front of the standing stone and looked into the sparkling water, The oak opposite formed with its reflection a complete circle of branches, as above, so below. As the ripples moved so it seemed one could look into the past and future. This was truly an ageless place.

A couple of days later I spoke about this wood to a local woman deeply involved in the Old Religion and especially devoted to the Goddess Bride. She told me this wood was known locally as once having hosted a training school for Druids! Later I described my experience to an elder of Druidry. He immediately told me I had been called by the Old Ones and should come to see him and swear the Druid oath. This I did at the first opportunity.

I do not see what happened to me as that special. I feel no inclination to boast of being a Druid. It surely is a path open to all whose religion is centres on the love of nature. I learn, as does a child, with imagination and the love of wild creatures. As for talking with trees, trees are as alive as are animals. They are part of a sentient and intelligent creation. They are woven from the same energies that created me. Christians recognise angels as God's messengers. Trees sometimes are this for me and more. They are part of the divine imagination, part of divinity.

The old wisdom of Druidry is partly recorded in a text called *The Triads of Britain*. It spoke of the duties of a Bard, an order of Druidry:

The three principal obligations of a Bard
One is to learn and collect sciences,
The second is to teach
And the third is to make peace
And to put an end to all injury;
For to act contrary to these things
Is not usual or becoming to a Bard.

Druidry had a high reputation in ancient times as a learned religion. We know that Continental Celts sent their Druid or Seers for training to the British Isles. The currents of magic and ritual were so strong here that

Pliny commented: "Even today Britain is still spell-bound by magic, and performs its rites with so much ritual that she almost seems to be the source of Persian ritual."[382] Indeed the Latin word for Druid was "Magi", the ancient Persian title.

The Enchantress

I went to the Prescilli Mountains intending to camp among them for three weeks. I stayed there for over three and a half months. It was only my obligation to a witchcamp in Lyminge Forest that brought me back to England. I learnt many things while there and longed to go back as soon as possible to continue my lessons. One was the use of chant as a way to listen to the voice of the earth, to my unconsciousness and to my inheritance of memories. This chantress path came to me out of my childhood experiences and out of my time with Aborigines, but it is something I have not directly learnt from anyone. I think of it as part of my own way of working.

I experience Nature as Divine and naturally want to sing to her my thanks and my joy. My song is also a way of returning something to the earth in gratitude. Australian Aborigines believe that they must put energy into their holy place to keep them alive and well. They thus repaint their ancient paintings, dance in the sacred places and travel the dreaming tracks singing the songs that recount the stories of creation. My fancy is that my own songs are helping to keep my own hills and bays sacred and that my descendants will feel in these places something of the love that others and I have put into them while we walked this land.

The chants I sing are often spontaneous, as you probably can guess from the few I have included. I do not consciously choose the words. These come from deep within. I have no control over them. As I sing, I learn from the words I sing. To give one example; I heard myself chanting one day on a cliff top, "In the root of my life, I support the great magic."

This was I thought a gift of Wisdom—and I sung it all the way back home lest I forget it. Yes, at the root of my life, I am now being true to the root of magic, the ecstatic love that I have long known. The flowing of ecstasy is deep. It is a dark river, strong and pure, flowing with pleasure through the ravines within me. This river is Bride, is Sophia, is the great magic of Creation and when I say; "I support the great magic" I am saying that I have made the conscious decision to be part of the flow of energy that sustains everything. Since then I found that Doreen Valiente said something very similar, that, at their core, all magical traditions are one in "the great work."

She wrote about the more erudite western traditions of magic including the Qabbalah and commented; "However it may well be asked what this has to do with the simple pagan and rural traditions of the old religion of witchcraft? We have already seen that countryside witches were often quite illiterate, like most of the common people of olden days. This is quite true; but, nevertheless, the old religion of witchcraft has its roots deep in the same soil as the rest of the western magical tradition. Indeed in basic ideas, the magical traditions of the whole world are interrelated at their deepest levels. Moreover, at the deepest levels magic and religion are also closely entwined about each other and are concerned with the same great theme; the marriage of heaven and earth, the union of macrocosm and microcosm, the Great Work."[383]

Of all the words describing people of magic that of chantress seemed to fit me better than most. I draw from within by using chants, I use them sometimes when weaving spells and as a priestess. But generally I am dubious about titles. The meaning of "witch" has been tainted by those who female magic. The title of "wise woman" seems conceited to adopt.

My final trip on the Welsh west coast was to the north, to one of my favourite great peaks. I went to visit what is for me the Great Circle of the Old Ones, to ask them for strength and to be simply with them in awe and wonder. This great circle is the cwm at the heart of Calder Idris.

I started climbing at dawn. It was not long before I was passing the great white quartz boulder that guards this high valley. Soon I was in sight of the deep blue lake at the top of the valley. From its grassy shore that day it reflected the mountain peaks around it as perfectly as a mirror.

The elements were set around me. I had climbed up from the east and that side alone was open to any breeze. The sun was rising into the south. It was the element of fire. The lake was the water in the west. The highest of all the peaks, Calder Idris, was the earth in the north. I acknowledged the presence of the Elders and Elements. There was no need to cast a circle. It was cast aeons ago by glaciers.

I asked to be allowed to listen to them. I bared my feet, exposed my skin to the mountain underneath and to its energy. I had come to remind myself of the strength of the powers with whom I am bonded; to remind myself that their strength is mine; to learn not to fear; to learn to trust. I spent much time meditating by the lake and thanking the spirits for the blessings I had received in Wales.

Meetings with Guardian Spirits

But before I left Wales there were other lessons for me. A medium took me to an ancient Celtic Christian sanctuary in a bay called Mwnt. She said she wanted to introduce me to its guardian spirit. While we were in the small old church she called on its guardian. I opened my senses, became as aware as I could of what was around me and seemed to feel the presence of a strong old male spirit. My companion told me that the Guardian had noted the anointed cross on the back of my hands, the mark of a person ordained among Christians, and said that I was most welcome. As we walked out of the gate of the round church enclosure, we both simultaneously noted a strong smell of honey although we could find no signs of bees or honeysuckle. I could have imagined possibly the old spirit but not this scent.

Later I returned alone to sing to this spirit. I knew in the old days many hermits travelled from this bay to the sacred islands. Mwnt was a sacred place from long before Christianity arrived, but the names people gave their religion did not matter. If people recognised the land's sacredness, the guardian spirits would have no quarrel with them. In the chapel I again seemed to sense a presence, and an image. It was of an ancient sailing ship with myself standing bright upon the shore. I found this disconcerting. It was, I felt, a challenge to do what I should, to share my bright love for what I knew. Afterwards, by the gate in the circular wall I smelt the honey again, a smell that was absent when I arrived.

A similar experience came when I stayed overnight with the mother of a child who had once camped with me in Lyminge and whom I had helped bury when she died tragically and accidentally. The mother woke me early, saying she had received a message to take me to a wild valley near Llangynog. There I was to visit a shrine to a 7th Century holy woman who had lived in the local woods, called St Melangell. The story went that a hunted hare took refuge under her skirts. When the hunters urged their hounds on, the hounds refused. The hunters thenceforth regarded that valley as belonging to Melangell and a community grew up around her. The locals still call hares "Melangell's Lambs" and many still see the valley as a refuge for wild creatures.

We found in this old chapel several miniature landscapes created for the feast of St Melangell. These were made out of moss, wood and stones and depicted the story of the saint and the hare. Sculptures of hares decorated the chapel's walls. There was an ark-like structure behind the altar containing her remains and behind this, a plain white chapel over her tombstone.

When we arrived, a woman was praying aloud in this chapel. She turned out to be the Vicar. She told us that her late husband, the previous Vicar, raised the money to rebuild this 12th century Welsh shrine. He was now buried in its graveyard. She showed us ancient standing stones and millennia-old yews in the graveyard, saying proudly that it had been a holy place from before Christian times. She told us that they had found the graves of the followers of Melangell contained white quartz crystals placed upon their bodies. White quartz has long been a precious stone used in healing and divining. Aborigines put it to use in healing.

She apologised for the spider webs in the church, saying that, as the chapel was dedicated to wild creatures, she was not removing cobwebs while the baby spiders were hatching. She also told of her delight when she saw a stoat in its winter coat in the churchyard at 4 a.m. that morning. Nearby was her centre for people with cancer. She said she could at least cure them of their fear. She was a real priestess. I thus felt able to tell her of my experiences in the oak wood. She then clasped my hands and greeted me as another on a sacred path.

When I spent time alone in Melangell's sanctuary, I suddenly smelt again the honey smell as at Mwnt and this time it did not have the same male feel, but felt as if associated with a female guardian. Some may wonder if I were imagining this? All I can say is that is how I perceived it. I am now used to trying to keep my senses open, to trying to keep myself aware of things that only faintly come to me. As for Melangell; among today's eco-warriors I have met spiritual women who lived in poverty in the woods in order to protect them and the wild creatures. One of these, a young woman called Sarah, presented me with my dog.

Many early Celtic Christians retained the wisdom they learnt from Druidry. Many kept their love for their lands and sacred places. One wise man who stopped by my wagon in Caebwr told me not to forget how much the members of the early Celtic Christian church had loved this land.

But our sacred inheritance from before Christian times is sadly not recognised in many Welsh parishes. I found churches with leaflets saying that they were built in sacred circles twice as old as Christianity. Some still had standing stones around them. But their leaflets suggested that the first truly spiritual people to arrive were Christians. They did not acknowledge the ancestral blessings that helped make these places sacred. Missionaries do much the same today on Aboriginal sacred lands.

There are still traces of ancient sacred places in London. On the first full moon of 1999, a month before Imbulc, I went with a friend to search out places in London once dedicated to the Goddess Bride. We went first to Brideswell in Wapping in the East End, by the former London docks. This was a well that supplied seamen with water as a gift of the Goddess Bride but today it can only be detected by its gurgles under a manhole cover.

We then went to an Anglican Church dedicated to St Bride, the patron "saint" of journalists. It stands near Fleet Street. Its board noted that the church was underpinned by a Roman building and by an ancient holy well. This was dedicated to the Goddess Bride before the Romans arrived. Springs were seen as the breasts of the goddess. Under the full moon my friend and I thanked the spirits of the place, asked for blessings for London and remembered our ancestors on this most ancient sacred place.

Bride was the threefold Goddess of poets, of metal workers and healers, a fine inheritance for journalists. The church board celebrated this place being Christian for 1,500 years. It did not honour the sacred gift of water in its well nor our pagan ancestors, whose energy and devotion had first made this a sacred place. The well and church are on a low hilltop beside the river Fleet, a tributary to the Thames. From Bride's Church we could see across this now hidden river to where St Paul's Cathedral stood on an opposite height. It too was built over an ancient shrine, reportedly dedicated in Roman times to the Goddess of witches, Diana.

When I was a child, my Catholic mother made sure I knew that the Anglican pre-Reformation churches were "stolen" from us by the greedy King Henry VIII. I have since always felt utterly at home in the marvels of the great Gothic Cathedrals with naves of great stone trees sometimes held together by keystone images of the Green Man. All of us have pagan ancestors who bequeathed to us much that they held sacred. The Church of England does not "own" the sacred spaces on which stand its most ancient churches. These are sacred also to Catholics and to Pagans. I hope that soon we will all be able to celebrate in all of our sacred places.

Our common spiritual inheritance

We need something new, millennial, an "even" balance between Pagan, Christian, and other religions that allows all of us to work together. We need to honour and share the different expressions of our innate religion, woven by different cultures with rich insights.

I acknowledge that I inherited knowledge of the mystical tradition from the Churches, and thus owe them a debt. I owe also to the religions of other continents that were part of the Mediterranean mixing pot at the time when Christianity was born. When Gnostic Christianity flourished, Buddhist missionaries had been in Alexandria for generations. The Brahmins of India had also shared their knowledge there.

I have been happy to see signs of change in Christianity in recent years. I was impressed by the "We Are Church" movement that grew in the 1990s in the European and American Roman Catholic Church. One of its leaflets stated: "We believe in a church which affirms the goodness of sexuality, the human rights of all persons regardless of sexual orientation, the primacy of conscience in deciding issues of sexual morality, for example birth control…We believe in a church where the people of God participate in the process of selecting their bishops and pastors. We believe in a church with equal rights for women, where women are full participants in all official decision-making and are welcomed in all ministries, including the deaconate and the ministerial priesthood…where priests may choose either a celibate or non-celibate way of life…We believe in a church which embraces and welcomes those who are divorced and remarried, married priests, theologians and others who exercise freedom of speech…"

At their conferences they discussed: "Creating Feminist Liturgies"…"Family Prayer: Opening Children to Feminine Images of God"; "In the Beginning Is Relationship: Human Sexuality as Energy for Love and Service"; "Remaking a Servant Church from the Bottom Up"; "New Millennium: Women Breaking through a Patriarchal Church." Unfortunately the Vatican did its best to obstruct this movement.

Some modern witches are anti-church perhaps because they have had bad experiences of churches or because they know how witches were once killed and tortured by church people. Others, including many in the old Craft family traditions, are not at all anti-Christian—as neither was Blandford. He wrote: "Let me assure you that we were not in any way anti-Church...we have always frequently attended services and even helped with their festivals...If truth be known, there have been more than one or two members of the clergy in our area who were as comfortable out on the wild moors as they were in the pulpit if you see what I mean. If there have been any problems with the Church, it has been only recently with the coming of the more evangelical clergy, those people who want everyone to bend to their beliefs and their beliefs only." What is not acceptable to me is intolerance of the religious views of others and using religion to gain power over others.

What he described as his own belief is a human experience open to everyone, not meant to be "occult". We inherit it by the very fact that we are human. He concluded by saying much the same: "I don't think I am giving away any secrets for the simple reason that there are none. Mystery, yes, but secrets, no. It is an open book if you are prepared to read it correctly...You have to experience, know and ultimately understand, in that order, these things, and I think the time has come when we have to understand them quickly, before it really is too late."

Behind all religions lies the innate human religion of our children. Our deepest wisdom lies in understanding the gifts we inherited as children. The truth is there from the beginning, within us, as is beauty, energy, spirit—and divinity. We humans are not born at random, not created purely for survival by Darwin's natural selection, but as part of a great work of music, of creation, of art and of love. Poets and scientists instinctively know that something is true if it fits into the great pattern of beauty. For me all nature is infused with divine spirit. All matter is also energy and spirit.

This is alike to the vision of the Jesuit mystic and palaeontologist Teilhard de Chardin, although he saw this fusion of spirit and matter as coming about through evolution rather than being always in existence. He wrote: "All that exists is matter becoming spirit. There is neither spirit nor matter in the world; the stuff of the universe is *spirit-matter*. No other substance but this could produce the human molecule."

He continued: "Life represents the goal of a transformation of great breadth, in the course of which what we call 'matter' turns about, furls in on itself, *interiorises* the operation, covering, so far as we are concerned, the whole history of the earth. The phenomenon of spirit is not therefore a sort of brief flash in the night; it reveals a gradual and systematic passage from the unconscious to the conscious, and from the conscious to the self-conscious. It is a cosmic *change of state*. This irrefutably explains the links and also the contradictions between spirit and matter."[384]

For me the Creating Energy of the universe both dreamt us and loves us. It gave birth to us and all other creatures because we have a role to lay in the great music of this universe, in what Plato called the chorus of the spheres. It gives to each one of us a destiny. Just as we share in the nature of the universe, we share in the nature of God. This is the "Force" that is really with us. Our bodies could not exist without the presence of this Creating Energy. This Energy is the Person who dreamt us, loves us and forms us in Her, His, own likeness. It is present in all creatures. It is both within and outside us.

The *Gospel according to Luke* reported Jesus as saying: "the kingdom of God is within you", not in some separate City of God, but here. This then is God's place, not just a vale of tears. The rediscovered *Gospel according to Thomas* reported Jesus as saying: "'If those who lead you say to you 'look the Kingdom is in the sky, then the birds will arrive there before you. If they say, "It is in the sea", then the fish will arrive before you...Rather the Kingdom is inside you and it is outside you." When Jesus was accused of committing blasphemy because he had said he was the Son of God, his response was that the scriptures said we are all gods!

Jesus then spelt out the consequence of this:

"When you come to know yourselves, then you will be known and you will realise that you are the sons of the living Father. But if you will not know yourselves, then you dwell in poverty and it is you who are that poverty."[385]

If the Gospel accounts are accurate, Jesus really laboured to get across to people that they already shared the divine nature, that they were naturally children of God. It is therefore most ironic and misleading that many "Christians" later insisted that Jesus alone was a Son of God, that Jesus alone shared in the divine nature; that we ourselves are guilty miserable sinners who become the children of God only through the Father's generosity, not through our nature, not as a birthright.

The *Gospel of St. Thomas* related that Jesus said, "I am not your master…He who will drink from my mouth will become as I am: I myself shall become he, and the things that are hidden will be revealed to him." This to my mind is the fruit of the Tree of Knowledge which Eve reached for and which the Jealous God, Jehovah, wanted to deny her. This is the knowledge denied to many Christians, leaving them struggling with guilt and fig leafs. Rather should we be singing:

> I am the daughter of God,
> I am the son of the Goddess
> This is the root of ecstasy,
> This is the root of magic
> To know to sing
> I am divine
> The world is divine
> I am the one who is.

I honour and learnt from the Christ that the priests killed and whose words they distorted. I am the daughter of God; I am she that is born of the Father, walking strong, warrior, mother, father, beyond time and gender, she who is being given birth to, she who gives birth.

I am also the Pagan, the spirit of nature, child of the Goddess, the one that was killed and tortured for centuries, born of the Mother of All.

We span the worlds, one with the mystics of all religions, one with the children of all races. We must realise and reflect the beauty that we possess so that our behaviour is a truthful match to our inner reality. It is our way to make the world more beautiful. When we accept who we really are, then we are rid of the divisions that fragment us. We accept with love the aspects of ourselves that we had rejected. We become complete. We become strong, able to self-fertilise, able to create.

This too was among the saying of Jesus kept by the Gnostics.

Jesus said; "When you make the two one, and when you make the inside like the outside and the outside like the inside, and the above like the below, and when you make the male and the female one and the same...then you will enter [the kingdom]."[386]

I remember the day when I conquered my fears enough to find my oneness. At that time I was wearing an ankh, the magical pagan Egyptian symbol also used by Coptic Christians, like a cross with a loop as its upper arm. When I first started wearing it, I told friends that I felt I was travelling the loop on top of the ankh back towards its centre. The day when I realised I had at last learnt to embrace both the male and female sides of myself without feeling that my self-identity as a woman was thereby threatened, I felt I had completed this journey to the centre. I was at the point from which the arms radiate out. I felt this meant the time had come for me to start teaching!

I also remember when I realised that I did not have to chose religions framed by others, that I could retain everything I valued, whether learnt from Christian or Pagan ancestors, without feeling that I was disloyal. Religions are not opposing football teams. I knew I was not abandoning what I have learnt and inherited when I sought a new synthesis. We carry our own truth within us. We do not need to be the label. We all have our own paths. There are many ways the Creatrix needs to be served, thus she makes many of us!

Some are called to serve the people as a teacher or as a representative in ritual of the sacred people and the Deity among us. I see this as more than serving the people by empowering them, by healing, and by keeping the balance. It is also to be completely wedded to the Deity. The Priestess in ritual must let the Divine energy pour into her. She becomes as one with the Deity. She learns to take this energy into her everyday life, as she eventually becomes an Elder or a Crone. Of course the same must apply to priests.

When working as a priestess, I sometimes experience a sense of timelessness. When I walk up the Avenue of Stones at Avebury, I feel I am the priestess who did this before, who has done it many times, and will do it many times. Many women have told me that they had the same experience. Perhaps this comes from the nature of our sacred work for in it we are all one.

When we work magically, when we walk the Avebury Stones Avenue, when we meditate, we may experience life beyond time. For me if one person can sense future events, then the future is in some way present now. I see the past, the present and the future as but different dimensions of the now. The gnostic scriptures record Jesus as teaching much the same, "Blessed is he who is before he came into being. For he who is, has been and shall be."[387] (There is also an interesting mathematical theory that explains part of the Chaos theory by positing that we cannot know the precise position of an electron because it is influenced by the future. It seems science and magic are again bedfellows, which is as it should be!)

I feel that my current work as a priestess, as a guardian of the wild, will continue to be my work after my death. It is not simply that this work is timeless in the sense I experienced at Avebury. It is rather that I will be going home to be with my Lover, not to go to sleep or to be blissed out, but to work with my Lover in sustaining this wonderful world.

I wrote the above paragraphs in the midst of rainstorm on Bodmin Moor, sheltered in a Land Rover near to The Hurlers, a stone circle. This is where I finished the first draft of this book. I needed wilderness to feed me and to sustain me for what I feel is a sacred task that is definitely in the present. Two days earlier I had watched the full eclipse of the sun, seeing it copy the moon in waning and waxing, creating midday darkness that awoke a bat roosting near me.

When the rainstorm on Bodmin Moor finished, I took a break from writing to climb to burial mounds set upon a summit where I talked to my ancestors and honoured them. On the way down, following no path, I found a stream issuing from a cave within a dark cleft. Within it there was a waterfall with a clear pool below it. The entrance was encircled with flowers, foxgloves, primroses, heather and gorse. It seemed to be a truly holy hidden place. I left in the flow of its natural blessings a healing wish for all that found her. My feet had unconsciously taken me here to do this. It is part of my work. This spring was nourishing many creatures. My own energy is now joined with the energy that was already there.

Working with death

My energy today is joined to a man who was with me on Bodmin Moor during the Solar Eclipse for he died of cancer in the following year, 2000. He helped me write this book. His name was Dick Swettenham. We worked together in the Craft as the High Priest and High Priestess of a coven and we were lovers, although he was many years older then I. When we first met, he had been over 35 years a member of the Bricket Wood Coven formed by Gerald Gardner. We met on the day when I raised energy for Lyminge Forest in a Circle of 120 witches. He was one of the 120. We found another common interest in that we both had large old wooden boats. Within a year we were working magic together. A group started to grow around us that the High Priestess of his old coven honoured by calling a "sister coven." We shared our ritual knowledge. I learnt much from him. We also organised the witchcamps together that I mentioned above. These camps kept a cauldron on the fire to feed all that came with or without money. He worked generously with eco-warriors, doing all he could to help.

Dick suspected within two months of the eclipse that his cancer had returned. A stomach cancer had been successfully removed some seven years earlier. He went for a check at the hospital. It gave him the all clear but his instincts were right. Some four months later the doctors found the cancer but it was much too late.

Dick then asked me to live with him so he might spend as much time as possible on his much loved boat. I agreed, and it was one of the most richly rewarding decisions of my life. I knew that he might not have much more than a few months left. We turned every day, every action, into a sacred ritual. When I lifted his feet up steps, it was "blessed be these feet that have honoured God and Goddess at the altar." When we stopped to watch the sunset for the final time, he ecstatically thanked the God for his blessing. All he thought needed to be done was done. Hurts were put right. He was stronger in his will than I had ever seen him before. He asked the Priest who presided over the last rites for Doreen Valiente the previous year to help me with performing his own last rites. He picked for his ashes the smaller stone ring on the crest of the hill at Stanton Drew in Somerset.

It was not a gloomy time. We celebrated each day. He was constantly designing some new piece of equipment to help himself move about. We went out for wonderful meals. We celebrated rituals in the woods, making seats for him against trees. As winter closed in, a local coven hosted us (as our own groups were far from his boat). We finally celebrated, as he wanted, his Third Degree Initiation, the Mystic Wedding. He glowed and was resplendent. He became again the fiery priest. Next day we visited for the last time the ancient stones of Stanton Drew. All was soon ready.

After a brief period in a local hospital, to which I was also admitted with an internal infection (a blessing for it kept us near to each other), he was admitted into a local hospice. The day I came out of hospital was a Friday, I later found he had jotted a note to himself that day saying that he would spend the weekend waiting for me, keeping himself busy with reading or working on his music business (in the 1960s he designed and made sound equipment for the Beatles and Rolling Stones.). When I reached the hospice, he gave me an enormous hug. He said. "You are alive. I am alive. It is good." My sheep dog, Storm, gave him a great lick. She was also his favourite. The hospice created a bed for the dog and I at the foot of Dick's bed. The nurses asked me how should they honour his religious beliefs? They said they had never knowingly had a Pagan there before. They willingly gave permission for an altar and religious pictures. These were put in place. I found Dick had no music. They found a radio and Classic FM took over his room.

Next morning there was a great change. It was as if he had decided that it was now time to die. He stopped being able to eat. He lay flat on his back, his eyes closed. He held my hand and conducted the music on the radio with his other hand, Sibelius, Beethoven, Mozart. Into the music I wove stories, meditations, pathworkings. He gave a sudden squeeze to my hand and a smile when I said: "I will be your rock. I am here as I said I would be. I will not go."

His secretary from the 1960s music business turned up. He delighted in her reminiscences. Shortly after she left, the energy in the room changed. I went barefoot. It was time for the final magic. It was time to take him to the river that borders this life.

Dick's sign was the Sun. His business was called after the sun. He had thus invoked south, the direction of the sun, at the final rites for Doreen Valiente. I could see in my mind a river sparkling with the light of the sun. I told him that I was taking him to the river. I lifted him, carried him out into the water. I felt him trust me. "Dick, the water is sparkling all around you. The sun is shining on it. It is in the water. The water is so clear. It is washing away your pain. Dick I am the Goddess. She is in me. I am here for you. I am at both sides of the gate. I will let you go, and I will catch you on the other side. I love you. Go my beloved. I love you."

I let him go, and he let go. Not long after this he peacefully stopped breathing, still holding my hand. His own hands were still very warm. It felt as if his spirit was strong at the time of death. It was not what I expected death to be like. It was some minutes before his hands started to cool. He lay there, looking so strong, his staff beside him. I strangely felt so very proud of him. He looked stronger than he had for many months, like an Elder of the Craft that had reached the apex of life and simply gone on. He had done what he wished in this life. It was time for the next. He seemed to have transcended all the cares that worried him, all the frailties of cancer that had so bothered and humbled him.

Dick wanted no one to waste money on a fine coffin so we got a cheap one and an artist friend of ours painted it. When he died he was wearing an ankh, so the coffin had an ankh painted on top. On its front there rode the sun. It was a gay boldly painted coffin for a person who loved life. Another friend accompanied me to the funeral parlour for the final preparation of his body. We wrapped him in a fine robe. We surrounded his face with ivy and flowers. He looked like the Green Man. Very much at rest. We stood at each end and blessed his body. "Blessed be those feet that carried him to the altar, blessed be those hands that lifted the Chalice, blessed be those lips that kissed the Goddess." Then we sealed the coffin.

Dick had wanted to come back for a last time to his boat, a 1905 motor ketch called Leonid, a Camper Nicholson named after a meteor shower, lying in Bristol Harbour. So we had the undertakers start the procession from the boat. We took the path of one of the final journeys undertaken by Dick and I. This took us down the Avon gorge and up to a yew wood on the cliff top. Here we conducted our Coven's last rite. It was very simple. We joined each of us around a yew tree with a golden cord. This symbolised the bond between Dick and us. We then used our ceremonial sword to cut this cord. The pieces we throw over the cliffs, wishing Dick's spirit to fly free.

The final rite at the Crematorium had as its Master of Ceremonies the Witch Priest who Dick had asked to help me with these rites. Strangely others picked him to be M.C. without knowing of his promise to Dick to help me in this. I was thus able to work with him, as Dick had wanted. We prepared the rite. I composed Quarter Calls and Invocations, trying to make them suitable for all that might come. These are the words we used.

Let us take a few deep slow breathes to prepare ourselves. Breathe deeply and remember the love you have for Dick and the joy he brought you. And so we begin.

East Spirits of the East, Powers of Air, we call you. Bring us bright memories of our beloved Dick and of the music that surrounded him. Blessed Be.

South Spirits of the South, Powers of Fire, we call you. Keep the fire of our love for Dick alive in the memory of this lover of the sun and of Helios. Blessed be.

West Spirits of the West, Powers of Water, we call you. Open our hearts; let our tears and love flow. Bring us healing and renewal. Remember this man who loved life, loved his friends and his magical family. Blessed Be.

North Spirits of the North, Powers of the Earth, we call you. From you we come; to you we return. Bring us Strength. Remember the Elder to whom you gave strength and wisdom and embraced in his passing. Blessed be.

I wrote this chant for this ritual.
We place our beloved in the river of life
The River is washing
The river is cleansing
The river is embracing
The river is sparkling with the Sun and new life
The river is carrying our beloved away
The river is filled with our love and our tears
The river is the Goddess and the God.

The final invocation before Dick's body went from the Chapel.
Goddess of fire,
Sun's fire, lightening,
Flame on the hearth,
Fire that cleanses and destroys,
Fire that purifies,
Now take our beloved Dick
Let him become flame and ash,
From Dick's spirit
A pure flame will arise
Go in Peace our beloved.

We finally thanked the Elements.
North:
Spirits of the North, Powers of the Earth thank you for the land that Dick walked upon, for the beauty in the plants and trees that gave him so much pleasure. Thank you for sustaining him.
Hail and Farewell
West:
Spirits of the West, Powers of Water. Thank you for quenching Dick's thirst, inspiring and washing him. Hail and Farewell
South:
Spirits of the South, Powers of Fire. Thank you the warmth of the summers he enjoyed and for the warmth of his heart. Hail and Farewell
East:
Spirits of the East, Powers of Air. Thank you for supporting Dick with every breath that he took, and may the last breathe that he took in this life become the first that he took in the next. Hail and Farewell

And in the summer, when the sun was high, on Dick's birthday, we carried out his final wishes by ceremonially spreading his ashes within the hilltop stone circle at Stanton Drew, where he and I had often worked; a place of magic very special to us. Although he had long loved the larger of the stone circles, we had discovered this separate ring together. During the rite it was as if the Old Ones were there with us. We set the circle together. We remembered him, told our special memories. We thanked him for his life. Then, when it felt right, I took the bag of ash, slit it with his athame (sacred dagger), and walked three times around the circle letting the ash flow freely. The Guardian spirits of the Stones seemed outlined in his fine ash as it blew in the wind across the stones. It was as he had asked. We knew he was one with the Old Ones.[388]

Dick's spirit seems to be still with us. I am writing this some twelve months after he died. His boat is being transformed, as he wanted. I feel he is delighting in watching it happen. I am living on her. Everyday I am sanding, filling, painting, putting my energy into her, loving her, turning a neglected orphan into a swan as I enter my 60th year. Her engine had not run for fifteen years, her masts have laid for the same period in the yard. Her wheelhouse was soggy with wet rot. But underneath I have found, as Dick said I would, a sound 44-foot teak hull built with great skill in 1905. I also found a shipwright, a friend of Dick's, who knew the boat well and who was willing to put much traditional skill into refitting her.

I have sold my own boat as Dick wanted and, as he suggested, I am using the money on his boat to turn it back into an elegant ketch. The 1952 engine is now working. A new wheelhouse is on her and her mast is up. Her oak ribs are sound. This work is a metaphor for the magic afoot. During the day I help turn an ugly duckling into a swan. At night I work finishing this book. Friends of Dick are dreaming of him and joining our magical group. We treasure his Book of Shadows. He is very precious to us. He has now taught me the lessons I needed to work as a Crone. I have now worked with death. It was for me the greatest privilege of my life. I am so very glad we did this together.

The myth we have as a birthright

There have been other mysteries that I only learnt to recognise in recent years. Our destiny is dreamt for us by our Creating Parent and revealed to us in our lives when we follow instincts and in the dreams that helped shape us.

I learnt of this when I found to my surprise that some of the most important events of my life were seemingly woven into a pattern that related to the ancestral myths of my people. This gave my life a structure and meaning that I had not intended. Was it by chance that the two key events in my gender transition happened on two of the four major ancient feasts of my ancestors, and in each case, happened on very appropriate feastdays, revealing a deeper meaning in what was happening to me?

By seeming chance, not then knowing the significance of the date, I took my first female hormone pill on August 1st, the feast of Lughnasadh or Llamas, a harvest festival when we celebrate the death of the corn king, a death needed that we might live. This was the day I too killed the willing male so that I, Jani, the daughter of God, might live. The pill contained hormones taken from a pregnant mare. She thus helped give birth to me. A white mare in ancient times signified the Goddess.

Next a hospital assigned me a date for the operation that would enable me to make love as a woman. They picked seemingly at random May 1st, the great feast of Beltane, when is celebrated the new life of spring, a time traditionally for much lovemaking. It was then too that I later first made love with a man.

Then I faced death at midnight on the great feast of Samhain or Halloween. Was it by chance that this assault happened at a time in Celtic traditions when the veil is said to be thinnest between the dead and living? It took me to the borderlands of death to listen to the Creating Spirit. Through it I came to put my sacred work at the centre of my life.

Finally, was it chance that my final initiation in the Craft was on the remaining quarter-year feast? I celebrated what is called the Great Rite, the mystic marriage, on the Celtic feast of Imbulc, the feast that celebrates the first signs of winter passing, when ewes beginning to have milk, serpents emerging from hibernation, when fires are lit to celebrate the day of Goddess Bridget. True I chose this day, but it was at a time when I was still unaware of this pattern in my life.

This suggested to me that some God, spirit or ancestor, with knowledge of the ancient myths of my ancestral lands, had helped weave my story for me. This Deity had dreamt me a life that gained meaning from these ancient myths. This would not have surprised Aboriginal Elders. They were used to their Land's spirits shaping their own lives.

There are many signs, many myths, within which I find myself dancing. My travelling way of life is like to that of the Gallae, the priestesses of Cybele. I did not choose this to mimic them. It came naturally. The Gallae apparently believed, as Jackie and I did when our children were young, that owning property was an obstacle to spiritual progress.[389] They travelled in caravans. I travel by a wooden boat or an old Land Rover with a cabin framed in wood. They took from one place to another a small shrine of the Goddess. I do the same. If a Gallae had a true home, it would be the mountain forests considered sacred to Cybele. Such places are my home. They ate meat believing, as I do, that all food was alive and died that we might live, therefore that all food is sacred. They preferred food gathered directly from nature. So do I.

The ancients believed that a Gallae, a transgendered priestess or shaman, was fulfilling a destiny ordained before birth and revealed by dreams or by the stars.[390] They believed we all have a destiny. We are free yet each one of us was brought into being for a specific purpose. This is set in the dreaming that began the process aeons ago that resulted in us now materialising as the humans of this planet.

Karl Jung held that our myths and dreams are tools that make conscious the secret knowledge concealed within in our unconsciousness. This contains "the almighty deposit of ancestral experience accumulated over millions of years". We share this as our "collective unconsciousness".³⁹¹ It combines 'the characteristics of both sexes, transcending youth and age, birth and death"³⁹². We are the richer, he held, the more we make conscious our unconsciousness. In a similar fashion the palaeontologist Teilhard de Chardin saw matter itself as naturally evolving to consciousness from unconsciousness. For Jung dreams and myths can better express the personal meaning of a truth than can objective scientific "facts", since personal truth cannot be defined, limited or be purely rational. Carl Jung like the Beguine Porete, held that the more our critical reason dominates our lives, the more impoverished our lives become.³⁹³

He said in his eighties: "My life is the story of the self-realisation of the unconscious. Everything in the unconscious seeks outward manifestation. The personality also desires to evolve out of its unconscious state and to experience itself as a whole…We can only express by way of myth what we are to our inward vision and what man appears to be sub specie aeterni-tatis. Myth is more individual and expresses life more precisely than does science. Science works with concepts of averages that are far too general to do justice to the subjective variety of an individual life. Thus I have now undertaken, in my 83rd year to tell my personal myth. I can only make direct statements, only "tell stories". Whether or not the stories are "true" is not the problem. The only question is whether what I tell is my fable, my truth."³⁹⁴

But it seemed to me that I was not the author of the myth I lived, nor was it simply a product of a collective unconsciousness, but rather this myth was created with me and tailored for me. It was the high dream that lures each of us, that differs for all yet enriches each one of us the more we make it concrete and understand it. Its realisation gave ecstasy.

Jung in his later years came to a similar understanding. He had earlier held that "myth is the natural and indispensable intermediate stage between unconscious and conscious cognition." But in his final writings he described myths that acted as bridges between our conscious thoughts and an imperishable world lying outside us beyond the laws of time and space. This was closer to my own experience.

He said his dreams gave him knowledge of this imperishable world: "In the end the only events in my life worth telling are when the imperishable world erupted into this transitory one. That is why I speak chiefly of inner experiences among which I include my dreams and visions. They form the basis of my scientific work."[395] "Myths are the earliest forms of science. When I speak of things after death, I am speaking out of inner promptings and can go no farther than to tell you dreams and myths."[396]

I became aware of my own myths when I wedded this imperishable world. Perhaps the wedding of the personal will to the Creating Spirit as an act of love, of self-giving, helps free the eyes and heart to see with imagination, helps frees the spirit to live the dream our divine mother had for us when she formed each one of us? Perhaps myths are in our lives because we were formed among divine dreams. If so, the myths that reveal these dreams have much to teach us.

The night before Jung's mother died, he had a dream in which a wolf tore past him as if on a hunt. He immediately recognised this beast as part of the Wild Hunt that seeks the souls of the dying, an ancient myth of his German people. When he later learnt of his mother's death, he thought this dream a pre-cognition from another world. At first the savagery of this vision dismayed him. But on reflection he saw an inner meaning that pleased him. She was taken "beyond Christian morality, taken into that wholeness of spirit and of nature in which conflicts are resolved". Later on he wondered why he was not beset with grief when he thought of her death but then realised that whenever he thought of her: "I continually heard gay dance music, laughter and jollity, as though a wedding were being celebrated." It was perhaps as if his mother was celebrating her mystic marriage.[397]

Jung looked to life after death to give a purpose to our lifetime's work, which he defined as making conscious our unconsciousness. He theorised that the more we make conscious, the more we take with us into the next world. "The maximum awareness which has been attained forms, so it seems to me, the upper limit of knowledge to which the dead can attain. That is probably why earthly life is of such great significance and why it is that what a human being "brings over" at the time of death that is so important. Only here, in life on earth, where the opposites clash together, can the general level of consciousness be raised."[398]

I am not so sure that this is right. Why can our consciousness and not our unconsciousness come with us into this other world? Why should we not be able to continue to explore the contents of our unconsciousness? What happens if we are reincarnated, as many believe? I should add, I am dubious about reincarnation being my own next step. I believe after my death I will continue to work with my Lover God in sustaining this Creation—for I am made to be a daughter and lover of my God and to work with Him.

In the very early days of Christianity, some were attracted to the message of Jesus because they found incarnated in the stories about him many of their most precious myths. These included mysteries celebrated for hundreds of years in the temples of Greece and Egypt. These celebrated a divine person who died so that we might live; who descended into the underworld and later rose back into life. In Egypt they celebrated the death of the God Osiris who died on a Friday to rise up again three days later.

In Mesopotamia they had the 5,000-year-old story of the Goddess Innana, who descended into the underworld, spent three days there and then reappeared in splendour. These myths honoured the death of plants that gave their lives that we might live, celebrated the rebirth of spring as well as that of the moon and finally, and most importantly, used these symbolisms to celebrate the rebirth of an individual to spiritual life. As I have said, none of these myths were thought of as real historical events, no one went hunting for relics of Osiris or pieces of his coffin. They were seen as embodying a far more abstract wisdom.

The later Christian account was of an historical person who uniquely lived these mysteries. Some Pagans suspected that the church embellished

Christ's life with mythological elements or that he was himself a myth. But there are elements of his story that suggest he was a real historical figure. His great friendliness to women was particularly an aspect unlikely to be invented by a patriarchal Church.

I think it was rather that the myths came into his life and shaped it; that he could not escape from living them. Perhaps this also happens to others who reveal aspects of Deity? He apparently lived and spoke as a person who was one with God, living a life dominated by sacred realities, so to me it is no wonder that sacred dreams and myths came to him, taught him, possessed him.

I see these sacred myths as the foundation lessons of human kind, part of our inherited wisdom, a divine gift. They have become stories woven into the sacred rituals of a thousand different nations. Some are so fundamental that they never really die, even when religious authorities deny their reality, but keep on resurfacing.

Thus the stories about Mary, the Virgin Mother, are woven deep with old pre-Christian myths and symbols. Male authorities may insist that she is not a Goddess, but she has been experienced as such since "Goddesses" was officially abolished in the Roman Empire. Her title "Stella Maris", Star of the Sea, was inherited from Isis. Her name Mary means "Of the Sea", the primordial female ocean, the womb of life from which Macha, the Goddess of Ulster, was born. I now see Mary as symbolising a Goddess, the Mother of the divine child, the Mother of the divine children, who refuses to be suppressed, refuses to die, refuses to leave her people's lives.

These ancient myths even came to inhabit our fairy stories—tales originally not of literature but of nature spirits. The ancient tale of Cinderella has the heroine watched over by the "Godmother", who symbolised our Source of Wisdom and Enlightenment, for she teaches Cinderella what to do to reach happiness. Cinderella also has to spend the ritual lunar three days in darkness before she can attain union with her Beloved in the Sacred Marriage.

A modern example of a myth coming to life, possessing someone, surely happened in the life and death of Princess Diana. I was brought up as a Northern Irish Republican. I did not apply for an Australian passport when I could because I had no wish to swear allegiance to the Queen. But something happened one morning when I woke up in the very early hours and put on the television because I could not sleep. The surprise was not so much the news that Diana was dying following a car crash. It was what happened when she died.

At that moment I found myself, to my astonishment, sitting bolt upright in bed and exclaiming "But you are good!" It was as if we had touched and I had felt her goodness. I was embarrassed at first to admit this; it seemed so strange. But many others experienced something similar. I wondered if this was because many were engrossed in her life and so created a great surge of emotional energy around her death? This does not mean that she did not touch us. The collective energy added strength to her appearance in our lives. However it happened, I cannot forget how real her touch felt.

Over the next week, I studied the accounts of her work for sick children and for land mine amputees, to see if my intimation were correct. I found she had really worked hard to fulfil the myth she felt she had been given, that she was meant to be the Queen of Hearts. She went frequently to hospitals unannounced, without the press, taking great pains with sick children. I was particularly impressed by a parent who told how her sick daughter wrote to Diana and received from her a hand-written reply. Some weeks later at a public event, this parent called out to Diana, thanking her for the reply. Diana immediately stopped, came back and asked about her daughter. The reply came that she was at a children's hospital and gravely ill. A day later, quite privately in the middle of the night, Diana turned up to see this child.

And thus I was thrilled when her brother took on the role of completing her myth, championing her in the Abbey at her funeral, saying she was named for the pagan Goddess Diana, and burying her on an island where she will be remembered as a sleeping beauty. I loved it all and hoped the people hold fast to this new working of an ancient myth. Why it should be given to us now, why Diana, that I do not know but her death was extraordinarily experienced by many. Tens of thousands left her flowers in a national outpouring of quite incredible grief. Maybe she was too earthy, too sexual, too honest ever be officially made a saint, but she would be if we still made saints by acclamation.

One lesson I learnt from this was that the divine way does not always to work through the poor and outcasts but may use popular myths, even a princess of the royal family! The divine way is of the people, not of an esoteric occult few.

We can make our own myths. Sometimes we do this by building on deep true instincts. Other times myths may be created for political ends. Such a creation with terrible consequences was the tale of Adam and Eve that taught us the world was a vale of tears given as a punishment for our first parents' sin, thus wrecking our inherited and instinctive delight in nature.

But looking at this myth more closely, it turns out to be a very muddled, cobbled together out of very different stories. Surely a Tree that gave us knowledge of Good and Evil was not a bad thing to have? Why were women and snakes so singled out for punishment? Were they punished because they had sacred knowledge learnt of trees, knowledge considered dangerous by the priestly author of Genesis? (Biblical scholars say that this story went through a priestly rewriting about 300-400 years before Christ.)

I have spent decades of my life helping people to deal with such evils as corporate greed, bad medicine, human rights violations, pollution, but all that I could achieve by doing this was to prevent a few evils. I often felt I was thereby simply plugging a few holes in a fragile dyke.

I now realise that there are other ways of tackling these problems that could be more effective. We must re-write the myths that have cursed us. The myth that God told us to "conquer" this world has served as a justification for carving up our common heritage for private profit and to make those who do so feel more comfortable at night. The myth that women were created to serve men justifies male chauvinism. The myth that we are weak sinful creatures helps to justify a milliard guilt complexes and our need for a priestly caste.

So, perhaps one of the most important things to us to do is to re-dream the myth of our Creation to make it reflect our deepest sacred instincts. If we love the World, then our myths about our creation will reflect that love and be beautiful. But if we fear nature, if we fear women, if we want to deny to others the knowledge of good and evil, then we will again find ourselves with a creation account like to the one in Genesis.

Let me start. Afterwards we all should embellish it, alter it, improve it, and make it more personal.

A Creation myth for our time

In a cave under the world lives the Mother who can make children by herself for she contained both male and female magic. She is in love with creating and is always refashioning herself by making children of every kind out of her own body. In four days she had made a galaxy out of one of her legs, a nova out of a breast and a spider out of the other breast. Her nose she had used to shape a cow, her eyes the planet Venus and jellyfish. She is a kaleidoscope of constantly shifting colours, lights and shapes.

And everything she creates is so full of her energy that it also dreams and creates. She is so alive, so much enjoying the detail of creation, that she is present everywhere, watching, seeing how it is going. Everything she has created is her family. She lives in them, sustaining them with her love. She creates a never-ending cycle of birth and death to allow creation to grow in an elegant sustainable way. She heals the wounds, cares for the dying. Nothing in her world is static. She is in the caves with the bats. For them she is a bat Goddess. She is on the moors with the wild ponies. For them she is a Pony Goddess. She is in the heavens. For the stars she is the

Goddess Mother of Galaxies. She is down the holes with the worms and they too know her as their Mother Goddess. All sing to her, all love her in their own way.

Creation matured and became self-aware. On the fifth day of creation the trees, the rocks, the earth dreamt of themselves and learnt that they were beautiful. The Goddess was delighted. Every mother likes it when her children appreciate her. The dreams of the trees, of the rocks, of the earth, were full of her divine energy as they too created out of themselves species that expressed other aspects of divinity. On the sixth day they dreamt a species with creative abilities in even its fingertips so, out of the earth, out of the plants, out of the animals and the snakes, out of their dreams, came humans.

The Goddess gave humans instincts that left them free to choose what they wanted to create. She gave them the choice of loving her or not. She had to trust them, for otherwise creation would never reflect her own freedom.

The trees and herbs, birds and insects, animals and rocks that helped create humans, promised to teach, house, feed and heal them when needed. She then gave humans a guide to help them in their own creating, the gift of a sacred tree that could teach them of the dangers of false gods. It was the Tree that knew both Good and Evil. She bade them eat of this tree and live wisely.

And so that humans would not think they were a species apart, she gave them a special guardian, the snake. It would remind them of the cycle of life and death every time it shed its skin. It also promised her to teach them magic, for; living close to the earth it was full of earth energy.

The Goddess knew that if humans fulfilled the dreams she shared with them, then they would become her Lovers and she would no longer be alone. So it was a risk she willingly took in making them free. And she made them male and female so they could mix their gene and have fun in doing so. She also created gays and bisexuals so all creatures had many ways of expressing love. Then she said the time had come to rest and make love, for her Garden of Eden was complete. It was now the day of love, the seventh day that was unending. This is the story of the Original Blessing and of how all things came about.

Some Fragments

Who Am I?

I let my own dreams speak.
A birthgift led me to become a shaman and priestess
With many lives in one.
My children they said were tainted.
I was taught shame and penitence,
To cry: "I am not worthy"
To a God who only wanted me to be His Lover.
His gifts to me were spurned.
I was flung from the temple steps.
As were the transgendered Gallae
In whose face spat St Augustine,
Whose words damned them to fire.
And now
I am she, who comes from the flames,
Who is now forged.

And I come in the armour gifted by my lover.
I come with sword of the almighty,
I come with the laughter and gaiety of the lover
To Christ who loved the Magdalene,
To Sophia, the Goddess of wisdom,
To Herne the Lord of Magic,
To Macha of my Irish blood,
To the Morrigan
To Brighid

On lowliness

I am the lowest of the low, for I have cast off all layers
Tore off the clothes, washed off the make-up.
Not now so afraid of being called a witch,
A not-a-woman, a freak, a fraud, a pretence,
For I am none of the things that you define your world by.
A voice in the wilderness perhaps,
But it is my voice, my wilderness.

On being feared

These words of my Lover are bitter true,
You will be persecuted,
Rejected at home.
These are the consequences…
This is the cost.
For living the dream.
Of your sexuality, gender and magic

You cast a big shadow
Whether you like it or not
Standing tall as a warrior,
In the light of the sun.

Some will fear being eclipsed by
The dark of your shadow
So ridiculously; inevitably.
They will hurt you
Because of a shadow
The sun gifts to your feet.

On Overcoming Fear

Nothing can scare us if we are one
With foxes and rabbits and bumps in the night,
So spin together the days of your life
With the mosquito, the fly and the beetle.
Weave them together into a fine fable
Then forget to be scared,
For the web you have woven
Leaves nothing outside it
And nothing is left to be scared of.

The tapestry of magic

As a priestess of the Earth, I am not of one path, but of all paths. I stand between them, accepting what each gives for me to weave into my tapestry. I weave knowing that my work is but one piece in a cosmic patchwork quilt. We, the Weavers, are of the humancraft, the inherited Old Wisdom. We weave the net that protects those who fall. We weave the thread that joins us. We weave the quilt that protects. We weave the beauty that inspires. We weave the magic of imagination and the tapestry of life.

The Unity at the End of Life

The next morning, Storm, my dog, wakes me before dawn. It is the start of the shortest day of the year. The sky is veiled in ever-changing waves of colour as she prepares the way for the golden sun. I welcome the rise with the sign of the Tree of Life drawn within the Circle of Life. It is the sign that unites me with my heritage, male and female, Christian and Pagan. I now am not confined. I have at last the confidence to be everything I have experienced. I am freed. My circle is complete.

Destiny

I invoke Herne. I play and work with him.
I invoke Macha. I flirt and work with her.
They are closer than my skin to my bones, my brain to my mind.
I touch my fingers
To their cheeks.
I weave their hair,
I share their dream.
Their Child and Lover

NOTES

1. For those who are interested in astrology, I was born in the morning of the 19th, in Aquarius, cusp with Pisces, the same signs as allotted to this age in astrology. Currently the equinoctial point is moving from within the constellation of Pisces to Aquarius in the solar 'Great Year" cycle that takes this point through 12 constellations over a period of 2160 years. The Grecian ancients used to crown their Goddess with 12 stars in honour of this Great Year—and the Virgin Mary is sometimes shown similarly crowned—a direct inheritance from pre-Christian days. To astronomers this is known as the "precession of the equinoxes". (Doreen Valiente *Witchcraft for Tomorrow* 11-12.) I do not know the relevance of this, outside that it seemed symbolically right for me as my life shares with this epoch a transition from the age of Patriarchy.

2. Diana Bell, (1998) *Ngarrindjeri Wurrunwarrin: a world that is, was, and will be,* Spinifex Press women@spinifexpress.com.au Melbourne, 1998, page 498.

3. Intersex Society of North America. (ISNA) From their website in 2000.

4. J N Zhou, M A Hofman, L Gooren & D F Swaab, 'A sex difference in the human brain and its relation to transsexuality', Nature, 2 November 1995, vol. 378: 6552, pp. 68-70 shows 'a female brain structure in genetically male transsexuals and supports the hypothesis that gender identity develops as a result of an interaction between the developing brain and sex hormones'. A paper by D de Cegli, J Dalrymple, L Gooren, R Green, J Money & R Reid, *Transsexualism: the Current Medical Viewpoint,* produced on 18 January 1996 for the UK Parliamentary Forum on Transsexualism chaired by Dr Lynne Jones MP, states 'the weight of current scientific evidence suggests a biologically-based, multifactorial etiology for transsexualism'." Also see *Brainsex: the real difference between Men*

and Women by Anne Moir and David Jessel, Mandarin Paperback, 1989, London.

5. J. Roberts, Ed.*Mapoon Book One*. International Development Action, Melbourne 1976.

6. Mudrooroo *Aboriginal Mythology* Thorsons 1994, 62

7. Connor *Blossom of Bone* HarperSanFrancisco 1993, 31

8. Ibid. 32

9. Ibid. 27

10. Ibid. 31

11. Ibid. 41

12. Ibid. 42-43

13. Ibid. 33

14. Ibid 43

15. Ibid note 62

16. Ben Stiles, "*Medieval Understanding of Women's Physiology*".

17. A marvellous description of this from the viewpoint of a participant can be found in Diane Bell's book *Daughters of the Dreaming*, Phee Gribble/Allen & Unwin, Melbourne, 207-225

18. Diane Bell *Daughters of the Dreaming* McGeorge Allen & Unwin, Sydney 169

19. Diane Bell *Ngarridnjeri Wurruwarrin: A world that is, was and will be* 511

20. Diana Bell "*The Daughters of the Dreaming*. 225

21. Chris Knight, *Blood Relations*, ISBN 0 300 06308-3 Yale University Press 95

22. Quoted on "*Mountain Man*" website.

23. Book of Genesis, The Bible. 17:10

24. Herodotus, *Histories 2*, 104 1-4

25. A view also endorsed by the Koran 2, 223

26. Lev. 12/1.

27. Dawson 1929 quoted in Cyril Adler in *The Adler Museum Bulletin*, Johannesburg. Vol 10 No 1. March 1984.

28. Philo 3: 48, 1971, 244

29. Ranke-Heinemann *Eunuchs for the sake of the Kingdom of Heaven: Women, Sexuality, and the Catholic Church* Penguin and Doubleday 1991 New York page 317

30. Jack Roberts and Joanne McMahon *The Sheela-na-Gigs of Britain and Ireland.* Bandia, Ireland 1997

31. Intersex Society Report

32. The Sciences, July/August 1993 quoted on Intersex Society of North America website.

33. Intersex Society of North America (ISNA) website.

34. J N Zhou, M A Hoffman, L Gooren and D F Swaab, 'A sex difference in the human brain and its relation to transsexuality', Nature, 2 November 1995, vol. 378:6552, pp 68-70.

35. Information supplied by ISNA.

37. *The Independent on Sunday*, UK 13/2/1998

38. Rev. Hey in the 1961 *Queensland Presbyterian Mission Message Stick*, quoted in *Mapoon Book Three* Ed. Jan Roberts.

39. In modern medicine there is a definition of the hermaphrodite that is quite different from its ancient sense. It focuses entirely on the genitals. It thus defines it only in terms of a genital condition, ignoring the person's gender identity and the hormone-shaped brain. In this book I use this word in its older sense.

39. *The Tain* translated by Thomas Kinsella, Oxford Paperbacks 66

40. Uta Ranke-Heinemann *Eunuchs for the Kingdom of Heaven* 323-4

41. Baring and Cashford *The Myth of the Goddess* 532, note 97.

42. Pagel *The Origin of Satan* 77

43. Baring and Cashford

44. St. Ignatius *Exercises.* Week One.

45. Baring and Cashford op.cit. 245

46. Plato *Symposium* 189e

47. Plato op.cit. 190a

49. Matthew Fox *Confessions-the making of a post-denominational priest* HarperSanFransisco 70

50. Romans 16/7 and commentary in Ranke-Heinemann op.cit.127

51. Mary Condren *The Serpent and the Goddess. Women, Religion and Power in Celtic Ireland* HarperSanFrancisco 1989160

52. Philip Haselton *Wiccan Roots* 133-140, 183

53. In this work I use the modern scholarly notation for dates. CE means "Current Epoch" and is used instead of AD as that format only had relevance to Christians. Likewise I use BCE, "Before Current Epoch" instead of BC.

54. Montague Summers Introduction to 1938 edition of *Malleus Mallificorum* XIV

55. Pagels *The Origin of Satan* 171

56. Pagels *The Gnostic Gospels,* Vintage Books, Random House, 1979 New York page 57

57. James Robinson (ed.) *The Nag Hammadi Library* HarperSanFrancisco 1990, page 209

58. Hans Kung *Christianity: The Religious Situation of Our Time* SCM Press 1995, London, page 160

59. Thomas Aquinas *Summa Theologica* lll q42 a 4 and 5

60. Thomas Aquinas S Th ll/ll q151 a3 and 2.

61. Thomas Aquinas Sum Th ll/ll q70 a3

62. Ibid. ll/ll q26 a10

63. Sth, suppl. Q64 a 5 ad2.

64. S Th Suppl. Q39 a1.

65. Tertullian *On Female Dress.*1 I

66. Galatians 3.28.

67. Documented in Elaine Pagels *The Gnostic Paul.*

68. J John Knox, Geneva, Published in 1558

69. Karen Armstrong, *The Gospel According to Women: Christianity's Creation of the Sex War in the West* ElmTree Books 1986 London page 34

70. Hans Kung 140

71. Elaine Pagels *The Gnostic Gospels* 42

72.Andrew Welburn *Gnosis—the mysteries and Christianity* 190

73. Baring and Cashford op.cit 631

74. Armstrong. op.cit. 42

75. Catholic Encyclopaedia.

76. Elaine Pagels *The Gnostic Gospels*

77. Prof. H.Koester, Harvard. I use the more religious neutral notation of CE for Current Epoch instead of AD, and BCE for Before Current Epoch instead of BC. This is now the practice of many scholars.

78. Robinson *The Nag Hammadi Library* 2-3. Also see Pagels *The Gnostic Gospels* 31

79. Baring and Cashford op.cit. 634

80. Armstrong op.cit 65.

81. Pagels 31-34

82.Jeremiah 44/16

83. Andrew Welburn. Op.cit. 32

84. Kung 306

85. Pagels *The Origin of Satan* 132

86. Pagels 57

87. Pagels 143

88. Some historians refused to recognise them as women and thus used for them the male term "galli"—as did the author of *"Blossom of Bone"*.

89. Conner *Blossom of Bone*. 100, 105, 125

90. Revelations 12/1

91. Quoted in Armstrong, op.cit 3.

92. Condren op.cit. 103

93. Armstrong op.cit. 36

94. I used the male pronoun for the deity at that time in public. I prefer now to use the female. But what is right for a divine person who is beyond gender? We need a new gender pronoun.

95. Daniel Berrigan *Consequences, Truth, and* 10

96. *Declaration on Some Questions in Sexual Ethics* 1975

97. Papel Encyclical *Redemptoris Mater*

98. Dr D. Zambaco. *"Onanism and Mental Disturbance in Two Little Girls"* L'Encephale 1882 cited in Uta Ranke-Heineman 218.

99. Armstrong op.cit 32

100. Augustine 2,12

101. *Casti Connubii,* 1930

102. Augustine *The City of God.* Book 7 Ch 21

103 Origen *Commentary on Matthew.* 15.3

104. Augustine Letters 243, 10.

105. Pliny *Natural History* 8/5

106. Seneca quoted on page 13 of Ranke-Heinemann op.cit.

107. Ranke-Heinemann op.cit. 12

108. ibid.

109. Ephesians, 5/22-32

110. Ephesians 5/22

111. I Cor 7/25

112. Ranke-Heineman op.cit.12

113. *Adversus Jovianian* 1/7

114. *Cambridge History of the Bible.* Vol. 2. Page 84

115. Cited by Pagel 73-75

116. Unfortunately many modern historians seemingly judged Gnosticism by the attacks on it launched by the Fathers, holding the Gnostics responsible for much that could perhaps be more rightly blamed on the Catholic Fathers. Thus Professor Ursula King in *"Christian Mystics"* (1998) wrote, "A certain depreciation of the body, of sexual relations and marriage developed which may well have been due to Eastern and Gnostic influences". (P40) She also denied the title of "Christian" to the gnostic Christians.

117. *Commentary on Genesis* 3/9 Luther 103

118. Freud, *An Outline of Psychoanalysis,* SE, XX111 193-4

119. Aristotle *On the generation of animals,* 2/3.

120. Eumenides, II 658-60, 736-65. Translated by Richmond Lattimore.

121. Riane Eisler *Chalice and the Blade*

122. Diane Bell *Daughters of the Dreaming* 132

123. Ibid. 29

124. Koran 2/223

125. Late 20th century scholarship suggested that there was never a mass migration of tribes into Britain bearing a "Celtic culture" from Central Europe as once thought, but that the "Celtic' culture of these islands is indigenous, although much influenced by immigrants, invaders and traders from mainland Europe. I use "Celtic" in this sense.

126. Armstrong 134.

127. Freud, *"Civilisation, Society and Religion,* Penguin Freud Library

128. Baring and Cashford op.cit. 278

129. Baring and Cashford op.cit. 279

130. Armstrong op.cit 73

131. Passion of Perpetua and Felicitas. Trans. P. Dronke in *Women writers of the Middle Ages.*

132. Ibid. 84

133. *Apocalypse of Peter* quoted on page 106 of Pagel. Op.cit.

134. Pagel op.cit 99.

135. Ranke-Heinemann op.cit 25

136. Jerome Commentary on Ezekiel 18- 6

137. Ranke-Heinemann op.cit. 22

138. Ranke-Heinemann op.cit. 22

139. Armstrong op.cit 64

140. Jones and Pennick, *A History of Pagan Europe* Routledge, London 1995, page 72

141. Augustine quoted in Baigent and Leigh *The Elixir and the Stone* 51

142. Pope Gregory Dialogues. 4/II

143. Cf. Kempt, in Jedin, *Hadbuch de Kirchengeschichte*, vol III 1966 407ff

144. *Decretum Gratiani*, pars II, dist XXXII, c10

145. C Will, *Acta et scripta quae de controversiis ecclesiae graecae et latinae* 1861 p126 (Ranke-Heinemann op.cit 107)

146. Ranke-Heinemann op.cit. 112

147. Hildergard Causes and Cures 2.8; k35-36; quoted on page 106 of Sabina Flanigan *Secrets of God. Writings of Hildegard of Bingen*.Shambhala Publications, Boston 1996

148. News report on the BBC's Radio 4 c. 5th July 2001

149. Mornes to Cardinal Farnese, *Mounumenta Vaticana*, ed. Laemmer 1861 p 312

150. C2000 Janine Roberts

151. Kahlil Gibran *The Prophet* page 20

152. Janine F. Roberts C2000

153. Karen Armstrong *A history of God*, page 184

154. Bede Griffiths *The Marriage of East and West* 14

155. Ibid. 14

156. Ibid. 203

157. Augustine *De Doctrina Christiana* 3/18

158. Nature Article reported in *The Independent on Sunday*, 24th Jan 99

159. Armstrong op.cit 224

160. Drane 56

161. Augustine, *On Marriage and Concupiscence* Chapter 22

162. Hans Kung in *Christianity* on page 420 maintained that in rejecting the Gnostic Christians, Christianity had remained non-syncratic—that is, not melded with elements of other faiths. But here we have a clear example of a pagan belief helping to shape a Christian doctrine.

163. I mentioned earlier how in the 20th Century many sacred books of the Manichaeans were discovered in Asia. Until then, most of what we knew of them came from the distorting accounts of their enemies. Their sacred books seem to have belonged to a much more tolerant and gracious religion than the one Augustine described.

164. J. Roberts ed. *Mapoon Book Three* International Development Action, Melbourne, 1976

165. Maire MacNeill, *The Festival of Lughnasa*, Oxford (1962), 3. The Anglo-Saxons also held a sacred harvest festival on the same day which they called Lammas or 'loaf-mass' celebrated with the first grain baked into sacred bread.

166. Ovid *Amores* 1, verse 8

167. Jerome *Commentary of the Epistle to the Ephesians* III, 5

168. Ambrose—*Exposition of the Gospel according to St Luke*, lib X, n.161

169. Karen Armstrong, *Gospel according to Women* p134

170. Ranke-Heinemann op.cit. 132.

171. Pagel op.cit44

172. Randy Connor *Blossom of Bone* 121, 125.

173. Augustine *City of God* Book 7 Chapter 28

174. Tertullian quoted on page 113 of Connor *Blossom of Bone.*

175. Isaiah 56:3-5.

176. Matt. 19:21

177. Deuteronomy 23:1

178. Germaine Greer in *"The Independent"*, "On why sex change is a lie". 22nd July 1989.

179. Randy Connor *Blossom of Bone* page 124 n124

180. Monica Sjoo and Barbara Mor *The Great Cosmic Mother: Rediscovering the religion of the Earth* Harper Collins 1987 P226

181. Monica Sjoo and Barbara Mor op.cit. 67

182. Charles Darwin 26

183. Sjoo and Moo op.cit. 33

184. St. Martin's Press

185. J. Roberts *Mapoon Book Three* International Development Action, Melbourne 1976

186. Norman Cohn *Europe's Inner Demons* Xii

187. Regine Pernoud *Hildegard of Bingen* 160

188. Ibid. 165
189. Professor Eva Pocs *Between the Living and Dead* Central European University Press, Budapest. ceupress@osi.hu
190. Eliade *Shamanism; Archaic Techniques of Ecstasy*
191. Pocs *Between the Living and Dead* 16
192. Ibid. 9
193. Ibid. 14
194. Hermaphroditism was defined by 20th Century doctors as if it referred only to the shape of genitals. I use it more broadly. My body had physical features of both genders, it was thus of both Hermes and Aphrodite.
195. Private communication, June 2001, from a practitioner of magic.
196. Diane Bell *Daughters of the Dreaming* 173-5
197. Ibid. 161
198. Ibid. 210
199. Baring and Cashford. *The Myth of the Goddess* Penguin 1993 103
200. Ibid. 10
201. J. Roberts. Ed. *Mapoon Book Two* 51
202. Bell op.cit 162
203. Hutton *The Triumph of the Moon* 98
204. Pocs op.cit
205. Bede *A history of the English Church and People* I, 30 86—7
206. Website on Anglo Saxon magic
207. Pocs op.cit. 75
208. Ibid. 155
209. Ibid. 150
210. Ibid. 151
211. Ibid. 152
212. Ibid. 14—refers to Wall 1980 and Ryan 1978
213. Ibid. 12
214. Eliade *Shamanism*, published in 1957 and Pocs op.cit. 77
215. Friedrich von Spee quoted on page 115 of Armstrong op.cit.

216. Quoted in *Witches and Witchcraft* by Rosemary Ellen Guiley.

217. Ibid. 18

218. Ibid. 30

219. Ronald Hutton *Stations of the Sun* 135

220. Cohn, op. cit 214

221. Ibid. 21

222. Miranda Green *Celtic Goddesses* 85

223. Witchcraft Museum, Boscastle, Devon

224. University of Michigan website—section on magic.

225. Norman Cohn *Europe's Inner Demons* 180 to 184

226. Ibid. 188.

227. Ibid. 176

228. Ibid. 198

229. Ibid. 203.

230. Pocs op.cit. 85

231. Aquinas *Summa Theological* Final Section or Appendix.

232. Ranke-Heinemann 227

233. Ibid. P229

234. Thomas Aquinas Iq. 3: q. 10

235. Ronald Hutton *The pagan religions of the British Isles* Blackwell 1991, page 68

236. Sprenger and Kramer *Malleus Maleficorum* Dover Publications, New York 1971 edition.

237. Ibid. 2

238. Ibid. 13

239. Ibid. 40.

240. Pagels *The Origin of Satan* 50

241. Ibid. cit. III q 34

242. Ranke-Heinemann 231

243. Sprenger and Kramer 41

244. Pocs op.cit. 107

245. Sprenger and Kramer 157

246. Ranke-Heinemann 233

247. Ibid. 233

248. Ibid. 234

249. Hutton *Triumph of the Moon* 379

250. Quoted in *The way of the Earth: Encounters with Nature in Ancient and Contemporary Thought* Simon and Schuster, New York 1994, page 108

251. HRT stands for Hormone Replacement Therapy

252. From the interview with him in our film, *Munda Nyuringu*.

253. c2000 Janine Roberts

254. Fr. Perez, *Kalumburu* 1977, p 122-3)

255. See "Saturday" for more about Daisy Bates

256. Janine Roberts c2000

257. Gimbutas *"Gods and Goddesses of Old Europe"*1974 and in her later *"The Language of the Goddess: Unearthing the Hidden Symbols of Western Civilization "* Harper & Row, 1989

258. William Osborn *The Women Warriors* 1997 http://www.linguafranca.com/9712/nosborne.html

259. Elizabeth Wayland Berber *Women's Work: the first 20,000 years"* (Women, Cloth and Textile in Early Times 1994 Norton. New York.

260. Diane Bell *Daughters of the Dreaming* 26

261. Ibid 173

262. Bell op.cit. 204

263. Janine Roberts *Massacres to Mining: the colonization of Aboriginal Australia* Dove Communications, 1981

264. Hildegard quoted on page 57 of Matthew Fox *The Original Blessing*

265. The criteria for membership of the Pagan Federation in 2001 were 1. Love for Kinship with Nature. Reverence for the life force and its ever-renewing cycles of life and death. 2. A Positive Morality, in which the individual is responsible for the discovery and development of their true nature in harmony with the outer world and community. This is often

expressed as: "Do what you will, as long as it harms none." 3 Recognition of the Divine, which transcends gender, acknowledging both the female and male aspect of Deity.

266. Geoffrey of Monmouth. *Vita Merlini* (quoted on P12 of Caitlin Matthews *The Celtic Tradition*)).

267. Ellis op. cit. 266

268. Lois Bourne *Dancing with Witch*es published by Robert Hale, London, 1998

269. There are different inheritances. By blood I identified with the land my mother told me my people mostly came from—Ulster and Western Scotland—to which I added the other strongly Celtic lands. By birth I identified with the land where I grew up as a child—Kent in England. But this did not stop me acknowledging a wider inheritance—first as a European and finally as a human born of Gaia or the Earth. Each of these inheritances was a gift—and a responsibility.

270. Thomas Aquinas *Summa Theo. Suppl* q 53 a3 ad 1

271. Marguerite Porete *The Mirror of Simple Souls* Translated by Ellen Babinsky 1993, Paulist Press, New York, page 80

272. Paul Verdeyen's article "Le Proces d'inquistion contra Marguerite Porete et Guiard Cressonessart" in Revue d'historire ecclesiastique 81 (1986); 47-94; quoted in the Introduction by Ellen Babinsky to Marguerite Porete *The Mirror of Simple Souls* Paulist Press, New York 1993

273. Ellen Babinsky op.cit. 12

274. Quoted in Matthew Fox *Original Blessing* 58

275. Quoted on page 69 of *Original Blessing* by Matthew Fox. This book is an excellent source of quotes from Beguine mystics. I have used it extensively.

276. Babinsky op.cit 5

277. Ekhardt *Miscellanies.*

278. Romans 10:170". Ranke-Heinemann op.cit. 241

279. Pocs. *Between the Living and the Dead*

280. Barbara Griggs *Green Pharmacy* 18

281. Hildegard *"On Causes and Cures"* 4.3; k 188. Translated by and quoted by Sabina Flanagan in *"Secrets of God; Writings of Hildegard of Bingen"*. 117

282. Briggs op.cit. 27

283. Peter Berresford Ellis *The Druids* 217

284. Griggs op.cit 48

285. Pocs op.cit. 108

286. Mary Condren *The Serpent and the Goddess* 52

287. Their persecution has continued. The New York Holocaust Centre estimated that some 500,000 to 1,500,000 Roma died at Nazi hands in what the Roma called "The Devouring". Today they make up many of the refugees fleeing from Eastern Europe.

288. PE 197-8

289. Particularly Ronald Hutton in *The Triumph of the Moon* and *The Pagan Religions of the British Isles.*

290. Vivienne Crowley *Wicca* 26

291. Hans Kung op.cit 611

292. Hans Kung op.cit 612-3

293. Trevor-Roper op.cit 146 n7

294. Hans Kung op.cit 614

295. Ronald Hutton *The Triumph of the Moon* Oxford Press, 1999, page 379

296. F von Spee *Cautio Criminalis—Legal Objections to the Witchtrials* 1631

297 N 914.

298. Janine Roberts *Massacres to Mining* 16

299. Thomas Merton op.cit. 34-36

300. Lee Carroll Pieper—quoted on page 286 of *Original Blessing* by Matthew Fox

301. Old Testament. Is. 45/7

302. *The Age*, Melbourne, Australia.

303. There is a photograph of such a stone arrangement on page 14 of Diane Bell's *Daughters of the Dreaming*

304. There is a photograph of a woman dancing with a men's board on page 203 of Bell's *Daughters of the Dreaming*

305. Condren 26

306. Condren 187

307. Lawrence Osborn op.cit.

308. William Blake Tyrrell, *Amazons; a study in Athenian Mythmaking.* John Hopkins University Press 1984. P. 86

309. Condren op.cit. 32

310. Jean Markale *Women of the Celts* Inner Traditions, Rochester, Vermont Page 38

311. Ibid. 27

312. *The Tain* op.cit. 7-8

313. Condren op.cit 36

314. Bell. op.cit. 37

315. Ibid. 182

316. Ibid. 204

317. Ibid. 119

318. Ibid. 143

319. I counted as Australian for I held an Australian resident's permit.

320. Karen Armstrong *Gospel according to Women* 231

321. See http://www.sparkle.plus.com

322. *Gospel According to Philip.* Gnostic Christian Text of around 100CE

323. Drawing in Caverne des Trois Freres in Arriege depicted in Margaret Murray's *God of the Witches* Oxford University Press (Plate 2)

324. David Clarke with Andy Roberts *Twilight of the Celtic Gods* 45

325. Capitularia Regum Francorum" 1677, quoted in *A History of Pagan Europe* by Prudence Jones and Nigel Pennick 104

326. Hutton *Triumph of the Moon, A history of Pagan Modern Witchcraft* 303-4

327. Ronald Hutton, *The Pagan Religions of the British Isles* 300

328. Hutton, *The Triumph of the Moon: A history of Pagan Modern Witchcraft* 3

329. Hutton,. The *Pagan Religions of the Ancient British Isles* 289

330. Ibid. 299

331. Ibid. 300

332. Eliade *Shamanism* op.cit. 5.

333. Hutton *The Pagan Religions of the British Isles* 340

334. Ibid. 308

335. Karen Armstrong *The Gospel according to Women* 111

336. Murray *God of the Witches* 57

337. Ibid. 38

338. Ibid. 89-93

339. Ibid. 122-126

340. Ibid. 138-139

341. Ibid. 114-117

342. Eva Pocs; *Between the living and the dead.* 50

343. Ibid. 86

344. Hutton op.cit. 340

345. Keith Thomas *Religion and the Decline of Magic.* 515-525

346. Pocs op.cit. 166

347. Richard Kieckhefer Pen, State Univ. 1999

348. *Capitularia Regum Francorum* 1677, quoted in *A History of Pagan Europe* by Prudence Jones and Nigel Pennick 104

349. Prudence Jones and Nigel Pennick 103

350. Ibid.105

351. Hutton *The Pagan Religions of the British Isles* 85

352. Hutton *Triumph of the Moon* 66

353. Ibid. 87

354. Ibid. 105

355. Ibid. 303-4

356. Philip Haselton, *Wiccan Roots* 205-216

357. Peter Berresford-Ellis, *The Druids*, 247

358. Caitlin and John Matthews *Encyclopaedia of Celtic Wisdom* 153

359. Quoted in Shirley du Boulay *Beyond the Darkness; A Biography of Bede Griffiths* Rider, Random House, page111

360. Anne Baring and Jules Cashford *The Myth of the Goddess* 382

361. Quoted in Johannes Fabricius's *Alchemy.* (The "bain-marie" is named after her—a method of cooking slowly over warm water)

362. Cherry Gilchrist. *The Elements of Alchemy* 15

363. Ron Heiser. *The Impact of Freemasonry on Elizabethan literature.*—From Internet.

364. Anne Baring and Jules Cashford *The Myth of the Goddess* 131

365. Numbers. 21:9

366. Baring and Cashford op.cit. 5

367. Ibid. 60

368. *The Way of the Earth* 222 Note 45, Aeschylus was born circa 525BCE

369. This story is documented in my book *"Glitter and Greed "* or *"Blood Diamonds"*

370. MMR stands for Measles, Mumps and Rubella

371. Carl Jung *Collected Works. Volume 16 The Practice of Psychotherapy* Para. 407 Quoted in Baring and Cashford *The Myth of the Goddess* 651

372. Meister Ekhardt, *Tractate* 11.

373. Quoted by M Laski in *Ecstasy* 201

374. Diane Bell *Ngarrindjeri Wurruwarrin: a world that is, was, and will be* 326-243

375. Pocs op.cit. 108

376. Matthews *Miscellany* 46

377. Bleddyng Fardd Elegy for Llywelyn ap Gruffuddd, the Last Prince in *Welsh Verse*, translated by Tony Congran 165

378. John Matthews *The Druid Source Book* Blandford Press, 1997, London, page 350

379. Anne Ross *Ritual and the Druids* in *The Celtic World* Ed. Miranda Green page 432

380. John Matthews op.cit 53

381. Christina Oakley, in her paper *Druids and Witches* in *The Druid Renaissance*, edited by Philip Carr-Gomm (1996), argued that Druids and Witches are two very separate traditions. She saw Druids as historically associated with supporting the governing powers, while witches only owed allegiance to their Gods and Goddesses. She noted that the Druid Carr-Gomm on the contrary has suggested that there might be an underlying historical unity between Druidry and Witchcraft, perhaps because there was a universal Pre-Christian religion that used no particular name. She dismissed this, quoting extensive research that showed a rich variation in early European pagan religions. But I think Carr-Gomm's argument cannot be so easily set aside. Caitlin Matthews and others have linked Druidry and Shamanism—and thus surely also linked it to Witchcraft. Whenever I hear Bobcat, a Chief of the British Druid Order, speak; I cannot distinguish her mystical nature-centred description of "Druidcraft" from my own experience in what many of my friends call Witchcraft. Perhaps we are practicing the one and the same Craft but giving it different names?

382. Quoted by Caitlin Matthews in *The Druid Renaissance* op.cit, 230.

383. Doreen Valiente, *Witchcraft for Tomorrow*, 112

384. Teilhard de Chardin, *The Phenomenon of Man*

385. Elaine Pagel *The Gnostic Gospels* 128

386. *Gospel According to Thomas*. Nag Hammidi text.

387. *Gospel According to Philip*. Gnostic Christian text.

388. Part of Dick's ashes were retained by his son with my agreement for later distribution in California, where Dick had many magical friends—and to which he had planned to take me for Beltaine. Part of me would travel with him there as we had put a little of my hair into the coffin.

389. Randy Connor *Blossom of Bone* 108

390. Ibid. 111

391. Ibid. 105
392. Baring and Cashford op.cit 41-2
393. Jung *Recollections* 302
394. Jung op.cit. 3
395. Ibid. 4
396. Ibid. 304
397. Ibid. 311, 313-4
398. Ibid. 311

0-595-23637-5

Printed in the United States
23049LVS00008B/26

9 780595 236374